INSPIRE / PLAN / DISCOVER / EXPERIENCE

USA

USA

CONTENTS

DISCOVER 6

EXPERIENCE THE USA 60

NEED TO KNOW 738

Left: Signs lining a sidewalk in Nashville, Tennessee
Previous page: Fog engulfing the Golden Gate Bridge, San Francisco
Front cover: Horseback riding in the Rocky Mountains

DISCOVER

Yosemite National Park, California

WELCOME TO
THE USA

Dramatic and diverse, the star-spangled super-power that is the USA offers everything in excess. From the bright lights of its cities and quaint charisma of its rural towns, to the natural majesty of its national parks, this is a country of contrasts. Whatever your American Dream entails, this DK Eyewitness travel guide is the perfect companion.

1 The snowy peak of Mount Rainier, Washington.

2 Bayou Classic Parade, New Orleans.

3 San Francisco's historic working trams.

4 Bustling 42nd Street, New York City.

Wherever you're heading, the past awaits you. American Indian culture permeates the USA, and nowhere more so than in the Southwest, where native heritage and spirituality is palpable. Follow in the footsteps of the Founding Fathers and discover New England for yourself, or pay homage to those who fought for Civil Rights in the Southeast and Deep South. Adventure calls, whatever the season; hike around the beguiling Grand Canyon in spring, kayak around the arcadian Florida Keys in summer, or watch the mystical Northern Lights dance across the skies of Alaska in winter.

Craving the bustle of a city? You're spoiled for choice. New York City has long been the gateway to America and remains a great starting point thanks to its plethora of super-lative restaurants, world-class museums, and iconic landmarks. There's much more waiting beyond the Big Apple. Perhaps you're after the political pull of Washington, DC, or the archi-tectural wonders of Chicago. Irresistible food and music continue to reign in New Orleans, while San Francisco is bursting with creativity and the arts. Then there's Boston, Los Angeles, Miami, Philadelphia – the list goes on.

With so many different regions and experiences on offer, the USA can seem over-whelming. We've broken the country down into easily navigable chapters, with detailed itineraries and comprehensive maps to help plan the perfect adventure. Add insider tips, and a Need to Know guide that lists all the essentials to be aware of before and during your trip, and you've got an indispensable guidebook. Enjoy the book, and enjoy the USA.

REASONS TO LOVE
THE USA

Its scenery is spectacular. Its cities pulse with energy. It's a diverse fusion of cultures. Ask any American and you'll hear a different reason why they love their country. Here we pick some of our favorites.

1 FOURTH OF JULY
Wherever you are, the US celebrates its Declaration of Independence with passion. Expect star-spangled parades, fireworks, and parties, particularly in the major cities.

NEW YORK CITY 2
The jewel in America's crown, New York City is chock-full of icons, from Times Square and the Statue of Liberty to pastrami on rye and Carrie Bradshaw's stoop.

3 AMERICAN INDIAN HERITAGE
Villages carved out of giant mesas, enigmatic petroglyphs, and lovely crafts: American Indian history dates back thousands of years, but is alive today and deserves attention.

FALL IN NEW ENGLAND 4

Come October, great forests of sugar maple, beech, yellow birch, and hemlock blaze with color from the Green Mountains of Vermont to the White Mountains of New Hampshire.

HIKING IN NATIONAL PARKS 5

America's national parks encompass everything from reserves of pristine wilderness and lofty volcanoes to wetlands hosting native animals. They're all calling out to be explored.

SOUTHERN SOUL FOOD 6

Shrimp and grits that melt in your mouth; chicken fried countless ways; collared greens and mac n cheese. Soul food emerged in the Deep South and it remains the most satisfying.

MARDI GRAS *7*

Colorful and decadent, Mardi Gras in New Orleans is unlike anything else. Celebrations include raucous parades with float riders tossing strings of beads into the crowds.

AMERICAN SPORTS *8*

Grab a hot dog and join baseball fans in summer. Cheer a touchdown at a gripping NFL game. Admire the action at a hockey match, or try to keep up with players at a basketball game.

9 THE PACIFIC COAST

America's epic Pacific Coast begins in the redwood forests of the northwest and ends at the southern deserts of California, passing misty cliffs and untouched beaches.

10 AMERICAN ROAD TRIPS

Road trips are a huge part of the American psyche. Driving coast to coast is a classic rite of passage, a route that takes in snowy peaks, broiling deserts, wide rivers, and roadside diners.

HOLLYWOOD AND THE SILVER SCREEN 11

Film studios and movie-themed attractions are a big part of Hollywood's appeal, but you'll recognize movie sets all over America – from the Empire State Building to Monument Valley.

MUSICAL LEGENDS 12

The blues, jazz, rock 'n' roll, country, hip-hop – the US has produced it all. Sample grunge in Seattle, punk in New York, techno and soul in Detroit, and country in Nashville.

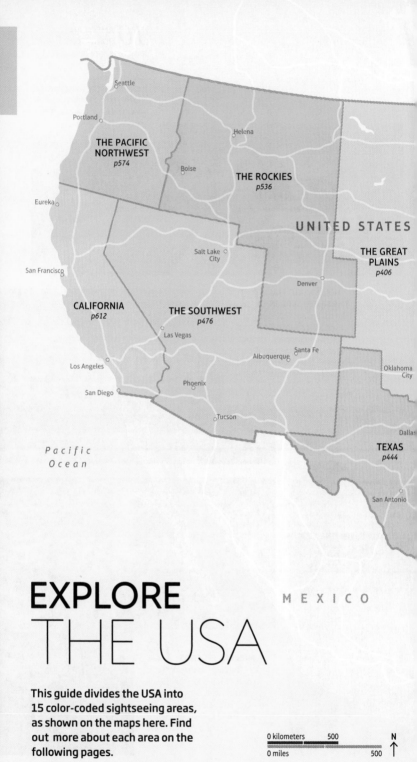

Seattle

Portland

**THE PACIFIC
NORTHWEST**
p574

Helena

Boise

THE ROCKIES
p536

Eureka

UNITED STATES

Salt Lake
City

**THE GREAT
PLAINS**
p406

Denver

San Francisco

CALIFORNIA
p612

THE SOUTHWEST
p476

Las Vegas

Los Angeles

Albuquerque

Santa Fe

Oklahoma
City

San Diego

Phoenix

Tucson

Dallas

*Pacific
Ocean*

TEXAS
p444

San Antonio

EXPLORE

M E X I C O

THE USA

This guide divides the USA into
15 color-coded sightseeing areas,
as shown on the maps here. Find
out more about each area on the
following pages.

0 kilometers   500

0 miles   500

N
↑

CANADA

Lake Superior

NEW
ENGLAND
p132

Portland

Minneapolis

Lake
Huron

Lake
Ontario

Boston

Lake Michigan

Milwaukee

Detroit

Buffalo

OF AMERICA

Lake
Erie

NEW YORK CITY
AND THE
MID-ATLANTIC
p62

New York City

Omaha

Chicago

THE GREAT LAKES
p360

Pittsburgh

Philadelphia

Indianapolis

Cincinnati

Baltimore

Kansas
City

St. Louis

WASHINGTON, DC AND
THE CAPITAL REGION
p192

Washington, DC

Memphis

THE SOUTHEAST
p238

THE DEEP SOUTH
p322

Atlanta

Charleston

Savannah

*Atlantic
Ocean*

Jacksonville

Houston

New
Orleans

FLORIDA
p276

*Gulf of
Mexico*

Miami

NORTH AMERICA

ALASKA
p686

CANADA

HAWAII
p710

UNITED STATES
OF AMERICA

*Pacific
Ocean*

MEXICO

GETTING TO KNOW
THE USA

The US is a vast nation of over 330 million people, and few countries have such a variety of landscapes. From the snowcapped Rockies and deserts of the Southwest, to the beaches of Florida and the endless prairies of Texas, each region has its own unique personality.

PAGE 62

NEW YORK CITY AND THE MID-ATLANTIC

New York City is the nation's cultural capital. It's a city that's constantly reinventing itself, where pizza slices compete with celebrity chefs; contemporary art meets mesmerizing graffiti; and the streets hum with honking horns and hip-hop. Upstate New York, New Jersey, and Pennsylvania form the Mid-Atlantic, an area rich in natural wonders, from the scenic byways of the Hudson River Valley and thundering Niagara Falls, to the tranquil trails of the Catskills and Adirondacks. There are great cities here too, including Philadelphia and Pittsburgh.

Best for
Iconic cities, skyscrapers, food, art and culture, outdoor adventures

Home to
New York City, Philadelphia, Niagara Falls

Experience
A scenic cruise around New York Harbor

NEW ENGLAND

PAGE 132

America's most historic region, New England is studded with charming clapboard houses, Revolutionary War sites, and handsome white-spired churches. There are festivals in the Berkshires, LGBT+ parties in Provincetown, and a plethora of hiking, rock-climbing, and sailing opportunities year-round. As for the fall foliage, it's truly magnificent, with swaths of bright red and gold glowing in the forest canopy. All of New England's tree-lined roads lead to Boston, a city loved for its rich heritage, successful sports teams, and illustrious universities.

Best for
Colonial history, seafood, beaches, fall foliage

Home to
Boston, Salem, Acadia National Park

Experience
The Red Sox playing at Boston's Fenway Park

WASHINGTON, DC AND THE CAPITAL REGION

PAGE 192

Capital of the nation, Washington, DC is crammed with world-class museums and grand monuments. The state of Virginia is rich in Colonial history and natural beauty, from the Blue Ridge Mountains to the sleepy backwaters of the Chesapeake. Gritty Baltimore has a lively waterfront, while Delaware features beaches and opulent country mansions. Rugged West Virginia is all about the Allegheny Mountains, white-water rivers, and wild forests.

Best for
National monuments, museums, Colonial and Civil War history

Home to
The White House, Colonial Williamsburg, Jamestown, Yorktown

Experience
The Blue Ridge Parkway's 469 miles (755 km) of snaking roads and awe-inspiring views

→

PAGE 238

THE SOUTHEAST

America's Southeast has transformed in the past 100 or so years. North and South Carolina, Georgia, Tennessee, and Kentucky now feature lively college towns, a growing number of stylish museums, Civil Rights monuments, and contemporary restaurants helmed by celebrity chefs. Its traditional charms remain, however; unspoiled Outer Banks beaches, charismatic churches, BBQ dinners, country music, and lively, musically rich cities such as Atlanta, Lexington, Nashville, and Memphis, the home of the blues, rock 'n' roll, and Elvis.

Best for
Southern food and BBQ, history, music

Home to
Charleston, Atlanta, Memphis

Experience
A country music show at the Grand Ole Opry, or a live blues show in Memphis

PAGE 276

FLORIDA

The aptly named "Sunshine State" is incredibly dynamic and diverse. The northern half of Florida features old-fashioned Southern charm, plus Daytona, Disney, and surfing to boot. The south, meanwhile, is home to ultra-hip cities such as Miami and Palm Beach, and a blossoming Latino culture. The watery grasslands of the Everglades, as well as the quirky, Caribbean-like communities on the Keys, feel like different countries altogether. Wherever you go, expect orange groves, grazing manatees, irresistible Key lime pie, conch fritters, and miles and miles of gorgeous, sugary sands.

Best for
Beaches, Latino and Cuban culture, theme parks

Home to
Miami, Walt Disney World® Resort, Universal Orlando Resort™

Experience
A simulated launch into orbit at the Kennedy Space Center

PAGE 322

THE DEEP SOUTH

The states of the Deep South – with their vast plantations draped in oak trees, soul food traditions, and a brutal history of slavery – offer a very different perspective on American life. Music lovers flock to the Mississippi Delta to dance to the blues, while history buffs head for the thought-provoking Civil Rights memorials dotting Alabama. Louisiana serves up Cajun culture, and New Orleans, one of the nation's most beautiful and fiercely idiosyncratic cities, seduces with its jambalaya, jazz, and indulgent culture of drinking, dancing, and general merry-making.

Best for
Southern food, music, Civil Rights and African American history

Home to
New Orleans, Alabama, Mississippi Civil Rights Museum

Experience
A hedonistic night out on Bourbon Street, New Orleans

→

PAGE 360

THE GREAT LAKES

The states of the Midwest hug the shores of the five Great Lakes, providing countless opportunities for boating, fishing, and sunbathing in summer. Outdoor adventures also dominate in lake- and forest-filled Wisconsin, Minnesota, and Michigan, though all three states further attract foodies thanks to their wonderful farmers' markets, cheeses, and microbrews. Illinois, Ohio, and Indiana feature vibrant cities, with Chicago in particular home to iconic artwork, live blues, giant skyscrapers, and those irresistible thick-crust pizzas. And don't forget Detroit, a city on the rise once more.

Best for
Architecture and skyscrapers, outdoor adventure, microbrews

Home to
Chicago, Detroit, Cincinnati

Experience
Craft beer trails in the likes of Wisconsin, Milwaukee, and Grand Rapids

THE GREAT PLAINS

PAGE 406

The heartland of the country is dominated by the Great Plains, home to iconic sights including Mount Rushmore, the Gateway Arch in St. Louis, and the Wild West town of Dodge City. Though often overlooked as the flat "flyover" states of conservative "Middle America," the landscape here is utterly stunning and road-trippers in particular will enjoy the scenery while motoring along Route 66. After passing through its rolling hills and vast grasslands, the likes of Omaha, Tulsa and St. Louis come into view, home to dynamic art and culinary scenes.

Best for
Road trips, American Indian culture, classic American food

Home to
Black Hills, Mount Rushmore, St. Louis

Experience
Route 66 as it sweeps through Americana

TEXAS

PAGE 444

Texas really is big – bigger than most European countries. It promises legendary BBQ restaurants and plenty of Stetson-wearing cowboys – and girls. Though the state is peppered with small towns, rolling plains, cattle ranches, and lesser-known sights such as Big Bend National Park, it's the cities that attract many. San Antonio brims with Mexican culture, while Austin is a liberal enclave loved for its live music. Dallas and Houston are sprawling, intensely modern cities, home to great art, restaurants, and America's fascinating space program.

Best for
BBQ, live music, cowboy culture

Home to
Dallas, Fort Worth, Austin, San Antonio, Houston

Experience
White-water rafting in Big Bend National Park

→

PAGE 476

THE SOUTHWEST

American Indian culture – Hopi, Navajo, and Apache among others – is especially prevalent in the Southwest, and the desert landscapes are home to some of the most mesmerizing scenery on the planet. Here lies the utterly mind-bending chasm of the Grand Canyon, the stunning Zion and Arches National Parks, and the gargantuan fingers of rock at Monument Valley. And who can forget the region's ancient Puebloan ruins, its clutch of charming Spanish cities, and the neon behemoth Las Vegas, where pleasure and hedonism reign.

Best for
American Indian culture, desert landscapes and canyons, national parks

Home to
Las Vegas, Grand Canyon

Experience
Hike to the bottom of the awe-inspiring Grand Canyon

PAGE 536

THE ROCKIES

Stretching from the Canadian border to the deserts of southern Colorado, America's rugged spine encompasses geyser basins, lava flows, arid valleys, magnificent snowcapped peaks, and huge sand dunes. Remote mountain ranges lace Montana, Idaho, and Wyoming, not forgetting the utterly magical Yellowstone National Park. Thrill-seekers come to America's playground for white-water rafting, hiking, and skiing, while those looking for a more relaxed experience can indulge in some of the country's best microbreweries and a burgeoning arts scene in Denver.

Best for
The great outdoors, skiing, craft beer

Home to
Yellowstone National Park, Grand Teton National Park, Denver

Experience
A thrilling jet-boat ride in Hell's Canyon National Recreation Area

PAGE 574

THE PACIFIC NORTHWEST

Oregon and Washington states are anchored by two enticing cities – pop-culture icon Seattle, star of the silver screen and home to coffee king Starbucks, and increasingly hip Portland, a leader in farm-to-table produce, organic wineries, and superb microbreweries. The real appeal of the Pacific Northwest, however, lies outdoors. Every way you turn you'll find pristine wilderness, glacier-fed lakes, forests of giant Douglas firs, and snow-topped mountains. Hike, bike, kayak, or climb in the likes of Columbia River Gorge, Crater Lake, Olympic National Park, or the lava-scraped landscapes of Mount St. Helens.

Best for
Coffee and craft beer, organic dining, cool cities

Home to
Seattle, San Juan Islands, Mount Rainier National Park

Experience
Modern masterpieces at Seattle Art Museum

→

PAGE 612

CALIFORNIA

The Golden State packs a real punch. California's coast is synonymous with surf and beach culture, while Los Angeles is the home of Hollywood, Disneyland, and Beverly Hills. To the south, San Diego has broad beaches and numerous museums, while the Victorian houses and steep hills of San Francisco make this one of the world's most distinctive cities. Inland things change dramatically, from the deserts of Death Valley and the craggy peaks of Yosemite, to the ghost towns of the Gold Country and the redwood forests of the north. Whatever you're after, you'll find it in California.

Best for
Beaches and surfing, food and wine, national parks

Home to
Los Angeles, San Diego, Death Valley National Park, San Francisco,

Experience
The local grape on a Napa Valley wine tour

ALASKA

PAGE 686

Far to the north is Alaska, a truly vast wonderland of great mountains, glaciers, and untouched wilderness. The charmingly remote islands and rugged coastline to the south can be reached only by air or sea, making for delightfully remote getaways. Visitors arrive here to take to the waters and explore its historic ports, ice sheets, and wonderful whale-rich bays. From Anchorage it's possible to travel to captivating Denali National Park by road, and even reach the Arctic Circle on the Dalton Highway. It's here that you might catch a glimpse of the Northern Lights.

Best for
Wilderness adventures, mountains and glaciers, sea cruises, wildlife

Home to
Anchorage, Denali National Park, Fairbanks

Experience
The truly breathtaking Northern Lights dance in the skies above Fairbanks

HAWAII

PAGE 710

Vibrant and verdant, Hawaii is America's holiday paradise, a chain of tropical islands cast in the central Pacific and famed for legendary surf breaks, Polynesian culture, and (very) active volcanoes. Most sun-seekers arrive by air in Honolulu on the island of O'ahu, the state capital, home to iconic Waikīkī Beach and Pearl Harbor. Small, lush Moloka'i and volcano-smothered Hawai'i itself – the biggest island – are more rustic destinations. Maui, meanwhile, excels at lively resorts and water sports, while Kaua'i arguably offers the most spectacular scenery.

Best for
Beaches and surfing, Polynesian culture, rest and relaxation

Home to
Pearl Harbor, Waikīkī Beach, Honolulu

Experience
O'ahu's North Shore from a surfboard

←

1 Fallingwater, by Frank Lloyd Wright.

2 Anish Kapoor's *Cloud Gate*.

3 Great Lakes Brewing, Cleveland.

4 Deep-dish pizza in Chicago.

This two-week road trip gives a taster of the USA's most iconic cities and landscapes, from the East to the West Coast. Starting in New York State and ending in Los Angeles, it passes along sections of the historic Route 66.

2 WEEKS

Coast to Coast

Day 1

Set out early – and with plenty of provisions – for the long drive from New York to Cleveland, taking a southern route (I-78 and I-76) across the densely wooded Allegheny Mountains. In the heart of rural Pennsylvania, stop at the Flight 93 National Memorial *(p129)*, a poignant tribute to those killed on September 11, 2001. Further on, check out celebrated architect Frank Lloyd Wright's Fallingwater house *(p129)* before continuing on to Cleveland.

Day 2

Spend a few hours exploring buzzing Cleveland's pride and joy, the Rock and Roll Hall of Fame and Museum *(p390)*. For a quick lunch grab a hot dog at Lucky Dogs *(1200 Lakeside Av East)*, or sit down for a classic German meal at Hofbräuhaus *(1550 Chester Av)*. Admire the Old Masters in the Cleveland Museum of Art. If the kids are in tow, take a peek at the dinosaurs at the Cleveland Museum of Natural History. In the evening, check out Warehouse District nightlife, or sample the craft beers at Great Lakes Brewing *(2516 Market Av)* across the river in Cleveland.

Day 3

It's a five-hour drive to Chicago *(p370)*, America's third city, home to stylish sky-scrapers and baseball. Tour Barack Obama's old neighborhood, Hyde Park, in the afternoon. Visit the DuSable Museum of African American History *(p376)*, and wander the leafy campus of the venerable University of Chicago *(p376)*. Finish up with a deep-dish pizza at Lou Malnati's Pizzeria *(p373)*.

Day 4

Start the day with a tour of Downtown Chicago, either on foot or on a boat along the river. Dazzling views of the city and Lake Michigan can be had at the top of super-tall Willis Tower *(p374)*. Stroll around Millennium Park and stare into the shiny surface of Anish Kapoor's Cloud Gate. After a classic Chicago lunch – Italian beef sand-wich or Chicago-style beef hot dog at Al's Italian Beef *(601 West Adams)* – spend the afternoon gazing at the wonders inside the Art Institute of Chicago *(p373)*. End the day with drinks and live blues at Buddy Guy's Legends *(700 South Wabash Av)* or B.L.U.E.S. *(2519 North Halsted St)*.

Day 5

Drive down to Springfield *(p380)*, the Illinois state capital, which is now a virtual shrine to Abraham Lincoln. The illuminating Abraham Lincoln Presidential Library and Museum and the wonderfully preserved Lincoln Home National Historic Site chronicle the life and times of the great man. Grab something light to eat in Springfield before continuing on to St. Louis, Missouri, in the evening.

Day 6

Spend the day exploring the frontier city of St. Louis *(p434)*. Start by taking the tram to the top of the Gateway Arch, a momentous feat of engineering by architect Eero Saarinen. After lunch at blues shrine Blueberry Hill *(6504 Delmar Blvd)*, walk to Forest Park. Highlights include the Missouri History Museum and St. Louis Art Museum.

→

Day 7

From St. Louis, drive southwest to Oklahoma City (*p442*) and take in the Americana-rich remaining stretches of iconic Route 66. Enjoy a classic diner lunch at Waylan's Ku-Ku Burger (*915 North Main St, Miami*), admire the Blue Whale at Catoosa, and peruse the exhibits at the road-themed Route 66 Interpretive Center (*400 East 1st St*) in Chandler. Just before Oklahoma City, grab a bite at POPS (*660 West Route 66*) in Arcadia.

Day 8

Leaving Oklahoma City, the Great Plains stretch out to the horizon: great swaths of corn studded with bright red barns and lonely grain elevators. The scenery is spectacular. It's 535 miles (860 km) to Santa Fe, New Mexico, via I-40, which will take you around 8 hours. Break the journey at the Oklahoma Route 66 Museum in Clinton (*2229 W Gary Blvd*), and grab lunch in Amarillo, in the Texas Panhandle (*p475*). Beyond Amarillo lies the New Mexico border and the vast deserts and mountains of the American West.

Day 9

After spending a day on the road, enjoy exploring Santa Fe (*p528*), the elegant state capital of New Mexico, a glorious ensemble of Spanish adobe and Baroque architecture. Begin with the New Mexico Museum of Art and Georgia O'Keeffe Museum, dedicated to the celebrated painter of the Southwest. Learn about the region's Puebloan cultures at the Museum of Indian Art and Culture, or its Spanish heritage at the San Miguel Mission and Palace of the Governors. Be sure to sample Southwestern or Mexican food here; La Plazuela (*100 East San Francisco St*) is a good bet.

Day 10

It's another long drive via I-40 from Santa Fe to Flagstaff (*p513*), Arizona, the gateway to one of the most mind-blowing natural wonders in the world – the Grand Canyon (*p514*). Be sure to stock up on picnic foods en route – you'll need them today and tomorrow. It's possible to make the 385-mile (620-km) trip in around seven hours, giving you time to enjoy the South Rim of the canyon before sunset.

1 Western Plains, Oklahoma.
2 St. Francis Cathedral, Santa Fe.
3 Red chili peppers in Santa Fe.
4 The bright lights of Las Vegas.
5 Sunset over the Grand Canyon.
6 Santa Monica Beach.

Day 11

You'll want a full day to experience the Grand Canyon in all its glory, either exploring the viewpoints along Hermit Road and Desert View Drive, or hiking part of the Bright Angel Trail (don't attempt the whole trail in one day). Remember to set off with plenty of food and drink.

Day 12

Around four hours' drive west of the Grand Canyon lies Las Vegas (p490), Nevada, a confection of mega-casinos in the middle of the desert. On foot it can take the best part of the day wandering through the labyrinthine hotels on the Strip, from the Luxor pyramid to the canals of the Venetian. You're spoiled for choice when it comes to food, but be sure you try one of the city's famous buffets, such as the Bacchanal at Caesar's Palace.

Day 13

From Vegas it's a five-hour drive to Downtown Los Angeles on busy I-15, but it's far more enjoyable to pick up Route 66 again, taking a full day to soak up sights in the Mojave Desert. The best section loops south off I-40 from Essex to Ludlow in California. Roy's Motel & Café (87520 National Trails Hwy, Amboy) is familiar from numerous movies and worth stopping at for coffee and photos. It's also worth stretching your legs in Barstow, home to the Bagdad Café, and the Route 66 "Mother Road" Museum. But Emma Jean's Holland Burger Café (17143 D St, Victorville) is the best place to eat traditional diner food.

Day 14

You've made it. Finish this epic coast-to-coast road trip the right way, by driving through Los Angeles to the Pacific Ocean to watch the sun set over Santa Monica Pier (p622). Take in the quirky scene on Venice Beach and soak up the iconic sights in Hollywood en route to the beach, where you'll be rewarded with a hard-earned rest on the beautiful golden sands. Sundowners are best enjoyed at the popular Art Deco-style Esters Wine Shop and Bar (p629).

Pass the Buck

The National Hockey League (NHL) season is October to May and games are notoriously boisterous, extremely fast, and often bruising - fights can break out among players. Teams compete for the venerable Stanley Cup. You can watch the likes of the Boston Bruins play at TD Garden *(www.tdgarden.com)* and the New York Rangers play at Madison Square Garden *(www.msg.com)*.

→

The Boston Bruins playing at TD Garden, Boston

USA FOR
SPORTS FANS

The USA is one of the world's great sporting nations, with American football, baseball, basketball, and ice hockey ruling the domestic sports scene. The country also hosts some of the world's biggest golf tournaments, horse and motor races, and tennis championships.

SPORTING EVENTS

Nothing beats the thrill of a live sporting event. The Masters takes place in April in Augusta, Georgia, the first major golf tournament of the year. The Kentucky Derby is a prestigious horse race that takes place in Louisville in May. Also in May is the Indy 500. This is the world's oldest major motor racing event, at Indianapolis Motor Speedway, Indiana. Down in Queens, the US Open Tennis thrills audiences around August and September, while the iconic New York Marathon, in November, is the world's largest, with 50,000 finishers.

Touchdown!

American football is the USA's No.1 sport, and the February Superbowl is *the* event to watch. New England Patriots, based in Boston *(p146),* continue to enjoy success, but there are plenty of other teams. Visit Hard Rock Stadium *(p290),* home to the Miami Dolphins, or kick back in a sports bar and enjoy a game.

→

New England Patriots facing the Los Angeles Rams

Cheer a Home Run

Cheering for the local baseball team, with a hot dog and cold beer, is a summer tradition. Iconic stadiums include Boston's Fenway Park *(p159)*, Chicago's Wrigley Field *(p376)*, San Francisco's Oracle Park, and Yankee Stadium *(p104)* in the Bronx, New York City. The National Baseball Hall of Fame can be found in Cooperstown, New York *(p111)*. Pioneering African American players are honored at the Baseball Museum in Kansas City *(p436)*. You can learn about the art of baseball bats at the Louisville Slugger Museum in Kentucky *(p274)*.

←

A baseball game at the packed Wrigley Field, Chicago

(p159), (p376), (p104), (p111), (p436), (p274)

TOP 4 SPORTS LEGENDS

"Babe" Ruth (1895–1948)
The greatest baseballer joined the Yankees from arch-rivals the Boston Red Sox in 1919.

Jesse Owens (1913–1980)
African American track and field athlete who won four gold medals at the 1936 Olympic Games.

Billie-Jean King (1943–)
Winner of 39 Grand Slam titles and an advocate for gender equality.

Michael Jordan (1963–)
A basketball star in the 1980s and '90s, winning six championships.

It's a Slam Dunk

The NBA (National Basketball Association) season runs October through June, and the Women's National Basketball Association (WNBA) starts in May and ends in September. Stadiums are typically smaller than those used for football or baseball. The Basketball Hall of Fame is in Springfield, Massachusetts *(p167)*.

↑ Alyssya Thomas of Connecticut Sun shoots against the New York Liberty

The Mother Road

Few road trips have captured popular imagination like Route 66. Stretching from Chicago *(p370)* to Santa Monica *(p622)*, it passes through eight states but – perhaps more potently – it transports roadtrippers back in time, thanks to the kitsch motels and faded road signs that punctuate the route.

$\rightarrow$

Driving through Canyonlands National Park, along Route 66

USA FOR
ROAD TRIPS

Road trips have been an indelible part of American culture since Henry Ford rolled off his first Model-T in 1908. Traveling across North America on wheels has been immortalized in books like Jack Kerouac's *On the Road* and movies such as *Thelma & Louise*. Where will the road take you?

Blue Ridge Parkway and Grandfather Mountain, North Carolina ↑

Beautiful Blue Ridge

The serpentine Blue Ridge Parkway *(p227 and p248)* crests the Appalachian mountains for hundreds of miles through Virginia and North Carolina. In the fall the slopes erupt in a blaze of gold, copper-colored, and ruby-red leaves, while the scent of barbecued pork wafts up from wooden roadside shacks. The route meanders past rugged mountains and through pastoral landscapes for some 469 miles (755 km), the southern end anchored by Great Smoky Mountains National Park *(p266)*.

Fabulous Florida

US-1 connects Key West (p321) to the Florida mainland, a tantalizing highway that seems to run straight toward the middle of the open sea. Long bridges glide over the enticing lagoons of the Florida Keys (p320), an island chain that juts into tropical waters just north of Cuba. Along the way you can snorkel and dive at the John Pennekamp Coral Reef State Park, sunbathe at Bahia Honda State Park, and spot deer on Big Pine Key.

→

The stunning Seven Mile Bridge, Florida Keys

Arresting Alaska

The vast, untouched wilderness of Alaska is prime road-trip country, with long, winding roads slicing through forests and skirting snowy peaks. The Alaska Highway itself lies mainly in Canada, but scenic Alaska Route 1 runs between Homer (p708), through the Chugach National Forest, all the way to Tok, on the road to Fairbanks (p696). It passes through Anchorage (p707) and snakes up the gorgeous Matanuska River valley.

←

Stopping to admire Alaska Matanuska Glacier

TOP 3 ONE DAY-DRIVES

Going-to-the-Sun Road
This 50-mile (80-km) route offers mesmerizing views as it cuts through Glacier National Park (p552).

Northern Pueblos Tour
This 45-mile (70-km) route snakes between Santa Fe and Taos, and passes eight American Indian pueblos.

Crater Lake Rim Drive
Dazzling ride around the entire rim of Crater Lake in Oregon, some 33 miles (53 km).

California's Captivating Coast

In California, Hwy-1 - aka the Pacific Coast Highway - makes a superb drive between Los Angeles (p622) and San Francisco (p648), with the sublime, canyon-cut landscape of the Big Sur (p670) coast as its undisputed highlight. Here the road twists and turns through dense pine forest, high above isolated beaches speckled with lounging seals and sea lions.

↑ Driving along the gorgeous Pacific Coast Highway, California

Great Sand Dunes National Park, Colorado

Just Deserts

The deserts of the Southwest are rich in myth, American Indian culture, and startling landscapes. Death Valley *(p642)* is a vast basin of sun-blasted rocks, saltpans, and furnace-like temperatures, while giant cacti star in Joshua Tree National Park *(p642)* and Arizona's Saguaro *(p518)*, part of the Sonoran Desert. Vast mountains of golden sand are piled within Great Sand Dunes National Park *(p571)*, Colorado.

USA FOR
NATIONAL
PARKS

From the jaw-dropping vistas of the Grand Canyon to the wetlands of Florida's Everglades, America's 61 national parks abound in captivating scenery. The immensity and diversity of the country's wide-open spaces are truly staggering – and they're waiting for you to explore.

TOP 5 NATIONAL PARKS

Acadia, Maine
This park teems with wildlife and rugged hills. Great for hiking *(p190)*.

Big Bend, Texas
This colorful wilderness is a white-water rafter's paradise *(p472)*.

Bryce Canyon, Utah
A colony of sandstone pinnacles *(p506)*.

Canyonlands, Utah
The Colorado and Green rivers thread through canyons and plateaus *(p504)*.

Crater Lake, Oregon
A beautiful lake in a volcanic caldera *(p610)*.

Incredible Canyons

The mother of all canyons is within Grand Canyon National Park *(p514)*, measuring a mind-bending one mile (1.6 km) deep and 277 miles (446 km) long. Further along the Colorado River, Canyonlands *(p504)* harbors smaller canyons. Utah also contains Bryce Canyon *(p506)* and Zion Canyon *(p508)*, while lovely Santa Elena Canyon lies in Big Bend National Park *(p472)*.

→

Hiking through Grand Canyon National Park

Tectonic Terrain

The godfather of mountain parks is Yosemite *(p684)*, studded with plunging granite monoliths and waterfalls. Grand Teton *(p558)* is laced with jagged, snow capped peaks, while Trail Ridge Road traverses Rocky Mountain National Park *(p568)*. Alaska's Denali *(p698)* is the nation's highest peak, at 20,310 ft (6,190 m). Out in the Pacific, Haleakalā National Park *(p736)* contains the giant East Maui Volcano, while lava and craters dominate Hawai'i Volcanoes National Park *(p731)*. Yellowstone *(p560)* is a huge volcanic caldera, littered with geysers and bubbling pools of mud and sulfur.

→

Glacier Point, Yosemite National Park

Forests and Wetlands

The leafy giants of Redwood National Park *(p677)* tower above California like skyscrapers, with trunks wider than buses. Sequoia and Kings Canyon national parks *(p685)* have their own super-sized sequoia groves. In the east, the Everglades *(p320)* of Florida contain forests of a different kind: tropical wetlands of hardwood hammocks, pines and cypress, sawgrass prairies, and mangroves.

←

Exploring Florida's lush and leafy Everglades

Caving In

New Mexico's Carlsbad Caverns National Park *(p534)* is a vast underground wonderland of chalky white calcite columns and spiky stalactites. Its "Big Room" limestone cave is an astounding 4,000 ft (1,219 m) long and 255 ft (78 m) high. Kentucky's Mammoth Cave *(p272)* is the longest known cave system in the world, a limestone labyrinth draped with flowstones melting into the cave walls.

→

The stunning Carlsbad Caverns National Park, New Mexico

I Love Rock 'n' Roll

Rock 'n' roll surfaced in the early 1950s, when the likes of Elvis Presley blended blues, gospel, and country. Memphis *(p270)* is home to Graceland, the lavish Presley home, the Memphis Rock-N-Soul Museum, and historic Sun Studio. Read up at Cleveland's Rock & Roll Hall of Fame *(p390)* or Seattle's Museum of Pop Culture *(www.mopop.org).*

→
Legendary Sun Studio, Memphis

↑
Inside the Johnny Cash Museum, Nashville

Take Me Home, Country Roads

Nashville *(p268)*, Tennessee, is the capital of country music. Its Grand Ole Opry and Country Music Hall of Fame serve as central pilgrimage points, while the Johnny Cash Museum *(www.johnnycashmuseum.com)* honors the life of the country superstar. Eastern Kentucky is also rich in country customs; Hwy-23 is known as the "Country Music Highway." The state is home to a style of country music called bluegrass.

USA FOR
MUSIC LOVERS

America has created some of the world's greatest musical genres, and they live on today. New Orleans for jazz; Nashville for country; Memphis for the blues and rock 'n' roll; Detroit for soul and techno; and New York City for everything else. Where will you tune in?

All That Jazz

Jazz emerged in New Orleans in the early 1900s. Blending African traditions with western techniques, it's a distinctly American art form. Louis Armstrong, Duke Ellington, and Billie Holiday remain household names. Jazz is still flourishing in New Orleans today *(p339)*, though scenes also exist in New York City and Chicago. The New Orleans Jazz Museum *(p339)* offers a great introduction.

→
Enjoying live jazz at Maison Bourbon, New Orleans

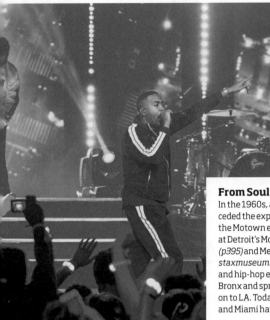

From Soul to Hip-Hop
In the 1960s, artists like Otis Redding preceded the explosion of talent that defined the Motown era of soul music. Learn more at Detroit's Motown Historical Museum *(p395)* and Memphis's Stax Museum *(www. staxmuseum.com)*. Then, in the 1970s, rap and hip-hop emerged on the streets of the Bronx and spread across New York City and on to LA. Today, Atlanta, Chicago, Houston, and Miami have cool hip-hop scenes.

←

Rapper Nas performing in New York City

TOP 3 BLUES FESTIVALS

B.B. King Homecoming Festival
One of the oldest and most popular of the many Deep South summer blues festivals, in May/June *(www. bbkingmuseum.org)*.

Chicago Blues Festival
A June festival featuring three days of performances by acclaimed blues musicians *(www.chicago.gov)*.

The Sunflower River Blues and Gospel Festival
This August festival is held in Clarksdale, Mississippi, the "Birthplace of the Blues" *(www. sunflowerfest.org)*.

Singing the Blues
The blues grew out of the African American experiences of slavery and poverty in the Mississippi Delta, with traditional African and gospel music merging in the late 19th century. By the 1930s the blues followed the Mississippi to Memphis, and on to other cities. Beale Street, Memphis *(p270)*, is still a live blues hub today. You can also visit the Delta Blues Museum in Clarksdale *(p350)* and the Chicago Blues Experience *(p372)*.

↑ The MC Daniel Band on stage at the Rum Boogie Cafe, Memphis

Idyllic Islands

Martha's Vineyard and Nantucket *(p165)* are short ferry rides off the coast of Cape Cod, with atmospheric whaling ports, cranberry bogs, and clapboard churches. Remote coastal islands in South Carolina and Georgia have quiet beaches and wildlife preserves. The Florida Keys *(p320)* are subtropical gems, a haven for snorkeling, diving, and seafood. On the West Coast, the tranquil San Juan Islands *(p588)* can be explored by bike, while California's Channel Islands *(p668)* offer pristine reserves.

↑ Picturesque scenery in the Florida Keys

USA FOR
COASTAL CHARM

The coast has always played a huge role in American life, from colonial harbors and whaling ports to modern beach resorts. Today the American seaboard features iconic beaches and surf breaks, wildlife preserves, wetlands, sand dunes, towering sea cliffs, and isolated fishing villages.

SURF'S UP

Hawai'ian legends such as Duke Kahanamoku introduced the ancient Polynesian sport of surfing to California in the 1920s. Modern surf culture went mainstream in Malibu, Huntington Beach, and Oceanside in the late 1950s. Movies like *Gidget* (1959) instigated the genre known as beach party films, as well as the surf music of Dick Dale and the Beach Boys. Today Hawai'i and California remain at the heart of the US surf scene, though you'll find plenty of surfers along the East Coast, from Florida up to New York and Rhode Island.

Life's a Beach

Southern California is especially linked with a laid-back beach culture, and beaches between San Diego *(p636)* and LA *(p622)* are crammed with sunbathers and volleyballers. Miami's South Beach *(p286)* is perhaps America's most glamorous beach resort. On the Gulf Coast, Pensacola *(p314)* and Padre Island *(p469)* attract boisterous students during Spring Break. Hawai'i, of course, is in a league of its own.

→ Sun soakers in Hanauma Bay in O'ahu, Hawai'i

Take to the Water

Windsurfing shouldn't be missed on Maui's Hookipa Beach and North Carolina's Outer Banks *(p251)*. South Padre Island *(p469)*, Texas, and even the Columbia River Gorge *(p602)* are also great for windsurfing. Glaciers make sea kayaking extraordinary in Alaska, and kayaking around the San Juan Islands *(p588)*, or along the Florida Keys *(p320)*, can be equally magical. Sailing is popular in Newport *(p171)* and San Francisco Bay.

→

Kayaking past the incredible Shoup Glacier, Alaska

Under the Sea

Whales can be spotted spyhopping off the coast of California or Washington. Gentle manatees bask along the coast of Florida, and you are likely to spot dolphin pods all along the coast, not to mention sharks and rays from the bridges of the Overseas Highway. Colonies of seals and sea lions are especially common along the New England and Californian coasts; you can even kayak with sea otters near Monterey *(p670)*.

←

Manatees in the crystal waters of Florida

Sensational Seafood

Delicious seafood is promised along the USA's coastlines. Crab is king in Maryland, with steamed blue crabs and spicy soft-shells around Chesapeake Bay, while stone-crab claws are a specialty in Miami *(p286)*. New Englanders feast on giant Maine lobsters, while any trip to Louisiana should see you slurping raw oysters. Monstrously sized salmon grace the menus of the Pacific Northwest, while giant spider crabs are renowned in Alaska.

→

A plate of oysters served in New Orleans, Louisiana

TOP 5 AMERICAN HEROINES

Abigail Adams (1744-1818)
Remarkable wife of John Adams.

Sacagawea (1788-1812)
Shoshone woman who helped European settlers while carrying a baby on her back.

Harriet Tubman (1822-1913)
An enslaved woman turned political activist.

Eleanor Roosevelt (1884-1962)
First Lady and delegate to the United Nations.

Toni Morrison (1931-2019)
Winner of the 1993 Nobel Prize in Literature.

The French Quarter of New Orleans ↑

Colonial America

St. Augustine *(p313)* was founded by the Spanish in 1565, and today its colonial architecture, old forts, and chapels are redolent of those early days. Little remains of the original English colonies at Plymouth *(p163)* and Jamestown *(p222)*, but both have fascinating historic sites. Williamsburg *(p224)* has been faithfully restored, with clapboard houses and immersive exhibits, while the French legacy is displayed in New Orleans' French Quarter *(p334)*.

USA FOR
HISTORY BUFFS

North America has been inhabited for at least 15,000 years but the United States was created relatively recently, in 1776. It might be a relatively "new" country, but there is much to be remembered, and wherever you go you'll find well-preserved buildings, battlefields, and museums.

Revisit the Revolution

America's defining moment is remembered at Independence Hall in Philadelphia, preserved as if time had stopped in 1776. Philly *(p118)* is packed with sites dedicated to the Revolutionary War, as is Boston *(p146)*; Bunker Hill, Minute Man National Historical Park, Paul Revere's Old North Church, to name a few. Key battle sites such as Saratoga *(p110)* and Yorktown *(p222)* have visitor centers to add context. If you're in New York City, hit Broadway show *Hamilton* provides a wonderfully entertaining education.

↑ Independence Hall, Philadelphia

Civil War Memorials

The US Civil War was another turning point in American history. All the major battle sites have been sensitively preserved, from Antietam and Bull Run to Shiloh and Chancellorsville, though Gettysburg (p128) is by far the biggest and most poignant. Vicksburg National Military Park (p351) commemorates the pivotal Mississippi siege. The illuminating National Civil War Museum stands in Harrisburg (p128). President Lincoln is memorialized in Springfield (p380), and also at the Lincoln Memorial in Washington, DC (p213). You can also visit Ford's Theatre, where he was shot (p213).

←

Gettysburg National Military Park, Pennsylvania

Wild Wild West

The Western Frontier played a major role in the culture of the US. To get into the spirit of the Wild West, visit Dodge City (p441) or Tombstone (p519). Cody (p559) is home to the Buffalo Bill Center of the West, which celebrates the cowboy legend. In Montana, Little Bighorn Battlefield National Monument (p554) remembers Custer's defeat at the hands of warriors like Crazy Horse.

→

A stage coach in Tombstone, Arizona

The Fight for Civil Rights

In the 1950s and '60s African Americans engaged in a monumental struggle for civil rights. Their legacy is preserved at the Martin Luther King, Jr. National Historical Park in Atlanta (p262), the Selma to Montgomery National Historic Trail, the National Civil Rights Museum in Memphis (p270), and the Rosa Parks Museum in Montgomery (p356). The heart-rending stories of Medgar Evers, Fannie Lou Hamer, and Vernon Dahmer are told at the Mississippi Civil Rights Museum (p352).

←

A vintage bus at the National Civil Rights Museum, Memphis

AMERICAN ARTISTS

America has long produced talented artists. Mary Cassatt (1844–1926) is known as one of "les trois grandes dames" of Impressionism, while Georgia O'Keeffe (1887–1986) was the mother of American Modernism and known for her abstract, sensual paintings of nature. Iconic Pop artist Andy Warhol (1928–87) changed the course of art history, and street art emerged soon after; a work by street artist Jean-Michel Basquiat (1960–88) sold for $110 million in 2017.

The Charles Engelhard Court at the Met, New York City ↑

USA FOR
ART LOVERS

American painters have been active since the 17th century, but the country's abstract art and Pop Art went global after World War II. Today the US is also one of the great storehouses of world art, with mammoth museums displaying great masterpieces and street art gracing its city streets.

Art on the Street

In the country that invented graffiti in the 1960s, street art has become a fully fledged artistic genre. In New York City, neighborhoods such as the East Village (p87) and Harlem (p102) are festooned with murals. Philadelphia (p118) is known as "the City of Murals" thanks to Mural Arts Philadelphia, the USA's largest public art program. The Grand River Creative Corridor in Detroit (p394) features 100 murals on 15 buildings, while Miami has the art-smothered Wynwood Walls (p292).

←

Pedal Thru by Paul Santoleri, Philadelphia

Monumental Museums

Almost every American city has at least one exceptional art museum. In New York alone you have the magical Met (p101), MoMA (p93), the Guggenheim (p94), the Whitney (p88), and the Frick (p95). LA has the phenomenal Getty Center (p623), plus the Norton Simon Museum in Pasadena (p633), home to European art. In Washington, DC, you'll find the National Gallery of Art (p206), while Chicago's legendary Art Institute (p373) contains Seurat's famous *Sunday Afternoon on the Grand Jatte*.

Did You Know?

The Met's mascot is an ancient Egyptian statue of a hippopotamus, called William.

Artist Abodes

Connecticut has various Impressionist homes, such as the Florence Griswold Museum *(www.florencegriswoldmuseum.org)*. In New York, the Pollock-Krasner House *(www.stonybrook.edu)* honors Jackson Pollock's legacy, and the Thomas Cole National Historic Site *(www.thomascole.org)* was the home of the 19th-century artist. Georgia O'Keeffe's New Mexico home *(www.okeeffemuseum.org)* is also open.

← Studio of painter Thomas Cole, New York State

TOP 4 AMERICAN ARTWORKS

American Gothic **(1930), Grant Wood** Art Institute of Chicago (p373).

Flag **(1954-55), Jasper Johns** MoMA, New York City (p93).

Nighthawks **(1942), Edward Hopper** Art Institute of Chicago.

Cow's Skull **(1931), Georgia O'Keeffe** The Met, New York City (p101).

↑ Sol LeWitt's *Zoran Orlić Campus Building 7 Wall Drawing 340*, MASS MoCA

Modern Art Powerhouses

You're spoiled for choice when it comes to modern art galleries. In the Berkshires, Massachusetts, MASS MoCA *(www.massmoca.org)* is a major showcase for contemporary art housed in a converted factory. A great place for Rothko's work is the Rothko Chapel in Houston (p462). The excellent Andy Warhol Museum (p131) in Pittsburgh commemorates the king of Pop Art.

Hike in the Wild

National and state parks offer a great opportunity for captivating hikes. At the Grand Canyon *(p514)*, make time for the two-day hike down to the Colorado River. Sensational mountain hikes include the Skyline Trail in Washington's Mount Rainier National Park *(p592)*, and the Hidden Lake Trail through the wildflowers of Glacier National Park *(p552)*. In California's Yosemite *(p684)*, climb the Half Dome for views over the valley.

→
Hiking the Skyline Trail in Washington

USA FOR
OUTDOOR ADVENTURES

The USA's natural landscapes are playgrounds for the intrepid and adventurous. Vast tracts of completely untouched wilderness, desert, and wetlands make for superb hiking, swimming, cycling, and skiing opportunities – all with unbeatable views. The possibilities are endless.

Exploring a Civil War shipwreck in Key Largo ↑

Into the Blue

From May to September, it's common to see turtles on the Florida coast, and the waters off the Florida Keys *(p320)* are especially rich in sea life. The underwater "Shipwreck Trail" is also here. The world's largest artificial reef lies off Pensacola *(p314)*, where USS Oriskany was sunk. You can also glimpse harbor seals and leopard sharks at Monterey Bay National Marine Sanctuary and Channel Islands National Park *(p668)* in California.

Take to the Slopes

The most celebrated ski resorts lie in the Colorado Rockies, while Utah is the connoisseur's choice, with no-frills Alta featuring pillowy soft powder plus a ban on snowboarders, so skiers have the slopes to themselves. Back country fans should instead head for Jackson Hole *(p558)*, in Wyoming. The East Coast can't compete in mountainous slopes, but Killington *(p178)* and Stowe *(p180)* in Vermont and Cannon Mountain in New Hampshire will keep most skiers happy.

$\longrightarrow$

A ski lift ascending a mountain in Aspen, the Colorado Rockies

We're Going to Need a Bigger Boat

It's hard to beat kayaking on Lake Tahoe *(p685)*, suitable for any level of ability and with endlessly blue scenery. Those with more experience should tackle the rapids on the Arkansas River or the Indian River Canoe Trail in Michigan. White-water rafting hot spots include the Yellowstone River in Montana, Cañon City in Colorado *(p570)*, Hartford in Tennessee, and best of all, Flagstaff *(p513)* in Arizona, for rafting the Grand Canyon *(p514)*.

$\longleftarrow$

Rafters enjoying the choppy waters of the Arkansas River

Pedal Through Pastures New

With masses of impressive trails across the US, renting a bike is a great way to explore. Long-distance bike routes include the highly scenic Tony Knowles Coastal Trail near Anchorage *(p707)*, while the Tahoe Rim Trail, Lake Tahoe *(p685)*, is arguably the most thrilling. The George S. Mickelson Trail cuts through the heart of the Black Hills *(p418)*.

↑ Cycling along the Tahoe Rim Trail, passing between California and Nevada

TOP 4 MOUNTAIN BIKING SPOTS

Sun Valley, Idaho
With more than 400 miles (640 km) of single-track trail.

Moab, Utah
Home of "The Whole Enchilada," a highly technical, 33-mile (53-km) route.

Oak Mountain State Park, Alabama
Famed for its 22-mile (35-km) Red Trail.

Tucson, Arizona
The Fantasy Island Mountain Bike Trail, some 20 miles (32 km) of trails in the city limits.

◁ United Steaks

Emotions run high when it comes to barbecue in America. The four main styles are Carolina (led by Lexington, North Carolina, and defined by its mix of condiments), Memphis (smoked over hickory wood), Kansas City (known for "burnt ends"), and Texas. If you fancy a juicy steak head for Texas, Montana, and Wyoming, or Chicago, Omaha, and Kansas City. New York City is known for posh but pricey steakhouses.

USA FOR
FOODIES

Food is big business in the US, a country where a deli sandwich can be a meal for two and where all-you-can-eat buffets are destinations in themselves. In cities you'll find just about every type of cuisine, while American staples, refreshing beers, and classic diners are found across the country.

▷ Wonderful Wine Country

American wines boomed after the 1976 "Judgment of Paris", where a panel of French wine experts chose Californian wines over their French counterparts. Today the Napa and Sonoma valleys *(p674)* are still the USA's prime wine regions, and California also has the Santa Ynez Valley *(p670)*. The state dwarves the rest in quality and production, though Washington State (notable for bright fruit flavors), New York (known for Rieslings), Pennsylvania, and Oregon are on the rise.

◁ Tasty Tex-Mex

Mexican food is wildly popular all over the US, but much of it is more properly defined as Tex-Mex. This hybrid adds more guacamole, melted cheese (or just "queso"), and chopped tomatoes with cilantro to classics like pinto beans and tortillas. Texas is also where you'll find the best chili – and scores of passionately fought chili cookoffs.

◁ Southern Soul

Southern soul food is the perfect comfort dining. Menus vary, but grits (ground corn cooked with butter and salt), collard greens, black-eyed peas and rice, fried chicken, and cornbread are classics. Sweet fruit pies round-out the experience. Georgia and South Carolina favor seafood and rice, while Cajun cooking emerged in southern Louisiana. This has similarities with Creole cuisine, its urban cousin, and you'll find spicy jambalayas and po-boy sandwiches served in New Orleans *(p334)*.

CLASSIC DINERS

Few American icons are so beloved as the roadside diner, where burgers, apple pie, and coffee are often served 24/7. The South Street Diner *(140 South St)* in Philly is a buzzing spot with a huge menu. In Chicago there's Lou Mitchell's *(www.lou mitchells.com)*, while LA boasts Rae's *(2901 Pico Blvd)*, and San Diego County has Ruby's *(p637)*. Route 66 drivers should look out for Waylan's Ku-Ku Burger in Oklahoma *(915 N Main St)* and 66 Diner in Albuquerque *(www.66diner.com)*.

△ The Craft Beer Revolution

Since the 1990s America has experienced a beer revolution, led by the Boston Beer Company and iconic Brooklyn Brewery in New York City. The West Coast has since developed a major craft beer scene, with California and Oregon especially rich in microbreweries. Beer capitals include San Diego, Grand Rapids, Milwaukee, and Denver.

◁ American Icons

New York and Chicago battle it out for who makes the best pizza (thin-crust or deep-dish). Nathan's Famous *(www. nathansfamous.com)* popularized the hot dog in New York, but you'll find local versions in Detroit and Chicago. The Philly cheesesteak is a sandwich of sliced beef and rich melted cheese. Even burgers vary: try the "Jucy Lucy" in Minnesota, onion burger in Oklahoma, and green chile burger in New Mexico.

Specific Reservations and Nations

Some 573 American Indian tribes are legally recognized by the Bureau of Indian Affairs. Most of these tribes are associated with a specific reservation, though some are simply "nations." Tribal lands are self-governing to a degree, and it's important to respect local rules and regulations. The Navajo Nation of Arizona, Utah, and New Mexico is the largest tribal land area, encompassing a host of attractions, from Monument Valley (p520) to the Rainbow Bridge National Monument. The Agua Caliente Band of Cahuilla Indians manages the Indian Canyons near Palm Springs (p645), while the Seminole Tribe of Florida pioneered gaming operations in the 1970s, and has owned most of the Hard Rock Cafe franchises since 2007.

→

Rainbow Bridge Monument, and Navajo sisters (inset)

USA FOR
AMERICAN INDIAN CULTURE

American Indian culture has a long and rich history in the US. European colonization in the 17th century took a devastating toll on indigenous cultures. Problems remain, but today increased political autonomy and new income streams have provided many tribes with greater economic freedom.

Living History

Many American Indian tribes have established illuminating cultural centers. Oklahoma is home to many, including the Cherokee Heritage Center (www.cherokeeheritage.org) and the Osage Nation Museum (www.osagenation-nsn.gov). The excellent Ah-Tah-Thi-Ki Museum (www.ahtahthiki.com) lies at the heart of the Big Cypress Seminole Reservation in Florida, while Wisconsin is home to the informative Ojibwe Museum (www.ldfmuseum.com). The Navajo Nation Museum (p523) can be found in Window Rock, Arizona.

↑ Exploring the Cherokee Heritage Center, Oklahoma

TOP 3 PUBLIC POW WOWS

The Gathering of Nations
The country's largest takes place in Albuquerque, New Mexico, on the fourth weekend in Apr.

Cherokee National Holiday Pow Wow
Honors the 1839 Cherokee constitution, in Tahlequah, Oklahoma, in late Aug/early Sep.

Denver March Pow Wow
Some 1,600 dancers from 100 tribes gather in late Mar.

THE FIGHT FOR CIVIL RIGHTS

1890 Wounded Knee Massacre and end of "Indian Wars."

1924 Indian Citizenship Act grants US citizenship to all American Indians.

1941-45 Some 44,000 American Indians serve in the US military during World War II.

1968 USA's first tribally controlled community college established, awarding degrees in areas important to the Navajo Nation.

1969 The Occupation of Alcatraz Island saw the Indians of All Tribes (IAT) group occupy Alcatraz for over a year.

1973 Oglala Lakota and American Indian Movement (AIM) activists occupy Wounded Knee, South Dakota.

2009 An "apology to all Native Peoples on behalf of the United States" is included in the Defense Appropriations Act.

Dancing at a pow wow at Mesa Verde National Park, Colorado ↑

Echoes of the Past

The remnants of great American Indian civilizations lie all over the US. The best known are the ancient Puebloan towns of the Southwest. Pueblo Bonito in Chaco Culture National Historical Park *(p526)*, the Navajo National Monument *(p523)*, and Mesa Verde National Park *(p572)* are spectacular examples. Learn about the advanced mound-building Mississippian culture at Cahokia Mounds, near St. Louis *(www.cahokiamounds.org)*. Ceremonial pipes were once made at the Pipestone National Monument *(p403)*, in southwestern Minnesota, while Mission San Luis in Tallahassee *(p314)* is one of the most spectacular reconstructions of an American Indian village in the country.

A YEAR IN
THE USA

JANUARY

△ **Rose Parade & Rose Bowl Game** *(Jan 1).* Pasadena, California, celebrates the new year with floral floats, marching bands, and the Rose Bowl – one of the major games in college football.
Martin Luther King, Jr. March *(second Mon in Jan).* San Antonio, Texas, holds the nation's largest MLK march, attracting some 300,000 people.

FEBRUARY

△ **Mardi Gras** *(Feb, sometimes early Mar).* The biggest and most raucous carnival celebration in the United States, with a major parade every day and several masquerade balls in New Orleans, Louisiana.

MAY

△ **Kentucky Derby** *(first Sat in May).* America's premier horse race is the climax of the two-week-long Kentucky Derby Festival in Louisville, known as much for its mint juleps and extravagant ladies' hats as for the races.

JUNE

Red Earth Festival *(early Jun).* One of the nation's biggest celebrations of American Indian culture includes a parade, art market, and Red Earth Pow Wow in Oklahoma City.
△ **Pride Week** *(various dates in Jun).* The biggest, most hedonistic celebrations of LGBT+ culture take place in the likes of New York City and San Francisco.

SEPTEMBER

△ **Monterey Jazz Festival** *(third weekend in Sep).* Epic jazz fest in California with around 500 artists performing on nine stages.
Texas State Fair *(late Sep–late Oct).* This 24-day extravaganza in Dallas is one of the USA's biggest state fairs, featuring parades, college football, auto shows, and a showground of exhibitors.

OCTOBER

△ **Halloween Parades** *(Oct 31).* America's largest Halloween parades take place in New York City and Florida's Key West, and feature spectacular costumes, giant puppets, and lots of parties.

MARCH

St. Patrick's Day *(Mar 17)* Major cities celebrate Ireland's national day with parades, parties, and boozing; Chicago even colors its river green.

△ **National Cherry Blossom Festival** *(late Mar–early Apr)*. Three weeks of cherry blossoms in Washington, DC, featuring kite-flying, martial arts, a street festival, fireworks, and a major parade.

APRIL

Coachella Music & Arts Festival *(mid-Apr)*. Music and arts festival on consecutive three-day weekends in Indio, California, including live performances from the biggest names in rock, R&B, hip-hop, and pop.

New Orleans Jazz & Heritage Festival *(late Apr–May)*. A ten-day cultural feast of live musical performances, local cuisine, and artisans demonstrating and selling their crafts.

△ **Tribeca Film Festival** *(late Apr–May)*. New York City's major indie movie festival, co-founded by Robert de Niro, screens over 1,500 movies.

JULY

△ **Independence Day** *(Jul 4)*. The 1776 US Declaration of Independence is commemorated with a massive firework display in New York City, plus fireworks and concerts in Boston and Washington, DC.

Newport Folk Festival *(late Jul)*. Legendary folk, alt-rock, and world music festival held in Rhode Island since 1959, hosting all the top global performers.

AUGUST

Alaska State Fair *(late Aug–early Sep)*. This state fair has the most picturesque location, in Palmer, and the biggest, record-setting vegetables.

Burning Man Festival *(late Aug–early Sep)*. Art festival in the middle of the Nevada desert.

△ **US Open** *(last Mon in Aug–early Sep)*. Crowds flock to Queens, New York, for this Grand Slam.

NOVEMBER

△ **Macy's Thanksgiving Day Parade** *(last Thu of Nov)*. Thanksgiving is primarily a family holiday in the US, but this fun annual tradition in New York City brings out the crowds and Macy's Thanksgiving Day Parade is televised coast-to-coast.

DECEMBER

△ **New Year's Eve** *(Dec 31)*. Millions watch on TV or cram Times Square in New York City or Mallory Square in Key West to count down the final minutes of the year. Major celebrations also take place in cities such as Chicago, Las Vegas, New Orleans, and San Francisco.

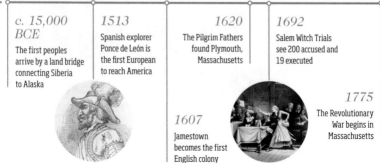

PHYSICAL MAP
OF THE
UNITED STATES

1

A BRIEF
HISTORY

Indigenous civilizations thrived for at least 15,000 years before Columbus arrived in 1492. European exploration began in earnest thereafter and the United States was founded in 1776, with the last of the 50 states joining the Union in 1959. The nation grew into one of the world's greatest superpowers.

Early Origins

Nomadic hunter-gatherers are thought to have entered Alaska from Siberia around 17,000 years ago, and within 1,000 years an estimated ten million people were living across the Americas. Indigenous cultures flourished in all corners of the land, with tribes having their own languages and customs, establishing complex trade routes and building cities and towns. When the Europeans arrived in the 16th century, they fought the American Indian tribal nations for land, but it was the diseases brought over by the Europeans that devastated the indigenous peoples; by the 17th century, just one million American Indians remained.

1 A 19th-century map of the USA.

2 Pilgrim fathers arriving in America.

3 *Signing of the Declaration of Independence* by John Trumbull (1817).

4 *The Trail of Tears* by Robert Lindneux (1942).

Timeline of events

c. 15,000 BCE
The first peoples arrive by a land bridge connecting Siberia to Alaska

1513
Spanish explorer Ponce de León is the first European to reach America

1607
Jamestown becomes the first English colony

1620
The Pilgrim Fathers found Plymouth, Massachusetts

1692
Salem Witch Trials see 200 accused and 19 executed

1775
The Revolutionary War begins in Massachusetts

Colonial America and the Revolutionary War

Though the Spanish and Dutch first founded colonies, it was the English who gained control in Jamestown, Virginia (1607), and Plymouth, Massachusetts (1620), after arriving on the Mayflower ship. Tobacco production and the exploitation of enslaved people from Africa meant Virginia's economy and European population swelled, and 13 colonies were established along the East Coast. In 1775, war broke out between Britain and its colonies (allied with France) following British abuses. Congress adopted the Declaration of Independence on July 4 1776. America prevailed after victories at Saratoga and Yorktown, and the war ended in 1783.

Birth of a Nation

George Washington became the first US president in 1789, after the US Constitution was officially adopted, and served until 1797. Under Thomas Jefferson, the 1803 Louisiana Purchase added a vast area of land west of the Mississippi. When Andrew Jackson was in office, from 1829, he had American Indian tribes deported from their ancestral lands; some 4,000 Cherokees died on the Trail of Tears. Meanwhile, millions of pioneers migrated west.

FOUNDING FATHERS

In a general sense the term "Founding Fathers" covers anyone who led the Revolutionary War, signed the Declaration of Independence, or partook in the Constitutional Convention. More specifically, it refers to the most famous figures: John Adams, Benjamin Franklin, Alexander Hamilton, John Jay, Thomas Jefferson, James Madison, and – of course – George Washington.

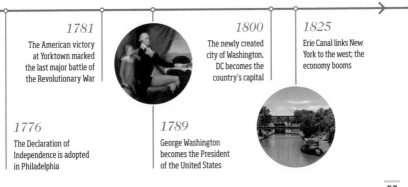

1781
The American victory at Yorktown marked the last major battle of the Revolutionary War

1776
The Declaration of Independence is adopted in Philadelphia

1789
George Washington becomes the President of the United States

1800
The newly created city of Washington, DC becomes the country's capital

1825
Erie Canal links New York to the west; the economy booms

1

2

The Mexican-American War and Gold Rush

In 1845, editor John L. O'Sullivan coined the phrase "Manifest Destiny" to describe the now common belief that America was destined to expand across the continent. The US annexed Texas in 1845, a move that sparked the Mexican-American War the following year. In 1848, Mexico yielded nearly half of its territory (California and much of the Southwest). The same year, gold was discovered in California, a seismic event that drew thousands into the new territory.

Civil War

By the 1850s, an industrialized society was emerging in the North, whereas the South was a less populous, agrarian society dependent on slavery. The nation was bitterly divided over the question of extending slavery into the newly forming western states. When Abraham Lincoln was elected president in 1860, Southern states began seceding from the Union to form the Confederate States of America. The Civil War began in 1861, and battles raged across the likes of Virginia, Maryland, South Carolina, Pennsylvania, Tennessee, Georgia, and Mississippi.

OPPRESSION OF AMERICAN INDIANS

Early European colonies often fought with eastern tribes. Shawnee warrior Tecumseh came close to unifying the tribes, but he was killed in 1813. The 1830 Indian Removal Act mandated the forced removal of all remaining southeastern tribes. As Europeans moved west, tribes were forced onto reservations – usually poor, desolate lands – where many still remain.

Timeline of events

1845

The US annexes Texas, previously part of Mexico

1846–48

Mexican-American War; US acquires Arizona, California, Utah, Nevada, and New Mexico

1848

Gold is discovered near Sacramento and the California Gold Rush begins

1861–65

Civil War between the Union (North) and Confederates (South)

1865

The 13th amendment abolishes slavery in the US

With their defeat at Gettysburg, in 1863, the Confederates were turned back and, in April 1865, General Lee finally surrendered to General Grant at Appomattox. The Civil War was over, but President Lincoln was assassinated soon after by Confederate sympathizer John Wilkes Booth.

America in the Gilded Age

After the war the north boomed in what Mark Twain dubbed the Gilded Age. Merchant princes such as the Vanderbilts (railroads), Andrew Carnegie (steel), John D. Rockefeller (oil), and J.P. Morgan (banking) created vast monopolies, and the pace of life was changed by the growth of railroads, the telephone, and the automobile. In the 1880s, over six million immigrants arrived in the US, and by the first decade of the 20th century a million people were arriving every year. In the West, the US Army battled American Indian tribes in the 1870s and 1880s, and resistance ended with the massacre at Wounded Knee, in 1890. The US acquired Alaska from Russia in 1867, took over Hawai'i in 1893, and occupied Puerto Rico and the Philippines after the Spanish-American War of 1898. Initially neutral, America was drawn into World War I.

① Gold washing in California, c. 1840s. ↑

② The Battle of Gettysburg, July 1863.

③ The assassination of President Lincoln.

④ Immigrants landing at Ellis Island, c. 1900.

$7,200,000
The amount the US paid Russia for Alaska, in 1867.

1890
Lakota Indians are killed by the army in the Wounded Knee Massacre

1892
Ellis Island opens its doors to immigrants, and sees 450,000 arrive in one year

1898
Spanish-American War; the US gains control of Puerto Rico

1907
Charles Curtis becomes the first American Indian Senator

1917
US enters World War I under President Woodrow Wilson

Boom and Bust

The 1920s, known as the Jazz Age or Roaring Twenties, saw an explosion of artistic creativity. Ironically, this coincided with Prohibition (1920–33), when the sale of alcohol was made illegal. The Wall Street Crash of 1929 shattered millions of dreams and left many Americans destitute and this was swiftly followed by the Great Depression which lasted for most of the 1930s. Elected in 1932, President Franklin D. Roosevelt established federal government relief programs to revitalize the economy. The Japanese attack on Pearl Harbor in 1941 brought the US into World War II.

The Cold War Era

The Cold War between the US and Soviet Union dominated the post war period. The Korean War (1950–53) was the first of many fought to stop the spread of Communism. Yet the 1950s and '60s were years of unprecedented economic growth. Not all civilians shared in this prosperity, especially in the segregated South, where African Americans could not use the same facilities as white people. Congress finally passed civil rights acts in the 1960s but, by the end of the decade, President Kennedy and Martin Luther

1 Duke Ellington, a pivotal figure of the Jazz Age. ↑

2 A 1950s family.

3 The poignant National September 11 Memorial.

4 Celebrating the increased presence of women in Congress, 2019.

1969
—
The year of New York's Stonewall Uprising, which inspired the gay rights movement.

Timeline of events

1920–33
Prohibition bans all alcohol; the Harlem Renaissance

1929
The Wall Street Crash plunges the country into the Great Depression

1941
Japanese attack on Pearl Harbor triggers entry into World War II

1959
Alaska and Hawai'i become the 49th and 50th states

1963
Assassination of President John F. Kennedy in Dallas

1964
The Civil Rights Act outlaws discrimination based on race, religion, or sex

King, Jr. had both been assassinated, race riots plagued big cities, and the Vietnam War divided opinions. The Watergate scandal led to President Nixon's resignation in 1974, and the post war boom ended with the energy crisis resulting in inflation and a recession.

The USA Today

The collapse of the Soviet Union ended the Cold War in 1991. Hopes for peace were soon dashed by conflict in Afghanistan and Iraq, which continues today. These invasions were US responses to 9/11, the devastating terrorist attacks on New York City and Washington, DC on September 11, 2001. Despite several recessions, most recently in 2008, the US economy has continued to expand. Yet divisions born in the 1960s have grown deeper, with the country divided into "blue" (Democrat) and "red" (Republican) states. Similarly, the election of Donald Trump in 2016 was bitterly divisive, his presidency characterized by attempts to roll back abortion laws and reduce immigration. In spite of political and cultural divisions, the Supreme Court legalized same-sex marriage in 2015, women's rights have increased, and a historic 117 women were elected or appointed to Congress in 2018.

THE SPACE RACE

The "Space Race" was launched by President John F. Kennedy in 1961. The USSR had just put the first man into space following its launch of the Sputnik satellite in 1957. Money and manpower were pumped into the National Aeronautics and Space Administration (NASA) and success came with the moon landing in July 1969 by Neil Armstrong and Buzz Aldrin in Apollo 11.

1991

The end of the Cold War after 40 years of tension

2008

Barack Obama becomes the country's first black president

2016

Donald Trump is elected president

2019

US wins the FIFA Women's World Cup for the fourth time

1968

Assassination of Martin Luther King, Jr. in Memphis

2001

Terrorist attacks on New York City and Washington, DC

AMERICAN TRAILBLAZERS

The US is so vast and diverse that it's no surprise the country has produced a number of remarkable figures. From the struggle for LGBT+ rights, women's rights, and Civil Rights, to technical innovation and political leadership, trailblazers punctuate America's history. Here are just a few of our favorites.

US history began long before Christopher Columbus or the Founding Fathers - indigenous peoples have lived here since 15,000 BC. Indian American tribes fought hard to defend their native lands, with chieftains such as Sitting Bull and Black Hawk famously leading the resistance against European settlers. The US has certainly produced significant leaders. George Washington led the War for Independence and became the first US president, with a line of influential presidents following him; from the 16th president Abraham Lincoln, who engineered the abolition of slavery, to the 44th president Barack Obama, the country's first African American leader. It's not all titles and power, however. Some of the most trailblazing figures were ordinary people who would change the course of history.

> **It's not all titles and power, however. Some of the most trailblazing figures were ordinary people who would change the course of history.**

↑ Barack Obama and his family on stage in Denver, 2008, having accepted the Democratic presidential nomination

Timeline

Sitting Bull (1831–1890)

Lakota chief who led Sioux resistance to the US government's occupation of traditional lands.

Helen Keller (1880–1968)

▽ The first deaf-blind person to earn a degree became an inspiring speaker and advocate for people with disabilities.

Frederick Douglass (1818–1895)

▲ Escaped slavery and championed abolition and social justice - including women's suffrage.

Thomas Edison (1847–1931)

The USA's greatest inventor created the phonograph, the movie camera, and the electric light bulb.

Amelia Earhart (1897–1937)

▲ Pioneer aviator who became the first woman to fly a plane solo across the Atlantic.

EQUAL RIGHTS AND GENDER EQUALITY

1 Susan B. Anthony (1820-1906)
Anthony became an activist in her teens, campaigning to abolish slavery. She co-founded the National Woman Suffrage Association in 1869, and was arrested for voting in 1872. The "Susan B. Anthony Amendment," which gave women the right to vote, was introduced to Congress in 1878, and became law as the 19th Amendment in 1920.

2 Harriet Tubman (1822-1913)
Born into slavery in Maryland and severely beaten as a child, Harriet Tubman not only managed to escape, but returned to rescue her family and many other enslaved people in the 1850s. During the Civil War she liberated others and became a champion for women's suffrage.

3 Victoria Woodhull (1838-1927)
Woodhull was the first woman to campaign for the US presidency, in 1872. She argued that a woman should be free to marry, divorce, and bear children without restriction – a radical proposition at the time. Woodhull and her sister were also Wall Street's first female stockbrokers.

4 Ruth Bader Ginsberg (1933-)
The second-ever female Supreme Court justice (appointed in 1993), the "Notorious R.B.G." has spent her career fighting for gender equality. The lawyer co-founded the Women's Rights Project at the American Civil Liberties Union in 1972, arguing six gender discrimination cases before the Supreme Court (she won five).

5 Gloria Steinem (1934-)
One of the world's leading feminists since the late 1960s, Steinem began her career as an investigative journalist, achieving prominence with articles such as "After Black Power, Women's Liberation" in 1969. She's been an advocate for a woman's right to reproductive choice, the Equal Rights Amendment, and even female movie superheroes.

Rosa Parks (1913–2005)

▽ Parks' rejection of bus segregation in Montgomery, Alabama, sparked the most dynamic period of Civil Rights activism in America.

Dolores Huerta (1930–)

Labor leader who founded the first national farm workers' union with fellow Latino activist Cesar Chavez.

Bill Gates (1955–)

▽ The Microsoft co-founder instigated the computer revolution of the 1980s. Philanthropy is his main focus today.

Martin Luther King, Jr. (1929–1968)

△ African American Baptist minister who led the struggle for Civil Rights in the 1950s and 1960s.

Harvey Milk (1930–1978)

LGBT+ trailblazer who became the first openly gay city supervisor in San Francisco.

EXPERIENCE

Santa Monica Boulevard, Los Angeles

NEW YORK CITY AND THE MID-ATLANTIC

A beach in the Hamptons, New York State

EXPLORE
NEW YORK CITY AND THE MID-ATLANTIC

This chapter divides the Mid-Atlantic into three sight-seeing areas, as shown on the map below. Find out more about each area on the following pages.

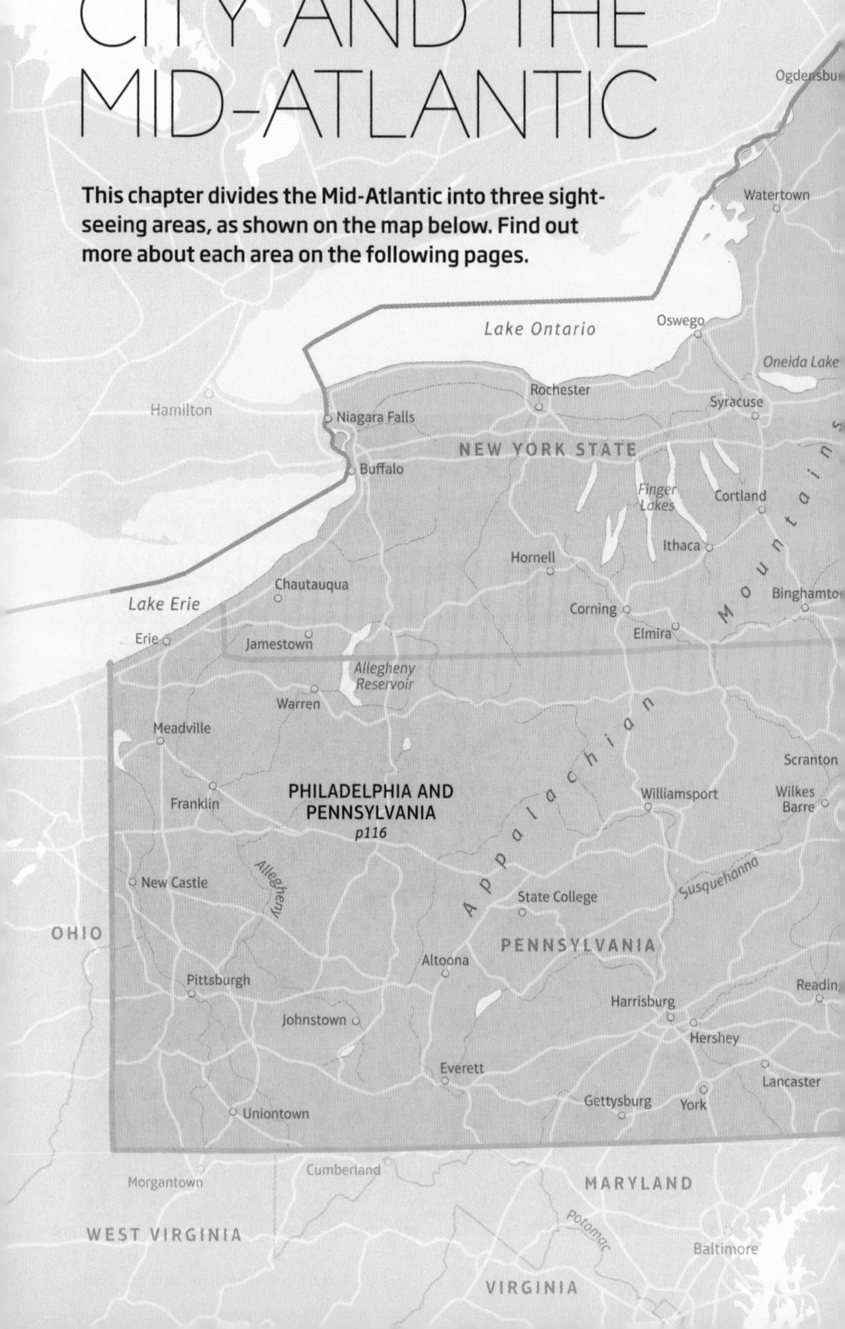

Ogdensbu
Watertown
Lake Ontario
Oswego
Oneida Lake
Hamilton
Niagara Falls
Rochester
Syracuse
Buffalo
NEW YORK STATE
Finger Lakes
Cortland
Mountains
Hornell
Ithaca
Chautauqua
Corning
Binghamto
Lake Erie
Elmira
Erie
Jamestown
Allegheny Reservoir
Warren
Meadville
Scranton
Franklin
PHILADELPHIA AND PENNSYLVANIA
p116
Williamsport
Wilkes Barre
New Castle
Allegheny
State College
Susquehanna
OHIO
PENNSYLVANIA
Altoona
Pittsburgh
Readin
Johnstown
Harrisburg
Hershey
Everett
Lancaster
Uniontown
Gettysburg
York
Morgantown
Cumberland
MARYLAND
Potomac
WEST VIRGINIA
Baltimore
VIRGINIA

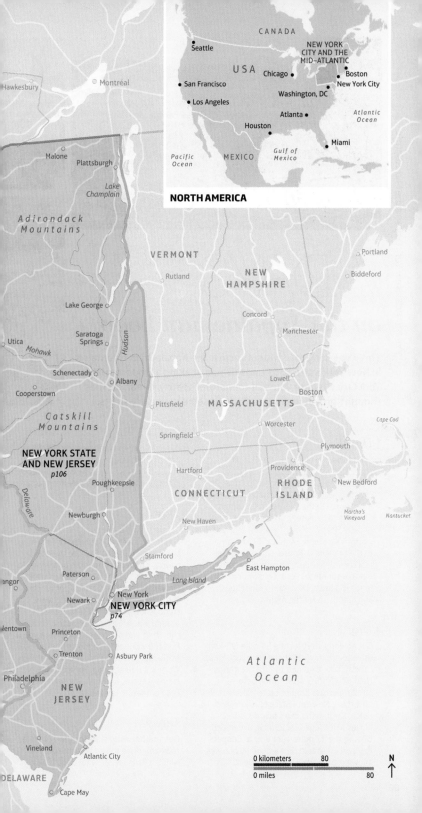

NORTH AMERICA

CANADA

USA

Seattle

San Francisco

Los Angeles

Houston

Atlanta

Miami

Washington, DC

Chicago

Boston

NEW YORK CITY AND THE MID-ATLANTIC

New York City

Pacific Ocean

MEXICO

Gulf of Mexico

Atlantic Ocean

Hawkesbury

Montréal

Malone

Plattsburgh

Lake Champlain

Adirondack Mountains

VERMONT

Rutland

NEW HAMPSHIRE

Concord

Manchester

Portland

Biddeford

Lake George

Saratoga Springs

Utica

Mohawk

Schenectady

Albany

Hudson

Cooperstown

Catskill Mountains

NEW YORK STATE AND NEW JERSEY
p106

Pittsfield

MASSACHUSETTS

Springfield

Lowell

Boston

Worcester

Cape Cod

Plymouth

Poughkeepsie

Hartford

Providence

New Bedford

RHODE ISLAND

Delaware

Newburgh

CONNECTICUT

New Haven

Martha's Vineyard

Nantucket

Stamford

Paterson

Long Island

East Hampton

angor

Newark

New York

NEW YORK CITY
p74

lentown

Princeton

Trenton

Asbury Park

Atlantic Ocean

Philadelphia

NEW JERSEY

Vineland

Atlantic City

0 kilometers   80

0 miles   80

N

DELAWARE

Cape May

7 DAYS

on the Appalachian Loop

This week-long road trip cuts across the Appalachian Mountains in New York State and Pennsylvania, making a loop from New York City. Prepare yourself for natural beauty, dynamic cities, thought-provoking museums, plus some very early starts.

Day 1

Spend the day exploring the bucolic Hudson River Valley *(p108)*. Start by touring Washington Irving's home in Sunnyside *(3 W Sunnyside Lane)* and then head a few miles north to the Old Dutch Reformed Church and cemetery that featured in his ghostly *Sleepy Hollow*. If you're a real bookworm, it's a scenic 54 miles (87 km) on to the Franklin D. Roosevelt Presidential Library and Museum *(www.fdrlibrary.org)*, but a detour into pretty Cold Spring for lunch is a must. Drive on to Rhinebeck and stop here for the night.

Day 2

Get an early start for the 58-mile (93-km) drive to Albany *(p109)*, the New York State capital. Take a guided tour of the gargantuan New York State Capitol, before strolling across Empire State Plaza to the absorbing New York State Museum. For lunch, sample the city's favorite snack at Gus's Hotdogs *(212 25th St, Watervliet)*. Driving the 77 miles (124 km) to Cooperstown *(p111)* should take around 90 minutes, allowing time to visit the National

Baseball Hall of Fame *(www.baseballhall. org)* at the birthplace of baseball itself. Try Cooperstown Diner *(www.cooperstown diner.com)* for a no-frills American supper.

Day 3

Cooperstown is just over 100 miles (161 km) from Ithaca, at the heart of the Finger Lakes region *(p110)*. Explore the downtown art galleries and indie bookstores before strolling the picturesque Cornell University campus. Grab a light lunch at the 1850s Carriage House Café *(www. carriagehousecafe.com)*. It should take around 1 hour to reach Seneca Falls at the other end of Cayuga Lake. Here you'll find the wonderful Women's Rights National Historical Park and the National Women's Hall of Fame. For a change of culinary scene, 84 Fall *(www.84fall.com)* is an authentic tapas bar.

Day 4

Get another early start for the 127-mile (204-km) drive to the breathtaking Niagara Falls *(p112)*, where you'll be

① Overlooking the Hudson River Valley.

② *When Anthony Met Stanton* statue, Seneca Falls.

③ Niagara Falls, on the US side.

④ An appetizer at Altius, Pittsburgh.

⑤ The towering buildings of modern Pittsburgh.

spending the day. Start with a visit to Niagara Falls State Park, for a scenic overview of the American Falls. You can also take the Cave of the Winds elevator ride to the base of the falls, and the famous *Maid of the Mist* boat.

Day 5

It's a long 250-mile (402-km) drive to Pittsburgh from Niagara (the fastest option is to take I-90 and I-79), but there's plenty to see on route. Make a pit-stop at the lakeside town of Erie (around halfway), where you can peruse the Erie Maritime Museum *(50 E Front St, Erie)* and grab a filling lunch at waterside Sloppy Duck Saloon *(www. sloppyducksaloon.com)*. The more leisurely route to Pittsburgh involves cutting across the heart of Allegheny National Forest (principally Hwy-219 and Hwy-66), stopping where the fancy takes you.

Day 6

Start your tour of Pittsburgh *(p130)* with a stroll around Point State Park to see where the Allegheny and Monongahela rivers come together to form the Ohio, and visit Fort Pitt Museum, to learn about the city's origins. The Andy Warhol Museum, a fine tribute to the local artist, is a must for any lover of modern art. It's also worth taking the city's historic incline railway to enjoy the sensational views from Mount Washington. Make sure you try a Primanti Bros. sandwich before leaving town, and splurge at Altius *(www.altiuspgh.com)* for a memorable dinner with truly stellar views.

Day 7

New York City is around 370 miles (595 km) from Pittsburgh, but with an early start you should be able to squeeze in a tour of Frank Lloyd Wright's utterly enchanting Fallingwater *(p129)* on the way. The poignant Flight 93 National Memorial, commemorating those lost on 9/11, is just 40 miles (64 km) further on, and the final stretch of I-78 in Pennsylvania cuts through Amish country *(p128)*. Have a traditional "Dutch" dinner at Deitsch Eck Restaurant *(www.the-eck.com)* before continuing 112 miles (180 km) on to New York City to end your fantastic week.

→

1 Morning in Central Park.

2 Artisan cheese sold at Eataly NYC Downtown.

3 The reflective pools of the National September 11 Memorial, overlooked by One World Trade Center.

4 Walkers enjoying the elevated High Line at dusk.

2 DAYS
in New York City

Day 1

Morning Start your day with a take out bagel and coffee in Central Park (p96). Try to arrive at the Met (p101) by opening time at 10am (from the southern end of the park, on 59th St, it takes around 40 minutes to walk to the museum). You could spend days marveling at the wonders inside the Met, but focus on the highlights over 2–3 hours; we suggest the European paintings section, plus the Temple of Dendur.

Afternoon Grab a cab or bus on Madison Avenue down to Grand Central (p92) for a quick seafood lunch at the Oyster Bar. From here walk (or take a bus) down to the Empire State Building (p91), to soak up the Art Deco splendor and those magnificent views. If you still have energy left, it's a 15-minute ride on bus #M34 to Hudson Yards and the northern end of the High Line (p88), which makes for a lovely stroll in the late afternoon or early evening light.

Evening Have dinner in the Meatpacking District (p87), at the southern end of the High Line.

Day 2

Morning Grab your camera and jump on a narrated cruise from the Seaport District's Pier 16 (p81) around Liberty and Ellis islands (p80). Afterward, walk or take a cab across to the National September 11 Memorial (p79), taking in the waterfalls and tranquil groves of oak.

Afternoon Have lunch at Eataly NYC Downtown, over in 4 World Trade Center, before walking down Broadway to Wall Street and the Stock Exchange (p78). From Pier 11, where Wall Street meets the East River, take the ferry across to the Fulton Ferry District in Brooklyn (p104). Grab an ice cream and enjoy wandering the streets of this historic district before strolling back across the Brooklyn Bridge (p80) for unmissable views of Manhattan.

Evening From the bridge it's a short walk to Chinatown (p84), where tasty dinners await at Joe's Shanghai (9 Pell St). Night owls should continue on to SoHo for evening drinks in one of the neighborhood's fashionable bars (p86).

The New York Deli

A city institution, the deli was traditionally a Jewish affair. Find smoked fish and bagels at Zabar's *(www.zabars.com)* and Russ & Daughters *(www. russanddaughters.com)*. Katz's Deli is famed for its giant pastrami sandwiches *(www.katzsdelicatessen. com)*. Alleva Dairy *(188 Grand St)* is a classic Italian deli, while Brooklyn's Sahadi's *(www.sahadis.com)* is a Middle Eastern specialist.

←

Salami and pickles galore at Katz's Deli in the Lower East Side

NEW YORK CITY FOR
FOODIES

Foodies are in for a treat in New York. Just about every type of cuisine is showcased here, from Colombian and Armenian to Korean and Senegalese, with prices ranging from $1 pizza slices to some of the world's most expensive and prestigious French gourmet and farm-to-table restaurants.

→

Irresistible desserts at Le Bernardin, Midtown West and the Theater District

BRUNCH IN NYC

Sunday brunch is a big deal in New York. Special brunch menus (which sometimes include booze) attract long lines at the most popular spots; traditionally in Greenwich Village *(p87)*, SoHo *(p86)*, and the Lower East Side, but now just as prevalent in Brooklyn *(p104)*. Carroll Gardens, Cobble Hill, and Williamsburg are especially busy. Reserve a table in advance to avoid disappointment.

America's Fine Dining Capital

Looking to splash out? Thomas Keller's Per Se *(www.thomas keller.com)* is an award-winner, while Eric Ripert's Le Bernardin *(www.le-bernardin.com)* has three Michelin stars. Chef's Table at Brooklyn Fare *(www.brooklynfare.com)* and Eleven Madison Park *(www.elevenmadisonpark.com)* are also stellar choices.

The New York Food Hall

With the success of Eataly *(www.eataly.net)* and Brooklyn food fair Smorgasburg *(www.smorgasburg.com)*, gourmet food halls are all the rage in New York. Le District *(www.ledistrict.com)* has a French theme, while Great Northern Food Hall in Grand Central Terminal *(p92)* is Scandinavian, and Plaza Food Hall *(www.theplazany.com)* is upscale. Dekalb Market Hall *(www.dekalbmarkethall.com)* has everything from sushi to key lime pie.

←

Drinkers and diners at
Dekalb Market Hall in Brooklyn

💬 INSIDER TIP
Food Tours

Food walking tours are a great way to see the city and fuel up in the process. Top tours include NoshWalks *(www.noshwalks.com)* and Scott's Pizza Tours *(www.scottspizzatours.com)*.

All American Icons

Lombardi's *(www.firstpizza.com)*, founded in 1905, was America's first pizzeria, but Patsy's *(www.patsys.com)* sold the first pizza slice in 1933. Polish-Jewish Nathan Handwerker popularized Coney Island's hot dog, now sold at Nathan's Famous *(www.nathansfamous.com)*, while German émigré Arnold Reuben invented New York-style cheesecake, best sampled at Junior's *(p105)*. Meanwhile the "cronut" (croissant-donut pastry) is sold at 189 Spring St.

↑ Nathan's Famous and "cronuts" *(inset)*, old and new American icons

→
Led Zeppelin tribute
concert at prestigious
Carnegie Hall

NEW YORK CITY
LIVE!

Although the glittering lights of Broadway are mesmerizing, New York offers countless forms of live entertainment across the city – from music and comedy to live TV recordings. Better still, there's something to suit every budget, from lavish concerts at Carnegie Hall to free jazz nights.

Comedy Clubs

New York's comedy clubs often feature artists you'll recognize and nightly shows. Carolines on Broadway *(1626 Broadway)* is one of the most famous, while Comic Strip Live *(1568 Second Av)* has been around since 1975, and Dangerfield's *(1118 First Av)* since 1969. The Gotham Comedy Club *(208 W 23rd St)* has starred in many shows. The West Village has more options *(p88)*.

Sydnee Washington ↑
performs stand-up at
Carolines on Broadway

Music

You're spoiled for choice when it comes to live music in the Big Apple. Arlene's Grocery *(95 Stanton St)* offers grungy rock and punk at its Lower East Side venue, which hosted big names such as The Strokes, Lady Gaga, and Arcade Fire in their early years. Prestigious Carnegie Hall (881 7th Av), meanwhile, is New York's *grande dame* of concert venues, and primarily hosts classical music. New York is one of the cradles of jazz. Major venues include the iconic Blue Note *(131 West 3rd St)* and Village Vanguard *(178 Seventh Av)* in Greenwich Village, and Birdland *(315 West 44th St)* in Midtown. Nuyorican Poets Café *(236 East 3rd St)*, in the East Village *(p87)*, is a Latino-oriented venue hosting hip-hop, perform-ance art, live poetry readings, and other theater performances.

← Live jazz performance at iconic Birdland in Midtown

TOP **5**
NEW YORK JAZZ LEGENDS

Louis Armstrong (1901-71)
The legendary trumpet player settled in Queens in 1943 and lived here for almost 30 years.

Duke Ellington (1899-1974)
Based in New York City from the mid-1920s, he had a famed residency at the Cotton Club.

Billie Holiday (1915-1959)
"Lady Day" began singing in Harlem jazz clubs in 1929.

Wynton Marsalis (1961-)
Trumpeter and current artistic director of Jazz at Lincoln Center.

Sonny Rollins (1930-)
The saxophonist grew up in Harlem and recorded live at Village Vanguard in 1957.

💬 INSIDER TIP
Free Live Music

Arlene's Grocery has free punk karaoke with a live band on Mondays. Sidewalk Café, Saint Vitus, Warsaw, and Otto's Shrunken Head are free indie venues. Marjorie Eliot's has free jazz 3:30–6pm Sundays.

Live Late-Night TV Show Tapings

To experience American TV up close, apply online for free tickets to be part of the "live audience" at shows taped in New York City. Comedy Central's *Daily Show with Trevor Noah* is recorded at 733 11th Av, while *The Late Show with Stephen Colbert* tapes at 1697 Broadway. NBC rival *The Tonight Show with Jimmy Fallon* shows at 30 Rockefeller Plaza. *Late Night with Seth Meyers* is also taped here.

↑ Bryan Cranston with host Stephen Colbert on *The Late Show with Stephen Colbert*

NEW YORK CITY

The USA's biggest city owes its existence mainly to the Dutch, who founded New Amsterdam at the mouth of the Hudson River in the 1620s. The region had previously been wilderness populated by the Lenape people, from whom the land was bought by the Dutch. The colony flourished as a fur-trade port, despite its capture by Britain in 1664, and it was renamed New York. The New York Stock Exchange got its start on Wall Street in 1792, and the opening of the Erie Canal in 1825 cemented New York's position as a premier entrepôt. After the Civil War the economy boomed again, led by the Astors, Morgans, Rockefellers, and Vanderbilts of the Gilded Age. Their lavish mansions were a stark contrast to the tenements inhabited by the millions of immigrants who were pouring in, creating the "melting pot" still in evidence today. In the 20th century, New York City became the nation's cultural as well as business capital, from Broadway musicals and the Harlem Jazz Age of the 1920s, to the Beat poets, Andy Warhol's Pop Art, and Bronx hip hop. It remains one of the world's most famous and visited cities.

NEW YORK CITY

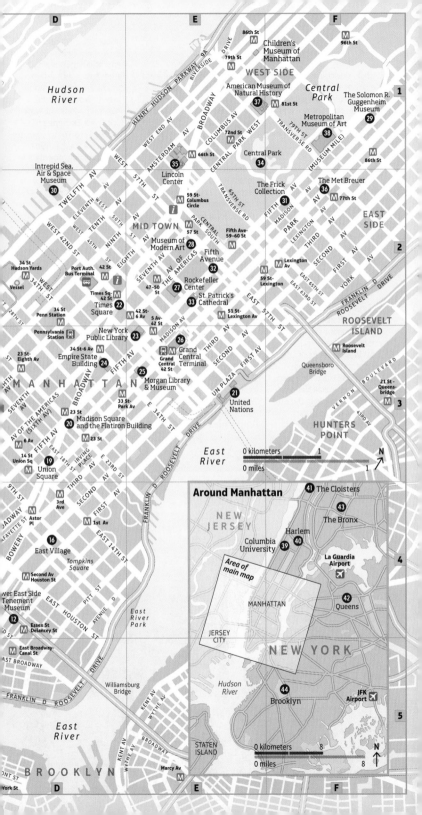

D
E
F

Hudson
River

86th St

Children's
Museum of
Manhattan

79th St

96th St

WEST SIDE

1

American Museum of
Natural History

Central
Park

The Solomon R.
Guggenheim
Museum

37 81st St

72nd St

Metropolitan
Museum of Art

38

29

Central Park

34

86th St

66th St

35 Lincoln
Center

59 St-
Columbus
Circle

The Frick
Collection

The Met Breuer

31

36

77th St

EAST
SIDE

MID TOWN

57 St

Museum of
Modern Art

28

59 St-
59–60 St

Fifth
Avenue

32

Lexington
Av

59 St-
Lexington

2

Intrepid Sea,
Air & Space
Museum

30

Port Auth.
Bus Terminal

34 St-
Hudson Yards

Vessel

42 St

Rockefeller
Center

47–50
St

27

St. Patrick's
Cathedral

33

51 St-
Lexington Av

Times Sq-
42 St

22

Times
Square

42 St-
6 Av

5 Av-
42 St

34 St
Penn Station

Pennsylvania
Station

New York
Public Library

23

26

Grand
Central
Terminal

Grand
Central
42 St

ROOSEVELT
ISLAND

Roosevelt
Island

Queensboro
Bridge

21 St-
Queensbridge

3

23 St-
Eighth Av

34 St-6 Av

Empire State
Building

24

FIFTH AV

25

Morgan Library
& Museum

33 St-
Park Av

United
Nations

21

HUNTERS
POINT

MANHATTAN

23 St

20

Madison Square
and the Flatiron Building

23 St

East
River

0 kilometers   1

0 miles   1

14 St-
Union Sq

19

Union
Square

3rd
Av

1st Av

Around Manhattan

41 The Cloisters

43

The Bronx

Astor
Pl

16

East Village

Tompkins
Square

NEW
JERSEY

Harlem

40

Columbia
University

39

La Guardia
Airport

4

Second Av
Houston St

wer East Side
Tenement
Museum

Area of
main map

MANHATTAN

42

Queens

12

Essex St
Delancey St

East
River
Park

JERSEY
CITY

NEW YORK

East Broadway-
Canal St

AST BROADWAY

Williamsburg
Bridge

Hudson
River

44

Brooklyn

JFK
Airport

5

East
River

STATEN
ISLAND

0 kilometers   8

0 miles   8

BROOKLYN

Marcy Av

D
E
F

MANHATTAN

With its skyscrapers and bright lights, the "Gateway to America" is a city of superlatives. Most of the major sights lie within Manhattan, with its glittering shops and museums lining the streets of Midtown and along Central Park. Dynamic and diverse, New York City offers everything in abundance; no wonder that, as the saying goes, it's a city so nice, they named it twice.

①

Wall Street

C5 **S** Wall St, Rector St

Named for the Dutch wall that kept rival colonists from England out of Manhattan, Wall Street is now the heart of the city's financial district. One of the prominent sites near here is the Federal Reserve Bank on Liberty Street. Inspired by the Italian Renaissance, this is a government bank for banks, where US currency is issued.

On Wall Street itself a bronze statue of George Washington sits on the steps of the Federal Hall National Monument, marking the site where the nation's first president took his oath of office in 1789. The current imposing structure was built between 1834 and 1842 as the US Custom House, and is one of the finest Greek Revival designs in the city.

At the head of Wall Street is **Trinity Church**. Built in 1846, this square-towered Episcopal church is the third one on this site, in one of America's oldest Anglican parishes, founded in 1697. Designed by British-American architect Richard Upjohn, it was one of the grandest churches of its day, marking the beginning of the most fertile period of Gothic Revival architecture in America. Its huge steeple was New York's tallest structure until 1883, when it was surpassed by the stone tower of the famous Brooklyn Bridge. Many famous New Yorkers are buried here, including Founding Father (and now hip-hop icon) Alexander Hamilton.

The hub of the world's financial markets, the **New York Stock Exchange** (NYSE) is housed in a 17-story building that was built in 1903. Initially, trading took place haphazardly in the area, but a small consortium of brokers signed an agreement in 1792 to deal only with one another, forming the basis of the NYSE. Membership was strictly limited, and a "seat" that cost $25 in 1817 can now cost several million dollars. The NYSE has weathered several slumps and booms over the years, and has seen advances in technology from ticker tape to electronic trading.

Trinity Church
Broadway at Wall St
7am–6pm daily trinity wallstreet.org

New York Stock Exchange
20 Broad St Visitors' gallery nyse.com

2

One World Trade Center and 9/11 Memorial

C4 **A** Greenwich St, between Fulton and Liberty sts **S** Cortlandt St, Rector St, WTC Station

The area known as Ground Zero after the 9/11 attacks has been utterly transformed. At its heart is the poignant **9/11 Memorial**, comprising a plaza of nearly 400 oak trees and twin pools that shimmer in the spaces where the Twin Towers once stood. The **9/11 Memorial Museum** looks at the history of the World Trade Center and the attacks, including personal testimonies and tributes.

At **One World Trade Center**, the tallest skyscraper in the US, high-speed elevators whisk visitors to the 102nd floor for unparalleled views of the city. The multi-billion-dollar complex includes five other skyscrapers and the Oculus, a futuristic subway station and mall whose steel ribs resemble a giant dinosaur skeleton.

FEARLESS GIRL AND THE BULL

In 2017, Wall Street's famous *Charging Bull* was challenged by another bronze sculpture known simply as the *Fearless Girl*. Designed by Kristen Visbal, the image of a small girl defiantly staring down the beast quickly became a feminist icon, despite being commissioned as part of a marketing campaign for a gender-diverse index fund. Mayor De Blasio agreed that *Fearless Girl* could stay for 11 months; in 2019, she was moved to a more accessible location in front of the New York Stock Exchange as the crowds milling around the statues on Broadway posed a traffic hazard.

KRISTEN VISBAL'S FEARLESS GIRL

9/11 Memorial & Museum
⊛ **C** Memorial: 7:30am–9pm daily; Museum: 9am–8pm Sun–Thu (last adm: 6pm), 9am–9pm Fri & Sat (last adm: 7pm) **W** 911memorial.org

One World Trade Center
⊛ ⊕ ⊕ ⊕ **C** Times vary, check website **W** oneworld observatory.com

3

The Battery

B5 **S** S Ferry, Bowling Green **W** thebattery.org

This 18th-century park, named for the British cannons that once protected New York, is one of the best places in the city for great views of the harbor. Its statues and monuments include Castle Clinton and the East Coast Memorial, dedicated to US servicemen killed in the Atlantic during World War II. Other attractions include the SeaGlass Carousel, an aquatic-themed merry-go-round, and the Pier A Harbor House, built as the New York Harbor Police headquarters in 1886 and now home to bars and restaurants.

On the east side of the park is the National Museum of the American Indian, housed in the stately US Custom House. The museum houses over a million artifacts along with photographs representing American Indian culture. On the west side, the Museum of Jewish Heritage stands as a memorial to the victims of the Holocaust, beginning with everyday Eastern European Jewish life pre-1930, moving through the the Holocaust, and ending with the establishment of Israel.

← One World Trade Center looming high over the city skyline

④ 🗺️ 💻 🏛️
Statue of Liberty

📍A5 🚇Liberty Island 🚇S Ferry, Bowling Green 🚌To S Ferry, then Statue Cruises from the Battery 🕐Jul-Aug: 9am-6pm daily; Sep-Jun: 9:30am-5pm daily 🚫Dec 25 🌐nps.gov/stli

The figure of Roman goddess Libertas presiding over New York harbor, titled *Liberty Enlightening the World*, has been the symbol of freedom for millions since her inauguration by President Grover Cleveland in 1886. A gift from the French to the American people to mark the centenary of the US Declaration of Independence in 1876, the statue was the brainchild of sculptor Frédéric-Auguste Bartholdi. In Emma Lazarus's poem, which is engraved on the base, Lady Liberty says: "Give me your tired, your poor, / Your huddled masses yearning to breathe free."

The 305-ft- (93-m-) high statue stands on a pedestal set within the walls of an old army fort. In one hand Liberty holds a torch with a 24-carat gold-leaf flame, while in the other is a book inscribed "July 4, 1776" in Roman numerals. The rays of her crown represent the seven seas and seven continents. The crown was closed to the public following the September 11 attacks, but reopened in 2009. Groups of 10 people at a time can now climb up the 377 steps from the main lobby to this level.

⑤
Governors Island

📍B5 🚇S Ferry, Bowling Green 🕐May-Oct: 10am-6pm Mon-Fri, 10am-7pm Sat & Sun 🌐govisland.com

With its village greens and colonial halls reminiscent of a college campus, this vast island in New York Harbor makes for a great day trip.

Between 1794 and 1966, the US Army occupied the island, and it was the US Coast Guard's largest base for the next 30 years. Since 2003, the island has been shared between the city and the National Park Service. On the northwest corner of the island, Castle Williams was built in 1811 to complement near-identical Castle Clinton in the Battery. Used as a prison until 1966, its cramped cells held up to 1,000 Confederate soldiers during the Civil War.

The island has plenty of green spaces, ideal for relaxing in on sunny days, and a breezy promenade. Along with the visitor center, there is a beach, Hammock Grove (featuring comfy red hammocks), the Hills (four man-made hills, rising high above the harbor), and a small museum, plus an ever-changing program of festivals, exhibitions, and other events.

⑥
Brooklyn Bridge

📍C5 🚇Chambers St; Brooklyn Bridge-City Hall (Manhattan side); High St, Brooklyn Bridge (Brooklyn side) 🚌

An engineering wonder when it was built in 1883, the Brooklyn Bridge linked Manhattan and Brooklyn, then two separate cities. At that time it was the

←

The 305-ft- (93-m-) high Statue of Liberty dominating the New York City harbor

↑ The spectacular steel cablework of the Brooklyn Bridge

world's largest suspension bridge and the first to be constructed of steel. The German-born engineer John A. Roebling conceived of a bridge spanning the East River while ice-bound on a ferry to Brooklyn. The bridge took 16 years to build, required 600 workers, and claimed over 20 lives, including Roebling's. Most died of caisson disease (known as "the bends") after coming up from the underwater excavation chambers. From the pedestrian walkway there are fabulous views of the city towers, seen through the artistic cablework.

7 🍴 🛍

Seaport District NYC

📍 C5 🏠 19 Fulton St
Ⓢ Fulton St 🕐 Times vary,
check website 🌐 seaport
district.nyc

This district of cobbled streets – part of New York's original working dockyards – has been preserved since 1966, and today houses all manner of shops and restaurants. Since Hurricane Sandy hit in 2012, the site has been transformed. An iPic

Theater opened in the Fulton Market building and **Pier 17** has been rebuilt, with a shopping mall, the Riverdeck (an outdoor bar with the best views of the Brooklyn Bridge), and the Rooftop, hosting the Summer Concert Series.

South Street Seaport Museum has a vast collection of maritime art and artifacts, and owns several historic ships docked nearby. Those open to visitors include the *Ambrose*, a 1908 lightship, the *Wavertree*,

a graceful tall ship built in Southampton, England, in 1885, and the *Pioneer*, which cruises the harbor in summer.

Pier 17
🏠 89 South St 🕐 Check
website 🌐 pier17ny.com

South Street Seaport Museum
♿ 🎫 🏠 12 Fulton St
🕐 11am–5pm Wed–Sun
🌐 southstreetseaport
museum.org

STONE STREET

Nestled away a few blocks from South Street Seaport Museum is narrow, cobbled Stone Street. Many of its charming Greek Revival houses were built after the Great Fire of 1835, which ravaged the area. Today, this is a great place to eat and drink. On summer nights it's a vast open-air beer garden, with bars like Ulysses and restaurants like Adrienne's Pizzabar covering the street with tables.

8 🌿 🏛 🍴 ☕ 🛍

ELLIS ISLAND

📍A5 🏛Ellis Island 🚇Bowling Green, Whitehall, then Statue Cruises from the Battery 🕐9:30am–5:15pm daily (extended hours during Federal hols) 🌐libertyellisfoundation.org

Almost 40 percent of the country's population can trace their roots to historic Ellis Island, the country's immigration depot from 1892 until 1954. The gateway to America is now a remarkable museum paying homage to the greatest wave of migration the world has ever known.

Ellis Island Immigration Museum

During its tenure, nearly 12 million people passed through Ellis Island's gates and dispersed across the country. Centered on the Great Hall, or Registry Room, the site today houses the three-story Ellis Island Immigration Museum. Its history is told with photographs and the voices of actual immigrants, and an electronic database traces ancestors. Outside, the American Immigrant Wall of Honor is the largest wall of names in the world, with more than 12,000 inscriptions. No other place explains so well the "melting pot" that formed the character of the nation.

Visit early to avoid the crowds. Entry to the museum is included in the ferry fare. The ferry generally departs every 20–30 mins but do check online in advance.

↑ The Medical Examining Rooms, where immigrants with contagious diseases could be refused entry

The architects were inspired by the French Beaux Arts style.

→ Ellis Island, New York City's immigration depot from 1892 to 1954.

The ferry office sold tickets to New Jersey.

← Some of the immigrants' meager possessions, held in the Baggage Room

GREAT HALL

Newly arrived immigrants were made to wait for "processing" in the huge, vaulted Great Hall on the second floor. Some days, over 5,000 people would wait to be inspected and registered; if required, medical and legal examinations also took place here. Once the scene of so much trepidation, today the room has been left imposingly bare, with just a couple of inspectors' desks, and original wooden benches.

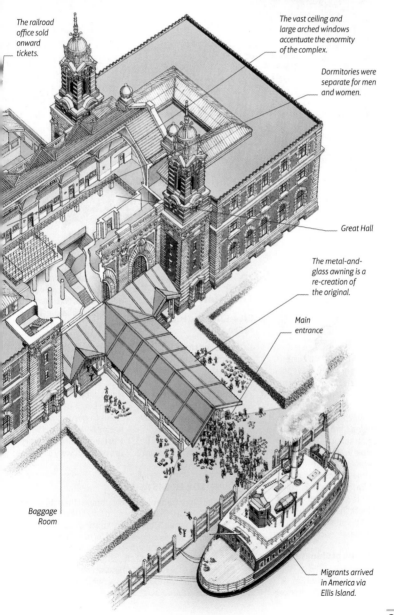

The railroad office sold onward tickets.

The vast ceiling and large arched windows accentuate the enormity of the complex.

Dormitories were separate for men and women.

Great Hall

The metal-and-glass awning is a re-creation of the original.

Main entrance

Baggage Room

Migrants arrived in America via Ellis Island.

A sign welcoming visitors to the Little Italy neighborhood ↑

⑨ 🍴 🏛

Chinatown

📍 C4 🏠 Around Mott St
Ⓢ Canal St ⓦ explore
chinatown.com

More than 200,000 Chinese Americans live in New York's largest and most colorful multi-cultural neighborhood. The shops and sidewalks overflow with exotic foods and gifts ranging from backscratchers to fine antiques, but most people visit to eat in one of the more than 200 restaurants.

Other sights here include the Eastern States Buddhist Temple and the **Museum of Chinese in America**, which provides an overview of the Chinese-American experience.

Museum of Chinese in America
♿ 🚫 📍 215 Center St
🕐 Tue–Sun ⓦ mocanyc.org

⑩ 🍴 🏛

Little Italy and Nolita

📍 C4 🏠 Around Mulberry St
Ⓢ Canal St

Little Italy and Nolita (short for "North of Little Italy") became home to southern Italian immigrants in the late 19th century. They preserved their language, customs, and food, making Mulberry Street lively with the colors, flavors, and atmosphere of Italy. Today the 10-day Feast of San Gennaro in September draws crowds of joyful celebrants. Some of the original cafés and *salumerias* (specialty food stores) survive nearby, such as Ferrara's at 195 Grand St and Di Palo's Fine Foods at 200 Grand St. Also on Mulberry Street is the Gothic-Revival style Basilica of St. Patrick's Old Cathedral. Nolita, meanwhile, is home to stylish boutiques and vintage stores frequented by well-heeled New Yorkers. The **New Museum of Contemporary Art** on the Bowery showcases

---

JEWISH LOWER EAST SIDE

Jewish immigrants have indelibly stamped their character on the LES. On East Houston, head to Katz's Deli for pastrami sandwiches, Yonah Schimmel for knishes, and Russ & Daughters for bagels; check out p70 for more. The Forward Building on East Broadway became the HQ of the Jewish daily *The Forward,* while Shtiebel Row is home to dozens of storefront *shtieblach* (small Jewish congregations). Find out about local tours at www.nycjewishtours.org.

① ⊘ ⓜ 🛍

Museum at Eldridge Street

🅠 C5 🏛 12 Eldridge St
Ⓢ E Broadway ⏰ 10am–
5pm Sun–Thu, 10am–3pm
Fri 🌐 eldridgestreet.org

This Moorish-style synagogue was the first large temple built in the US by Jewish immigrants from Eastern Europe, from where 80 percent of American Jews came. At the turn of the century, it was the most flamboyant temple in the neighborhood, and as many as 1,000 people attended services here. As congregants left the area, attendance waned and the temple closed in the 1950s. The synagogue is now a National Historic Landmark and houses exhibitions of ritual objects, archival documents, and other artifacts.

② ⊘ ⓜ

Lower East Side Tenement Museum

🅠 D4 🏛 97 Orchard St
Ⓢ Canal St, Delancey St, Essex St ⏰ Times vary, check website 🌐 tenement.org

This 1863 building provides a rare opportunity to view the cramped living conditions experienced by immigrants and migrants in the crumbling interior of a tenement building. The apartments have been re-created to reflect the lives of its tenants in the mid-19th century, when indoor toilets were rare and there was no plumbing, electricity, or heat, to the mid-20th century, when many families ran cottage industries out of their homes. The building's past is brought to life by guided tours.

the city's most avant-garde art. The building is as much of an attraction as the shows inside.

New Museum of Contemporary Art
⊛ ⓜ 🛍 🏛 235 Bowery
🗓 Mon 🌐 newmuseum.org

EAT

Chinese Tuxedo
Hip Chinese restaurant serving inventive dishes and cocktails.

🏛 5 Doyers St
🌐 chinesetuxedo.com

$⑤$

Dirt Candy
Stylish vegetarian and vegan food from lauded chef Amanda Cohen.

🏛 86 Allen St 🗓 Mon
🌐 dirtcandynyc.com

$⑤$

Ferrara Café
Traditional Italian café with a vast range of Italian pastries.

🏛 195 Grand St
🌐 ferraranyc.com

$⑤$

Ivan Ramen
No-frills joint serving noodles, ramen, and steamed buns.

🏛 25 Clinton St
🌐 ivanramen.com

$⑤$

←
The stunning interior of the Museum at Eldridge Street, a former synagogue

13

Washington Square

C4 **Greenwich Village** **W 4 St**

Today one of New York's most vibrant open public spaces, Washington Square was once a marshland that was filled to form a park. Stanford White's magnificent Washington Memorial Arch, completed in 1895, replaced the original wooden version that marked the centenary of George Washington's inauguration. In 1916, a group of artists led by John Sloan and Marcel Duchamp broke in, climbed atop the arch, and declared the "free and independent republic of Washington Square, the state of New Bohemia." Today most of the buildings surrounding the park are part of New York University (NYU).

THE STONEWALL RIOTS

The Stonewall Inn dates back to the 1840s, but after becoming a gay bar in 1966 it suffered regular police harassment. During a police raid on June 28, 1969, protestors fought back against the police for the first time, resulting in several arrests and some injured police officers. The event informally inaugurated the gay-rights movement. In 2016, the "Stonewall National Monument" was dedicated to the ongoing efforts for LGBT+ rights.

14

SoHo

C4 **S of Houston St; Greene St** **Canal St, Spring St, Prince St**

The largest concentration of cast-iron architecture in the world survives in this former industrial district. SoHo was saved from demolition in the 1960s, and by the 1980s it had developed its own vibrant art scene. It now chiefly serves as

a large outdoor shopping mall, scattered with bars and bistros, with Broadway its main drag. Its historic heart is Greene Street, where 50 cast-iron buildings are stretched out over a five-block area. The finest are those at Nos 72–76, the "King," and Nos 28–30, the "Queen." Over on Broadway, the Singer Building was built by Ernest Flagg in 1904. This ornate 12-story building was an office and warehouse for the Singer sewing machine company. SoHo's legacy of fine art galleries is maintained at the Drawing Center at No 35 Wooster Street, with changing exhibitions of historical and contemporary drawings. The

Leafy Washington Square Park, home to the Washington Memorial Arch *(inset)*

innovative Leslie-Lohman Museum of Gay and Lesbian Art at No 26 Wooster Street has a permanent collection of over 30,000 objects, spanning over three centuries of LGBT+ art.

Greenwich Village

🅚 C3 🅐 N of Houston St & S of 14th St 🅢 W 4 St-Washington Sq, Christopher St-Sheridan Sq, 8 St

"The Village" has been a bohemian haven and home to many celebrated writers, artists, and musicians. Later, it became a popular LGBT+ district, whose cafés, theaters, and clubs come alive at night. A stroll through its narrow old-fashioned lanes reveals charming row houses, hidden alleys, and leafy courtyards. The 15 Italianate houses lining the north side of St. Luke's Place date from the 1850s. Poet Marianne Moore lived here, and Theodore Dreiser wrote *An American Tragedy* at No 16. The heart of the Village is Sheridan Square, where seven streets meet in a maze known as "The Mousetrap."

Reveling in the lively atmosphere of Bua bar, the East Village

Jefferson Market Courthouse was built in 1877 and turned into a library in 1967. Opposite is Patchin Place, a group of 19th-century houses where playwright Eugene O'Neill and poets John Masefield and E. E. Cummings lived. Northwest of Greenwich Village lies the fashionable Meatpacking District, crammed with clubs, bars, and restaurants.

East Village

🅚 D4 🅐 14th St to Houston St 🅢 Astor Pl, 1 Av

Prominent New Yorkers lived in this fomer Dutch enclave until they moved uptown in the mid-19th century. Thereafter, it was home to German, Jewish, Irish, and Ukrainian immigrants. In the 1960s it became a haven for hippies and punks. Today, it is home to bohemian cafés, lively restaurants, vintage stores, and indie movie houses.

The six-story Cooper Union was set up in 1859. Its Great Hall was inaugurated in 1859 by Mark Twain, and Abe Lincoln delivered his "Right Makes Might" speech there in 1860. The 1832 **Merchant's House Museum**, a remarkable Greek Revival brick town house, is a time capsule of a vanished way of life. The English-style Tompkins Square Park was the site of America's first organized labor demonstration in 1874, the main gathering place during the neighborhood's hippie era and, in 1988, an arena for riots when the police tried to evict the homeless occupants.

Merchant's House Museum
🅐 29 E Fourth St 🕐 Noon–5pm Mon & Fri–Sun, noon–8pm Thu 🌐 merchantshouse.org

DRINK

Death & Company
Lauded cocktail bar with a charming, speakeasy theme and a huge menu of creative drinks with names such as "Cloud Nine" and "Clockwork Orange."

🅐 433 E Sixth St
🌐 deathandcompany.com

Ghost Donkey
Cozy tequila and mezcal cocktail bar. Nachos and other Mexican-inspired bar snacks served.

🅐 4 Bleecker St
🌐 ghostdonkey.com

Bua
Open-fronted (in summer) for people-watching, this bar has a great happy hour.

🅐 122 St. Mark's Pl
🌐 buabar.com

↑ Admiring the view while walking along the elevated High Line

17 ⊘ Ⓜ 🍴 🛍

Whitney Museum of American Art

📍 C3 🏠 99 Gansevoort St
Ⓢ 14 St ⏰ 10:30am–6pm
Mon, Wed, Thu & Sun;
10:30am–10pm Fri & Sat
🚫 Some Federal hols
🌐 whitney.org

The Whitney showcases a range of American art from the 20th and 21st centuries in a stunning setting. The museum was founded in 1930 by sculptor Gertrude Vanderbilt Whitney. Having moved around the city, it settled in its present building, designed by Renzo Piano, in 2015.

The sixth and seventh floors showcase pieces from the permanent collection, while temporary exhibitions occupy the first, fifth, and eighth floors. Highlights include Alexander Calder's sculpture *Circus* (1926–31), and works by Edward Hopper, whose *Early Sunday Morning* (1930) depicts the emptiness of American city life.

The Whitney Biennial, a long-running exhibition of the latest breakthroughs in American art, is held here in even years.

18

High Line

📍 C3 🏠 Gansevoort St, 14th St, 16th St, 18th St & every 2–3 blocks to 34th St Ⓢ 23 St, 14 St ⏰ 7am–11pm daily (winter: to 7pm) 🌐 the highline.org

A fantastic reconstruction of what was once an elevated rail track, this ambitious urban renewal project links Chelsea, Midtown, and the Meatpacking District. The structure stands as an elevated promenade and public park, about 30 ft (9 m) in the air.

Built between 1929 and 1934, the rail line lay abandoned for a number of years before two locals created the "Friends of the High Line" organization in 1999. The aim was to save the structure from demolition. Today, the High Line offers incredible views of the city, and a variety of gardens to explore on route. The walk offers a subtle water feature between 14th and 15th streets, and an amphitheater with cinematic views of Tenth Avenue. The last fraction of the High Line curves around the shiny skyscrapers of the new Hudson Yards development toward the river.

Look out for "The Vessel," a monumental art installation by British designer Thomas Heatherwick, standing like giant honeycomb.

NIGHTLIFE AND COMEDY IN THE WEST VILLAGE

Its leafy parks and bustling squares aside, the West Village is a great place for a night out. The Comedy Cellar *(117 MacDougal St)* is one of the city's most iconic comedy clubs. Live jazz is also flourishing at the Village Vanguard *(178 Seventh Av)* and Blue Note *(131 W 3rd St)*. SOB's *(204 Varick St)* showcases hip-hop, Brazilian, West Indian, Caribbean and World Music acts; Terra Blues *(149 Bleecker St)* is an old-school blues club. Cabaret and piano bars such as Marie's Crisis *(59 Grove St)* and Duplex *(61 Christopher St)* continue to attract boisterous crowds.

---

⑲

Union Square

◉ D3 ⑤ 14 St-Union Sq
🖱 unionsquarenyc.org

Originally opened in 1839 before being redesigned in 1872, this park has served as the base for a long list of historical events, from the first Labor Day parade in 1882 through workers' rallies in the 1930s, to the first Earth Day in 1970. It eventually deteriorated into a somewhat seedy hangout until renovations transformed the area into a flourishing hub of Manhattan life, with markets, art vendors, street performers, and locals just taking it easy.

Beginning with just a handful of farmers in 1976, GrowNYC's Greenmarket now fills the square several times a week. The square is also ringed by a wide variety of cafés, bars, restaurants, and shops.

The park was designated a National Historic Landmark in 1997, and you can find several statues depicting historic figures such as George Washington, Abraham Lincoln, and Mahatma Gandhi dotted around the place.

---

⑳

Madison Square and the Flatiron Building

◉ D3 ⑤ 23 St ◷ Madison Square Park: 10am–9pm daily

Created in 1847 as the focus of Madison Square, leafy Madison Square Park is full of gardens, statues and contemporary art, while the original outpost of burger icon Shake Shack stands at its center. Today the park lies in the Flatiron District, named after the adjacent Flatiron Building. This skyscraper, its shape conforming to the triangular plot of land at the intersection of Fifth Avenue and Broadway, has intrigued New Yorkers since it was built by Chicago architect David Burnham in 1902. It became known as the "Flatiron" for its triangular shape, but some called it "Burnham's Folly," predicting that winds created by the building's shape would knock it down. It has, however, withstood the test of time and is now as much of a New York landmark as any other.

Opposite stands **Eataly NYC Flatiron** *(200 Fifth Av)*, a vast Italian food emporium packed with restaurants, espresso bars, gelato carts, and a charming beer garden on its roof. On the east side of Madison Square is the spectacular New York Life Insurance Company building *(51 Madison Av)* with its gold-leaf roof, completed in 1928 to a design by Cass Gilbert. Next door is the Appellate Division of the Supreme Court of the State of New York *(27 Madison Av)*, a marble palace designed by James Brown Lord in 1900. During the week, the public can admire the gorgeous interior, including the courtroom when it is not in session. Also on the east side of the square is the 54-story Metropolitan Life (or MetLife) Tower *(1 Madison Av)*. Built in 1909, it was the tallest building in the world until it was surpassed by the **Woolworth Building** on Wall Street in 1913.

Eataly NYC Flatiron
⌂ 200 Fifth Av ◷ 7am–11pm daily 🖱 eataly.com

Woolworth Building
⌂ 233 Broadway ◷ Daily for tours 🖱 woolworthtours.com

> Leafy Madison Square Park is full of gardens, statues, and contemporary art, while the original outpost of burger icon Shake Shack stands at its center.

←

Madison Square Park, in the heart of the Flatiron District

21

United Nations

📍 E3 🔼 First Av at 46th St
🚇 42 St-Grand Central 🚌
🕐 9am–4:45pm Mon–Fri
🚫 Federal hols, Eid 🌐 visit.
un.org

When New York was chosen as the UN headquarters in the 1940s, philanthropist and multimillionaire John D. Rockefeller, Jr. donated $8.5 million for the purchase of the East River site. This complex was the creation of American architect Wallace Harrison and a team of international consultants.

Currently 193 members meet each year from mid-September to mid-December in the General Assembly. The most powerful body is the Security Council, which strives to achieve peace and security, intervening in international crises, and is housed in the Conference Building.

Daily guided tours show visitors the various council chambers and the General Assembly hall, offering a behind-the-scenes view of the organization at work.

22 🚇

Times Square

📍 D2 🚇 42 St-Times Sq
🌐 timessquarenyc.org

Named for the New York Times Tower, Times Square is the city's most famous intersection. Although the *New York Times* has moved from its original headquarters at the square's southern end, the crystal ball still drops at midnight on New Year's Eve, as it has since 1906.

Since 1899, when Oscar Hammerstein built the Victoria and Republic theaters, this has also been the heart of the city's theater district. Other attractions include a Madame Tussauds at 42nd Street, a massive Disney Store, a traffic-free plaza, and M&M's World at 1600 Broadway.

Old-world Broadway glamor rubs shoulders with modern entertainment. MTV has its studios here, and E-Walk is a vast entertainment and retail complex. Exciting structures like the Bertelsmann Building and the minimalist 4 Times Square sit alongside classic establishments such as Sardi's and the Lyceum Theater.

23 🚇 🏛

New York Public Library

📍 E3 🔼 Fifth Av & 42nd St
🚇 42 St-Grand Central
🕐 10am–6pm Mon, Thu–Sat,
10am–8pm Tue & Wed,
1–5pm Sun 🚫 Federal hols
🌐 nypl.org

This library's white marble Beaux Arts edifice fulfilled its first director's vision of a light, quiet, airy place, where millions of books could be stored and yet be available to readers as promptly as possible. Built on the site of the former Croton Reservoir, it opened in 1911 to immediate acclaim. The architects' genius is best seen in the massive Main Reading Room, a vast paneled space as majestic as a cathedral, extending almost two city blocks. Below it are 88 miles (140 km) of shelves, holding over seven million volumes. The Periodicals Room holds 10,000 current periodicals from 128 countries. On its walls are murals by Richard Haas, honoring New York's great publishing houses. The original library combined the collections of John Jacob Astor and James Lenox. Its collections today range from Thomas Jefferson's handwritten copy of the original Declaration of Independence to T. S. Eliot's typed copy of "The Waste Land." Visit the Children's

---

💬 INSIDER TIP
TKTS

The Times Square TKTS booth, at Broadway and West 47th Street, is the go-to spot for discount tickets to Broadway shows. Lines are shorter at the TKTS booth in the Seaport District *(p81)*, at 190 Front Street.

←
Times Square glowing with neon lights and billboards as traffic hurries past

ENCOUNTERS IN THE SKY

The Empire State Building has starred in many movies, but the finale from the 1933 *King Kong* is the most iconic, with the giant ape straddling the spire. In 1945, a bomber flew too low over the city in fog and struck the building just above the 78th floor. The elevator operator made a lucky escape as she plunged 79 floors.

Center to see the real stuffed toy animals that inspired the beloved Winnie-the-Pooh stories by A. A. Milne, acquired by the library in 1987.

24 ⊗ ⊕

Empire State Building

⊙ D3 ⬚ 350 Fifth Av ⓢ 34 St, 33 St 🚌 ⊙ Observatories: 8am–2am daily (last elevators 1:15am) ⓦ esbnyc.com

The Empire State Building is still New York's most iconic skyscraper. Construction began in March 1930, not long after the stock market crash, and, by the time it opened in 1931, space was so difficult to rent that it was nicknamed the "Empty State Building." Only the immediate popularity of the observatories saved the building from bankruptcy – to date, they have attracted more than 120 million visitors – but the building soon became a symbol of the city the world over. It took only 410 days to build this 102-story limestone-and-brick skyscraper, with an average of four and a half stories added every week. The 102nd floor can be visited for an additional fee. The annual Empire State Run-Up is held each February, when 150 competitors race up the 1,576 steps from the lobby to the 86th floor in 10 minutes.

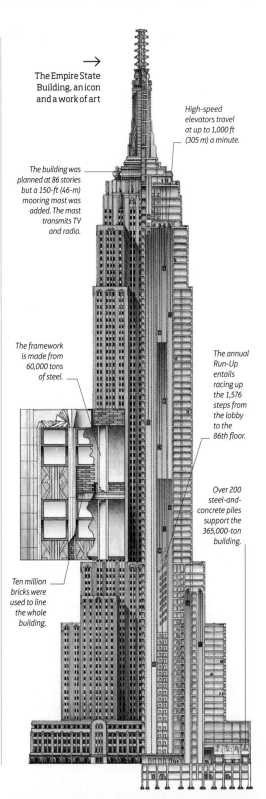

→
The Empire State Building, an icon and a work of art

High-speed elevators travel at up to 1,000 ft (305 m) a minute.

The building was planned at 86 stories but a 150-ft (46-m) mooring mast was added. The mast transmits TV and radio.

The framework is made from 60,000 tons of steel.

The annual Run-Up entails racing up the 1,576 steps from the lobby to the 86th floor.

Over 200 steel-and-concrete piles support the 365,000-ton building.

Ten million bricks were used to line the whole building.

25

Morgan Library & Museum

Q E3 **A** 225 Madison Av
S 33 St, 5 Av, Grand Central
O 10:30am-5pm Tue-Thu,
10:30am-9pm Fri, 10am-
6pm Sat, 11am-6pm Sun
(free 7-9pm Fri) **Q** Mon, Jan
1, Thanksgiving, Dec 25
W themorgan.org

This magnificent palazzo-style building was designed in 1902 to house the private collection of banker J. P. Morgan (1837–1913), one of the great collectors of his time. Established in 1924 as a public institution by Morgan's son, J. P. Morgan, Jr., it has a splendid collection of rare manuscripts, prints, books, and bindings.

The complex includes the original library and J. P. Morgan, Jr.'s home. Morgan, Sr.'s opulent study and his original library contain some of his favorite paintings, objets d'art, and a wide variety of cultural artifacts. Among the exhibits are one of the 11 surviving copies of the Gutenberg Bible (1455), printed on vellum, and six

surviving leaves of the score for Mozart's Horn Concerto in E-flat Major, written in different-colored inks.

The Garden Court, a three-story skylit garden area, links the library with the house. Exhibits are changed regularly.

26

Grand Central Terminal

Q E3 **A** E 42nd St at Park
Av **S** Grand Central
O 5:30am-2am daily
W grandcentralterminal.
com

One of the world's great rail terminals, this outstanding Beaux Arts building dates from 1913. Its glory is the main concourse, dominated by three great arched windows that fill the space with natural light. The high-vaulted ceiling is decorated with twinkling constellations. The information booth here is surmounted by a wonderful four-faced clock, while the Grand Staircase is styled after the staircase in Paris's Opera House.

→

The ornate interior of Grand Central's magnificent main hall

Today, Grand Central is an attraction in its own right, with a museum, over 40 shops, a gourmet food market, and fine restaurants, including the famed Oyster Bar. Also worth visiting is the Campbell bar, in a beautiful space that was formerly the private office of tycoon John W. Campbell.

27

Rockefeller Center

Q E2 **A** 630 Fifth Av
between 49th & 52nd sts
S 47-50 sts

This massive Art Deco complex has been at the very heart of Midtown since the 1930s. Today it encompasses Radio City Music Hall, 30 Rockefeller Plaza (or "30 Rock"), an underground shopping mall, and the Rainbow Room bar and restaurant. Perhaps it is most famous for its viewing deck –one of the city's highest – and much-loved holiday ice rink and Christmas tree. 30 Rock has long been the home of the

---

MIDTOWN MANHATTAN

Midtown Manhattan's skyline is graced with some of the city's most spectacular towers, from the familiar beauty of the Empire State Building's Art Deco pinnacle to the dramatic wedge of Citibank's modern headquarters. As the shoreline progresses uptown, the architecture becomes more varied. The United Nations complex dominates a long stretch, before Beekman Place begins a strand of exclusive residential enclaves, and the Chrysler Building looms over the stunning Grand Central Terminal.

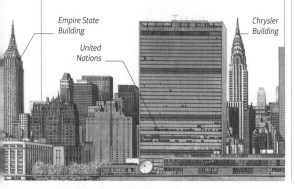

Empire State
Building

United
Nations

Chrysler
Building

50,000

The number of lights on the Rockefeller Center's annual Christmas tree.

NBC television network. See where *Saturday Night Live*, *The Tonight Show Starring Jimmy Fallon*, and *The Today Show* are filmed on the NBC Studio Tour. You can be a part of the *Today Show* outdoor audience simply by turning up before 7am on a weekday.

The center was originally commissioned by tycoon John D. Rockefeller, Jr. and designed by architect Raymond Hood. Rockefeller had leased the site in 1928, seeing it as a new home for the Met Opera, but the 1929 Depression scuttled those plans, and Rockefeller went ahead with his own development. The 14 buildings erected between 1931 and

1940 provided jobs for up to 225,000 people during the Depression; by 1973, there were 19 buildings.

Museum of Modern Art

📍E2 🚇11 W 53rd St
🚇5 Av-53 St 🚌 🕐10:30am-5:30pm Sat-Thu, 10:30am-8pm Fri (free for under 16s; free entry for all 4-8pm Fri)
🚫Thanksgiving, Dec 25
🅦moma.org

Founded in 1929, the Museum of Modern Art (MoMA) set the standard for other museums of its kind, and is now one of the world's most comprehensive collections of modern art. It was the first art museum to include utilitarian objects in its collection, from ball bearings and silicon chips to ordinary household appliances.

In 2019, MoMA reopened after a major renovation, with stunning new galleries and spaces for performance and events. The building provides

gallery space over six floors. MoMA's collection includes more than 150,000 works of art, ranging from Impressionist classics to an unrivaled collection of modern and contemporary art, including paintings, sculptures, prints, drawings, photographs, and graphic designs. Some of the highlights of the collection include well-known works, such as Picasso's *Les Demoiselles d'Avignon* (1907), van Gogh's *Starry Night* (1889), and Monet's *Water Lilies* (1920).

SHOP

Macy's
The merchandise inside the "world's largest store" includes any item you could imagine in every price range.

🏠151 W 34th St
🅦macys.com

The Solomon R. Guggenheim Museum

⑨F1 📍1071 Fifth Av at 89th St 🚇86 St 🚌
🕐10am–5:30pm Mon, Wed–Fri & Sun, 10am–8pm Tue & Sat 🚫Thu, Jan 1, Dec 25
🌐guggenheim.org

One of the world's finest collections of modern and contemporary art is housed in a building that is considered one of the great architectural achievements of the 20th century. The only New York building to be designed by the celebrated American architect Frank Lloyd Wright, it was completed after his death in 1959. Its shell-like facade is a New York landmark – its curves and asymmetry being in stark contrast to the surrounding Manhattan city grid – while the interior is dominated by a spiral ramp that curves down and inward from the dome. Not everyone was impressed when it first opened, however: one critic described it as "an indigestible hot cross bun."

The museum was named for its founder, a mining magnate, art collector, and proponent of "nonobjective" art – art that doesn't depict physical objects. The museum has continued to grow since it opened, housing works by the likes of Kandinsky, Calder, Picasso, Pollock, Degas, Cézanne, van Gogh, and Manet. Guggenheim was Kandinsky's biggest fan, buying many of his works, which are exhibited in the Kandinsky Gallery.

Today the Great Rotunda features special, temporary exhibitions. The Small Rotunda is dedicated to Impressionism and Post-Impressionism. The Tower galleries (also known as the Annex) exhibit works from the permanent collection as well as contemporary pieces. The permanent collection is shown on a rotating basis.

Intrepid Sea, Air & Space Museum

⑨D2 📍Pier 86, W 46th St 🚌 🕐Apr–Oct: 10am–5pm Mon–Fri, 10am–6pm Sat, Sun & federal hols; Nov–Mar: 10am–5pm daily
🌐intrepidmuseum.org

This ship museum chronicles military and maritime history and traces the progress of flight exploration, as well as being home to a variety of retired air and sea vessels from across the US armed forces. Exhibits on board this historic World War II aircraft carrier include fighter planes from the 1940s, the Lockheed A-12 Blackbird spy jet, and the USS *Growler*, a guided-missile submarine launched in 1958 at the height of the Cold War.

The workings of today's supercarriers are traced in Stern Hall, while Technologies Hall showcases the rockets of the future and includes two flight simulators. Mission Control offers live coverage of NASA shuttle missions and the Space Shuttle Pavilion houses the space shuttle *Enterprise* from 1972.

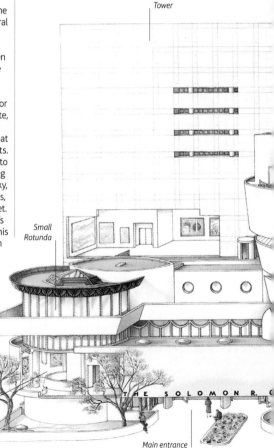

Tower

Small Rotunda

The Solomon R. Guggenheim Museum

Sackler Center for Arts Education

THE SOLOMON R.

Main entrance

The Frick Collection

F2 **E 70th St** **S 68 St** **10am-6pm Tue-Sat, 11am-5pm Sun; "Pay What You Wish" 2-6pm Wed** **Federal hols; children under 10** **frick.org**

The priceless art collection of steel magnate Henry Clay Frick (1849–1919) is exhibited in a residential setting amid the furnishings of his opulent mansion, providing a rare glimpse of how the wealthy lived in New York's gilded age. Frick intended the collection to be a memorial to himself and bequeathed the house to the nation in his death.

The collection includes a suberb display of Old Master paintings, French furniture, and Limoges enamel. Of special interest is the skylit West Gallery, offering oils by Hals, Rembrandt, and Vermeer, whose *Officer and the Laughing Girl* (1655–60) is a fine example of the Dutch painter's use of light and shadow. The Oval Room features Whistler, while the Library and Dining Room are devoted to English works. In the Living Hall are works by Titian, Bellini, and Holbein.

Fifth Avenue

E2 **S 5 Av-53 St, 5 Av-59 St** **visit5thavenue.com**

Today, the stretch of New York's best-known street, from the Empire State Building *(p91)* to the Grand Army Plaza, is lined by the famous stores that have made Fifth Avenue synonymous with luxury goods throughout the world.

The Cartier store, at 52nd Street, is housed in a 1905 Beaux Arts mansion, originally the home of banker Morton F. Plant, who supposedly traded it for a perfectly matched string of pearls. Other well-known jewelry and accessory stores include Tiffany's, made famous by Truman Capote's 1958 novel *Breakfast at Tiffany's*, and Harry

↑ The Gothic Revival St. Patrick's Cathedral in Midtown Manhattan

Winston. The Apple store's iconic glass cube entrance can be found near Central Park.

St. Patrick's Cathedral

E2 **Fifth Av & 50th St** **S 51 St, 5 Av** **7:30am-8:30pm daily** **saint patrickscathedral.org**

New York's finest Gothic Revival building was completed in 1878. This was also the largest Catholic cathedral in the US and seats more than 2,500 people. When Archbishop John Hughes decided to build here in 1850, many criticized his choice of a site so far from the city center.

CLASSIC DEPARTMENT STORES

Bloomingdale's department store, founded in 1872, remains synonymous with the good life. Bergdorf Goodman, luxurious, elegant, and understated since 1928, sells contemporary European designer fashions at high prices. Saks Fifth Avenue has been known for style and elegance since 1924, while Lord & Taylor is the place for classic, conservative fashions.

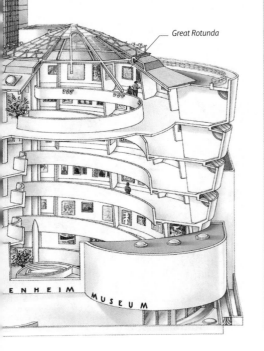

Great Rotunda

E 88

ENHEIM MUSEUM

34 Ⓜ ⑪

CENTRAL PARK

Ⓠ E1 Ⓐ Between 59th St, Fifth Av, 110th St and Eighth Av Ⓢ 59 St-Columbus Circle, 5 Av-59 St, 72 St Ⓒ 6am–1am daily Ⓦ centralparknyc.org

Few New Yorkers today could imagine their home city without this expansive and beloved park, which lies at the heart of New York. With a wealth of green spaces, numerous sights and attractions to explore, and various activities to entertain, Central Park has something for everyone, and a different story to tell with each season.

Central Park is a green paradise for both New Yorkers and visitors to the city. It attracts bird-watchers and naturalists, swimmers and skaters, picnickers and sunbathers, runners and cyclists, and festival-goers in the summer. Frederick Law Olmsted and Calvert Vaux were chosen to create Central Park in the 1850s. The area had been largely desolate, pockmarked with shantytowns and pig farms, and the trans-formation was a huge undertaking. It opened to the public in 1876 under the proviso that it was a "people's park." Today the southern section of the park contains most of the popular attractions, including the open formal spaces of Bethesda Terrace, the Delacorte Theater, where Shakespeare in the Park is staged, and the Wollman Rink during the holiday season. But the northern tract (above 86th Street) is well worth a visit for its wilder natural setting and a dramatically quieter ambience.

Green and leafy ↑
Central Park contrasting
with the city skyline

↑ The Sheep Meadow, in the southern part of Central Park

Seasonal Guide

Spring

The park returns to life at the end of March, with cherry trees blossoming around the Reservoir and birds chirping on their spring migration. Check out model boat races at the Boat Pond (10am-1pm Sat).

Summer

The park becomes a shady respite in summer, while sunbathers bask in the Sheep Meadow. For many, it's all about the free festivals: Shakespeare in the Park, SummerStage, the Met Opera Summer Recital Series, and New York Philharmonic Concerts.

Fall

With 20,000 trees turning red and gold, plus milder temperatures, Central Park is at its most beautiful in the fall. Birds again visit, with hawks best spotted from Belvedere Castle.

Winter

Most of the trees are bare and the winds are biting cold, but winter can be a magical time in Central Park. Snow often blankets the lawns and woods long after it has melted from the streets, and you'll have large swaths of the park to yourself. Don't miss ice-skating at the Wollman Rink or Lasker Rink (Oct-Mar).

← Cyclists enjoying Central Park in the warm summer months

① The Dairy
🕐 **10am–5pm daily**
Central Park's visitor center is the place to begin. Maps and event information can be obtained here, and visitors can rent chess sets too.

② Strawberry Fields
This is Yoko Ono's tribute to her husband, John Lennon. Gifts for the garden came from all over the world.

↑ Pedestrians crossing Bow Bridge, while boaters enjoy the lake

③ Belvedere Castle
🕐 **10am–5pm daily**

This stone castle atop Vista Rock, complete with tower and turrets, offers some of the best views of the park. Inside is the Henry Luce Nature Observatory, with a delightful exhibit about the surprising variety of wildlife to be found in the park.

④ Bow Bridge
This is one of the park's original cast-iron bridges, and was designed as a bow tying together sections of the lake. In the 19th century, when the lake was used for skating, a hoisted red ball signaled that the ice was safe. The bridge offers expansive park views.

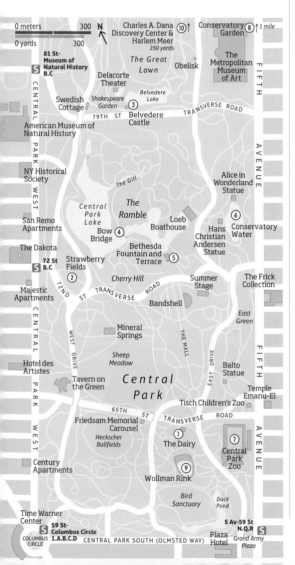

```
0 meters          300
0 yards           300
```
N

81 St-Museum of Natural History B.C

Charles A. Dana Discovery Center & Harlem Meer ⑩↑ 350 yards

Conservatory Garden ⑧ ↑1 mile

The Great Lawn

Obelisk

The Metropolitan Museum of Art

FIFTH AVENUE

Delacorte Theater

Swedish Cottage

Shakespeare Garden

Belvedere Lake

American Museum of Natural History

79TH ST Belvedere Castle ③

TRANSVERSE ROAD

CENTRAL PARK WEST

NY Historical Society

The Gill

Central Park Lake

The Ramble

Alice in Wonderland Statue

San Remo Apartments

Bow Bridge ④

Loeb Boathouse

Hans Christian Andersen Statue

Conservatory Water ⑥

The Dakota

72 St B.C

Strawberry Fields ②

Bethesda Fountain and Terrace ⑤

Cherry Hill

Majestic Apartments

72ND ST TRANSVERSE ROAD

Summer Stage

The Frick Collection

CENTRAL PARK WEST

Bandshell

East Green

Mineral Springs

THE MALL

Sheep Meadow

WEST DRIVE

Hotel des Artistes

Tavern on the Green

Central Park

EAST DRIVE

Balto Statue

FIFTH AVENUE

65TH ST TRANSVERSE ROAD

Tisch Children's Zoo

Temple Emanu-El

Friedsam Memorial Carousel

Heckscher Ballfields

The Dairy ①

Central Park Zoo ⑦

CENTRAL PARK WEST

Century Apartments

Wollman Rink ⑨

Bird Sanctuary

Duck Pond

AVENUE

Time Warner Center

59 St-Columbus Circle 1.A.B.C.D

COLUMBUS CIRCLE

CENTRAL PARK SOUTH (OLMSTED WAY)

5 Av-59 St N.Q.R

Plaza Hotel

Grand Army Plaza

TOP 3 CENTRAL PARK BIKE RENTALS

Bike and Roll
451 Columbus Av, at W 82nd St; www.bikeandroll.com

Master Bike Shop
265 W 72nd St; www.masterbikeshop.com

Bike Rental Central Park
1391 Sixth Av; and 9 W 60th St; www.bikerentalcentralpark.com

⑤ Bethesda Fountain and Terrace

Between the lake and the Mall, this is the architectural heart of the park. The fountain was dedicated in 1873 and the statue, *Angel of the Waters*, marked the opening of the Croton Aqueduct system in 1842, bringing the city its first supply of pure water; its name refers to a biblical account of a healing angel at the pool of Bethesda in Jerusalem.

⑥ Conservatory Water

Better known as the Model Boat Pond, this is where model yacht races occur every weekend and birdwatchers gather here in spring to see the city's famous red-tailed hawk, Pale Male, nest on the roof of 927 Fifth Avenue. At the north end of the lake, a sculpture of Alice in Wonderland is popular with kids. It was commissioned by George T. Delacorte, who is immortalized as the Mad Hatter. Delightful free story hours take place at H. C. Andersen's statue.

Did You Know?

The opening credits of sitcom *Friends* were filmed in L.A., not in a Central Park fountain.

⑦ Central Park Zoo

🕒 Apr–Oct: 10am–5pm daily (to 5:30pm Sat, Sun & federal hols); Nov–Mar: 10am–4:30pm daily

This zoo has won plaudits for its creative and humane use of small space. More than 150 species are represented.

⑧ Conservatory Garden

The Vanderbilt Gate on Fifth Avenue gives entry to three gardens, each with a landscape style; the Central Garden recreates an Italian style, the South Garden is English, and the North Garden is French.

⑨ Wollman Rink

🕒 Oct–Mar

The Wollman Rink has offered the city's most atmospheric ice-skating since 1949. The location is perfect, providing thrilling views of the park and the skyscrapers along Central Park South. The rink transforms into Victorian Gardens, a small amusement park (Jun–Sep).

⑩ Charles A. Dana Discovery Center & Harlem Meer

This center has exhibits on the park's ecology and overlooks Harlem Meer, where catch-and-release fishing is allowed (fishing poles are loaned out).

Snow-covered statue in Central Park's Conservatory Garden →

35 Lincoln Center

E1 **Broadway between W 62nd & W 65th Sts** **66 St** **w** lincoln center.org

A giant cultural complex begun in the 1950s, the Lincoln Center was conceived when both the Metropolitan Opera House and the New York Philharmonic needed homes. Today, the center includes the David H. Koch Theater, home to the acclaimed New York City Ballet and American Ballet Theater in the fall. The Metropolitan Opera House, the focal point of the plaza, opened in 1966 with five great arched windows overlooking the opulent foyer and two radiant murals by Marc Chagall. The other two key institutions here are the Lincoln Center theater complex and David Geffen Hall, home to the New York Philharmonic, America's oldest orchestra. The best way to see this complex is by guided tour.

The **American Folk Art Museum** features an excellent and extensive collection of traditional folk art, including quilts, carvings, and paintings, dating from the 18th century to the present.

American Folk Art Museum

2 Lincoln Sq **Mon** **w** folkart museum.org

MUSEUM MILE

There's a lot to explore along Museum Mile *(Fifth Av along Central Park)*. Dedicated to German and Austrian art, the Neue Galerie *(1048 Fifth Av)* is home to Klimt's famous *Portrait of Adele Bloch-Bauer I*. The Jewish Museum *(1109 Fifth Av)* houses one of the world's largest collections of Judaica. The Museum of the City of New York *(1220 Fifth Av)* chronicles local history. Finally, the Museo del Barrio *(1230 Fifth Av)* is devoted to Latin American art.

36 The Met Breuer

F2 **945 Madison Av** **77 St** **10am-5:30pm Tue-Thu & Sun, 10am-9pm Fri & Sat** **Jan 1, Thanksgiving, Dec 25** **w** met museum.org

The Met Breuer opened in 2016, as an extension of the Metropolitan Museum of Art, in the old premises of the Whitney Museum. Created by the Hungarian modernist architect Marcel Breuer (also famous for designing the tubular steel "Wassily chair"), the building's Brutalist design was a controversial addition to the town houses of the Upper East Side in 1966, but today it is one of the city's most recognizable landmarks.

The Met Breuer provides further exhibition space for the Met's collection of 20th- and 21st-century art, along with educational programs, performances, and artist residencies. There are plans underway to move the collection back to the Met's Fifth Avenue building.

37 American Museum of Natural History

E1 **Central Park W at 79th St** **81 St** **10am-5:45pm daily** **Thanksgiving, Dec 25** **w** amnh.org

This is one of the largest natural history museums in the world. Since it opened in 1877, the complex has grown to cover four city blocks, and now holds over 30 million specimens and artifacts. The most popular areas are the dinosaurs, and the Milstein Family Hall of Ocean Life.

Enter at Central Park West onto the second floor to view the Barosaurus display and exhibits on African, Asian, Central and South American peoples. First-floor collections include ocean life and meteors. Exhibits on American Indians, birds, and reptiles occupy the third floor. Dinosaurs and early mammals are kept on the fourth floor.

↑ The Lincoln Center, the world's most prestigious performing arts complex

→

Classical sculpture in the stunning Great Hall of the Metropolitan Museum of Art

38

Metropolitan Museum of Art

F1 📍 **1000 Fifth Av**
🚇 **86 St** 🚌 🕐 **10am-5:30pm Sun-Thu, 10am-9pm Fri & Sat** 🚫 **Jan 1, 1st Mon in May, Thanksgiving, Dec 25**
🌐 **metmuseum.org**

Founded in 1870 to rival the great art institutions of Europe, the Met houses treasures that span 5,000 years of culture from all over the world. It began with three private European collections and 174 paintings. Today, its holdings number over two million, and the original 1880 Gothic Revival building has been expanded many times. Additions include huge windows overlooking Central Park and the breath-taking Medieval Art Galleries under the Grand Staircase.

Most of the collections are housed on the two main floors. On the first floor is the Robert Lehman Collection, including Old Masters, Dutch, Spanish, and French artists, Fauvists, and Post-Impressionists, as well as ceramics and furniture. Also on the first floor are the American Wing, European Sculpture and Decorative Arts, Egyptian Art, and the Michael C. Rockefeller Wing, with a superb collection of over 1,600 primitive artworks from Africa, the Pacific Islands, and the Americas. Among the African works are outstanding ivory and bronze sculptures from Benin (Nigeria). Also on view are pre-Columbian gold, ceramics, and stonework from Mexico and Central and South America.

The American Wing has one of the world's finest collections of American paintings, including several by Edward Hopper. Prize exhibits include Gilbert Stuart's first portrait of George Washington, John Singer Sargent's notorious portrait of *Madame X*, and the monumental *Washington Crossing the Delaware* by Emanuel Leutze. There are also period rooms, including one designed by Frank Lloyd Wright.

The Met has one of the largest collections of Egyptian art outside Cairo. Objects range from the fragmented jasper lips of a 15th-century BC queen to the massive Temple of Dendur. Many of the objects were discovered in the early 20th century.

The Lila Wallace Wing holds the museum's growing Modern and Contemporary Art collection, including Picasso's *Portrait of Gertrude Stein* (1905) and Jackson Pollock's *Autumn Rhythm* (1950).

The heart of the museum, however, is its awe-inspiring collection of 3,000 European paintings on the second floor. Its highlights are Dutch and Flemish masterpieces such as Bruegel's *The Harvesters* (1565) and Rembrandt's *Self-Portrait* (1660). Among the finest Impressionist and Post-Impressionist paintings is

Cypresses (1889), painted by Vincent van Gogh the year before he died.

The second floor also has a comprehensive collection of textiles, sculpture, and ceramics from China, Japan, Korea, India, and Southeast Asia. The Ming-style Chinese scholar's garden in the Astor Court was built by craftspeople from Suzhou. The Cantor Roof Garden has superb annual shows of 20th-century sculpture, displayed against the dramatic backdrop of the city skyline.

TOP 5 **UNMISSABLE ARTWORKS AT THE MET**

Madonna and Child
Duccio (c. 1290-1300). Delicately crafted, early-Renaissance piece.

Harvesters
Pieter Bruegel the Elder (1565). This captures an agricultural scene.

Washington Crossing the Delaware
Emanuel Leutze (1851). Shows Washington's surprise attack in 1776.

Bridge over a Pond of Water Lilies
Claude Monet (1899). The Met's most popular Impressionist painting.

White Flag
Jasper Johns (1955). This was inspired by a dream.

> Founded in 1870 to rival the great art institutions of Europe, the Met houses treasures that span 5,000 years of culture from all over the world.

AROUND MANHATTAN

There's more to the Big Apple than Manhattan alone. Upper Manhattan and the four other boroughs that together comprise New York City are each unique in feel and spirit, and offer respite from the bustle of the inner city; even residents describe a trip to Manhattan as "going into the city." The likes of the Bronx, Queens and Brooklyn feature stunning educational institutions, botanical gardens, museums, churches, beaches, and huge sports arenas galore.

39 Columbia University

F4 W 116th St & Broadway S 116 St ℹ 213 Low Library, 535 W 116th St; www.columbia.edu

One of the oldest Ivy League universities, Columbia was founded as King's College in 1754. The present campus was begun in 1897 and placed on a terrace, with the classical, columned Low Library dominating the central Quadrangle.

Eastward across the campus on Amsterdam Avenue, and bestrewn with hand-carved gargoyles, lies the Neo-Gothic **Cathedral of St. John the Divine**. Begun in 1892 and only two-thirds completed, it is said to be the largest in the world.

Cathedral of St. John the Divine

1047 Amsterdam Av at W 112th St S Cathedral Pkwy (110 St) 9am-5pm Mon-Sat, 12:30-2pm Sun stjohndivine.org

40 Harlem

F4 N of 110th St & Central Park S 125 St

Harlem has been at the heart of African American culture since the 1920s, when poets, activists, and jazz musicians came together during the Harlem Renaissance. Today the neighborhood is home to West African eateries, Sunday gospel choirs, a vibrant local jazz scene, and some of the prettiest blocks in the city.

The area around Malcolm X Boulevard, between West 118th and 124th streets, is known as the Mount Morris Park Historic District, and is crammed with elegant brownstones and churches. The stretch of 125th Street between Broadway and Park Avenue is Harlem's main drag. The Apollo Theater opened in 1913 as a whites-only opera house. It rose to fame in 1934 when entrepreneur Frank Schiffman took over and made

Did You Know?

Originally a Dutch village founded in 1658, Harlem is named after the city of Haarlem in the Netherlands.

it accessible to all races. He converted it into one of the city's most well-known venues, hosting the likes of Billie Holiday, Duke Ellington, and Dinah Washington.

Harlem's culinary scene has blossomed over the years with newcomers like Red Rooster, not far from Sylvia's, Harlem's best-known soul-food restaurant. Beloved African American poet Langston Hughes lived in an aging brownstone at 20 East 127th St from 1948 until his death in 1967. Now known as **Langston Hughes House**, the I, Too Arts Collective has since opened parts of it to the public. The tiny **National Jazz Museum** honors Harlem's musical history, with displays of valuable memorabilia.

Just north, at 138th Street, is the **Abyssinian Baptist Church**. Founded in 1808, the church gained fame through its pastor, Adam Clayton Powell, Jr. (1908–72), a congressman and civil-rights leader, and is known for its uplifting gospel music. The Schomburg Center for

←

One of the intersections in Harlem, lined with a row of colorful buildings

Research in Black Culture, on Malcolm X Boulevard, is the largest center dedicated to black and African culture in the country. The collection was assembled by the late Arthur Schomburg (1874–1938), a black man of Puerto Rican descent, who was once told by a teacher that there was no such thing as "black history."

St. Nicholas Historic District, better known as "Striver's Row," comprises two blocks of beautiful houses on either side of West 138th and West 139th streets, between Adam Clayton Powell Jr. Boulevard and Frederick Douglass Boulevard. A contrast to the surrounding streets, the houses here were built in 1891, when Harlem was considered a neighborhood for New York's gentry. Further uptown is the **Hamilton Grange National Memorial** in St. Nicholas Park, where the 1802 mansion built by Alexander Hamilton has been relocated and restored.

Langston Hughes House
🏠 20 E 127th St 🕐 Noon–5pm Tue, Thu & Sat 🌐 itooarts.com

National Jazz Museum
♿ 🏠 58 W 129th St 🕐 11am–5pm Thu–Mon 🚫 Federal hols 🌐 jazz museuminharlem.org

Abyssinian Baptist Church
🏠 132 Odell Clark Pl 🕐 Visitors: 11:30am service 🚫 Check website 🌐 abyssinian.org

Hamilton Grange National Memorial
♿ 🏠 414 W 141st St 🕐 9am–5pm Wed–Sun 🚫 Thanksgiving, Dec 25 🌐 nps.gov/hagr

> #### ALEXANDER HAMILTON
> Founding Father Alexander Hamilton (c. 1755–1804) was born in the West Indies and moved to New York in 1772. He served under Washington in the Revolutionary War and later set up the First Bank of the United States. His strong views gained him enemies and he was killed in a duel by Vice-President Aaron Burr in 1804. Inspired by his life, Lin-Manuel Miranda created the musical *Hamilton* in 2015.

↑ Stained glass glowing above the tombs in the Cloisters' Gothic Chapel

41 ⬦ Ⓜ 🖼 🏛
The Cloisters

📍 F4 🏠 Ft Tryon Pk Ⓢ 190 St 🚇 🕐 Mar–Oct: 10am–5:15pm daily (Nov–Feb: to 4:45pm) 🚫 Jan 1, Thanksgiving, Dec 25 🌐 metmuseum.org

This world-famous branch of the Metropolitan Museum *(p101)*, devoted to medieval art, resides in a building that incorporates medieval cloisters, chapels, and halls. The museum, organized in chronological order, starts with the Romanesque period (AD 1000) and moves to the Gothic (1150 to 1520). It is noted for its exquisite illuminated manuscripts, its striking stained glass, metalwork, enamels, and ivories, and its beautifully preserved tapestries. Perhaps the most engaging exhibits in the Cloisters are the gardens, planted according to horticultural information found in medieval treatises and poetry. Performances of music from the Middle Ages and the Renaissance are given regularly and are very popular. Reserving tickets is advised.

42
Queens

◉ F4 ⑤ ▥

New York's largest borough has a trove of cultural attractions, from the Steinway & Sons piano factory and the Queens Museum in Flushing Meadows–Corona Park, to sculpture parks and Louis Armstrong House. It's a melting pot of cultures, and the aromas of Greek, Thai, and Indian food fill the streets.

In Astoria, the **Noguchi Museum** is devoted to works by sculptor Isamu Noguchi (1904–88), while the Socrates Sculpture Park was created by Expressionist Mark di Suvero. The **Museum of the Moving Image** displays memorabilia from the Kaufman Astoria Studio, opened in 1920. Its Jim Henson Exhibition celebrates all things Muppet-related.

MoMA PS1 in Long Island City is dedicated to contemporary art. Traveling exhibitions are hosted alongside permanent works and interactive pieces.

Noguchi Museum
⊘⊘ ◨9-01 33rd Rd ⑤ Bdwy ◷Mon, Tue, Jan 1, Thanksgiving, Dec 25 ▥ noguchi.org

Museum of the Moving Image
⊘⊘☺ ◨36-01 35th Av at 36th St, Astoria ⑤36 St ◷Mon, Tue, 4 July ▥ movingimage.us

---

43
The Bronx

◉ F4 ⑤ ▥

Once a prosperous suburb for the wealthy, then a borough with a reputation, parts of the Bronx are making a comeback. New Yorkers flock to Yankee Stadium, home of the New York Yankees baseball team since 1923. Games take place between April and September, while tours run all year.

The **Bronx Zoo** opened in 1899 and is the largest urban zoo in the US. The park is a leader in the perpetuation of endangered species and is home to more than 4,000 animals, which live in realistic imitations of their natural habitats. A shuttle train takes visitors around the sprawling woods, streams, and parklands.

Across the road, visitors can experience the beauty of the **New York Botanical Garden**. One of the oldest and largest of its kind in the world, it has 48 specialty gardens and plant collections, the Thain Family Forest, vast Children's Adventure Garden, and the Enid A. Haupt conservatory, with its interconnected glass galleries.

Bronx Zoo
⊘⊘☺◨ ◨Fordham Rd ◷Apr–Oct: 10am–5pm daily (to 5:30pm Sat & Sun); Nov–Mar: 10am–4:30pm daily ▥ bronxzoo.com

New York Botanical Garden
⊘⊘☺◨ ◨Kazimiroff Blvd ◷10am–6pm Tue–Sun ▥ nybg.org

44
Brooklyn

◉ F5 ⑤ ▥

Arguably the most fashionable borough in the city, Brooklyn offers a multitude of experiences, plus cool bars, top-rated restaurants, and groundbreaking galleries. Among its diverse neighborhoods are the historic districts of Fort Green, Park Slope, and Brooklyn Heights, all tree-lined enclaves with Victorian houses and cafés. Brooklyn Heights Promenade offers stunning views of the Manhattan skyline. Inland, the Brooklyn Historical Society chronicles the history of the borough, while the New York Transit Museum displays transport-related exhibits in an old subway station.

Between Manhattan Bridge and Brooklyn Bridge is the ritzy neighborhood of Dumbo, short for "Down Under the Manhattan Bridge Overpass." Primarily industrial in the 19th century, its brick factories have been converted into art galleries, eateries, condos, and

→
Fall colors saturating the Thain Family Forest in the Bronx

↑ Brooklyn Bridge, with Manhattan's skyline beyond

artsy malls, such as Empire Stores. It's also home to Sunday's Brooklyn Flea market.

Williamsburg is one of the city's most popular neighborhoods, with culinary attractions like Brooklyn Brewery and Smorgasburg, a trendy food market held on Saturdays between April and November. Not far from Smorgasburg is Bedford Avenue, which is lined with cafés, boutiques, record stores, bars, and restaurants.

To the south, transformed in recent years from a near-derelict site, the Brooklyn Navy Yard now contains over 300 businesses, from Brooklyn Grange Farms to Steiner Studios (where hit comedy-drama *Girls* was filmed). Get oriented at the Brooklyn Navy Yard Center at BLDG 92, which charts the history of the site.

The 1897 **Brooklyn Museum** is one of the most impressive cultural institutions in the US, with a permanent collection of some one million objects. Highlights include a collection of ancient Egyptian and Middle Eastern artifacts, and some works of American and European contemporary art.

On the edge of the giant Prospect Park (where the Sunday Smorgasburg takes place), the modest Brooklyn Botanic Gardens is a great place to spend a few hours. It features one of North America's largest rose collections, an Elizabethan-style herb garden, and a stunning Japanese-style garden. Over on the waterfront, Red Hook is a surprising blend of brick warehouses, cycle paths, cobblestoned blocks, and stores, and its laid-back vibe makes it unlike any other part of the city. At the borough's southern point lies the old-fashioned seaside resort of Coney Island. It remains a popular option for day trips, with a wide beach, Nathan's "famous" hot dogs, the Wonder Wheel and the iconic Cyclone roller coaster. The New York Aquarium and Coney Island's boardwalk are also popular attractions.

Brooklyn Museum

🎨🎨🎨🎨 📍200 Eastern Pkwy, Brooklyn 🕐11am–6pm Wed, Fri-Sun, 11am–10pm Thu 🗓Federal hols 🌐brooklynmuseum.org

EAT

Fette Sau
BBQ specialist with industrial chic.

📍345 Metropolitan Av
🌐fettesaubbq.com

$$$

Frankies 457 Spuntino
Refined Italian-American cuisine.

📍457 Court St
🌐frankiesspuntino.com

$$$

Junior's
Venerable diner famous for NY cheesecake.

📍386 Flatbush Av
🌐juniors cheesecake.com

$$$

Peter Luger Steak House
Heavenly porterhouse and lunchtime burgers.

📍178 Broadway
🌐peterluger.com

$$$

Arguably the most fashionable borough in the city, Brooklyn offers a multitude of experiences, plus cool bars, top-rated restaurants, and groundbreaking galleries.

NEW YORK STATE AND NEW JERSEY

Though today large parts of New York State and New Jersey serve as bedroom communities for New York City, it wasn't always that way. The region was the homeland of the Iroquois Confederacy before the arrival of Europeans. The Dutch established Albany in 1614, but colonization was generally restricted to the Hudson River Valley until the Erie Canal opened up the interior in 1825. In the 19th century, both states became heavily industrialized. Inventor Thomas Edison worked in Menlo Park, and Paterson, Buffalo, Rochester, and Syracuse boomed as manufacturing hubs. After a long period of decline, these cities are reinventing themselves, though it's the states' untouched mountains that attract many.

NEW YORK STATE

Stretching north to Canada and west to the Great Lakes, the "Empire State" is a world away from the city. Long Island is the largest island adjoining the continental US, with miles of suburbs, farmland, and beaches; the Hudson River Valley is an area of opulent mansions and small towns; and Albany marks the start of the upstate area, comprising rural farmland and vibrant cities.

❶ Hudson River Valley

🚆🅿🚌 ℹ3 Neptune Rd, Poughkeepsie; www. dutchesstourism.com

From its source high in the Adirondacks, the Hudson courses past bustling riverport towns and the dramatic Catskill and Taconic mountain ranges to its mouth at New York City harbor. Strikingly beautiful and strategically located, the valley has played a pivotal role in North American military, economic, and cultural history.

Settled by the Dutch in the 1620s, the area's heritage survives in the names of places such as Catskill, Kinderhook, and Claverack, as well as in the writings of Washington Irving (1783–1859), whose tales of *Rip Van Winkle* and *The Legend of Sleepy Hollow* made him an international star. Irving's modest but eclectic Hudson River home, **Sunnyside**, is now a tourist attraction.

The Hudson's strategic advantages also made it valuable to British and American forces during the Revolutionary War. Fort Putnam, built in 1778, is now part of the **US Military Academy** at West Point. Established in 1802, the academy has trained such leading military officers as Civil War generals Ulysses S. Grant and Robert E. Lee, and World War II commanders Douglas MacArthur and Dwight D. Eisenhower.

In the 19th century, many of New York's emerging elite built seasonal retreats along the Hudson. The largest of these is the Beaux Arts **Vanderbilt Mansion** in Hyde Park. The **Home of Franklin D. Roosevelt National Historic Site** includes an extensive museum and library detailing his leadership during the Great Depression and World War II.

Sunnyside

⊛⊛ 🅰3 W Sunnyside Ln, off Rte 9, Irvington 🕐May-mid-Nov 🌐hudsonvalley.org

US Military Academy

⊛⊛ 🅰West Point Hwy (Thayer Rd), West Point 🕐Hours vary, check website 🚫Jan 1, Thanksgiving, Dec 25 🌐westpointtours.com

Vanderbilt Mansion

⊛ 🅰119 Vanderbilt Park Rd, Hyde Park 🕐9am-4pm daily 🌐nps.gov/vama

Home of Franklin D. Roosevelt National Historic Site

⊛⊛⊜ 🅰4097 Albany Post Rd, Rte 9, Hyde Park 🕐9am-5pm daily, for guided tours only 🚫Jan 1, Thanksgiving, Dec 25 🌐nps.gov/hofr

Did You Know?

New York State is home to some 70,000 miles (112,650 km) of rivers and streams.

↑ George Washington's Montauk Point Lighthouse on Long Island

2

The Hamptons & Montauk

⊕🏠🚌 **w** discoverlong island.com

At Riverhead, Long Island splits into two peninsulas: the mostly pastoral North Fork and the more urban South Fork, where beaches and attractions are concentrated in the trendy summer retreats of the Hamptons and Montauk.

Most New Yorkers associate the Hamptons (from west to east: Westhampton Beach, Hampton Bays, Southampton, Bridgehampton, East Hampton, and Amagansett) with the celebrities and fashionistas who migrate here during the summer. However, the area has a rich historical heritage, including the 19th-century whaling town of Sag Harbor, to the north of Bridgehampton.

The easternmost Long Island community, Montauk, is a busy summer resort, and a jumping-off point for the area's nature trails and beaches. Other activities include golf, horseback riding, cycling, surfing, and fishing. Montauk State Park contains the Montauk Point Lighthouse, commissioned by George Washington in 1792.

←

Bear Mountain Bridge stretching across the Hudson River at sunrise

3

Albany

⊕🏠🚌 *i* 25 Quackenbush Square; www.albany.org

Albany has been a central force in New York State since 1614, when the Dutch established a fur-trading post, Fort Nassau (later known as Fort Orange), at the northernmost navigable point on the Hudson River. When the British took over in 1664, they changed its name to Albany. In 1797 Albany was selected as the state capital, and its future was secured. The city expanded dramatically in the 1830s with the completion of the Erie Canal, which linked the Hudson to the Great Lakes. When canal traffic declined in the 1850s, Albany retained its commercial dominance, rapidly evolving into a railroad terminus and manufacturing center.

While transportation and industry are still important to the local economy, government is the main concern in today's Albany. The majestic **New York State Capitol**, built over 30 years and completed in 1898, occupies a central location near downtown. The massive stone building is an amalgam of Italian and French Renaissance and Romanesque, replete with ornamented stairways, soaring arches, and an ornate Senate chamber embellished with granite, marble, stained glass, onyx, and mahogany.

The **New York State Museum** chronicles New York's rich heritage, beginning with its American Indian occupants and incorporating the stories of its many settlers.

New York State Capitol

⊛ 🏠 Empire State Plaza 🕙 Mon-Sat 🚫 Most Federal hols **w** empirestateplaza. ny.gov

New York State Museum

⊚⊛🏠 Cultural Education Center, 222 Madison Av 🕙 9:30am–5pm Tue-Sun 🚫 Jan 1, Thanksgiving, Dec 25 **w** nysm.nysed.gov

↑ Stunning fall foliage at Heart Lake in the Adirondack Mountains

④
Adirondack Mountains

🚌 𝒊 2608 Main St, Lk Placid; www.visitadirondacks.com

Spanning almost a quarter of the state, the Adirondacks encompass untrammeled wilderness, rugged peaks, and hundreds of lakes and rivers. Mount Marcy is the highest peak, with a tough but straight-forward 7.4-mile (12-km) hike to the top. Much of the region is within **Adirondack Park**. The **Adirondack Interpretive Center** features exhibits on the park's flora and fauna, plus 3 miles (4.8 km) of interpretive trails. The southern end of the region is anchored by the town of Lake George, where you can cruise on the eponymous lake or visit the Fort William Henry Museum, a reconstruction of the fort from the French and Indian War (1754–63).

Lake Placid hosted the 1932 and 1980 Winter Olympic Games, and its Olympic Museum is packed with sport-ing memorabilia. To the west, Saranac Lake and Tupper Lake offer canoeing and kayaking, while Fort Ticonderoga lies on the Hudson River to the southeast. The fully restored 18th-century fort was the site of a key battle during the US Revolutionary War.

Adirondack Park

🏠 1 mile (0.5 km) N of Rte 86/Rte 30, & 14 miles (22 km) E of Long Lake, Rte 28N
🕙 9am–5pm daily
🚫 Thanksgiving, Dec 25
🌐 visitadirondacks.com

Adirondack Interpretive Center

🏠 5922 State Route 28N, Newcomb 🕙 9am–5pm Wed-Sun 🚫 Nov & Dec 🌐 visit adirondacks.com

Did You Know?

New York - or the Empire State - is the fourth most populated state in the US.

⑤
Saratoga Springs

🏠🚌 𝒊 28 Clinton St; www.saratoga.org

This town has been known for its horse racing, gambling, and high society since the 19th century, when the therapeutic waters at **Saratoga Spa State Park** sparked an influx of tourists seeking relief from various ailments. Other distrac-tions were offered by the lavish casinos and racing facilities. One of Saratoga's original gambling establishments, the elegant Canfield Casino, is now part of Congress Park. The gabled grandstand of the Civil War-era Saratoga Race Track is still in use, attracting large crowds in August. For a glimpse of the area's tempestuous Revolutionary War past, **Saratoga National Historical Park**, 15 miles (24 km) southeast, was the site of the 1777 Battle of Saratoga. Here, American commander Horatio Gates led Colonial forces to a victory over 7,000 British, Hessians, and American Indians. The victory ensured control of the Hudson River corridor, and prompted the French King Louis XVI to send troops to the colonists' aid.

Saratoga Spa State Park

♨ 🏠 I-87, exit 13N 𝒊 19 Roosevelt Dr; www.nysparks.com/parks/saratogaspa

Saratoga National Historical Park

♨🕙 🏠 Rte 4, 8 miles (13 km) S of Schuylerville 🕙 9am–5pm daily 🚫 Jan 1, Thanksgiving, Dec 25 🌐 nps.gov/sara

⑥
Finger Lakes

🏠🚌🚂 𝒊 904 E Shore Dr, Ithaca; www.visitithaca.com

According to the Iroquois, the Finger Lakes were created when the Great Spirit placed his hand on the region, leaving behind a series of slender lakes. Seneca Lake is the deepest, at 630 ft (192 m), while Cayuga Lake is the longest, stretching 40 miles (64 km) north from the lively town of Ithaca, home to Cornell University. The picturesque Cornell campus contains Ithaca Falls Natural Area and the Johnson Museum of Art, with its exceptional collection of Asian ceramics, sculpture, and scroll paintings. Downtown Ithaca features a diverse array of art galleries, bookstores, and restaurants. **Taughannock Falls State Park**, north of Ithaca, is a wooded oasis, with waterfalls tumbling into a cool, green pool, where swimming is allowed in season. At the northern end of Cayuga Lake, Seneca Falls was the location of the first American Women's Rights Convention in 1848, commemorated at the National Women's Hall of Fame and Women's Rights National Historical Park. The surrounding Finger Lakes Wine Country is sprinkled with wineries and tasting rooms.

Taughannock Falls State Park

⊛ ⌂10 miles (16 km) N of Ithaca, Rte 89 ☒Some trails in winter ⓦparks.ny.gov

---

❼
Letentworth State Park

⌂🚻 🛈1 Letchworth State Park, Castile ⏰6am–11pm daily ⓦparks.ny.gov

The "Grand Canyon of the East" is a lesser-visited gem, encompassing a deep gorge along the Genesee River, three major waterfalls (the Upper, Middle, and Lower Falls), and lush forests laced with 66 miles (106 km) of hiking trails. Other activities include whitewater rafting, kayaking, and even hot-air ballooning. The **Humphrey Nature Center** offers interactive exhibits highlighting the geology, wildlife, and ecology of the park. The thundering Middle Falls are the largest in the park, with a 107ft (33 m) drop.

Humphrey Nature Center

⌂6773 Trailside Rd, Castile ⏰May–Oct: 10am–5pm daily; Nov–Apr: 10am–5pm Thu–Mon ☒Thanksg. ⓦparks.ny.gov

---

❽
Cooperstown

� 🛈20 Chestnut St; www.thisiscooperstown.com

Overlooking Otsego Lake, this little village is the birthplace of baseball and home of the **National Baseball Hall of Fame**, an engaging shrine and museum paying homage to all the greats from the last 100-odd years. Founded in 1786, Cooperstown also has a superb collection of American Indian artifacts, folk art, and Hudson River School paintings in the Fenimore Art Museum. The adjacent Farmers' Museum features exhibits on 19th-century rural life.

National Baseball Hall of Fame

⊛ ⌂25 Main St ⏰Check website ☒Jan 1, Thanksg., Dec 25 ⓦbaseballhall.org

↑ Celebrating America's pastime inside the National Baseball Hall of Fame in Cooperstown, and the main entrance *(inset)*

❾

Niagara Falls

🚗🅿️♿ 🛈 10 Rainbow Blvd;
www.niagara-usa.com

Louis Hennepin, the French priest who was one of the first Europeans to feast their eyes upon Niagara Falls in 1678, wrote that "the Universe does not afford its parallel." Even today the three waterfalls here, which plunge nearly 200 ft (61 m) into a rocky gorge, are as awe-inspiring as they were over 300 years ago. Despite the rampant development on both the US and Canadian sides of the Niagara River (which separates the Canadian province of Ontario from New York State), the sheer spectacle of Niagara Falls still provides enough

drama, mist, and romance to lure more than 10 million visitors every year.

Visitors on the American side often start their exploration with a visit to **Niagara Falls State Park**, from which the 240-ft (73-m) Prospect Point Observation Tower provides a fabulous scenic overview of the falls. For a closer look, there are a number of paid excursions available, such as the **Cave of the Winds** elevator ride to the base of the falls, and the **Maid of the Mist** boat ride, which departs from Prospect Park and passes directly in front of the falls and into the river's Horseshoe Basin, for a closer view of the more dramatic Canadian falls.

The pedestrian-friendly Rainbow Bridge provides quick passage from downtown

Niagara Falls to the Canadian side, where most of the area's commercial attractions are located. At night, the falls are dramatically illuminated by electricity generated by the Niagara Power Project, New York State's biggest electricity producer. Its insightful Niagara Power Vista visitor center traces the development of hydropower in the area and features interactive, animated exhibits for all ages.

Niagara Falls State Park
⊘ 🎫 🍴 ♿ 🕐 Dawn-dusk daily 🛈 323 Prospect St; www.niagarafallsstate park.com

Cave of the Winds
⊘ 🕐 May-Oct; times vary, check website 🌐 niagara fallsstatepark.com

Maid of the Mist
⊘ 🎫 Prospect Park 🕐 Mid-May-Oct: 9am-5pm daily (times vary, check website) 🌐 maidofthemist.com

> The sheer spectacle of Niagara Falls still provides enough drama, mist, and romance to lure more than 10 million visitors every year.

The **National Susan B. Anthony Museum & House** is the former home of the legendary civil rights leader and headquarters of the National American Woman Suffrage Association. The interior is kept in period style, with tours led by enthusiastic docents.

George Eastman Museum
♿🔊🎧 📍900 East Av
🕐10am–5pm Tue–Sat, 11am–5pm Sun 🚫Mon, Jan 1, Thanksgiving, Dec 25
🌐eastman.org

National Susan B. Anthony Museum & House
♿🔊 📍17 Madison St
🕐11am–5pm Tue–Sun
🌐susanbanthonyhouse.org

HISTORIC WOMEN

New York has a history of trailblazing women. Elizabeth Cady Stanton (1815–1902) and Susan B. Anthony (1820–1906) held the first American Women's Rights Convention in 1848. Stanton's home and the chapel in which the convention took place have been preserved in Seneca Falls. Anthony's base in Rochester is also a museum. Learn more at the National Women's Hall of Fame in Seneca Falls (p111).

↑ *Maid of the Mist* sailing alongside the dramatic Niagara Falls

10
Rochester
🚉🚌🚗 ℹ️45 East Av; www.visitrochester.com

Founded on the southern shore of Lake Ontario, Rochester boomed in the 19th century thanks to the milling industries that developed around the Genesee River's High Falls. It remains a wealthy city, with a revitalized downtown of parks and museums, and the East End entertainment district. The Center at High Falls offers scenic views of the still-roaring cascades, a display on local history, and a tour of the 1816 Triphammer Forge. The **George Eastman Museum** is where the eccentric founder of Kodak lived until his death in 1932. It is now an intriguing museum centered on film and cameras.

→
Ancient classical sculpture at the Albright-Knox Art Gallery in Buffalo

11
Buffalo
🚉🚌🚗 ℹ️403 Main St; www.visitbuffaloniagara.com

Buffalo flourished in the 19th century when it became the western terminus of the Erie Canal. It's New York State's second city, its downtown a cluster of skyscrapers overlooking Lake Erie. The waterfront features the Canalside development and the Buffalo & Erie County Naval & Military Park includes access to the missile cruiser, destroyer and WWII submarine moored on the river nearby. Delaware Park contains the Buffalo History Museum, with exhibits on the town's rich industrial heritage. The nearby **Albright-Knox Art Gallery** displays works by Picasso, de Kooning, and Pollock. Also nearby is Frank Lloyd Wright's Martin House. Buffalo's Anchor Bar invented the Buffalo-style chicken wing in 1964, and the Buffalo Bills, the city's football team, play outside Buffalo at New Era Field in Orchard Park.

Albright-Knox Art Gallery
♿🔊🎧♿ 📍1285 Elmwood Av, off Rte 198 🚫Mon, Jan 1, Thanksgiving, Dec 25
🌐albrightknox.org

NEW JERSEY

In spite of the industrial image earned by manufacturing and railroad towns, such as Newark and Hoboken, the "Garden State" really does live up to its moniker. Outside the urban corridor that lies across the Hudson River from New York City all the way into Philadelphia, New Jersey is a gentle landscape of green and small towns, pine forests, and stretches of white sandy beaches.

⓬ Atlantic City

🚗🚆🚌 *ℹ* Boardwalk Information Center at Mississippi Av; www. atlanticcitynj.com

Called the "Queen of the Coast" by generations of beachgoers, Atlantic City (or more familiarly, AC) has been a favored vacation spot since the mid-1800s. The first casino opened on the boardwalk in 1978, and since then the town has become one of the most popular destinations on the Eastern Seaboard.

All gambling takes place in the large, ostentatious casino-hotels that lie within a block of the boardwalk and the beach. Although the casinos are justly famous for their nightlife, families will find plenty of other entertainment during the day. Atlantic City's boardwalk, lined with shops and amusement arcades, is always busy with people enjoying a stroll at any time of day or night. Another way to see the boardwalk is in a "rolling chair," a rickshaw-like wicker chair on wheels that seats up to three people. Rolling chairs have been plying the AC boardwalk since 1887. Beyond the boardwalk, sandy beaches beckon sunbathers and swimmers. At one time, Atlantic City was known mainly for hosting the Miss America pageant, which was founded here in 1921 and is still held annually at Boardwalk Hall to this day.

In nearby Margate City, some 5 miles (8 km) south of Atlantic City, **Lucy the Elephant** stands tall in celebration of American marketing ingenuity. Built in 1881 by real-estate developer James Lafferty to draw attention to his holdings, "Lucy" has served as a restaurant, office, hotel, and tavern over the years. Today, guided tours take visitors into the 90-ton (90,000-kg) structure for views of the Jersey Shore from Lucy's howdah (carriage).

Lucy the Elephant
♿ 🏠 9200 Atlantic Av, Margate City ⏰ Times vary, check website 🌐 lucythe elephant.org

THOMAS EDISON AND MENLO PARK

Perhaps America's greatest inventor, Thomas Edison (1847–1931) developed many devices, from the phonograph to the electric light bulb. He was born in Ohio but lived most of his life in New Jersey. In 1876 he established his first laboratory in Menlo Park, about 25 miles (40 km) north of Princeton; today this is the Thomas Edison Center. In 1887 he built a laboratory in West Orange, preserved as the Thomas Edison National Historical Park.

The sun setting behind Atlantic City's Steel Pier Amusement Park ↑

⓭ Princeton

🏛🚌 ℹ️ Princeton-Mercer Regional CVB, 182 Nassau St; www.visitprinceton.org

The once-sleepy central New Jersey village of Princeton saw considerable activity during the Revolutionary War, changing hands between British forces and the Continental Army. The former agricultural village is now a pleasant tree-lined town, combining sophisticated shops, lodgings, and restaurants with one of America's most prestigious Ivy League universities.

The center of Princeton's shopping and dining area is Nassau Street. The Historical Society of Princeton (at 354 Quaker Road) offers walking tours, highlighting the town's fine 18th-century architecture. Palmer Square is home to the Nassau Inn, a 1930s replica of a colonial inn and Princeton's premier hotel.

The College of New Jersey, one of the 14 original Colonial colleges, moved to Princeton in 1756 and was renamed **Princeton University** in 1896. Landmark Nassau Hall was the site of the initial meeting of the New Jersey State Legislature in 1776, and renowned physicist

↑ The historic 18th-century East Pyne Hall at Princeton University

Albert Einstein spent his final years here at the Institute for Advanced Study. The grounds include sculptures by Pablo Picasso, Henry Moore, and Louise Nevelson. The Art Museum in McCormick Hall specializes in ancient pre-Columbian, Asian, and African art as well as modern works. The University Chapel is one of the world's largest – note the superb Gothic architecture, stained-glass windows, and 16th-century French pulpit and lectern. Some 30 gargoyles decorate the buildings on campus, including the Firestone Library, which houses a small museum of works by Beatrix Potter, the Brothers Grimm, and Hans Christian Andersen.

Princeton University Visitor Center

♿ 🅿️ Welcome Desk, First Campus Center 🚫Federal hols 🌐princeton.edu

⓮ Cape May

🏛🚌 ℹ️ Cape May Welcome Center, 609 Lafayette & Elmira sts, Cape May; www.capemay.com

First explored by Cornelius Mey for the Dutch West India Company in 1621, Cape May is one of the oldest seashore resorts on the Atlantic Coast. Visited by a number of US presidents, including James Buchanan, Ulysses S. Grant, and Benjamin Harrison, it was

popular with socialites from New York and Philadelphia during the late 1800s. Since then, it has continued to enjoy a fine reputation among beach lovers. A small boardwalk and sandy beach afford splendid views of the Atlantic sunrise.

The area is characterized by the Victorian building boom. The central district is made up of so-called "cottages": two- and three-story summer homes built in styles popular at the turn of the century. Most of the homes have been restored, and some are open to the public, including for B&B lodgings. Several tours are available, including a special trolley tour.

The **Historic Cold Spring Village** is a living museum where costumed interpreters portray 19th-century rural New Jersey life, and demonstrate trades and crafts such as pottery making, bookbinding, and blacksmithing.

Historic Cold Spring Village

♿☕🎁 🅿️720 US 9, Cape May 🕐Late Jun–Labor Day: 10am–4:30pm Tue–Sun; Labor Day–late Jun: 10:30am–4:30pm Mon–Fri, 11am–3pm Sat 🌐hcsv.org

Benjamin Franklin Bridge, Philadelphia

PHILADELPHIA AND PENNSYLVANIA

Founded by Quaker William Penn in 1680, Pennsylvania thrived thanks to its fertile soil and industrious colonists. Its capital, Philadelphia, was at the heart of the fight for US Independence (Benjamin Franklin was based here). The city hosted the first two Continental Congresses, and the Constitutional Convention of 1787. It continued to challenge New York as commercial capital well into the 19th century. Pennsylvania boomed in the 1800s with steel production, coal mining, and textile production, but the state fell into industrial decline after World War II. Philly and Pittsburgh are booming again, and much of the state remains an economic and political bellwether.

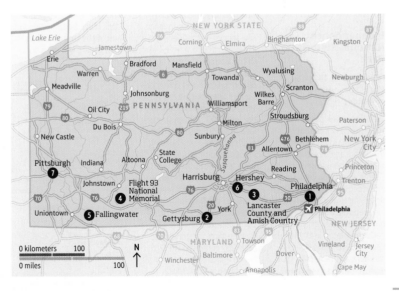

❶

PHILADELPHIA

"The City of Brotherly Love" served as an early capital of the fledgling United States, with the Declaration of Independence being signed here in 1776. The city's neighborhoods reflect a lively ethnic mix, and its rich history, world-class museums, and fine restaurants make it one of America's most popular destinations.

①

Independence National Historical Park

🚇 2 St, 5 St 🚌 ❼ 6th & Market Sts; www.nps.gov/inde

This urban park preserves key structures associated with Philadelphia's crucial role in the American Revolution. Start at the Independence Visitor Center, where you can watch introductory films and pick up tickets for timed entrance to **Independence Hall**, a Georgian building at the heart of the park, completed in 1753 as the Pennsylvania State House. It was here on July 4, 1776, that representatives from the 13

American colonies signed the Declaration of Independence, the document that declared America's freedom from the British Empire. The evocative Assembly Room, Pennsylvania Supreme Court, and Governor's Council Chamber are furnished simply, as they were during the late 1700s. Eleven years later, the US Constitution was drafted in the same building.

Independence Hall's West Wing is home to the must-see Great Essentials exhibit, displaying original printed copies of the Declaration of Independence, the Articles of Confederation, and the US Constitution. Congress Hall, originally completed in 1789 as the Philadelphia County Court House next door

↑ Grand and impressive Independence Hall, Philadelphia

(5th and Chestnut sts), served as the meeting place of the US Congress from 1790 to 1800. Completed in 1791, the austere Old City Hall served as the temporary Supreme Court of the United States from 1791 to 1800, with most of the furnishings from that period.

One block east, the **Second Bank of the United States** is now a gallery with over 150

EAT

City Tavern

Authentic replica of the 1773 tavern where the Founding Fathers wined and dined during the Revolutionary War. Today staff in period dress serve the delicious old-fashioned dishes.

🏠 138 S 2nd St 🕐 Sun
🌐 citytavern.com

$$$

---

portraits of celebrated 18th- and 19th-century political leaders, military officers, explorers, and scientists, many by preeminent artist Charles Willson Peale. Built in 1819–24, the building is one of America's finest examples of Greek Revival architecture.

The large brass bell that once hung in Independence Hall is now reverently displayed in the Liberty Bell Center (526 Market St). In 1846, a small crack developed and the bell could no longer be sounded. However, it remains the go-to symbol of the Colonial struggle for self-governance. The center incorporates fascinating displays that highlight the bell's importance to the story

of America's independence. Benjamin Franklin (p121) lived and worked in Franklin Court, though only a "ghost house" now marks the outline of Franklin's home, just outside the Benjamin Franklin Museum (317 Chestnut St). Also here is the Franklin Court Printing Office (which features a working 18th-century printing press), and the Fragments of Franklin Court exhibit of artifacts found here.

Independence Hall

Ⓧ 🏠 420 Chestnut St
🕐 9am–5pm daily (summer: to 7pm); timed tickets required Mar–Dec 🕐 Dec 25
🌐 nps.gov/inde

Second Bank of the United States

Ⓧ 🏠 520 Chestnut St
🕐 Memorial Day–Labor Day: 11am–5pm daily; rest of year: 11am–5pm Wed–Sun 🕐 Dec 25
🌐 nps.gov/inde

---

② 🚲 🎭 🍴 ☕ 🛍

National Constitution Center

🏠 525 Arch St 🚇 5 St 🚌
🕐 9:30am–5pm Mon–Sat, noon–5pm Sun 🕐 Jan 1, Thanksgiving, Dec 25
🌐 constitutioncenter.org

At the northern end of the Independence National Historical Park, this slick,

interactive museum tells the story of the US Constitution, drafted in Philadelphia in 1787. *Freedom Rising* in the Kimmel Theater is a 17-minute multimedia dramatization of the American fight for freedom from 1787 to the present day, while Signers' Hall features 42 life-size bronze statues of the Founding Fathers. The center also owns an original copy of the first public printing of the momentous Constitution.

↑ Historical heavy-weights at the National Constitution Center

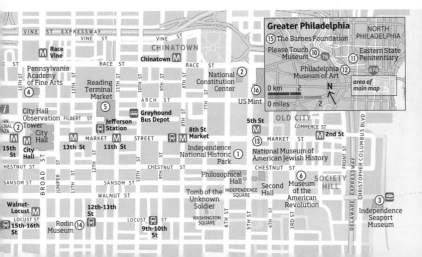

③

Independence Seaport Museum

🏠 211 S Columbus Blvd
Ⓢ 2 St 🚌 🕐 10am–5pm daily (summer: to 7pm Thu–Sat) 🚪 Jan–Mar: Mon; Jan 1, Thanksgiving, Dec 25
🌐 phillyseaport.org

Quartered in a stunningly modern building on the waterfront, the vast Independence Seaport Museum's mandate is to preserve US maritime history and tradition, with a particular focus on Chesapeake Bay and the Delaware River and its tributaries. Displays combine art and artifacts with hands-on computer games, large-scale models, and audio-visual attractions.

In "River Alive!", a 4,000-sq-ft (372-sq-m) interactive exhibit, the first floor of the museum has been transformed into an area devoted to the Delaware River. The installation lets you take a closer look at how the river weaves through the every-day lives of millions of people, the wildlife that populates the waters, and the threats to the river's ecology.

> Quartered in a stunningly modern building on the waterfront, the vast Independence Seaport Museum's mandate is to preserve US maritime history and tradition.

Other highlights include "Tides of Freedom," which focuses on the history of African presence on the Delaware River, and "Seafarin' Saturdays," with activities designed for kids.

The World War II submarine *Becuna*, which was commissioned in 1943 and fought battles in the South Pacific, and the *Olympia*, Admiral George Dewey's flagship in the Battle of Manila (1898), are berthed next to the museum.

---

④ 🧭 🖥 🛍

Pennsylvania Academy of Fine Arts

🏠 118 N Broad St at Cherry St Ⓢ 15 St 🚌 🕐 10am–5pm Tue–Fri (to 9pm Wed), 11am–5pm Sat & Sun 🚪 Federal hols 🌐 pafa.org

The collection of this museum and school, founded in 1805, spans the history of American painting. Galleries display works by some of the art world's best-known denizens. One of them, the Classical stylist Benjamin West (1738–1820), a Quaker who grew up in Springfield, Pennsylvania, helped organize the British Royal Academy in 1768, and four years later was named Historical Painter to the King. Impressionist and former Academy of Fine Arts student Mary Cassatt (1844–1926), and modern abstractionist Richard Diebenkorn (1922–93), among others, share wall space.

For well over a century, the Annual Student Exhibition has been one of Philadelphia's most anticipated cultural events. Each spring, students from the academy showcase their work, and people flock to buy pieces from the up-and-coming talents of the art world (notable PAFA alumni include Maxfield Parrish, Mary Cassatt, and David Lynch).

↑ The *Olympia* warship and the *Becuna* submarine docked at the Independence Seaport Museum

↑ Fresh flowers and hanging plants at Reading Terminal Market

This distinctive building is considered one of the finest examples of Victorian-Gothic architecture in America, and is especially striking in contrast with Claes Oldenburg's *Paint Torch*, a 51-ft (15-m) sculpture of a paintbrush, staked outside.

⑤
Reading Terminal Market

🏛️51 N 12th St 🚇City Hall, 13 St, Juniper St 🚍 🕐8am-6pm daily 🚫Federal hols 🌐readingterminalmarket.org

This particular market was created under an elevated train shed after two farmers' markets were leveled to make space for a new terminal in 1893. So modern was the market that people came from as far as the New Jersey Shore to buy fresh produce brought in from Lancaster County. Reading Terminal Market declined over the years and was nearly destroyed in the 1970s. Today, however, it has been revitalized, and fish-mongers, butchers, bakers, florists, and greengrocers vie for space. Here you'll also find stands run by Amish women selling delicious dairy and baked goods.

⑥ 🎨 🎭 🍴 💻 🛍️
Museum of the American Revolution

🏛️101 S 3rd St 🚇30 St 🕐10am-5pm daily (mid-Jun-mid-Sep: 9:30am-6pm) 🚫Jan 1, Thanksg., Dec 25 🌐amrevmuseum.org

One of the city's most recent additions, this absorbing interactive museum chronicles the history of the American Revolution, from colonial unrest in the 1760s to the decisive Patriot victory at the siege of Yorktown in 1781. Beginning with the 15-minute film *Revolution*, the museum features Revolution-era weapons, personal items, letters, diaries, interactive digital displays, and immersive installations (including a life-size reproduction of the Boston Liberty Tree and a replica of a privateer ship).

⑦ 🎨 🍴 🛍️
The Franklin Institute Science Museum

🏛️222 N 20th St 🚇Suburban 🕐9:30am-5pm daily 🚫Thanksgiving, Dec 24 & 25 🌐fi.edu

This fun, hands-on museum is a big hit with kids. Among the museum's attractions are Electricity Hall, which show-cases Benjamin Franklin's discovery of electricity, "Your Brain," which offers a glimpse into the inner workings of the human brain, the Escape Rooms, where participants have to solve puzzles and riddles to escape before the time runs out, and the Giant Heart, a walk-through exhibit that lays out the anatomy and physiology of the human body. The Fels Planetarium is a particular favorite, where cutting-edge astronomical presentations are projected onto a 60-ft (18-m) dome. Shows are put on throughout the day and are included in general admission. Films shown in the immersive 79-ft (24-m) Tuttleman IMAX Theater are extra.

BENJAMIN FRANKLIN IN PHILLY

Politician, philosopher, and inventor, Benjamin Franklin (1705-1790) was born in Boston but fled to Philadelphia at the age of 17. He became a respected newspaper editor and printer, a legacy explored at the Franklin Court museums *(p119)*. Franklin was also a founder of the Philosophical Society in 1743, commemorated today at the American Philosophical Society Museum next to Independence Hall. Franklin is buried in the nearby Christ Church Burial Ground and honored by a statue at the Benjamin Franklin National Memorial, located in the rotunda of the Franklin Institute Science Museum *(222 N 20th St)*.

⑧ 🛹

Mütter Museum of the College of Physicians of Philadelphia

📍 19 S 22nd St 🇸 22 St 🚌
🕐 10am–5pm daily 🚫 Jan 1, Thanksgiving, Dec 24 & 25
🌐 muttermuseum.org

Founded in 1787 for the "advancement of the science of medicine," the still-active college is a well-known source of health information. This is provided by the institute's C. Everett Koop Community Health Information Center, through its library, videotapes, and computer system.

The Mütter Museum, on the first floor of one of the college's buildings, is a fascinating collection of preserved specimens, skeletal constructions, and wax figures. These were originally used for educational purposes in the mid-19th century, when diseases and genetic defects were generally identifiable only by patients' physical manifestations. Some of the afflictions on display here are quite grotesque and

may not be suitable for small children or those who are easily upset.

The museum also contains medical instruments, exhibits on the history of medicine over the last 100 years, a re-creation of a doctor's office from the early 20th century, and a medicinal plant garden. It also holds exhibits of contemporary art, photography, and other subjects.

---

⑨ 🛹 Ⓜ

One Liberty Observation Deck

📍 1650 Market St 🇸 15 St
🕐 May–Aug: 10am–9pm daily; Sep–Apr: 10am–8pm daily 🌐 phillyfromthe top.com

Sensational views of the city and the Delaware River await at the observation deck of the 57th floor of One Liberty Place, on the corner of Market and 17th streets. The 945-ft (288-m) skyscraper was completed in 1987 to a design by Chicago-based architect Helmut Jahn,

Did You Know?

A typical 7-inch Philly cheesesteak has 520 calories, 0.8 oz of fat, and 1,047 mg of sodium.

who was heavily influenced by the Art Deco style and used the Chrysler Building in New York City as a reference point. This influence is most obviously seen in the step-like recession of the uppermost floors and the huge spire on top. It was also the first building in Philadelphia to break the "gentleman's agreement" not to build any structure higher than the statue of William Penn on top of Philadelphia City Hall (completed in 1901), and was for many years the tallest building in the city, until it was surpassed by the Comcast Center in 2008.

In addition to the striking panoramic views, One Liberty also features installations

→ Giant sculpture of Benjamin Franklin at One Liberty Observation Deck

→

A long walk down a crumbling cell block at Eastern State Penitentiary

such as a giant green sculpture of Benjamin Franklin, listening stations, and touch screens. Entrance includes the "Philly from the Top" tour, where guides point out iconic sites that are visible from the observation deck.

⑩ 🤸 🖥 🎒
Please Touch Museum

📍 4231 Av of the Republic
Ⓢ 22 St 🚌 🕐 9am-5pm
Mon, Tue & Thu-Sat, 10am-5pm Wed, 11am-5pm Sun
🚫 Thanksgiving, Dec 25
Ⓦ pleasetouchmuseum.org

Philadelphia's premier museum for children is aimed at kids aged under eight, with several exhibits that enhance a child's ability to learn, discover, and play. The "Alice's Adventures in Wonderland" exhibit is based on the popular classic story

and includes many settings from the book to encourage problem-solving and language skills. The SuperMarket has checkouts, shopping carts, and toy food items, while Barnyard Babies teaches children about life on a farm. Other activities include the absorbing interactive theater performances, with musicians, dancers, and storytellers.

⑪ 🤸 Ⓜ
Eastern State Penitentiary

📍 2027 Fairmount Av at 22nd St 🚌 🕐 10am-5pm daily 🚫 Jan 1, Thanksg., Dec 25 Ⓦ easternstate.org

Nicknamed "The House" by inmates and guards, the Eastern State Penitentiary, established in 1829, was a revolutionary concept in criminal justice. Prior to this, criminals were thrown together in despicable conditions and punished by physical brutality. The Philadelphia Quakers proposed an alternative – a place where criminals could be alone to ponder and

become penitent for their actions. During incarceration, with sentences seldom less than 5 years in length, inmates literally never heard or saw another human being for the entire duration of their stay. The prison had one entrance and 30-ft- (9-m-) high boundary walls. Each solitary cell had a private outdoor exercise yard contained by a 10-ft (3-m) wall. Eastern State's many "guests" included bootlegger and crime lord Al Capone. It was officially closed in 1971.

💬 INSIDER TIP
Best Philly Cheesesteaks

Philadelphia's most iconic food is the Philly cheesesteak – a grilled steak sandwich slathered with provolone or Cheez Whiz and onions. Pat's King of Steaks (1237 E Passyunk Av) was the originator and still serves one of the best, along with Geno's Steaks (1219 S 9th St), both of which are open 24 hours a day.

↑ Vincent van Gogh's *Sunflowers* at the Museum of Art

⑫ 🚲 🅼 🍴 🖥 🏛

Philadelphia Museum of Art

📍 26th St & Ben. Franklin Pkwy 🚇 Spring Garden 🚌 🕐 10am–5pm Tue–Sun 🚫 Mon, 4 July, Thanksg., Dec 25 🌐 philamuseum.org

This museum attracts major exhibitions to supplement its permanent collection which ranges from 15th-century illuminated manuscripts to modern sculpture by Constantin Brancusi. The full-scale medieval cloister courtyard and fountain on the second floor is a favorite, as are the French Gothic chapel and a pillared temple from Madurai, India. A collection of Pennsylvania Dutch and American decorative arts adjoins galleries that feature paintings by American artists.

Associated facilities nearby are the Perelman Building and the Rodin Museum. This venue is also famous for its notable appearance in the 1976 movie *Rocky*, where the title character bounds up the museum's steps as he trains for his upcoming title match with Apollo Creed.

📷 PICTURE PERFECT
"Rocky" at the Museum of Art

Don't miss the famous Rocky Statue at the bottom of the "Rocky Steps" in front of Philly's Museum of Art. Created for a scene in *Rocky III* (1982), the sculpture celebrates the city's favorite fictional son, boxer Rocky Balboa, played by Sylvester Stallone in the movies.

⑬ 🚲 🅼 🖥 🏛

National Museum of American Jewish History

📍 101 S Independence Mall 🚇 5 St 🕐 10am–5pm Tue–Fri, 10am–5:30pm Sat & Sun 🚫 Jan 1, Passover, Rosh Hashanah, Yom Kippur, Thanksg. 🌐 nmajh.org

This museum celebrates the history of Jews in America. The museum was founded by the Congregation Mikveh Israel, established here in 1740 and known as the "Synagogue of the American Revolution" (many of the congregation's members served in the Revolutionary War). The museum owns some 30,000 artifacts, from rare Civil War letters and a Torah scroll and ark (from 1761), to a precious manuscript prayer from 1789. The museum's Hall of Fame honorees include composer Irving Berlin, Albert Einstein, entrepreneur Estée Lauder, and singer Barbra Streisand.

⑭ 🚲 🅼

Rodin Museum

📍 2151 Ben. Franklin Pkwy 🚇 Spring Garden 🕐 10am–5pm Wed–Mon 🚫 4 July, Thanksgiving, Dec 25 🌐 rodinmuseum.org

This small but exquisite gallery is one of the city's lesser-visited treasures. Open since 1929, it contains the largest collection of sculptor Auguste Rodin's works outside Paris (some 150 bronzes, marbles, and plasters). The museum was the brain-child of local tycoon and "King of cinema" Jules Mastbaum, who donated his Rodin collection to the city and had the Beaux-Arts style building specially created to house it. Highlights include the towering *Gates of Hell*, a plaster model of a naked Honoré de Balzac, and the poignant *Young Mother in the Grotto*.

⑮ 🚲 Ⓜ 🍴 🖥 🛍

The Barnes Foundation

🏛 Philadelphia Campus, 2025 Ben. Franklin Pkwy Ⓢ Spring Garden 🚍 🕐 11am-5pm Wed-Mon 🚫 4 July 🌐 barnesfoundation.org

Established in the year 1922 to share the private collection of pharmaceutical magnate Albert C. Barnes with "people of all socioeconomic levels," this museum has one of the world's premier displays of French modern and Post-Impressionist paintings. Originally housed in Barnes's personal museum in suburban Pennsylvania, the collection was relocated in 2012 to a 93,000-sq-ft (8,600-sq-m) limestone-clad building in downtown Philadelphia. Crowned by a translucent light box, the two-story building was conceived as "a gallery in a garden and a garden in a gallery," providing visitors with an unusual experience.

Among 800 or so works on display, there are dozens by Auguste Renoir, Paul Cézanne,

↑ The elegant Barnes Foundation building reflected in water

and Henri Matisse, and many more by Picasso, Modigliani, van Gogh, Seurat, Rousseau, and almost every other noteworthy artist of that era. Other exhibits include ancient Greek and Egyptian art, medieval manuscripts, African sculpture, American furniture, ceramics, and handwrought ironwork. The art is displayed to highlight artistic affinities between diverse works. For instance, the Barnes Collection is arranged in accordance with the unique specifications Albert Barnes left after his death, where all of the paintings, sculptures, and craft pieces are grouped into distinct ensembles, without labels and with very little regard to the chronology of the works themselves.

← Auguste Rodin's *Three Shades* sculpture at the Rodin Museum

⑯

US Mint

🏛 151 N Independence Mall East Ⓢ 5 St 🕐 Summer: 9am-4:30pm Mon-Sat; winter: 9am-4:30pm Mon-Fri 🚫 Federal hols 🌐 usmint.gov

The Philadelphia mint, the oldest in the United States, makes the majority of the coins that Americans use every day, and also produces gold bullion coins and national medals. The first US coins, minted in 1793, were copper pennies and half-pennies intended solely for local commerce. Today, 24 hours a day, 5 days a week, hundreds of machines and operators in a room the size of a football field blank, anneal, count, and bag millions of dollars' worth of quarters, dimes, and pennies. Commemorative coins are available in the gift shop along with a variety of collectibles, books, and games. Tours are self-guided and take around 45 minutes to complete (no reservations are necessary).

A SHORT WALK
INDEPENDENCE NATIONAL HISTORIC PARK

Distance 1 mile (1.5 km) **Time** 20 minutes
Nearest subway Chinatown

If it's history you're after history, this walk is a must. Known locally as Independence Mall, this urban park encompasses several well-preserved 18th-century structures associated with the American Revolution. The Declaration of Independence that heralded the birth of a new nation was signed in this historic area. Dominated by the tall brick tower of Independence Hall, the park includes the oldest street in Philadelphia, the US Mint, and several special-interest museums exploring Philadelphia's Colonial and seafaring past as well as its ethnic heritage.

Arch St. Friends Meeting House

Christ Church Burial Ground, *where Benjamin Franklin and other notables are buried.*

National Constitution Center

The **National Museum of American Jewish History** *celebrates the history of Jewish people in America (p124).*

Inspirational stories of the city's famous African American citizens are displayed at the **African American Museum**.

RACE STREET

ARCH ST

5TH STREET

MARKET STREET

7TH STREET

6TH ST

Independence Visitor Center

● **START**

The **Atwater-Kent Museum** *traces Philadelphia's history, from its infancy as a small country town to current times.*

Inscribed with the words, "Proclaim Liberty throughout all the Land," the **Liberty Bell** *was rung when the Declaration of Independence was adopted.*

←
The beloved symbol of American independence, the Liberty Bell

Elfreth's Alley *is the city's oldest residential street and is lined with 18th-century houses, many of which are now shops.*

Betsy Ross House, *a restored 18th-century home, is a memorial to Betsy Ross, who is credited with stitching the first American flag.*

Locator Map
For more detail see p118

PHILADELPHIA

Independence National Historic Park

Christ Church

2ND STREET

3RD STREET

↑ Gorgeous brick buildings in historic Elfreth's Alley

City Tavern *was the venue of frequent debates during Colonial times. It still serves food and drink today (p119).*

Benjamin Franklin lived and worked in the buildings in what is now **Franklin Court** *(p119). Here you'll find the B. Free Franklin Post Office and Benjamin Franklin Museum.*

4TH ST

FINISH

This 18th-century garden, created by the **Pennsylvania Horticultural Society** *(1827), was the first of its kind in the US.*

CHESTNUT STREET

WALNUT STREET

An extensive collection of portraits of luminaries involved in the military, diplomatic, and political events of 1776 is on display at the Grecian-style **Second Bank of the US** *(p118)..*

Did You Know?

The Liberty Bell, which was originally cast in London, cracked when it was first rung.

Independence Hall *(p118) is the centerpiece of the park and a World Heritage Site. It was here that the Declaration of Independence was signed on July 4, 1776.*

Washington Square Park

0 meters   500   N
0 yards   500

PENNSYLVANIA

Pennsylvania has it all – vivid history, beautiful scenery, and irresistible dining. Philadelphia might be the state's city with dramatic history, but Pittsburgh is a sparkling cultural gem. Most of the state is rural and bucolic, a green patchwork of farms, embroidered with Appalachian forests and streams, tidy fields, and cute towns.

❷ Gettysburg

🏛🚆 ℹ 1195 Baltimore Pike; www.destination gettysburg.com

A pivotal confrontation of the Civil War (p54) took place near the small farming community of Gettysburg in early July 1863. Nearly 100,000 Union soldiers under General George Meade fought 75,000 Confederates led by Robert E. Lee. After three days of fighting, a staggering 50,000 soldiers lay dead or wounded, and the Confederates were turned back. To honor their sacrifice, President Abraham Lincoln dedicated the Gettysburg National Cemetery with his inspirational Gettysburg Address. Several monuments have been placed throughout the battlefield, now the **Gettysburg National Military Park**. Start at the Museum and Visitor Center, which includes showings of *A New Birth of Freedom*, a film narrated by Morgan Freeman, a museum featuring relics of the battle, and the Cyclorama, a giant circular mural painted in 1884. The mural dramatizes Picket's Charge, where over 6,000 Confederate soldiers were killed or wounded.

For more on the Civil War, head to state capital Harrisburg, 40 miles (64 km) north. Here the National Civil War Museum chronicles the conflict with artifacts owned by President Lincoln, as well as average soldiers.

THE AMISH

The Amish trace their roots to the Swiss Anabaptist ("New Birth") movement of 1525, an offshoot of the Protestant Reformation, whose creed rejected the formality of established churches. Today's Old Order Amish disdain any device that would connect them to the larger world, such as electricity, phones, and cars. Conspicuous because of their plain attire and horse-and-buggy mode of transportation, the Amish in America are little changed from their 17th-century ancestors who came to the US.

Gettysburg National Military Park

⊗ ⏱ Apr-Oct: 6am-10pm daily; Nov-Mar: 6am-7pm daily; Visitor Center: 8am-5pm daily (Apr-Oct: to 6pm) ⏱ Jan 1, Thanksg., Dec 25 🌐 nps. gov/gett

Gettysburg Eternal Light Peace Memorial on the Gettysburg Battlefield, and the circular Cyclorama mural *(inset)*

③ Lancaster County and Amish Country

🅰️🚍 ℹ️ 501 Greenfield Rd, Lancaster; www.cityof lancasterpa.com

Pennsylvania is a bastion of the Amish and Mennonite religious communities, the so-called "Pennsylvania Dutch." Actually deriving from early German immigrants ("Deutsch," or German, became "Dutch"), the "Old Order Amish" Christians live and work without modern conveniences like electricity. It's common to see them riding in horse-drawn buggies in their distinctive 17th-century clothes, though it's extremely disrespectful to take photographs. Lancaster County is at the heart of Pennsylvania Dutch Country, studded with covered bridges, one-room schools, and so-called "Dutch buffets."

The Amish Farm and House and Amish Village both give fascinating insights into Amish culture. There are also local, specialized guided tours in and around Lancaster. Jacob's Choice at the Amish Experience Theater is an immersive 40-minute movie

dramatizing the story of the Fishers, an Old Order Amish family. The movie screens daily every hour, on the hour, (10am–5pm).

In the western part of the state, scenic Lawrence County and the town of New Castle is at the center of a quilt of Amish and Mennonite farms, parks, and villages.

---

④ Flight 93 National Memorial

🅰️ 6424 Lincoln Hwy, Stoystown 🌐 nps.gov/flni

The calm of this remote corner of rural Pennsylvania was torn apart on September 11, 2001, when hijacked United Airlines Flight 93 crashed here, killing all 40 passengers and crew. Today the site is marked by a poignant memorial, comprising the white marble "Wall of Names" and an engraved boulder at the actual point of impact. The concrete-and-glass Visitor Center overlooking the site pays tribute to the heroic actions of the passengers, who tried to storm the cockpit before the plane reached what was thought to be its eventual destination – Washington, DC.

---

⑤ Fallingwater

🅰️ 1491 Mill Run Rd, Mill Run ⏰ 8am–4pm Thu–Mon ⏰ Jan, Feb, Thanksgiving, Dec 24, Dec 25 🌐 fallingwater.org

One of the most spectacular homes ever designed by American architect Frank Lloyd Wright, Fallingwater sits on the edge of a waterfall deep in the Pennsylvania woods. The incredibly picturesque house was designed in 1935 for the family of Pittsburgh department store owner Edgar J. Kaufmann, perfectly

↑ The traditional Amish Village at Lancaster County and Amish Country

showcasing Wright's famous architectural philosophy of creating a harmonious union of art and nature. The highly illuminating tours take in all the wonderfully preserved rooms – it's also the only major Wright building with its original furnishings and artwork intact. Advance tickets are essential, and can be purchased online.

EAT

Good 'n' Plenty
Family-style eatery with "world famous" fried chicken and cracker pudding.

🅰️ 150 Eastbrook Rd, Smoketown 🌐 goodnplenty.com

⑤⑤⑤

Shady Maple Smorgasbord
One of the most popular Pennsylvania Dutch all-you-can-eat buffets, with superb home-cooked meals all day.

🅰️ 129 Toddy Dr, East Earl ⏰ shady-maple.com

⑤⑤⑤

6

Hershey

101 Chocolate World Way; www.hersheypa.com

Its name a dead giveaway, this factory town and wildly popular tourist destination revolves around chocolate. Even its streetlights are shaped like silver-foil-wrapped Hershey's Kisses. The town's main attraction is **Hershey's Chocolate World**, which features a 4D Chocolate Mystery Show, Create Your Own Candy Bar, Hershey's Chocolate Tour, and Hershey's Unwrapped, an interactive experience revealing Hershey's chocolate-making process. A free sample awaits at the end, while a series of shops sell souvenirs and every Hershey product available. Nearby is **Hersheypark**, a vast amusement park offering 80 rides, including five waterslides and one of the finest Philadelphia Toboggan Company four-row carousels in existence today.

Hershey's Chocolate World

SR 743 & US 422, Hershey 9am–5pm daily (times vary, check website) hersheys.com/chocolate world

Hersheypark

100 W Hersheypark Dr Times vary, check website hersheypark.com

7

Pittsburgh

120 Fifth Av; www.visitpittsburgh.com

Located at the point where the Allegheny and Monongahela come together to form the Ohio River, Pittsburgh is an American success story. It grew from a frontier outpost to become an industrial giant, home to the huge mills of the US Steel conglomerate as well as the food company Heinz and the Westinghouse electric company. From the Civil War through World War II, Pittsburgh thrived, but in the 1950s and 1960s the city's fortunes faded and Pittsburgh became run-down. However, times have changed and Pittsburgh is today a dynamic, buzzing metropolis, home to various cultural institutions and tempting restaurants.

Known as the Golden Triangle, Downtown Pittsburgh is thriving once more, with a lively Cultural District and its historic Market Square lined with restaurants. Point State Park covers the spot where the rivers meet, marked by a fountain. The park was also the site of French and British forts in the 18th century, commemorated at the Fort Pitt Museum and the 1764 Fort Pitt Blockhouse. Just east of Downtown, you'll find the thriving Strip District, a half-mile strip of land bordered by

the Allegheny on the north side. Head here for affordable and fun foodie experiences, or immerse yourself in an eclectic mix of markets, boutiques, and street vendors.

The history of Pittsburgh is chronicled at the **Senator John Heinz History Center**. The enlightening "Pittsburgh: A Tradition of Innovation" exhibit focuses on the city's movers and shakers, from George Westinghouse to Andrew Carnegie. Other highlights include sets from *Mister Rogers' Neighborhood*, and an exhibit on local ketchup legend Heinz.

Endowed by famous steel magnate Andrew Carnegie, the **Carnegie Museum of Art** offers a brilliantly lit suite of galleries chockfull of treasures and masterpieces, with exhibits ranging from ancient Egyptian sculptures to Impressionist and modern American art, including works by Roy Lichtenstein and Alexander Calder. The Carnegie Museum of Natural

←

Shopping for chocolatey treats to take home at Hershey's Chocolate World

↑ Pleasure boats puttering around Point State Park in front of the impeccable Pittsburgh skyline

History, found in the same complex, opens out on a central gallery and relies on filtered natural light as a part of its architectural charm. Exhibits change from time to time, but most of the displays consist of dioramas made up of taxidermy specimens.

The 42-story **Cathedral of Learning** houses the University of Pittsburgh's Nationality Classrooms, which seek to reflect the different ethnic groups that contribute to the city's heritage. It's a city landmark, and shouldn't be missed. Founded in the 1930s, each of the 31 rooms is trimmed with authentic decor and furnishings, depicting a unique time and place from 5th-century BC Greece to 16th-century Poland. Audio tours provide great insights into the cathedral.

In the city's north side, the tile-clad exterior of the **Andy Warhol Museum** reflects the workaday character of the neighborhood. The former warehouse conceals a brightly illuminated and ultramodern interior dedicated to the Pittsburgh-born founder of American Pop Art, Andy Warhol (1928–87). Its extensive collection, housed across 17 galleries, includes thousands of the artist's paintings, prints, sculptures, photographs, and films. There is also a calendar of special exhibitions.

Mount Washington, on the bank of the Monongahela, offers sensational views. The historic **Incline Railway** is a charming funicular that carries passengers from Carson Street up to the overlooks on Grandview Avenue.

Senator John Heinz History Center
⊗ ⊜ ⌂ 1212 Smallman St
🕐 10am–5pm daily
Ⓦ heinzhistorycenter.org

Carnegie Museum of Art
⊗ ⊜ ⊜ ⌂ ⌂ 4400 Forbes Av
🕐 10am–5pm Mon & Wed–Sun (to 8pm Thu) 🚫 Federal hols
Ⓦ cmoa.org

> **Times have changed and Pittsburgh is today a dynamic, buzzing metropolis, home to various cultural institutions and tempting restaurants.**

EAT

S&D Polish Deli
As well as stocking the largest selection of Polish products in the city, S&D is the go-to spot for authentic pierogi, borsch, and haluski.

⌂ 2204 Penn Av
Ⓦ sdpolishdeli.com

$⑤$⑤$⑤

Cathedral of Learning
⌂ 4200 Fifth Av 🕐 9am–2:30pm Mon–Sat, 11am–2:30pm Sun Ⓦ nationalityrooms.pitt.edu

Andy Warhol Museum
⊗ ⊜ ⊜ ⌂ 117 Sandusky St
🕐 10am–5pm Tue–Sun (to 10pm Fri) Ⓦ warhol.org

Incline Railway
⊗ ⌂ 1197 West Carson St
🕐 5:30am–12:45am Mon–Sat, 7:45am–midnight Sun & federal hols

NEW ENGLAND

A misty valley in rural Vermont

EXPLORE NEW ENGLAND

This chapter divides New England into four sightseeing areas, as shown on the map below. Find out more about each area on the following pages.

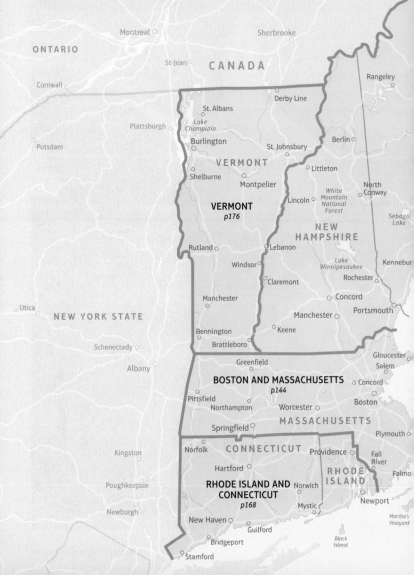

QUEBEC

ONTARIO

Montreal

Sherbrooke

St-Jean

CANADA

Cornwall

Rangeley

Derby Line

St. Albans

Lake Champlain

Plattsburgh

Burlington

St. Johnsbury

Berlin

Potsdam

VERMONT

Littleton

Shelburne

Montpelier

White Mountain National Forest

North Conway

Lincoln

VERMONT
p176

NEW HAMPSHIRE

Sebago Lake

Rutland

Lebanon

Windsor

Lake Winnipesaukee

Kennebur

Utica

Claremont

Rochester

NEW YORK STATE

Manchester

Concord

Portsmouth

Bennington

Manchester

Schenectady

Keene

Brattleboro

Gloucester

Albany

Greenfield

Salem

BOSTON AND MASSACHUSETTS
p144

Concord

Pittsfield

Northampton

Worcester

Boston

MASSACHUSETTS

Springfield

Plymouth

CONNECTICUT

Norfolk

Providence

Kingston

Hartford

Fall River

Falmo

RHODE ISLAND

RHODE ISLAND AND CONNECTICUT
p168

Norwich

Poughkeepsie

Newburgh

Newport

Mystic

Martha's Vineyard

New Haven

Guilford

Block Island

Bridgeport

Stamford

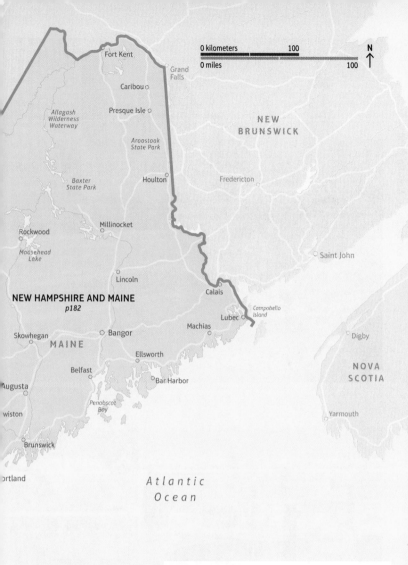

←

1 Boston's dynamic skyline.

2 Boats in Provincetown marina, Cape Cod.

3 Mookie Betts, playing for Boston Red Sox, Fenway Park.

4 Interior of The Breakers.

2 WEEKS
in New England

Day 1

Embrace Boston's history by walking the Freedom Trail *(p156)*, tracing the American Revolution. After touring Faneuil Hall, enjoy lunch in the food hall of adjacent Quincy Market and shopping in the surrounding Faneuil Hall Marketplace buildings *(p151)*. Continue to the North End to see the Paul Revere House and Old North Church *(p150)* before concluding in Charlestown *(p161)*. You'll be wowed by the panoramic view atop Bunker Hill Monument. Backtrack to the North End for an Italian dinner on Hanover Street.

Day 2

You'll be covering a lot of ground today, so start with the 9am tour of Fenway Park *(p159)*, the most venerated field in Major League Baseball. From Fenway, stroll through the green paths of the Back Bay Fens to the Museum of Fine Arts *(p159)* and marvel at the American masters, such as Winslow Homer and John Singer Sargent. Then take the MBTA to Harvard Square for a free student-led tour of Harvard Yard before perusing bookstores and enjoying dinner near the university *(p160)*.

Day 3

Rise early and drive the length of Cape Cod *(p164)* to Provincetown – a trip of around 2.5 hours (following Route 6). Rent a bicycle and pedal through the dramatic dunelands before spending quality beach time at Race Point or Herring Cove; the light here is astonishing. Back in town, visit some of the quirky contemporary art galleries along Commercial Street before enjoying a seafood dinner overlooking the fishing village's sheltered harbor.

Day 4

Head back toward mainland Massachusetts by following Route 6A from the Orleans circle to Sandwich. Scenic saltwater villages, antiques dealers, and workshops of contemporary potters, jewelers, and other artists punctuate this road, known as the Old King's Highway. Stop in Barnstable to explore the birdlife and beaches of Sandy Point before entering Sandwich, where you'll spend the night.

Day 5

The 90-minute drive to Newport *(p171)*, Rhode Island, brings you to one of America's top yachting harbors and the most glittering mansions on the East Coast. Park at your hotel or the waterfront visitor center and take the RIPTA trolley to Bellevue Avenue to see the "summer cottages" built for the barons of the Gilded Age. Soak up the lavish lifestyle on a tour of The Breakers *(p171)* before clearing your head on an afternoon sailing cruise from the harbor and dinner at the docks.

Day 6

Follow Route 138 west from downtown Newport to cross Narragansett Bay on the soaring Pell Bridge. Continue for about an hour to the town of Mystic *(p174)*, Connecticut, to explore maritime history. Amble around Mystic Seaport and eat lunch at Mystic Pizza *(p175)*, the inspiration for the 1988 film of the same name. It's only an hour to Hartford, where the flamboyant home of novelist and humorist Mark Twain is now a museum. End the day with a comedy show and dinner at City Steam Brewery and Cafe in downtown Hartford.

→

Day 7

Your destination today is the Berkshires (p165), western Massachusetts, New England's epicenter of summer theater and outdoor music. If the kids are with you, stop at the Springfield Museums (p166), with its enchanting sculpture garden of Dr. Seuss characters. Continue to Stockbridge to see the work of American illustrator, at the Norman Rockwell Museum. Nearby Lenox is the hub of shopping and dining in the southern Berkshires – and home to Tanglewood, summer venue of the Boston Symphony Orchestra.

Day 8

Rise early and drive an hour north to Lanesborough to corkscrew up Mount Greylock where, on clear days, you can see parts of four states (the ranger station has maps of hiking routes). Continue north for an hour to Bennington (p178), Vermont, to ascend the Battle Monument and visit the Bennington Museum, best known for paintings by "Grandma Moses." The stoneware of Bennington Potters may tempt you to buy another suitcase.

Day 9

After a classic roadfood breakfast at the Blue Benn Diner in Bennington, drive north on Route 7 to Manchester (p178) to check out the upscale designer outlet stores. Veer east to connect to Route 100 north, one of the best fall foliage roads in Vermont. Follow Route 4 to the country squire village of Woodstock (p179). Its quintessential charm is perfectly captured at the Billings Farm and Museum and the Woodstock Inn, both creations of the Rockefeller family.

Day 10

From Woodstock, pick up the I-91 north for a striking 40-mile (65-km)drive along the Connecticut River Valley. At Exit 17, follow Route 302 east through the White Mountains to connect with I-93 south toward Franconia Notch State Park (p185). It's worth exploring the Flume Gorge and riding the aerial tramway at Cannon Mountain for another jaw-dropping view. Dine and spend the night in Lincoln or Woodstock in the midst of the White Mountain National Forest (p184).

1 Norman Rockwell Museum.
2 Blue Benn Diner, Bennington.
3 Kancamagus Highway.
4 Franconia Notch State Park.
5 Maine lobster.
6 Bradley Wharf in Rockland.
7 On Cadillac Mountain,
Acadia National Park.

Day 11

In the morning, pick up Route 112 in Lincoln to drive east through the White Mountains on the exhilarating Kancamagus Highway – one of America's premier scenic byways and a sure boost to your adrenaline. Purchase a parking permit at the ranger station so you can explore the roadside trails. When you reach the end in Conway, pick up Route 302 east to Portland (p188), Maine, about a 90-minute drive. Enjoy the seaside ambiance of the Old Port shopping and dining district.

Day 12

You're finally experiencing the long, rugged midcoast of Maine as you drive Route 1 north to reach Rockland. Don't hurry – the maritime villages on the peninsulas dribbling off the coast are some of the most scenic in New England. Rockland is the lobster-fishing capital of Maine and a cruise aboard a lobster boat is a fascinating way to see the coast. Some of Maine's greatest painters have major works in the city's Farnsworth Art Museum. For dinner, eat lobster anywhere in town.

Day 13

You'll circle Penobscot Bay on Routes 1 and 3 on your way to Bar Harbor, a two-hour drive. The town is the hub of Mount Desert Island and gateway to Acadia National Park (p190). Explore the park on the 27-mile (44-km) Loop Road, taking special note of Thunder Hole and Cadillac Mountain and the unmatched land – and seascapes. Break for tea and popovers on the lawn at the Jordan Pond House. In the evening, cap your lobster dinner with pie made from wild Maine blueberries.

Day 14

Start the day early with a brisk constitutional along the Shore Path and marvel at dawn breaking across the dark waters of the Gulf of Maine. After a hearty breakfast, visit the Abbe Museum, which details the continuous 10,000 years of American Indian culture here. Aboard an afternoon whale-watching cruise out into the Gulf – you might spy several species of whales feeding on the shoals. Come evening, it's only appropriate to order another lobster dinner.

A Burgeoning Food Scene

A pioneer city in the foodie revolution, Boston continues to roll out the gastronomic carpet for new ideas and taste sensations. The armada of food trucks along the Rose Kennedy Greenway, bounding the Waterfront *(p152)*, serves everything from Korean *bulgogi bibimbap* (a rice dice with various toppings) to Mexican *tortas* and grilled cheese sandwiches. Chinatown *(p148)* has enough to satisfy all food cravings and set taste buds alight, with *pho* and dumplings being lunchtime standbys. Eat scrod or baked beans at Boston's oldest restaurant, Union Oyster House *(p151)*, founded 1832, or savor Boston-bred superchef Barbara Lynch's upscale pastas at the modern and stylish Sportello *(www.sportelloboston.com)* in the Seaport.

→

Chefs preparing and serving shellfish at the Union Oyster House

NEW ENGLAND FOR
FOODIES

From the sweet lobster hauled from the sea in summer to the tangy crunch of apples picked in the fall, New England has a signature taste in every season. You can find the flavors at the source by connecting with the foragers, farmers, and fishermen whose skills bring them to the table.

King Crustaceans

Lobster shacks all along coastal New England serve steamed whole lobster, usually with melted butter and corn on the cob. The most simple shacks give you a lobster and a fist-sized rock to crack the shell. If you're less ambitious, go for a lobster roll. Abbott's Lobster in the Rough *(www.abbottslobster.com)* in Noank, Connecticut, serves it hot and grilled in butter.

INSIDER TIP
Food Tours

Walk and sample your way through Boston's North End on the "Little Italy" North End Market Tour, led by Boston Food Tours *(www.bostonfoodtours.com)*.

↑ Lobster served with butter

CLAM CHOWDER: CLEAR, WHITE, OR RED?

This is the question that you might be asked when you order clam chowder, a New England delicacy. All three versions contain onions, clams, and potatoes, but the traditional version uses roux-thickened milk or cream. Manhattan clam chowder (culinary heresy in much of New England) substitutes tomatoes for the milk. "Clear" is a Rhode Island variant using clear broth, bacon instead of butter, many chopped clams, and potatoes.

From Farm to Fork

As diners seek authentic local food, New England farmers often cut out the middleman. Rural roads are lined with farmstands that range from a table with cucumbers and tomatoes to small barns filled with bins of produce. Farmers' markets like those in Portland, Maine *(www.portlandmaine farmersmarket.org)* and Bennington, Vermont *(www. benningtonfarmersmarket. org)* are great places to pick up picnic fare. You may even be shopping alongside chefs from hot local restaurants.

→

Fresh produce at a Farmers' Market in Massachusetts

Syrupy Sweetness

When winter's first thaw makes the maple sap rise, New England sugar houses boil the juice into thick syrup. Some sugar houses also cook big farm breakfasts with pancakes. Maple Sugar and Vermont Spice *(www.vtsugarandspice.com)* in Mendon, Vermont, and Heritage Farm Pancake House *(www.heritagefarmpancakehouse.com)* in Sanbornton, New Hampshire, are local favorites.

→

Pancakes drizzled in maple syrup

NEW ENGLAND'S CONTEMPORARY WRITERS

Even today, New England remains fertile literary ground. Richard Russo (Pulitzer Prize) and Stephen King are closely associated with Maine. Andre Dubus III writes from his roots on the Massachusetts North Shore. The elite universities also harbor award-winning writers with global roots. Jamaica Kincaid (American Book Award), Junot Diaz (Pulitzer Prize), and Ha Jin (National Book Award) live and teach in New England.

Murals above the famous Brattle Book Shop in Boston ↑

NEW ENGLAND FOR
BOOKWORMS

America's first publisher set up in Cambridge, Massachusetts, in 1639, and New Englanders haven't stopped writing since. The region is the undeniable birthplace of American literature, and book-lovers will enjoy the regular festivals and literary events that honor these luminaries.

Literary Festivals

Beat Generation author Jack Kerouac draws fans to his hometown for the Lowell Celebrates Kerouac Festival (www.lowellcelebrates kerouac.org). The Boston Book Festival (www. bostonbookfest.org) features readings by top authors, while four days of readings and talks highlight Vermont's Brattleboro Literary Festival (www.brattleboroliterary festival.org). All three take place in October.

←

Authors discuss the craft of memoir at the 2018 Boston Book Festival.

Book-Mad Boston

Follow in the footsteps of Boston's greatest authors on a literary walking tour (www.boston byfoot.org), or go on a self-guided walk around the city's many bookstores. Harvard Bookstore (www.harvard.com) anchors the extensive Cambridge scene, which includes the all-verse Grolier Poetry Book Shop and the graphic novel riches of Million Year Picnic. The Brattle Book Shop (www.brattlebookshop.com) is Boston's leading source for used and antiquarian volumes - the largest in the country. Meanwhile, Trident (www.tridentbookscafe. com) is bibliophile heaven in Back Bay.

Did You Know?

Boston-based Anne Bradstreet became the first published writer from the American colonies in 1650.

Birthplace of American Literature

In the mid-1800s, writers around Ralph Waldo Emerson launched a new American literature. Visit Emerson House (p163) to see where they gathered. At nearby Orchard House (p163), Louisa May Alcott wrote *Little Women*, and Nathaniel Hawthorne was inspired by his home to write *The House of Seven Gables (p162)*. The Mark Twain House (p172) honors Twain at his peak.

←
The desk where author Louisa May Alcott wrote

Frost Country

The quintessential New England poet, Robert Frost etched the region's rural landscape and hardscrabble life in his immortal lines. Learn more about the master and his career at the Frost Place Museum (p185) in Franconia Notch, New Hampshire. You can also pay homage to him at the Old Burying Ground in Bennington (p178), Vermont.

→
A busy poetry event at The Frost Place Barn.

Experience

BOSTON AND MASSACHUSETTS

For many, Massachusetts is where modern America was born. The English Pilgrims established Plymouth in 1620, and Boston was founded just ten years later. Resistance to British rule was strongest here, led by the Sons of Liberty, and the Revolutionary War began at Concord in 1775. After Independence, whaling boomed in Nantucket and New Bedford; Boston and Salem grew rich from international trade; and Lowell became the birthplace of America's Industrial Revolution. The state also led a cultural renaissance, from the writings of Emerson, Wharton, and Thoreau to abolitionists such as William Lloyd Garrison. Though industry declined in the 20th century, today the state remains a wealthy and progressive bastion, fueled by tech industries and institutions such as Harvard and MIT.

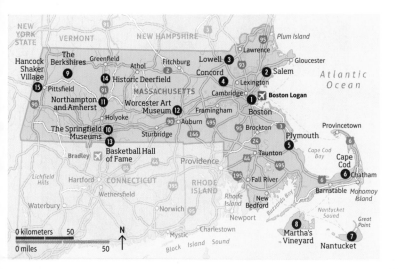

1

BOSTON

All New England roads lead to Boston, on the northeastern Atlantic Coast on Massachusetts Bay. This is the region's hub of culture, dining, and nightlife, where the city's streets are imbued with Revolutionary history. The city is focused around the harbor on the Shawmut Peninsula, while Greater Boston encompasses the surrounding area.

1

Old State House

⌂ Washington & State sts
Ⓣ State ◷ 9am–5pm daily
(Jun–Aug: to 6pm)
🅦 bostonhistory.org

This was the seat of the British Colonial government between 1713 and 1776 and the royal lion and unicorn still decorate the east facade. It was from a balcony here that the Declaration of Independence was first read to the public in 1776. After independence, the legislature took possession of the building, and it has had many uses since, including a market, Masonic Lodge, and City Hall. Its wine cellars now function as a subway station. Inside, exhibits include a multimedia presentation about the Boston Massacre and the restored royal Council Chamber.

2 Ⓜ

Black Heritage Trail

⌂ Tours begin at Boston Common ◷ Spring–Fall
🅦 nps.gov/boaf

During the 1800s, Boston's large free African American community lived principally on the north slope of Beacon Hill and in the West End. Free walking tours of the Black Heritage Trail depart from the Shaw Memorial on Boston Common. Sights include safe houses for escaped enslaved people and the **Museum of African American History**, which houses the preserved African Meeting House, the country's oldest black church.

Museum of African American History
⊛⊛ ⌂ 46 Joy St ◷ 10am–4pm Mon–Sat ◷ Federal hols
🅦 maah.org

←

The 18th-century Old State House, where past and present merge seamlessly

The tower is a classic example of Colonial style.

A gilded eagle, symbol of America, is on the west facade.

The east facade still has the royal British lion and unicorn symbol on each corner. It is adorned with a beautiful clock dating to the 1820s.

The Declaration of Independence was read from this balcony in 1776.

Keayne Hall displays exhibits that depict events from the American Revolution.

Entrance

The Central Staircase, with its two spiraling wooden handrails, is a fine example of 18th-century workmanship.

Council Chamber

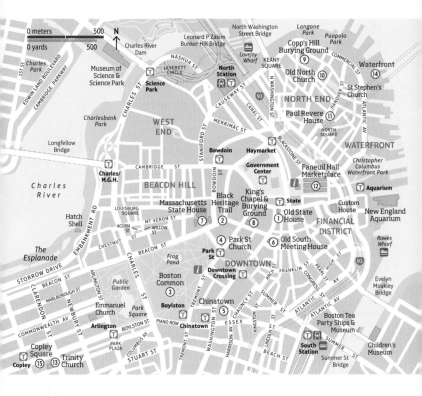

↑ Walkers enjoying the colors of fall on Boston Common

③

Boston Common & Public Garden

🅐 Charles St 🚇 Park St, Boylston St, Arlington
🕒 24 hrs 🌐 boston.gov/parks/boston-common

The city's most beautiful green space, Boston Common was established in 1634. For over two centuries it served as a common pasture, gallows site, and a military camp. By the 19th century, it had become a center for open-air civic activity and remains so to this day. At the northeastern edge of the common is the Robert Gould Shaw Memorial, with a magnificent relief depicting the first free black regiment during the Civil War, and their white colonel, Robert Gould Shaw. In the south-eastern corner is the Central Burying Ground, dating from 1756, with graves of both British and American casualties from the Battle of Bunker Hill in 1775.

Southwest of the common is the smaller and more formal Public Garden, designed in English style in 1869. Amid its beautifully tended lawns and flower beds is a superb bronze equestrian statue of George Washington. A path leads from the statue to a serene lagoon, spanned by the ornamental Lagoon Bridge. Paddling about in the garden's delightful Swan Boats is a great way to spend a sunny afternoon.

DRINK

The Black Rose
Head here for Guinness stew, lobster rolls, and live Irish music.

🅐 160 State St
🌐 blackroseboston.com

Mr. Dooley's Tavern
This is a firm favorite with local musicians for its impromptu sessions.

🅐 77 Broad St
🌐 mrdooleys.com

Hennessy's
Choose from a strong list of whiskeys at this great conversation bar.

🅐 25 Union St
🌐 hennessysboston.com

④ Park Street Church

🏠 1 Park St 🚇 Park St
🕐 9:30am–3pm Tue–Sat
🌐 parkstreet.org

Since its dedication in 1810, the Park Street Church has been one of Boston's most influential pulpits. In 1829, the firebrand crusader for the abolition of slavery, William Lloyd Garrison, gave his first abolition speech here; and in 1893 the anthem "America the Beautiful" debuted at Sunday service in this church. The church, with its 217-ft (65-m) steeple, was designed by the English architect Peter Banner, who actually adapted a design by the earlier English architect Christopher Wren.

Adjacent to the church, on Tremont Street, is the mid-17th-century **Old Granary Burying Ground**, which was once the site of a grain storage facility. Among those buried in this historic cemetery are three important signatories to the Declaration of Independence – Samuel Adams, John Hancock, and Robert Treat Paine – as well as one of the city's most famous sons, Paul Revere.

Old Granary Burying Ground

🏠 Tremont St
🕐 9am–5pm daily

↑ Grand entrance to Boston's Chinatown, lit up at dusk

⑤ 🍴 🖥 🛍 Chinatown

🏠 Bounded by Kingston, Kneeland, Washington, & Essex sts 🚇 Chinatown

Boston's Chinatown is the third largest in the US, after those in San Francisco and New York. Pagoda-topped telephone booths set the tone of the neighborhood, which is packed with great places to eat and stores selling everything from traditional garments to Chinese medicine. Boston's Chinese colony was fully established by the turn of the 19th century, and the area's population has since swelled with new arrivals from Korea, Vietnam, and Cambodia.

⑥ Old South Meeting House

🏠 310 Washington St
🚇 Park St, State, Government Center 🕐 Apr–Oct: 9:30am–5pm daily; Nov–Mar: 10am–4pm daily
🌐 osmh.org

Built for Puritan religious services in 1729, this edifice, with a tall octagonal steeple, had Colonial Boston's biggest capacity for town meetings. From 1765 on, it became the venue for large and vociferous crowds, led by a group of merchants called the "Sons of Liberty", to gather in protest against British taxation and the widely detested Stamp Act. During a protest rally on December 16, 1773 – with some 5,000 people in attendance – the fiery speechmaker Samuel Adams uttered the famous words, "This meeting can do nothing more to save the country," a covert signal that led to the Boston Tea Party at Griffin's Wharf several hours later, cementing the Old South's place in American history. The British retaliated by gutting the building, filling it with dirt, and using it as a

stable for army horses. Today, the Meeting House holds lectures and exhibitions, and has an audio program that relives the events. The shop sells "Boston Tea Party" tea and books on the history of Boston and New England.

The Great Hall, used for state functions, is the latest addition to the State House.

The Sacred Cod hangs over the gallery in the House of Representatives.

The Wings, added in 1917, sit rather incongruously with the rest of the structure.

⑦ Massachusetts State House

🏠 Beacon St 🚇 Park St
🕐 10am–3:30pm Mon–Fri (reservations advised)
🌐 sec.state.ma.us/trs

The cornerstone of this Charles Bulfinch designed center of state government was laid in 1795 by Paul Revere and Samuel Adams. Completed in 1798, the State House served as a model for the US Capitol

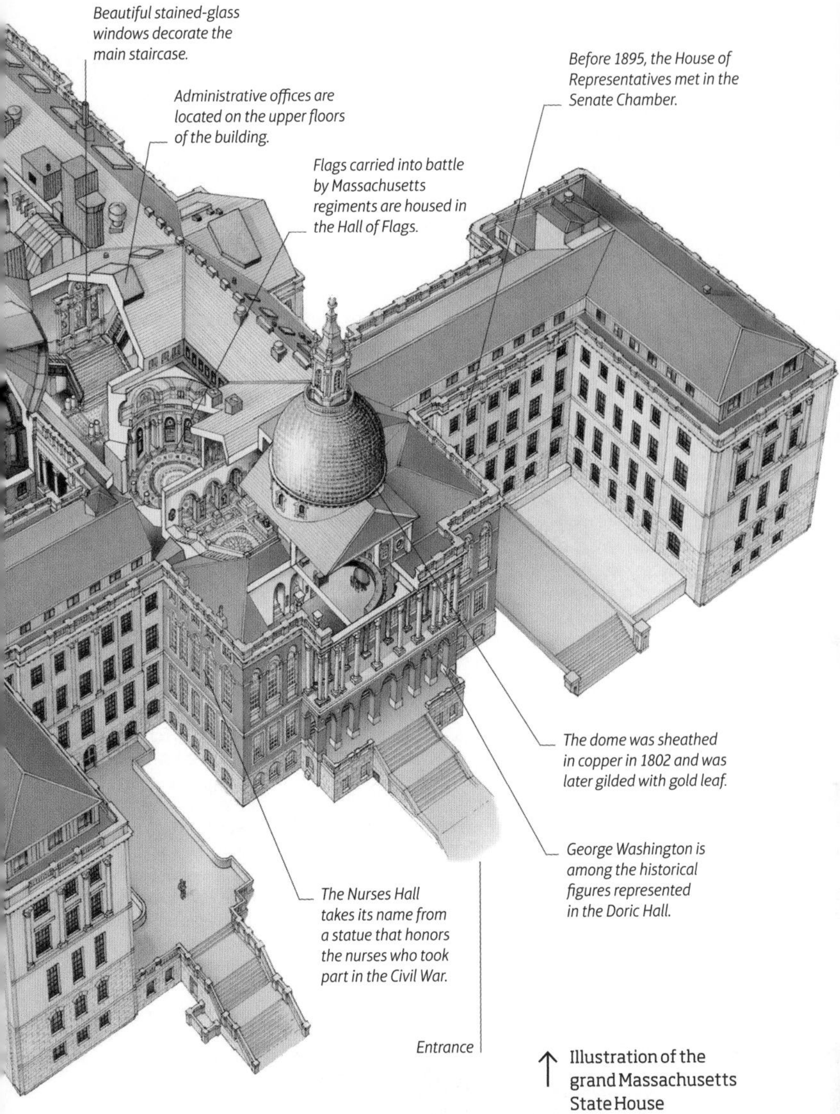

Beautiful stained-glass windows decorate the main staircase.

Administrative offices are located on the upper floors of the building.

Flags carried into battle by Massachusetts regiments are housed in the Hall of Flags.

Before 1895, the House of Representatives met in the Senate Chamber.

The dome was sheathed in copper in 1802 and was later gilded with gold leaf.

George Washington is among the historical figures represented in the Doric Hall.

The Nurses Hall takes its name from a statue that honors the nurses who took part in the Civil War.

Entrance

↑ Illustration of the grand Massachusetts State House

building in Washington and as an inspiration for many other state capitols throughout the United States. Later additions were made, but the original building remains the archetypal American government building. Its 23-carat gilded dome serves as the zero-mile marker for Massachusetts. Various portraits, murals, and statues are in and around its grounds.

THE BOSTON TEA PARTY AND MASSACRE

The 18th century was a key period of American history. A marker below the balcony on the east facade of the Old State House (p146) indicates the site of the 1770 Boston Massacre. This saw an angry mob of colonists taunt British guardsmen with insults, rocks, and snowballs. The soldiers opened fire, killing five. A number of related articles are exhibited inside the Old State House. The notorious Boston Tea Party of 1773 saw colonists, some disguised as American Indians, rebel against the British by dumping 342 chests of tea into the city habor.

⑧ King's Chapel & Burying Ground

🏠 58 Tremont St 🚇 Park St, State, Government Center 🕐 10am–5pm Mon–Sat (to 4:30pm Wed), 1:30–5pm Sun 🌐 kings-chapel.org

The first chapel on this site was built in 1689, but the present granite edifice was begun in 1749 and constructed around the original wooden chapel. High ceilings and open arches enhance the sense of spaciousness inside the chapel. Its other notable features include a pulpit shaped like a wine glass, which dates back to 1717, and a huge bell that was recast by the foundry of Revolutionary hero Paul Revere. The adjacent cemetery, Boston's oldest, contains the graves of 12-time Colonial governor John Winthrop, and Mary Chilton, the first woman to step off the *Mayflower*.

⑨ Copp's Hill Burying Ground

🏠 Charter & Hull sts 🚇 N Station 🕐 9am–5pm daily

Established in 1659, Copp's Hill is the second-oldest cemetery in Boston, after the one by King's Chapel. Among those at rest here are Robert Newman, who hung Paul Revere's signal lanterns in the belfry of the Old North Church, as well as many enslaved people.

During British occupation, King George III's troops used the slate headstones at Copp's Hill for target practice, and pockmarks from their musket balls are still visible. Copp's Hill Terrace, directly across Charter Street, is where, in 1919, a 2.3-million-gallon tank of molasses exploded, drowning 21 people in a huge tidal wave.

⑩ Old North Church

🏠 193 Salem St 🚇 N Station Haymarket, Aquarium 🕐 Apr–Oct: 9am–6pm daily; Nov–Mar: 10am–4pm daily 🌐 oldnorth.com

Old North Church, which dates from 1723, is Boston's oldest surviving religious edifice. The church was made famous on April 18, 1775, when sexton Robert Newman hung a pair of lanterns in the belfry to warn the patriots in Charlestown of the westward departure of British troops.

An imposing marble bust of George Washington, dating from 1815, adorns the church interior. The tower contains the first set of church bells made in North America, cast

Did You Know?

Between 1659 and 1681, Christmas was banned in Boston as Puritans declared it a corrupt holiday.

in 1745. One of the church's first bellringers was a teenage Paul Revere.

⑪ Paul Revere House

🏠 19 N Square 🚇 Aquarium, Haymarket 🕐 Mid-Apr–Oct: 9:30am–5:15pm daily; Nov–mid-Apr: 9:30am–4:15pm daily 🕐 Jan–Mar: Mon 🌐 paulreverehouse.org

As well as being one of Boston's oldest surviving buildings, this unassuming clapboard house is historically significant, for it was here in 1775 that Paul Revere began his legendary horseback ride to warn his compatriots in Lexington *(p161)* of the impending arrival of British troops. This event was immortalized by Henry Wadsworth Longfellow in his epic poem which begins, "Listen, my children, and you shall hear of the midnight ride of Paul Revere."

A versatile gold- and silver-smith, Revere lived here from 1770 to 1800. Small leaded windows, an overhanging upper story, and a nail-studded front door make the house a fine example of 18th-century American architecture. Two rooms in the house contain artifacts from the Revere family. In the courtyard is a large bronze bell cast by Revere himself, who is known to have made nearly 200 church bells.

← Slate headstones at Copp's Hill Burying Ground

↑ Dining at Quincy Market in Faneuil Hall Marketplace, and the Greek Revival-style entrance *(inset)*

⑫ 🍽 🛍

Faneuil Hall Marketplace

📍 Between Chatham & Clinton sts 🚇 Haymarket, State 🕐 10am-9pm Mon-Sat, 11am-7pm Sun (winter: to 6pm) 🌐 faneuilhall marketplace.com

This popular shopping and dining complex adjacent to historic Faneuil Hall attracts millions of people every year. It was developed from the old buildings of the city's meat, fish, and produce markets, which were lovingly restored in the 1970s. The Greek Revival-style Quincy Market is now filled with fast-food stands

and tables, sheltered under a spectacular central rotunda. Completing the ensemble are the twin North and South Market buildings, refurbished to house boutiques, restaurants, and offices.

A short distance southeast of Faneuil Hall Marketplace is **Custom House**, whose tower is also in Greek Revival style. The 495-ft (150 m) tower was built in 1915. For much of the 20th century it was Boston's only skyscraper, until it was exceeded by the Prudential Tower. There is a display of local history in the rotunda. Take a tour of the tower for spectacular city and harbor views (check www.marriott. com for details).

Custom House
◈ 📍 3 McKinley Square

> The marketplace was developed from the old buildings of the city's meat, fish, and produce markets, which were lovingly restored in the 1970s.

EAT

Union Oyster House
Serving up Boston seafood classics a stone's throw from Quincy Market.

📍 41 Union St
🌐 unionoyster house.com

$ $ $

Salty Dog Seafood Grille & Bar
Established in 1972, a culinary landmark and one of the original vendors at Faneuil Hall.

📍 206 Faneuil Hall Marketplace
🌐 saltydogboston.biz

$ $ $

Legal Harborside
Choose from casual dishes, fine dining, and sushi at this vast seafood hot spot.

📍 270 Northern Av
🌐 legalseafoods.com

$ $ $

⑬ Ⓢ Ⓜ

Trinity Church

📍 Copley Sq 🚇 Copley
🕐 10am-4:30pm Wed-Sat,
12:15-4:30pm Sun 🌐 trinity
churchboston.org

Routinely voted one of
America's ten finest buildings,
Henry Hobson's Trinity Church
is a masterpiece dating from
1877. The church is a beautiful
granite and sandstone Romanesque structure, standing on
wooden piles driven through
mud into bedrock. John
LaFarge designed the interior,
while some of the windows
were designed by Edward
Burne-Jones and executed
by William Morris.

---

⑭ 🍴 🖼 🏛

Waterfront

📍 Atlantic Av 🚇 Aquarium

Boston's waterfront is one of
the city's most fascinating
areas. Fringed by wharves and
warehouses – a reminder of
the city's past as a key trading
port – its attractions include
a famous aquarium and
two fine museums.
One of the largest

wharves is Long Wharf,
established in 1710. Once
extending 2,000 ft (610 m)
into Boston Harbor and lined
with shops and warehouses, it
provided secure mooring for
the largest ships of the time
and is today a departure
point for ferries.

Harbor Walk connects
Long Wharf with other
adjacent wharves, dating
from the early 1800s.
Most of them have now
been converted to
fashionable
harborside

apartments. Rowes Wharf,
to the south of the waterfront,
is a particularly fine example
of such revitalization. This
modern red-brick devel-
opment, with condominiums,
a hotel, and offices, features
a large archway that links
the city to the harbor.

The waterfront's prime
attraction is the **New
England Aquarium**, which
dominates Central Wharf.
Designed in 1969, the
aquarium's core
encloses a vast
four-story ocean
tank, which
houses a
Caribbean

> **Routinely voted one of America's
> ten finest buildings, Henry Hobson's
> Trinity Church is a masterpiece dating
> from 1877.**

On the wall of the
chancel are a series
of gold bas-reliefs.

Bell tower

The North Transept
Windows were designed by
Edward Burne-Jones and
executed by William Morris.

The pulpit features
carved scenes from the
life of Christ and portraits
of great preachers
through the ages.

The present-day
chancel was
designed by
Charles Maginnis.

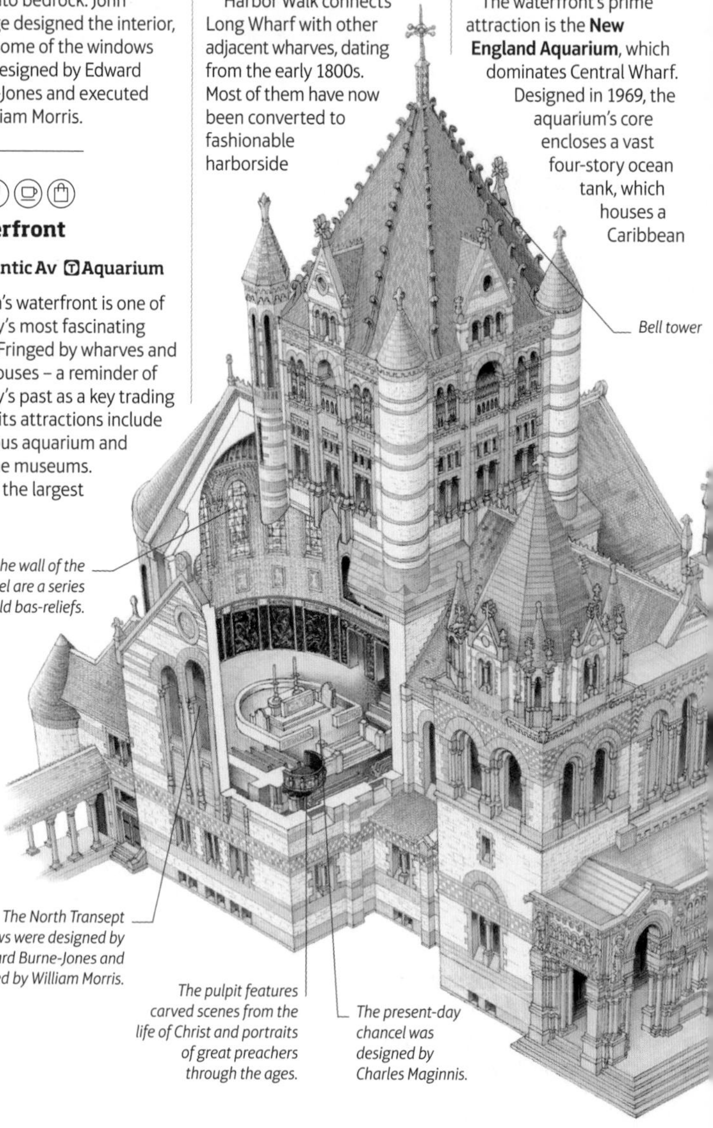

coral reef and a wide array of marine creatures such as sharks, moray eels, barracudas, and sea turtles, as well as exotic and brightly colored tropical fish. A curving walkway runs around the outside of the aquarium tank from top to bottom, and provides different viewpoints at many levels.

A popular section of the aquarium is the Penguin Exhibit Pool, which runs around the base of the ocean tank, while the west wing has an outdoor tank with a lively colony of harbor seals. The Simons IMAX® Theater on the wharf presents changing programs of 3D films on a giant screen. A highlight of the aquarium's programs is the boat trip from Boston Harbor, which takes visitors to the whale-feeding grounds far offshore. The aquarium also has a gift shop and a café with a beautiful view of the harbor. Griffin's Wharf, where the Boston Tea Party took place on December 16, 1773, was long ago buried beneath land-fill. Anchored nearby on Fort Point Channel, the **Boston Tea Party Ships and Museum** replicates the

John LaFarge's lancet windows show Christ in the act of blessing.

The West Portico was modeled on that of St. Trophime in Arles, France.

Main entrance

British East India Company ships involved in the Tea Party protest (*p149*). At Fan Pier, the light-flooded galleries, performance space open to harbor views, and cutting-edge media center highlight the landmark building of the **Institute of Contemporary Art**, where the exhibitions place strong emphasis on electronic media and performance art.

Overlooking Fort Point Channel is a rejuvenated 19th-century wool warehouse that houses the **Children's Museum**, one of the best in the country. Its many attractions and interactive exhibits include a climbing wall, a hands-on art studio, and a "construction zone" with child-scaled trucks and blocks. Kids can also follow a giant maze or act in KidStage plays. An international flavor is added by a visit to the silk merchant's house, which has been transplanted from Kyoto in Japan.

New England Aquarium

🎦 🎭 🎫 🅰 Central Wharf
🚇 Aquarium 🕐 Jul-Aug: 9am-6pm; Sep-Jun: 9am-5pm Mon-Fri, 9am-6pm Sat & Sun 🌐 neaq.org

Boston Tea Party Ships and Museum

🎦 🅰 306 Congress St
🚇 S Station 🕐 9am-6pm daily (winter: to 5pm)
🌐 bostonteapartyship.com

Institute of Contemporary Art

🎦 🅰 25 Harbor Shore Dr
🚇 Courthouse 🕐 10am-5pm Tue, Wed, Sat & Sun; 10am-9pm Thu & Fri 🌐 icaboston.org

Children's Museum

🎦 🅰 300 Congress St
🚇 S Station 🕐 10am-5pm daily (to 9pm Fri)
🌐 bostonkids.org

← The breathtaking Trinity Church, with its bell tower and interior

↑ Dazzling tropical fish at the New England Aquarium on the Boston Waterfront

⑮

Copley Square

🚇 Copley

Named after the famous painter John Singleton Copley, Copley Square took on its present form in the late 20th century. This inviting plaza is an open space of trees and fountains, and a hive of civic activity, with farmers' markets and concerts.

Formerly known as the John Hancock Tower, **200 Clarendon** was constructed in 1975 and anchors the southeastern side of the square. The tallest building in New England, the tower's mirrored facade reflects Trinity Church and the original Hancock Building that stand next to it. West of 200 Clarendon, across Copley Square, is the Italian palazzo-style **Boston Public Library**. A marvel of fine wood and marble, the library has huge bronze doors, and murals by John Singer Sargent in a third-floor gallery. The vast Bates Hall on the second floor is notable for its soaring barrel-vaulted ceiling.

200 Clarendon

🅰 200 Clarendon St
🔒 To the public

Boston Public Library

🎦 🅰 Copley Square 🕐 9am-9pm Mon-Thu, 9am-5pm Fri & Sat, 1-5pm Sun 🔒 Federal hols 🌐 bpl.org

A SHORT WALK
BEACON HILL

Distance 1 mile (1.5 km) **Time** 15 minutes
Nearest subway Park Street

The south slope of Beacon Hill was, from the 1790s to the 1870s, Boston's most sought-after neighborhood, until its wealthy elite decamped to the more exclusive Back Bay. Many of the district's houses were designed by the influential architect Charles Bulfinch (1763–1844) and his disciples, and the south slope evolved as a textbook example of Federal architecture. Elevation and view were everything, resulting in the finest homes on Boston Common or perched near the top of the hill. Earlier developers set houses back from the street, but the economic depression of 1807–12 resulted in row houses being built right out to the street. As you walk around Beacon Hill look out for these elegant houses.

Did You Know?

The area is named for a wooden beacon that once stood on the hill to warn residents of attack or fire.

Built in the 1830s, **Louisburg Square** is still Boston's most desirable address.

PINCKNEY STREE

LOUISBURG SQUARE

MOUNT VERNON STREET

CEDAR STREET

CHESTNUT STREET

CHARLES STREET

Charles Street Meeting House was built in the early 19th century to house a congregation of Baptists.

Between Cedar Street and Willow Street, beautiful **Old Acorn Street** takes visitors back in time to Colonial Boston.

← Vintage Christmas lights illuminating Charles Street during the holidays

↑ Low light on Old Acorn Street, the most photographed street in Boston

BOSTON

Beacon Hill

Locator Map
For more detail see p147

Nichols House Museum *offers an insight into the life and times of Beacon Hill resident Rose Nichols, who lived here from 1885 to 1960.*

Described in the 19th century as "the most civilized street in America," **Mount Vernon Street** *is where developers of Beacon Hill chose to build their own homes.*

MOUNT VERNON STREET

WALNUT STREET

START

SPRUCE STREET

FINISH

Elegant in their simplicity, the three Bulfinch-designed **Hepzibah Swan Houses** *were wedding gifts for the daughters of a wealthy Beacon Hill proprietress.*

BEACON STREET

The finest houses on Beacon Hill were invariably built on **Beacon Street**. *Grand, Federal-style mansions, some with ornate reliefs, overlook the city's beautiful green space, Boston Common.*

0 meters	50
0 yards	50

N
↑

A LONG WALK
THE FREEDOM TRAIL

Distance 2.5 miles (4 km) **Time** 1 hour
Terrain Generally flat and paved; the route is clearly marked by a painted red line on sidewalks **Stopping point** Quincy Market

Boston has more sites directly related to the American Revolution than any other city. The most important of these sites, as well as some that relate to other freedoms gained by Bostonians, form "The Freedom Trail," starting at Boston Common and ending at Bunker Hill in Charlestown. The first section weaves its way through the central city and Old Boston. Distances begin to stretch out on the second half as the trail meanders through the narrow streets of the North End to Charlestown, where Boston's settlers first landed. For more details on this historic route, visit www.thefreedomtrail.org.

The towering granite obelisk above the Charlestown waterfront is Bunker Hill Monument (p161), which commemorates those lost in the battle of June 17, 1775 that ended with a costly victory for British forces.

An iron bridge over the Charles River links the North End with Charlestown.

Revere Landing Park

Charlestown Bridge

Continuing along Tremont Street, you will come to King's Chapel and Burying Ground (p150).

On School Street, a hopscotch-like mosaic embedded in the sidewalk commemorates the site of the first public school, established in 1635. At the bottom of the street is the Old Corner Bookstore, a landmark associated with Boston's literary flowering.

A bulwark of the anti-slavery movement, Park Street Church (p148) took the place of an old grain store facility, which gave its name to the Old Granary Burying Ground.

↑ The gold dome of the Massachusetts State House illuminated at dusk

Before reaching the Massachusetts State House (p149), the trail passes the Robert Gould Shaw and the 54th Massachusetts Infantry Regiment memorial, which honors the first African American volunteer unit in the American Civil War.

Massachusetts State House

Old Granary Burying Ground

Park Street Church

Boston Common

START

Downtown Crossing

DOWNTOWN

Boylston

The Freedom Trail starts at the Visitor Information Center on Boston Common (p147), where angry colonials rallied against their British masters. Political speakers still expound from their soapboxes here, and the Common remains a center of civic activity.

Chinatown

156

Charlestown Navy Yard (p161) *is home to the USS Constitution, one of the most famous ships in US history.*

USS *Constitution* in Charlestown Navy Yard

→

CHARLES-TOWN

USS *Constitution* Museum

Charlestown Navy Yard

USS *Constitution*

USS *Cassin Young*

Boston Inner Harbor

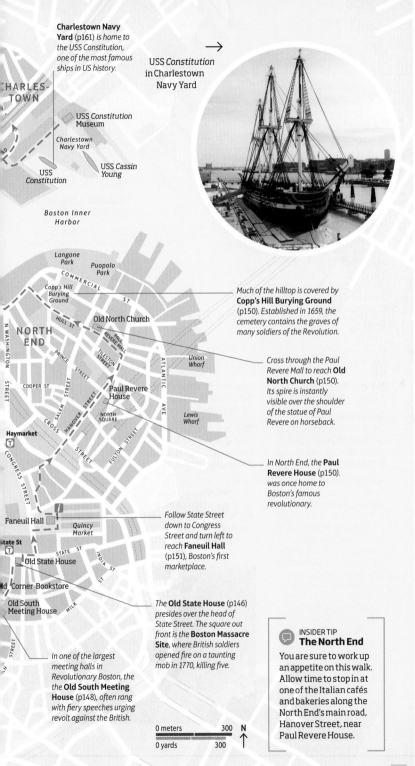

Langone Park

Puopolo Park

COMMERCIAL ST

Copp's Hill Burying Ground

HULL ST

NORTH END

N WASHINGTON STREET

PRINCE STREET

COOPER ST

SALEM STREET

HANOVER STREET

CROSS STREET

TILESTON STREET

PAUL REVERE MALL

Old North Church

Paul Revere House

NORTH SQUARE

ATLANTIC AVE

Union Wharf

Lewis Wharf

FULTON STREET

Haymarket Ⓣ

CONGRESS STREET

Faneuil Hall

Quincy Market

State St Ⓣ

Old State House

Old Corner Bookstore

Old South Meeting House

STATE ST

INDIA ST

MILK

Much of the hilltop is covered by **Copp's Hill Burying Ground** *(p150). Established in 1659, the cemetery contains the graves of many soldiers of the Revolution.*

Cross through the Paul Revere Mall to reach **Old North Church** *(p150). Its spire is instantly visible over the shoulder of the statue of Paul Revere on horseback.*

In North End, the **Paul Revere House** *(p150). was once home to Boston's famous revolutionary.*

Follow State Street down to Congress Street and turn left to reach **Faneuil Hall** *(p151), Boston's first marketplace.*

The **Old State House** *(p146) presides over the head of State Street. The square out front is the* **Boston Massacre Site**, *where British soldiers opened fire on a taunting mob in 1770, killing five.*

In one of the largest meeting halls in Revolutionary Boston, the the **Old South Meeting House** *(p148), often rang with fiery speeches urging revolt against the British.*

0 meters	300
0 yards	300

N ↑

💬 INSIDER TIP
The North End

You are sure to work up an appetite on this walk. Allow time to stop in at one of the Italian cafés and bakeries along the North End's main road, Hanover Street, near Paul Revere House.

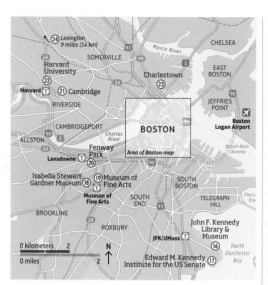

Museum, this institute was opened in 2015 to celebrate his contribution to American politics. A re-creation of his office provides a personal look at the "Lion of the Senate," while interactive exhibits and a full-scale reproduction of the Senate Chamber offer insights on the legislative process.

Isabella Stewart Gardner Museum

🏛 25 Evans Way 🚇 MFA
🕐 11am–5pm Wed–Mon (to 9pm Thu) 🚫 Jan 1, Thanksgiving, Dec 25
🌐 gardnermuseum.org

This Venetian-style palazzo, completed in 1903, houses a remarkable collection of over 2,500 works of art, including Old Masters and Renaissance pieces. The wealthy and strong-willed Isabella Stewart Gardner began collecting art in the late 19th century and acquired masterpieces by Titian, Rembrandt, and Matisse as well as the American painters James McNeill Whistler and John Singer Sargent. Her acquisitions are still displayed as Mrs. Gardner arranged them, in galleries around a flower-filled central courtyard.

The striking modern wing includes galleries, a café, and a performance space for the acclaimed concert series.

AROUND BOSTON

John F. Kennedy Library & Museum

🏛 Columbia Point, Dorchester 🚇 JFK/U Mass
🕐 9am–5pm daily 🚫 Jan 1, Thanksgiving, Dec 25
🌐 jfklibrary.org

Housed in a dramatic white-concrete and black-glass building, this museum chronicles the 1,000 days of the Kennedy presidency. The combination of video and film footage, papers, and memorabilia evoke the euphoria of "Camelot" as well as the numb horror of the assassination. Some of the key chambers in the White House, including the Oval Office, are re-created here.

The house at 83 Beals Street in Brookline, where the late president was born in 1917, is now the John F. Kennedy National Historic Site. The Kennedy family moved to a larger house in 1921; in 1966 they repurchased this house, and restored it to how it would have looked in 1917. It is open during the summer and fall.

Edward M. Kennedy Institute for the US Senate

🏛 Columbia Pt, Dorchester 🚇 JFK/U Mass 🕐 10am–5pm Tue–Sun 🚫 Federal hols
🌐 emkinstitute.org

For almost half a century, Ted Kennedy honed his skills as one of the most talented negotiators in the US Senate. Standing adjacent to the John F. Kennedy Library and

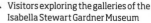
↑ Visitors exploring the galleries of the Isabella Stewart Gardner Museum

↑ Beaux Arts-style exterior of the Museum of Fine Arts

(19) (image icons)

Museum of Fine Arts

📍 Avenue of the Arts, 465 Huntington Av 🚇MFA
🕐10am–5pm Sat–Tue, 10am–10pm Wed–Fri
🚫Federal hols 🌐mfa.org

The largest art museum in New England, the Museum of Fine Arts – or MFA – has a permanent collection of some half a million objects, ranging from Egyptian artifacts to modern paintings. Though founded in 1876, the MFA's original Beaux Arts-style building dates from 1909 and was augmented in 2010 and 2011.

The MFA's excellent collection of ancient Egyptian and Nubian Art derives primarily from the joint MFA–Harvard University excavations along the Nile, which began in 1905. It also includes a wonderful collection of mummies.

Among the highlights of the Classical Art collection are Greek vases, Etruscan sarcophagi, and Roman busts, as well as wall-panel paintings unearthed in Pompeii in 1901.

The Asian Art collections are said to be the most extensive under one roof anywhere in the world. They include Indian sculpture and narrative paintings, and exhibitions of Islamic miniature paintings that keep changing.

A highlight of the museum is the serene Japanese Temple Room, known for its exquisite examples of Buddhist art.

The European Art collections date from the 7th to the 20th centuries and feature paintings by Rembrandt, El Greco, Titian, and Rubens.

The museum has several works by 19th-century French artists such as Millet, Manet, Renoir, and Degas. It also has various paintings by van Gogh and Monet.

Among the highlights of the American Painting collection are portraits by John Singleton Copley and John Singer Sargent. Twentieth-century American masters represented include Stuart Davis, Jackson Pollock, and Georgia O'Keeffe.

The Decorative Arts exhibit features silver tea services by Paul Revere (p150), 18th-century Boston-style clocks, and numerous ship models. Period rooms include three in the Neo-Classical style (c.1800) from a Peabody mansion.

(20) (image icons)

Fenway Park

📍 4 Jersey St 🚇Kenmore
🕐Check website for events
🌐redsox.com

Whatever their loyalties, sports fans from all over the world flock to this civic icon, home of the Boston Red Sox. Opened in 1912, this is the oldest Major League baseball park still standing and a shrine to the national pastime.

Tickets to games during the baseball season (April through October) can be hard to come by, but tours are offered daily. The venue is also a popular concert space, hosting big-name acts such as Bruce Springsteen and the Rolling Stones.

> 💬 INSIDER TIP
> **Fenway Tours**
>
> Behind-the-scenes tours of Fenway Park Stadium run on the hour, 9am–5pm daily (www.mlb.com/redsox/ballpark/tours). On game days, the last tour departs three hours before the game begins.

㉑
Cambridge

Ⓣ Harvard ☐ 𝑖 4 Brattle St; www.cambridge-usa.org

As well as having two world-famous universities – the Massachusetts Institute of Technology (MIT) and Harvard – Cambridge was a hotbed of the American Revolution. Among the historic sights is the house on Brattle Street, known as Longfellow House–Washington's Headquarters National Historic Site, George Washington's headquarters during the Siege of Boston.

Harvard Square is the area's main shopping and entertainment district, where Harvard's large student population is much in evidence.

Cambridge Common, north of Harvard Square, was used as an army encampment from 1775 to 1776. Today, its tree-shaded lawns and playgrounds are popular with families.

Among the masterpieces of modern architecture on the MIT campus along the Charles River is the Wiesner Building, which houses a collection of avant-garde art. Art and science are blended in the MIT Museum.

㉒
Harvard University

Ⓣ Harvard 𝑖 30 Dunster St; www.harvard.edu

Founded in 1636, the country's oldest institution of higher learning has touched every corner of American cultural, political, professional, and business life. At the heart of the vast campus is the Old Harvard Yard, dotted with student dormitories. Its focal point is the statue of its most famous benefactor, the cleric John Harvard. To the right of the statue is the imposing Widener Library, the third largest in the US. Another impressive building in the yard is the Memorial Church, whose steeple is modeled on that of the Old North Church (p150).

1775
—
The year Continental troops melted down the Cambridge Christ Church organ pipes to cast musket balls.

Standing out amid Harvard's Georgian-style buildings is the Carpenter Center for Visual Arts.

The **Harvard Art Museums** are a major draw for visitors. The university's main art facility brings the collections of the university's three major art museums under one roof. The Fogg Art Museum focuses on European art from the late Middle Ages to the present; the Busch-Reisinger Museum concentrates on Germanic art, particularly of the 20th century; the Sackler Museum houses a rich collection of ancient Greek and Roman, Asian, Indian, and Near Eastern art.

The **Harvard Museum of Natural History** is the public face of three Harvard institutions: the Botanical Museum, the Museum of Comparative Zoology, and the Mineralogical and Geological Museum. Highlights include the exhibits of dinosaurs and whales, and the "Glass Flowers" – 3,000 botanically correct models of 850 plant species in handblown glass, created between 1887 and 1936 by father and son artisans Leopold and Rudolph Blaschka. Don't miss the spectacular geodes or the collections of mysterious meteorites.

↑ Students strolling across Harvard Yard on a sunny afternoon

The **Peabody Museum of Archaeology and Ethnology**, at the opposite side of the building from the Natural History Museum, has impressive collections of Egyptian, North American Indian, and Central American artifacts as well as objects from the South Pacific Islands. Outstanding exhibits include totem carvings by Pacific Northwest tribes, Navajo weavings, artifacts from the Lewis & Clark Expedition, and casts of objects unearthed at Chichén Itzá in Mexico and Copán in Honduras.

Harvard Art Museums
⊛ ⊛ ⌂ 32 Quincy St ⌚ 10am–5pm daily ⌧ Federal hols ⓦ harvardartmuseums.org

Harvard Museum of Natural History
⊛ ⊛ ⌂ 26 Oxford St ⌚ 9am–5pm daily ⌧ Jul 4, Thanksgiving, Dec 24 & 25 ⓦ hmnh.harvard.edu

Peabody Museum of Archaeology and Ethnology
⊛ ⊛ ⌂ 11 Divinity Av ⌚ 9am–5pm daily ⌧ Jan 1, Jul 4, Thanksg., Dec 24 & 25 ⓦ peabody.harvard.edu

㉓
Charlestown

ⓣ Community College 🚌 🚢 From Long Wharf

Historic Charlestown, its streets lined with Colonial houses, is the site of the pivotal Battle of Bunker Hill (June 17, 1775) between British and Colonial troops. The Bunker Hill Monument, dedicated in 1843, commemorates this event. Nearly 300 stone steps lead to the top, which has spectacular views of Boston Harbor and the Zakim Bridge.

Charlestown Navy Yard is the home of America's most famous warship, the USS *Constitution*. Built in 1797, she is the oldest warship afloat and a veteran of 42 sea battles. The ship is taken out into the harbor on the Fourth of July each year to reverse her position at the pier.

㉔
Lexington

ⓣ Alewife 🚌 ℹ 1875 Massachusetts Av; www.tourlexington.us

The Colonial town of Lexington, 16 miles (26 km) northwest of Boston, is the site of a bloody skirmish between armed colonists, known as Minutemen, and British troops on April 19, 1775. This battle, together with the Battle of Concord (*p163*), acted as a catalyst for the Revolutionary War (*p53*). The Lexington Battle Green, with *The Minute Man* statue, is the focal point of the town. Three historic buildings associated with the battle are maintained by the local Historical Society and are open to visitors from spring to fall.

← *The Minute Man*, a statue commemorating the fierce Battle of Lexington in 1775

MASSACHUSETTS

Of all the New England states, Massachusetts may have the most diverse mix of natural and man-made attractions. Scenic seascapes and picturesque villages beckon along the eastern seaboard and Cape Cod. Venturing inland, visitors will find well-preserved historic towns. In the west, green mountains and valleys, and rich culture characterize the Berkshire Hills.

❷
Salem

🚗🚆From Boston's Long Wharf ℹ️2 New Liberty St; www.salem.org

This coastal town, founded in 1626, is best known for the infamous witch trials of 1692. The Salem Witch Museum traces the history of witchcraft to the present day.

In the 18th and 19th centuries, Salem was one of New England's busiest ports, its harbor filled with ships from around the globe. The

Peabody Essex Museum has deep holdings of Asian art and artifacts, as well as other treasures brought back from around the globe. The Yin Yu Tang exhibit is the only Qing Dynasty house outside China. New galleries and a garden opened in late 2019.

The town's waterfront has been preserved as the Salem Maritime National Historic Site. It offers tours and maintains the 1819 Custom House and a re-created 1797 East Indiaman, *Friendship*.

Fans of author Nathaniel Hawthorne should make a pilgrimage to the **House of Seven Gables Historic Site**. The Salem-born writer was so taken with the charming 1668 Colonial home that

House of Seven Gables Historic Site *(inset)*, and the great kitchen fireplace
↓

THE SALEM WITCH TRIALS

In 1692 Salem was swept by a wave of feverish fear in which 200 citizens were accused of practicing witchcraft. In all, 150 people were jailed and 20 were hanged. Unsurprisingly, when the governor's wife became a suspect, the trials came to an abrupt end.

he used it as the setting of his novel *The House of Seven Gables* (1851).

Marblehead, just 4 miles (6 km) from Salem, is a picturesque seaport village with historic buildings, mansions, and cottages, most notable of which are Abbot Hall and the Jeremiah Lee Mansion.

Peabody Essex Museum
♿🅿️☕ 🏠East India Sq
🕐10am–5pm Tue–Sun
🌐pem.org

House of Seven Gables Historic Site
♿🅿️☕ 🏠115 Derby St
🕐10am–5pm daily (Nov–mid-May: 10am–4pm Wed–Sun)
📅1st 2 wks Jan, Thanksg., Dec 25 🌐7gables.org

→ North Bridge, site of the opening battle in the Revolutionary War

③
Lowell

✈ Boston 🚩 61 Market St; www.merrimackvalley.org

Lowell paved the way for the American Industrial Revolution in the early 19th century but, in the 1920s, companies moved south in search of cheap labor. The final death knell came with the Great Depression, leaving Lowell a ghost town.

In 1978, the **Lowell National Historical Park** was established to rehabilitate the downtown buildings and preserve the city's unique history. On Market Street, the Market Mills Visitor Center offers screenings, maps, guided walks, and summer tours of the waterways. In summer and fall, antique trolleys take visitors to the **Boott Cotton Mills Museum**, which traces the Industrial Revolution and the growth of the labor movement.

While Lowell is best known for its industrial history, author Jack Kerouac and painter James McNeill Whistler, most famous for his portrait of his mother, were born here. The latter's birthplace is now the **Whistler House Museum of Art** and a number of the old mills have been turned into galleries.

Lowell National Historical Park

◈ ⚐ ⚑ 246 Market St
🕐 Times vary, check website
ⓦ nps.gov/lowe

Boott Cotton Mills Museum

◈ ⚑ 115 John St 📞 (978) 970-5000 🕐 Late Mar–Nov: 9:30am–5pm daily

Whistler House Museum of Art

◈ ⚑ 243 Worthen St
🕐 11am–4pm Wed–Sat
ⓦ whistlerhouse.org

④
Concord

✈ 20 miles (32 km) W of Boston 🚆 🚩 58 Main St; www.concordchamberof commerce.org

The Battle of Concord took place on April 19, 1775, marking the start of the Revolutionary War. The **Minute Man National Historical Park** preserves the site of the battle, where the Minutemen drove back British troops at North Bridge, where a wooden replica now stands.

In the 19th century, Concord blossomed into the literary heart and soul of the country. Nathaniel Hawthorne lived briefly in the Old Manse, and Ralph Waldo Emerson lived at Emerson House. Orchard House was where Louisa May Alcott wrote *Little Women* in 1868. **Concord Museum** holds decorative arts from the 17th, 18th, and 19th centuries.

Also in Concord is Walden Pond, immortalized by author and naturalist Henry David Thoreau.

Did You Know?

The Alcotts were vegetarians, and talked of abolitionism, women's suffrage, and social reform.

Minute Man National Historical Park

⚑ 174 Liberty St 🕐 Dawn–dusk ⓦ nps.gov/mima

Concord Museum

◈ ⚑ 53 Cambridge Turnpike
🕐 Times vary, check website
ⓦ concordmuseum.org

⑤
Plymouth

✈ 🚌 Provincetown (Jun–Sep) 🚩 130 Water St; www. seeplymouth.com

The ship *Mayflower* sailed into Plymouth Harbor in 1620 and established the first permanent European settlement in New England. Today the town bustles with visitors exploring the sites of America's earliest days, including the **Plimoth Plantation**. At the harbor is Plymouth Rock, where the Pilgrims are said to have first stepped ashore. Moored by it is the *Mayflower II*, a replica of the 17th-century ship. Many of the Pilgrims are buried on Coles Hill, overlooked by a statue of Massasoit, an American Indian chief who became an ally of the survivors. The Pilgrim Hall Museum has a vast collection of Pilgrim-era furniture, armor, and art.

Plimoth Plantation

◈ ⓗ ⚑ 137 Warren Av
🕐 Late Mar–Nov: 9am–5pm daily ⓦ plimoth.org

6

Cape Cod

🚌🚐215 Iyannough Rd,
Hyannis 🚢Ocean St,
Hyannis; Cowdry Rd, Woods
Hole ℹ️Jct Rtes 132 & 6,
Hyannis; Rte 3, Plymouth;
www.capecodchamber.org

> **Millions of people arrive each summer to enjoy the boundless beaches, natural beauty, and quaint Colonial villages of Cape Cod.**

Millions of people arrive each summer to enjoy the boundless beaches, natural beauty, and quaint Colonial villages of Cape Cod. The Cape extends some 70 miles (113 km) into the Atlantic, severed from the mainland by the Cape Cod Canal. Whale-watching is offered by outfits all along the Cape (April–mid-October). Bikers and hikers can tackle the Cape Cod Rail Trail, a 22-mile (35-km) bikeway that runs from South Dennis to Wellfleet.

Sandwich, the oldest town in the Cape and just across the canal, is straight off a postcard: The First Church overlooks a picturesque pond, fed by a brook that powers the waterwheel of a Colonial-era Dexter Grist Mill. The town's most unusual attraction is **Heritage Museums & Gardens**, featuring American Indian relics and a 1912 carousel.

Hiking trails, salt marshes, tidal pools, and beaches attract visitors to Falmouth. It also has the 3-mile (5-km) Shining Sea Bike Path, with vistas of beach, harbor, and woodland.

Hyannis is the main transportation hub for the region and is also famous for the summer home of the celebrated political dynasty, the Kennedys. The **John F. Kennedy Hyannis Museum** tells the story of the family here. It is also the home of Cape Cod Beer and Cape Cod Potato Chips – both offer fun factory tours. One of the most popular draws is the Cape Cod Central Railroad, a scenic 2-hour round trip to the Cape Cod Canal.

Upscale Chatham offers fine inns, attractive shops, and the Monomoy Theatre (open in summer). The 1877 Chatham Lighthouse is open for taking in wonderful views of the area in the summer. The Railroad Museum, housed in a Victorian train station, exhibits vintage memorabilia and railroad cars.

Cape Cod National Seashore, stretching from Provincetown to Chatham, is famed for its horseshoe-shaped dunes, white beaches, salt marshes, glacial cliffs, and woodlands. Historical structures are scattered among the area's beautiful natural sights.

The Pilgrims first landed in Provincetown in 1620 before pushing on to the mainland, commemorated by the huge granite Pilgrim Monument. Provincetown is especially vibrant during the summer, when it becomes a leading LGBT+ resort. Since the early 20th century, the town has also had a bustling artists' colony, counting among its famous residents the painters Mark Rothko and Jackson Pollock, and the writers Eugene O'Neill and Tennessee Williams.

Heritage Museums & Gardens

♿ 🏠67 Grove St, Sandwich
🕐Mid-Apr-Oct: 10am-5pm daily 🌐heritagemuseums andgardens.org

John F. Kennedy Hyannis Museum

♿ 🏠397 Main St, Hyannis
🕐Times vary, check website 🌐jfkhyannismuseum.org

Cape Cod National Seashore

♿ 🏠Rte 6, Cape Cod ℹ️Salt Pond Visitor Center, Rte 6, Eastham; www.nps.gov/caco

←

The elegant façade of the John F. Kennedy Hyannis Museum in Cape Cod

↑ Colors of fall punctuating the landscape across the Berkshire Hills

7

Nantucket

Hyannis 25 Federal St, Nantucket Town; www.nantucket-ma.gov

The gently windswept island of Nantucket, a 14-mile- (22-km-) long enclave of tranquility with only one town, remains a largely untamed world of kettle ponds, quiet beaches and fields of wild grapes and blueberries, punctuated by the odd house. Nantucket was a prosperous center of the whaling industry in the early 1800s, and the mansions of sea captains and merchants reflect those glory days. The **Nantucket Historical Association (NHA)** operates 11 historical buildings in town, one of which houses the fascinating Whaling Museum. A popular spot, 8 miles (13 km) from town, is the village of Siasconset, which is famous for its rose-colored bluffs and lanes with tiny cottages.

Nantucket Historical Association (NHA)

15 Broad St Times vary, check website nha.org

8

Martha's Vineyard

Woods Hole 24 Beach St, Vineyard Haven; www.mvy.com

Just a 45-minute boat ride away from the mainland, this small island combines dazzling natural beauty with the charms of an old-fashioned resort. Each town has a distinctive atmosphere and architectural style. On the eastern shore is Edgartown, with the gracious 19th-century homes of the town's wealthy sea captains and merchants. The **Martha's Vineyard Museum** is housed in the Thomas Cooke House (c. 1730), filled with family possessions and other exhibits. From here, a short ferry ride will take you to Chappaquiddick Island, or "Chappy," known for its beaches and nature reserves and a Japanese garden. North of Edgartown is Oak Bluffs, with its gingerbread cottages, while the western shoreline is rural with pristine beaches.

Martha's Vineyard Museum

59 School St, Edgartown Times vary, check website mvmuseum.org

9

The Berkshires

66 Allen St, Pittsfield; www.berkshires.org

Wooded hills, green valleys and waterfalls surround this region's small towns and villages. Pittsfield, beneath Mount Greylock, was the home of Herman Melville (1819–91), author of *Moby Dick*. Lenox has the grand estates of Edith Wharton and others. Stockbridge was immortalized by resident Norman Rockwell (1894–1978), whose paintings can be seen in the **Norman Rockwell Museum**.

Especially attractive to nature lovers is the Mount Washington State Forest and nearby Bash Bish State Park.

Norman Rockwell Museum

Rte 183 Check website nrm.org

TOP 5 BERKSHIRES FESTIVALS

Berkshire Opera Festival
Great Barrington berkshireoperafestival.org
Classic operas performed in various venues (Aug).

Jacob's Pillow
Becket jacobspillow.org
The most famous US dance festival (Jun–Aug).

Shakespeare & Company
Lenox shakespeare.org
Full season (May–Nov) of plays by Shakespeare.

Tanglewood
Lenox bso.org
Home of the Boston Symphony Orchestra (Jul–Aug).

Williamstown Theatre Festival
Williamstown wtfestival.org
At the Williams College campus (Jun–Aug).

The Cat in the Hat with Dr. Seuss in his Memorial Sculpture Garden, Springfield

⑩
The Springfield Museums

🏛 21 Edwards St, Springfield ⏰ 10am–5pm Mon–Sat, 11am–5pm Sun 🌐 spring fieldmuseums.org

Founded along the banks of the Connecticut River in 1636, Springfield lies some 90 miles (145 km) west of Boston. The Springfield Museums comprise five institutions set around the tree-lined Quadrangle. The George Walter Vincent Smith Art Museum focuses on Asian decorative arts, including a spectacular collection of Chinese cloisonné. The Museum of Fine Arts is especially good for American paintings (it has the largest collection of John George Brown paintings in the world). The Springfield Science Museum is fun for kids, while the Museum of Springfield History showcases the city's post-Civil War industrial history. The Amazing World of Dr. Seuss Museum pays homage to the Springfield-born children's author, and has an adjacent memorial sculpture garden.

⑪
Northampton and Amherst

✈ Bradley 🚉 Springfield ℹ 210 Main St, North-ampton; www.north-amptonma.gov

Artsy Northampton is home to Smith College, founded in 1871 and still a prestigious women-only college. On its leafy campus, the excellent Smith College Museum of Art includes works by the likes of Claude Monet, Georgia O'Keeffe, and Frank Stella. The college library holds the Sylvia Plath Collection, including drafts of *Ariel* and *The Bell Jar*. Don't leave town without

grabbing a cone at Herrell's Ice Cream (8 Old South St), a local institution.

Nearby, Amherst is home to the **Emily Dickinson Museum**, dedicated to one of America's greatest poets. The museum comprises two houses: the Homestead, which was her birthplace and home, and the Evergreens, the home of her brother. The Mead Art Museum at Amherst College features works by Frederic Church, Thomas Cole, John Singleton Copley, Thomas Eakins, and Winslow Homer.

Emily Dickinson Museum
♿ 🔊 👓 🏛 280 Main St, Amherst ⏰ 10am–5pm Wed–Mon 🌐 emilydickinson museum.org

⑫
Worcester Art Museum

🏛 55 Salisbury St, Worcester ⏰ 10am–4pm Wed–Sun 🌐 worcesterart.org

Some 40 miles (64 km) west of Boston, Worcester is the second-largest city in Massachusetts, best known for its world-class art museum. Its vast holdings include a Romanesque chapter house from the 12th century, ship-ped from France, El Greco's *Repentant Magdalen*, and an early *St. Bartholomew* by Rembrandt. There are also pieces from Monet, including examples of his *Waterloo Bridge* and *Water Lilies* series, plus beguiling American art, while the museum also holds the USA's oldest Colonial portraits.

EMILY DICKINSON

Born in Amherst in 1830, Emily Dickinson (1830–86) attended nearby Mount Holyoke College, but loneliness drove her back to her home – now the fascinating Emily Dickinson Museum. Sometime in the 1850s, she began to write startling and beautiful poetry. Dickinson's work was collected and published posthumously in 1890 by her sister, but she wasn't widely read until the 1950s. She is now regarded as one of the greatest American poets.

13

Basketball Hall of Fame

📍 1000 Hall of Fame Av, Springfield ⏰ 10am–5pm daily 🌐 hoophall.com

In 1891 Canadian-born James Naismith created the rules for basketball in Springfield, now the site of the entertaining and insightful Basketball Hall of Fame. Inside, the Honors Ring marks all those players and coaches that have been inducted here (new Hall of Famers are inducted every August). Other highlights include a virtual hoop game, a super shot arcade and a rebound machine, a copy of Naismith's original rules, and his original wooden peach basket. There's also special exhibits on local heroes the Boston Celtics and legendary player Michael Jordan.

14

Historic Deerfield

📍 84B Old Main St, Deerfield ⏰ Mid-Apr–Nov: 9:30am–4:30pm daily; Dec–mid-Apr: 9:30am–4:30pm Sat & Sun 🌐 historic-deerfield.org

Some 16 miles (26 km) north of Northampton, Historic Deerfield is a beautifully preserved open-air museum, frozen in time, incorporating virtually all of Old Deerfield, including 65 or so 18th- and 19th-century structures on either side of Old Main Street (the main drag, running parallel to US-5). Several of the houses here are open to the public, in addition to a couple of engaging museums. Highlights include Sheldon House, which illustrates the life of a middle-class farming family from 1755 to 1802, and the Flynt Center of Early New England Life, with an artfully presented ensemble of furniture, textiles, dresses, and powder horns.

> Historic Deerfield is a beautifully preserved open-air museum, frozen in time, incorporating virtually all of Old Deerfield.

15

Hancock Shaker Village

📍 1843 West Housatonic St, Pittsfield ⏰ Mid-Apr–late Jun: 10am–4pm daily (late Jun–Oct: to 5pm) 🌐 hancock shakervillage.org

From 1790 until 1960, Hancock Shaker Village was an active community of Shakers, who were a branch of the Quakers that fled England and came to America in 1774. They were named for the convulsive fits of joy they experienced when worshiping. Known for their simple but elegant furniture, the Shakers disappeared during the 20th century, largely due to the members' vows of celibacy. Hancock comprises 18 preserved buildings, including the ingenious Round Stone Barn and the enormous Brick Dwelling (1830), where up to 100 Shakers slept and ate.

The Round Stone Barn in Hancock Shaker Village, where traditional crafts *(inset)* are practiced

Experience

RHODE ISLAND AND CONNECTICUT

Both long inhabited by American Indian tribes, Connecticut and Rhode Island were colonized by Europeans in the 1630s, and Rhode Island uniquely established religious tolerance from the start. After the Revolutionary War, both states enjoyed a flourishing economy, driven by shipbuilding, maritime commerce, and fishing. New technologies were born, with Samuel Slater building the nation's first water-powered textile mill in Pawtucket, and Eli Whitney inventing the cotton gin in New Haven. Manufacturing was central to the states' cities in the 19th century, but today Rhode Island and Connecticut are much loved for their rural charm.

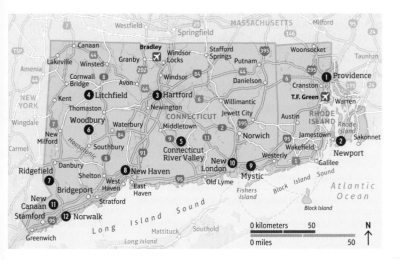

↑ The tree-lined walkways of Providence Waterplace Park and Riverwalk

RHODE ISLAND

The smallest state in America, Rhode Island is not an island at all but has a shoreline dotted with lovely islets and beaches. Although known as the Ocean State, half of Rhode Island is woodland, ideal for nature walks and camping. The state's two major cities are Providence, the lively capital, and Newport, which has some of New England's most opulent mansions.

❶ Providence

✈ Warwick 🚆 Providence Station 🚍🚌 Point St (to Newport) 🛈 1 Sabin St; www.goprovidence.com

Sandwiched between Boston and New York, Providence started life as a small farming community. It flourished as a seaport in the 17th century and evolved into a hub of industry in the 19th century. Downtown Providence has undergone several renewal phases since the 1980s, helping to inject vitality into the city.

The buildings along Benefit Street's Mile of History each tell a story. The **RISD Museum** houses a collection of art, from Ancient Egyptian to contemporary American. The elegant 1838 Greek Revival **Providence Athenaeum** is where Edgar Allan Poe found inspiration for his poem *Annabel Lee* (1849). Other architectural gems include the First Unitarian Church, which contains a bell cast by Paul Revere, and the First Baptist Church in America, built in 1774–5.

Founded in 1764, Brown University on Prospect Street is a rich blend of Gothic and Beaux Arts styles. Buildings of note include University Hall, where French and Colonial troops were quartered during the American Revolution, and the List Art building, housing classical and contemporary art.

John Brown House was built in 1786 for merchant and ship-owner John Brown (1736–1803). This lavish Georgian mansion introduced many new architectural elements, including the the Doric portico and the Palladian window above it.

Perhaps the brightest addition to downtown Providence is Waterplace Park and Riverwalk on Memorial Boulevard, where you can stroll along the park's cobblestone paths, float under footbridges in a gondola, or enjoy a free concert. High-end boutiques and restaurants can be found at the Arcade on nearby Weybosset Street.

Dominating the city landscape is the imposing **Rhode Island State House** (1904). The bronze *Independent Man* statue, a longtime symbol of Rhode Island's free spirit, stands atop the magnificent building.

Federal Hill is known for its Italian delis, bakeries, and its charming old-world piazza.

RISD Museum

♿◉ 🛇 20 North Main St 🕐 10am-5pm Tue-Sun, 10am-9pm third Thu 🚫 Federal hols 🌐 risdmuseum.org

Providence Athenaeum

🛇 251 Benefit St 🕐 10am-7pm Mon-Thu, 10am-6pm Fri & Sat, 1-5pm Sun 🚫 Summer: Sat pm, Sun 🌐 providence athenaeum.org

John Brown House

♿◉🛇 🛇 52 Power St 📞 (401) 273-7507 🕐 Apr-Nov: 1-3pm Tue-Fri, 10am-3pm Sat; Dec-Mar: 10am-3pm Sat

Rhode Island State House

♿◉🛇 🛇 82 Smith St 📞 (401) 222-3983 🕐 8:30am-4:30pm Mon-Fri 🚫 Federal hols

❷

Newport

🚗🚌 **Gateway Center,
23 America's Cup Av**
🚢 **Perrotti Pk (to Providence)**
ℹ️ **23 America's Cup Av;
www.discovernewport.org**

A center of trade, culture, and military activity for more than 300 years, Newport is a true sightseeing mecca. The main attractions are its mansions, most of them located on Bellevue Avenue on the southeastern side of the city, and built between 1748 and 1902. Modeled on European palaces and decorated with the finest artworks, the mansions served as summer retreats for the country's wealthiest families. The architecture and ostentation of the Gilded Age of the late 1800s reached its pinnacle with **The Breakers**, owned by the railroad magnate Cornelius Vanderbilt II (1843–99). Built in 1895, the four-story, 70-room mansion was modeled after 16th-century palaces in Turin and Genoa, and its interior is adorned with marble, stained glass, gilt, and crystal.

Newport is also home to the oldest synagogue in US. The **Touro Synagogue** (1763) is an outstanding example of 18th-century architecture. It is found just east of Washington Square, where a number of historic Colonial buildings remain. Among them is the Brick Market Museum and Shop, housed in the market, the center of commerce in Colonial times. Also on the square is the White Horse Tavern, which opened in 1673, making it the oldest tavern in America.

Apart from its mansions and historic sites, Newport also has numerous outdoor attractions. South of Washington Square is **Fort Adams State Park**, with Fort Adams as its centerpiece. No longer in use as a garrison, the fort is surrounded with facilities for swimming and other sports. Each year, Newport's famous Jazz Festival is held here.

Another popular site is the 3.5-mile- (5.5-km-) long Cliff Walk, which offers fine views of the Gilded-Age mansions. The Forty Steps, each named for someone lost at sea, lead to the ocean. **Easton's Beach**, along Memorial Boulevard, has a vintage carousel and is a great spot for surfing.

The Breakers

🚶🚶 📍 44 Ochre Point Av
⏰ Mid-Mar–mid-Nov: 9am–5pm daily (winter: times vary: check website)
🚫 Thanksg., Dec 24 & 25
🌐 newportmansions.org

Touro Synagogue

🚶🚶🚶 📍 85 Touro St
⏰ Times vary, check website
🌐 tourosynagogue.org

Fort Adams State Park

🚶🚶 📍 Harrison Av ⏰ Dawn–dusk 🌐 fortadams.org

ROGER WILLIAMS

Williams (1603–83) was a friend of Rhode Island's indigenous peoples and believed everyone should be free to worship as they liked. Banished for his outspoken views, he established his own colony, obtaining land from the Narrangansett Indians so that "no man should be molested for his conscience sake."

Mrs. Vanderbilt's Bedroom is sumptuously decorated in Louis XVI style.

The Music Room was the scene of many grand dances and recitals.

The Great Hall rises two full stories.

The Dining Room, a two-story room, has a stunning arched ceiling and two huge crystal chandeliers.

The Upper Loggia has enchanting views of the Atlantic Ocean.

The Billiard Room features several costly wall marbles.

← Magnificent Newport mansion, The Breakers

The Morning Room's ceiling is adorned with paintings of the four seasons, the mahogany doors with the four elements.

The sculpted archways are inspired by Italian Renaissance-style palazzos.

CONNECTICUT

Although compact, Connecticut has plenty of enticing treasures. Along its magnificent shoreline are beaches, marinas, and the remarkable maritime museum at Mystic Seaport. Inland, the Connecticut River Valley and the Litchfield Hills are dotted with scenic and historic villages. Hartford, the bustling capital, and New Haven, home of Yale University, are its main cities.

❸ Hartford

✈ Bradley Intl Airport
🚌🚉 Union Station 🛈 100 Pearl St; www.hartford.com

Hartford became a vibrant cultural hub in the 19th century, thanks to resident authors such as Mark Twain. In recent years, a revitalization program has breathed new life into the city, with the Mortensen Riverfront Plaza and Riverwalk opening access to the river downtown.

Dominating the cityscape is the gleaming gold-leaf dome of the 1878 Victorian-Gothic Connecticut State Capitol, in Bushnell Park. Opposite lies the Museum of Connecticut History, home to the 1662 Connecticut Royal Charter. The 1796 Old State House is the country's oldest capitol building and a superb example of Federal architecture. To its south is the Wadsworth Atheneum, the oldest public art museum in the US. Closer to the river, the Connecticut Science Center is crammed with entertaining exhibits.

West of downtown is the 1874 **Mark Twain House and Museum**, a Gothic-style masterpiece. Of special interest is the tranquil Billiard Room where Twain wrote some of his best-known works, including *The Adventures of Tom Sawyer*. Next door is the Harriet Beecher Stowe Center, where the author of antislavery novel *Uncle Tom's Cabin* (1852) lived. The house is adorned with gingerbread ornamentation, while the interior shows off Beecher Stowe's lesser-known talent as a decorator.

Mark Twain House and Museum

ⓐⓑ 🏠 351 Farmington Av
🕐 9:30am–5:30pm daily
🚫 Jan–Feb: Tue; Federal hols
🌐 marktwainhouse.org

---

❹ Litchfield

🏠 30 miles (48 km) W of Hartford 🚌 🌐 litchfield hills.com

This picturesque and historic town is at the center of the Litchfield Hills region in north-western Connecticut. A village green marks the center, over-

← *Genius of Connecticut* statue at the State Capitol in Hartford

looked by the white steeple of the Congregational Church (1828). Worthwhile sights include the 1784 Tapping Reeve House and Law School, the country's first law school. The Litchfield History Museum chronicles the development of the town from 1719 to today. To appreciate the natural beauty of the hills, visit the White Memorial Foundation & Conservation Center, a pristine reserve that includes much of the Bantam Lake shoreline and 35 miles (56 km) of leafy trails. The attached Nature Museum is housed in the summer home ("Whitehall") of conservationist Alain White and his sister May, built in the 1860s.

---

❺ Connecticut River Valley

🏠 6 miles (10 km) S of Hartford 🚌🚉 Hartford 🌐 ctvisit.com/hartford

The Connecticut River Valley is dotted with picture-postcard towns and villages. The charming town of **Wethersfield** is a good example of 18th–20th century American architecture. Especially worth visiting is the Webb-Deane-Stevens Museum, which depicts

↑ Fall foliage rising above a mist-shrouded lake in the Litchfield Hills region of Connecticut

Did You Know?

Mark Twain was born shortly after a visit by Halley's Comet in 1835. He died in 1910, a day after it returned.

the lifestyles of 18th-century Americans. Just outside of East Haddam is the bizarre **Gillette Castle**. Built in 1919, the medieval-style mansion is packed with oddities such as homemade trick locks. Picturesque Old Lyme is known for the **Florence Griswold Museum**, housing works by America's leading artists in an 1817 mansion.

Wethersfield
Greater Hartford Tourism District, 1 Constitution Plaza, Hartford; www.ctvisit.com

Gillette Castle
67 River Rd, off Rte 82, E Haddam (860) 526-2336 May-Sep: 10am-5pm daily

Florence Griswold Museum
96 Lyme St, Old Lyme Times vary, check website flogris.org

6

Woodbury

40 miles (65 km) SW of Hartford woodburyct.org

Woodbury was first settled in 1672 and is now the antiques capital of New England. The main street is lined by 18th- and 19th-century houses that have been converted into boutiques and antiques shops. The premier attraction is Glebe House Museum & Gertrude Jekyll Garden, which combines a 1740s Colonial home with the only remaining garden in the US designed by celebrated English landscaper Gertrude Jekyll (1843–1932). Samuel Seabury, the first Episcopal bishop, was elected here in 1783, signaling the foundation of the Episcopal church.

7

Ridgefield

40 miles (65 km) W of New Haven 13 Grove St; www.destinationridgefield.com

Picturesque Ridgefield was founded in 1708. Today, the Ridgefield Playhouse is one of many highly regarded theaters in the area. The stylish Aldrich Contemporary Art Museum is devoted to up-and-coming artists from all over the world. Ridgefield's history is highlighted at the Keeler Tavern Museum, built in 1713. Weir Farm National Historic Site displays the studio and work of Impressionist J. Alden Weir (1852–1919).

TOP 4 CONNECTICUT VINEYARDS

Haight-Brown Vineyard, Litchfield
haightbrownwine.com
The state's first vineyard, growing Chardonnay and Riesling grapes.

Hopkins Vineyard, Warren
hopkinsvineyard.com
Stunning location at Lake Waramaug.

DiGrazia Vineyards, Brookfield
digraziavineyards.com
Adds blueberries, pears, and honey to wines.

Stonington Vineyards, Stonington
stoningtonvineyards.com
Top wines near the coast.

New Haven

🛪 Tweed NH 🚉 Union Stn 🚌
ℹ 1008 Chapel St; www.
visitnewhaven.com

Founded in 1638, New Haven is best known as the home of the prestigious **Yale University**, whose alumni include four US presidents. Founded in 1701, Yale has made New Haven a leading center for education, research, and technology, and has enriched its culture as well.

The main area of the town is New Haven Green. Three beautiful early 19th-century churches are located here, of which the First Church of Christ, with a Tiffany stained-glass window, is a masterpiece of American Georgian style. Much of downtown is covered by the Yale campus, dotted with Georgian and Neo-Gothic buildings. Major landmarks include the beautiful Gothic-style Memorial Quadrangle and the Harkness Tower.

The **Yale Center for British Art** has the largest collection of British art outside the UK and includes paintings by Gainsborough, Hogarth, and Turner. The treasures of the **Beinecke Rare Book and Manuscript Libraries** include one of the world's few remaining Gutenberg Bibles. The **Yale**

University Art Gallery houses works by Picasso, van Gogh, Manet, and Monet, while the Peabody Museum of Natural History is famous for its dinosaur fossils. A must for the musically inclined is the Yale Collection of Musical Instruments, whose centuries-old violins and harpsichords are still played at concerts held here today.

Lighthouse Point Park on Long Island Sound has nature trails, a bird sanctuary, an 1840 lighthouse, and a carousel.

Yale University
🏛 149 Elm St 🌐 yale.edu

Yale Center for British Art
🚫 ♿ 🏛 1080 Chapel St
🕙 10am–5pm Tue–Sat, noon–5pm Sun ⊘ Federal hols
🌐 britishart.yale.edu

Beinecke Rare Book & Manuscript Libraries
🏛 121 Wall St 🕙 Times vary, check website ⊘ Federal hols
🌐 beinecke.library.yale.edu

Yale University Art Gallery
🚫 ♿ 🏛 1111 Chapel St
🕙 10am–5pm Tue–Fri (Sep–Jun: to 8pm Thu), 11am–5pm Sat & Sun ⊘ Federal hols
🌐 artgallery.yale.edu

💬 INSIDER TIP
New Haven Pizza

New Haven's pizzas are seriously authentic. Pepe's *(www.pepes-pizzeria.com)* was founded in 1925 by Italian chef Frank Pepe. Frank's nephew, Salvatore Consiglio, opened Sally's Apizza *(www.sallys apizza. com)* in 1938.

9 Mystic

🏛 55 miles (88 km) E of New Haven 🚉 🚌
ℹ 62 Greenmanville Av; www.mysticchamber.org

Nestled along the Mystic River, the two sides of the small town of Mystic are connected by its photogenic 1922 Bascule Bridge. Gravel Street, on the west bank of the river, is lined with handsome Cape Cod, Greek Revival, and Italianate homes once owned by wealthy sea captains and merchants.

One of the nation's largest maritime museums, **Mystic Seaport** lies on a wedge of riverfront once occupied by shipyards. It features the 1841 *Charles W. Morgan*, a enormous wooden whaling ship, as well as old-style workshops and stores reflecting life in a late 19th-century seafaring village. Other highlights include the Mystic River Scale Model, a 50-ft (15-m) representation of the town c. 1850–70, and the Figureheads exhibition. The splended Mystic Aquarium has a huge gallery of penguins, stingrays, sharks, and beluga whales. To the north lies Olde Mistick Village, designed to represent life in 18th-century New England.

Mystic Seaport

⊛ ⌂ 75 Greenmanville Av (Rte 7) ⌚ Ships and exhibits: 9am–5pm daily ✆ Dec 24 & 25 🌐 mysticseaport.org

↑ Admiring the variety of sea life at the Maritime Aquarium at Norwalk

🔟 New London

⌂ 48 miles (77 km) E of New Haven 🚆🚌 ℹ Trolley Info Ctr, Eugene O'Neill Dr; www.newlondonmainstreet.org

A major whaling port in the 19th century, New London is a dynamic, multicultural working city today. Downtown has been spruced up with a new promenade and waterfront district along the Thames River, while Starr Street is lined by handsome 19th-century Greek Revival and Italianate homes. The US Coast Guard Academy stands on a leafy red-brick campus overlooking the Thames. Its US Coast Guard Museum charts two centuries of Coast Guard history. The Lyman Allyn Art Museum specializes in American arts and crafts, with a special focus on Paul Revere silverware and paintings from the Connecticut Impressionists and the Hudson River School, including work by Frederic Church.

Overlooking the Thames just south of downtown,

←

Dwight Hall, formerly the college library at Yale University Old Campus

Monte Cristo Cottage preserves the memory of Eugene O'Neill (1888–1953), one of America's most beloved playwrights and winner of the Nobel Prize for Literature in 1936. O'Neill spent his summers here, and it was the setting for two of his works, *Long Day's Journey into Night* and *Ah, Wilderness!*

🔟 New Canaan

⌂ 37 miles (60 km) W of New Haven 🚆🚌 🌐 explore newcanaan.com

Set in a landscape of woods, sleepy New Canaan, is most spectacular in fall. From the 1940s to the 1960s, it became a training ground for the "Harvard Five," architects and designers Philip Johnson, Marcel Breuer, Landis Gores, John M. Johansen, and Eliot Noyes. Many of the homes they built still stand, Johnson's **Glass House** being the best example. Built in 1949 of glass and charcoal-painted steel, it's regarded as one of America's most intriguing buildings.

The Glass House

⊛ 🈲 ⌂ 199 Elm St ⌚ May–Nov: Mon & Thu–Sun (last tour 2:30pm) 🌐 theglass house.org

🔟 Norwalk

⌂ 33 miles (53 km) W of New Haven 🚆🚌 ℹ 125 East Av; www.norwalkct.org

Norwalk has historic buildings, shops, and cafés along its waterfront, as well as hip South Norwalk ("SoNo"). The Maritime Aquarium features the varied marine life of Long Island Sound, including sharks, harbor seals, and jellyfish. The city's past is chronicled at the Norwalk Museum, with a focus on oysters and hat-making, as well as Raggedy Ann dolls. The Lockwood-Mathews Mansion Museum was constructed in 1864 for insurance and railway tycoon LeGrand Lockwood.

VERMONT

Before European settlers arrived, this region was occupied by the Iroquois, Mahican, and Wabanaki confederacies. In 1770, businessman and patriot Ethan Allen formed the Green Mountain Boys, who protected settlers' rights and resisted New York's attempted rule. This free-spirited nature stuck. Vermont remained an independent state for 14 years, joining the US in 1791. It also enacted the world's first constitution to forbid slavery and grant universal (male) suffrage. Its progressive nature aside, Vermont's wooded hills and pretty villages have attracted tourists since the 19th century.

Experience

1 Bennington
2 Manchester
3 Killington
4 Shelburne Museum and Farms
5 Woodstock
6 Lake Champlain
7 Stowe
8 Burlington
9 Ben & Jerry's Ice Cream Factory

↑ A snowboarder spraying powder at Sugarbush in the Green Mountains

VERMONT

Villages and natural splendors are abound in Vermont, and its residents are famed for their political and social conscience. In the south is the lovely town of Bennington, while in the northwest Lake Champlain provides a backdrop for the lively college town of Burlington, and the ski resorts perched in the mountains. In fall, Vermont's leaf colors are particularly spectacular,

1 Bennington

📍💻 🚩100 Veterans Memorial Dr; www.bennington.com

In the southwest corner of the Green Mountain National Forest lies Bennington, home to the small but prestigious Bennington College. The town's most prominent landmark is the Bennington Battle Monument, a granite obelisk commemorating the 1777 defeat of the British by Colonial forces. The monument looms over the Old Bennington Historic District, which has a village green ringed by Federal-style buildings. The 1806 First Congregational Church is particularly striking, with its vaulted plaster and wood ceilings. Next door is the Old Burying Ground where one of America's most loved poets, Robert Frost, is buried. The **Bennington Museum** has an impressive collection of Americana, with a gallery devoted to folk artist Anna Mary "Grandma" Moses, (1860–1961). A farmer's wife with no formal art training, Grandma Moses started painting landscapes as a hobby when she was in her mid-seventies.

Bennington Museum

🎨🏛 🚩75 Main St 🕙10am-5pm Thu-Tue (Jun-Oct: daily) 🚫Jan, Thanksgiving, Dec 25 🌐benningtonmuseum.org

2 Manchester

🚂Rutland 🚌 🚩18 Depot St; www.manchestervermont.com

Ringed by mountains, this scenic town is a favorite of both shoppers and skiers. Clusters of outlets scattered around the villages here offer branded goods at significant discounts. Visitors also enjoy the Equinox Skyline Drive, with its panoramic views from the crest of Mount Equinox. The town has two major ski areas – Stratton, with more than 90 trails and a hillside ski village with shops and restaurants, and Bromley, a busy, family-oriented ski area.

Manchester has been a resort since the 19th century, and its mansions evoke that era. One of the most elegant is **Hildene**, a 24-room Georgian manor built by Robert Todd Lincoln, son of Abraham Lincoln. Among its notable features is a 1,000-pipe organ.

Hildene

🎨🏛 🚩Rte 7A 🕙9:30am-4:30pm daily 🌐hildene.org

3 Killington

🚂Rutland 🚩Rte 4, West Killington; www.killington.com

Sporty types who like outdoor adventure and a lively social

1777

The year that Vermont abolished slavery.

life head for this year-round resort. Killington operates the largest ski center in the eastern United States, with 212 runs for skiing and snowboarding spread across seven peaks, including nearby Pico Mountain. It also has cross-country ski areas at Mountain Top Inn and Mountain Meadows.

Killington itself is the second -highest peak in Vermont. The ski season here lasts 8 months, the longest in Vermont. In summer as well as fall, a gondola ferries visitors up to the peaks from where, on clear days, there are views of five states and distant Canada.

4 Shelburne Museum and Farms

📍 Rte 7, 7 miles (11 km) S of Burlington 🕐 Mid-May-late Oct: 10am–5pm Mon-Sat, noon–5pm Sun 🕐 Late Oct–May, Thanksg., Dec 25 🌐 shelburnemuseum.org

Shelburne Museum's 39 exhibition buildings constitute one of America's finest museums. Its eclectic collection celebrates three centuries of American ingenuity, including folk art, circus memorabilia, and paintings by artists such as Winslow Homer and Grandma Moses.

Among the historic buildings on view are the Circus Building, and an 1890 Railroad Station. Visitors can also explore an 1871 Lake Champlain lighthouse and the *Ticonderoga*, a former Lake Champlain steamship. The Pizzagalli Center is open all year for art workshops, lectures, film screenings, and musical performances.

At Shelburne Farms, there are tours of the dairy, and areas where children can pet and play with the animals.

→ Children watching cows grazing at Billings Farm and Museum in Woodstock

5 Woodstock

🚹 🚻 ℹ️ 3 Mechanic St; www.woodstockvt.com

Even in Vermont, where historic, picturesque villages are commonplace, Woodstock stands out. The town is an enclave of Georgian houses, many of them beautifully restored. At the working **Billings Farm and Museum**, the 1890 farmhouse has been restored, and visitors can attend seasonal events such as apple cider pressing in the fall and plowing competitions in the spring. The museum's exhibits include vintage farm implements and butter churns. At the farm you can reserve tours of the Marsh-Billings-Rockefeller National Historical Park, encompassing the 19th-century mansion of three generations of ground-breaking conservationists. George Perkins Marsh (1801–1882) was born here, later campaigning against deforestation. The house was bought in 1869 by lawyer Frederick Billings (1823–90), who put Marsh's ideas into practice. Wealthy philanthropist Laurence Rockefeller (1910–2004) opened the Billings Farm section of the property and donated the rest to the National Park Service in 1992.

East of town is the stunning Quechee Gorge. The best view is on Route 4, which crosses the gorge via a steel bridge. Hiking trails lead down through forests to the surrounding Quechee Gorge State Park along the river.

Billings Farm and Museum
♿ 🍴 📍 River Rd 🕐 Times vary, check website 🌐 billingsfarm.org

EAT

Hen of the Wood
Locally grown and foraged food in an intimate setting.
📍 55 Cherry St, Burlington
🌐 henofthewood.com

$$$

Farmhouse Tap & Grill
Gastropub with locally sourced food and 30 taps of local craft beer.
📍 160 Bank St, Burlington
🌐 farmhousetg.com

$$$

❻
Lake Champlain

✈ Burlington 🚌 ℹ 60 Main St, Burlington; www.lake champlainregion.com

Sometimes called the sixth Great Lake, Lake Champlain has 500 miles (800 km) of shoreline and some 70 islands. At the northern end is Isle La Motte, which has a statue of French explorer Samuel de Champlain. On nearby Grand Isle is Vermont's oldest log cabin (1783). The lake has its western shore in New York State, and seasonal ferries run between Burlington and Port Kent, New York.

Some of the lake's treasures are underwater in a marine park where scuba divers can explore shipwrecks resting on sandbars and at the bottom of the clear water.

Lake Champlain Maritime Museum at Basin Harbor gives a complete overview of the region's marine history.

Lake Champlain Maritime Museum

⊛ 🏠 4472 Basin Harbor Rd, Vergennes ⏰ Late May–mid-Oct: 10am–5pm 🖥 lcmm.org

Did You Know?

Lake Champlain is said to be the home of "Champ," a water serpent similar to the Loch Ness Monster.

❼
Stowe

↗ Burlington ℹ 51 Main St; www.gostowe.com

This mountain-ringed village is the skiing capital of New England and draws hordes of visitors in winter. Mountain Road begins in the village and is lined with chalets, motels, restaurants, and pubs; it leads to the area's highest peak, Mount Mansfield.

In summer there are plenty of outdoor activities on offer. Visitors can hike, rock-climb, fish, canoe, bike, or skate along the paved, meandering 5.5-mile (8.5-km) Stowe Recreational Path, which winds from the village church across the West Branch River, then through green woodlands.

Stowe's other claim to fame is as the home of the musical Von Trapp family, who were the inspiration behind the 1965 movie *The Sound of Music*. After their daring escape from Austria during World War II, they chose Stowe as their new home. Their Trapp Family Lodge is set in a 4-sq-mile (11-sq-km) estate. This giant wooden chalet is now one of the most popular hotels in the area.

SKIING IN VERMONT

Vermont boasts two world-famous slopes at Killington and Stowe Mountain. In the south, Bromley and Stratton mountains are easily accessible, while Mount Snow lies in the Green Mountains. In the north, the Jay Peak and Burke Mountain resorts are the least crowded and most challenging. Two great locations for cross-country skiers and snowshoers are the Catamount Trail and the Trapp Family Lodge Ski Center.

Stowe's charming village church, amid magnificent fall colors ↑

8 Burlington

King St Dock 60 Main St; www.vermont.org

Burlington is Vermont's largest city and one of the most popular tourist destinations in the state. Half of the population of this lively town is made up of students from the University of Vermont and the city's four colleges. As well as grand old mansions and historic landmarks, Burlington is also Vermont's center of commerce and industry, and is scenically located on the shores of Lake Champlain.

The center of Burlington is compact and easy to explore on foot. It includes the Historic District, at the core of which is the four-block section known as Church Street Marketplace. The neighborhood has been converted into a pedestrian mall, complete with trendy boutiques, patio restaurants, and crafts shops. Many of them are housed in Queen Anne–style buildings from the late 1800s. The historical attractions in this neighborhood include the 1861 First Unitarian Church, the oldest house of worship in Burlington, and the City Hall, which marks the southern boundary of the marketplace. This graceful building, built of local brick, marble, and granite, dates to 1928. City Hall Park is a popular outdoor concert venue, and in summer street performers and musicians add color and action to the area.

On the waterfront is Battery Park, where a battle between US soldiers and the British Royal Navy took place in 1813. Today, the park is a peaceful place, from where there are captivating views of Burlington Bay and the backdrop of the Adirondack Mountains on the other side of Lake Champlain. Just south of the park is the Burlington Boat House; here the *Spirit of Ethan Allen III* takes visitors on a 90-minute trip around the lake, while the captain regales them with tales of the Revolutionary War.

The **Fleming Museum of Art**, on the campus of the University of Vermont, is on a hillside overlooking the city. Artifacts in this elegant 1931 Colonial Revival building range from ancient Mesopotamian objects to European artwork and American Indian crafts. Visitors can enjoy a coffee while browsing the book store.

Fleming Museum of Art

61 Colchester Av
Times vary, check website
uvm.edu/fleming

9 Ben & Jerry's Ice Cream Factory

Rte 100, Waterbury
Times vary, check website benjerry.com/waterbury

Although Ben Cohen and Jerry Greenfield hail from Long Island, New York, they have done more than any other "flatlanders" to put Vermont's dairy industry on the map. In 1978, these childhood friends paid $5 for a correspondence course on making ice cream, and parlayed their knowledge into an enormously successful ice cream franchise. No longer privately owned, the factory uses the richest dairy products to produce the ice cream and frozen yogurt.

↑ Contemplating different flavors at Ben & Jerry's Ice Cream Factory

Tours of the factory start every 30 minutes and run for 30 minutes. Visitors learn all there is to know about making ice cream. They are given a bird's-eye view of the factory floor, and at the end of the tour they get a chance to sample the products and sometimes taste new flavors.

INSIDER TIP

Vermont Cheese and Maple Syrup

Vermont is famous for its cheddar cheese - sample it at Cabot Creamery *(www.cabotcheese.coop)*. Vermont is also the largest producer of maple syrup in the US. Pick some up at Morse Farm Maple Sugarworks *(www.morsefarm.com)*.

Mature bull moose in Baxter State Park, Maine

Experience

1. White Mountain National Forest
2. Bretton Woods
3. Franconia Notch
4. Lake Winnipesaukee
5. Concord
6. Manchester
7. Portsmouth
8. Canterbury Shaker Village
9. Portland
10. The Kennebunks
11. Penobscot Bay
12. Acadia National Park
13. Bethel
14. Campobello Island

NEW HAMPSHIRE AND MAINE

"Live Free or Die" is the motto of New Hampshire, summing up a belief in rugged individualism that applies just as much to Maine. European settlement began in the 1620s, though the interior remained the preserve of the people of the Wabanaki confederacy for decades. In 1776, New Hampshire became the first state to declare independence, while Maine remained part of Massachusetts until 1820. By this time, Portsmouth and a few towns in Maine were thriving ports, thanks mostly to shipbuilding. New Hampshire also thrived as a manufacturing center in the 19th century.

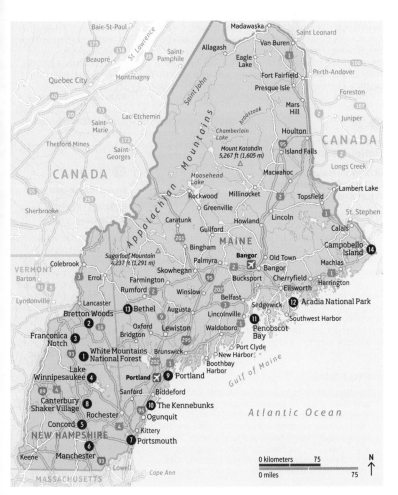

Winter hikers brave the snow near Lion Head in the White Mountains ↑

NEW HAMPSHIRE

New Hampshire's natural beauty has little changed since the American Revolution, and is evident all over the state – from the tall peaks of the White Mountains range in the north to the spectacular chasm of Franconia Notch. The main cities – historic Concord and lively Portsmouth, with its scenic Atlantic coastline – nestle amid the tranquil farmlands of the south.

❶

White Mountain National Forest

🚹 71 White Mountain Dr, Campton; www.visitwhite mountains.com

New Hampshire's most beautiful area of wilderness has an abundance of wildlife, including a large moose population, which can often be seen from the road. Outdoor activities in this region range from bird-watching and rock climbing to skiing and kayaking. But even less sporty travelers will revel in the spectacular scenery: pine forests, waterfalls, rocky outcrops, and soaring summits. An especially scenic stretch is the White Mountains Trail, which loops across Mount Washington Valley through Crawford Notch and Franconia Notch. In fall, the brilliant foliage transforms the rugged countryside into a flaming palette of reds, golds, and maroons.

Another popular route is the **Kancamagus Highway**, the most beautiful road in New England. This short run from Lincoln to Conway offers exceptional vistas as it climbs through the Kancamagus Pass. The road descends into the Saco Valley and joins up with the Swift River, where you'll find campgrounds and picnic areas along the highway. Well-marked trails allow you to stretch your legs amid the beautiful scenery – try the short loop that leads to the delightful Sabbaday Falls.

Kancamagus Highway

🚗 Rte 112 between Lincoln & Conway 🕸 kancamagus highway.com

---

❷

Bretton Woods

🚗🚹 99 Ski Area Rd; www. brettonwoods.com

This tiny enclave has an unusual claim to fame. In 1944, with the need for stability after the economic upheavals of World War II, it hosted the United Nations conference that led to the establishment of the IMF and, later, the World Bank. The setting for this historic meeting was the magnificent **Omni Mount Washington Resort**, with its striking white-and-crimson exterior.

The Mount Washington Valley, in which Bretton Woods is located, is dominated by Mount Washington, which has the distinction of having the worst weather of any mountain in the world. On clear days, however, brave souls hike to the summit by one of the many

---

FALL FOLIAGE

Thousands of visitors head for New England in the fall, to gaze in wonder at the annual changing of leaf colors. In New Hampshire especially, the White Mountain National Forest and the woods around Lake Winnipesaukee erupt in a riotous display of shades of yellow, orange, crimson, and maroon. The peak period for "leaf-peeping" varies from early October in northern New England to late October in the south, but this can differ, depending on the weather.

trails, drive cars, or puff slowly to the top aboard the **Mount Washington Cog Railroad**, which opened in 1869.

Omni Mount Washington Resort
🍴🏨 📍Rte 302, Bretton Woods 🌐omnihotels.com

Mount Washington Cog Railroad
🎫🍴🏨 📍Off Rte 302, Marshfield Base Station 🕐Apr–Nov: check website for timetable 🌐thecog.com

---

STAY

Wolfeboro Inn
Waterfront inn perched on Lake Winnipesaukee. Rooms range from comfy modern suites to vintage rooms.

📍90 N Main St (Rte 109), Wolfeboro 🌐wolfeboroinn.com

💲💲💲

3
Franconia Notch

📍I-93, Franconia Notch Pkwy 🌐nhstateparks.org

This spectacular mountain pass is home to some of the state's most stunning natural wonders. Foremost among them was the Old Man of the Mountain, a rocky outcrop that resembled a man's profile until the nose and forehead fell down in May 2003. Profile Lake reflects the brilliant colors of fall foliage on the slopes of Cannon Mountain. A boardwalk and stairways lead through the Flume Gorge, a narrow chasm whose granite walls tower overhead, while an aerial tramway speeds you to the summit of Cannon Mountain.

Robert Frost (1874–1963), one of America's best-loved poets, settled here in 1915. The Frost Place Museum includes a nature trail with plaques displaying Frost's poems.

The Omni Mount Washington Resort in Bretton Woods, and nearby Cog Railroad *(inset)* ↓

4
Lake Winnipesaukee

📍Lakes Region Association; www.lakesregion.org

This stunning lake, ringed by mountains and scattered with islands, has the state's largest waterfront. The prettiest of all its resort towns is Wolfeboro. Leaving from Weirs Beach, the MS *Mount Washington* offers the best scenic cruise in New England. To the north are the upscale lakeside homes of Meredith. North of Meredith is pristine Squam Lake, ideal for boating and fishing. Surrounded by woodland, the town of Center Sandwich on the north shore is a favorite fall destination. On the eastern shore, the Castle in the Clouds mansion crowns the crest of a hill.

5

Concord

49 S Main St; (603) 224-2508

New Hampshire's capital is a quiet little town, dominated by its impressive State House. Built in 1819 from granite and marble, it is one of the oldest state houses in the US. In its heyday, the Eagle Hotel on Main Street hosted the likes of presidents Andrew Jackson and Benjamin Harrison, as well as aviator Charles Lindbergh, and former First Lady Eleanor Roosevelt. Another landmark is the giant glass pyramid of the **McAuliffe-Shepard Discovery Center**, named after Concord teacher Christa McAuliffe (1948–86), who died in the space shuttle *Challenger* accident in 1986, and New Hampshire native Alan B. Shepard, Jr. (1923–98), the first American in space. The astronomy and space exploration exhibits include a Mercury space capsule, a large-scale model of a space shuttle, and a planetarium with multimedia shows such as a recap of the Apollo Moon Landing program.

McAuliffe-Shepard Discovery Center
2 Institute Dr
Times vary, check website
starhop.com

6

Manchester

54 Hanover St; (603) 666-6600

Once a major center of the textile industry, with its many mills powered by water from the Merrimack River, today Manchester is famous as the home the **Currier Museum of Art**, with its excellent collection featuring such European masters as Claude Monet and Henri Matisse. The entire second floor is dedicated to 18th- and 19th-century American painters such as Andrew Wyeth (1917–2009) and Georgia O'Keeffe (1887–1986). Also part of the museum is the Zimmerman House, designed in 1950 by pioneering American architect Frank Lloyd Wright (1867–1959) as an exemplar of his style of home. Shuttles take visitors from the museum to the house, and guided tours (by advance reservation mid-April through January) of its interior highlight textiles and furniture designed by Wright.

The indoor Mall of New Hampshire features more than 100 shops and restaurants.

Currier Museum of Art
150 Ash St
11am-5pm Mon, Wed-Fri & Sun, 10am-5pm Sat
currier.org

DRINK

Smuttynose Brewing Co.

One of New England's most celebrated craft brewers, Smuttynose is based just outside Hampton. Tour the facility before sampling the selection of beers in the tasting room.

105 Towle Farm Rd
smuttynose.com

$$$

7

Portsmouth

10 Ladd St 500 Market St or Market Sq; www.goportsmouthnh.com

Girded by the Piscataqua River and North and South Mill ponds, historic Portsmouth is small enough to be explored on foot. Established in 1623, it became a prosperous hub of maritime commerce by the 18th century and was a hotbed of revolutionary fervor.

A number of Portsmouth's historic buildings are in the downtown core, especially along Market Street. Historic

Admiring the works on display at Manchester's Currier Museum of Art ↑

The distinctive belfry contains a bell made by Revere and Sons.

Dormer rooms were used for summer sleeping.

The Chapel Wing was added in 1837.

Exhibits show the simple hand tools that Shakers used to produce their spare but elegant furniture.

This display shows how a uniformity of design was maintained within and across all of the Shaker communities.

The dining room once held as many as 60 Shakers per sitting.

↑ Canterbury Shaker Village's communal Dwelling House

houses and gardens can also be found along the Portsmouth Harbor Trail, a walking tour of the Historic District. Especially worth visiting is the elegant Moffatt-Ladd House on Market Street (1763), an early example of Federal-style architecture. The Wentworth-Gardner House on Mechanic Street is one of the finest Georgian-style buildings in the country.

Interactive exhibits are the highlight of the **Children's Museum of New Hampshire**, where children can interact with a sound sculpture or command a submarine. You can explore the real thing at Albacore Park, where the USS *Albacore* submarine is docked.

Portsmouth's most popular attraction is **Strawbery Banke**. This outdoor museum contains more than 40 buildings that depict life from 1695 to 1954. It also has the Colonial Revival Aldrich Garden, planted with flowers mentioned in the poetry of Portsmouth native Thomas Bailey Aldrich.

Children's Museum of New Hampshire
⊛ ⌂ 6 Washington St, Dover ◷ 10am-5pm Tue-Sat (summer: also Mon), noon-5pm Sun 🌐 childrens-museum.org

Strawbery Banke
⊛ Ⓣ ⊕ ⊞ ⌂ 14 Hancock St ◷ May-Oct: 10am-5pm daily 🌐 strawberybanke.org

 ⑧ ⊛ ⓜ Ⓣ ⊟ ⊞

Canterbury Shaker Village

⌂ 288 Shaker Rd, Canterbury ◷ May-Aug: 10am-4pm Tue-Sun; Sep-late Oct: 10am-5pm daily; late Oct-late Nov: 10am-4pm Sat & Sun 🌐 shakers.org

Founded in 1792, this village was occupied by Shakers for 200 years. The Shakers were a sect that broke away from the Quakers and fled to America to escape religious persecution in Britain in the mid-18th century. Their theology of ecstatic worship was balanced by their strict practice of celibacy and this eventually led to their demise. As well as having several buildings open to visitors, the site is further punctuated by millponds, nature trails, and traditional gardens. Skilled artisans can be seen re-creating distinctive Shaker crafts, which were known for their simple lines and beautiful workmanship.

MAINE

New England's largest state is truly the Great Outdoors. Its most popular attractions are found along the spectacular coastline, beginning in Maine's largest and liveliest city, Portland. World-class skiing, hiking, and mountain-biking opportunities are found inland, while maritime museums and lighthouses along the coast symbolize the state's seafaring history.

9

Portland

Commercial & Franklin sts 14 Ocean Gateway Pier; www.visitportland.com

This historic city sits on the crest of a peninsula, with expansive views of Casco Bay and the Calendar Islands. Once a flourishing port, Portland was devastated by four major fires, the last one in 1866. Nevertheless, the city still has a number of sturdy Victorian buildings.

The West End has several fine mansions and a splendid promenade overlooking the water. Portland's liveliest area, however, is around the Old Port. This restored neighborhood's narrow streets are filled with shops, restaurants, and art galleries. Dominating the area is the former United States Custom House, with its gilded ceilings, marble staircases, and chandeliers. From the docks, ships offer cruises to the Calendar Islands, harbor tours, and deep-sea fishing trips.

West of the Old Port, the **Portland Museum of Art** displays works by the area's most famous artist, Winslow Homer (1836–1910), as well as by European masters such as Gauguin and Picasso. The **Children's Museum and Theatre of Maine** is filled with interactive exhibits, opportunities to dress up and examples of traditional crafts.

Several fine historic houses are open to visitors, including the Wadsworth-Longfellow House (1785), where poet Henry Wadsworth Longfellow grew up, and the Victoria Mansion, with its trompe l'oeil walls. Portland's signature landmark is the Portland Head Light, surrounded by beach and picnic areas at Fort Williams Park. The keeper's house is now a museum.

1791

The year the Portland Head Light was first illuminated at Fort Williams Park.

Portland Museum of Art
7 Congress Sq Late May-Oct: 10am-6pm daily (to 8pm Thu & Fri); Nov-late May: 11am-6pm Wed-Sun (to 8pm Thu & Fri) portlandmuseum.org

Children's Museum and Theatre of Maine
142 Free St 10am-5pm Tue-Sun Federal hols kitetails.org

← Portland Head Light at Fort Williams Park guiding ships safely into the city

⑩ The Kennebunks

 ✉ 🛈 16 Water St, Kennebunk; www.visitthe-kennebunks.com

Once a thriving shipbuilding center and port, this affluent summer retreat is made up of two villages, Kennebunk and Kennebunkport.

Kennebunkport's historic village is graced by several Federal and Greek Revival structures. Some 200 antique streetcars are housed at the **Seashore Trolley Museum**. Tours of the countryside are offered on restored trolleys. The scenic drive along Route 9 offers views of Cape Arundel, while at Cape Porpoise you can sample lobster fresh from the Atlantic. Kennebunk is famous for its beaches, and seasonal walking tours of its historic area are offered by the **Brick Store Museum**.

Seashore Trolley Museum

♿ 🚗 195 Log Cabin Rd, Kennebunkport ⏰ Check website 🌐 trolleymuseum.org

Brick Store Museum

♿ 🚗 117 Main St, Kennebunk ⏰ 10am–5pm Tue–Fri, 10am–4pm Sat, noon–4pm Sun 🌐 brickstoremuseum.org

⑪ Penobscot Bay

🚌

Penobscot Bay is picture-book Maine, with wave-pounded cliffs and sheltered harbors. It's also famous for its islands, which can be reached by boat from the mainland.

The bay's commercial center is the fishing town of **Rockland**, whose lobster festival is held on the first full weekend of August. **Camden** village is dotted with spired churches and elegant homes, and Camden Hills State Park offers breathtaking views of the bay. **Searsport** has busy summer flea markets and boasts the Penobscot Marine Museum, recalling its port era.

The eastern shore leads to the village of **Castine**. Fort George, built by the British in 1799, was witness to the American Navy's worst defeat in the Revolutionary War.

Deer Isle, reached by bridge from the mainland, is a series of small islands. From the scenic town of Stonington, it is an 8-mile (13-km) boat ride to the wooded Isle au Haut. Monehgan Island is a favored retreat for birders and hikers.

Rockland
🛈 1 Park Dr; www.camdenrockland.com

Camden
🛈 2 Public Landing; www.visitcamden.com

Searsport
🛈 14 Main St; www.searsport.me.gov

Castine
🛈 67 Court St; www.castine.me.us

Deer Isle
🛈 114 Little Deer Isle Rd; (207) 348-6124

⑫ 🚵 🥾

Acadia National Park

🚌 Bangor–Bar Harbor at Hulls Cove 🛈 Hulls Cove Visitor Center, off Rte 3 in Hulls Cove; www.nps.gov/acad

Located primarily on Mount Desert Island, off the southeast Maine coast, Acadia National Park is a wild, unspoiled paradise where wave-beaten shores and inland forests await.

Relaxing on the top of Cadillac Mountain, Acadia National Park, and people visiting the mighty Thunder Hole *(inset)* ↑

The Loop Road, a scenic 27-mile (43-km) drive (closed Dec–mid-Apr), climbs and dips with the pink granite mountains of the east coast. Among the sights is Cadillac Mountain, the highest point on the Atlantic Coast. The road continues south to the idyllic Sand Beach, but the icy water discourages many swimmers. Farther south is the natural phenomenon known locally as Thunder Hole – when the tide rises during heavy winds, air trapped in this crevice is compressed and then expelled with a resounding boom. The Loop Road continues inland, swinging past Jordan Pond, Bubble Pond, and Eagle Lake.

On the southern shore of the park is the village of Bass Harbor, where an 1858 lighthouse is perched on the rocky coastline, offering magnificent views of the ocean. For a more intimate look at the park's flora and fauna, travel on foot, bike, or horseback along the 45 miles (72 km) of old carriage roads that wind through the park.

Cutting through the center of the island is Somes Sound, a finger-shaped natural fjord that juts 5 miles (8 km) inland. It separates the quiet village of Southwest Harbor from Northeast Harbor, the center of Mount Desert Island's social scene, with its upscale shops and handsome mansions.

The elegant resort town of **Bar Harbor**, on Mount Desert Island's northeastern shore, is a lively tourist center and a good base from which to explore Acadia National Park. More than 5 million visitors each year pass

EAT

Red's Eats

Few delicacies can compete with the classic lobster roll served at this no-frills white-and-red shack.

📍 41 Water St (Rte 1), Wiscasset

🌐 redseatsmaine.com

$⑤$⑤$⑤

through Bar Harbor on their way to the wilds of the park. Attractions include the Abbe Museum, which celebrates Maine's American Indian heritage with displays of tools, crafts, art, artifacts, and archaeology. A seasonal branch of the museum is located at Sieur de Monts Spring in the park next to the Wild Gardens of Acadia. The museum sponsors the American Indian Festival each summer.

Bar Harbor Oceanarium, situated 8.5 miles (14 km) northwest of the town, is an inviting spot for families to walk along a salt marsh and to learn about marine life. The facility includes the Lobster Fishing Program, and a lobster hatchery, where eggs grow until the lobsters are large enough to be released.

Bar Harbor
🏠 2 Cottage St, Bar Harbor; www.visitbarharbor.com

13
Bethel

🚇🏠 8 Station Place; www.bethelmaine.com

A picturesque historic district, a major ski resort, and proximity to the White Mountains give Bethel its year-round appeal. First settled in 1796, the town was a farming and lumbering center until the coming of the railroad in 1851 made it a popular resort. The lineup of classic clapboard mansions on the town green includes the Federal-style **Moses Mason House** (c. 1813), restored and furnished with period pieces.

There are scenic drives in all directions, taking in unspoiled Colonial hamlets such as Waterford to the south, and beautiful mountain terrain to the north. **Sunday River Ski Resort**, 6 miles (10 km) north of town in Newry, has more than 130 ski trails. **Grafton Notch State Park** has spectacular scenery along its drives and hiking trails. The park's best spots include waterfalls and sweeping views of the surroundings from Table Rock and Old Speck Mountain.

Moses Mason House
⊗⊗ 🏠 10–14 Broad St 📞 (207) 824-2908 ⏰ Jul–Aug: 1–4pm Thu–Sat; Sep–Jun: by appointment only

Sunday River Ski Resort
⊗ 🏠 Off Rte 2 in Newry 🌐 sundayriver.com

Grafton Notch State Park
⊗ 🏠 Rte 26 NW of Newry 🌐 maine.gov/graftonnotch

---

14 ⏯

Campobello Island

🏠 Roosevelt Campobello International Park; (506) 752-2922

At the northeast tip of the US, Campobello Island is a place of tranquil seclusion and natural beauty. The island's main settlement of Welshpool was where Franklin D. Roosevelt spent most of his summers. The **Roosevelt Campobello International Park** was established in 1964 as a memorial to the president.

INSIDER TIP
Sugarloaf Mountain

Maine's highest ski resort, Sugarloaf, offers more than 150 trails. In summer, the emphasis shifts to golf, boating, and hiking. The resort is also famous for its mountain-biking trails.

The highlight of the park, which actually lies in Canada and is the only international park in the world, is Roosevelt Cottage. Built in 1897, this sprawling wood-frame summer home displays furnishings and mementos that belonged to FDR and his family.

At the island's southern tip is Liberty Point, where a pair of observation decks perched on the rugged cliffs offer far-ranging views of the Atlantic.

A short distance inland from here is Lower Duck Pond Bog, a prime habitat for the great blue heron, killdeer, and the American black duck.

On the island's western shore is Mulholland Point, with an 1885 lighthouse and a picnic site offering views of the FDR Memorial Bridge.

Roosevelt Campobello International Park
⊗⊗ ⏰ Mid-May–mid-Oct (ID required for international border crossing) 🌐 fdr.net

→
FDR's summer residence in Roosevelt Campobello International Park.

WASHINGTON, DC AND THE CAPITAL REGION

The United States Capitol at dawn

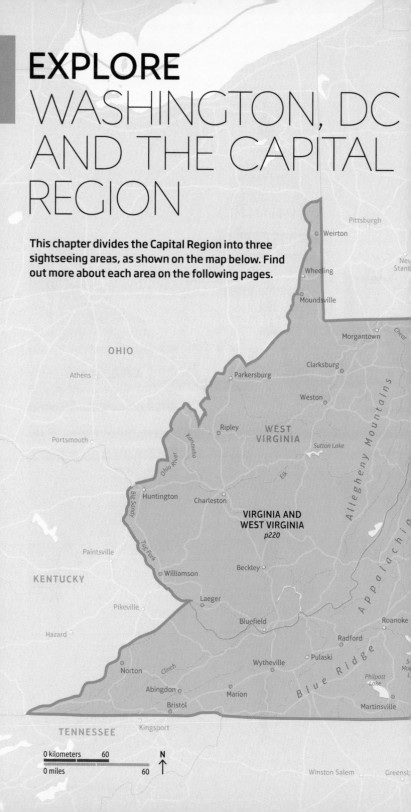

EXPLORE
WASHINGTON, DC AND THE CAPITAL REGION

This chapter divides the Capital Region into three sightseeing areas, as shown on the map below. Find out more about each area on the following pages.

Pittsburgh

Weirton

New Stant

Wheeling

Moundsville

Morgantown

Cheat

OHIO

Clarksburg

Athens

Parkersburg

Weston

Allegheny Mountains

Ripley

WEST VIRGINIA

Sutton Lake

Portsmouth

Elk

Kanawha

Ohio River

Huntington

Charleston

Big Sandy

VIRGINIA AND WEST VIRGINIA
p220

Appalachia

Paintsville

Tug Fork

KENTUCKY

Williamson

Beckley

Pikeville

Laeger

Hazard

Bluefield

Roanoke

Radford

Norton

Clinch

Wytheville

Pulaski

Blue Ridge

Philpott Lake

S Mo L

Abingdon

Marion

Martinsville

Bristol

TENNESSEE   Kingsport

0 kilometers   60

0 miles   60

N ↑

Winston Salem   Greenst

CANADA

Seattle

USA   Chicago   Boston
                             New York City
San Francisco   WASHINGTON, DC AND   Washington, DC
                 THE CAPITAL REGION
Los Angeles
                     Atlanta   Atlantic
                                          Ocean
          Houston
Pacific   Miami
Ocean   MEXICO   Gulf of
                    Mexico

NORTH AMERICA

PENNSYLVANIA

DuBois

Johnstown   Harrisburg

      Everett   Philadelphia

                                              Wilmington
                                              New Castle

umberland   Aberdeen   NEW JERSEY
           Potomac River   MARYLAND
                    Frederick   Baltimore
S. Branch Potomac   Harpers   Columbia   Dover
                     Ferry
          Winchester   Silver   Annapolis
                               Spring
            Front   WASHINGTON, DC   Lewes
            Royal   p202
       Alexandria   St.   Easton
Mountains   Michaels   DELAWARE
   Dale City   DISTRICT OF
Shenandoah   COLUMBIA
                                   Cambridge
       Culpeper   Ocean
                                             City
                               Salisbury
Staunton   Chesapeake Bay
         VIRGINIA   Fredericksburg   Crisfield
   Charlottesville   Chincoteague
                    Bowling Green   Rappahannock
    James
         Dillwyn
Lynchburg   Richmond
   Farmville
      Crewe   Petersburg   Williamsburg   Yorktown
                         James   Hampton
                    Newport News   Norfolk
                                          Virginia Beach
            Emporia   Suffolk   Portsmouth
   Roanoke John H. Kerr Lake
            Reservoir   Gaston
Dan
                              Elizabeth City
    NORTH CAROLINA   Edenton
                              Albemarle Sound
   Durham   Rocky Mount   Plymouth

MARYLAND AND
DELAWARE
p230

←

1 Planes at the National Air and Space Museum.

2 Calder's *Cheval Rouge* (1974), Sculpture Garden.

3 Van Gogh's *Self Portrait* (1889), National Gallery of Art.

4 Blues Alley, Georgetown.

2 DAYS
in Washington, DC

Day 1

Morning Start your day rocketing into space on an Apollo mission or soaring on simulators at the National Air and Space Museum *(p206)*. Arrive early and be sure to see the Wright Flyer, the *Spirit of St. Louis*, and the Lunar Module. Afterward, walk across the Mall to the Sculpture Garden at the National Gallery of Art *(p206)* to admire works by Chagall and Calder. Enjoy lunch on the patio of the Pavilion Café, overlooking the garden.

Afternoon Spend a couple of leisurely hours strolling around the world and through time inside the National Gallery of Art. Choose from Byzantine, Renaissance, and Impressionist collections, or visit the East Building for modern art. Next, walk east along the Mall and north around the White House *(p214)*. Enjoy the iconic views and linger for a while in Lafayette Square. Then it's back to the Mall and the Lincoln Memorial *(p213)* to stand at the feet of the statue and read the Gettysburg Address engraved on the wall.

Evening Head to Washington Harbour and Farmers Fishers Bakers *(www.farmersfishers bakers.com)* for a farm-to-table dinner. Top off the evening at Gypsy Sally's, one of Georgetown's livelier nightspots, offering a varied menu of rock and blues.

Day 2

Morning A stroll through the beautiful, dew-laden Enid A. Haupt Garden is a great way to start the morning before you head across the Mall to the National Museum of Natural History *(p207)*. There is a lot to see here, including the towering dinosaur skeletons, the Hope Diamond (and hundreds of other dazzling gems), and the powerfully reconstructed faces of our early ancestors in the Hall of Human Origins.

Afternoon Pause for lunch at the United States Capitol Cafe, whose gleaming serving stations provide far more delicious fare than its name suggests. If you haven't reserved your Capitol *(p209)* tour online, go to the information booth, where there may still be timed-entry tickets available. After your tour, head over to the Library of Congress *(p208)*, a house of worship for book lovers and a truly breathtaking building in itself.

Evening Not far away is the elegant marble building that once housed the *Washington Star* newspaper. Here the Fogo de Chão Brazilian Steakhouse offers paleo-style dining *(www.fogodechao.com)*. Finish your evening at Georgetown's Blues Alley *(www.bluesalley.com)*, one of the oldest jazz venues in the country.

8 DAYS

in Washington, DC and around

This eight-day road-trip covers the most enticing parts of historic Virginia within easy reach of Washington, DC. You can rent a car in the city or at central Ronald Reagan Washington National Airport.

Day 1

Make the short trip to what is now a suburb of DC, Mt Vernon. When George Washington lived here in the 18th century it was completely rural, and his home and estate, Mount Vernon itself *(p222)*, is a wonderfully preserved memorial to the first US president. Round off the experience with lunch at the Colonial-themed Mount Vernon Inn Restaurant, on site. It's just under 100 miles (160 km) from here to Richmond.

Day 2

Spend the day touring Richmond *(p227)*, the historic capital of Virginia. Peruse the Civil War artifacts in the Museum of the Confederacy, before visiting the elegant Virginia State Capitol, where you can grab a quick lunch on site at Meriwether's. In the afternoon, pop into the charming Edgar Allan Poe Museum.

Day 3

It's just 50 miles (80 km) from Richmond to Williamsburg, home of venerable William & Mary College and Colonial Williamsburg *(p224)*. This preserved 18th-century town is the world's largest living history museum, and is studded with clapboard houses, churches, and work-shops manned by costumed interpreters. Eat at one of four alehouses, such as Christiana Campbell's Tavern, allegedly George Washington's favorite for seafood.

Day 4

Scenic Colonial Parkway connects Williamsburg with two of Virginia's most portentous historic sites. Spend the morning at Historic Jamestowne *(p222)*, the first permanent English settlement in the US and now an archaeological site. Eat at the cozy Dale House Café, before driving 15 miles (24 km) to Yorktown. This was where the decisive battle of the American Revolutionary War took place in 1781, and tours of the battlefield add context.

Day 5

It's around 125 miles (201 km) from Williamsburg to Monticello *(p226)*, the home and estate of Thomas Jefferson.

1 Monticello house, Virginia.

2 Colonial Williamsburg.

3 Statue of George Washington in Richmond's State Capitol building.

4 Cityscape of Richmond, Virginia.

5 Skyline Drive snaking through Shenandoah National Park.

It's easy to spend the best part of a day here, taking in the main house and gardens, enhanced by a variety of illuminating tours that don't shirk the darker side of plantation life. The Hemings Family Tour explores this, as well as the president's scientifically proven relationship with Sally Hemings. Nearby Charlottesville is the best place to stay and eat; try cool New American restaurant The Local *(www.thelocal-cville.com)*.

Day 6

Spend the whole day traversing gorgeous Skyline Drive *(p226)* through Shenandoah National Park, on the crest of the Blue Ridge Parkway *(p227)*. The route begins a short drive west of Charlottesville and ends at Front Royal, around 105 miles (170 km) in all. Be sure to stop at scenic viewpoints such as Pinnacles Overlook, and make time for short hikes off the road (we recommend Whiteoak Canyon Trail, which features six waterfalls). Grab an old-fashioned burger at Spelunker's (116 South St) in Front Royal or hit one of the town's old-school diners.

Day 7

Drive along the Shenandoah River valley to Harpers Ferry *(p228)* in West Virginia, some 42 miles (68 km) north. Much of this pretty Victorian town is preserved within Harpers Ferry National Historic Park, where the Shenandoah meets the Potomac in a picturesque valley. In addition to browsing the independent shops, visit John Brown's Fort to learn about the fateful raid conducted by the famous abolitionist here in 1859. Spend the night in one of the town's lovely B&Bs, enjoying a locally sourced dinner in the Canal House Café *(226 Washington St)*.

Day 8

It's around 70 miles (113 km) back to DC from Harpers Ferry, but it's worth taking a slight detour to visit Frederick, over in Maryland. The old town center is crammed with antiques stores and quaint cafés, while the National Museum of Civil War Medicine offers fascinating insight. Grab a Southern lunch at the Black Hog BBQ Bar *(www.blackhogbbq.com)*. It's around 50 miles (80 km) to Ronald Reagan Washington National Airport from here.

Founders and Foundations

The city owes its location to George Washington, who chose the site as the capital. He also participated in the design of the Capitol *(p209)* and set its cornerstone. Thomas Jefferson also helped, and after the city was burned in 1814, he sold his library to the government to rebuild the collection of the Library of Congress *(p208)*.

←

George Washington, wearing his Masonic apron, placing the cornerstone of the Capitol

WASHINGTON AS A
PRESIDENTIAL POWERTOWN

Most Americans know stories of their presidents, and many presidents are honored by monuments and memorials in Washington. Where can you follow in the footsteps of legendary presidents, and which of their passions and efforts helped to shape the city we see today?

A PRESIDENTIAL CANAL

Few landmarks have had more presidential attention than the Chesapeake and Ohio Canal. Started by George Washington's Patowmack Company, it had its first spade of earth turned by John Adams. Dwight D. Eisenhower declared the canal a National Monument, while Richard Nixon made it a National Historic Park. The reconstruction of the canal was a milestone of Lyndon Johnson's presidency.

Unfinished Business

In the mid-1800s America was struggling financially, especially after the Civil War. But Ulysses S. Grant saw to it that work was restarted on the Washington Monument *(p211)*, which for years had been just an unfinished stub on the Mall *(p218)*. And the Mall only became the cultural hub it is today when Theodore Roosevelt initiated the completion of L'Enfant's original grand design.

→

Theodore Roosevelt at Washington's Union Station in May 1914

The War Years

During World War II, Franklin D. Roosevelt oversaw the design and construction of the Pentagon *(p217)*, the world's largest office building, which took only 16 months to build. After the war, Harry Truman conceded that the White House *(p214)* was in a terrible state, saying, "The damned place is haunted, sure as shootin'." He moved out with his family into a nearby row house while the Executive Mansion was gutted back to the walls and completely re-created, room by room, from scratch.

Did You Know?

The Pentagon has 17 miles (27 km) of corridors and 150 acres (60 ha) of enclosed space.

↑ The Pentagon, built in 1941-42 to house the Department of Defense

The 21st Century

Presidents continue to build and change the US capital. The National Museum of African American History and Culture (NMAAHC) *(p210)* was brought into being by George W. Bush and officially opened by Barack Obama. Not far away, the elegant Old Post Office was purchased and turned into an exclusive hotel by billionaire developer Donald Trump, who, shortly thereafter, became the 45th president of the United States.

↓ Barack Obama speaking at the opening of the NMAAHC

↑ An 1852 plan showing proposed improvements to the Washington Monument

The Rotunda at the United States Capitol

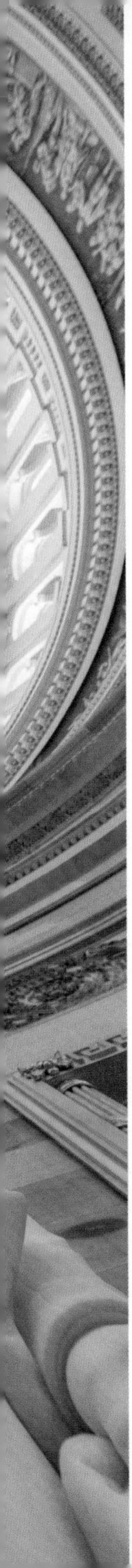

WASHINGTON, DC

Indigenous peoples occupied this region for some 6,000 years before European settlers arrived from the 17th century onward. It's perhaps fitting that America's capital was created by a secret political deal. The Compromise of 1790 (engineered by Founding Fathers James Madison, Alexander Hamilton, and Thomas Jefferson) gave the capital to the Southern states, with land donated by Virginia and Maryland. Congress officially arrived in 1800. Despite grand plans, DC was a swampy, underdeveloped backwater for years, with dirt roads and poor housing. It did, however, attract a sizeable African American population, especially after the Civil War and again after World War I, becoming a center for African American culture. Sadly, the city also gained a reputation for poor management. Blighted areas surrounded the center until the early 1900s, and it wasn't until the 1930s that the grand buildings and attractions that exist today started to appear. In the last few decades many downtown neighborhoods have been revitalized, and the city is massively popular with tourists, welcoming tens of millions every year.

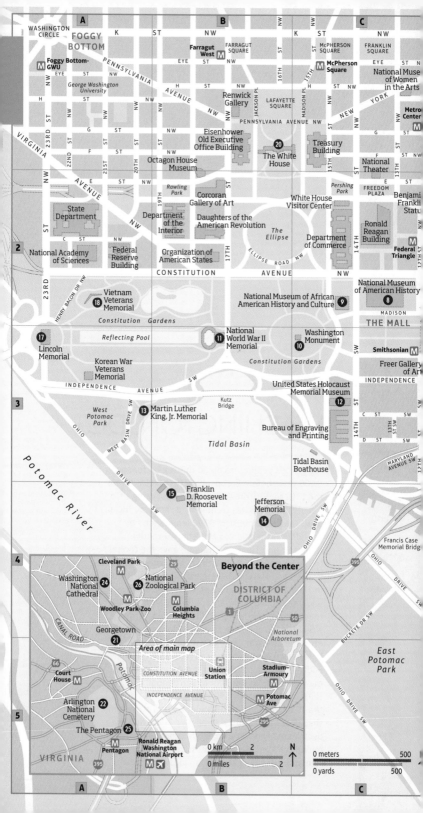

WASHINGTON, DC

1. National Air & Space Museum
2. National Gallery of Art
3. National Museum of Natural History
4. US Supreme court
5. Library of Congress
6. United States Capitol
7. Smithsonian American Art Musuem & National Portrait Gallery
8. National Museum of American History
9. National Museum of African American History and Culture
10. Washington Monument
11. National World War II Memorial
12. United States Holocaust Memorial Musuem
13. Martin Luther King, Jr. Memorial
14. Jefferson Memorial
15. Franklin D. Roosevelt Memorial
16. Newseum
17. Lincoln Memorial
18. Vietnam Veterans Memorial
19. Ford's Theatre
20. The White House
21. Georgetown
22. Arlington National Cemetery
23. The National Archives Museum
24. Washington National Cathedral
25. The Pentagon
26. National Zoological Park

WASHINGTON, DC

Museums filled with wonders. Galleries bursting with master-works. Lush, verdant parks and gardens. And everywhere famous views that every visitor knows by heart. This is a city in renaissance, a grand dream of marble and art, of substance and spectacle. Washington is a small gem, but so full of things to see and do that it can be hard to know where to start.

1

National Air and Space Museum

🔲 D3 🏛 601 Independence Av, SW Ⓜ Smithsonian 🚌
🕙 10am–5:30pm daily
🚫 Dec 25 🌐 nasm.si.edu

Opened on the US Bicentennial on July 1, 1976, the flagship National Air and Space Museum is the most visited sight in Washington, DC. The museum's entrance leads into

the lofty Milestones of Flight gallery, which displays many of the firsts in air and space travel in the United States. These include the 1903 Wright Flyer, the first ever powered, heavier-than-air machine to achieve controlled, sustained flight, built by the Wright brothers; the *Spirit of St. Louis*, in which Charles Lindbergh made the first transatlantic solo flight in 1927; and the Apollo 11 Command Module, which carried astronauts Buzz Aldrin, Neil Armstrong, and Michael Collins on their historic mission to the moon in 1969. An eye-catching exhibit in the

Pioneers of Flight gallery is the red Lockheed Vega in which Amelia Earhart became the first woman to make a solo transatlantic flight in 1932. The popular World War II Aviation gallery displays fighter aircraft from the American, British, German, and Japanese air forces.

Check the museum's website for updates on what's on view, as the museum is undergoing major renovations until 2023, with partial closures.

2

National Gallery of Art

🔲 E2 🏛 Constitution Av & 4th St, NW Ⓜ Archives, Navy Mem'l, Penn Qtr 🚌
🕙 10am–5pm Mon–Sat, 11am–6pm Sun 🚫 Jan 1, Dec 25 🌐 nga.gov

One of Washington's top draws, this museum was first estab-lished when financier Andrew Mellon bequeathed his collec-tion of European art. Spurred on by his example, other collectors left art to the National Gallery of Art.

Of the two main buildings, the stately Neo-Classical-style

Vintage planes on show at the National Air and Space Museum, and Amelia Earhart's Lockheed Vega (inset)

→ The National Museum of Natural History's Neo-Classical exterior

West Building, opened in 1941, features European art from the 13th to the 19th centuries. The National Gallery of Art's modern East Building is a bright and inviting public space with a stunning roof terrace and sculpture garden.

Matching wings flank a central rotunda in the West Building. West of the rotunda are the galleries displaying Italian, Dutch, Flemish, and Spanish art. The Italian paintings include works by Giotto, Botticelli, Raphael, and da Vinci; other masterpieces on display include works by Rembrandt, Van Dyck, Rubens, Goya, El Greco, and Velásquez. The sculpture galleries here display decorative arts from the Middle Ages to the 20th century. Galleries east of the rotunda house an outstanding collection of French Impressionist and Post-Impressionist art. Among its highlights are pieces by Monet, Degas, and Toulouse-Lautrec. Portraits by John Singer Sargent and James McNeill Whistler are among the gallery's collection of American paintings. Adjacent to the West Building is a charming Sculpture Garden with a café. The fountain here is transformed into an ice-skating rink in winter.

The huge East Building is designed to accommodate large pieces of modern art. Centered in its courtyard is a giant red, blue, and black

mobile by Alexander Calder, completed in 1976. Near the entrance is a sculpture by Henry Moore; the atrium displays a 1977 tapestry by Joan Miró.

> The National Gallery of Art's modern East Building is a bright and inviting public space with a stunning roof terrace and sculpture garden.

National Museum of Natural History

📍 D2 🏛 Constitution Av & 10th St, NW Ⓜ Smithsonian ⏰ 10am–5:30pm daily 🚫 Dec 25 🌐 nmnh.si.edu

Established in 1910, this vast museum's collection of some 120 million artifacts includes samples from the world's diverse cultures, as well as fossils and living creatures. The museum's entrance leads into the lofty Rotunda, where visitors are greeted by the impressive sight of a massive African bush elephant. To the right of the Rotunda is one of the most popular areas of the museum, the Fossil Hall. Also on the ground floor is Ocean Hall, which explores the magnificence of the ocean.

On the second floor is the Gems and Minerals collection, the highlight of which is the 45.52-carat Hope Diamond. The largest deep-blue diamond in the world and famed for its stunning color and clarity, it once belonged to Louis XVI of France. Also on the second floor is the Butterfly Pavilion and Insect Zoo, with its giant hissing cockroaches and large leaf-cutter ant colony.

EAT

Ben's Chili Bowl
Ben's pork and beef dogs, milkshakes, and ice creams are the ultimate comfort foods.

🏠 1213 U St, NW
🌐 benschilibowl.com

$$$

Old Ebbitt Grill
A hospitable tavern with mouthwatering oysters, crab cakes, and hanger steak.

🏠 675 15th St, NW
🌐 ebbitt.com

$$$

Federalist Pig
Arguably the city's best BBQ, with must-try brisket, chicken wings, and mac n cheese.

🏠 1654 Columbia Rd, NW
🚫 Mon, Tue
🌐 federalistpig.com

$$$

Oyamel Cocina Mexicana
Authentic Mexican cuisine, with diverse ceviches and tacos.

🏠 401 7th St, NW
🌐 oyamel.com

$$$

The stunning main reading room in the Library of Congress ↑

Supreme Tips

Visitors may watch the court in session October through April - check the website. Admission is on a first-come, first-served basis. When the court is not in session, public lectures are held every hour on the half hour in the Courtroom.

4

US Supreme Court

📍 F2 🏛 1st St between E Capitol St & Maryland Av, NE Ⓜ Capitol S 🕐 9am–4:30pm Mon-Fri 🔒 Federal hols 🌐 supremecourtus.gov

The judicial branch of the US government and the highest court in the land, the Supreme Court is the last stop in the disposition of the nation's legal disputes and issues of constitutionality. Ground-breaking cases settled here include *Brown v. Board of Education*, which abolished racial segregation in schools, and *Miranda v. Arizona*, which declared that crime suspects were entitled to a lawyer before they were interrogated.

As recently as 1934, the Supreme Court met in various sections of the US Capitol.

Then, at Chief Justice William Howard Taft's urging, Congress authorized the construction of a separate, dedicated building. The result was a magnificent Corinthian edifice designed by Cass Gilbert that opened in 1935. Allegorical sculptures depicting the Contemplation of Justice and the Authority of the Law stand beside the steps.

The Great Hall that leads to the courtroom is an expanse of marble, lined with columns and the busts of former chief justices. The elegant court chamber itself has a coffered plaster ceiling decorated with gold leaf, and a frieze running around the walls that depicts both real and allegorical legal figures. The exhibit hall has displays on legal systems from around the world and an array of judges' robes.

5 🅜 🍴

Library of Congress

📍 F3 🏛 10 1st St, SE Ⓜ Capitol S 🚌 🕐 10am–5:30pm Mon-Sat (photo ID essential for reading rooms) 🔒 Federal hols 🌐 loc.gov

The Library of Congress holds the largest collection of books, manuscripts, microfilms, maps, and music in the world. First established in the Capitol in 1800, the original library was

destroyed during the burning of Washington by the British in 1814. Thomas Jefferson then sold the library his personal collection as a replacement, and from this seed the collection grew. Since 1897, it has been housed in the grand Italian Renaissance-style main building, now known as the Thomas Jefferson Building. In front of it is a fountain with a striking bronze statue of the Roman sea god Neptune.

One of the highlights of this marvel of art and architecture is the Great Hall, with its

House Chamber, home of the House of Representatives.

The Hall of Columns, lined with statues of notable Americans.

splendid marble arches and columns, grand staircases, bronze statues, rich murals, and stained-glass skylights.

Equally impressive is the Main Reading Room, where huge marble columns and towering personifications of human endeavors dwarf the reading desks beneath the soaring domed ceiling.

The landing near the Visitors' Gallery, overlooking the Main Reading Room, is dominated by a beautiful marble mosaic figure of Minerva.

The library's treasures include one of only three perfect vellum copies of the 15th-century Gutenberg Bible, the first book printed using movable metal type.

6 Ⓜ 🛍
United States Capitol

📍 F3 🏛 Beneath E Front Plaza at 1st & E Capitol sts Ⓜ Capitol South, Union Station, Federal Center SW 🕐 8:30am–4:30pm Mon-Sat 🚫 Federal hols 🌐 visitthe capitol.gov

One of the world's best known symbols of democracy, the US Capitol has been the legislative heart of America for over 200 years. Every year about four million visitors come to admire the breathtaking building and learn how America creates and passes the laws that govern the nation. The cornerstone of this grand Neo-Classical

building was laid by George Washington in 1793, and by 1800 it was occupied, though unfinished. The British burned the Capitol in 1814 during the invasion of Washington, and in 1815 work began on its restoration. Many architectural and artistic features, such as the Statue of Freedom, were added later.

The Capitol also marks the center of Washington, DC. The city's four quadrants radiate out from the middle of the building, defined by a point directly below the dome.

While waiting for a free tour (reserve ahead), explore the Exhibition Hall, where artifacts and documents tell the story of Congress and the Capitol.

Cast-iron dome, originally built of wood and copper.

The 180-ft- (55-m-) high Rotunda, capped by Brumidi's fresco The Apotheosis of Washington.

The Senate Chamber, completed in 1859.

National Statuary Hall, with two statues for each state.

Brumidi Corridors

Old Senate Chamber, occupied by the Senate until 1859, and then by the Supreme Court until 1934.

The Crypt, with a central star denoting the city's quadrants.

Columbus Doors, made of solid bronze.

↑ The United States Capitol building, the legislative heart of Washington

Did You Know?

The Capitol has its own exclusive subway system, and the car passes a flag of every US state.

7 Smithsonian American Art Museum and National Portrait Gallery

D1 Museum: 8th & G sts NW; Gallery: 8th & F sts NW Gallery Place-Chinatown 11:30am-7pm daily Dec 25 americanart.si.edu; npg.si.edu

Nowhere in Washington is the city's penchant for copying Greek and Roman architecture more obvious than in the former US Patent Office building, now the home of the Smithsonian American Art Museum and the National Portrait Gallery. The art museum contains a wealth of works by American artists, reflecting the history and culture of the country. The highlight of the American folk art collection is an amazing piece of visionary art called *Throne of the Third Heaven of the Nations' Millennium* (c. 1950–64), created out of light bulbs, silver and gold foil, and old furniture by a Washington janitor by the name of James Hampton. Among the 19th- and early 20th-century works, the Western landscapes by Albert Bierstadt stand out. Especially dramatic is his painting *Among the Sierra Nevada, California*, which captures the vastness of the American West. Fine works by Jasper Johns, Andy Warhol, and Robert Rauschenberg are among the other treasures of this museum.

The National Portrait Gallery is America's very own family album, featuring paintings, sculptures, etchings, and photographs of thousands of famous Americans. Assembled here are such diverse works as Gilbert Stuart's famous portrait of George Washington (which features on the one-dollar bill), busts of Dr. Martin Luther King, Jr. and the poet T. S. Eliot, and photographs of actress Marilyn Monroe.

Did You Know?

Judy Garland's ruby slippers from *The Wizard of Oz* are kept at the National Museum of American History.

8 National Museum of American History

C2 14 St & Constitution Av, NW Smithsonian-Federal Triangle 10am-5:30pm daily Dec 25 americanhistory.si.edu

The fascinating and diverse exhibits here cover the USA's cultural, social, technological, and political history, from science to objects representing the offices of the presidency, to popular culture exhibits.

The first floor's east wing is devoted to America's history of transportation and technology. Displays range from a Model T Ford to ancient gold coins.

Popular exhibits elsewhere include the actual kitchen of beloved American cook Julia Child (1912–2004), first ladies' gowns, and Jackie Kennedy's haute couture outfits.

Of great historical and cultural significance is the "Star-Spangled Banner" that flew over Fort McHenry in 1814, displayed on the second floor.

9 National Museum of African American History and Culture

C2 1400 Constitution Av NW Federal Triangle 10am-5:30pm daily Dec 25 nmaahc.si.edu

The NMAAHC is one of the only museums devoted solely to the documentation of African American history and culture. Displays elucidate on a wide array of topics, including the horrors of slavery and the path to freedom, as well as key figures in the struggle for civil rights, including Rosa Parks and Martin Luther King, Jr.

←

An array of American icons in the Great Hall of the National Portrait Gallery

↑ The National World War II Memorial and Washington Monument at night

Don't miss the Contemplative Court, a memorial room on the lowest floor in which to meditate on the slavery exhibit before moving on to exhibits on progress and culture.

Cultural explorations cover music, dance, athletics, cuisine, crafts, and more. Standout items in the collection include a shawl given to Harriet Tubman by Queen Victoria, an invitation to President Obama's inauguration, and Chuck Berry's red Cadillac. The museum café is superb and showcases traditional and modern African American cuisine.

The exhibits are popular, and you may need to register for timed-entry passes on the museum's website.

---

⑩

Washington Monument

◙ C3 🏛 Independence Av at 17th St, SW Ⓜ Smithsonian
🚌 🕒 9am–4:45pm daily
🗓 Jul 4, Dec 25 🌐 nps.gov/wamo

Constructed from some 36,000 pieces of marble and granite, the 555-ft- (170-m-) tall Washington Monument is clearly visible from almost all over the city. Conceived of as a

tribute to the first president of the US, its construction began in 1848, but stopped in 1858 when funds ran out. A slight change in the color of the stone indicates where construction resumed in 1876.

Cleaned to a gleaming white, the monument has a capstone weighing 3,300 lbs (2,000 kg). It is topped by an aluminum pyramid and surrounded by 50 flagpoles. There are stunning views across the city from the top (admission is free, but timed tickets are required).

---

⑪ ⓂⓈ

National World War II Memorial

◙ B3 🏛 17th St, NW, btwn Constitution Av & Independence Av Ⓜ Smithsonian, Federal Triangle 🕒 24 hrs daily 🌐 nps.gov/nwwm

This 7.5-acre (3-ha) memorial was built to honor US veteran soldiers and civilians of World War II. It includes two pavilions, bas-relief panels, and 56 granite pillars, one for each of the country's states and territories. These are adorned with bronze wreaths of oak and wheat, which symbolize the nation's agricultural and industrial strength.

⑫

United States Holocaust Memorial Museum

◙ C3 🏛 100 R. Wallenberg Pl, SW Ⓜ Smithsonian 🚌
🕒 10am–5:30pm daily (Mar–Jun: 10am–6:30pm Mon–Fri)
🗓 Yom Kippur & Dec 25
🌐 ushmm.org

The US Holocaust Memorial Museum bears witness to the systematic persecution and annihilation in Europe of six million Jews and other "undesirables" by the Third Reich. Within the exhibition space, which ranges from the claustrophobic to the majestic, are thousands of photographs and artifacts, video monitors, and interactive stations that force visitors to confront the horrors of the Holocaust. Starting from the top, the fourth floor documents the early years of the Nazi regime. The third floor exhibits are devoted to the "Final Solution."

On the second floor is the Hall of Remembrance, which houses an eternal flame, while the first-floor Hall of Witness features temporary exhibits.

At the Concourse Level is the Children's Tile Wall, a memorial to the 1.5 million children murdered in the Holocaust.

13

Martin Luther King, Jr. Memorial

⊙ A3 **🏛 1964 Independence Av, SW** **Ⓜ Smithsonian** **🚌**
🕐 24 hrs daily **🌐 nps.gov/mlkm**

The Martin Luther King, Jr. Memorial is located at the northwest corner of the Tidal Basin, in a quiet space surrounded by cherry trees, and is aligned along the axis of the Jefferson Memorial and Lincoln Memorial.

The centerpiece, a 30-ft- (9.1-m-) high relief of Martin Luther King, Jr., is based on a line from his famous "I Have a Dream" speech: "Out of a mountain of despair, a stone of hope." Rangers are on hand to answer queries 9:30am–11:30pm daily.

14

Jefferson Memorial

⊙ B4 **🏛 S bank, Tidal Basin, SW** **Ⓜ Smithsonian**
🕐 9:30am–11:30pm daily **🚫 Dec 25** **🌐 nps.gov/thje**

When this Neo-Classical-style memorial to the third US president, Thomas Jefferson (1743–1826), was completed in 1943, it was dismissed as far too "feminine" for so bold and influential a man who had played a significant part in drafting the Declaration of Independence in 1776. The dome of this round, colonnaded building covers a majestic 19-ft (6-m) statue of Jefferson, and a museum is housed in the basement. The memorial stands on the banks of the Tidal Basin. In the 1920s Japanese cherry trees were planted along its shores, and the sight of them in bloom is one of the most photographed in the city. Peak blooming time is mid-March to mid-April. Rental paddle-boats are available.

15

Franklin D. Roosevelt Memorial

⊙ B4 **🏛 W Basin Dr, SW** **Ⓜ Smithsonian** **🚌** **🕐 8am–midnight daily** **🚫 Dec 25** **🌐 nps.gov/fdrm**

FDR's memorial is a mammoth park of four granite open-air rooms, one for each of his terms in office. The first room has the visitor center, and a bas-relief of Roosevelt's first inaugural parade. In the second room is a sculpture titled *Hunger*, recalling the hard times of the Great Depression. A controversial statue in the third room shows the disabled president sitting in a wheelchair hidden by his Navy cape. Dramatic waterfalls cascade into a series of pools in the fourth room, which also has a statue of Roosevelt's wife, Eleanor, and a relief of his funeral cortege carved into the granite wall. The water symbolizes the peace that Roosevelt was so eager to achieve before his death.

← The granite centerpiece of the Martin Luther King, Jr. Memorial

↑ Cherry blossoms framing the Jefferson Memorial at the Tidal Basin

decades of Pulitzer Prize-winning photographs. Other galleries deal with the history of the Berlin Wall and 9/11. A favorite is the newsroom, where you can read the news in front of a live TV camera. There is also a moving memorial to journalists who have lost their lives in the line of duty.

16

Newseum

⚐E2 ⌂555 Pennsylvania Av, NW Ⓜ Archives/Navy Memorial-Penn Quarter ⏰9am-5pm Mon-Sat, 10am-5pm Sun ⊘Jan 1, Thanksg., Dec 25 🌐newseum.org

This museum is dedicated to the role that journalism plays in defending democracy. On the front of the building, the First Amendment, which guarantees freedom of speech, is engraved six stories tall.

The museum's collections span five centuries of news history. One of the most popular galleries features

↑ Panels from the Berlin Wall at the Newseum, representing the value of a free press

---

17

Lincoln Memorial

⚐A3 ⌂900 Ohio Drive, SW Ⓜ Smithsonian, Foggy Bottom ⏰24 hrs 🌐nps.gov/linc

The Lincoln Memorial is one of Washington's most awe-inspiring sights, with the seated figure of President Abraham Lincoln in his Neo-Classical "temple," looming over a reflecting pool.

The site chosen for the memorial was a swamp, and it had to be drained before building began in 1914. Concrete piers were poured for the foundation so that the building could be anchored in bedrock. As the memorial neared completion, architect Henry Bacon realized that the statue of Lincoln would be dwarfed inside the huge edifice, and the original 10-ft (3-m) statue was doubled in size. Engraved on the wall are the words of Lincoln's famous Gettysburg Address.

🔍 HIDDEN GEM
Dwight D. Eisenhower Memorial

Unveiled in 2020, this memorial honors Eisenhower's legacy as a military general and as president, with bas reliefs, sculptures, and depictions of the cliffs of Normandy.

18

Vietnam Veterans Memorial

⚐A2 ⌂21 St & Constitution Av, NW Ⓜ Foggy Bottom ⏰24 hours 🌐nps.gov/vive

Powerful in its symbolism and dramatic in its simplicity, the Vietnam Veterans Memorial consists of two triangular black walls, set at an angle of 125 degrees, one end pointing to the Lincoln Memorial and the other to the Washington Monument. The walls are inscribed with the names of Americans who died in the war, in chronological order from 1959 to 1975. Rangers are on hand to answer queries 9:30am–11:30pm daily.

19

Ford's Theatre

⚐D1 ⌂511 10th St, NW Ⓜ Gallery Place-Chinatown, Metro Ctr ⏰9am-4:30pm daily with timed pass (check website) 🌐fords.org

John T. Ford built this small jewel of a theater in 1863. On April 14, 1865, Abraham Lincoln was shot here by John Wilkes Booth while watching a performance. After the tragedy, it was left to spiral into decay for nearly a century until the government restored it to its original splendor. Today, it stages productions and offers tours. Across the street, visitors can tour Petersen House, where Lincoln died the next morning.

20 (M) (P)

THE WHITE HOUSE

B1 🏛 White House: 1600 Pennsylvania Av, NW Ⓜ Federal
Triangle 🕐 White House: Tue-Sat (appt only) 🚫 White House:
federal hols, official functions; visitor center: federal hols
ℹ 1450 Pennsylvania Av, NW; open 7:30am-4pm daily;
www.whitehouse.gov

With every US president except George Washington
having called the White House home, this Neo-
Classical mansion has been the seat of
executive power for over 200 years.

One of the most famous residential landmarks
in the world, the White House was built to
reflect the power of the presidency. Although
George Washington commissioned the
mansion, President John Adams was its first
occupant, in 1800. Burned by the British in
1814, the partially rebuilt edifice was
reoccupied in 1817. In 1901,
President Theodore Roosevelt
renamed it the White House and
ordered the West Wing to be
built. The East Wing was added in
1942, completing the building as it
is today. Bedecked with period
furniture, antiques, and paintings,
the White House attracts more than
1.5 million visitors every year.

*The West Terrace leads
to the West Wing and
the Oval Office, the
president's official office.*

*The stonework
has been painted
over and over
to maintain
the building's
white facade.*

*Able to seat as many as 140
people, the State Dining Room
was enlarged in 1902. A
portrait of President Lincoln,
by George P.A. Healy, hangs
above the mantel.*

→
The White House, both a
presidential residence and
a working office building

FLIPPING THE WHITE HOUSE

On Inauguration Day, the White House must be
changed over for the incoming president in
just five hours. At 10:30am the outgoing family
leaves for the inauguration, and the carefully
choreographed chaos begins. The outgoing
family's moving trucks park on South Portico's
west side, and the incoming family's on the
east. The rooms are scrubbed, rugs and
curtains cleaned, repairs made, all personal
belongings placed, and the Oval Office painted.
At 3:30pm the new First Family arrives, and
the Chief Usher says, "Welcome to your new
home, Mr. President."

President Lincoln used this room as his Cabinet Room, then turned it into a bedroom, furnishing it with contemporary decor. Today it is used as a guest room.

The East Terrace leads to the East Wing.

The East Room is used for large gatherings such as concerts and press conferences.

The Treaty Room

The ivory Vermeil Room houses seven paintings of First Ladies, including a portrait of Eleanor Roosevelt by Douglas Chandor.

The Green Room was first used as a guest room before Thomas Jefferson turned it into a dining room.

The Blue Room

The Diplomatic Reception is used to welcome friends and ambassadors. It is furnished in the Federal Period style (1790–1820).

One of four reception rooms, the Red Room is furnished in red in the Empire Style (1810–30).

Did You Know?

570 gallons (2,100 liters) of paint are needed to cover the exterior of the White House.

[1] Every president personalizes the Oval Office – Barack Obama added a bust of Martin Luther King, Jr., while Donald Trump added a bust of Winston Churchill and military flags.

[2] The State Dining Room mantel has a portrait of President Lincoln.

[3] The Red Room, decorated by Jacqueline Kennedy, is used as a sitting room and for small parties.

↑ Painted Colonial town houses lining the streets of Georgetown

21

Georgetown

A4

One of Washington, DC's most attractive neighborhoods, Georgetown is lined with elegant townhouses, many of which have been converted into upscale bars, restaurants, and boutiques. Its two main business streets are Wisconsin Avenue and M Street. On the latter is the historic **Old Stone House** (built in 1765), which may be the only building in Washington that predates the American Revolution. N Street has an array of 18th-century Federal-style mansions and fine Victorian town houses.

More Federal houses can be seen lining the banks of the Chesapeake and Ohio Canal, whose ingenious transportation system of locks, aqueducts, and tunnels fell out of use with the arrival of the railroad in the 19th century. It is now a protected national park, offering many recreational facilities. Park rangers in period costume guide tours of the canal in mule-drawn barges, and boating is also popular here, especially between Georgetown and Violette's Lock. The towpath along the canal is ideal for walks and bike rides.

A major center of activity in this district is **Georgetown University**, founded in 1789. Among the historic buildings on its campus is the Gothic-inspired Healy Hall, topped by a fanciful spire.

The superbly landscaped gardens of the **Dumbarton Oaks** estate surround a grand Federal-style mansion, which houses a priceless art collection. The historic Dumbarton Oaks Conference, attended by President Franklin Roosevelt and British Prime Minister Winston Churchill, was held here in 1944, laying the groundwork for the establishment of the United Nations.

The house now serves as a library, research institution, and museum, with a superb collection of Byzantine art, pre-Columbian masks, gold jewelry from Central America, and Aztec carvings.

Old Stone House

3051 M St, NW ☐ Noon-5pm Wed-Sun ☑ nps.gov/olst

Georgetown University

37th & O sts, NW ☐ Times vary, check website ☑ georgetown.edu

Dumbarton Oaks

1703 32nd St, NW ☐ 2-6pm Tue-Sun (winter: to 5pm) ☐ Federal hols ☑ doaks.org

22

Arlington National Cemetery

A5 ☐ Arlington, VA ☐ Arlington National Cemetery ☐ Apr-Sep: 8am-7pm daily; Oct-Mar: 8am-5pm daily ☐ Dec 25 ☑ arlingtoncemetery.mil

A sea of simple headstones covers Arlington, marking the graves of around 400,000 American servicemen killed in the nation's major conflicts – from the Revolution onward. The focus of the cemetery is the Tomb of the Unknown Soldier, honoring those whose bodies were never found or identified. Nearby is the Memorial Amphitheater, which has hosted many state funerals, and where services are held on Memorial Day.

North of the Tomb of the Unknown Soldier, an eternal flame burns at the grave of

Did You Know?

The guard at Arlington's Tomb of the Unknown Soldier takes 21 steps and stops for 21 seconds.

> **The National Archives Museum is home to the most important documents in US history - the Declaration of Independence, the Constitution, and the Bill of Rights.**

John F. Kennedy, lit by his wife Jacqueline on the day of his funeral in November 1963. She and their infant son Patrick and an unnamed stillborn daughter are buried next to the late president. His brother Robert F. Kennedy is nearby.

The grand Georgian-Revival mansion at the top of the hill, above the Kennedy grave, is Arlington House, which was the home of the Confederate general Robert E. Lee (1807–70). When Lee left his home in 1861 to lead Virginia's armed forces during the Civil War, the Union confiscated the estate for a military cemetery. The house, now a memorial to the general, is open to visitors.

㉓

National Archives Museum

⦿ D2 **☖ 701 Constitution Av, NW** **Ⓜ Archives-Navy Mem'l-Penn Qtr** **⏰ 10am-5:30pm daily (to 7:30pm Wed)** **⊘ Thanksg., Dec 25** **🆆 museum.archives.gov**

As well as some three billion other items, the National Archives Museum is home to the most important documents in US history – the Declaration of Independence, the Constitution, and the Bill of Rights.

The Public Vaults journey deeper into the archives. Over a thousand documents are on display, showcasing the sheer breadth of American democracy. The David M. Rubenstein Gallery is home to Records of Rights, summarizing American debate around key issues such as citizenship, voting rights, equal opportunity, and free speech. Another must-see is one of four surviving originals of the 1297 Magna Carta.

㉔

Washington National Cathedral

⦿ A4 **☖ Massachusetts & Wisconsin avs, NW** **⏰ 10am-3:30pm Mon-Sat, 12:45-4pm Sun** **🆆 national cathedral.org**

This is the world's sixth-largest cathedral, and uses building techniques of the Gothic style of architecture, evident in the pointed arches, rib vaulting, and exterior flying buttresses. Inside, sculpture, wrought iron, and carvings depict US history and biblical scenes.

Above the west entrance is a splendid relief of *The Creation* by Frederick Hart. Above the south entrance is an exquisite stained-glass Rose Window, while another stained-glass window in the nave commemorates the Apollo 11 space flight. By the Children's Chapel, built to the scale of a six-year-old, is a statue of Jesus as a boy.

㉕

The Pentagon

⦿ A5 **☖ 1000 Defense Pentagon, Hwy 1-395, Arlington, VA** **Ⓜ Pentagon** **⏰ 10am-4pm Mon-Thu, noon-4pm Fri** **🆆 pentagon. afis.osd.mil**

The Pentagon is almost a city in itself. This enormous edifice houses 23,000 people who work for the US Department of Defense, including the Army, Navy, and Airforce. Despite its enormous size, the building's efficient design ensures that it takes no more than seven minutes to walk between any two points in the Pentagon. Designed by army engineers, the building was completed in 1942 at a cost of $83 million.

The headquarters of the US military establishment and the ultimate symbol of America's military might, the Pentagon was one of the targets of terrorists who flew a hijacked plane into the building on 9/11, killing 189 people. It has now been completely restored.

㉖

National Zoological Park

⦿ A4 **☖ 3001 Connecticut Av, NW** **Ⓜ Cleveland Park, Woodley Park-Zoo** **⏰ Times vary, check website** **⊘ Dec 25** **🆆 natzoo.si.edu**

Located in a sprawling park designed by Frederick Law Olmsted (the landscape designer of New York's Central Park), the National Zoo was established in 1887. Since 1964 it has been part of the Smithsonian Institution, which has developed it as a dynamic "biopark" where animals are studied in environments that replicate their natural habitats. The zoo's most famous residents are the giant pandas. Equally popular with visitors are the gorillas and orangutans, rare Komodo dragons, red pandas, and sloth bears. Other rare creatures include the endangered golden lion tamarins and red wolves.

↑ A playful California sea lion at the National Zoological Park

A SHORT WALK
THE MALL

Distance 1.5 miles (2.5 km) **Time** 30 minutes
Nearest Metro Smithsonian

This 1-mile (1.5-km) boulevard, between the Capitol and the Washington Monument, is the city's cultural heart, with the many different museums of the Smithsonian Institution set along this green strip. At the northeast corner of the Mall is the National Gallery of Art and its pleasant Sculpture Garden. Standing directly opposite the gallery is one of the most popular museums in the world – the National Air and Space Museum, a vast, soaring construction of glass and steel. Both the National Museum of American History and the National Museum of Natural History, on the north side of the Mall, draw huge numbers of visitors.

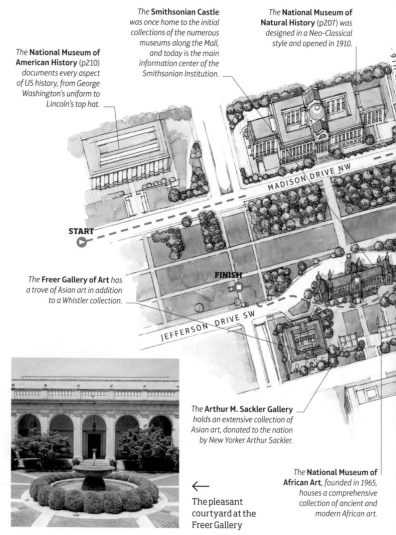

The **Smithsonian Castle** was once home to the initial collections of the numerous museums along the Mall, and today is the main information center of the Smithsonian Institution.

The **National Museum of Natural History** (p207) was designed in a Neo-Classical style and opened in 1910.

The **National Museum of American History** (p210) documents every aspect of US history, from George Washington's uniform to Lincoln's top hat.

MADISON DRIVE NW

START

The **Freer Gallery of Art** has a trove of Asian art in addition to a Whistler collection.

FINISH

JEFFERSON DRIVE SW

The **Arthur M. Sackler Gallery** holds an extensive collection of Asian art, donated to the nation by New Yorker Arthur Sackler.

The **National Museum of African Art**, founded in 1965, houses a comprehensive collection of ancient and modern African art.

← The pleasant courtyard at the Freer Gallery

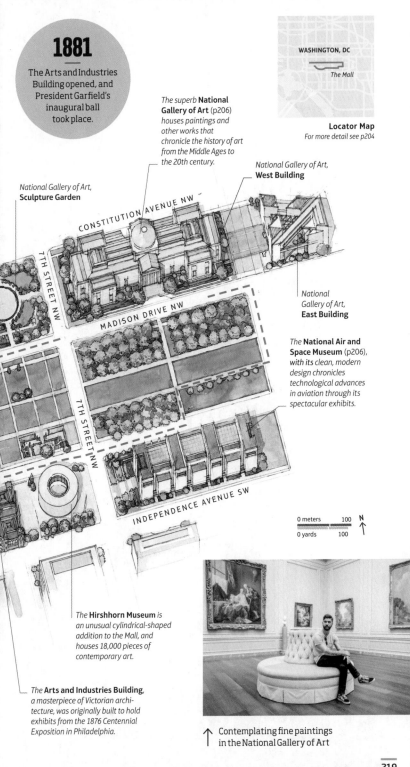

1881

The Arts and Industries Building opened, and President Garfield's inaugural ball took place.

The superb **National Gallery of Art** (p206) houses paintings and other works that chronicle the history of art from the Middle Ages to the 20th century.

WASHINGTON, DC

The Mall

Locator Map
For more detail see p204

National Gallery of Art, **West Building**

National Gallery of Art, **Sculpture Garden**

CONSTITUTION AVENUE NW

7TH STREET NW

MADISON DRIVE NW

7TH STREET NW

National Gallery of Art, **East Building**

The **National Air and Space Museum** (p206), with its clean, modern design chronicles technological advances in aviation through its spectacular exhibits.

INDEPENDENCE AVENUE SW

0 meters   100
0 yards   100

N

The **Hirshhorn Museum** is an unusual cylindrical-shaped addition to the Mall, and houses 18,000 pieces of contemporary art.

The **Arts and Industries Building**, a masterpiece of Victorian architecture, was originally built to hold exhibits from the 1876 Centennial Exposition in Philadelphia.

↑ Contemplating fine paintings in the National Gallery of Art

VIRGINIA AND WEST VIRGINIA

Home of the first permanent English colony in the Americas (Jamestown, in 1607), Virginia was also the first to develop tobacco – and to import enslaved people from Africa. As the wealthiest and most populous colony, Virginia played a key role in the Revolutionary War: presidents George Washington, Thomas Jefferson, James Madison, and James Monroe were all from Virginia. Richmond became capital of the Confederacy during the Civil War and saw some of the bloodiest battles. After its defeat, Virginia never recovered its former prominence. During the war, Unionists carved out West Virginia as a separate state, with the economy revolving around timber and coal. Both states remain rural, cashing in on their scenery and historical appeal.

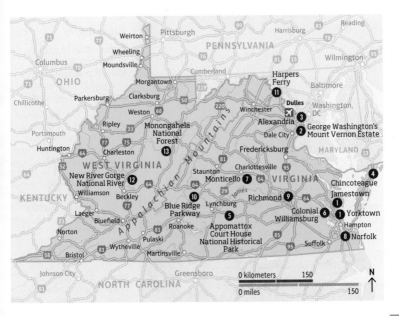

VIRGINIA

Virginia's history and natural beauty will satisfy the most avid sightseer. Bucolic Mount Vernon, home of President Washington, is conveniently close to Washington, DC. The old capital, Williamsburg, is a living museum found in eastern Virginia, while the state capital, Richmond, retains a charming Old South aura. To the west is the spectacular landscape of Shenandoah National Park.

❶ Jamestown and Yorktown

🚗 Jamestown: 52 miles (83 km) SE of Richmond; Yorktown: 63 miles (101 km) SE of Richmond 🚌 🖥 historyisfun.org

Jamestown, established in 1607, was the first permanent English settlement in the US. Disease, famine, and Algonquin attacks all took their toll, and in 1699 the colony was abandoned. The **Jamestown Settlement** is a re-creation of the colony, complete with costumed interpreters and replicas of James Fort, an American Indian village.

On the opposite side of the peninsula, Yorktown was the site of the decisive battle of the American Revolution, in 1781. Battlefield tours at Colonial National Historical Park explain the siege at Yorktown, which ended with British surrender.

Jamestown Settlement

🎫 🏠 1368 Colonial Pkwy, 🕒 9am–5pm daily 🖥 historicjamestowne.org

❷

George Washington's Mount Vernon Estate

🚗 George Washington Memorial Pkwy 🚇 Huntington 🚌 🕒 9am–5pm daily (Nov–Mar: to 4pm) 🖥 mountvernon.org

This country estate on the Potomac River was George Washington's home for over 45 years. The house is largely furnished as it would have been during Washington's presidency (1789–97), and the grounds still retain aspects of the original farm, such as the flower and vegetable gardens, the sheep paddock, and quarters for the enslaved people who worked the plantation.

❸ Alexandria

🚉 Union Station, 110 Callahan St 🚇 King St 🛈 Ramsay House Visitor Center, 221 King St; www.visitalexandriava.com

Old Town Alexandria has kept its historical flavor, dating back to its incorporation in 1749. Accessible by Metro from Washington, Alexandria is still a busy port with a lively Market Square. Its tree-lined streets are filled with elegant, historic buildings, among them the 1753 **Carlyle House**, a Georgian Palladian mansion on Fairfax

← Replica of a 17th-century colonists' ship docked at Historic Jamestowne

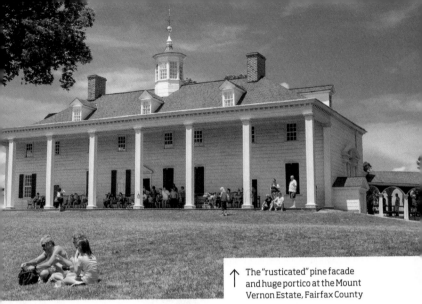

↑ The "rusticated" pine facade and huge portico at the Mount Vernon Estate, Fairfax County

INSIDER TIP
Watching History

Watch reenactments at Mount Vernon Estate, including exciting restagings of wars and battles and a re-creation of George Washington's funeral. Check the website for details.

Street. On the same street is the 1792 Stabler Leadbeater Apothecary Shop. It was closed in 1933 with everything intact.

The **Lee-Fendall House Museum** is rich with artifacts, from the Revolution to the 1930s Labor Movement. To its south is the 1773 Christ Church, where George Washington's and Robert E. Lee's pews are still preserved.

On Union Street is the **Torpedo Factory Art Center**, displaying the work of local artists and craftsmen. From the nearby waterfront, there are boat tours on the Potomac.

Carlyle House

 ⌂ 121 N Fairfax St
🕐 10am-4pm Tue-Sat, noon-5pm Sun (Nov-Mar: last adm 4pm) ⊡ novaparks.com

Lee-Fendall House Museum

⌂ 614 Oronoco St 🕐 1-4pm Fri & Sun, 10am-4pm Sat 🔒 Dec 25-Jan 31 (except 3rd Sun) ⊡ leefendallhouse.org

Torpedo Factory Art Center

⌂ 105 N Union St 🕐 10am-6pm daily (to 9pm Thu) 🔒 Jan 1, Easter, Thanksg., Dec 25 ⊡ torpedofactory.org

④ Chincoteague

⌂ 190 miles (300 km) SE of Richmond 🅘 4099 Bradley Ln; www.chincoteague.com

The main tourist attraction on Virginia's Eastern Shore, Chincoteague draws fishermen, bird-watchers, and beach-combers. The town itself caters primarily to visitors bound for the **Chincoteague National Wildlife Refuge**. A driving tour loops through the refuge, but the best way to see the numerous birds found here is by walking or paddling in a canoe.

Chincoteague National Wildlife Refuge

⌂ 8231 Beach Rd 🄲 (757) 336-6122 🕐 6am-6pm daily

⑤ Appomattox Court House National Historical Park

⌂ 95 miles (152 km) W of Richmond, 111 National Park Dr, Appomattox 🕐 9am-5pm daily 🔒 Major hols ⊡ nps.gov/apco

This National Historical Park, located 3 miles (5 km) northeast of Appomattox, re-creates the spot where Confederate General Robert E. Lee surrendered to US General Ulysses S. Grant to signal the end of the Civil War. Today, markers trace the last skirmishes of the war, and reconstructed and restored buildings replicate the scene where the two leaders put an end to the war, on April 9, 1865. The terms of surrender were generous, since Union leaders hoped to promote reconciliation. When the Confederates laid down their arms, the Union soldiers saluted their opponents.

Much of the original setting was destroyed in battle or later dismantled by souvenir hunters. Most of what stands here today was reconstructed by the National Park Service in the 1940s.

⑥ 🗺 Ⓜ 🍴 🖼 🛍

COLONIAL WILLIAMSBURG

🏠 155 miles (250 km) S of Washington, DC 🚗🚌 ⏰ 8.45am–5pm daily
🌐 colonialwilliamsburg.com

Now the world's largest living history museum, this 18th-century Colonial town takes visitors back to when the idea of the United States was being born and the nascent country's ideals were being defined.

As Virginia's capital from 1699 to 1780, Williamsburg was the hub of the British colony. After the colony moved to Richmond (p227), the town went into decline until John D. Rockefeller embarked on a restoration project in 1926. Today, in the midst of the modern-day city, the 18th-century town has been re-created. Costumed interpreters bring history alive, craftsmen show off their skills, horse-drawn carriages clatter through the streets, and fife and drum bands play, vividly evoking America's past.

→

The reconstructed Governor's Palace, originally built in 1720

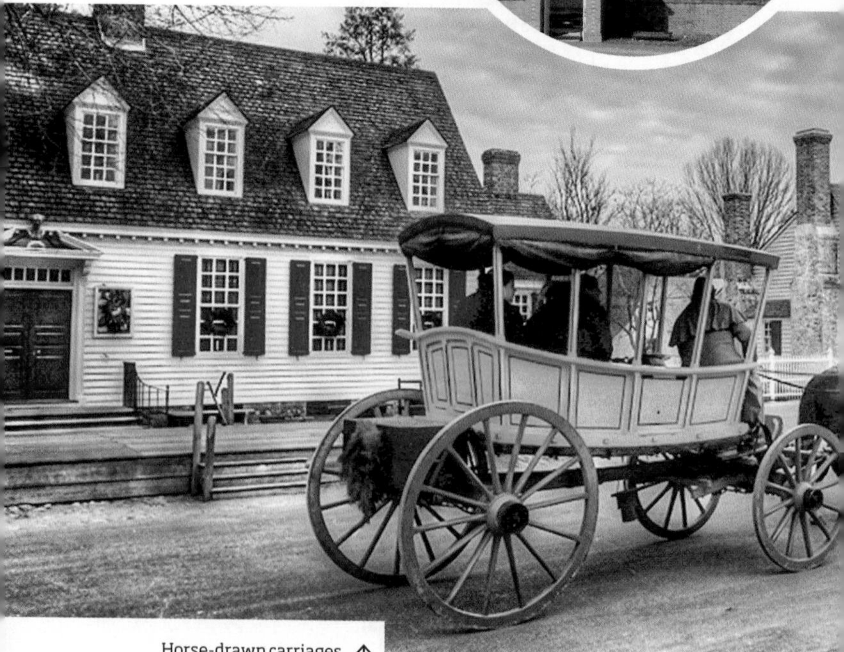

Horse-drawn carriages guiding passengers into Williamsburg's past ↑

Governor's Palace

The courthouse, built in 1770–71 and home of the county court for more than 150 years.

The milliner shop, originally stocking imported clothes, jewelry, and toys.

The Raleigh Tavern, once an important center for social, political, and commercial gatherings.

The Capitol, with the government in its West Wing, and General Court in its East Wing.

The nursery, where costumed interpreters use replica tools and original techniques.

Market Square, where reenactors read official proclamations.

The Print Office, now a store selling authentic 18th-century foods.

NASSAU STREET

PALACE STREET

PALACE STREET

NORTH ENGLAND ST

NICHOLSON STREET

QUEEN ST

COLONIAL ST

DUKE OF GLOUCESTER STREET

← The historic area within the modern city of Williamsburg

Did You Know?

Buildings with a Grand Union flag in front are open to the public; all others are private.

Monticello, Jefferson's
Palladian masterpiece
in Charlottesville ↓

East
portico

The entrance hall, a
natural history museum
and also where visitors
were received.

North
piazza

Jefferson's bed,
between his cabinet
(office) and bedroom.

The greenhouse,
used by Jefferson
to cultivate a
variety of plants.

7 🌀 Ⓜ 🏛

Monticello

🏠 Route 53, 3 miles (5 km)
SE of Charlottesville 🚗🚌
🕙 10am–5pm Mon–Sat
(from 8:30am Sun) 🚫 Dec
25 🌐 monticello.org

As well as the University of
Virginia, Thomas Jefferson's
hometown of Charlottesville is
dominated by his Palladian-
style home, Monticello, which
he began building in 1769 and
took him 40 years to complete.
The entrance hall doubled as a
private museum, and the
library held a collection of
around 6,700 books. The
remains of the slave quarters
still stand; nearly 200 enslaved
people worked the estate's
plantations. An exhibit studies
the life of the enslaved Sally
Hemings, who bore at least
six of Jefferson's children
from age 16.

8

Norfolk

🚇🚗🚌 ℹ 232 E Main St;
www.visitnorfolk
today.com

This historic Colonial port is
located at the point where
Chesapeake Bay meets the
Atlantic Ocean. Norfolk is a
busy maritime center with the
world's largest naval base, and
the downtown waterfront
centers on the battleship USS
Wisconsin at **Nauticus, The
National Maritime Center**.

Another top attraction is the
Chrysler Museum of Art, which
displays the eclectic collection
of automobile tycoon Walter
Chrysler, Jr., including paintings
by Rubens, Degas, and Renoir.

SKYLINE DRIVE

One of the most beautiful and pastoral drives on America's
east coast, the 105-mile (170-km) Skyline Drive runs along
the backbone of the Shenandoah National Park's Blue
Ridge Mountains. Deer, wild turkey, bears, and bobcats
inhabit the park, and wildflowers, azaleas, and mountain
laurel are abundant. The park's many hiking trails and its
75 viewpoints offer stunning natural scenery. The drive is
best experienced in mid-October for fall leaf colors, and
spring and summer for wildflowers.

> **Richmond retains an aura of the Old South, and its Victorian mansions and brownstones testify to the area's postwar prosperity.**

Neighboring Virginia Beach (18 miles or 29 km west of Norfolk) is a flourishing seaside city with stunning beaches, a bustling boardwalk, excellent restaurants and bars, and plenty of family-friendly attractions, including the Virginia Aquarium and Marine Science Museum. It is also the site of the 18th-century lighthouse at Cape Henry, where the English first landed in 1607.

Nauticus, The National Maritime Center

⊛ ⊕ 🏠 1 Waterside Dr
🕐 10am–5pm Tue–Sat (summer: also Mon), noon–5pm Sun 🚫 Jan 1, Thanksg., Dec 24 & 25 🌐 nauticus.org

⑨
Richmond

🏛️ 🚌 ℹ️ 401 N Third St; www.visitrichmond va.com

As the former capital of the Confederacy, Richmond retains an aura of the Old South, and

its Victorian mansions and brownstones testify to the area's postwar prosperity.

Civil War artifacts, including General Robert E. Lee's coat and sword, are among the exhibits at the Museum of the Confederacy. The graceful Neo-Classical State Capitol dominating downtown houses a life-size sculpture of George Washington by Jean Antoine Houdon. Palmer Chapel offers superb views of James River and Belle Isle. Farther uptown is the **Virginia Museum of Fine Arts**, whose highlight is the priceless Pratt Collection of Imperial Russian Art, including five fabulous Fabergé eggs.

Virginia Museum of Fine Arts

⊛ ☺ 🏛️ 🏠 200 North Blvd
🕐 10am–5pm Wed–Sun (to 9pm Thu & Fri) 🌐 vmfa. museum

⑩
Blue Ridge Parkway

📞 (828) 670-192
🌐 blueridgeparkway.org

Stretching for hundreds of miles along the crest of the Appalachian Mountains, the Blue Ridge Parkway extends from the southern border of Shenandoah National Park all the way to North Carolina *(p248)*, ending finally at Great

Smoky Mountains National Park. Mileposts along the way help travelers discover the points of interest along the route. Some of the highlights include a crossing of the James River at milepost 63 and the lakefront lodge in the Peaks of Otter section near milepost 86. The historic Mabry Mill at milepost 176 was in use as a sawmill and blacksmith shop until 1935.

The parkway passes through Asheville, North Carolina, and Roanoke, Virginia. Open all year, the peak season is fall.

TOP 5 VIRGINIAN FOODS

Pimento Cheese
Spread of cheese, mayo, and sweet peppers.

Fried Pie
Old-fashioned, fruit-filled dough crescents.

Ham & Biscuits
Smoked country ham in a buttery biscuit.

Peanut Pie
Salty, sweet, and sticky.

Chesapeake Oysters
Raw, steamed, or fried (Chesapeake means "great shellfish Bay" in Algonquin).

← European devotional artworks at the Chrysler Museum of Art in Norfolk

↑ Harpers Ferry glowing beside the Potomac and Shenandoah rivers

WEST VIRGINIA

Set entirely within the Appalachian Mountains, this "Mountain State" remains largely forested, despite centuries of aggressive lumbering and mining. Today West Virginia is known for its woodworking, quilting, and basketry crafts, and traditional Appalachian music and dancing, and is a great destination for outdoor activities, such as fishing and mountain biking.

⓫
Harpers Ferry

🅰 63 miles (101 km) NW of Washington, DC 🚊🚌
🚆 171 Shoreline Dr; www. nps.gov/hafe

Nestled at the confluence of the Potomac and Shenandoah rivers, where West Virginia meets Virginia and Maryland, is the tiny town of Harpers Ferry. Named after Robert Harper, the Philadelphia builder who built a ferry here in 1761, most of the historic downtown area is today the Harpers Ferry National Historical Park. It was here, in 1859, that Maryland abolitionist John Brown led an ill-fated raid on the federal arsenal. Although his attempt failed, it ignited the Civil War two years later.

The town looks much as it did in the 19th century, and several historic buildings, including John Brown's Fort and the arsenal, are open to visitors.

The famous Appalachian Trail, which runs through town, has its headquarters at the **Appalachian Trail Conservancy**. The trail is a 2,000-mile (3,220-km) footpath that stretches along the spine of the Appalachian Mountains from Georgia to Maine. Harpers Ferry is just an hour's train ride from Washington, DC, making the region easily accessible.

Appalachian Trail Conservancy

🅰 799 Washington St
🕑 9am–5pm daily
🌐 appalachiantrail.org

Did You Know?

West Virginia is known as the southernmost northern state, and the northernmost southern state.

⓬
New River Gorge National River

🅰 59 miles (95 km) SE of Charleston 🚆 US Hwy 19, Lansing; www.nps.gov/ neri

The New River courses through a deep gorge in the south-eastern corner of the state, and its compact set of Class V rapids are some of the best whitewater adventures in the eastern US. The modern Canyon Rim Visitor Center and gorge bridge provide easy access to panoramic overlooks and rim hiking trails. The visitor center also distributes comprehensive lists of local rafting outfitters, while the nearby **Hawk's Nest State Park** offers modest lodge rooms and operates an aerial tram down to the river for boat rides during summer. The former mining town of Fayetteville is also a popular base for rafters and outfitters, while the old industrial town of Hinton holds a grittier appeal and is easily accessible to visitors via Amtrak.

Hawk's Nest State Park

♿ 🅰 Hwy 60, Ansted
🕑 Tram/boat rides: check website for days and hours
🌐 hawksnestsp.com

⑬
Monongahela National Forest

⌂ 137 miles (220 km) E of Charleston 🛈 200 Sycamore St, Elkins; www.fs.udsa.gov/mnf

The eastern half of the state lies deep within the Allegheny Mountains, a part of the longer Appalachian Range. Much of this rugged terrain is protected as the Monongahela National Forest, which encompasses five wilderness areas and serves as the headwaters for six major river systems. The forest's trails attract hikers, mountain bikers, and skiers.

The small town of Elkins makes a convenient base from which to explore the area. The Augusta Heritage Center hosts summer programs on traditional folklife and arts, as well as bluegrass and mountain music dances and concerts.

Northeast of Elkins, a short stretch of the Allegheny Trail links the Canaan Valley Resort State Park, a downhill ski resort, and Blackwater Falls State Park,

a good place for backcountry ski touring. Farther south, Snowshoe Mountain Resort is the state's largest downhill resort in winter and a mountain biking center from spring to fall. The nearby **Cass Scenic Railroad State Park** organizes vintage steam train rides across the mountaintops. Southeast of Elkins, the **Spruce Knob-Seneca Rocks National Recreation Area** draws rock-climbers up Seneca Rocks, an hour's drive away. The 75-mile (121-km) Greenbrier River Trail, from White Sulphur Springs in the south all the way to the Cass Scenic Railroad State Park in the north, is a converted "rails-to-trails" rail-bed route, popular for bicycle tours.

Cass Scenic Railroad State Park
⌂ Route 66/Main St, Cass 🕐 Late May–Oct ⓦ cassrailroad.com

Spruce Knob-Seneca Rocks National Rec. Area
📞 (304) 567-2827 🕐 May–Sep: 9am–4:30pm Wed–Sun; Oct–Apr: 9am–4:30pm Sat–Sun

EAT

Hillbilly Hotdogs
Slinging dogs, slaw, and burgers served up from a wooden bus.

⌂ 6951 Ohio River Rd, Lesage ⓦ hillbilly hotdogs.com

$⑤$$

Pies & Pints
Known for the state's best stone-hearth pizzas and craft ales.

⌂ 222 Capitol St, Charleston
ⓦ piesandpints.net

$$⑤

Thyme Bistro
Tiny bistro that excels at elevated comfort food and daily specials.

⌂ 125 Main Av, Weston 🕐 Sun, Mon ⓦ thyme-bistro.business.site

$$⑤

Bluegrass Kitchen
Laid-back local grub elevated to sublime.

⌂ 1600 Washington St E, Charleston 🕐 Sun ⓦ bluegrasswv.com

$$$⑤

Lot 12 Public House
Fine dining in a lovingly restored historic home, ideal for a romantic evening.

⌂ 117 Warren St, Berkeley Springs 🕐 Mon, Tue, Wed ⓦ lot12.com

$$$

← Looking into Blackwater Canyon in Monongahela National Forest

MARYLAND AND DELAWARE

Experience

The Dutch first colonized Delaware in the 1630s, quickly followed by the Swedish. The state eventually fell to the British, and it was governed as part of Pennsylvania until 1701. The only state to offer religious freedom for Roman Catholics, Maryland was settled by the English from 1634. Its plantation society was otherwise very similar to Virginia – both Maryland and Delaware were slave states, but both sided with the Union during the Civil War. Baltimore became one of the nation's largest and richest cities – its finest hour was during the War of 1812, fending off British attacks and inspiring "The Star-Spangled Banner." Since World War II, industry in both states has declined, but the economy has been boosted by tourism and biotech jobs.

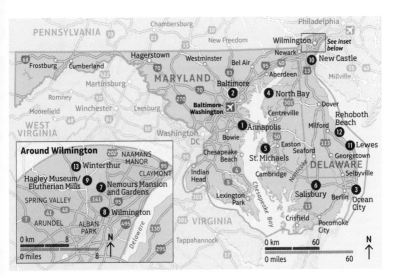

MARYLAND

Maryland has a wealth of natural and historical sites. The rolling farmlands of Antietam in the west are rich in Civil War heritage. Southern Maryland's Chesapeake Bay is the longest inland shoreline in the US, attracting foodies looking to indulge in the local specialty – blue crabs. The Delmarva Peninsula is graced by the wild beauty of Assateague and Chincoteague islands.

❶

Annapolis

🚗🚌 ℹ️ **Annapolis & Anne Arundel County Visitors Bureau, 26 West St; www. visitannapolis.org**

The capital of Maryland, Annapolis is the jewel of Chesapeake Bay, defined by the nautical character that comes with its 17 miles (27 km) of shoreline. A walk down Main Street leads past the 200-year-old Maryland Inn and endless seafood restaurants to the City Dock. It is then a short walk to the 150-year-old **US Naval Academy**. Inside the visitor center is the *Freedom 7* space capsule piloted by Alan Shepard, the first American in space. The **Maryland State House**,

completed in 1779, is the oldest state capitol in use. It was here that the Treaty of Paris was ratified in 1784, ending the Revolutionary War.

Annapolis teems with Colonial-era buildings. The 1765 **William Paca House**, home of Governor Paca, a signatory to the Declaration of Independence, is a fine Georgian mansion with an enchanting garden. The 1774 Hammond Harwood House, a masterpiece of Georgian design with exceptionally fine woodcarving, is a short walk west of the State House on Maryland Avenue. Worth exploring are Cornhill and Duke of Gloucester streets, examples of the city's historic residential streets. Bus and walking tours are on offer, but the best way to view the city is from the water, on a sightseeing boat, schooner, or kayak.

US Naval Academy

♿ 🏛️ **52 King George St**
🕐 9am–5pm daily (photo ID required) 🌐 usna.edu

Maryland State House

♿ 🏛️ State Circle 🕐 Jan–Feb: 9am–4pm daily; Mar–Dec: 9am–5pm daily (photo ID required) 🌐 msa.maryland. gov

William Paca House

♿ 🏛️ **186 Prince George St**
🕐 Apr–Dec: 10am–5pm Mon–Sat, noon–5pm Sun
🌐 annapolis.org

🔍 HIDDEN GEM
Fort McHenry

In 1814, this star-shaped fort held off the British during the Battle of Baltimore. A survivor, 35-year-old Francis Scott Key, wrote the national anthem "The Star Spangled Banner" after watching bombs burst over his head.

↑ Maryland State House rising above Main Street in Annapolis

②

Baltimore

🚗🚌 **ℹ** 100 Light St (12th Floor); www.baltimore.org

There is much to do and see in this port city, stacked with buzzy restaurants, antiques, arts, monuments, and pleasure boats. A good place to start is the Inner Harbor, the city's redeveloped waterfront, filled with harborside shops and restaurants. The centerpiece is the **National Aquarium**, whose collection includes a seal pool and a dolphin sanctuary. Historic Ships, a floating museum, gives an on-deck glimpse of the city's maritime history. To the east, waterside Fells Point is famous for its hipster pubs and sea-food spots. The cobblestoned streets are lined with independent shops, ranging in theme from records to fashion and art. The Frederick Douglass-Isaac Myers Maritime Park

→ The eclectic collection at the Walters Art Museum in Baltimore

Museum explores Baltimore's African American nautical history. The Baltimore Water Taxi is a swift and scenic way to zip around the harbor.

Uptown, the famous modern art collection at the **Baltimore Museum of Art** includes works by Matisse, Picasso, Degas, Van Gogh, and Warhol. Also impressive is the **Walters Art Museum** on the elegant Mount Vernon Square. The gallery's collection includes Greek and Roman classical art, Southeast Asian and Chinese artifacts, Byzantine silver, pre-Columbian carvings, and jeweled objects by Fabergé.

Downtown, literary pilgrims descend upon poet Edgar Allan Poe's final resting place in Westminster Burying Ground, while Little Italy is known for its knockout Italian restau-rants and the games of *bocce* (Italian lawn bowling) played around Pratt and Stiles streets on warm evenings.

National Aquarium

♿🚭 🅰 501 E Pratt St, Pier 3 ⏰ Times vary, check website 🌐 aqua.org

Baltimore Museum of Art

♿🚭🚭 🅰 10 Art Museum Dr ⏰ 10am-5pm Wed-Sun 🌐 artbma.org

Walters Art Museum

♿🚭 🅰 600 N Charles St ⏰ 10am-5pm Wed-Sun (to 9pm Thu) 🌐 thewalters.org

---

EAT

L. P. Steamers
Get your hands dirty cracking local crabs with cheap beer and sweeping rooftop views of the bay.

🅰 1100 E Fort Av, Baltimore 🌐 locustpoint steamers.com

$$$$$

Iron Rooster
All-day breakfasts with crab-cake eggs benedict, house-made "pop tarts," and bacon Bloody Marys.

🅰 12 Market Space, Annapolis 🌐 ironroosterallday.com

$$$$$

The Point
The top-choice waterfront crab joint in the state, serving heaps of blue crabs and seasonal specials.

🅰 700 Mill Creek Rd, Arnold 🌐 thepoint crabhouse.com

$$$$$

3

Ocean City

🏠 30 miles (48 km) E of Salisbury 🚌 ℹ️ 4001 Coastal Hwy; www.ococean.com

Soft beige sand extends endlessly along the Ocean City peninsula, fronted by miles of hotels. In summer, brightly colored umbrellas provide shade, while at night, the beach boardwalk that stretches from the inlet north past 27th Street is lively with strolling couples, friends, and families.

At the inlet, on the southern border of Ocean City, the **Ocean City Life-Saving Station Museum**, housed in a decommissioned 1891 Life-Saving Station, relates the history of Ocean City and the US Life-Saving Service.

At the northern end of the boardwalk, **Trimper's Rides** began operating in 1902 with a steam-powered, 45-animal carousel. Today, Trimper's includes a 1905 Herschel-Spellman merry-go-round glittering with brilliant jewels and fantasy animals, Ferris wheels, bumper rides, mechanized fortune-tellers, and a host of other entertainments.

Ocean City also has many miniature golf courses: visitors can play beneath plaster polar bears, bask in the tropics, or putt around rubber sharks.

Ocean City Life-Saving Station Museum

♿ 🏠 813 South Atlantic Av ⏰ Times vary, check website 🌐 ocmuseum.org

Trimper's Rides

♿ 🏠 Baltimore Av & S 1st St on the boardwalk ⏰ Summer: 1pm–midnight Mon–Fri, noon–midnight Sat & Sun; fall–spring: limited hours 🌐 trimpersrides.com

---

4

North Bay

🏠 38 miles (61 km) NE of Baltimore 🚌 ℹ️ 121 N Union St, Ste B, Havre de Grace; (410) 939-2100

At the far northern end of Chesapeake Bay, the delightful town of Havre de Grace is home to the Concord Point Lighthouse. Popular with artists and photographers, the lighthouse has been in continuous operation since the mid-1800s. The **Havre de Grace Decoy Museum** has a fine collection of working decoys and chronicles how the craft evolved from a purely practical wildfowl lure into a highly sophisticated form of American folk art. The Havre de Grace Maritime Museum, situated at the point where the Susquehanna River meets Chesapeake Bay, tells the story of this region's rich maritime heritage.

Across the bay to the east, the lush forests of **Elk Neck State Park** cover the tip of a peninsula crowned by Turkey Point Lighthouse, one of the bay's oldest. The park offers a sandy beach for swimming, boat rentals, and hiking trails.

Northeast of the park across the Elk River is Chesapeake City, where rooftops appear much as they did 100 years ago when the village grew to service the Chesapeake and Delaware Canal. Today, the village is a "boutique town," with fine shops and restaurants. The **C & D Canal Museum**, in the canal's original pumphouse, has working models of canal locks, the original steam power plant, and a giant waterwheel.

Havre de Grace Decoy Museum

⊘ ⌂ 215 Giles St
◷ 10:30am–4:30pm Mon-Sat, noon–4pm Sun ⦿ Federal hols ⊞ decoymuseum.com

Elk Neck State Park

⌂ End of Route 272 ☎ (410) 287-5333

C & D Canal Museum

⌂ End of 2nd St ☎ (410) 885-5622 ◷ 8am–4pm Mon-Fri, 11am–4pm Sat & Sun
⦿ Federal hols

5

St. Michaels

⌂ 50 miles (80 km) SE of Annapolis via US-50
⊞ stmichaelsmd.org

St. Michaels, founded in 1677, was once a haven for ship builders, privateers, and blockade-runners. Today, the town is a destination for pleasure boaters and yachts flying international colors. Excellent B&Bs, shops, and restaurants abound.

Chesapeake Bay Maritime Museum is one of Maryland's top cultural attractions. The museum features interactive exhibits on boat building, historic boats, decoys, and various other aspects of life

↑ Boatyard workshop at the Chesapeake Bay Maritime Museum, St. Michaels

in maritime Chesapeake Bay. Several vessels unique to the area are anchored right on the property, and the Hooper Strait Lighthouse, a fully restored screwpile wooden structure from 1879, is open for exploration by the public.

Chesapeake Bay Maritime Museum

⊘ ⌂ 213 North Talbot St
◷ 10am–5pm daily (summer: to 6pm; winter: to 4pm)
⊞ cbmm.org

6

Salisbury

⌂ 88 miles (142 km) SE of Annapolis via US-50 ⊞
ℹ 8480 Ocean Hwy; www.salisbury.md

The largest city on the Eastern Shore, Salisbury is known for its fine antiques shops. It developed as a mill community in 1732 and soon became the principal crossroads of the southern Delmarva Peninsula. Salisbury's **Ward Museum of Wildfowl Art** houses the world's premier collection of decorative and antique decoys. Here, wood is expertly carved

and painted to resemble wild birds in natural settings. The museum looks at the history of the art, from antique working decoys to contemporary sculptural carvings.

Pemberton Historical Park is the site of Pemberton Hall, built in 1741 for Isaac Handy, a British Army colonel. The grounds are threaded by self-guided nature trails, and the manor house contains a small museum maintained by the local historical society.

Ward Museum of Wildfowl Art

⊘ ⌂ 909 S Schumaker Dr
◷ 10am–5pm Mon-Sat, noon–5pm Sun ⊞ wardmuseum.org

SHOP

Season's Best Antiques

This 50-dealer, 10,000-sq-ft (930-sq-m) antiques mall is stuffed with charming antiques, collectibles, and quirky odds and ends.

⌂ 104 Poplar Hill Av, Salisbury
☎ (410) 860-8988

← Taking a stroll down Ocean City's lively beach boardwalk

↑ The impeccable landscaped gardens of Nemours Mansion

DELAWARE

Delaware's importance in industry, banking, and technology far exceeds its size. This is mainly due to the laissez-faire tax and corporation laws that have encouraged several large companies to set up shop here. Along with a significant history, stately country homes, and some of the nation's best museums, Delaware also boasts miles of sandy beaches along the Atlantic Ocean.

7 ⬡ ⬡

Nemours Mansion and Gardens

🏠 850 Alapocas Dr, Wilmington 🚌 🕐 May–Dec: 10am–5pm Tue–Sat, noon–5pm Sun 🚫 Federal hols 🌐 nemoursmansion.org

Built by Alfred I. du Pont in 1909–10, this Louis XVI-style château is named after the north-central French town that Pierre Samuel du Pont de Nemours, Alfred's great-great-grandfather, represented as a member of the French Estates General in 1789. The Nemours Mansion's 102 rooms are opulently decorated with Oriental rugs, tapestries, and paintings dating from the 15th century onward. The 300-acre (120-ha) gardens are landscaped in the classic *jardin à la française* style, and are the largest formal French gardens in the US.

8

Wilmington

🚌 ℹ 100 W 10th St; www. visitwilmingtonde.com

This former Swedish colony is home to the **Delaware Art Museum**, whose outstanding collections contain works by several notable 19th- and 20th-century American artists as well as paintings and decorative arts from the English pre-Raphaelite movement, led by Dante Gabriel Rossetti.

Delaware Art Museum
♿ 🏠 2301 Kentmere Parkway 🕐 10am–4pm Wed–Sun (to 8pm Thu) 🌐 delart.org

9 ⬡ ⬡ ⬡ ⬡

Hagley Museum/ Eleutherian Mills

🏠 200 Hagley Creek Rd, Wilmington 🚌 🕐 10am–5pm daily (Nov–mid-Mar: to 4pm) 🚫 Thanksgiving, Dec 25 🌐 hagley.org

Picturesquely located on the banks of the Brandywine River, Hagley Yard is the origin of the du Pont fortune in America. In spring the river banks are ablaze with purple and pink rhododendrons and azaleas.

Eleuthere du Pont established an explosives factory here in 1884, and the factory buildings are now open to the public. Hagley Museum, at the entryway to the property, explores the history of the sites with exhibits and dioramas.

Eleutherian Mills, the modest du Pont family home overlooking the powder works, contains many original furnishings. The gardens are verdant with a variety of native plant life, shrubs, and trees.

> **The Nemours Mansion's 102 rooms are opulently decorated with Oriental rugs, tapestries, and paintings dating from the 15th century onward.**

⑩ New Castle

📧 ℹ️ 220 Delaware St;
www.newcastlecity.
delaware.gov

Delaware's former capital is now a well-preserved historic site, with restaurants, shops, and residential areas. The **New Castle Courthouse** illuminates the town's Swedish, Dutch, and British origins. Several historic homes lie a short stroll from each other. One, the elegant Amstel House (1738), was the home of Governor Van Dyke and its most famous guest was George Washington.

New Castle Courthouse

🏛️ 211 Delaware St 📞 (302) 323-4453 🕐 10am–3:30pm Tue-Sat, 1:30–4:30pm Sun 📅 Federal hols

---

⑪ Lewes

📧 ℹ️ 114 E Third St; www.
lewes.com

Once known as Zwaanendael ("Swan Valley"), Delaware's original Dutch settlement in 1631, Lewes is a quiet town with a small beach and sophisticated restaurants and shops. The **Zwaanendael Museum**, built in 1931, is a striking replica of the Town Hall of Hoorn, home of most of the settlers.

In 1682, the British Crown granted the colony of Delaware to Englishman William Penn, who set aside Cape Henlopen for the citizens of Lewes. Besides a bay and beaches, **Cape Henlopen State Park** contains Gordon's Pond Wildlife Area, with hiking trails, interpretive displays, a pier, camping, and swimming.

Zwaanendael Museum

🏛️ 102 Kings Hwy
🌐 history.delaware.gov

Cape Henlopen State Park

🏛️ 42 Cape Henlopen Dr
🌐 destateparks.com

⑫ Rehoboth Beach

📧 ℹ️ 229 Rehoboth Av;
www.cityofrehoboth.com

A strip of restaurants and shops here stretches along Rehoboth Avenue, meeting Funland on the boardwalk. The Outlets, between Lewes and Rehoboth Beach, feature every major outlet store.

Three miles (5 km) south of the beach, **Delaware Seashore State Park** covers the strip of land between the Atlantic and Rehoboth Bay. Millsboro, west of Rehoboth Bay, is home to the Nanticoke tribe, who hold a pow-wow in mid-September to preserve their heritage and explain their beliefs. South of the park, the 1852 Fenwick Island Lighthouse marks the Delaware–Maryland border.

Delaware Seashore State Park

🏛️ 39415 Inlet Rd, Rehoboth Beach; www.destate parks.com

---

⑬ 🚲 🚶 Winterthur

🏛️ SR 52 🕐 10am–5pm Tue-Sun 📅 Thanksgiving, Dec 25
🌐 winterthur.org

Originally the home of Evelina du Pont and James Biderman,

Winterthur was named after the Biderman ancestral home in Switzerland. Henry Francis du Pont inherited the house in 1927. Du Pont's exhaustive collection of furniture at Winterthur is one of the most impressive assemblages of early American decorative arts in the world.

Winterthur showcases the du Pont family's fascination with American decorative arts and horticulture. The grounds are beautifully landscaped, with miles of paths and scenic woodland trails. The museum consists of two buildings, 175 period rooms, and two floors of exhibition galleries.

↑ A period room at Winterthur, showcasing the du Pont family's fascination with American decorative arts

THE SOUTHEAST

The midtown skyline of Atlanta, Georgia

EXPLORE THE SOUTHEAST

This chapter divides the Southeast into three sightseeing areas, as shown on the map below. Find out more about each area on the following pages.

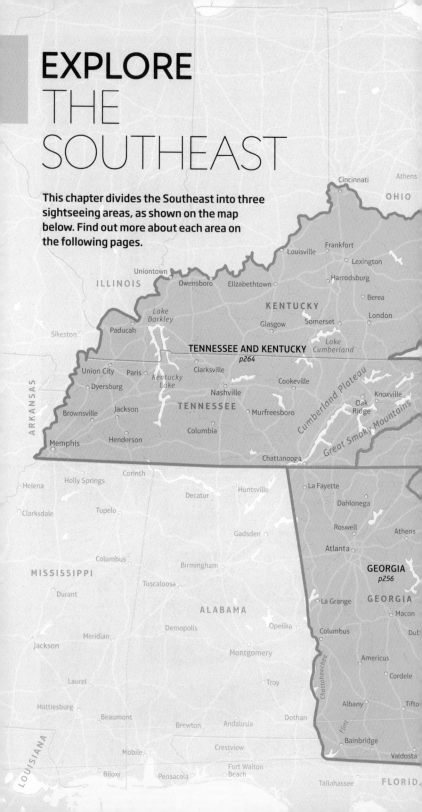

Cincinnati
Athens
OHIO
Louisville
Frankfort
Lexington
Harrodsburg
Uniontown
ILLINOIS
Owensboro
Elizabethtown
Berea
KENTUCKY
Lake
Barkley
Glasgow
Somerset
London
Sikeston
Paducah
Lake
Cumberland
TENNESSEE AND KENTUCKY
p264
Union City
Paris
Kentucky
Lake
Clarksville
Cookeville
Knoxville
Dyersburg
Nashville
Oak
Ridge
Cumberland Plateau
TENNESSEE
Murfreesboro
Brownsville
Jackson
Columbia
Great Smoky Mountains
Memphis
Henderson
Chattanooga
Corinth
Holly Springs
Huntsville
La Fayette
Helena
Decatur
Dahlonega
Clarksdale
Tupelo
Gadsden
Roswell
Athens
Atlanta
Columbus
Birmingham
GEORGIA
p256
MISSISSIPPI
Tuscaloosa
GEORGIA
Durant
ALABAMA
La Grange
Macon
Demopolis
Opelika
Columbus
Dub
Jackson
Meridian
Americus
Montgomery
Cordele
Laurel
Troy
Albany
Tifto
Hattiesburg
Beaumont
Dothan
Brewton
Andalusia
Chattahoochee
Flint
Bainbridge
Valdosta
LOUISIANA
Mobile
Crestview
Biloxi
Pensacola
Fort Walton
Beach
Tallahassee
FLORID
ARKANSAS

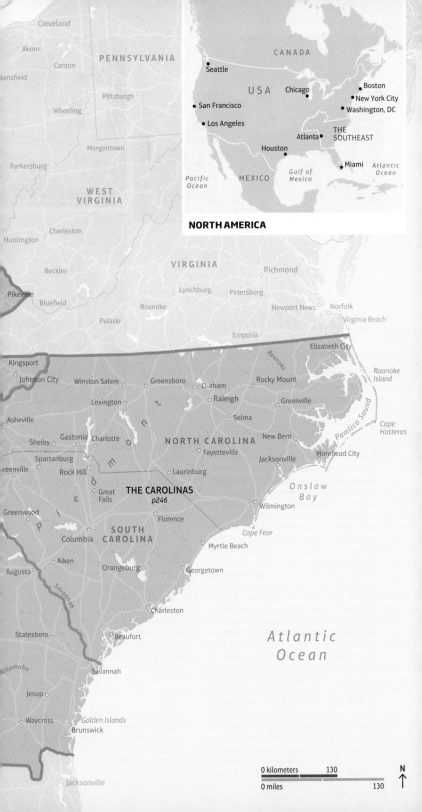

THE CAROLINAS
p246

2

3

7 DAYS

A Musical Tour

This road trip takes in the eclectic music traditions of the Southeast, from Kentucky bluegrass to Elvis. The tour can be completed as a loop from Memphis, or as a one-way trip to Macon or nearby Atlanta.

Day 1

Start your time in Memphis *(p270)* with a pilgrimage to Sun Studio, which launched the careers of Elvis, B.B. King, Johnny Cash, and many others, before heading down to Beale Street and the W. C. Handy House Museum, home of the father of the blues. From here it's a short walk to the Memphis Rock-N-Soul Museum and the adjacent Gibson Guitar factory, which offers a great tour. Fuel up with a soul food lunch at Blues City Café *(www.bluescitycafe.com)* or Miss Polly's Soul City Café *(154 Beale St)*. Afterward, take a taxi or drive south to the Stax Museum of American Soul Music, in the legendary old Stax Records recording studio. Spend your evening taking in a live show on Beale Street (Jerry Lee Lewis' Cafe & Honky Tonk is a good bet).

Day 2

Dedicate this morning to the shrine to all things Elvis Presley: Graceland. Aficionados should take the guided tour then pay extra to see Elvis's car collection, his two airplanes, and an exhibit focusing on his love for the state of Hawaii. From here, it's

about a 3.5-hr drive to Nashville *(p268)*. Whatever time you arrive in the capital of country, make sure to sample the city's famous "hot chicken" – the spicy delicacy was invented by Prince's Hot Chicken Shack *(www.princeshotchicken.com)*.

Day 3

Start the day by getting a Nashville music primer at the Country Music Hall of Fame and Museum, before making a pilgrimage to the Ryman Auditorium, former home of the Grand Ole Opry and still a major concert venue (tours are available). In the afternoon, drive out to the Grand Ole Opry House itself for a backstage tour. Get dinner at the Bluebird Cafe *(www.blue birdcafe.com)* then see a show at Tootsies Orchid Lounge *(www.tootsies.net)*.

Day 4

Kentucky *(p272)* is the birthplace of bluegrass music, and today's itinerary is a long, winding route through the heart of bluegrass country. It's 135 miles (217 km) to the Bluegrass Music Hall of Fame and

1 Beale Street, Memphis.

2 Interior of Graceland.

3 Trombone Shorty performing in Asheville.

4 Country Music Hall of Fame, Nashville.

5 Renfro Valley Entertainment Center.

Museum in Owensboro, where you can learn all about the state's mountain music. Next up is the Bill Monroe Museum, dedicated to the "Father of Bluegrass." Finally, drive 165 miles (265 km) to the Kentucky Music Hall of Fame in Mount Vernon, before taking in a show at Renfro Valley Entertainment Center (www.renfrovalley.com).

Day 5

Get up early to drive across the mountains to Asheville, North Carolina (p249). Asheville's music scene is rooted in old-time mountain music and bluegrass, but you'll hear a huge variety of genres in its many live venues. During the day, check out Thomas Wolfe State Historic Site, dedicated to the local author, and peruse the galleries and stores in the River Arts District. Eat tacos for lunch at the Grey Eagle Taqueria (www.greyeagle tacqueria.com) inside the seminal indie venue Grey Eagle Music Hall. In the evening, reserve dinner and a bluegrass show at the Isis Music Hall, or opt for a more laid-back night of listening to local musicians jam at Asheville Guitar Bar.

Day 6

It's about a 3-hr drive from Asheville to Athens (p260), Georgia, the city that gave us bands such as REM, the B-52s, Drive-By Truckers, and Widespread Panic. Grab a free copy of the weekly Flagpole Magazine (www.flagpole.com) to see what's going on. Follow in the footsteps of REM with a trip to Wuxtry Records, where the band first met, and sample soul food at Weaver D's (www.weaverds.com), whose slogan inspired REM's album, Automatic for the People. In the evening, a visit to the iconic 40-Watt Club is a must (www.40watt.com).

Day 7

Just two hours from Athens, Macon (p260) – home of Otis Redding and Little Richard – maintains a lively musical tradition. Visit the Allman Brothers Band Museum to learn about the early years of the iconic rock band, then indulge in dinner at the atmospheric Tic Toc Room (www.thetictocroom. telwink.com), a former nightclub where Little Richard got his start in the 1950s. End your trip by catching a live gig at the 1923 Macon City Auditorium (415 First St).

→ Preparing a barbecue dish in North Carolina

BOURBON WHISKEY

American bourbon – whiskey made primarily from corn – is synonymous with Tennessee and Kentucky, where it's been distilled since the 18th century. Bardstown (p275), Kentucky is the "Bourbon Capital of the World," home to an annual Bourbon Festival. Other big Kentucky names include Jim Beam (Clermont), Maker's Mark (Loretto), and Wild Turkey (Lawrenceburg). Jack Daniel's (Lynchburg) is the giant of Tennessee whiskey.

Barbecue Basics

The Southeast is home to two styles of barbecue. Memphis-style traditionally features pork, slow-cooked in a hickory and charcoal pit. Sample the smoky, delicious end-product at Corky's BBQ (p270). North Carolina barbecue is subdivided into Lexington style (using red sauce) and Eastern style (vinegar and pepper sauces only). Of numerous joints, try Pit Authentic Barbecue (328 W Davie St, Raleigh) and Skylight Inn (4618 Lee St, Ayden).

THE SOUTHEAST FOR
FOODIES

Foodies are in for a treat in the Southeast. Southern cuisine has deep roots here, blending indigenous, African, and European flavors and ingredients. Experiences run the gamut from barbecue served at roadside shacks to farm-to-table dishes in gourmet restaurants in Charleston and Savannah.

Finger Lickin' Good

Humble fried chicken is an art form in the Southeast, where it's a crispy, juicy treat. KFC really was founded by "Colonel" Harland Sanders in Corbin, Kentucky, in the 1930s. Hot chicken was finessed in Nashville – spicy fried chicken seasoned with cayenne pepper. Try it at Prince's Hot Chicken Shack (p268) or Hattie B's Hot Chicken (www.hattieb.com), both in Nashville. In Memphis there's Gus's Fried Chicken (www.gusfriedchicken.com).

←

A plate of Gus's Fried Chicken, Memphis

Lowcountry Cuisine

Lowcountry cuisine developed along the South Carolina and Georgia coasts. It features plenty of fresh seafood in addition to a strong African influence from the Gullah culture (p255). Dine on she-crab soup, catfish stew, shrimp and grits. In Charleston, try them at High Cotton (199 E Bay St), Poogan's Porch (72 Queen St) or Magnolias (p254).

→

Poogan's Porch restaurant in Charleston, South Carolina

INSIDER TIP
Food Tours

Food walking tours are a great way to enjoy the Southeast's foodie cities. Try Charleston Culinary Tours (www.charleston-culinarytours.com), and Savannah Taste Experience (www.savannah-tasteexperience.com).

Cooked by Celebrity Chefs

Chef Sean Brock is one of Charleston's biggest names, with the likes of Husk (p254). Orchid Paulmeier runs One Hot Mama's American Grille (www.onehotmamas.com) also in South Carolina. In Atlanta, Richard Blais runs FLIP Burger (www.flipburgerboutique.com), Kevin Gillespie cooks at Gunshow (p263), and Anne Quatrano oversees Bacchanalia (www.starprovisions.com). Paula Deen's The Lady and Sons (www.ladyandsons.com) rules in Savannah.

↑ Husk's Sean Brock inspecting dishes, like pig's ear lettuce wraps (inset)

Experience

THE CAROLINAS

Named for Charles I, the English colony of Carolina was settled in the 1670s and divided in two in 1729. Both became slave states, dominated by plantations, and both joined the Confederacy in the Civil War; South Carolina was the first state to secede and the war began here. Segregation lasted until the 1960s – in North Carolina, the peaceful Greensboro sit-in protests helped to end it. The state remains a leading tobacco producer, and finance, technology, and research are booming. North Carolina is a swing state, and South Carolina is reliably Republican. In 2011, Nikki Haley became South Carolina's first female governor.

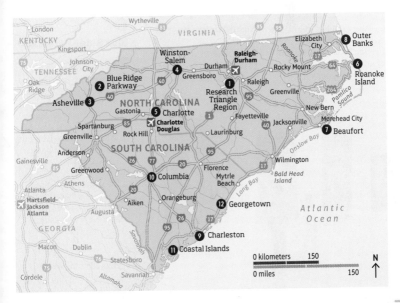

NORTH CAROLINA

Although the population today is mainly based in cities, green fields of tobacco remain the classic image of North Carolina. Though tobacco-growing farms dominate the state's center, the east is lined by miles of pristine Atlantic Ocean beachfront, and the western mountains are among the most majestic found east of the Rockies.

❶

Research Triangle Region

🔗🅿️🚻 *i* 212 W Main St, Durham; www.discover durham.com

The state capital of Raleigh forms a geographic triangle with the university towns of Durham and Chapel Hill. This region is the state's intellectual center, and has spawned the high-tech Research Triangle Park, a corporate campus located between the three cities.

Primarily a business hub, the Triangle does offer some interesting sights. Raleigh is known as the "City of Oaks" for the many oak trees lining its streets. Downtown Raleigh has a handful of modern museums, including the Sports Hall of Fame, the Museum of Natural Sciences, and the **North Carolina Museum of History**. The latter is well known for a Civil War exhibit on the state's divided loyalties. Just north, the **North Carolina Museum of Art** holds three floors of statuary and paintings.

Of the two university towns, the smaller Chapel Hill is significantly more quaint, with its wooded **University of North Carolina (UNC)** campus, Morehead Planetarium, art museum, and genteel Carolina Inn. Downtown Durham, wedged between **Duke University** campuses, has a reputation for innovation, and is home to the Durham Bulls minor-league baseball team. Alumni and students of the two universities enjoy the lively rivalry between their respective sports teams – Duke's Blue Devils and UNC's Tar Heels. Another landmark is the Duke Lemur Center, home to the largest population of lemurs outside Madagascar.

North Carolina Museum of History

🏛 5 E Edenton St, Raleigh 🕐 9am–5pm Mon–Sat, noon–5pm Sun 🌐 ncmuseumof history.org

North Carolina Museum of Art

🏛 2110 Blue Ridge Rd, Raleigh 🕐 10am–5pm Tue–Sun (to 9pm Fri) 🌐 ncartmuseum.org

Mountains and greenery bounding the city of Asheville ↑

UNC Visitor Center

🏛 250 E Franklin St, Chapel Hill 🕐 9am–5pm Mon–Fri 🚫 Federal hols 🌐 unc.edu

Duke University Visitor Center

🏛 2138 Campus Dr, Durham 🕐 8:30am–4:30pm Mon–Fri, 8:30am–12:30pm Sat 🌐 duke.edu

❷

Blue Ridge Parkway

🌐 nps.gov/blri

This scenic two-lane highway runs 469 miles (755 km) south from Virginia (*p227*) along the Blue Ridge Mountain ridge-line. Its most scenic stretches lie in North Carolina, where the road meanders past peaks, waterfalls, and the towering, Mount Mitchell.

The route is the National Park Service's most popular destination, with over 16 million visitors every year, and has a

←

Visitors admiring works in the North Carolina Museum of Art

EAT

Dame's Chicken and Waffles
Serving up irresistible Southern classics with a modern spin.

🏠 530 Foster St, Durham
🌐 dameschicken
waffles.com

$ $ $

The Pit Barbeque
Authentic pit-cooked barbecue dishes are served in a restored 1930s warehouse.

🏠 328 W Davie St, Raleigh
🌐 thepit-raleigh.com

$ $ $

strictly enforced speed limit of 45 mph (72 km/h).

The parkway ends at the entrance to Great Smoky Mountains National Park, north of Cherokee (p266). Here a museum relates the history of the Cherokee people, focusing on the tribe's forcible removal to Oklahoma in 1838. The town of Cherokee itself has a large American Indian-run casino.

---

❸
Asheville

 🛈 36 Montford Av; www.exploreasheville.com

Surrounded by mountains, downtown Asheville evokes

 HIDDEN GEM
Thomas Wolfe Memorial

"Dixieland" boarding-house, described by local author Thomas Wolfe in his novel *Look Home-ward Angel*, is today preserved as this historic site (*www. wolfememorial.com*) in Asheville.

the period of local author Thomas Wolfe (1900–38), who wrote about his hometown in his novels. It is said to be among the healthiest cities in the country, with many health-food stores, cafés, organic restaurants, and a vibrant arts scene. It is also considered one of the beer capitals of the US, with a wealth of craft breweries.

Beyond this, Asheville is probably best known for its 250-room **Biltmore Estate**. This French Renaissance-style mansion is the largest residence in America, and holds a collection of 18th- and 19th-century art and sculpture. The splendid estate also has a winery, a brand new hotel, a deluxe inn (*see p276*), and gardens designed by Frederick Law Olmsted, who also designed New York's Central Park. Visitors should expect long lines, as the estate attracts huge crowds. Asheville also makes a great base for exploring the surrounding mountain region.

Biltmore Estate
♿ 🏠 1 Lodge St ⏰ Times vary, check website
🌐 biltmore.com

❹

Winston-Salem

🚆🚌 🛈 200 Brookstown Av; www.visitwinstonsalem. com

Moravian immigrants first settled here in 1766. Their descendants celebrate their roots at **Old Salem**, a restoration of a Colonial village, where costumed guides relate the story of this Protestant sect's journey from Moravia. Traditional Moravian wares can be purchased at the gift shop.

Adjacent to the village is the **Museum of Early Southern Decorative Arts**, which exhibits antebellum furnishings and artifacts from across the region. There is also a museum for children downstairs.

Old Salem
♿ 🏠 900 Old Salem Rd
⏰ 9:30am–4:30pm Tue–Sat, 1–4:30pm Sun 🌐 oldsalem.org

Museum of Early Southern Decorative Arts
🏠 924 S Main St ⏰ 9:30am–4:30pm Tue–Sat 🌐 mesda.org

The Harvey B. Gantt Center for African-American Arts + Culture in Charlotte

by African American artists comprise the Center's permanent collection, which also offers a community outreach program. Nearby is the **Bechtler Museum of Modern Art**, housing an impressive collection of artists such as Miró, Picasso, and Warhol.

Levine Museum of the New South

📍 200 E 7th St 🖥 museumofthenewsouth.org

Harvey B. Gantt Center for African-American Arts + Culture

📍 551 S Tryon St
🖥 ganttcenter.org

Bechtler Museum of Modern Art

📍 420 S Tryon St
🖥 bechtler.org

---

⑤
Charlotte

ℹ️ 501 S College St; www.charlottesgotalot.com

Thanks to an influx of banking and insurance firms, which revitalized the city in the 1990s and early 2000s, Charlotte is a booming city, and the second largest in the Southeast after Jacksonville, Florida (p313).

The **Levine Museum of the New South** explores the history of North Carolina – from the Civil War, to slavery, to the Civil Rights Movement – and gives an overview of the region. The fabulous **Harvey B.Gantt Center for African-American Arts + Culture**, named for the first African American mayor, honors the contributions that Africans and African Americans have made in the South. Fifty-eight works

⑥
Roanoke Island

ℹ️ 1 Visitors Center Circle, Manteo; www.outerbanks.org

This marsh island was the site of the first English settlement in North America. The first expedition to these shores, sponsored by Sir Walter Raleigh, was in 1584. In 1587, another ship carrying more than 100 colonists disembarked at the island. But when the next group arrived three years later, no trace of the earlier colonists was found. To-

day, the **Fort Raleigh National Historic Site**, the adjacent Elizabethan Gardens, and the nearby theme park all relate the story of this legendary "Lost Colony."

At the northern tip of the island, Fort Raleigh preserves the ruins of the colony's original disembarkation point. A short drive south, the **Roanoke Island Festival Park** tells the story of the first ship through tours of a re-creation of the *Elizabeth II*, while a museum relates the region's American Indian and European history.

Fort Raleigh National Historic Site

♿ 📍 1401 National Park Dr, Manteo 🕐 9am–5pm daily 🖥 nps.gov/fora

Roanoke Island Festival Park

♿ 📍 Port of Manteo 🕐 Jun-Sep: 9am–5pm daily; Oct–May: 9am–5pm Mon–Fri, noon–5pm Sat 🖥 roanokeisland.com

---

⑦
Beaufort

ℹ️ 701 Front St; www.beaufortsc.org

Beaufort's considerable charms lie in its historic B&B inns, seafood markets, and

> ## HARVEY BERNARD GANTT
>
> Harvey Bernard Gantt was the first African American student to attend Clemson University. It is here that he met his wife, Lucinda Brawley, who was the first African American woman to attend the university. Gantt has worked on iconic projects in Charlotte, and has remained an activist for equal rights throughout his lifetime.

Did You Know?

The first documented gold discovery occurred in Charlotte in 1799, triggering the nation's Gold Rush.

restaurants. The highlight of this coastal resort's waterfront is the **North Carolina Maritime Museum**, which interprets the boating, fishing, and pirate history of the area. A robot of Edward "Blackbeard" Teach, a notorious pirate (1680–1718), welcomes visitors to the site.

At the docks, private ferries take passengers out to the deserted sands of Lookout Island, preserved from development as the **Cape Lookout National Seashore**. The ecology of the island is similar to Cape Hatteras, but limited access makes it more remote.

North Carolina Maritime Museum

🏠315 Front St ⏰9am–5pm Mon–Fri, 10am–5pm Sat, 1–5pm Sun 🚫Jan 1, Thanksgiving, Dec 25 🌐ncmaritime museums.com

Cape Lookout National Seashore

🛈Beaufort Town Hall, 701 Front St, Beaufort; www.nps.gov/calo

8
Outer Banks

🛈1 Visitors Center Circle, Manteo; www.outerbanks.org

North Carolina's Atlantic coastline is made up of a long chain of narrow barrier islands known as the Outer Banks. Most of this coast is protected as part of the Cape Hatteras National Seashore, where long stretches of pristine beach, dune, and marsh shelter wild ponies, sea turtles, and numerous waterbirds. The coastline's historic lighthouses and pirate lore are as important a part of the Outer Banks' maritime heritage as its seafood industry.

Among the dozens of lighthouses, the 1872 Bodie Island Lighthouse is the only one still in operation. A free ferry transports cars and passengers between Hatteras Island and Ocracoke Island. Hatteras's distinctive black-and-white lighthouse, built in 1870, is the tallest brick lighthouse in the US. The village of Ocracoke has a good selection of inns

and restaurants, and visitors can connect with ferries here.

In addition to the sun, surf, and sand, this tourist region offers many historic attractions and family amusements, in the town of Kill Devil Hills. The "First in Flight" slogan found on coins and the state's license plates commemorates the Wright Brothers' historic first flight, which took place here. The **Wright Brothers National Memorial** stands at the very site where Orville and Wilbur Wright launched *Flyer* in 1903. At Jockey's Ridge State Park, hang-gliders participate in a modern version of the Wright Brothers' adventures, while "sandboarders" ride the largest sand dune on the East Coast. Fewer people venture to the inland side of the island, where a slow kayak ride or a walk through the scenic maritime forest at **Nags Head Woods Ecological Preserve** hold a quieter appeal.

Wright Brothers National Memorial

♿ 🏠1000 North Croatan Hwy, Kill Devil Hills ⏰9am–5pm daily 🌐nps.gov/wrbr

Nags Head Woods Ecological Preserve

♿ 🏠701 W Ocean Acres Dr, Kill Devil Hills 📞(252) 441-2525 ⏰Dawn–dusk daily

↑ Dusty pink skies as the sun sets over Bodie Island Lighthouse, Outer Banks

↑ Charleston's skyline at sunset with its tall church steeples

SOUTH CAROLINA

South Carolina's part in national and world events is interpreted in its museums and monuments but there is much more to the state aside from its history. Many visitors head straight for its miles of gorgeous beaches, others preferring to explore its lush forests and mossy swamps. Here you can also discover Gullah culture, unique to South Carolina.

9
Charleston

🛫🚂🚌 🄸 375 Meeting St; www.charlestoncvb.com

One of the South's loveliest cities and South Carolina's first capital, Charleston is situated on the tip of a peninsula between the Ashley and Cooper rivers. Named after King Charles II of England, the city was founded in 1670 and soon became a wealthy colony of tobacco, rice, and indigo plantations. The first shot of the Civil War was fired just off the city's harbor, where people gathered to watch the Confederate siege of Fort Sumter.

Today, Charleston retains much of its period architecture and is a popular destination for antebellum house-and-garden tours and delicious Southern cuisine.

The historic district's well-preserved architecture evokes the city's Colonial and early American past. The civic and religious buildings vary hugely in style, while among the city's highlights are distinctive Charlestonian residences, set perpendicular to the street with grand piazzas running along their lengths. The only high structures are the church steeples. Horse-and-carriage rides along tree-lined streets provide a graceful overview.

A trip south from Old City Market to the Battery takes in many highlights along Church Street, including the old magazine, the Gothic French Huguenot Church, and the Heyward-Washington House, now part of the **Charleston Museum**. This 1772 house was built by rice planter Daniel Heyward and has a collection of locally made furniture. The rest of the museum is on Meeting Street, and presents a comprehensive overview of the city's history from pre-Colonial days. Its most distinctive exhibits are in the American Indian and Natural History galleries; the former has dugout canoes and costumed mannequins, and the latter has a number of mounted skeletons of pre-historic animals. A half-block east of the Heyward-Washington House is the Old Slave Mart, once one of the busiest in the American colonies. At the Battery, the **Edmondston-Alston House** features two floors of an opulent 1825 mansion overlooking the harbor. White Point Gardens Park lies to the south, while in the north, Waterfront Park stands across from the popular restaurant row. West of the park, the **Gibbes Museum of**

> **Charleston retains much of its period architecture and is a popular destination for antebellum house-and-garden tours and delicious Southern cuisine.**

Art reveals local history in its landscape pieces and portraits of famous South Carolinians.

Picturesquely set overlooking the harbor, the **South Carolina Aquarium** is a great introduction to the indigenous creatures found within the state's aquatic habitats. These range from Appalachian rivers and blackwater swamps, to salt marshes and coral reefs.

An embarkation point for boat tours to **Fort Sumter**, the visitor center relates the story of the Civil War's first battle. The fort, which stands on an island at the entrance to Charleston harbor, was controlled by Union troops. In April 1861, the Confederate army besieged the fort. When Union troops tried to bring in supplies, the Confederates, who had occupied nearby Fort Johnson, unleashed a 34-hour bombardment. Union forces surrendered on April 14, 1861, and the fort remained under Confederate control until 1865. Ironically, General Beauregard, the Confederate leader, was a student of the defending Union commander, Major Robert Anderson, at the US Military Academy at West Point, New York. Fort Sumter has been preserved unchanged since the end of the war as a National Monument.

Within a short drive upriver, three historic house tours provide a glimpse of Charleston's plantation life. The grandest is **Middleton Place**, with its 1755 mansion located on a bluff overlooking the oldest landscaped gardens in the US. Nearby **Drayton Hall** is one of the country's finest examples of Colonial architecture. Built in 1738, the Georgian Palladian mansion has been preserved in its original condition without electricity or plumbing. A 30-minute program about the plantation's contentious relationship with slavery is shown daily. **Magnolia Plantation** is a more modest house with acres of informal gardens.

↑ Portraiture lining the walls of the Gibbes Museum of Art

Charleston Museum

⊛ 🚩 360 Meeting St; Heyward-Washington House: 87 Church St 🕔 9am-5pm Mon-Sat, 11am-5pm Sun 🔲 Major Federal hols 🅦 charlestonmuseum.org

Edmondston-Alston House

⊛ 🚩 21 E Battery 🕔 10am-4:30pm Tue-Sat, 1-4:30pm Sun & Mon 🔲 Major federal hols 🅦 edmondstonalston.org

Gibbes Museum of Art

⊛ 🚩 135 Meeting St 🕔 10am-5pm Mon-Sat (to 8pm Wed), 1-5pm Sun 🔲 Major federal hols 🅦 gibbesmuseum.org

South Carolina Aquarium

⊛ 🚩 100 Aquarium Wharf 🕔 9am-4pm daily 🔲 Thanksgiving, Dec 25 🅦 scaquarium.org

Fort Sumter Visitor Center

⊛ 🚩 340 Concord St 🕔 Daily, check website for boat times 🔲 Jan 1, Thanksgiving, Dec 25 🅦 nps.gov/fosu

Middleton Place

⊛ 🚩 4300 Ashley River Rd 🕔 9am-5pm daily 🔲 Dec 25 🅦 middletonplace.org

Drayton Hall

⊛ 🚩 3380 Ashley River Rd 🕔 9:30am-3:30pm Mon-Sat, 10:30am-3:30pm Sun 🔲 Jan 1, 1st week Feb, Thanksgiving, Dec 24, 25 & 31 🅦 draytonhall.org

Magnolia Plantation

⊛ 🚩 3550 Ashley River Rd 🕔 9am-5:30pm daily (to 4:30pm Nov-Feb) 🅦 magnoliaplantation.com

PLANTATIONS AND SLAVERY

A sadly central part of Charleston and the Southeast's history is slavery, with the city a trade center for the industry. Plantations are synonymous with this dark period of history. Most held large numbers of enslaved people, who worked long hours in awful conditions, living on site in sparse accommodations. There were more enlightened plantation owners, who hired workers and paid them a small wage, but they were few and far between.

←

Visitors walking through the trees of Congaree National Park, near Columbia

South Carolina State Museum

⊕ ⌂301 Gervais St
🕐10am-5pm Mon-Fri (to 10pm Tue), 10am-6pm Sat, noon-5pm Sun ⊘Easter, Thanksgiving, Dec 25
🅦scmuseum.org

South Carolina Confederate Relic Room & Museum

⊕ ⌂301 Gervais St 🕐10am-5pm Tue-Sat; 1-5pm first Sun of month 🅦crr.sc.gov

---

EAT

Husk

A spot renowned for its superb modern interpretations of traditional Southern dishes.

⌂76 Queen St, Charleston
🅦huskrestaurant.com

$\$\$\$

Soda City Market

From Italian to Mexican or Brazilian, there's a wonderful choice of eating places at this weekly farmers' market.

⌂1300-1600 Main St, Columbia
🅦sodacitysc.com

$\$$

Magnolias

Head here for regional classics - think fried green tomatoes and carpetbagger filet - and excellent service.

⌂185 E Bay St, Charleston 🅦magnolias charleston.com

$\$\$\$

---

⑩ Columbia

🚌🚍 ℹ1120 Lincoln St; www.columbiacvb.com

Situated at the fall line of the Congaree River, this city was declared the state capital over Charleston in 1786. Although General William T. Sherman destroyed most of Columbia during the Civil War, the State House managed to survive intact. Today, six bronze stars mark the spots where Union cannonballs hit the 1855 copper-domed building.

On the banks of the river, the **South Carolina State Museum** is housed in an artfully recycled textile mill built in 1894, and offers informative exhibits on the state's natural, cultural, and industrial history. The adjacent **South Carolina Confederate Relic Room & Museum** maintains a huge collection of artifacts that trace the military history of South Carolina's participation in US wars from the Civil War onward, as well as an exhibit on the history and controversial meanings of the Confederate flag.

A 20-minute drive south of town, the Congaree National Park offers visitors a close-up look at the biodiversity found in a cypress swamp ecosystem.

⑪ Coastal Islands

ℹLowcountry Visitors Center & Museum, Frampton Plantation House, Yemassee; www.south carolinalowcountry.com

The vast, remote islands of the Lowcountry are a semitropical region with a rich natural and cultural history.

Shifting dunes, dense maritime forests of live oak, and numerous lagoons and marshes harbor a mix of wildlife.

The area's African American history evolved around enslaved people brought here from West Africa to cultivate the rice crop. Isolated on these islands, Lowcountry Africans were able to perpetuate their cultural traditions over generations. Today, their "Gullah" heritage remains distinct in the local language, music, and food.

On St. Helena Island, to the east of Beaufort, the renowned **Penn Center** is a touchstone of Gullah culture. A former school established by Pennsylvanian abolitionists during the Civil War, the center has a distinguished history. National leaders such as Martin Luther King, Jr. met here to advance the Civil Rights Movement. A museum located in the schoolhouse relates the center's history through visual displays.

Beyond St. Helena, **Hunting Island State Park** preserves a natural barrier island environment. Its highlights include a pleasant, uncrowded beach, a coastside campground, and a 19th-century lighthouse.

Hilton Head Island is South Carolina's premier beach resort. It is dominated by several deluxe complexes, including the Westin Resort, Crowne Plaza, Hyatt Regency, Disney, and, of course, the Hilton. Recreational activities include golf, tennis, horseback riding, fishing, boating, sailing, and a variety of other water sports.

Penn Center

🏵 🗺 16 Penn Center Circle W, St Helena Island 🕐 9am–4pm Tue–Sat 🗓 Federal hols 🌐 penncenter.com

Hunting Island State Park

🏵 🗺 2555 Sea Island Pkwy, Hunting Island 🕐 6am–6pm daily (Apr–Oct: to 9pm) 🌐 south carolinaparks.com

---

12
Georgetown

🚌 🛈 531 Front St; www. visitgeorge.com

Georgetown was the center of the state's lucrative rice trade, producing almost half the rice grown in the US in the 1840s. Downtown's **Rice Museum**, housed in the 1842 Old Market building, explains how the rice industry influenced almost every facet of life here.

Just south of Georgetown, Hampton Plantation State Park is an unfurnished 1750 Georgian house. Visitors can explore the mansion, which overlooks the old rice fields, and the well maintained grounds.

Rice Museum

🏵 🗺 633 Front St 🕐 10am–4:30pm Mon–Sat 🗓 Federal hols 🌐 ricemuseum.org

↑ A brightly striped lighthouse on the coastal island of Hilton Head

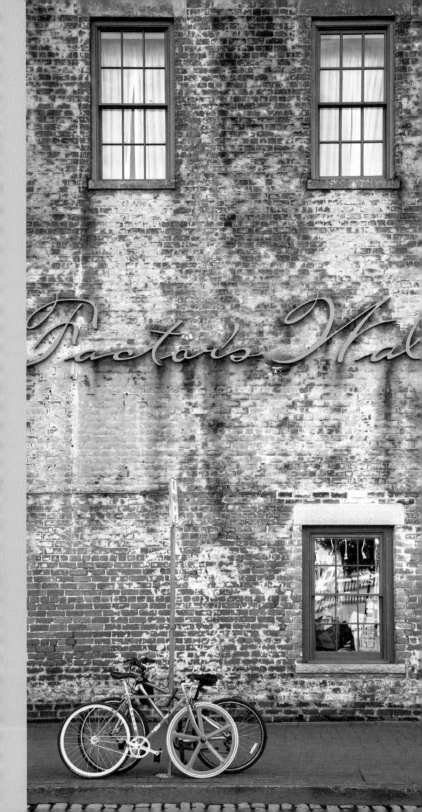

GEORGIA

James Oglethorpe established Georgia (named for George II) in 1733. The Cherokee resisted for years, but were forcibly removed in 1838 on the "Trail of Tears." The colony flourished thanks to rice, sugar-cane, and cotton plantations, worked by enslaved people. During the Civil War, Georgia was a Confederate stronghold and provided inspiration for Margaret Mitchell's *Gone With the Wind*. Segregation lasted into the 1960s; Atlanta was the base for Martin Luther King, Jr. in the Civil Rights era. Since hosting the 1996 Olympics, the state's capital city has further emerged as an economic powerhouse and hub for African American culture.

Experience

1. Savannah
2. Golden Isles
3. Okefenokee Swamp National Wildlife Refuge
4. Macon
5. Athens
6. Americus
7. Dahlonega
8. Atlanta

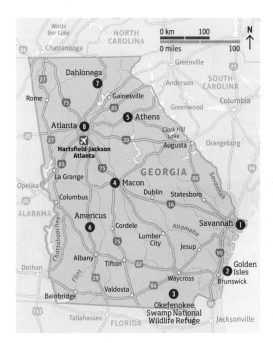

GEORGIA

The last of the 13 original colonies – and named after King George II – Georgia is the largest state east of the Mississippi. Its history is complex and its landscape is similarly multi-faceted, with the likes of sprawling Atlanta and picture-postcard Savannah, cypress-shaded swamps and gorgeous sandy beaches. Here you'll also find totally irresistible food, best washed down with a refreshing glass of iced tea.

HIDDEN GEM
Bonaventure Cemetery

Well-known Savannah figures are buried here, such as singer Johnny Mercer, but the cemetery is most famous as a setting in *Midnight in the Garden of Good and Evil* (both the book and film).

❶
Savannah

🚗🚲🚌 🛈 **301 Martin Luther King, Jr. Blvd; www.visit savannah.com**

The lushly landscaped parks and gracious homes of Savannah have earned it a reputation for scenic beauty and sophistication. It was established in 1733 on the banks of the Savannah River, and its founder, James Oglethorpe, laid out a town grid dotted with small squares. His design remains intact, with the squares now serving as pretty parks filled with statues and fountains.

The city has one of the largest urban historic districts in the US, which thrives as the city's downtown commercial center. Horse-and-carriage tours provide an introduction to historic Savannah, though walking is the best way to explore the area. River Street is one of the city's central entertainment districts, lined with restaurants, raucous taverns, and souvenir shops. A few blocks in from the river, City Market is another lively district, housed in a series of historic buildings.

Further history is found in the city's places of worship. These include the Congregation Mickve Israel, an active synagogue that dates from 1878. The First African Baptist Church is even older, built in 1850 for the first black Baptist congregation in North America.

Notable house museums throughout Savannah shed light on the city's past. The **Davenport House** is considered one of the country's finest examples of Federal-style architecture, while the nearby **Owens-Thomas House**, built in 1816, is among the finest Regency buildings.

There is also a handful of interesting museums. The **Telfair Academy**, in the historic district, displays a fine collection of Impressionist paintings and decorative arts within an 1818 Regency-style mansion.

At the western edge of the district, the **Ships of the Sea Maritime Museum** holds ship models of all shapes and sizes within the palatial 1819 Scarborough House.

Many more attractions await in the surrounding Lowcountry. A drive east along Hwy 80, towards Tybee Island, passes the Bonaventure Cemetery and the behemoth brick **Fort Pulaski National Monument**, rising like a medieval fortress at the mouth of the Savannah River.

Davenport House
⊘ 🏠324 E State St 🕐10am-4pm Mon-Sat, 1-4pm Sun 🌐davenporthousemuseum.org

Owens-Thomas House
⊘⊘ 🏠124 Abercorn St 🕐10am-5pm Tue-Sat, noon-5pm Sun & Mon 🌐telfair.org

Telfair Academy
⊘ 🏠121 Barnard St 🕐10am-5pm Tue-Sat, noon-5pm Sun & Mon 🌐telfair.org

Ships of the Sea Maritime Museum
⊘ 🏠41 Martin Luther King, Jr. Blvd 🕐10am-5pm Tue-Sun 🌐shipsofthesea.org

Fort Pulaski National Monument
⊘ 🏠Hwy 80 E 🕐9am-5pm daily 🌐nps.gov/fopu

←

A bustling pub on River Street, in one of Savannah's liveliest districts

↑ Canoeists in Okefenokee Swamp National Wildlife Refuge, which is home to alligators (inset)

❷ Golden Isles

🚗 ℹ️ 529 Beachview Dr, St. Simons Island; www. goldenisles.com

The Spanish called the barrier islands off Georgia's southern coast "the Golden Isles," a term that tourism promoters revived. Primarily beach resorts, the islands do retain a number of historic sights. Fort Frederica National Monument, located on St. Simons, holds the ruins of a fortified village built by James Oglethorpe in 1736. South of Fort Frederica is an expanse of marsh, where the Battle of Bloody Marsh was fought in 1742. This battle between English and Spanish forces determined which Colonial power would control this part of the American continent.

At the turn of the 20th century, Jekyll Island was the preserve of the nation's premier industrialists, such as the Vanderbilts and Rockefellers. With the dawn of World War II, however, the island was deemed unsafe and the families moved elsewhere. Today its historic district comprises the "cottages," as the millionaires' mansions were known, and the Jekyll Island Club. The cottages have been restored and operate as museums or inns.

❸ Okefenokee Swamp National Wildlife Refuge

🏠 Hwy 121, Folkston 🚗
🕐 Dawn–5:30pm daily (summer: to 7:30pm)
🚫 Thanksgiving, Dec 25
🌐 fws.gov/refuge/okefenokee

In the remote southeastern corner of the state, the Okefenokee Swamp is an exotic, primeval landscape of blackwater and cypress that harbors alligators, softshell turtles, otters, and all kinds of birdlife. Boat tours provide a close-up view at three sections of the swamp, including the Okefenokee Swamp Park near Waycross, and the wildlife refuge headquarters at Folkston, which provides details about overnight paddling trips into the swamp. Fargo, near the swamp's western entrance, is the nearest town to the Stephen C. Foster State Park, 18 miles (29 km) to the northeast. Camping facilities and cabins are available here.

EAT

Leopold's Ice Cream
This spot has been serving up the cold stuff since 1919, with dozens of flavors. Look out for seasonal favorites.

🏠 212 E Broughton St, Savannah 🌐 leopolds icecream.com

$ $ ⑤

The warm brick exterior and impressive porch of Macon's Hay House Museum

⑤ Athens

🚌 ℹ️ 300 N Thames St; www.visitathensga.com

Home to the **University of Georgia** (UGA), Athens is well known as the state's literary and intellectual center. It has also gained repute as the originator of alternative music. Local bands such as REM, the B-52s, and Widespread Panic have made it big, and the annual Athfest in June continues the tradition. The city is largely deserted in summer, but overflows with Georgia Bulldog fans in fall for home football games. The visitor center provides details about house and garden tours.

University of Georgia

📷 Four Towers Building, 405 College Station Rd 🌐 uga.edu

⑥ Americus

🚌 ℹ️ 123 W Lamar St; (229) 928-6059

Off the beaten track in south Georgia, the tidy county seat of Americus lies in a region of diverse attractions. **Habitat for Humanity**, a worldwide organization offering "self-build" housing for the poor, has its headquarters downtown. Its Global Village and Discovery Center includes an international marketplace and up to 40 examples of habitat homes built around the world, including Papua New Guinea, Botswana, and Ghana.

Located 10 miles (16 km) north of town, Andersonville is the National Prisoner of War (POW) Museum. This marks a spot that was a notorious prisoner-of-war camp during the Civil War, which later

④ Macon

🚌 ℹ️ 450 Martin Luther King, Jr. Blvd; www.maconga.org

Founded on the Ocmulgee River in 1823, Macon was laid out in a grid of avenues, which still exist in its downtown. Uphill from here is one of the city's highlights, the Intown Historic District. This area has some of the city's loveliest homes, a few of which are open to the public. The 1855 **Hay House Museum**, built in the Italian Renaissance style, features period characteristics such as *trompe l'oeil* marble, a ballroom, and hidden hallways. Guided tours begin at the visitor center. The city also has a vibrant musical history and was home to such greats as Little Richard and Otis Redding. The Big House Museum houses the Allman Brothers Band Museum, which honors the ultimate Southern rock band.

Also of note is the **Tubman Museum**, which was founded in 1981 and is one of the largest museums in the US dedicated to the art, history and culture of African Americans. Across the river from downtown, the Ocmulgee National Monument marks a mound complex built around 1100 AD as the capital of the Creek Confederacy.

Hay House Museum

🎟️ 📷 934 Georgia Av ⏰ 10am–4pm Tue–Sat, 1–4pm Sun 🚫 Sun (Jan, Feb, Jul, Aug), federal hols 🌐 hayhouse macon.org

Tubman Museum

🎟️🧒 📷 310 Cherry St ⏰ 9am–5pm Tue–Sat 🌐 tubmanmuseum.com

TOP 5 GEORGIA FOODS

Fried Green Tomatoes
A Southern classic, which even inspired a book and movie.

Georgia Pulled Pork
Slow-cooked for hours, it's incredibly moreish.

Chicken and Dumplings
Georgia cooks its chicken slow in a crock-pot, then serves with dumplings.

Peaches
The reason why Georgia is called the Peach State.

Pecan Pie
Georgia is the USA's prime pecan producer, so this hits most menus.

became a veterans' cemetery. Almost 13,000 of the camp's inmates died from the terrible living conditions. Housed in a structure built to resemble a concentration camp, the museum's disturbing exhibits commemorate American POWs in conflicts from the Civil War to the Gulf and Iraqi wars.

The local high school in Plains, west of Americus, is part of the Jimmy Carter National Historic Site. It was here that a teacher predicted that her student would become president. Carter proved her right, and the school is now dedicated to the life of the Plains-area peanut farmer's son who was elected as the 39th president in 1976, in the wake of Nixon's resignation. The former president, and recipient of the Nobel Peace Prize in 2002, lives here and teaches Sunday school at the Maranatha Baptist Church when he is in town. Carter is also a vocal supporter of Habitat for Humanity.

Did You Know?

President Jimmy Carter, Martin Luther King, Jr., Ray Charles, and Kanye West were all born in Georgia.

Habitat for Humanity

⊘ ⌂ 121 Habitat St at W Lamar St 📞 (229) 924-6935 🕓 9am–5pm Mon–Fri

---

❼
Dahlonega

🛈 13 S Park St; www.dahlonega.org

The legendary Blue Ridge Mountain range extends across the state's northeastern corner. The region is well known for its cultural heritage of outstanding folk arts such as quilt-making, woodworking, and bluegrass music. The discovery of gold in the main town of Dahlonega in 1828 precipitated the nation's first gold rush, two decades before California's famous "Forty-Niners." The state's **Dahlonega Gold Museum**, housed in the 1836 courthouse in the town square, displays mining equipment, nuggets, and mining lore. The town also offers gold-panning and gold-mine tours as well as exhibiting a complete set of coins minted in the US Mint that operated here from 1838 to 1861.

About 18 miles (29 km) from Dahlonega, the Amicalola Falls State Park is the gateway to the southern terminus of the Appalachian Trail, a hiking route that leads from the top of Springer Mountain in

↑ A visitor panning for gold in the Dahlonega Gold Museum

Georgia north to Mount Katahdin, deep in Maine. Less ambitious hikers can head to the park's Len Foote Hike Inn, which offers ecologically sensitive, comfortably rustic overnight accommodations. East of Dahlonega, the federally designated "Wild and Scenic" Chatooga River is considered one of the most daunting rivers to navigate in the eastern US.

Dahlonega Gold Museum

⊘ ⌂ 1 Public Square 🕓 9am–4:45pm Mon–Sat, 10am–4:45pm Sun 🚫 Jan 1, Thanksgiving, Dec 25 🌐 gastateparks.org

↑ A prisoner of war memorial at Andersonville, near Americus

Dusk falling across Atlanta's 1996 Olympic Park

⑧ Atlanta

✈ 🏛 🚌 𝒊 233 Peachtree St, NE; www.atlanta.net

In 1837, Atlanta was founded as a terminus for two railroad routes, but its importance as a transportation hub made it a Union target during the Civil War. After a 75-day siege, General William T. Sherman broke the Confederate defenses and set most of the town ablaze, a history recounted in Margaret Mitchell's *Gone with the Wind*. Today, the city claims to be the "Capital of the New South" and is considered more brash and faster paced than its Southern neighbors.

This cosmopolitan city is home to many industrial giants, including Coca-Cola. Its entrepreneurial spirit led to an economic boom that lasted two decades, capped by a successful bid to host the 1996 Olympics. Downtown's attractions and the city's remaining Olympic landmarks are within easy reach, and can be covered in a Peachtree Trolley tour.

World of Coca-Cola is home to the world's largest collection of Coke-themed memorabilia. Visitors see a production line in operation and sample from a range of 60 products. **Georgia Aquarium** is great for children and is one of the world's largest. Don't miss the Ocean Voyageur, which features manta rays and whale sharks.

A guided tour of **CNN Studio** takes visitors behind the scenes at the world's first 24-hour news station. The gift shop sells merchandise ranging from Atlanta Braves paraphernalia to films of major world events.

The **Martin Luther King, Jr. National Historic Site** is a moving tribute. Situated in a long reflecting pool beside an eternal flame, the crypt of the Nobel Peace Prize-winner is a pilgrimage site for people from all over the world. Nearby is the original Ebenezer Baptist Church, over which Martin Luther King, Jr., his father, and grandfather presided. The Martin Luther King, Birth Home and the National Park Service Visitor Center, which houses portraits and exhibits

that relate to the area's role in the Civil Rights Movement, are both down the street. It's also worth visiting the **National Center for Civil and Human Rights**. One of its permanent exhibits relays the life of Dr. Martin Luther King, Jr., using his personal effects. Other galleries focus on aspects of international human rights.

Margaret Mitchell (1900–1949) wrote *Gone with the Wind* in Atlanta, and literature lovers will enjoy a visit to the **Margaret Mitchell House and Museum**, which tells the story of the writer. Mementos from the famous film, such as Scarlett O'Hara's bonnet, are also on display. The **High**

Did You Know?

Margaret Mitchell wrote *Gone With the Wind* to occupy herself while recovering from an ankle injury.

present contrasting examples of rural and urban life.

Located on a hilltop site 2 miles (3 km) from downtown Atlanta, the **Jimmy Carter Library and Museum** highlights the humanitarian successes of President Carter's administration. A popular attraction is an exact replica of the Oval Office at the White House as used by President Carter from 1977 to 1981.

World of Coca-Cola
♿ 😊 🏠 121 Baker St
🕐 Times vary, check website
🌐 worldofcoca-cola.com

Georgia Aquarium
♿ 😊 🏠 225 Baker St, NW
🕐 Times vary, check website
🌐 georgiaaquarium.org

CNN Studio
♿ 🏠 Centennial Olympic Park Dr NW 🕐 9am-5pm daily 🌐 cnn.com/tour

Martin Luther King, Jr. National Historic Site
🏠 450 Auburn Av 🕐 9am-5pm daily 🌐 nps.gov/malu

National Center for Civil and Human Rights
♿ 🏠 100 Ivan Allen, Jr. Blvd, NW 🕐 10am-5pm Mon-Sat, noon-5pm Sun
🌐 civilandhumanrights.org

Margaret Mitchell House and Museum
♿ 🏠 979 Crescent Av, NE
🕐 10am-5:30pm Mon-Sat, noon-5:30pm Sun 🌐 atlantahistorycenter.com/mmh

High Museum of Art
♿ 🏠 1280 Peachtree St, NE
🕐 10am-5:30pm Tue-Sat (to 9pm Fri), noon-5pm Sun
🌐 high.org

Jimmy Carter Library and Museum
♿ 😊 🏠 441 Freedom Pkwy
🕐 9am-4:45pm Mon-Sat, noon-4:45pm Sun 🌐 jimmycarterlibrary.gov

Museum of Art lies in the city's arts district and is housed in a strikingly modern Richard Meier structure. Its extensive collection careens from regional folk art and 19th-century American art to 18th-century Asian ceramics and sub-Saharan artifacts. The center consists of a museum and two historic houses, which

Visitors studying tanks of fish at the Georgia Aquarium, Atlanta ↑

TENNESSEE AND KENTUCKY

American folk hero Daniel Boone began exploring these Appalachian states in 1767. Kentucky's American Indian tribes strenuously opposed the encroachment of European settlers but, in 1775, Boone nevertheless led settlers from Virginia through the Cumberland Gap on the Wilderness Road. Tennessee's first British settlement was built in 1756, followed by the 1779 establishment of Fort Nashborough – a forerunner to Nashville. Both became slave states, though Kentucky stayed in the Union during the Civil War. In 1960, the Nashville sit-ins played a crucial role during the Civil Rights movement, but Memphis gained notoriety for the assassination of Martin Luther King, Jr. at the Lorraine Motel in 1968.

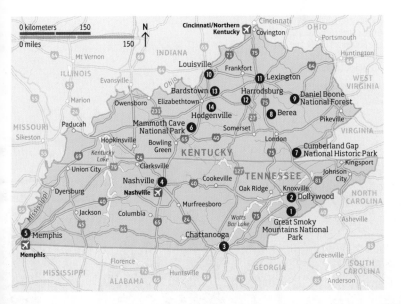

TENNESSEE

Tennessee is made up of three distinct regions. Memphis anchors the western lowlands; Nashville, the state capital, heads the central plateau; and the east is dominated by the Appalachian Mountains, with Knoxville as its urban base. Tennessee is known for its tremendous contribution to American roots music – from bluegrass, country, gospel, and blues, to rockabilly, rock 'n' roll, and soul – and its musical spirit lives on today.

❶
Great Smoky Mountains National Park

🕐 Times vary, check website 🚩 1420 Little River Road, Gatlinburg; www.nps.gov/grsm

The "Smokies," which earn their name from the smoke-like haze that clings to the ridge, hold some of the highest peaks in the eastern US and support a diversity of plant life. With more than 11 million visitors each year, this is the country's most visited national park. Established in 1934, half of it is in Tennessee and the other half in North Carolina. The Tennessee entrance is through Gatlinburg and Hwy 441, which bisects this sprawling park along the Newfound Gap Road and meets up with the Blue Ridge Parkway (p248) on the North Carolina side. Of the 800 miles (1,287 km) of trails, the most popular is the Appalachian Trail, which straddles the state border through the park. Trails to the park's many scenic waterfalls are also popular. The hike to Mount LeConte offers panoramic views, and hikers can stay overnight at LeConte lodge, which is only accessible by foot. The 6,643-ft (2,025-m) Clingman's Dome, Tennessee's highest peak, has an observation tower that offers fine views of the surrounding landscape. At the western end of the park, Cades Cove still preserves the historic farm buildings that were erected back in the 1820s. These include log cabins, barns, and a gristmill that's still in use. Cycling, horseback riding, fishing, and whitewater rafting are some of the popular activities available to adventurous tourists in this beautiful park and its surrounding region.

❷
Dollywood

🏠 2700 Dollywood Parks Blvd, Pigeon Forge 🕐 Times vary, check website 🌐 dollywood.com

Dollywood is the biggest ticketed tourist attraction in Tennessee, sprawling 50 percent bigger than Disneyland, and its many awards indicate that it is not merely cashing in on Dolly Parton's celebrity. There are ten themed areas with typical theme-park thrills, including the world's fastest wooden roller coaster. An interactive museum houses Parton's awards, personal items, and of course her stage outfits. Entertainment plays a large part and there are several theatres, while nightly fireworks wrap up the activities.

💬 INSIDER TIP
Local Whiskey

Tennessee whiskey isn't only about big names like Jack Daniel's, as good as it is. Aficionados should also watch out for creative craft distillers, like Corsair (www.corsairdistillery.com).

❸ Chattanooga

🚗🚌 **ℹ** 215 Broad St; www.chattanoogafun.com

Located on the banks of the Tennessee River, Chattanooga is surrounded by several high landmasses – the plateaus of Lookout Mountain, Signal Mountain, and Missionary Ridge. Founded as a ferry landing by the Cherokee Chief John Ross in 1815, Chattanooga was later occupied by white settlers after the Cherokees were forced out from here along the tragic "Trail of Tears."*(p53)*. The railroad leading to Atlanta was a natural target for the Union Army during the Civil War, and several battles were fought on this terrain.

Downtown Chattanooga is today a revitalized center with many of the city's most popular attractions. These include the Chattanooga Regional History Museum, which covers local American Indian, Civil War, and cultural history; the attractive Riverwalk promenade; and the pedestrian-only Walnut Street Bridge that spans the river to Coolidge Park and Carousel. At the **Tennessee**

← Hikers pausing to take in the scenery of Great Smoky Mountains National Park

Aquarium, visitors can trace a single drop of water from its origins in the Smoky Mountains through rivers, reservoirs, and deltas, and out into the Gulf of Mexico. Over 9,000 species of fish, amphibians, reptiles, mammals, and birds illustrate the state's varied habitats and ecosystems.

South of downtown, the Battles for Chattanooga Electric Map and Museum tells the story of local Civil War battles with 5,000 miniature soldiers and a series of tiny lights on large boards. At the foot of Lookout Mountain is the start point for the **Lookout Mountain Incline Railway**. The train climbs a gradient of 72.7 percent up the mountainside for panoramic views. It was built in the 1890s to bring tourists up to the hotels that were once located on top. The **Chickamauga and Chattanooga National Military Park** of Point Park is a three-block walk away. This site commemorates all the Confederate and Union soldiers who fought here during the 1863 Battle Above the Clouds. This battle took place after Union forces were able to reverse an earlier Confederate victory and planted the US flag on the top of Lookout Mountain.

At **Ruby Falls**, 3 miles (5 km) away, visitors descend by elevator to the floor of a cave, then walk past stalactites and stalagmites to the waterfall.

On the Georgia side of Lookout Mountain, Rock City Gardens has natural limestone rock formations beautified by the Enchanted Trail, with little gnomes peering out from the crevices.

Tennessee Aquarium
⊛ 🏠 1 Broad St 🕐 10am–6pm daily 🚫 Thanksgiving, Dec 25 🅦 tnaqua.org

↑ The dramatically lit Ruby Falls, near Chattanooga

Lookout Mountain Incline Railway
⊛ 🏠 827 E Brow Rd
🕐 8:30am–9:30pm daily
🅦 ridetheincline.com

Chickamauga and Chattanooga National Military Park
🏠 3370 LaFayette Rd, Fort Oglethorpe 🕐 Dawn–dusk daily 🅦 nps.gov/chch

Ruby Falls
⊛ 🏠 1720 South Scenic Hwy
🕐 8am–8pm daily
🅦 rubyfalls.com

EAT

Dolly Parton's Stampede
Visitors flock here for the show rather than the food, but the four-course menu won't disappoint.

🏠 3849 Pkwy, Pigeon Forge
🅦 dpstampede.com

$ $ $

---

❹

Nashville

▶🚌 ℹ Broadway at Fifth St; www.visitmusiccity.com

Best known today as the capital of country music, Nashville is a friendly and incredibly fun place to visit. Its musical history dates to 1927, when a radio broadcaster introduced a popular Barn Dance show as the "Grand Ole Opry." A musical legend was thus born and has flourished ever since. The city, however, has more to it than just music. It was founded as Fort Nashborough in 1779 and was named the state capital of Tennessee in 1843. It is also the financial center of the region and home to Vanderbilt University, one of the country's most prestigious institutions.

Most of Nashville's major attractions are within walking distance of each other, and plenty of restaurants, cafés, and nightclubs lie in the surrounding area, locally known as "the District."

Nashville's vibrant downtown area is anchored by the **Country Music Hall of Fame and Museum.** This site honors scores of such outstanding musicians as Patsy Cline, Merle Haggard, and Hank Williams in a huge rotunda. In keeping with its exhibits, the building itself was designed to resemble the black and white keys of a giant piano. Inside is a beloved collection of vintage guitars, costumes, cowboy boots, famous lyrics composed on bar napkins, and the celebrated golden Elvis Cadillac. A country music primer explains the academic distinctions between the subgenres of bluegrass, Cajun, honky-tonk, and rockabilly.

Known as the Mother Church of Country Music, the city's landmark **Ryman Auditorium** has hosted some of the biggest names in music history, including Elvis Presley, Patsy Cline and Johnny Cash. The live radio and TV show Grand Ole Opry was broadcast from here for 31 years, before moving to the new **Grand Ole Opry House** in 1974. Daytime tours are available, but the best way to see the 2,362-seat theater is by taking in a show. A few

Neon signs lighting up the streets of Nashville's busy downtown area ↑

blocks away, Bridgestone Arena and a number of nightclubs also feature all kinds of music. Learn all about the musicians who created the greatest recordings of all time at the **Musicians Hall of Fame at Nashville Municipal Auditorium**. Visitors can see guitars, drums, and other instruments played by stars such as Jimi Hendrix, as well as those played by lesser-known session musicians.

Although the main focus of the **Tennessee State Museum** is the Civil War, it also covers other aspects of the state's past, including local American

---

EAT

Prince's Hot Chicken Shack
Head here for an authentic taste of Nashville – though be warned, their spicy fried chicken is hot!

🏠 123 Ewing Dr #3
📞 (615) 226 9442 🕐 Sun

💲💲💲

Etch
Showing off the city's gourmet side, Etch has earned many awards for its exotic, international flavors.

🏠 303 Demonbreun St
🕐 Sun 🌐 etch restaurant.com

💲💲💲

→ A clapboard building within Nashville's Belle Meade Plantation

Indian history, early pioneer life, slavery, and the Civil Rights Movement. There is also a large collection of 19th-century decorative arts.

East of downtown Nashville, in a development called Music Valley, the 4,400-seat modern Grand Ole Opry House offers the "world's longest running radio show." A Who's Who of country music grace the stage of this legendary institution (live broadcast on 650 AM/ WSM), and visitors can take a backstage tour during the day. The complex also contains the fabulous Gaylord Opryland Resort and Convention Center, with its spectacular indoor gardens.

Southwest of downtown, **Belle Meade Plantation** is among the state's best-preserved antebellum estates. The Greek Revival mansion, built in the 1840s, was once the centerpiece of a vast plantation and has been restored to its former splendor. Costumed guides offer tours of the mansion and grounds. **Andrew Jackson's Hermitage** was the home of Tennessee's foremost political and military hero. After distinguishing himself as a military leader in the War of 1812, Jackson became the state's single Congressional representative. He was elected the seventh president of the United States in 1828 and re-elected in 1832.

Originally a series of American Indian trails, the **Natchez Trace Parkway**, which links Nashville with Natchez in Mississippi, is today a 450-mile (724-km) national historic parkway *(p353)*. Its northern terminus lies 15 miles (24 km) southwest of town. Here, the contour of the Trace is more rolling and deeply forested than farther down in Mississippi.

Country Music Hall of Fame and Museum
222 Fifth Av S · 9am-5pm daily · countrymusicandhalloffame.org

Ryman Auditorium
116 Fifth Av N · Tours: 9am-4pm · ryman.com

Musicians Hall of Fame at Nashville Municipal Auditorium
401 Gay St · 10am-5pm Mon-Sat · musicianshalloffame.com

INSIDER TIP
Goo Goo Clusters

Even if you don't have a sweet tooth, make an exception for Goo Goo Clusters - round candies with marshmallow, caramel, and peanuts, all coated in chocolate. They've been made in Nashville since 1912.

Tennessee State Museum
505 Deaderick St · 10am-5pm Tue-Sat (to 8pm Thu), 1-5pm Sun · tnmuseum.org

Grand Ole Opry House
2804 Opryland Dr · Times vary, check website · opry.com

Belle Meade Plantation
525 Harding Pike · 9am-5pm daily · bellemeadeplantation.com

Andrew Jackson's Hermitage
4580 Rachel's Lane · Times vary, check website · thehermitage.com

Natchez Trace Parkway
nps.gov

⑤

Memphis

🚆🏛️🚌 ℹ️ **3205 Elvis Presley Blvd; www.memphis travel.com**

Memphis sits on the banks of the Mississippi River, where it meets the states of Arkansas and Mississippi. The city is closely linked with two very different American icons – Civil Rights leader Dr. Martin Luther King, Jr., and Elvis Presley.

Since the early 20th century, Memphis has been synonymous with music. The city celebrates this legacy in its many nightclubs and saloons, and out on the streets. Even its festivals are mostly music-based. Highlights include Elvis's birthday on January 8; "Memphis in May," a month-long series of concerts and cookouts (the city is also famed for its barbecue); the W.C. Handy Heritage Awards, the blues' answer to the Grammys; and the Music and Heritage Festival on Labor Day weekend.

Beale Street is a thriving commercial center famed for its music connections. Beale Street's heyday was in the first half of the 20th century. After a period of decline, the street was resurrected as the heart of a vibrant entertainment district, rivaling New Orleans' Bourbon Street *(p338)* in popularity. Close by, W.C. Handy's Home, a tiny white shotgun shack, is now a museum to the man often called the "Father of the Blues." At the center of the strip stands the A. Schwab's Dry Goods Store at 163 Beale, which dates from 1876. Many nights Beale Street is closed to traffic, and people come to listen to live music emanating from every door. A short walk from Beale Street, AutoZone Park is the red-and-green stadium of the Memphis Redbirds baseball franchise. It lies across from the landmark Peabody Hotel, where famous ducks march twice a day to and from the lobby fountain.

The **National Civil Rights Museum** was once the Lorraine Motel, where Dr. Martin Luther King, Jr. was tragically assassinated on April 4, 1968. Room 306 is preserved as it was on the day of his killing. Across the street, the assassination scene is re-created in the bathroom from which James Earl Ray apparently fired his fatal shot.

The intersection between history and race, and its expression in song, is explained with outstanding musical accompaniment at the **Memphis Rock-N-Soul Museum**. The exhibit is sponsored by the Smithsonian Institution and examines the blues and country roots of rock 'n' roll through displays, a movie, and audio tour. If you love music, you'll also enjoy the Blues Hall of Fame and the Memphis Music Hall of Fame.

Mud Island is home to the Mississippi River Museum, which tells the story of the

---

EAT

Corky's BBQ

There are now branches of Corky's throughout the South, but this is the original. Whether you order BBQ or ribs, you'll leave licking your fingers.

🏠 **5259 Poplar Av**
🌐 **corkysbbq.com**

Ⓢ Ⓢ ⓢ

A display at the National Civil Rights Museum, housed in the former Lorraine Motel

river through artifacts such as an 1870 steamboat replica. The museum also has many American Indian exhibits and galleries on the origins of the blues. The most engaging exhibit, however, is located outside, where water courses through a huge replica of the Mississippi, ending at a swimming pool shaped like the Gulf of Mexico.

A touchstone for all that is authentically Southern, the **Center for Southern Folklore** offers a folk art gallery and a stage for shows, with plenty of blues, soul, folk, rock, and gospel thrown in. It also sponsors the acclaimed Music and Heritage Festival.

Famous musicians from all over the world come to record in the legendary **Sun Studio** that launched the careers of Elvis, B.B. King, Johnny Cash, Jerry Lee Lewis, and many more. Founded in 1954 by Sam Philips, the studio's exhibits include Elvis's original drum set and microphone. Souvenirs are on sale, and visitors can make their own keepsake recordings.

Graceland attracts more than 700,000 visitors each year to the estate that Elvis Presley bought as a 22-year-old superstar and called home until his death in 1977. Starting at the grand visitor complex, guests are taken up to the house to view the front rooms and Memorial Gardens, where Elvis is buried. Across the road,

there are additional charges to see Elvis's car collection, his two airplanes, and the "Elvis Presley's Memphis" exhibition.

The Reverend Al Green left a successful recording career in the 1970s (his hits included "Let's Stay Together") to pursue his calling. He often presides over Sunday services at the **Full Gospel Tabernacle Church** in Southside Memphis. Do show respect by dressing appropriately, donating a little, and staying for the entire service.

National Civil Rights Museum

⊕ 🏛 450 Mulberry St
🕐 9am–6pm Wed–Mon
🌐 civilrightsmuseum.org

Memphis Rock-N-Soul Museum

⊕ 🏛 191 Beale St
🕐 9:30am–7pm daily
🌐 memphisrocknsoul.org

Mud Island

⊕ 🏛 125 N Front St
🕐 Dawn–dusk daily
🌐 mudisland.com

Center for Southern Folklore

⊕ ⊕ ☺ 🎨 🏛 119 S Main St 🕐 Times vary, check website 🌐 southern folklore.com

Sun Studio

⊕ 🏛 706 Union Av
🕐 10am–6pm daily
🌐 sunstudio.com

Graceland

⊕ 🏛 3734 Elvis Presley Blvd
🕐 9am–5pm Mon–Sat, 10am–4pm Sun 🚫 Dec–Feb: Tue
🌐 graceland.com

Full Gospel Tabernacle Church

⊕ 🏛 787 Hale Rd
📞 (901) 396-8040

HEART OF SOUL

Memphis is associated so much with blues and rock 'n' roll that its soul music heritage gets overlooked. The Stax Records building where artists such as Otis Redding *(right)* and Rufus Thomas recorded, with the house band of Booker T. & the MGs, has been torn down, but the Stax Museum was built on the same spot and includes a replica of the original recording studio.

←

The skyline of downtown Memphis, lit up as the evening draws in

←

A man wandering through the dramatic passages of Mammoth Cave National Park

KENTUCKY

With its Appalachian Mountain landscapes and rolling rural pasturelands, Kentucky is easily one of the most picturesque states in the country. Kentucky is widely known for its horses, its downhome style of country music, and the state's famous spirit: Kentucky Bourbon. Budding connoisseurs should follow the Kentucky Bourbon Trail.

6

Mammoth Cave National Park

🚗 I-65 exit 53 🕐 Mar-mid-Aug: 8am-6:30pm daily; mid-Aug-Oct: 8am-6pm; Nov-Feb: 8:30am-4:30pm 🌐 nps.gov/maca

Halfway between Louisville (p274) and Nashville (p268), Mammoth Cave National Park offers guided tours of one of the world's largest known cave systems, formed by underground rivers that left a dramatic and eerie landscape of stalactites and stalagmites. Guests can choose from tours such as "Frozen Niagara" or "Wild Cave Tour" (helmets provided). Evidence suggests that the cave had been inhabited as far back as 4,000 years ago. The Green River runs its course above Mammoth Cave, an area that is criss-crossed by several hiking trails.

7

Cumberland Gap National Historic Park

🚗 91 Bartlett Park Rd, Middlesboro 🕐 Times vary, check website 🌐 nps.gov/cuga

Situated in the southeastern corner where Kentucky meets the states of Virginia and Tennessee, the Cumberland Gap is a natural pass through the Cumberland Mountains, once used by migrating deer and bison. It was first explored by Dr. Thomas Walker in 1750 on behalf of a land company. Five years later, frontiersman Daniel Boone ran his Wilderness Road through the Gap, thus opening the way for some 200,000 pioneers to establish homesteads in the interior wilderness.

This rugged area is thickly forested, and many sights, such as the Sand Cave

sandstone overhang, are accessible only by hiking trails. The forests shelter wild turkeys, white-tailed deer, and many varieties of songbirds.

The Gap was also a strategic location in the Civil War. It was held alternately by Confederate and Union forces, and fortifications can still be seen throughout the park. Today, a four-lane Interstate Highway and a railroad tunnel run through the Gap. A drive up to Pinnacle Overlook leads to a trail for a view of three states.

8

Berea

ℹ 3 Artist Circle; www.berea.com

Home to Berea College, which is dedicated to educating disadvantaged Appalachian youth, Berea is known as a highlands crafts center. Typical

---

COUNTRY AND BLUEGRASS MUSIC

The stretch of eastern Kentucky (along with West Virginia) is home to the greatest proportion of country music artists in America. British, Irish, and Scottish immigrants brought Elizabethan ballads, rhythms, and instruments to the area, which they then forged into a distinctly American style known as "country." Kentucky's vast bluegrass pasturelands defined one type of country music known as "bluegrass." This acoustic folk style evolved in the late 1940s and remains popular in the region today.

crafts include woodworking, pottery, and textiles. The town hosts the Kentucky Guild of Artists Fair, as well as the Berea Craft Festival. Public tours of artisans' studios – such as **Weaver's Bottom**, founded in 1989 – are available.

Weaver's Bottom
140 N Broadway (859) 986-8661 9am-5pm Mon-Sat Federal hols

9 Daniel Boone National Forest

1700 Bypass Rd, Winchester fs.usda.gov/dbnf

Named after the illustrious pioneer and frontiersman Daniel Boone, who lived in Kentucky, this National Forest protects some of the most dramatic scenery in the state. The dense forest provides shelter to more than 35 endangered species, including red-cockaded woodpeckers, big-eared bats, and bald eagles. The Sheltowee Trace National Recreation Trail runs across the entire length of the forest, from Morehead in the north to Pickett State Rustic Park in Tennessee. Also near Morehead, Cave Run Lake is a popular venue for boating, while the Zilpo Road National Scenic Byway offers a good chance to see the forest's rich variety of wildlife on a short drive. The central area east of Stanton features the Natural Bridge State Resort Park, a naturally occuring archway, and the picturesque Red River Gorge. Great hiking, canoeing, and white-water rafting opportunities can be found at both the park and gorge.

Visitors to the southern portion of the park might want to detour to Corbin, off I-75. The city is notable as the original home of Kentucky Fried Chicken, where Colonel Harland Sanders first served the special recipe that went on to become a global franchise. The kitchen where the famous spices were first put together is on display, along with KFC artifacts.

At the southern end, **Cumberland Falls State Resort Park** offers lodging, camping, and swimming.

Cumberland Falls State Resort Park
7351 Hwy 90, Corbin Daily parks.ky.gov

DRINK

The Garage Bar
This converted gas station is now a cool bar with a huge outdoor patio. There's a wide selection of craft beers and, of course, bourbon. If you're peckish, the pizzas are excellent.

700 E Market St, Louisville garageonmarket.com

Daniel Boone National Forest, home to a large population of woodpeckers *(inset)*

10
Louisville

 301 S Fourth St;
www.gotolouisville.com

Founded in 1788, Louisville is home to one of the world's most famous horse races, the Kentucky Derby. Since it began in 1875, three-year-old horses have run the track at Churchill Downs on the first Saturday in May, with the high society of Kentucky turning out to watch. The adjacent **Kentucky Derby Museum** showcases horse-racing history and offers tours through the track. A couple of blocks from the waterfront district, the **Louisville Slugger Museum** produces the world-class baseball bat in a factory marked by a towering bat.

The **Speed Art Museum** has a large collection of Renaissance paintings and sculpture. At the Riverfront Plaza on the banks of the Ohio River at Main and Fourth streets, the oldest operating river steamboat in the US tours the area. The surrounding historic district's old warehouses now house cafes, restaurants, galleries, and distilleries.

The **Muhammad Ali Center** sits in the city's West Main District. It is dedicated to the life and legacy of Louisville-born Ali (1942–2016), and exhibits introduce his life through six values: confidence,

The Louisville
Slugger Museum,
marked by a bat

INSIDER TIP
Hot Browns

Try this open toasted sandwich, which was created in Louisville's Brown Hotel in 1926. It's a great breakfast pick-me-up and hangover cure with turkey, bacon, and a Mornay sauce.

---

conviction, dedication, giving, respect, and spirituality.

Kentucky Derby Museum
704 Central Av
9am–5pm Mon–Sat (mid-Mar–Nov: from 8am), 11am–5pm Sun First Fri & Sat in May, Thanksgiving, Dec 24 & 25 derbymuseum.org

Louisville Slugger Museum
800 W Main St 9am–5pm Mon–Sat, 11am–5pm Sun (extended hours in summer) sluggermuseum.com

Speed Art Museum
2035 S Third St
10am–5pm Wed–Sat (to 8pm Fri), noon–5pm Sun speedmuseum.org

Muhammad Ali Center
144 N Sixth St
9:30am–5pm Tue–Sat (from noon Sun) alicenter.org

11
Lexington

215 W Main St;
www.visitlex.com

Kentucky's second-largest city, Lexington is also the unofficial capital of the state's horse country. The countryside is lined with thoroughbred stud farms, where many Kentucky Derby winners are bred, reared, and trained. Most farms are open to visitors. Just north of

Horses in a field at the Shaker Village of Pleasant Hill, near Harrodsburg

town lies the **Kentucky Horse Park**, a state-operated working farm that serves as an equestrian theme park, with live shows, and pony and trail rides. The park's International Museum of the Horse honors the role of the horse in the development of human history. The adjacent American Saddlebred Museum focuses on America's first registered horse breed. In town, the 1803 Mary Todd Lincoln House preserves the girlhood home of Abraham Lincoln's wife.

Kentucky Horse Park
4089 Iron Works Pkwy
Apr–Oct: 9am–5pm daily; Nov–Mar: 9am–5pm Wed–Sun Jan 1, Thanksg., Dec 24, 25 & 31 kyhorsepark.com

---

12
Harrodsburg

488 Price Av;
www.harrodsburgky.com

Many New England Shaker families relocated in and around Harrodsburg in 1805

and established a farming community renowned for its handicrafts. It grew to a population of around 500 in 1830 and then, in part due to the Shaker belief in celibacy, it grew less cohesive and became scattered by 1910. The area's chief attraction is the **Shaker Village of Pleasant Hill**, America's largest and most completely restored Shaker community and living-history museum. The site reflects the spare style that typifies Shaker values. Artisans demonstrate crafts such as woodworking.

Shaker Village of Pleasant Hill

⊘ ⌂ 3501 Lexington Rd
🕐 10am–5pm Mon–Thu & Sun, 10am–8pm Fri & Sat 🗓 Dec 24 & 25 🌐 shakervillageky.org

---

⑬

Bardstown

🛈 1 Court Square; www. visitbardstown.com

Bardstown is surrounded by the state's largest whiskey distilleries, which have earned Kentucky its reputation as the whiskey-making center of the US. Close to Bardstown is both the area's most popular distillery, Jim Beam, and the famed Maker's Mark site, which was the first distillery in the US to be placed on the National Register of Historic Places. However, Bardstown's most popular attraction is **My Old Kentucky Home State Park**. Guides lead visitors through the historic mansion that allegedly inspired composer Stephen Foster to write the state's beloved anthem.

My Old Kentucky Home State Park

⊘ ⌂ 107 E Stephen Foster Av 🕐 9am–5pm daily
🗓 Jan–mid-Mar: Mon & Tue; Jan 1, Thanksgiving, Dec 24, 25 & 31 🌐 parks.ky.gov

---

⑭

Hodgenville

🛈 60 Lincoln Square; (270) 358-3411

Hodgenville is the base for the **Abraham Lincoln Birthplace National Historic Site**, located 3 miles (5 km) to its south. The site commemorates the 16th US president's Kentucky roots by preserving his childhood home. Here, 56 steps representing the years of Lincoln's life lead up to a granite-and-marble Memorial Building built around a 19th-century log cabin, where the president was born in 1809. The site also encompasses a large portion of the original Lincoln family farmland.

Abraham Lincoln Birthplace National Historic Site

⌂ 2995 Lincoln Farm Rd
🕐 9am–5pm daily 🗓 Jan 1, Thanksgiving, Dec 25
🌐 nps.gov/abli

Did You Know?

95 percent of the world's Bourbon is made in Kentucky.

FLORIDA

Sunrise in Downtown Miami

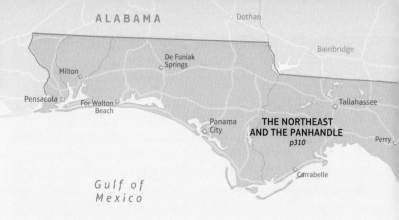

THE NORTHEAST AND THE PANHANDLE
p310

EXPLORE
FLORIDA

This chapter divides Florida into four
sightseeing areas, as shown on the map
above. Find out more about each area
on the following pages.

NORTH AMERICA

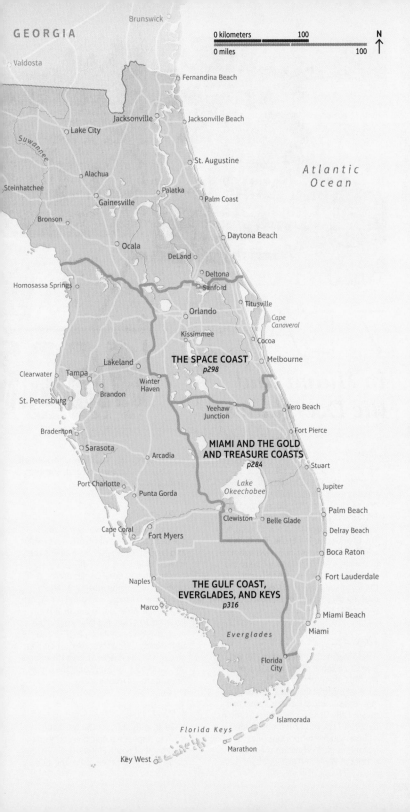

GEORGIA

Brunswick

0 kilometers   100
0 miles   100

N

Valdosta

Fernandina Beach

Suwannee

Jacksonville

Lake City

Jacksonville Beach

St. Augustine

Atlantic
Ocean

Alachua

Steinhatchee

Palatka

Gainesville

Palm Coast

Bronson

Ocala

Daytona Beach

DeLand

Homosassa Springs

Deltona

Sanford

Titusville

Orlando

*Cape
Canaveral*

Kissimmee

Cocoa

Lakeland

THE SPACE COAST
p298

Melbourne

Clearwater

Tampa

Winter
Haven

Brandon

St. Petersburg

Yeehaw
Junction

Vero Beach

Bradenton

Fort Pierce

Sarasota

Arcadia

MIAMI AND THE GOLD
AND TREASURE COASTS
p284

Stuart

Port Charlotte

*Lake
Okeechobee*

Jupiter

Punta Gorda

Palm Beach

Cape Coral

Clewiston

Belle Glade

Delray Beach

Fort Myers

Boca Raton

Naples

THE GULF COAST,
EVERGLADES, AND KEYS
p316

Fort Lauderdale

Marco

Miami Beach

Everglades

Miami

Florida
City

Islamorada

Florida Keys

Marathon

Key West

7 DAYS

in Miami and the Everglades

Day 1

Arriving in Miami, take a leisurely day to ease into the Floridian lifestyle. Spend the day exploring South Beach *(p286)*, first of all with a stroll along Ocean Drive. Start at the Art Deco Welcome Center and walk around, taking in the architecture – The Breakwater, The Leslie, The Carlyle, and The Cavalier are all perfect examples of the city's Art Deco legacy. Spend the afternoon on the beach itself, watching the surfers around 5th Street, before an evening cocktail and bite to eat along the waterfront on Ocean Drive.

Day 2

A morning in Little Havana *(p290)* will give you a sense of the influence of Miami's Cuban community. The streets are always full of life, and operate to an ambient soundtrack of salsa and Latin music. Calle Ocho is the liveliest stretch, between 11th and 17th avenues. After a Cuban sandwich from Versailles restaurant *(p293)*, head to the artistic district of Wynwood *(p292)*, where there's

vibrant street art, 70 galleries, an open-air art museum and a wealth of dining and nightlife options.

Day 3

A short drive from Downtown Miami, the neighborhoods of Coral Gables *(p290)* and Coconut Grove *(p292)* are among the region's oldest and most affluent communities. A Coral Gables driving tour takes in the striking Alhambra Water Tower, The Biltmore Hotel, and the French City Village. After lunch, stop in at the Lowe Art Museum and take a dip in the evocative Venetian Pool *(p292)*. Or head to the lively CocoWalk outdoor shopping center, and the nearby Vizcaya Museum and Gardens *(p293)*, arguably the city's finest historical residence.

Day 4

Make an early start for the two-hour drive to Naples, a scenic beach city on the west coast of South Florida, buying a packed lunch to eat en route. The journey

1 Ocean Drive, Miami.

2 Playing volleyball on a beach in Naples.

3 The Biltmore Hotel, Coral Gables.

4 Wynwood Kitchen and Bar, Wynwood Arts District.

5 Kayaking in a mangrove forest in Everglades National Park.

there can be leisurely, spending the morning exploring the Big Cypress Swamp (p320). Arrive in Naples for a late afternoon on its white, sandy beaches and head for a seafood dinner and cocktails at the Tommy Bahama restaurant (p307).

Day 5

Follow Route 41 southeast from Naples to Homestead, where you'll find the main entrance to the Everglades National Park (p320) and the Ernest F. Coe Visitor Center – a great place for orientation about the park. Less than an hour from here by car is Flamingo, an outpost of the park. The late afternoon is the perfect time to rent a kayak and explore the mangrove waterways here. Flamingo has a well-equipped camp ground if you fancy sleeping beneath the stars.

Day 6

Drive to the Shark Valley Visitor Center, considered to be the true heartland of the Everglades. There's a 15-mile (24-km) loop that takes in some of the best views of the park. You can hop on a tram at the Visitor Center, or rent a bike and follow the trail yourself. After a hearty lunch at Miccosukee Restaurant (www.gladeseats.miccosukee. com), the Visitor Center can point you in the direction of a local airboat tour company, which will take you into the parts of the park that can't be reached by foot or car. Spend the night back in Homestead.

Day 7

It's just a short drive to Key Biscayne (p295) and the Biscayne National Park, one of the most scenic coastal parks in the region. Coral reefs, islands, and mangrove forests characterize the area, and at the Biscayne National Park Institute, you can reserve a guided tour of the park's natural wonders. In the afternoon, try your hand at fishing as a crew takes you out into the park's sustainable fishery resources, where you'll likely see dolphins and turtles. Downtown Miami (p291) is just an hour away for a final night of live salsa music at Mango's Tropical Café (www.mangos.com).

Hike the Trails

Woodlands and forests cover a large proportion of Florida's landscape, so it's little wonder that hiking is such a popular activity. The state has 5,000 miles (8,000 km) of hiking trails, with something for all abilities. For stunning scenery, Big Cypress Swamp (p320) has rugged beauty, while the Disney Wilderness Preserve (p307) is a calm contrast to the hubbub of Walt Disney World Resort.

←

Walking through Big Cypress National Preserve on a hot day

FLORIDA
OUTDOORS

The state's warm climate means that most of Floridian life is led outdoors. Days lounging at the beach are hugely popular, but there are plenty of opportunities to be more active, with water sports aplenty. For inland activities, you can discover world-class golf courses or scenic hiking trails.

Wet and Wild

Florida's abundant coastline and inland waterways mean that there's plenty of opportunities for swimming and deep-sea fun. Scuba divers and snorkelers can explore clear waters and shipwrecks in Key West (p321), with Key Largo having some of the best dive sites in the US.

→

Diver exploring the incredible Benwood Wreck site at Key Largo

INSIDER TIP
Take a Hike

If you're big on outdoor sports and activities, the best time of year to visit Florida is from January through March, when the weather is not too hot or cold.

Set Sail

Most coastal cities and towns around Florida have boat trips on offer, and you can enjoy everything from dolphin watching to relaxing on luxury yachts. Pensacola *(p314)* is one of the state's main sailing centers, and Fort Lauderdale *(p296)* is chock-full of enviable yachts.

→

Enjoying the beautiful sunset from a sailboat in the Gulf of Mexico

A Golfer's Paradise

Florida has more golf courses than any other US state, and the climate makes it a joy to play at any time of year. Many clubs are open to the public and some have wonderful coastal views. Check out TPC Sawgrass *(www. tpc.com)* and World Woods *(www.worldwoods.com)*.

←

A golfer playing on a sunny day

Fishing Fever

Florida is a hot spot for fishing fans from all over the world, offering everything from high-adrenaline fishing out on the ocean, to more tranquil days spent off a pier or jetty. Key West *(p321)* and Key Largo are great for tarpon, and utterly incredible deep-sea fishing awaits off Cocoa Beach *(p300)*.

→

Deep-sea fishing off Key West

MIAMI AND THE GOLD AND TREASURE COASTS

After colonization, the native Tequesta, Jaega, and Ais peoples gradually died out from disease. The state was under Spanish rule until the 19th century, when it was viewed as a wile frontier. Much of Downtown Miami began life as a citrus farm, but the railroad completion in 1896 cleared the way for the 1920s property boom; Fort Lauderdale became "the Venice of America" and Palm Beach was a stomping ground for the wealthy. During the 1950s, celebrities flocked to Miami Beach while Cuban exiles began arriving, creating the basis for today's dynamic Latin American city.

Experience

1 Miami
2 Fort Lauderdale
3 Boca Raton
4 Palm Beach
5 Arthur R. Marshall Loxahatchee National Wildlife Refuge

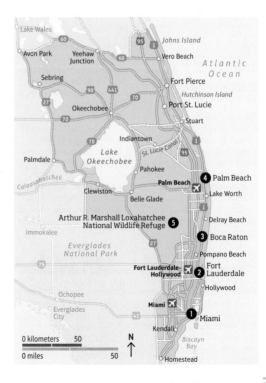

❶

MIAMI

With its world-class beaches, pastel-colored Art Deco architecture, and pulsating nightlife, Miami has come a long way from the small trading post it was over a century ago to become Florida's most glamorous city. There's also a robust cultural scene, with Little Havana adding a vibrant Cuban influence, and up-and-coming neighborhoods like Wynwood keep the city moving.

①
South Beach

🚌 ℹ️ 1001 Ocean Dr; (305) 763-8026

This trendy district, also known as SoBe, extends from 6th to 23rd streets between Lenox Avenue and Ocean Drive. A hedonistic playground enlivened by local fashionistas, bodybuilders, and drag queens, SoBe is also home to the largest concentration of well-preserved Art Deco buildings in the world.

The 800-odd buildings along Ocean Drive were once modest hotels constructed in the 1930s by architects such as Henry Hohauser and L. Murray Dixon, who famously used inexpensive materials to create the impression of stylishness. The present use of bright colors, known as Deco Dazzle, was introduced in the 1980s by

designer Leonard Horowitz. Collins and Washington avenues, too, have their fair share of Art Deco buildings, such as the classic Marlin Hotel at 1200 Collins Avenue, one of the finest representations of Streamline Moderne. Farther north is the luxury Delano Hotel, with its striking non-Deco interior of billowing white drapes, cabanas, and sunbeds around the pool. Other buildings of interest are the 1920s Mediterranean Revival Old City Hall and the austere

Did You Know?

Miami is the only US city founded by a woman: local entrepreneur Julia Tuttle, the "Mother of Miami."

Miami Beach Post Office on Washington Avenue. Inside is a mural showing the arrival of Juan Ponce de León, the Spanish conquistador who arrived in Florida in 1513. Also on Washington Avenue is the Wolfsonian Museum–FIU, built in the 1920s, housing a collection of fine and decorative arts from the period 1885–1945, focusing on the aesthetic, political, and social significance of design around the turn of the 20th century. Built in 1936, Miami Beach's first synagogue reopened in 1995 as the Jewish Museum of Florida. Colorful stained-glass windows and other Art Deco features make it almost as memorable as the exhibitions that are staged here.

Between Washington and Drexel avenues is Española Way, a small, pretty enclave of Mediterranean Revival buildings, where ornate arches, capitals, and balconies adorn salmon-colored, stuccoed frontages. Built from 1922–25, this street is said to be the inspiration for Addison Mizner's Worth Avenue in Palm Beach (p297). Offbeat art galleries and boutiques line this leafy street, and on weekends craft booths are set up here.

The pedestrian Lincoln Road Mall is one of Miami's cultural corners and is dominated by

Buzzing Miami's Ocean Drive in South Beach, glowing at dusk

the ArtCenter South Florida. The galleries here are usually open in the evenings, when the mall comes alive as theatergoers frequent the restored Art Deco Colony Theatre. After a heavy dose of modern art, the stylish restaurants and cafés, such as Books & Books (No. 927), just across from the ArtCenter, offer respite.

The Beach evolved into a spectacular winter playground after the bridge connecting the island with the mainland was built in 1913, and the vast stretches of imported sand are still impressive. Surfers predominate up to 5th Street; beyond is an extension of SoBe's lively persona, with colorful lifeguard huts and posing bathers.

The stretch north of 23rd Street, known as Central Miami Beach, is home to the eye-catching Fontainebleau Hotel (pronounced "Fountainblue"), an interpretation of a French château, whose grandeur made it the ideal setting for the 1960s James Bond movie classic *Goldfinger*.

---

②

Bass Museum of Art

🏠 2100 Collins Av
🚌 🕙 10am–5pm Wed–Sun
🚫 Federal hols 🌐 thebass.org

This Mayan-influenced 1930s Deco building has an excellent collection of European paintings, sculptures, and textiles donated in 1964 by the philanthropists John and Johanna Bass. The collection, dating from the 15th to the 18th centuries, includes Renaissance pieces, paintings from the northern European schools, including works by Rubens and Bol, and huge 16th-century Flemish tapestries.

EAT

Stiltsville Fish Bar
Specializes in local fish and cocktails inspired by Hemingway's Key West lifestyle.

🏠 1787 Purdy Av
🌐 stiltsvillefishbar.com

$$$

Joe's Stone Crab
Try the local stone crab claws at this legendary SoBe institution, open since 1913.

🏠 11 Washington Av
🕙 Oct–May
🌐 joesstonecrab.com

$$$

③ Maurice A. Ferré Park

🅰 Biscayne Blvd
Ⓜ Museum Park 🚌

This large park has a water-front baywalk and promenade from Biscayne Boulevard to Biscayne Bay, giving access to the **Pérez Art Museum Miami** and the **Patricia and Phillip Frost Museum of Science**. The Pérez museum's collection consists of 20th-century and contemporary international art, with an emphasis on the art of the Americas.

The Frost Museum of Science opened in the summer of 2016, and the white globe of its planetarium is a landmark on the Miami skyline.

Pérez Art Museum Miami

🔵🔵🔵🔵 🅰 1103 Biscayne Blvd 🕐 10am–6pm Mon, Tue, Thu–Sun (to 9pm Thu)
🔗 pamm.org

Patricia and Phillip Frost Museum of Science

🔵🔵🔵🔵 🅰 3280 S Miami Av 🕐 9:30am–6pm daily (Jun–Aug: to 7:30pm Sat & Sun)
🔗 frostscience.org

④ Biscayne Bay Boat Trips

🅰 Bayside Marketplace
Ⓜ College/Bayside 🚌

A leisurely way to view the sprinkling of exclusive private island communities around Biscayne Bay is to take one of the many cruises embarking from Bayside Marketplace. Tours, such as "Millionaire's Row" run by **Island Queen Cruises**, leave regularly throughout the day and last about 90 minutes.

MIAMI'S DECO STYLE

Across the water from Maurice A. Ferré Park is Ocean Drive, which illustrates Miami's unique interpretation of the Art Deco style, popular across the world in the 1920s and 1930s. Florida's version, often called Tropical Deco, uses motifs such as flamingos, sunbursts, and jaunty nautical features, appropriate to South Beach's seaside location. Three main styles exist: traditional Art Deco, futuristic Streamline Moderne, and Mediterranean Revival, inspired by European architecture. A spirited preservation campaign, led by author and activist Barbara Capitman in the 1970s, made this area the first 20th-century district to be added to the country's National Register of Historic Places.

The corners of the building are beautifully rounded.

The terrazzo floor in the bar is a mix of stone chips and mortar – an inexpensive marble that brought style at minimal cost.

Cardozo (1939)
A late Henry Hohauser work, this Streamline gem replaces traditional Art Deco details with curved sides and aerodynamic racing stripes.

← Awe-inspiring marine life at the Frost Museum of Science in Maurice A. Ferré Park

Tours begin by sailing past Dodge and Lummus islands, where the world's busiest cruise port is situated. This port, which contributes an annual income of more than $5 billion to the local economy, impressively handles more than 3 million cruise passengers a year.

Near the eastern end of MacArthur Causeway is the US Coastguard's fleet of high-speed craft. Opposite lies the unbridged Fisher Island, separated from South Beach by Government Cut, a water channel dredged in 1905. Named after Carl Fisher, the developer of Miami Beach, the island is an exclusive residential enclave and resort with prices beginning at around $4 million. The tour then heads north around the man-made Star, Palm, and Hibiscus islands, where real estate lots were sometimes sold "by the gallon." Among the lavish mansions are the former homes of singer Frank Sinatra and gangster Al Capone, as well as more recent residents such as Oprah Winfrey.

Other boat trips include nighttime cruises, deep-sea fishing excursions, and a tall-ship cruise. **Duck Tours** take place on a state-of-the-art "Hydra-Terra" amphibious bus that departs several times a day from South Beach, from the corner of Lincoln Road and James Avenue. The tour takes in points of interest in South Beach and heads into Miami before "splashing" into Biscayne Bay for a closer look at the homes of the rich and famous on Star Island. Bayside Marketplace is a fun complex with several shops, bars, and restaurants, including the Hard Rock Café. Nearby, at Bayfront Park is the Torch of Friendship, commemorating President John F. Kennedy. A plaque from the city's Cuban exiles thanks the US for allowing them to settle here.

Island Queen Cruises
⌖ ⌂401 Biscayne Blvd; www.islandqueencruises.com

Duck Tours
⌖ ⌂1661 James Av; www.ducktourssouthbeach.com

→ The haunting four-story-high sculpture at the center of the Holocaust Memorial

⑤
Holocaust Memorial

⌂1933–45 Meridian Av
🚌 ⏰9:30am–dusk daily
🌐holocaustmemorial miamibeach.org

Miami Beach has one of the largest populations of Holocaust survivors in the world. The centerpiece of Kenneth Treister's memorial, unveiled in 1990, is a colossal bronze arm and hand stretching skyward, representing the final grasp of a dying person. It is stamped with a number from Auschwitz and covered with life-size statues of people in the throes of grief. Titled *A Sculpture of Love and Anguish*, this is one of the most powerful contemporary sculptures in Florida. Around the central plaza is a tunnel lined with the names of Europe's concentration camps, a graphic history of the Holocaust, and a granite wall inscribed with the names of thousands of victims who perished.

Terra-cotta roof tiles.

A veranda is a prerequisite for most Ocean Drive hotels.

A flamingo is etched into the glass doors in the Beacon's lobby.

Adrian (1934)
Its Mediterranean tones and subdued colors make for a striking building.

Beacon (1936)
Horowitz's Deco Dazzle brightens the abstract flourishes above the first-floor windows.

⑥ 🚶

Miami-Dade Cultural Plaza

📍 **101 West Flagler St**
Ⓜ **Government Center** 🚌

Designed by the celebrated American architect Philip Johnson in 1982, the Miami-Dade Cultural Plaza is a large complex, with a Mediterranean-style courtyard and fountains. It includes a museum and a library. The **HistoryMiami Museum** concentrates on pre-1945 Miami. Besides displays on the Spanish colonization and Seminole culture, there is a fascinating collection of old photographs bringing Miami's early history to life.

History Miami Museum

🚶♿ 📍 **101 West Flagler St**
🕙 **10am–5pm Tue–Sat, noon–5pm Sun** ♻️ **Federal hols**
🌐 **historymiami.org**

___

⑦ 🚶

Coral Gables

Ⓜ **Douglas Rd** 🚌
ℹ️ **coralgables.com**

Aptly named the City Beautiful, this is a separate city within

> ### MIAMI SPORTS
>
> Floridians love their home sports teams. The Miami Dolphins play out of the Hard Rock Stadium in the NFL (AFC East Division) and have enjoyed much success over the years. The Miami Heat, who play at the American Airlines Arena, are considered one of basketball's more exciting teams, and have won three NBA championships. The Miami Marlins have won the World Series of Baseball twice and play out of Marlins Park, in Little Havana.

↑ American Indian sculpture in the Lowe Art Museum

Greater Miami. Regulations ensure that new buildings in Coral Gables follow the same part-Italian, part-Spanish style adopted in the 1920s. Major landmarks here include the Spanish Baroque Coral Gables Congregational Church, the Spanish Renaissance Coral Gables City Hall, and the **Lowe Art Museum**, the first in South Florida, located on campus at the University of Miami.

Its main shopping street was named Miracle Mile in 1940. Nearby, at Salzedo Street and Aragon Avenue, is the Old Police and Fire Station. This 1939 building houses part of the Coral Gables Museum, which offers a wide variety of exhibitions about the area. Along with the main building, the museum complex includes beautiful outdoor spaces.

Lowe Art Museum

🚶♿ 📍 **1301 Stanford Dr**
Ⓜ **University** 🚌🕙 **10am–4pm Tue–Sat, noon–4pm Sun** ♻️ **Federal hols**
🌐 **lowe.miami.edu**

___

⑧

Little Havana

Ⓜ **Brickell, then bus** 🚌

As its name suggests, the small area comprising Little Havana has been a surrogate home for Cuban immigrants since the 1960s. The atmosphere here is vibrant, reflecting the Cuban way of life. Spanish is spoken everywhere, while a salsa beat emanates from every other shop, and *bodegas* (canteens) sell Cuban specialties. The area's beating heart is Calle Ocho (Southwest 8th Street), with its liveliest stretch between 11th and 17th avenues. Here, the highly respected **El Titan de Bronze** stocks traditional handcrafted Cuban cigars. The Cubaocho Museum and Performing Arts Center, also on 8th Street, is a colorful bar and community center that celebrates Cuban culture through exhibitions and events.

The district's nationalistic focal point, Cuban Memorial Boulevard, as Southwest 13th Avenue is known, is dotted with memorials of Cuban heroes. The most prominent is the Brigade 2506 Memorial's eternal flame, commemorating the disastrous

Bay of Pigs invasion in 1961. On April 17, people gather here to remember the Cubans who died in the attempt to overthrow Fidel Castro's regime. Beyond are other memorials to heroes who fought against Cuba's Spanish colonialists in the 1880s. Along Calle Ocho, between 12th and 17th avenues, stars on the sidewalk honor modern-day Latin celebrities such as Julio Iglesias and Gloria Estefan in Little Havana's own Walk of Fame.

North of Calle Ocho, at West Flagler Street and Southwest 17th Avenue, the Plaza de la Cubanidad has a map of Cuba sculpted in bronze. There's a flourish of banners advertising the headquarters of Alpha 66, Miami's most hard-line anti-Castro group.

Also in this district are the tiny Máximo Gómez Park, or Domino Park, and Woodlawn Cemetery. The nearby Versailles restaurant (p293) is a Cuban cultural and culinary bastion.

El Titan de Bronze
⊛ ⊗ 🏠 1071 SW 8th St
🕐 9am–5pm Mon–Sat
🅦 titandebronze.com

⑨
Downtown

Ⓜ Arena/State Plaza 🚍

The futuristic skyscrapers of Miami's financial district are a monument to the banking boom of the 1980s, when the city emerged as a major trade center. The Metromover, a driverless shuttle launched in 1986, provides a swift overview of the area.

Among the most striking high-rises here are the Four Seasons Hotel in Brickell area, Southeast Financial Center, and the Miami Tower. Older structures include the Alfred I. DuPont Building (1938) and the Ingraham Building (1927), a Neo-Classical/Renaissance Revival work.

The 1931 **US Federal Courthouse** is an imposing Neo-Classical building with a Mediterranean-courtyard. It has hosted a number of high-profile trials, including that of

> Regulations ensure that new buildings in Coral Gables follow the same part-Italian, part-Spanish style adopted in the 1920s.

former Panamanian president Manuel Noriega in 1990. Entry is often restricted.

Built in 1925, Gesu Church on Northeast 2nd Street is Miami's oldest Catholic parish. It is noted for its fine Bavarian stained-glass windows. The Freedom Tower, on Biscayne Boulevard, is loosely modeled on the Giralda in Seville, and was the reception center for Cuban exiles in the 1960s. Macy's is on Flagler Street.

US Federal Courthouse
🏠 301 N Miami Av Ⓜ Arena/ State Plaza 📞 (305) 523-5100 🕐 8am–5pm Mon–Fri 🚫 Federal hols

↑ The mural on Calle Ocho welcoming visitors to Little Havana

Swimming in the waters of the Venetian Pool, Coral Gables ↑

⑩ Venetian Pool

🏠 2701 De Soto Blvd
Ⓜ Douglas Rd 🚌 ⏲ Times vary, check website ⏳ Mon (Sep–May); Jan 1, Thanksg., Dec 24 & 25 �W coralgables.com

Perhaps the most beautiful swimming pool in the world, the Venetian Pool was ingeniously fashioned from a coral rock quarry in 1923 by Denman Fink and Phineas Paist. Pink stucco towers and vine-covered loggias, candy-cane Venetian poles, a cobblestone bridge, fountains, waterfalls, and caves surround crystal-clear, spring-fed waters. The pool was once one of the most fashionable social spots in Coral Gables – in the lobby you'll find photographs of 1920s beauty pageants. It's worth a visit, especially for a swim.

Did You Know?

Johnny Weissmuller (famous for playing Tarzan) swam world records in the Biltmore Hotel pool.

⑪ Coconut Grove Village

Ⓜ Coconut Gr 🚌

Miami's oldest community, Coconut Grove was a fabled hippie hangout in the 1960s. Today, "the village," as it is known, is famous for its cafés and restaurants, especially at night or on weekends. This is also the city's most relaxed shopping area, with many boutiques and two malls: the outdoor CocoWalk and the stylish Streets of Mayfair. In contrast are the food stalls of the colorful farmers' market, held every Saturday at 3300 Grand Avenue.

On Grand Avenue, too, are the simple homes of the local Bahamian community, descendants of the Wreckers, who lived here from the mid-1800s. The lively Goombay Festival, a party with a parade, great food, and Caribbean music, is held here in summer.

In a shady, affluent neighborhood just south of Coconut Grove along Main Highway is the Barnacle, home of Ralph Monroe, a Renaissance man who made his living from ship-building and wrecking. At 3400 Devon Road is the picturesque Plymouth Congregational Church, built in 1916.

⑫ Biltmore Hotel

🏠 1200 Anastasia Av
Ⓜ Douglas Rd 🚌
W biltmorehotel.com

During its heyday in the 1920s, this hotel hosted figures such as Al Capone, Judy Garland, and the Duke and Duchess of Windsor. During World War II, it served as a military hospital. Its most striking feature is its replica of Seville Cathedral's La Giralda, also the model for Miami's Freedom Tower. Inside is a grand lobby, lined with Herculean pillars. It also has one of the largest hotel swimming pools in the US.

⑬ Wynwood Arts District

🏠 NE 20–29 sts, E of I-95 🚌
W wynwoodmiami.com

Wynwood is known for its vibrant outdoor arts scene, where blocks of gray industrial buildings have seen a rebirth through colorful murals and graffiti, promoting the opening of galleries and performing arts spaces. Restaurants and cafés followed, bringing more creative businesses. Now it is one of Miami's cultural hot spots. Wynwood features food tours, art walks, shops, design companies, office space, and much more. At its heart is the project that started it all: the Wynwood Walls. The late Tony Goldman's creative spotlight turned to the street art in the area and transformed the community.

Vizcaya Museum and Gardens

🏠 3251 S Miami Av
Ⓜ Vizcaya 🚌 🕐 9:30am-4:30pm Wed-Mon
🚫 Thanksgiving, Dec 25
🌐 vizcaya.org

Florida's grandest residence was completed in 1916 as the winter retreat for millionaire industrialist James Deering.

His vision was to replicate a 16th-century Italian estate, but one that had been altered by succeeding generations. As a result, Vizcaya and its opulent rooms come in a variety of styles from Renaissance to Neo-Classical, furnished with the fruits of Deering's extravagant shopping sprees around Europe. The formal gardens, a rarity in Florida, beautifully combine Italian and French garden features with tropical foliage. They are dotted with sculptures and quaint buildings, including a Japanese tea house. Deering would always ask of his architect: "Must we be so grand?" fearing that Vizcaya would be too costly to support. After Deering's death in 1925, it proved to be so until it was bought by Miami-Dade County in 1952. The house and gardens were opened to the public thereafter.

Top Cuban restaurants.

Versailles
🏠 3555 SW 8th St
🌐 versaillesrestaurant.com

$$$

Enriqueta's Sandwich Shop
🏠 186 NE 29th St
📞 (305) 573 - 4681

$$$

Palomilla Grill
🏠 6890 W Flagler St
📞 (305) 261 - 3424

$$$

The Music Room is arguably the loveliest room in the house. It is lit by a striking chandelier.

Deering Bathroom has marble walls, silver plaques, and a canopied ceiling.

The Courtyard, now protected with glass, was once open to the sky.

An overview of Vizcaya Museum and Gardens

The Swimming Pool, visible outside, is approached from a grotto behind the house.

The Living Room is a grand Renaissance hall with the curious addition of a specially made organ.

GREATER MIAMI

---

(17) (♿) (🚋)

Fairchild Tropical Botanic Garden

🏠 10901 Old Cutler Rd
Ⓜ Douglas Rd 🚌
🕐 Office: 8am–5pm daily; gardens: dawn–dusk daily
🚫 Dec 25 🌐 fairchild garden.org

Established in 1938, this beautiful tropical garden is also a major botanical research institution. One of the world's largest collections of palm trees stands around a series of man-made lakes. The garden also has an impressive array of cycads – relatives of palms and ferns that bear unusual giant red cones – as well as countless other trees and plants, including a comical-looking sausage tree.

Guides on the 40-minute tram tours describe how plants are used to manufacture medi-cines and perfumes (flowers from the ylang-ylang tree, for example, are used in Chanel No. 5). **Matheson Hammock Park** is on the waterfront next door to the tropical garden. Its highlight is the Atoll Pool, a salt-water swimming pool circled by sand and palm trees along-side Biscayne Bay.

Matheson Hammock Park

🏠 9610 Old Cutler Rd
📞 (305) 665-5475
🕐 Dawn–dusk daily

---

(15)

North Beaches

🏠 Collins Av 🚌
🌐 miamiandbeaches.com

The Barrier Islands to the north along Collins Avenue are occu-pied mainly by posh residential areas and inexpensive resorts, popular with package tours. A quiet strip of sand between 79th and 87th streets divides Miami Beach and Surfside, a simple community popular with French Canadians. At 96th Street, Surfside merges with Bal Harbour, a stylish enclave known for its flashy hotels and one of Miami's swankiest malls, Bal Harbour Shops. To the north is the pleasant Haulover Park, with a marina on the creek side and a "clothing-optional" beach facing the ocean.

---

(16) (✈️)

Ancient Spanish Monastery

🏠 16711 W Dixie Hwy
🚌 🕐 10am–4:30pm Mon-Sat, 11am–4:30pm Sun
🚫 Federal hols 🌐 spanish monastery.com

Built in Spain between 1133 and 1141, these monastery cloisters were bought in 1925 by news-paper tycoon William Randolph Hearst, who had their 35,000 stones packed into crates, but the stones were mixed up en route. Once in New York, they remained there until 1952, when it was decided to piece together "the world's largest and most expensive jigsaw puzzle." The cloisters resemble the original, but a pile of unidentified stones remains.

↑ Crescent shapes sculpted into coral rock by Edward Leedskalnin, Coral Castle

💬 HIDDEN GEM
Robert Is Here

A 15-minute drive from Coral Castle is this fruit market, which has a long history and a selection of tropical fruits. People travel for miles to pick up jackfruit, dragonfruit, and guanabana.

⑱ 🏛

Coral Castle

🏠 28655 S Dixie Hwy, Homestead Ⓜ Dadeland South 🚌 🕐 9am-6pm daily 🌐 coralcastle.com

From 1920 to 1940, Latvian immigrant Edward Leedskalnin crafted these castle-like sculptures out of coral rock using tools made from automobile parts. He sculpted most of the stones in Florida City before moving them to the site. Some, such as a working telescope, represent their creator's great passion for astrology. Others, such as a heart-shaped table, remember his Latvian fiancée Agnes, who canceled their wedding a day beforehand.

⑲ 🏛 🏍

Deering Estate

🏠 16701 SW 72nd Av 🕐 10am-5pm daily 🌐 deeringestate.com

Charles Deering was a wealthy businessman, philanthropist, and art collector who from 1922 to 1927 lived on these sprawling grounds, surrounding a beautiful three-story stone mansion called the Richmond Cottage. Visitors can enjoy hiking, nature trails, and kayaking as well as the chance to see some of Deering's art collection and enjoy the wealth of cultural events that take place on the grounds.

⑳

Key Biscayne

🏠 7 miles (11 km) SE of downtown 🚌 🕐 Daily 🌐 floridastateparks.org

The view of Downtown from the Rickenbacker Causeway, connecting the mainland to Virginia Key and Key Biscayne, is one of Miami's best. Views aside, this has some of the city's top beaches. The most impressive is at Crandon Park in the upper half of the Key, which is 3 miles (5 km) long and enormously wide, with palm trees and picnic areas. At the southern end, the white dunes and boardwalks of **Bill Baggs Cape Florida State Park** are crowned by the majestic Cape Florida Lighthouse.

Bill Baggs Cape Florida State Park

🏠 1200 S Crandon Blvd
📞 (786) 582-2673

← Cape Florida Lighthouse at the tip of Bill Baggs Cape Florida State Park

THE GOLD AND TREASURE COASTS

Named for the booty found in wrecked Spanish galleons, these are two of Florida's wealthiest regions. To the north, the Treasure Coast is characterized by wild sweeping beaches and small communities while, to the south, the Gold Coast is unremittingly built up, save for scattered golf courses and parks. Vacations center on the pencil-thin barrier islands along the coast.

② Fort Lauderdale

✈ 🚆 🚌 ⛴ 🅸 101 NE 3rd Av, #100; www.sunny.org

Fort Lauderdale's character is defined by its waterways, which branch from the New River and the Intracoastal Waterway. The area around the mouth of the river is known as the Isles. This is the city's prime area, filled with fine mansions and luxurious yachts. Millions of visitors head for the barrier islands lying along the coast.

The bustling Las Olas Boulevard is lined with eateries and boutiques and has some of the liveliest beaches on the Gold Coast at its eastern end.

Downtown is Fort Lauderdale's business and cultural center. Riverwalk, a short stretch along the New River's north bank, links most of the city's historical and cultural landmarks. The Historic District runs along Southwest 2nd Avenue and has several buildings from the early 1900s, such as those in the Fort Lauderdale History Center. The NSU Art Museum (1 E Las Olas Blvd) is best known for its works by the CoBrA artists, a group of 20th-century Expressionist painters. The Museum of Discovery and Science (401 SW 2nd St) is one of the largest and best of its kind in Florida. Here, a multitude of creatures appear in recreated "ecoscapes."

INSIDER TIP
Baseball Spring Training

In March, many Major League Baseball teams travel south to train, and some sessions are open to the public. The Gold and Treasure coasts traditionally play host to the New York Mets, the St. Louis Cardinals, and the Houston Astros.

③ Boca Raton

🅿 🅸 1555 Palm Beach Lakes Blvd; www.visitflorida.com

Affluent Boca Raton was once a sleepy town that architect Addison Mizner (1872–1933) envisaged as the "greatest resort in the world." The nucleus of his vision was the luxurious Cloister Inn (1926), now part of the exclusive Boca Raton Resort and Club. Weekly tours for nonresidents are arranged by the Boca Raton Historical Society, based at the Mizner-designed Town Hall.

The skyline and waterways of Fort Lauderdale, lit up as dusk falls

↑ Colorful buildings and palm-lined roads in Florida's Palm Beach

Just opposite is the dazzling Mizner Park open-air mall. Located in a spectacular setting within Mizner Park is the **Boca Raton Museum of Art**, with world-class exhibitions and displays of contemporary art.

The verdant and historic Old Floresta Historic District, a mile (1.6 km) west of the Town Hall, has 29 Mediterranean-style houses built by Mizner.

Boca Raton's long, wild beach is best reached via Red Reef Park, which also has the informative Gumbo Limbo Nature Center. The most northerly and attractive of the city's parks, Spanish River Park has pleasant picnic areas shaded by pines and palm trees. It also has a delightful lagoon on the Intracoastal Waterway, next to an observation tower.

Boca Raton Museum of Art

⊗ ⌂ 501 Plaza Real, Mizner Park ⏰ 10am–5pm Tue-Fri (to 8pm Thu), noon–5pm Sat & Sun 🗓 Federal hols ⓦ bocamuseum.org

④ Palm Beach

✗ 🚆 🚌 ℹ 400 Royal Palm Way, #106; www.palmbeachchamber.com

Essentially a winter resort for the rich and famous, Palm Beach was created at the end of the 19th century by the railroad baron Henry Flagler.

The major sights can be found in the area between Cocoanut Row and South County Road. Of these, the **Henry Morrison Flagler Museum** has a grand marble entrance hall, an Italian Renaissance library, and a Louis XV ballroom.

To the south, the Society of the Four Arts has two libraries, an exhibition space, and an auditorium for concerts and films. Other buildings of note include the 1926 Town Hall, the Mizner Memorial Park, and the Breakers, a mammoth Italian Renaissance-style hotel.

Stretching from Palm Beach Docks to the Atlantic Ocean, Worth Avenue is the epitome of Palm Beach's opulence, with glitzy boutiques, galleries, and shops, connected by a set of interlinking pedestrian alleys, and with the Esplanade mall at the eastern end.

Palm Beach's suburban mansions were built by Mizner and his imitators in the 1920s, but hundreds of others have since proliferated in styles from Neo-Classical to Art Deco.

The Norton Museum of Art in West Palm Beach is known for its exquisite collection of American, French, and Chinese art, including Impressionist works and Buddhist sculpture.

Henry Morrison Flagler Museum

⊗ ⊗ ⊗ ⊗ ⌂ 1 Whitehall Way ⏰ 10am–5pm Tue-Sat, noon–5pm Sun 🗓 Jan 1, Thanksg., Dec 25 ⓦ flaglermuseum.us

⑤ Arthur R. Marshall Loxahatchee National Wildlife Refuge

⌂ 10216 Lee Rd 🚆 Boynton Beach 🚌 ⏰ Refuge: daily; 🗓 Thanksg., Dec 25 ⓦ loxahatcheefriends.com

The northernmost part of the Everglades, this refuge is known for its superb wildlife. The best time to visit is in winter, when migrating birds arrive here from the north. The visitor center, off Route 441, has displays that explain the Everglades' ecology and provides the starting point for two memorable trails. The Cypress Swamp Boardwalk is lined with wax myrtle trees, and the longer Marsh Trail is a bird-watcher's paradise, with ibis, herons, and anhingas. Visitors can also spot turtles and alligators. Those with canoes can embark on the 5.5-mile (9-km) canoe trail.

The engines of the *Saturn V* rocket at the Kennedy Space Center

THE SPACE COAST

Orlando started out as an army post, established by General Andrew Jackson when he invaded Florida during conflict with the Seminole tribe in 1817. The army post grew into a town, but Orlando was small, sleepy, and dependent on cattle and the citrus crop even in the early 20th century. The "Great Freeze of 1894–95" wiped out many local farms, and thereafter the area served as a winter resort. In the 1950s, Patrick Air Force Base was established on the coast around Cape Canaveral; NASA was founded in 1958, and this became its primary launch site, ensuring the subsequent development of the "Space Coast." Similarly, Orlando's future was secured when Walt Disney announced plans to build a theme park in 1965.

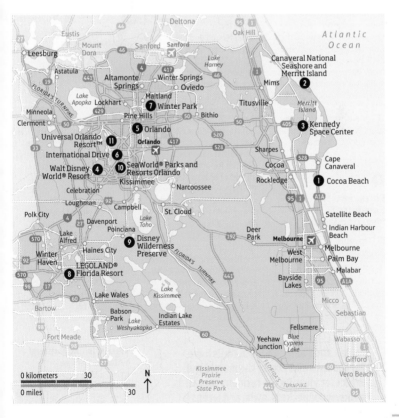

THE SPACE COAST

NASA has been an exciting presence in Florida since the late 1960s, and the area stretching from the Canaveral National Seashore to Melbourne Beach has since been named the Space Coast. However, the region also has a subtle beauty as well. The barrier islands across the Indian River boast 72 miles (116 km) of stunning beaches, and there are two nature preserves.

❶
Cocoa Beach

🚗 30 miles (48 km) SE of Titusville 🚌 Merritt Island
ℹ️ 400 Fortenberry Rd;
www.cocoabeach.com

For some, this large, no-frills seaside resort – the closest to Orlando – is the quintessential beach town and calls itself the East Coast's surfing capital. Surfing festivals set the tone, along with win-your-weight-in-beer competitions. Motels, restaurants, and gift shops characterize the main street. The dazzling Ron Jon Surf Shop has surfboards galore (for sale and rent) and a huge T-shirt collection. You'll also find opportunities for eco-tours, deep-sea fishing, golf, and kayaking, and there is a handful of museums and historic sites to explore. The beaches offer great viewing spots for the rocket launches from Cape Canaveral.

❷
Canaveral National Seashore & Merritt Island

🚌 Titusville
🌐 nps.gov/cana

These adjacent preserves on the Space Coast share an astounding variety of fauna and a range of habitats, including estuaries and hardwood hammocks. Visitors can often see alligators and the endangered manatee, but the real highlight is the rich birdlife.

The **Canaveral National Seashore** has an immaculate 24-mile (39-km) stretch of beach, where several endangered species, including sea turtles, find refuge. Apollo Beach at the northern end and Playalinda Beach to the south are fine for sunbathing, but swimming can be hazardous, and there are no lifeguards. Climb to the top of Turtle Mound and you'll find splendid views of Mosquito Lagoon (be sure to bring plenty of repellent in spring and summer).

Route 402 to Playalinda Beach offers views of the launch pads at the Kennedy Space Center. It also crosses the **Merritt Island National Wildlife Refuge**, which covers an area of roughly 220 sq miles (570 sq km). However, much of the refuge lies within the Space Center and is out of bounds. Winter is arguably the best season to visit. To view the local wildlife, follow the Black Point Wildlife Drive, which has the 5-mile (8-km) Cruickshank Trail. Be sure to pick up the informative leaflet at the drive's entrance. The Visitor Information Center has displays on the habitats and wildlife in the refuge. One mile (1.6 km) farther east, the Oak and Palm Hammock trails have short boardwalks across the marshland, perfect for viewing the resident songbirds, hawks, woodpeckers, owls, and wrens, as well as some of the local mammals.

Canaveral National Wildlife
♿ 🚗 Rte A1A, 20 miles (32 km) N of Titusville or Rte 402, 10 miles (16 km) E of Titusville 📞 (321) 267-1110 🕐 6am–8pm daily (winter: to 6pm)

Merritt Island National Wildlife Refuge
🚗 Rte 406, 4 miles (6.5 km) E of Titusville 📞 (321) 861-5601 🕐 Dawn–dusk daily

> The Oak and Palm Hammock trails have short boardwalks across the marshland, perfect for viewing the resident songbirds, hawks, woodpeckers, owls, and wrens.

↑ Blue skies at waters of Cocoa Beach, a popular spot for surfing *(inset)* and watching rocket launches

3 ⊘ Ⓜ 🍴 🛍

Kennedy Space Center

🏠 Brevard Co. 🚌 Titusville
🕐 From 9am daily (closing time varies by season, check website) 🚫 Dec 25
🌐 kennedyspacecenter.com

When Cape Canaveral was chosen as the site for the National Aeronautics and Space Administration (NASA) space program in the 1960s, the area came to be known as the Space Coast. The Kennedy Space Center on Merritt Island was the launching place for the *Apollo 11* mission to the moon and shuttle flights to the International Space Center until 2011. Today the complex welcomes around 1.5 million guests per year and stretches over 130 sq miles (335 sq km). It's a comprehensive space experience for guests, with artifacts and spacecraft combined with multimedia presentations. One of the best exhibits is the *Atlantis Orbiter*, complemented by the Shuttle Launch Experience,

a breathtaking, immersive simulator. The Apollo/Saturn V Center also has actual rockets on display and a re-creation of a control room. The Astronaut Hall of Fame and the Rocket Garden are both fascinating and look at the work of NASA from its inception, with "NASA: Now and Next" highlighting upcoming missions, some of which are enhanced further at the center's IMAX cinema.

Behind the Gates is the center's guided bus tour – it's included in the price of daily admission and grants visitors exclusive access to launch pads and other behind-the-scenes exhibits. At additional cost are two special-interest tours: the Explore Tour with its enhanced photo opportunities and the Cape Canaveral Early Space Tour, recommended for space buffs who want to step back in time and learn more about the history of the space program.

The Kennedy Space Center will occasionally close for operational reasons; always check the website.

Timeline of American Space Exploration

1958
First American satellite, the *Explorer 1*, is launched (Jan 31)

1961
▷ Alan Shepard becomes the first American in space (May 5)

1962
John Glenn orbits the earth in *Mercury* spacecraft

1969
▷ Neil Armstrong and Buzz Aldrin (*Apollo 11*) walk on the moon (Jul 20)

1975
American *Apollo* and Russian *Soyuz* vehicles dock in orbit (Jul 17)

1981
Columbia is the first shuttle in space (Apr 12)

1986
▽ *Challenger* explodes, killing its crew (Jan 28)

1996
Mars Pathfinder is sent to gather data from the surface of Mars

2011
Final flight of *Atlantis* marks the end of the 30-year Space Shuttle Program

2015
◁ A new era, with SpaceX and other commercial rockets

2019
First binary star explored by a spacecraft

④ 🏷️ 🍴 💻 🛍️

WALT DISNEY WORLD® RESORT

📍 Walt Disney World Resort®, Orlando 🕐 Times vary, check website
🌐 disneyworld.disney.go.com

Welcome to the happiest place on earth. Since opening in 1971, Walt Disney World® Resort has exploded from a single theme park into an American icon, dripping with nostalgic charm. The resort comprises four parks – the Magic Kingdom®, Epcot®, Animal Kingdom®, and Hollywood Studios® – all with their unique character.

① MAGIC KINGDOM®

This is the essential Disney theme park. Visitors arrive on Main Street, U.S.A.®, a wistful vision of turn-of-the-century America, chockfull of souvenir stores and cute cafés. Liberty Square is set in post-Colonial America; feast on nightly Thanksgiving dinners at Liberty Tree Tavern or board the Liberty Belle, a tri-level steam-powered river boat. Adventureland® is exotic and tropical, home to rides such as the Jungle Cruise, Pirates of the Caribbean®, and Magic Carpets of Aladdin. Frontier-land® is an idealized version of the Wild West where you'll discover the thrilling Big Thunder Mountain Railroad and Splash Mountain®. Fantasyland® is a wonderland of magical adventures and, most famously, Cinderella Castle. Finally, Tomorrowland® is both retro and futuristic, and punctuated by Space Mountain® and Buzz Lightyear's Space Ranger Spin.

② DISNEY'S ANIMAL KINGDOM

Disney's Animal Kingdom is part theme park, part animal sanctuary. Guests enter into Oasis, a land of greenery and hidden creatures; you'll spot the likes of wallabies, giant anteaters, and barking deer foraging in the area's foliage. Fans of Avatar will enjoy discovering the mythical land of Pandora, while Dinoland U.S.A. transports visitors back to primeval times. Asia is an evocative section of the theme park where majestic Sumatran tigers roam palace remnants within the Maharajah Jungle Trek® and passengers aboard the Expedition Everest – Legend of the Forbidden Mountain™ relish traveling across the re-created slopes of the Himalayas. Over in Africa, board a truck on Kilimanjaro Safaris® and look out for hippos, rhinos, and giraffes, before watching the acrobatic Festival of the Lion King. No visit is complete without a pilgrimage to the magnificent Tree of Life® on Discovery Island.

←

Admiring the imposing Tree of Life® in Disney's Animal Kingdom

↑ Bustling Main Street U.S.A.® leading to Cinderella Castle, in the Magic Kingdom®

A PLAYGROUND FOR ADULTS

Disney has plenty to entertain adults. Celebrity chefs provide fine dining at Disney Springs® *(www.disney springs.com)* plus tempting food festivals at Epcot®. There's plenty of nightlife, too, such as burlesque and DJ nights in Disney Springs®. For more music, swing by Raglan Road or the House of Blues, and don't miss the Rock 'n' Roller Coaster® Starring Aerosmith in Hollywood Studios. All parks except Epcot® offer Disney After Hours events.

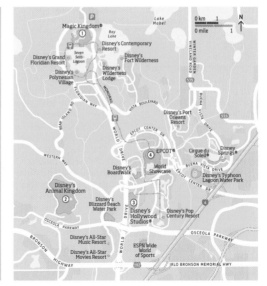

③ DISNEY'S HOLLYWOOD STUDIOS®

This is the place to experience Disney-helmed films in person, and Hollywood Boulevard provides a glamorous welcome to the movie magic. Here delightful Art Deco-styled buildings vie with a replica of Grauman's Chinese Theatre to present an idealized image of Hollywood. Shop for high-quality souvenirs at the many boutiques lining the park's entrance and you might even encounter the overzealous Citizens of Hollywood, who enact pop-up scenes throughout the day.

On Sunset Boulevard you'll find the stomach-plunging Rock 'n' Roller Coaster® Starring Aerosmith, a wild indoor ride with a nearly 60mph (100 km/h) launch that plays the band's hits at random and contains the only upside-down inversion in Walt Disney World®. Nearby is the unmissable lightning-ravaged and decrepit Hollywood Tower Hotel home to Orlando's scariest ride – The Twilight Zone Tower of Terror™.

Echo Lake has thrills and spills aplenty, thanks to the Indiana Jones™ Epic Stunt Spectacular! This show re-creates well-known movie scenes jam-packed with daredevil feats. Head to the Commissary Lake afterward for relaxation and refreshment.

One of the newest stars of the show is the *Star Wars: Galaxy's Edge* zone, which opened in 2017. Set within a trading post on planet Batuu, this themed land brings all manner of experiences from the film franchise, including Millennium Falcon: Smugglers Run, where passengers can pilot the fictional ship as it embarks on a secret mission.

On Grand Avenue the Muppet*Vision 3D continues to entertain, while Animation Courtyard offers insight into the history and process of animation, drawing back the curtain on the likes of *Monsters, Inc.* Finally, Toy Story Land includes the Slinky Dog Dash family coaster and Toy Story Mania! 4D interactive ride among its attractions. You might also bump in Woody, Jessie, and Buzz as you explore.

↑ The Twilight Zone Tower of Terror™ on Sunset Boulevard (© Disney), and *(inset)* Toy Story Mania! (© Disney)

💬 INSIDER TIP
Play Disney Parks App

This digital app, which launched with the opening of Toy Story Land in 2018, provides interactive games to keep you entertained while waiting in attraction lines. Interact with droids in *Star Wars: Galaxy Edge* and test your Disney trivia.

This is the place to experience Disney-helmed films in person, and Hollywood Boulevard provides a glamorous welcome to the movie magic.

④ EPCOT®

Imagined as a utopian "Experimental Prototype Community of Tomorrow" by Walt Disney himself, Epcot opened in 1982 as a world's fair, intent on blending education with entertainment. The park is divided into two halves: Future World and World Showcase.

Future World, which retains a science and technology edge, is home to a number of thrills and spills. One of its most popular rides is Test Track®, where you'll put your prototype vehicle head-to-head with other passengers in a series of road tests. On Mission: SPACE® take a journey beyond the horizon in a four-seat capsule that culminates with a landing on Mars. The emblematic Spaceship Earth – the landmark and symbol of the park – hosts an utterly delightful journey through the history of communication.

Those looking for something more earth-based will enjoy Soarin' Around the World™, one of the resort's finest attractions. Nearby is Living with the Land, a

↑ Views at the Soarin' Around the World™ attraction (© Disney)

greenhouse cruise providing lessons in sustainability and supplying produce to select Disney restaurants. Kids will love The Seas with Nemo and Friends, where they can embark on a journey into the sea aboard "clamobiles."

World Showcase represents and celebrates the culture and cuisine of countries from around the world. Specifically, eleven pavilions embody a country: Canada, Mexico, Norway, China, Germany, Italy, Japan, Morocco, France, the US, and the UK. Stroll past pyramid temples in Mexico, wooden churches in Norway, and towering minarets in Morocco. You're spoiled for choice when it comes to food.

Restaurants like Le Cellier Steakhouse in Canada and France's Monsieur Paul provide some of the best fine dining in all of Walt Disney World®, while bars aplenty have encouraged guests to sip sake in Japan and black & tan in the UK. The entertainment is also superb – stop to watch a Chinese acrobatic troupe or Mexican mariachi – and Disney characters make appearances, such as at the Frozen Ever After boat ride in Norway.

↓ Epcot®'s International Flower and Garden Festival (© Disney)

5

Orlando

🖼️🏨🚆 ℹ️ **8723 International Dr; www.visit orlando.com**

Orlando was just a sleepy provincial town until the 1950s, when its proximity to Cape Canaveral and the growth of theme parks transformed it into a burgeoning business center. Downtown Orlando, with its glass-sided high-rises, comes to life at night, when visitors and locals flock to the many bars and restaurants around Orange Avenue, the town's main street.

During the day, Lake Eola, east of Orange Avenue, offers a peaceful midtown oasis for visitors and families. The residential districts north of downtown have many parks and museums, including the serene Harry P. Leu Gardens and Loch Haven Park, which houses a trio of museums. The most highly regarded of these is the **Orlando Museum of Art**, whose collections include pre-Columbian artifacts, African art, and American paintings from the 19th and 20th centuries. Also in Loch Haven Park, the Mennello Museum of American Art houses a large collection of American art from across genres and time periods.

The **Orlando Science Center** promotes the spirit of learning and curiosity with a wide range of exciting state-of-the-art interactive exhibits, movies, and educational programs.

Orlando Museum of Art

♿ 🅿️ **N Mills Av at Rollins St**
🕐 Tue–Sun 🚫 Federal hols
🌐 omart.org

Orlando Science Center

♿🍽️📷🎬 **777 E Princeton St**
🕐 10am–5pm Thu–Tue
🚫 Federal hols 🌐 osc.org

6

International Drive

🅿️ Orlando 🚌 Orlando
ℹ️ **8723 International Drive; (407) 363-5872**

A stone's throw from Walt Disney World®, "I Drive" is a 3-mile (5-km) ribbon of hotels, shops, and theaters. Its most popular attraction is the ICON Orlando, a giant Ferris wheel that offers breathtaking views.

Other highlights include Ripley's Believe It or Not!, filled with fantastic objects, illusions, and footage of strange feats. WonderWorks is an interactive attraction combining science-based education and entertainment. *Titanic: The Artifact Exhibition* displays artifacts, movie memorabilia, and re-creations of the ship's interior. If you like the idea of skydiving try the iFLY indoor skydiving center. Two blocks away is Orlando's Official Visitor Center, which has coupons for discount admission and meals.

↑ The ICON Orlando Ferris Wheel, International Drive

7

Winter Park

🅿️🚌 ℹ️ **151 W Lyman Av; www.winterpark.org**

North of Orlando, this town took off in the 1880s when wealthy northerners came south to build winter retreats. The **Charles Hosmer Morse Museum of American Art** has one of the finest collections of works by Art Nouveau craftsman Louis Comfort Tiffany, with superb examples of his jewelry, lamps, and windows. Rollins College, just off Park Avenue, is dotted with 1930s Spanish-style buildings, including the Knowles Memorial Chapel. The **Scenic Boat Tour** explores nearby lakes and canals.

Charles Hosmer Morse Museum of American Art

♿ **445 Park Ave N**
🕐 Tue–Sun 🚫 Federal hols
🌐 morsemuseum.org

Scenic Boat Tour

♿ **312 E Morse Blvd**
🚫 Dec 25 🌐 scenicboat tours.com

> **Downtown Orlando, with its glass-sided high-rises, comes to life at night, when visitors and locals flock to the many bars and restaurants around Orange Avenue.**

8

LEGOLAND® Florida Resort

⌂ 1 Legoland Way, Winter Haven ⊟ Winter Haven ⊙ 10am–5pm daily ⟳ Tue & Wed in slow periods ⓦ florida.legoland.com

An action-packed day of adventure and education awaits at LEGOLAND® Florida Resort, just 45 minutes from both Walt Disney World® and Tampa, in the city of Winter Haven. The park contains 14 different themed zones, plus a water park and a botanical garden, including a Banyan tree planted in 1939, ensuring an exciting experience for every family member. The on-site resort hotel, with rooms built around LEGO® themes, is a favorite with LEGO® fans.

A detailed LEGO model of New York City, and life-size *LEGO® Movie™* characters *(inset)* at LEGOLAND®

9

Disney Wilderness Preserve

⌂ 2700 Scrub Jay Trail, 12 miles (18 km) SW of Kissimmee ⊟ Kissimmee ⊞ Kissimmee ⊙ 9am–5pm daily ⟳ Jun–Sep: Sat & Sun ⓦ nature.org

Orlando's finest wilderness preserve is a haven for native plants and animals, and for people wanting to get away from the crowds. Unlike other Disney attractions, there are no thrill rides here, but there is still plenty to do. There is an off-road buggy tour on Sundays, and three hiking trails that lead to Lake Russell. The interpretive trail is only 0.8 miles (1.2 km) long, and visitors can learn about nature along the way. The longer trails are mostly unshaded, so bring sunscreen, a hat, plenty of water, and insect repellent.

EAT

JB's Fish Camp & Restaurant
Seafood joint with an extensive fish and shellfish menu.

⌂ 859 Pompano Avenue ⓦ jbsfishcamp.com

$$$

10

SeaWorld® Parks and Resorts Orlando

⌂ 7007 SeaWorld Dr ⊟ ⊙ Times vary, check website ⓦ seaworld.com

SeaWorld® Orlando's family-friendly aquatic theme park is known for its water-themed rides, animal encounters, and live shows. Despite its rehabilitation program, negative aspects of the park have come to light since the 2013 documentary *Blackfish*, directed by Gabriela Cowperthwaite.

UNIVERSAL ORLANDO RESORT™

🏠 6000 Universal Blvd 🚌 21, 37, 40 from Orlando 🕐 9am–6pm daily; extended evening opening in summer and on federal hols 🌐 universalorlando.com

Universal Orlando Resort™ is home to three thrilling theme parks – Volcano Bay™, Universal's Islands of Adventure™ and Universal Studios Florida™, where animated characters and action films come to life. Disney may think it has a stronghold on this town, but The Wizarding World of Harry Potter™ is an unmissable sight for any Orlando vacation.

Sip a Duff Beer in Moe's Tavern before entering Krustyland, meet SpongeBob SquarePants, and fight alongside Optimus Prime – here, experiences that are only available on screen become reality. The rides range from tame to towering roller coasters, so the parks offer attractions catering to thrill-seekers young and old.

When the parks are open until late in the summer and on federal holidays, two full days are just about long enough to see everything. When the parks close early – the only disadvantage of visiting off season – you need three or four days. Advance booking is advised.

TACKLING THE PARKS

The busiest seasons are Christmas and Easter. During the off-season, check with Guest Services for deals on tickets. Arrive early to combat the long lines for rides (gates open an hour in advance for on-site guests). Arrive 15 minutes early for shows to ensure a seat. There are child-friendly rides: ET Adventure®, Woody Woodpecker's Nuthouse®, A Day in the Park with Barney™, and Seuss Landing™.

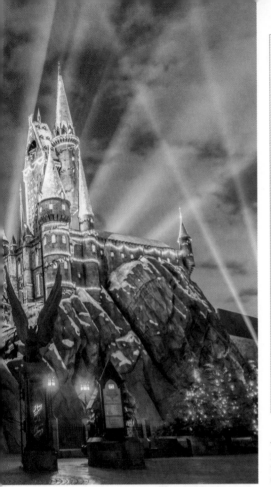

Waterslide down Krakatau™ Volcano
Snake through the volcano on a four-person canoe then dive down a glistening waterfall.

Sit front row on The Incredible Hulk Coaster®
It's worth the wait to be the first one catapulted out at intense speeds.

Choose-Your-Own Music on Hollywood Rip Ride Rockit™
Control the soundtrack to your ride by selecting from a list of songs.

Survive the Jurassic Park River Adventure™ drop
Come face to face with a T-rex and brace yourself for an 85-ft (26-m) pitch-black plummet.

←

Hogwarts Castle, Universal Studios Florida™, during the Christmas light show

Theme Parks

Universal Studios

This cinematic park is a must for all movie lovers. Little kids will love attractions themed around Shrek and Despicable Me, while big kids might prefer Men in Black™ – Alien Attack™ and Revenge of the Mummy™. Look out for your favorite characters in Universal's Superstar Parade.

Islands of Adventure™

▽ Eight themed lands centering around your favorite comic, book, and movie franchises - from Jurassic Park and King Kong to Seuss Landing™ and all things Marvel®. As its name implies, adventures abound here. Where will you begin?

Volcano Bay™

△ Arguably Universal's most beautiful park, Volcano Bay™ is a mythical oasis. Thrill-seekers will love the water park's plunging slides, while those looking for relaxation can enjoy a dip in Waturi Bay™ or float around the tranquil Kopiko Wai Winding River™.

Wizarding World of Harry Potter™

Experience the wizarding world for yourself. Stock up on chocolate frogs in Diagon Alley™, board the Hogwarts™ Express on Platform 9¾™, explore Hogwarts™ castle before riding the family-friendly Flight of the Hippogriff™ coaster.

THE NORTHEAST AND THE PANHANDLE

America's first permanent European colony was St. Augustine, founded by the Spanish in 1565. Franciscan missions were built across the Panhandle to convert the Apalachee, Timucua, and other tribes; Pensacola was founded in 1698, becoming the capital of West Florida, while St. Augustine remained in control of the east. War and disease virtually wiped out local American Indian tribes, and Spain ceded Florida to the US in 1819, with Tallahassee as its capital. Strong ties to the Deep South meant this part of Florida maintained segregation well into the 1960s. Today both regions are loved for their luxury coastal resorts.

THE NORTHEAST

The Northeast offers up fishing villages, former plantations, and country towns that recall old-time Florida. Broad, sandy beaches flank the popular resort of Daytona. West of the St. Johns River is the expansive Ocala National Forest, blending with the rolling pastures of Marion County. Nearby, charming towns and villages such as Micanopy have been virtually untouched by modernity.

❶
Daytona Beach

📍 **126 E Orange Av; www.daytonabeach.com**

Extending south from Ormond Beach is brash and boisterous Daytona Beach. As many as 200,000 students visit every Spring Break, and its famous 23-mile (37-km) beach is one of the few in the state where cars are allowed on the sands, a hangover from the days when motor enthusiasts raced on the beaches. The Boardwalk still retains some of its arcades and carnival-style atmosphere, but the area has been regenerated and offers updated rides, including a roller coaster.

Downtown Daytona, known simply as "Mainland," lies just across the Halifax River from the beach. Here, the Daytona International Speedway draws huge crowds, especially in February, March, and October. Halifax Historical Museum occupies a grand 1910 bank building. Local history displays include a scale model of the Boardwalk in about 1938, with chicken-feather palm trees and a Ferris wheel. To the west, the **Museum of Arts and Sciences** has exhibits from 1640 to 1920 and a planetarium.

Museum of Arts & Sciences
🏛 **1040 Museum Blvd**
🕐 Daily ❌ Federal hols
🌐 moas.org

❷
Ocala National Forest

🏛 **53 miles (87 km) W of Daytona Beach** 🕐 **Daily**
📍 **45621 State Rd 19, Altoona; www.fs.usda.gov/ocala**

Between Ocala and the St. Johns River, the world's largest sand pine forest is crisscrossed by rivers and hiking trails. One of the last refuges of the Florida black bear, it is also home to deer and otter, and a variety of birds such as bald eagles, barred owls, wild turkey, and several wading birds. Hiking trails vary from boardwalks and short loop trails to the 66-mile (106-km) stretch of the National Scenic Trail. Bass fishing is popular on the many lakes scattered through the forest, and there are swimming holes, picnic areas, and campgrounds at the recreation areas of Salt Springs, Alexander Springs, and Fore Lake.

Canoe rental is widely available; the 7-mile (11-km) canoe run down Juniper Creek from the Juniper Springs Recreation Area is one of the finest in Florida. The Salt Springs trail is especially good for bird-watching. There are guides at the main visitor center on the forest's western fringe or at the centers at Salt Springs and Lake Dorr, on Route 19.

3

Fernandina Beach

Jacksonville
961687 Gateway Blvd, Suite 101 G; www.fbfl.us

The town of Fernandina Beach on Amelia Island was famous as a pirates' den until the early 1800s. Today, it is better known as a charming Victorian resort. Considered the birthplace of Florida's shrimp industry, picturesque boats can still be seen and shrimp can be eaten at the annual Isle of Eight Flags Shrimp Festival in April.

Occupying a large section of the town's Historic District, the Silk Stocking District was named after the affluence of its original residents, who built turreted Queen Anne houses, graceful Italianate residences, and fine Chinese Chippendale structures, such as the Beech Street Grill. The 1878 Palace Saloon on Centre Street still serves a wicked Pirate's Punch at a mahogany bar adorned with hand-carved caryatids. Farther south, the **Amelia Island Museum of History** occupies the former jail and offers guided history tours recounting the island's turbulent past.

Amelia Island Museum of History
233 S 3rd St
Daily Federal hols
ameliamuseum.org

4

Jacksonville

Duval Co
550 Water St; www.visitjacksonville.com

Jacksonville, founded in 1822 and named after one General Andrew Jackson, boomed as a port and rail hub in the 1800s.

←
The Boardwalk at Daytona Beach, with its roller coaster and psychedelic Ferris wheel

Today the sprawling city spans the St. Johns River, and has an impressive commercial district.

East of downtown, half a dozen beaches stretch along the shore. Jacksonville Beach is the busiest spot, and is home to Adventure Landing, a year-round entertainment complex and summer water park. By far the nicest spot in the region is Kathryn Abbey Hanna Park, with its fine sand beach, woodland trails, and camping areas.

The **Cummer Museum of Art** and Gardens stands in exquisite formal gardens. Its 12 galleries exhibit a small but satisfying selection of both decorative and fine arts.

Cummer Museum of Art
829 Riverside Av
Times vary, check website
cummermuseum.org

5

St. Augustine

52 San Marco Av
10 Castillo Dr; www.floridashistoriccoast.com

America's oldest continuously occupied European settlement burned down in 1702 but was soon rebuilt in the lee of the **Castillo de San Marcos**, the largest Spanish fort in the US.

St. Augustine's historic heart is easy to explore on foot, but horse-drawn carriage tours also depart from Avenida Menendez, north of the Bridge of Lions. The 18th-century City Gate is the entrance to the Old Town. Its focus is the pedestrianized St. George Street, lined with attractive stone buildings. Attractions here include the Colonial Quarter, a re-creation of an 18th-century garrison town, and the Oldest Wooden Schoolhouse, built in the mid-1700s. At the heart of the settlement on Plaza de la

→
Flags hanging in St. George Street, the historic heart of St. Augustine

Constitution, the splendid Flagler College started out as a hotel, built by Henry Flagler in 1883. Flagler also built the Alcazar Hotel, a three-floor Hispano-Moorish structure, now the **Lightner Museum**. Its Gilded Age exhibits include glass works by Louis Tiffany, and its Grand Ballroom houses an eclectic exhibit of "American Castle" furniture.

Castillo de San Marcos
1 S Castillo Dr
8:45am-5:15pm daily
Dec 25 nps.gov/casa

Lightner Museum
75 King St 9am-5pm daily Dec 25
lightnermuseum.org

DRINK

St Augustine Distillery
Former ice factory now producing premium spirits. Fascinating tours include tasting sessions.
112 Riberia St, St. Augustine
staugustinedistillery.com

THE PANHANDLE

There is a saying in Florida that "the farther north you go, the farther south you get." Certainly, the Panhandle's history and sensibility are closer to its Deep South neighbors than the rest of the peninsula. Climate, history, geography, and even time (the western Panhandle is one hour behind the rest of the state) distinguish this intriguing region from other parts of Florida.

↑ Colorful buildings at the Seville Quarter complex in Historic Pensacola

6 Tallahassee

🔗🏛🚌 ℹ️ 106 E Jefferson; www.visittallahassee.com

Encircled by the gently rolling Red Hills, Florida's dignified state capital is gracious and uncompromisingly Southern.

Tallahassee grew dramatically during the plantation era, and the elegant town houses built in the 1800s can still be seen around Park Avenue and Calhoun Street.

A major landmark, the Neo-Classical Old Capitol Building in downtown Tallahassee has been beautifully restored to its 1902 state. Once inside, guests can visit the Supreme Court chamber and the Senate. The high-rise New Capitol Building behind it offers a fabulous view of the city.

During the 19th and 20th centuries, the region had a flourishing cotton-growing industry, and the old Cotton Trail takes in former cotton plantations and cattle pastures from this era. The Goodwood Museum and Gardens retains its exquisite 1830s mansion; Bradley's Country Store, set up in 1927, still serves its famous home-made sausages; and the open-air Tallahassee Museum shows how early settlers lived and worked among some of the state's most beautiful scenery. Mission San Luis, a national historic landmark and living history site, reconstructs a 17th-century Spanish mission with costumed interpreters and re-created period buildings.

Located 15 miles (24 km) south of Tallahassee, **Wakulla Springs State Park** has one of the world's largest freshwater springs. Here, visitors can swim or snorkel or ride in a glass-bottomed boat.

Wakulla Springs State Park

♿ 🏠 550 Wakulla Park Dr, Wakulla Springs 🕐 Daily 🌐 floridastateparks.org

7 Pensacola

🔗🏛🚌 ℹ️ 1401 E Gregory St; www.visitpensacola.com

One of Florida's earliest Spanish settlements, Pensacola is marked by its diverse architectural styles, from Colonial cottages to elegant Classical-Revival homes. Over its first 300 years the city was occupied by the Spanish, French, English, and the Americans. The 1800s were a period of prosperity ushered in by the timber boom, and much of today's downtown dates from this time.

The city's oldest quarter, Historic Pensacola, has a number of museums and houses built by wealthy pioneers and traders. There are daily tours from Tivoli House on Zaragoza Street. Forming a backdrop to the Museum of Commerce is a cleverly constructed Victorian

---

EAT

Aegean Breeze

A Greek restaurant where the fresh seafood is the perfect complement to the coastal ambience.

🏠 913 Gulf Breeze Pkwy #20, Gulf Breeze
🌐 myaegeanbreeze.com

$$(\$)(\$)(\$)$$

Café Tango

A romantic, intimate nook in a vine-covered cottage. Mediterranean menus include chorizo-encrusted fish.

🏠 14 Vicki St, Santa Rosa Beach
🌐 cafetango30-a.com

$$(\$)(\$)(\$)$$

The Jellyfish

Seafood rules at this Perdido Key institution, with sushi rolls and shrimp in high demand.

🏠 13700 Perdido Key Dr, Perdido Key
🌐 thejellyfishbar.com

$$(\$)(\$)(\$)$$

💬 INSIDER TIP
Cedar Key

On the other side of Apalachee Bay from Apalachicola is this quaint fishing village, with wooden waterside houses on stilts. The pioneering feel will charm any visitor.

streetscape, complete with a printer's workshop, a saddlery, and an old-time music store. Florida's earliest church, the Old Christ Church (1832), stands in leafy Seville Square shaded by oaks and magnolia trees.

The Seville Quarter entertainment complex, decorated in the Victorian style with furniture salvaged from historic local buildings, houses seven themed rooms under one roof.

The **TT Wentworth, Jr., Florida State Museum**, set in a Spanish Renaissance Revival building, has an eclectic collection including oddities such as a shrunken head and vintage Coca-Cola bottles.

TT Wentworth, Jr., Florida State Museum

♿ 🏠 330 S Jefferson St
🕐 Tue-Sat 🚫 Federal hols
W historicpensacola.org

⑧ Apalachicola

🚉 Tallahassee
ℹ 122 Commerce St, Franklin County; www. apalachicolabay.org

A riverside customs station set up in 1823, Apalachicola's first 100 years were its finest. It flourished first with the cotton trade, then sponge divers and lumber barons made their fortunes here. Today, pines and hardwoods still stand in the Apalachicola National Forest, where you'll find hiking trails, canoeing routes, and campgrounds. Oystering in the Apalachicola River began in the 1920s. Oyster boats still pull up at the dockside, which is lined with refrigerated seafood houses and old brick-built cotton warehouses. Among the seafood houses on Water Street there are several places to sample fresh oysters.

Walking through Tate's Hell State Park, Apalachicola National Forest, and *(inset)* the entrance ↓ to the forest

TOP 4

BEACHES OF THE PANHANDLE

Panama City Beach
W visitpanamacitybeach.com
Tourist-friendly with family attractions.

Pensacola Beach
W visitpensacolabeach.com
Eight miles (13 km) of varied and alluring coastline.

Grayton Beach
W floridastateparks.org
Natural beauty abounds at this State Park.

Perdido Key
W visitperdido.com
Expect acres of sand dunes and endless boardwalks.

A walking map of the old town, available at the Chamber of Commerce, takes in buildings from the cotton era, such as the 1838 Greek Revival Raney House. The John Gorrie State Museum houses a model of Gorrie's patent ice-making machine (1851), the vanguard of modern refrigeration.

THE GULF COAST, EVERGLADES, AND THE KEYS

The area around Tampa remained isolated until the 1880s, when the railroad was built, and the region subsequently became a booming port and tobacco-processing center. The Depression hit the region hard, but Tampa grew considerably as a result of World War II. The Everglades was largely ignored – a wilderness inhabited solely by the Seminoles, driven here in the 19th century – until it became a national park in 1934. Piracy was the main activity on the Keys prior to Florida joining the US in 1821. By the 1850s Key West was the country's wealthiest city, and developers sought to welcome tourists.

Experience

1. Tampa
2. Sarasota
3. St. Petersburg
4. Lee Island Coast
5. Big Cypress Swamp
6. Everglades National Park
7. The Keys
8. Key West

THE GULF COAST

In the late 1800s, the promise of winter sunshine lured wealthy travelers to the Gulf Coast, and the 361 days of sunshine a year still helps to attract great hordes to its miles of beaches bathed by the warm, calm waters of the Gulf of Mexico. Visitors can also kick the sand from their shoes and visit some of Florida's most interesting cities, or explore untouched wildernesses.

❶ Tampa

🚗🚉🚌✈ ℹ 401 E Jackson St; www.visittampabay.com

Tampa is one of the fastest-growing cities in Florida. Modern skyscrapers have replaced many of the original buildings, but vestiges of a colorful history remain.

Tampa's downtown area is centered around Franklin Street, home to the historic Tampa Theatre. To its southeast, on North Ashley Drive, is the Tampa Museum of Art, with Greek, Roman, and Etruscan antiquities as well as 20th-century American art. The Tampa Bay History Center on Riverwalk has three floors of galleries highlighting 12,000 years of Florida's history.

The Henry B. Plant Museum is the city's premier landmark, its Moorish minarets visible from all over the city. The interior retains the original 18th-century French furniture.

The Florida Aquarium on Channelside Drive displays a variety of creatures such as seabirds, otters, and alligators.

Located 3 miles (5 km) east of downtown, the historic Latin quarter of Ybor City was established in the 1800s by Spanish cigar manufacturer Vicente Martinez Ybor. His legacy is still visible in the shops, clubs, and restaurants on 7th Avenue, with their Spanish tiles and wrought-iron balconies.

Northeast of downtown is Tampa's biggest attraction – **Busch Gardens** theme park, which has a zoo, shows, rides, and more.

Busch Gardens

♿🅿 🏠 Busch Blvd ⏰ 10am–6pm daily, extended hours for summer & hols
🅦 buschgardens.com

❷ Sarasota

🚗🚌 ℹ 655 N Tamiami Trail; www.visitsarasota.com

Sarasota's affluence is often credited to the millionaire circus owner John Ringling, who invested much of his fortune in the area. His legacy is best seen at his house and in his splendid collection of European art. The Ringling Museum Complex comprises the Museum of Art, the Circus Museum, and the Ca' d'Zan – Ringling's winter residence overlooking Sarasota Bay. Ringling had a particular love

↑ Tampa's skyscrapers overlooking the Hillsborough River

for Italy, and his Italian Baroque paintings are the cornerstone of his collection.

Sarasota has an attractive waterfront setting, settled by numerous artists and writers. The restored storefronts in the downtown area around Palm Avenue and Main Street house many antiques shops, bars, and restaurants. The nearby barrier islands – Longboat Key, Lido Key, and Siesta Key – have great beaches and excellent accommodations. South Lido Park Beach on Lido Key has a fine woodland trail. The broad Siesta Key Beach is rather lively, while Turtle Beach is quieter and has the only campground on these Keys. Longboat Key is well known for its golf courses.

❸
St. Petersburg

🚇 🚌 ℹ 100 2nd Av N; www. visitstpeteclearwater.com

Established in 1875, "St. Pete's" claim to fame is the prestigious **Salvador Dalí Museum**, which has the largest private collection of the Spanish artist's work in the world. The pieces here range from Dalí's early figurative oil paintings to his first experiments in Surrealism, as well as his "masterworks."

The St. Petersburg Museum of History has exhibits ranging from mastodon bones and native pottery to a replica of the seaplane that made the world's first paid flight in 1914.

The modern Palladian-style Museum of Fine Arts, near the bay, is famous for its collection of European, American, and Asian works. Supreme among the French Impressionist paintings are *A Corner of the Woods* (1877) by Cézanne and Monet's classic *Parliament, Effect of Fog, London* (1904).

Entered through an artificial sandstone canyon in downtown St. Petersburg, the James Museum of Western and Wildlife Art has contemporary and traditional paintings and sculpture evoking the Old West.

Salvador Dalí Museum
⊘ ⊘ 🕐 🏠 1 Dalí Blvd
🚌 🕐 10am–5:30pm Mon–Sat (to 8pm Thu), noon–5:30pm Sun 🚫 Thanksgiving, Dec 25
🌐 thedali.org

🔍 HIDDEN GEM
Chihuly Collection

The Morean Arts Center in St. Petersburg celebrates the vivid colors and magical designs of glass sculptor Dale Chihuly (*www.morean artscenter.org*).

❹
Lee Island Coast

🚇 🚌 ℹ 1159 Causeway Rd, Sanibel; (239) 472-1080

This coastline offers an irresistible combination of sandy beaches, beautiful sunsets, spectacular seashells, and exotic wildlife. Of the two most popular islands, Sanibel has manicured gardens and rows of shops and restaurants along Periwinkle Way, the town's hub. The majority of the beaches with public access are along Gulf Drive, the best being Turner and Bowman's beaches.

The Sanibel Captiva Conservation Foundation on Sanibel-Captiva Road protects a chunk of the island's wetland. It has 4 miles (6 km) of boardwalk trails and an observation tower, a good vantage point for viewing birds. The **JN "Ding" Darling National Wildlife Refuge** occupies two-thirds of Sanibel. The popular scenic "Wildlife Drive" can be covered by bike or car. Paths and canoe trails are lined with red mangrove and sea grape. Canoes and boats are available to rent.

Captiva Island is less developed, but the old-fashioned South Seas Plantation Resort has a busy marina, the starting point for trips to the beautiful, untouched Cayo Costa Island. Other less developed islands lie close by and can easily be explored by boat.

JN "Ding" Darling National Wildlife Refuge
⊘ ⊘ 🏠 1 Wildlife Dr, Sanibel
📞 (239) 472-1100 🕐 Sat–Thu
🚫 Federal hols

↑ Renaissance artwork on display in the Ringling Museum of Art, Sarasota

EVERGLADES AND THE KEYS

The Everglades, a broad expanse of wetland dotted with tree islands, possesses a peculiar beauty and is a paradise for its prolific wildlife. Running southwest off the tip of the Florida peninsula are the Keys, a chain of jewel-like islands protected by North America's only coral reef. They say that the Keys are more about a state of mind than a geographical location.

Beachfront dining by torchlight in the Florida Keys

⑤

Big Cypress Swamp

🅐 Collier Co., Monroe Co.
🆆 nps.gov/bicy

Home to hundreds of species of plants and animals, a third of this vast wetland basin is covered by cypress trees. The Tamiami Trail (US 41) stretches from Tampa to Miami and cuts directly through the swamp. **Big Cypress National Preserve** is its largest protected area. Stop at the Oasis Visitor Center for information and enjoy the views from US 41. **Fakahatchee Strand Preserve State Park** lies to the west. The few remaining specimens of old-growth cypresses are found at Big Cypress Bend. Route 846 leads to the **Corkscrew Swamp Sanctuary**, a nesting area for endangered wood storks.

Big Cypress National Preserve

🕙 🆔 33000 Tamiami Trail E, Ochopee; www.nps.gov/bicy

Fakahatchee Strand Preserve State Park

🕙 🅐 137 Coast Line Dr, Copeland 🕗 8am–dusk daily 🆆 floridastateparks.org

Corkscrew Swamp Sanctuary

🕙🕙🕙 🅐 375 Sanctuary Rd W 🕗 7am–5:30pm daily 🆆 corkscrew. audubon.org

⑥

Everglades National Park

🅐 Collier Co., Monroe Co., Miami-Dade Co. 🆔 40001 State Rd, Homestead; www.nps.gov/ever

The Everglades form one of the most enduring images of Florida, and the National Park is the ideal place to explore this famous natural wonder.

The park's main entrance lies 10 miles (16 km) west of Florida City. Most of the trails here are boardwalks; some are suitable for bicycles. Boats and canoes can be rented. The best time to visit is during winter. South of the entrance is the Royal Palm Visitor Center and two boardwalk trails.

A short distance to the west, Long Pine Key's campground is beautifully situated. Several shady trails lead off from it: do not stray from the paths as the bedrock has "solution holes," which are difficult to spot.

Shark Valley lies north of Long Pine Key, near the park boundary. The area is best visited by taking a tram tour or a bicycle along the 15-mile (25-km) loop road. A tower at its end offers great views. The valley is home to the Seminole people, who were driven here in the 19th century.

Did You Know?

Beloved children's author Judy Blume is a long-time resident of Key West.

Flamingo offers activities such as hiking, fishing, boating, and wildlife viewing. The Visitor Center has information about ranger-led activities. Canoeing is the best way to explore the watery trails.

Visitors should bring insect repellent and sun protection. Follow park rules and respect all wildlife. Some plants and animals are poisonous. Do not wander off the pathways, and drive slowly as animals often venture onto the road.

⑦

The Keys

🚌 Miami 🆆 fla-keys.com

Running southwest off the tip of the Florida peninsula, this chain of fossilized coral islands

↑ See you later, at the Big Cypress National Preserve

is connected by the Overseas Highway and bordered by North America's only coral reef.

The largest of the Upper Keys is Key Largo, whose **John Pennekamp Coral Reef State Park** is famed for its diving and snorkeling. Islamorada, south of Key Largo, is known for its big game fishing.

Long Key Bridge marks the beginning of the Middle Keys, The primary appeal of the main center, Marathon Key, lies in its fertile fishing grounds. Crane Point Hammock is covered with tropical forest and mangroves, while the Crane Point Museum explains the islands' history, geology, and ecology.

The Lower Keys are more rugged – the vegetation is more wooded and supports a different flora and fauna. The most striking change, however, is in the languid pace of life.

Across the Seven Mile Bridge, Bahia Honda State Park has the finest beach in the Keys. The adjacent Looe Key National Marine Sanctuary is a spectacular dive location.

The second-largest island, Big Pine Key is the Lower Keys' main residential community and is great for watching deer and other wildlife.

John Pennekamp Coral Reef State Park

⊘ 🅰102601 Overseas Hwy
🄮8am–dusk daily
🅆floridastateparks.org

---

⑧
Key West

✈🚗🚢 🅸402 Wall St; www.fla-keys.com

Key West is a magnet for those who want to escape the mainland. Most of the sights are within a few blocks of Duval Street, the main axis of Old Key West. The Oldest House on Duval Street, built in 1829, displays eccentric maritime influences. At the northern edge of the Old Town is Mallory Square, which comes to life at sunset. The nearby Shipwreck Museum gives an insight into the lives of "wreckers."

The Bahama Village on the western fringe of the Old Town has a lively Caribbean flavor with a number of brightly painted clapboard buildings.

The Spanish-Colonial style **Hemingway Home** is where novelist Ernest Hemingway lived from 1931 to 1940. The room where he penned some

of his most famous works, such as *To Have and Have Not* (set in Key West), is above the carriage house.

The Mel Fisher Maritime Museum on Green Street displays fabulous shipwreck treasures salvaged from Spanish galleons in 1985. The Conch Train and the Old Town Trolley Tour are convenient options for exploring the town.

Hemingway Home

⊘ 🅰907 Whitehead St
🄮9am–5pm daily
🅆hemingwayhome.com

THE DEEP
SOUTH

A swamp in Mississippi

EXPLORE
THE DEEP SOUTH

This chapter divides the Deep South into three sightseeing areas, as shown on the map below. Find out more about each area on the following pages.

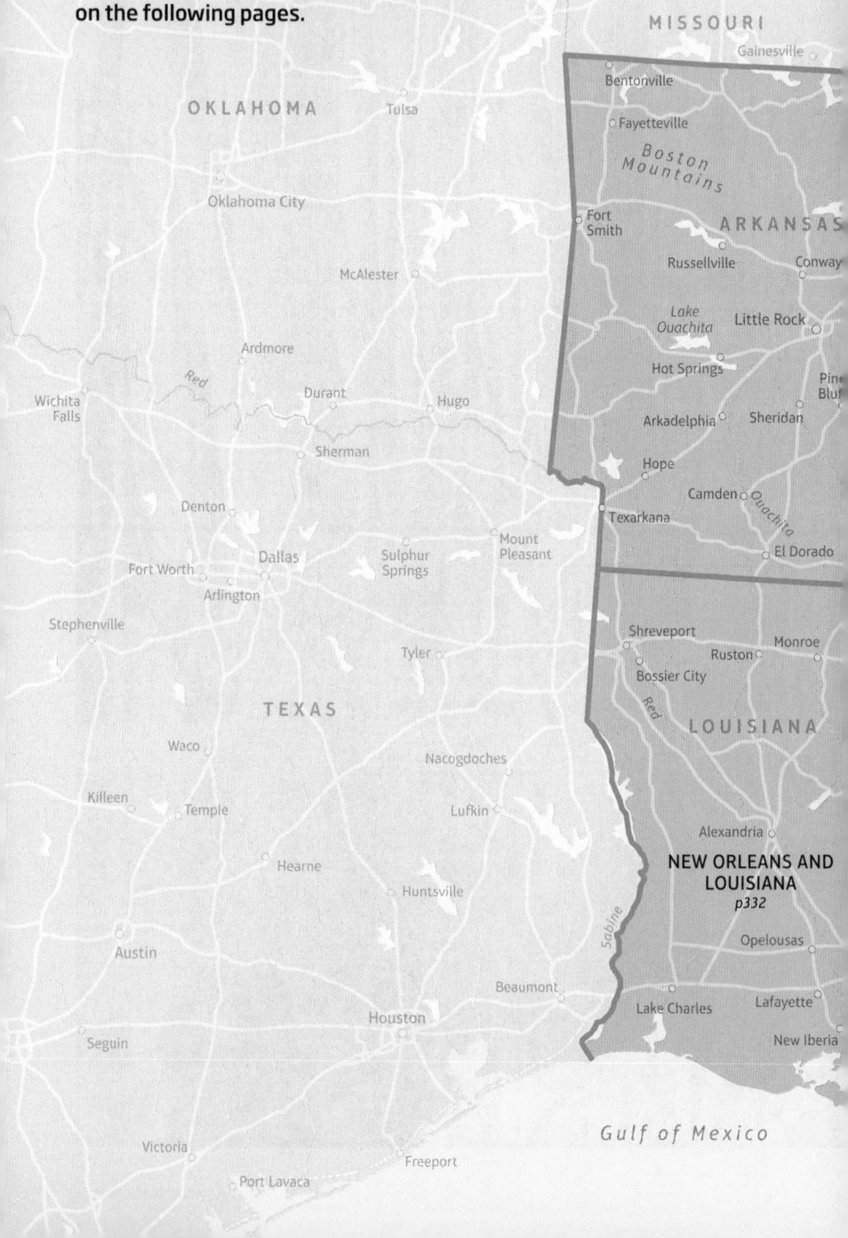

MISSOURI

Gainesville

Bentonville

Fayetteville

Boston Mountains

Fort Smith

ARKANSAS

Russellville   Conway

Lake Ouachita   Little Rock

Hot Springs   Pine Bluff

Arkadelphia   Sheridan

Hope

Camden   *Ouachita*

Texarkana

El Dorado

OKLAHOMA

Tulsa

Oklahoma City

McAlester

Ardmore

Red   Durant   Hugo

Wichita Falls

Sherman

Denton

Dallas   Sulphur Springs   Mount Pleasant

Shreveport   Monroe
Ruston

Bossier City

Fort Worth
Arlington

Stephenville

Red

LOUISIANA

Tyler

TEXAS

Waco

Nacogdoches

Killeen

Temple

Lufkin

Alexandria

Hearne

Huntsville

NEW ORLEANS AND LOUISIANA
p332

Opelousas

Austin

Sabine

Lafayette

Beaumont   Lake Charles

New Iberia

Seguin

Houston

Victoria

Freeport

Port Lavaca

Gulf of Mexico

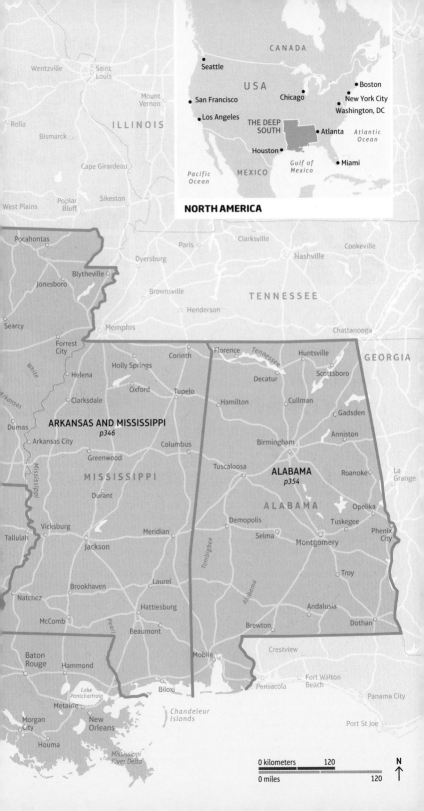

Wentzville
Saint Louis
Mount Vernon
Rolla
ILLINOIS
Bismarck
Cape Girardeau
West Plains
Poplar Bluff
Sikeston

Pocahontas
Paris
Clarksville
Cookeville
Nashville
Dyersburg
Blytheville
Jonesboro
Brownsville
TENNESSEE
Henderson
Chattanooga
Searcy
Memphis
Forrest City
Corinth
Florence
Tennessee
Huntsville
GEORGIA
Helena
Holly Springs
Decatur
Scottsboro
White
Oxford
Tupelo
Hamilton
Cullman
Gadsden
Clarksdale
Arkansas

ARKANSAS AND MISSISSIPPI
p346
Birmingham
Anniston
Dumas
Columbus
Arkansas City
Greenwood
Tuscaloosa
ALABAMA
p354
Roanoke
La Grange
Mississippi
MISSISSIPPI
ALABAMA
Opelika
Durant
Demopolis
Tuskegee
Vicksburg
Meridian
Selma
Phenix City
Tallulah
Jackson
Montgomery
Tombigbee
Brookhaven
Laurel
Troy
Natchez
Alabama
Andalusia
McComb
Hattiesburg
Dothan
Beaumont
Brewton
Pearl
Mobile
Crestview
Baton Rouge
Hammond
Pensacola
Fort Walton Beach
Panama City
Metairie
Lake Pontchartrain
Biloxi
Chandeleur Islands
Port St Joe
Morgan City
New Orleans
Houma
Mississippi River Delta

CANADA
Seattle
USA
Chicago
Boston
San Francisco
New York City
Washington, DC
Los Angeles
THE DEEP SOUTH
Atlanta
Atlantic Ocean
Houston
Pacific Ocean
MEXICO
Gulf of Mexico
Miami

NORTH AMERICA

0 kilometers   120
0 miles   120
N

8 DAYS

The Delta to the Ozarks

Day 1

Start your day in the historic French Quarter of New Orleans *(p334)*. Spend the morning browsing the stalls of the French Market, stopping in for beignets and *café au lait* at the Café du Monde *(p336)*. Then walk along the banks of the Mississippi River, down to the dock to the Steamboat *Natchez (p338)*. An afternoon cruise gives you a chance to take in some of the historic battle sites down river. Back on dry land, there's time to shop for antiques along Royal Street before a night of live jazz at Fritzel's *(www.fritzelsjazz.net)*.

Day 2

Arrive at the National WWII Museum *(p341)* as it opens, and spend the morning wandering its world-class exhibits before an early lunch at the site's atmospheric American Sector diner. Afterward, catch the streetcar along St. Charles Avenue to take in the lovely mansions of the city's Garden District *(p341)*. Drive on to Baton Rouge for the night *(p342)*, stopping off for a Creole dinner.

Day 3

Make an early start for the 4-hr drive to Shreveport *(p345)* – if there's time, take the road past the outskirts of the Kisatchie National Forest. After lunch, enjoy an educational afternoon at the Sci-Port Discover Center, an interactive science museum with dynamic exhibits and a planetarium. The Red River District is the town's nightlife hub; from here you can walk along the riverfront and risk a bet at one of the casinos if you're feeling lucky.

Day 4

Another early 3-hr drive can take you to Hot Springs National Park, Arkansas *(p348)*, by mid-morning. The visitor center within the Fordyce Bathhouse has information on some fascinating local history, and you can still experience some of the restorative benefits of the town at Buckstaff Bathhouse, a modern-day operational spa. If you're up for more driving, the scenic observation point at Hot Springs Mountain will result in some stunning photos. End your evening by

1 Mississippi River waterfront, New Orleans.

2 National WWII Museum, New Orleans.

3 Foliage in the Ozark Mountains.

4 The Superior Bathhouse, Hot Springs.

5 Tupelo Hardware Store.

relaxing at the Superior Bathhouse, now a lovely craft brewery.

Day 5

It's a 2-hr drive to the Mount Magazine State Park; take your own lunch and stop in sporadic scenic spots to drink in the beauty of the Ozark Mountains. Three hours farther through the splendor of the Ozark National Forest will bring you to Blanchard Springs Caverns, where you can take a tour of some of the world's most spectacular developed caves. Overnight just south of here, in Mountain View.

Day 6

The St. Francis National Forest is another 3-hr drive, so again it's worth setting an early alarm. It's one of the smallest but most diverse forests in the country, with a wealth of wildlife along its walking trails. The most popular spot is Bear Creek Lake, where you can picnic, swim, fish, or boat in the vast body of water. As darkness falls, drive to Little Rock (p348) for dinner.

Day 7

Little Rock is probably most famous for being the home town of former President of the United States, Bill Clinton. Clinton's Presidential Library is fascinating, and includes a replica of the Oval Office and the Clinton Presidential Park. After lunch at the library, head on to Clarksdale (p350), Mississippi, where you can end the day with down-home cooking and live blues the Ground Zero Blues Club (p351).

Day 8

Make a more leisurely start this morning and follow the Blues Trail markers to Oxford (p351), Mississippi. Here, at the campus of the University of Mississippi, the world's most extensive collection of blues recordings and related material is housed. You can also visit St. Peter's Cemetery, where the novelist William Faulkner is buried. Drive on to Tupelo, the birthplace of Elvis Presley. Pop into the hardware store where he bought his first guitar, before treating yourself to an indulgent dinner.

←

1 The French Market.

2 Bright lights of the grand Saenger Theatre.

3 An elegant lunch at Ralph's on the Park.

4 Dancing at the Spotted Cat on Frenchmen Street.

3 DAYS
in New Orleans

Day 1

Morning Beat the crowds with an early start at the French Market *(p334)*. Breakfast is coffee and a pastry from the food stalls, followed by a wander through the busy flea market. When you've picked up some souvenirs, aim for Jackson Square *(p336)* where you'll peak inside St. Louis Cathedral to glimpse the beautifully carved Baroque altar *(p336)*.

Afternoon For lunch, stop by Café du Monde *(p336)* and savor a few delicate beignets beside the Mississippi. Refreshed, hop on the Esplanade Avenue bus to Mid-City for a walk along the tranquil Bayou St. John. Cross Magnolia Bridge to reach City Park and the New Orleans Museum of Art *(p340)*.

Evening Enjoy a light supper of fresh, farm-to-table fare at Ralph's on the Park *(www.ralphsonthepark.com)*. Take the Canal Streetcar back to your hotel to freshen up for the evening. Then head to the plush Sazerac Bar *(www.winoschool. com)* for a nightcap of New Orleans' signature rye whiskey cocktail.

Day 2

Morning After breakfast at your hotel, ride the St. Charles Avenue Streetcar to the Garden District *(p341)*. Stroll the leafy streets and admire grand mansions such as Gothic Revival Briggs-Staub House and Greek-columned Robinson House, before exploring the wide avenues of elaborate stone mausoleums in walled Lafayette Cemetery.

Afternoon Take a stroll down Magazine Street and dip into trendy boutiques, before stopping in at Joey K's for a taste of homestyle Creole cooking *(www.joeyks restaurant.com)*. Reboard the streetcar and continue uptown to Audubon Aquarium of the Americas, home to all manner of underwater creatures *(p339)*.

Evening Ride the streetcar back to the Warehouse District in time for a contemporary Caribbean dinner at Compère Lapin *(www.comperelapin.com)*. Take a cab to the Spotted Cat on Frenchmen Street for late-night jazz *(www.spottedcatmusicclub.com)*.

Day 3

Morning Start the day with a bang-up breakfast at the Ruby Slipper Cafe *(www. therubyslippercafe.net)*, before spending a few hours in the huge National WWII Museum touring numerous impressive military displays *(p341)*. Grab a light lunch at the museum café, Jeri Nims Soda Shop.

Afternoon Catch a fresh breeze with a walk along the Mississippi. Wander through Woldenberg Riverfront Park, with its sculptures and gardens, and take a seat on the water's edge to watch the boats go by.

Evening Suitably chilled, head to modern Cajun restaurant Cochon for an early dinner of fine charcuterie and a glass or two of old-world wine *(www. cochonrestaurant.com)*. Then make for the beautiful Italianate Saenger Theatre and end your day with a spectacular Broadway show *(www.saengernola.com)*.

Contagious Cajun

Cajun music is a fiddle-driven country sound that's sure to get you dancing. The Acadians, or "Cajuns," were originally French immigrants to Canada, exiled by the British in 1755. Many settled in Louisiana and brought their traditions with them. To hear live Cajun bands, head to Lafayette (p344). The roadhouse restaurant Prejean's (www.prejeans.com) is a good bet.

→

A Cajun performance in Henderson, Louisiana

THE DEEP SOUTH FOR
MUSIC FANS

The Deep South has been a cradle for almost every great American musical genre since the early 20th century. Here, European folk blended with the soulful gospel and blues traditions passed down within the African American community. The result? Some of your favorite household names.

↑ King of rock'n'roll, Elvis Presley

Rock'n'Roll Stars

Blues, country, and the sound of the electric guitars merged in the 1950s to create high-tempo, rhythm-driven music. Though Memphis (p270) was the epicenter of rock in the 1950s, many of the early artists, including Elvis, grew up in the Deep South. Arkansas-born Sister Rosetta Tharpe (1915-73) was an early pioneer, while Fats Domino (1928-2017), the French Creole pianist from New Orleans, inspired a generation of artists.

THE KING OF ROCK'N'ROLL

Few rock stars can match the fame of Elvis Presley (1935-77), who dominated the charts in the 1950s and early 1960s, and whose tragic early death was mourned by much of the planet. Known for his smooth, baritone voice, good looks, and scandalously gyrating hips ("Elvis the pelvis"), he knocked out hits such as Jailhouse Rock, Love Me Tender, Blue Suede Shoes, and Hound Dog. Yet "The King" was born into very humble circumstances in Tupelo (p350). His simple home is now the Elvis Presley Birthplace (www.elvispresleybirthplace.com).

Barstool Blues

Lost love, oppression, murder, and deals with the devil – the blues has it all. The genre emerged in the African American communities of the Mississippi Delta, where African rhythms, work chants, and spirituals merged. The "Father of the Blues" was Alabama-born W. C. Handy (1873–1958), who published the landmark *Memphis Blues* in 1912, but most of the musicians hailed from Mississippi. To learn more, see a show at Ground Zero Blues Club *(www.ground zeroblues club.com)* or visit the Delta Blues Museum *(www.delta bluesmuseum.org)*, both in Clarksdale *(p350)*.

←

Jax Nassar performing at Ground Zero Blues Club

Soul Heaven

Early pioneers of soul were Arkansas-born Little Willie John (1937–68) and New Orleans artist Allen Toussaint (1938–2015). The "King of Soul" Sam Cooke (1931–64) was born in Clarksdale *(p350)*. Wilson Pickett (1941–2006) sang in Alabama church choirs before making it big with *Mustang Sally*. Lionel Richie (1949–) is also from Alabama *(p355)*. Arkansas-born Reverend Al Green (1946–) is best known for his soul hits of the 1970s.

←

Al Green performing during New Orleans Jazz & Heritage Festival

Hear That Dixieland Jazz Band Play

The birthplace of jazz, New Orleans *(p334)* remains a showcase for live perform-ances. "Dixieland" jazz can be heard most nights at Preservation Hall and the Jazz Playhouse, on Bourbon Street *(p335)*. Jazz was pioneered by locals such as Buddy Bolden (1877–1931). Learn more about the genre at the New Orleans Jazz Museum *(p339)*.

→

A performance in Preservation Hall, New Orleans

NEW ORLEANS AND LOUISIANA

Explorer René La Salle claimed Louisiana for France in 1682. Natchitoches was established in 1714, and New Orleans in 1718. Louisiana reverted to Spanish rule in 1763 before it was sold to the US in 1803, but French influence remains strong; Acadians fleeing French Canada created "Cajun" culture in the late 18th century. Enslaved Africans were imported to work cotton and sugar plantations; Louisiana joined the Confederacy in 1861, and remained segregated until the 1960s. The state experienced the full force of Hurricane Katrina in 2005, and is steadily recovering.

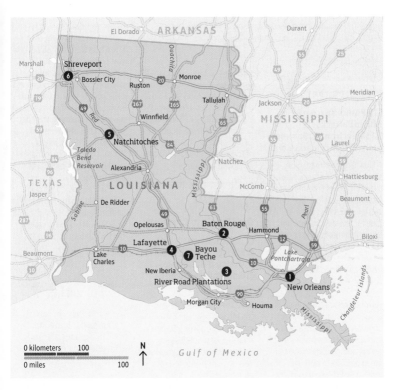

1

NEW ORLEANS

Located in southeast Louisiana, this is the "Crescent City," set in a sultry curve of the Mississippi River, where a history of strong European, Caribbean, and African influences has shaped a local culture like no other. This heady mix results in a daily celebration of life, reflected in the city's food, music, and many traditions.

1

French Market

🏠 N Peters St, from St. Ann to Barracks sts 🚌🚊 Riverfront 🕐 9am–6pm daily 🌐 frenchmarket.org

A New Orleans institution since 1791, this area served as a trading place for American Indians long before European settlement. Officially five blocks between St. Ann and Barracks streets, in daily use, the "French Market" usually denotes the open-air markets from St. Philip to Barracks streets, which stock many New Orleans specialties. The Farmers Market (beginning at Ursulines Street) offers fresh Louisiana produce, seafood, and spices. Strawberries in the spring and pecans in the fall are especially prized. The majority of the space is now given over to the Flea Market, where items such as jewelry, pottery, and crafts are sold at the stalls around the French Market buildings. The nearby Bazaar Market was built in 1870 by Joseph Abeilard, one of the country's first African American architects.

2

Old Ursuline Convent

🏠 1112 Chartres St 🚌🚊 Riverfront 🕐 10am–4pm Mon–Fri, 9am–3pm Sat 🌐 oldursulineconvent museum.com

This, the oldest building in the Mississippi Valley, was built in 1752, some 25 years after the Ursuline Sisters first arrived in New Orleans. With its steep-pitched roof punctuated by dormers and chimneys, it is a typical French Colonial structure and one of the few to remain from that period. In the 1820s, the nuns moved to new quarters, and the convent became the first official residence for the bishops and archbishops of New Orleans, and the home of the archdiocesan archives.

The current chapel, now known as Our Lady of Victory, was consecrated in 1845. Inside visitors can admire the splendid pine and cypress ceiling, two superb Bavarian stained-glass windows, and a window depicting the Battle of New Orleans, beneath an image of Our Lady of Prompt Succor. The nuns' old kitchen and laundry is now the rectory.

A formal French garden containing a handsome iron gazebo lies in front of the building, accessed via the porter's lodge.

Did You Know?

Various city buildings are said to be haunted, including Lafitte's Blacksmith Shop.

←

Bourbon Street in the French Quarter, humming with activity day and night

③
Bourbon Street

🅰 Between Canal St & Esplanade Av 🚌

Its reputation as a decadent party hub aside, this legendary street's name has nothing to do with the whiskey, despite the string of bars lining the thoroughfare; rather, it refers to the French royal family of Bourbon. While its infamy is not entirely unearned (during Mardi Gras, the balconies above the sidewalks sag from the weight of drunken revelers), Bourbon Street is a great spot for dining, architecture, and, of course, music.

The cozy **Fritzel's European Jazz Pub** has attracted the best musicians since 1969. Just a few minutes away, **Preservation Hall** has helped preserve New Orleans jazz since its inception in 1961. Named after the pirate brothers Jean and Pierre Lafitte, **Lafitte's Blacksmith Shop** is one of the finest bars in New Orleans. Constructed some time before 1772, it is a good example of the brick-between-posts French-style of building.

Fritzel's European Jazz Pub
🏠 733 Bourbon St
🌐 fritzelsjazz.net

Preservation Hall
⊛ 🏠 726 St. Peter St
🌐 preservationhall.com

Lafitte's Blacksmith Shop
🏠 941 St. Peter St
🌐 lafittesblacksmithshop.com

NEW ORLEANS IRONWORK

Among the city's most recognizable features are the elaborate iron balconies. Cast-iron patterns are romantic, with floral designs. Wrought iron is less complex but more dynamic. Both kinds of ironwork can be seen in the French Quarter; look up as you explore.

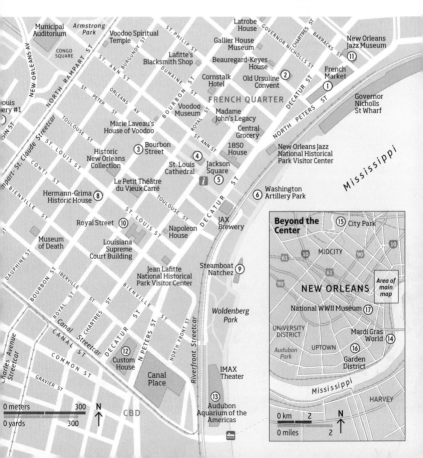

EAT

Café Beignet

Casual café on Royal Street, perfect for refreshment after a busy day antiques hunting. It can fill up quickly in the mornings but afternoons are generally quieter.

📍334 Royal St
🌐cafebeignet.com

$ $ $

Café du Monde

This legendary grazing spot serves sweet French beignets 24 hours a day, best enjoyed with a *café au lait*. There is plenty of seating, but expect lines at peak times (9am-9pm).

📍800 Decatur St
🌐cafedumonde.com

$ $ $

---

④ 🖼 🗺 🏛

St. Louis Cathedral, Cabildo & Presbytère

📍Jackson Sq 🚋🚊St. Charles Av, Canal ⏰St. Louis Cathedral: 8:30am-4pm daily; Cabildo & Presbytère: 10am-4:30pm Tue-Sun
🌐stlouiscathedral.org

St. Louis Cathedral, which stands on the site of two earlier churches, is the oldest Catholic cathedral in continuous use in the US. The current building, begun in 1789, was dedicated as a cathedral in 1794. Inside are superb murals and a carved-wood Baroque altar.

The Cabildo, designed by Guilberto Guillemard, was built in 1795 and served as a capitol for the legislative assembly of the Spanish Colonial government and subsequently as the City Hall. From 1853 to 1911 it housed the state Supreme Court. The Louisiana Purchase *(p53)* was signed in the Sala Capitular in 1803.

The Presbytère (or Casa Curial) was built between 1794 and 1813 and used as a courthouse until 1911. It now houses the Mardi Gras Museum.

---

⑤

Jackson Square

🚋🚊Riverfront

Today, an attractive and lively meeting place, this square was named the Place d'Armes in the early French colony, when it was little more than a muddy field. Here, the troops were drilled, criminals were placed in the stocks, and executions were carried out. In 1850, it was renamed for the hero of the Battle of New Orleans (1815), after the Baroness Micaela Pontalba laid out the gardens and pathways of the square in a radial pattern, with walkways stemming out from the center. Under her auspices, the Pelanne brothers designed the handsome wrought-iron fence that encloses the square. At the center stands a statue of General Andrew Jackson, astride a rearing horse. The inscription "The Union must and shall be preserved," on the plinth, was added by General Benjamin "Beast" Butler, when he occupied the city during the American Civil War *(p54)*.

The palatial St. Louis Cathedral rising above Jackson Square ↓

Today, there are plenty of benches where visitors can sit and enjoy the charm of the historical houses that surround the square. Outside the park, artists rent space and hang their works on the enclosing fence, and on the flagstones around the square, tarot card readers, jazz players, and clowns entertain visitors throughout the week.

→ A memorial Civil War cannon in Washington Artillery Park

⑥
Washington Artillery Park and Moon Walk

◪ Decatur St, between St. Ann St & St. Peter St
🚌🚊 Riverfront

Washington Artillery Park faces Jackson Square from Decatur Street. Inside the park is an austere concrete amphitheater with a central staircase leading to the Moonwalk. This community boardwalk was named after former New Orleans Mayor Maurice "Moon" Landrieu, who approved the construction of flood walls that made the riverfront area accessible to the public.

The park was built in 1976 and was once used as a military training ground, but today the amphitheater and Moonwalk are favored by street performers. Enthusiastic crowds often gather to enjoy performances by musicians, including guitarists, clarinettists, saxophonists, trombonists, and steel drummers, who play with an open case at their feet.

The breeze along the waterfront can provide a welcome break from the humidity of the city, and it's also the perfect vantage point from which to see the river, Jackson Square, and the surrounding area. Stone steps lead down to where you can dangle your feet in the whiskey-colored water or watch the steamboats, ocean-going barges, and other river traffic float past. Don't attempt to stand in the river, however, as the current is deceptively powerful.

⑦ Ⓜ
St. Louis Cemetery #1

◪ 425 Basin St between St. Louis & Conti sts ☎ (504) 482-5065 🚌 ◷ 9am-3pm Mon-Sat, 9am-noon Sun
🎭 Mardi Gras

The city's oldest surviving cemetery was established in 1789. This fascinating place, with its rows of mausoleums, is the resting place of many legendary local residents. The most famous of all is probably Marie Laveau, the voodoo priestess. Crowds visit her tomb, marking it with an "X" (symbolically requesting that she grant a particular wish). Many of the city's 19th-century Creole aristocracy are buried here in ornate mausoleums.

Under new rules, all visitors to St. Louis Cemetery #1 must be accompanied by a licensed tour guide. Tours by Save Our Cemeteries (*saveourcemeteries. org*) and Two Chicks (*twochicks walkingtours.com*) provide excellent local information.

⑧ ◈ Ⓜ
Hermann-Grima Historic House

◪ 820 St Louis St 🚌
◷ 10am-3pm Mon, Tue & Thu-Sat ◷ Federal hols
🌐 hgghh.org

This gabled brick house is one of the French Quarter's few examples of American Creole–style architecture. It was built in 1831 by William Brand for Samuel Hermann, a German-Jewish merchant who lost his fortune in 1837 and sold the house to Judge Felix Grima. It features a central doorway with a fanlight and marble steps; another window with a fanlight graces the second floor. Inside, the floors and doors are made of cypress. The three-story service quarters are in a building off the parterre garden behind the house. They contain a kitchen with a rare four-burner stove with a beehive oven.

VOODOO WORSHIP

Voodoo arrived in New Orleans from Africa, where it originated as a form of ancestor worship among West African tribes brought here as slaves. Voodoo queen Marie Laveau (c 1794–1881) used Catholic elements like incense and saints in her rituals, which she opened to the public for a fee.

The stylish *Natchez* paddle steamer, pride of the Mississippi River ↑

⑨ Steamboat Natchez

Woldenberg Riverfront Park wharf Riverfront **Jazz Cruises: 11:30am & 2:30pm daily; dinner cruise: 7pm daily** steamboatnatchez.com

A reminder of the old days of river travel, the Steamboat *Natchez* is typical of the 19th-century steamboats that traveled the length of the Mississippi, taking 3–5 days to sail from Louisville, Kentucky, to New Orleans. The boatmen, notorious brawlers in search of women and liquor at the end of a trip, cemented New Orleans' reputation as the "City of Sin." In their heyday, from 1830 to 1860, some 30 steamboats lined up at the levee. The steamboat era ended at the close of the 19th century with the development of railroads and highways. Today, the *Natchez* can be seen gliding along the river on daily two-hour jazz cruises, and every so often, competing in a paddle steamer race.

⑩ Royal Street

St. Charles Av

Running through the historic heart of the city, Royal Street is the pride of the French Quarter. Many of its beautiful buildings date back to the 18th century, when the thorough-fare was the city's financial center and most fashionable street. Today, it is alive with antiques shops, restaurants, and bars. Many of the landmarks here have been transformed into museums and galleries. LaBranche House, which was constructed in 1835 for sugar planter Jean Baptiste LaBranche, is among the city's

Did You Know?

Steamboat *Natchez* is named after an American Indian tribe native to southern Mississippi.

most photographed buildings, known as it is for its fine oak-leaf ironwork and attractive hanging ferns.

The **Historic New Orleans Collection**, born of one couple's interest in the Battle of New Orleans (1815), is housed in a complex of houses built for Jean François Merieult and his wife in 1792. The collectors were General L. Kemper and Leila Moore Williams, who lived in the residence at the rear of the courtyard from the 1940s to the 1960s.

The main Royal Street campus comprises seven restored properties and features changing exhibits. The 13 Louisiana History Galleries, on the main campus, trace the region's develop-ment. Highlights include original documents from the transfer of the Louisiana Purchase and items from the Battle of New Orleans. Nearby, the Williams Research Center houses three centuries of art and artifacts.

Also on Royal Street is Rumors, a gift shop that sells Mardi Gras souvenirs all year long – masks, beads, Krewe costumes, and posters are all available for sale here. Farther away are Gallier House Museum, an attractive 19th-century residence combining Creole and American architectural elements, and LaLaurie Mansion, an otherwise delightful building that is rumored to be one of the most haunted houses in New Orleans.

Historic New Orleans Collection

533 Royal St 9:30am-4:30pm Tue-Sat hnoc.org

(11)

New Orleans Jazz Museum

400 Esplanade Av Riverfront 10am-4:30pm Tue-Sun Federal hols louisianastate museum.org

This Greek Revival building, built in 1835, functioned as a mint until 1909, turning out a variety of coinage, including Confederate and Mexican currency. It then became a federal prison and was later used by the Coast Guard. In the late 1970s, it was taken over by the state and converted into a museum to house the vast New Orleans Jazz Collection. The exhibit tells the story of jazz through a collection of original musical instruments, vintage photographs, and historic documents. Among the instruments displayed are the clarinet George Lewis used to record "Burgundy Street Blues," and the cornet Louis Armstrong learned to play on. At the entrance are a series of photographs of early bands and musicians, as well as a scale model of a steamboat.

The building also houses the History of the Old US Mint Exhibition, which displays gold and silver coins formerly minted here. On the third floor, the New Orleans Mint Performing Arts Center offers live musical and theatrical performances for a modest fee.

(12)

Custom House

423 Canal St Canal Daily Federal hols auduboninstitute.org

Perhaps the most important Federal-style structure in the South, this architectural landmark took 33 years to complete (1848–81). The Marble Hall is a dramatic space under a glass ceiling supported by Egyptian Revival marble columns. The building is also home to the Audubon Butterfly Garden and Insectarium.

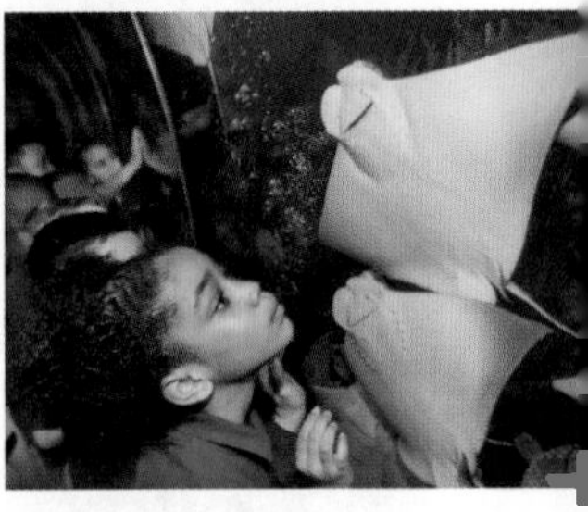

↑ Meeting stingrays at the Audubon Aquarium of the Americas

(13)

Audubon Aquarium of the Americas

Canal St at Mississippi River Riverfront 10am-5pm daily Mardi Gras, Thanksg., Dec 24 & 25 audubon institute.org

The collection at the Audubon Aquarium of the Americas spans the underwater world, from the Caribbean and the Amazon Rainforest, to the waters that give New Orleans its lifeblood – the Mississippi River and the Gulf of Mexico. Highlights of the complex, which features some 600 species of marine life, include the 30-ft- (9-m-) long tunnel to the Great Maya Reef exhibit of a submerged city of the Yucatan Peninsula, with ruins, lion fish, sponges, moray eels, spiny lobsters, and many other exotic sea creatures that inhabit a coral reef. In the Amazon Rainforest, piranhas lurk in the waters that flow under a forest canopy alive with tropical birds, wild orchids, and an anaconda. Sharks, stingrays, and sea turtles swim in the Gulf of Mexico, the aquarium's largest tank, which holds 400,000 gallons (150,000 liters) of water.

NEW ORLEANS JAZZ

Jazz is America's original contribution to world culture. Its roots lie in the entire spectrum of music that was played in 19th-century New Orleans, including African work chants and spirituals, as well as European and American folk melodies. The sound evolved slowly and almost imperceptibly in a number of places - at balls, parades, dances, and funerals - a perfect reflection of New Orleans' unique blend of cultures.

← Anthony, Cleopatra, and Elvis welcoming visitors to Blaine Kern's Mardi Gras World

⑭ 🛇 🛇 ▭ 🏛
Mardi Gras World

🏠 1380 Port of NO Place
🕐 9:30am–4:30pm daily
🌐 mardigrasworld.com

Blaine Kern is often called "Mr. Mardi Gras" because many of the massive floats that roll through the streets during Carnival are built here in his company warehouses. A tour begins with a short film showing the floats in parades and the stages of their production, from the original drawings to the manufacture of the final pieces. You can try on some of the costumes that Krewe members have worn in past parades and wander through one of the warehouses to view gigantic papier-mâché figures.

⑮ 🛇
City Park

🏠 Between Robert E. Lee Blvd & City Pk Av, & Orleans Av & Wisner Blvd 🚌
🕐 10am–6pm Tue–Sat (to 6pm Sat), 11am–5pm Sun

The fifth largest urban park in the US, City Park is a New Orleans institution, where visitors can relax and enjoy the semitropical Louisiana weather. The New Orleans Botanical Garden and the prestigious **New Orleans Museum of Art** (or NOMA) share this space with moss-draped live oaks, lagoons for boating and fishing, and the championship Bayou Oaks Golf Course.

Housed in an impressive Beaux Arts building, the museum has an astonishingly varied collection. Originally the Delgado Museum of Art, it was founded in 1910 when Isaac Delgado, a millionaire bachelor, donated the original $150,000 to construct an art museum in City Park. In 1971 it was renamed the New Orleans Museum of Art in deference to some of its newer benefactors. The New Orleans Botanical Garden was created in the 1930s. Then, it was primarily a rose garden, but today there are more than 2,000 varieties of plants from around the world organized as themed gardens. Highlights include the Conservancy of Two Sisters, the Butterfly Walk, the Lord and Taylor

MARDI GRAS

Spanning across several days and culminating on the day before Ash Wednesday - Mardi Gras - Carnival festivities in New Orleans are celebrated with lavish balls and parades, presented by "Krewes." The tradition of throwing souvenir coins and beads from the floats to the crowds began in 1881.

Rose Garden, and the Historic Train Garden with miniature trains and streetcars moving through a tiny New Orleans made of plant materials.

New Orleans Museum of Art (NOMA)

⊕ ⊛ 🅰 1 Collins Diboll Circle 🕐 10am–6pm Tue–Thu, 10am–9pm Fri (select dates), 10am–5pm Sat, 11am–5pm Sun 🔒 Federal hols 🌐 noma.org

---

⑯

Garden District

🅰 Between Jackson & Louisiana avs, & St. Charles Av & Magazine St 🚋 St. Charles 🚌

When the Americans arrived in New Orleans after the Louisiana Purchase in 1803, they settled upriver from the French Quarter. The area is referred to as the Garden District because of the lush gardens planted with magnolia, camellia, azalea, and jasmine. A residential neighborhood, it is filled with large mansions built by wealthy city planters and merchants. Some of the grand residences here are the Robinson House and Colonel Short's Villa, which has a handsome cast-iron cornstalk fence.

For a more romantic New Orleans experience, take a ride on the slow-moving St. Charles Avenue Streetcar to uptown New Orleans. The last of the sort that featured in Tennessee Williams' *A Streetcar Named Desire*, it travels from Canal Street to Carrollton Avenue. Along the way it passes many famous landmarks, the most prominent being the Greek Revival Gallier Hall, the Gothic Revival Christ Church, Touro Synagogue, the Latter Public Library, and Loyola and Tulane Universities.

Just off St. Charles Avenue is one of the most alluring urban parks in the country, filled with ancient oaks, a lagoon, running tracks, picnic shelters, and playgrounds. Audubon Park was originally a sugar plantation and was the location of the 1884 World Exposition before it opened as a public park in 1898.

> The area is referred to as the Garden District because of the lush gardens planted with magnolia, camellia, azalea, and jasmine.

DRINK

Old New Orleans Rum Distillery

This is the oldest premium rum distillery in the US. The tour includes a cocktail and a tasting session.

🅰 2815 Frenchmen St 🌐 oldneworleans rum.com

---

⑰ ⊛

National WWII Museum

🅰 945 Magazine St 🕐 9am–5pm daily 🔒 Federal hols 🌐 nationalww2museum.org

This hugely impressive archive honors the role played by the US military in WWII. The Home Front, the European and Pacific Theaters, and D-Day are the principal exhibits, combining news reports, personal stories, and some of the era's vehicles and weapons. There's also a local connection: New Orleans shipbuilder Andrew Higgins built many of the US landing craft used in the war.

← Admiring Renaissance paintings in the New Orleans Museum of Art

LOUISIANA

Renowned for its moody landscape of bayous and swamps, plantation homes, jazz music, fine food, and colorful Mardi Gras festivities, Louisiana is a state richly steeped in history. The state has come a long way since the Civil War, and the painful struggle for Civil Rights, and today, preserves both its Colonial history as well as its distinct Creole and Cajun heritage.

Did You Know?

Louisiana law says it is illegal for a person to "gargle" in public.

2

Baton Rouge

359 Third St; www.visitbatonrouge.com

Established by the French in 1699 to control access to the Mississippi River, Baton Rouge ("Red Stick") was named for the spikes hung with bloody fish heads that marked the boundary between two American Indian territories. The capital of Louisiana since 1849, Baton Rouge's population grew dramatically after Hurricane Katrina in 2005 as people from New Orleans, suddenly homeless, relocated here. North of downtown, the State Capitol was built in 1932 under the tireless direction of ex-governor and US senator Huey Long (1893–1935). Ironically, Long was assassinated in the building in 1935. This 34-story structure, the country's tallest capitol, offers superb views from its 27th-floor observation deck. To the south, Long's penchant for lavish buildings is further reflected in the Old Governor's Mansion, built in 1930 and modeled on the White House. Today, this restored Greek Revival structure displays such memorabilia of past governors as Jimmie Davis's guitar and Huey Long's pajamas. The ornate 1849 Gothic Revival **Louisiana Old State Capitol**, to the southwest, holds interactive exhibits on the state's tumultuous political history. Outside, a plaza overlooks the river, where the World War II-era destroyer USS *Kidd* offers public tours. Farther south, you can get a feel of the antebellum era first hand at the 1791 Magnolia Mound Plantation, a French Creole-style home.

A short drive southwest from downtown leads to the attractive, tree-shaded Louisiana State University campus and the **LSU Rural Life Museum**. Unlike the grand plantation restorations, this museum reveals how the common farming families lived in the 19th century.

Louisiana Old State Capitol
100 North Blvd 10am-4pm Tue-Fri, 9am-3pm Sat
Sun, Mon & Federal hols
louisianaoldstatecapitol.org

LSU Rural Life Museum
I-10 exit 160, at 4650 Essen Ln 8am-5pm daily
Some major hols
lsu.edu/rurallife

←

The stained-glass rotunda of the Louisiana Old State Capitol, Baton Rouge

↑ Strolling through the tunnel of trees at Oak Alley Plantation on the River Road

3

River Road Plantations

🏛 50 miles (80 km) NW of New Orleans 🚌

The River Road is a 70-mile (130-km) corridor that follows the Mississippi River toward Baton Rouge. In the 1850s, hundreds of antebellum mansions lined this stretch, owned by wealthy planters who profited from trading sugarcane, processed by a captive labor force of enslaved people. Today, the road meanders past petrochemical plants and surviving plantation houses, a few still surrounded by slave quarters and sugar mills. Some of these residences have been given a new lease on life as small museums, where visitors can learn about the history of plantations and the enslaved people who lived on them.

Located near Wallace in St. John the Baptist Parish, the **Whitney Plantation** Historic District is now an exceptional museum dedicated to those enslaved at the plantation. The original plantation dates back to 1752, though the main part of the house, built in a French-Creole raised style, was built in 1803. Curated by a Senegalese historian specializing in the history of the slave trade, the exhibits recount the

histories of some of the last survivors of slavery, recorded by the Federal Writers Project in the 1920s, and see Woodrow Nash's sculptures of these last survivors, who were children at the time of emancipation. There are poignant memorials listing names of the people enslaved here, and specially commissioned works of art.

The name **Oak Alley** comes from the 28 live oaks that line the entrance to this former sugar plantation. They were planted over 300 years ago, before the house was built by enslaved laborers for Creole planter Jacques Telesphore Roman III in 1837. Oak Alley was established as a sugar-cane plantation, but pecans were also harvested here: Antoine, an enslaved gardener, developed the first commercial variety of pecan nut, the "Paper Shell," on the property. There are exhibits on the process of sugar production and slavery, and visitors can wander the plantation's main house and grounds, which have been used in several movies.

Revolutionary War veteran Guillame Duparc was given a large land grant, and built the **Laura Plantation**'s French Creole-style house in 1805. After he died, four generations of women ran the plantation. The enslaved people at this

estate – who later became tenant farmers – are thought to be the source of various Senegalese folk tales, including the famous *Br'er Rabbit* stories. Guided tours of the main house and surviving outbuildings explore the history of the plantation.

Whitney Plantation
♿🚫 🏛 5099 Louisiana Hwy 18, Edgard ⏰ 9:30am-4:30pm Wed-Mon 🌐 whitney plantation.com

Oak Alley
♿ 🏛 3645 Hwy 18, Vacherie ⏰ 9am-5pm daily ✖ Jan 1, Mardi Gras, Thanksgiving, Dec 25 🌐 oakalley plantation.com

Laura Plantation
♿ 🏛 2247 Hwy 18 ⏰ 9am-5pm daily ✖ Federal hols 🌐 lauraplantation.com

EAT

Baton Rouge's most iconic restaurants.

Elsie's Plate and Pie
🏛 3145 Government St
🌐 elsiespies.com

$$$

———

Curbside Burgers
🏛 4158 Government St
🌐 curbside-burgers.com

$$$

———

Louie's Cafe
🏛 3322 Lake St
🌐 louiescafe.com

$$$

———

Bellue's Fine Cajun Cuisine
🏛 3225 Perkins Rd
🌐 parrains.com

$$$

↑ The towering Cathedral of St. John the Evangelist in Lafayette

Acadian Cultural Center

🏠501 Fisher Rd 🕘9am–4:30pm Tue–Fri, 8:30am–noon Sat 🔒Mardi Gras, federal hols 🌐nps.gov/jela

---

5

Natchitoches

🚌 🛈780 Front St; www.natchitoches.com

Louisiana's oldest settlement, Natchitoches ("Nack-a-tish") was founded on the banks of the Cane River in 1714. The town's compact riverfront district retains much of its 18th-century Creole architecture. South of downtown, Fort St. Jean Baptiste re-creates a 1732 frontier outpost designed to deter Spanish expansion.

The surrounding Cane River National Heritage Area offers several plantation house tours. Of these, **Melrose Plantation** was visited by such writers as John Steinbeck and William Faulkner. The **Louisiana Sports Hall of Fame and Northwest Louisiana History Museum** showcases Louisiana athletes and sports figures and explores the area's cultural traditions.

4

Lafayette

🚗🚌 🛈1400 NW Evangeline Thruway; www.lafayettetravel.com

The unofficial "Capital of French Louisiana" is a great introduction to Cajun life. It evolved from an Acadian settlement, set up in 1821 around what is now the Cathedral of St. John the Evangelist. Today, the town is distinguished by its unique cultural heritage.

Lafayette's living history museum, **Vermilionville** (the original name of the town), evokes 19th-century Acadiana with its French-style architecture. The **Acadian Cultural Center** features demonstrations on the skills needed to survive in 18th- and 19th-century Louisiana.

Vermilionville

♿ 🏠300 Fisher Rd 🕘10am–4pm Tue–Sun 🔒Mon, Jan 1, Mardi Gras, Thanksg., Dec 24, 25 & 31 🌐vermilionville.org

THE ACADIANS - CAJUN COUNTRY

The Acadians, or "Cajuns," were French immigrants who founded a colony in Nova Scotia, Canada, in 1604, naming it l'Acadie after the legendary Greek paradise, Arcadia. Exiled by the British in 1755, they finally settled along the bayous of Louisiana, where they developed a rich culture rooted in its music and cuisine. Acadian culture is best seen in the region's many festivals. Of these, the Courir de Mardi Gras, literally "Fat Tuesday Run," is a distinctly Cajun take on Mardi Gras. Acadiana is a 22-parish region comprising the wetlands area near New Orleans, the prairies north of Lafayette, and the remote southwestern coast.

Melrose Plantation

⊛ 🅰 3533 LA Hwy 19
🕐 10am–5pm Tue–Sun
🆆 melroseplantation.org

Louisiana Sports Hall of Fame and Northwest Louisiana History Museum

🅰 800 Front St 🕐 10am–4:30pm Tue–Sat 🆆 louisiana statemuseum.org

---

Shreveport

🚆 🅸 505 Travis St; www.shreveportla.gov

Situated near the Texas border, Shreveport was founded on the Red River in 1839. At the turn of the 20th century, it became a booming oil town, but declined after the industry moved offshore. The riverfront now has a number of casinos and museums, as well as the annual Louisiana State Fair, in late October/early November.

About 165 miles (265 km) east of Shreveport, the town of Epps retains the **Poverty Point National Monument**, a series of earth works built around 1700–1100 BC.

Poverty Point National Monument

⊛ 🅰 Hwy 577 🕐 9am–5pm daily 🆇 Jan 1, Thanksgiving, Dec 25 🆆 nps.gov/popo

---

7

Bayou Teche

🅰 Hwy 31, Breaux Bridge to New Iberia 🅸 2513 Hwy 14; www.iberiatravel.com

Bayou Teche ("Tesh") meanders north to south from Lafayette to the Atchafalaya Swamp. The 25-mile (40-km) stretch of Highway 31 between Breaux Bridge and New Iberia offers a true flavor of the region.

The town of Breaux Bridge, the self-proclaimed "Crawfish Capital of the World," hosts the annual Crawfish Festival in May.

At Lake Martin, the Nature Conservancy's Cypress Island Preserve offers hiking trails and boat tours.

Farther south, St. Martinville's famous Evangeline Oak marks the spot where Evangeline and her lover Gabriel were supposed to be reunited in *Evangeline*, Henry Wadsworth Longfellow's 1847 poem.

1844

The year Lafayette was named for the French Marquis de Lafayette.

Outside town, the evocative **Longfellow-Evangeline State Historic Site** offers tours of an 18th-century sugar plantation house. A detour to Avery Island brings you to the **McIlhenny Tabasco Company**, a popular stop for gourmands, where a guide presents information about the company's history and manufacturing. You can also tour the adjacent Jungle Gardens, a natural swamp.

Longfellow-Evangeline State Historic Site

⊛ 🅰 1200 N Main St, St. Martinville 🕐 9am–5pm Tue–Sat 🆆 crt.state.la.us

McIlhenny Tabasco Company

🅰 Avery Island 🕐 Daily 🆆 tabasco.com/avery-island

↓ The twinkling lights of downtown Shreveport on the banks of the Red River

ARKANSAS AND MISSISSIPPI

French explorers established the first outposts here in the late 17th century. Mississippi gained US statehood in 1817, Arkansas in 1836. Plantation economies reliant on the labor of enslaved people dominated, and Mississippi was the nation's top cotton producer by 1860. Both joined the Confederacy in the Civil War. Left poor in the aftermath, the states were hard hit by the Great Mississippi Flood of 1927 and the Depression. More suffering followed, with violence hampering the desegregation of Little Rock Central High School in 1957, the assassination of Civil Rights activist Medgar Evers in 1963, and the 1964 Freedom Summer murders in Mississippi.

Experience

1. Hot Springs
2. Little Rock
3. Mountain View
4. Eureka Springs
5. Clarksdale
6. Tupelo
7. Oxford
8. Vicksburg
9. Jackson
10. Natchez Trace Parkway
11. Natchez

ARKANSAS

Aptly known as the "Natural State," Arkansas abounds in mountains, valleys, woodlands, and fertile plains. Its two mountain ranges, the Ozarks and the Ouachita, are separated by the Arkansas River, which flows through the state capital, Little Rock. This former frontier state remains largely wild even today, with vast areas of natural beauty, famous for adventure sports.

INSIDER TIP
Clinton Origins

Arkansas has more Bill Clinton connections outside of Hot Springs and Little Rock. Head to 117 South Hervey Street, in Hope, to see the house the president was born in and pop into visitor center.

1

Hot Springs

📧 🇮 134 Convention Blvd; www.hotsprings.org

In the early 20th century, this was a popular resort for people seeking restorative cures from the thermal springs of Hot Springs Mountain. "Bathhouse Row" is now a National Historic Landmark District within **Hot Springs National Park**. The visitor center is housed in the Spanish Renaissance-style 1915 Fordyce Bathhouse. Only the **Buckstaff Bathhouse** remains in operation. The Ozark Bathhouse is a grand Spanish colonial building built in 1922, and hosts a wealth of programs. A scenic drive to the summit of Hot Springs Mountain leads to a tower offering panoramic views of the Ouachita Mountains, the city, and the forests and lakes that surround it.

Hot Springs National Park

🏠 369 Central Av 🕐 9am–5pm daily 🚫 Jan 1, Thanksg., Dec 25 🌐 nps.gov/hosp

Buckstaff Bathhouse

◈ 🏠 509 Central Av, Bathhouse Row 🕐 Check website 🚫 Jan 1, Easter, Jul 4, Thanksg., Dec 25 🌐 buckstaffbaths.com

2

Little Rock

➡️🚉📧 🇮 101 S Spring St; www.littlerock.com

Founded on the Arkansas River, Little Rock was another small Southern state capital until native son Bill Clinton was elected 42nd US president in 1992. A center for much activity is the Little Rock River Market District, lined with lively clubs, restaurants, cafés, and shops. Adjacent to the district is the **William J. Clinton Presidential Center**, which houses a library and museum telling the inside story of his presidency. The **Old State House Museum**, west of Main Street, is where Clinton celebrated his 1992 and 1996 presidential victories.

In 1957, the contentious desegregation of Little Rock Central High School catapulted the city to the forefront of the national struggle for Civil Rights. Today, the **Little Rock Central High School National Historic Site** documents its incredible story.

William J. Clinton Presidential Center

◈ 🏠 1200 Pres Clinton Av 🕐 9am–5pm Mon–Sat, 1–5pm Sun 🌐 clintonlibrary.org

Old State House Museum

🏠 300 W Markham St 🕐 9am–5pm Mon–Sat, 1–5pm Sun 🌐 oldstatehouse.com

Little Rock Central High School National Historic Site

🏠 2120 Daisy L. Gatson Bates Dr 🕐 9am–4:30pm daily 🌐 nps.gov/chsc

Fall foliage surrounding the peaceful Beaver Lake, Eureka Springs

❸

Mountain View

🛈 100 miles (161 km) N of Little Rock; www.your placeinthemountains.com

Nestled deep in the hills and valleys of the remote Ozark Mountains, Mountain View is a haven for outdoor enthusiasts. A short drive north is the **Ozark Folk Center State Park**. The park celebrates the region's cultural heritage with living history exhibits, crafts demonstrations, festivals, and traditional music at the state park theater. It also offers hiking trails and a lodge open year-round. The nearby "Wild and Scenic" Buffalo National River is highly popular for fishing and canoeing.

←

Historic Fordyce Bathhouse, now housing the Hot Springs National Park Visitor Center

About 15 miles (24 km) northwest of Mountain View, via Hwy 14, lie **Blanchard Springs Caverns**, which feature an extensive collection of cave formations and an underground stream offering an unforgettable experience.

Ozark Folk Center State Park
⊗ 🏠 1032 Park Av ⏰ Apr-late Nov: 10am-5pm Tue-Sat 🌐 ozarkfolkcenter.com

Blanchard Springs Caverns
⊗ 🏠 Off Hwy 14 ⏰ Times vary, check website 🌐 blanchardsprings.org

---

❹

Eureka Springs

🛈 516 Village Circle; www. eurekasprings.org

The seven-story-high statue of "Christ of the Ozarks" towers above this former resort town.

EAT

Brave New Restaurant
Beautifully presented mouthwatering food, with stellar river views.

🏠 2300 Cottondale Ln #105, Little Rock ⏰ Sun 🌐 bravenew restaurant.com

$$$

The Root Café
Light lunches with ingredients sourced from local farms.

🏠 1500 Main St, Little Rock ⏰ Sun 🌐 therootcafe.com

$$$

Vino's
Pub food, beer, and live music - great for a fun dinner out.

🏠 923 W 7th St, Little Rock 🌐 vinosbrewpub.com

$$$

After decades of decline, the town has benefited from its development as an artists' community, as a romantic getaway, and by the country music performances at the Hoe-Down and Pine Mountain Jamboree. For almost 30 years running, the Great Passion Play – depicting the last days of Christ – has been performed at the Sacred Arts Center.

The **Bible Museum** has collected some 6,000 editions in 625 languages. The Eureka Springs Historic Gardens and a scenic railroad are the town's other attractions.

Bible Museum
⊗ 🏠 935 Passion Play Rd ⏰ Apr-Oct: check website 🌐 greatpassionplay.org

MISSISSIPPI

Mississippi is a state with a complex history, known for blues music, antebellum plantation homes, and a lamentable Civil Rights history. The state capital, Jackson, sits in the central plain. Today, this largely rural state offers Vegas-style casinos on the Gulf Coast and the Mississippi River, excellent Vietnamese seafood, and ferry rides to deserted beaches.

⑤ Clarksdale

🚌🚂 Greenwood 🛈 1540 DeSoto Av, Hwy 49; www.visitclarksdale.com

The Mississippi Delta, a vast, alluvial basin, is the birthplace of the blues. Downtown, the **Delta Blues Museum** is the touchstone for music lovers from around the world. Set up in a renovated 1920s freight depot, this museum is a repository of blues music, with personal belongings, photographs, instruments, and videos of such legends as Muddy Waters, Robert Johnson, and Howlin' Wolf. Exhibits include the wooden "Muddywood" guitar created by Z.Z. Top with planks from the original House of Blues, the birthplace of Muddy Waters. The Sunflower River Blues and Gospel Festival is held outside in August. The Delta's creative legacy extends beyond music. The annual Tennessee Williams festival celebrates the work of the famous playwright who spent his childhood in Clarksdale.

About 55 miles (88 km) south, the **Museum of the Mississippi Delta** in Greenwood documents the history of the cotton industry that fueled the region. A 24-mile (38-km) drive farther south brings you to Greenville, the largest town in the Delta. The **Mississippi Delta Blues and Heritage Festival** is held here every September. Other sights include the tiny museum in Leland honoring Jim Henson, creator of the Muppets, and Indianola, the hometown of B. B. King, who is honored with a museum in his name.

Delta Blues Museum

🚲 🏠 1 Blues Alley 🕐 Mar-Oct: 9am-5pm Mon-Sat; Nov-Feb: 10am-5pm Mon-Sat 🌐 deltabluesmuseum.org

Museum of the Mississippi Delta

🚲 ♿ 🏠 1608 Hwy 82 W, Greenwood 🕐 9am-5pm Mon-Sat 🌐 museumofthemississippidelta.com

Mississippi Delta Blues and Heritage Festival

🚲 🌐 deltabluesms.org

⑥ Tupelo

🏠 117 miles (188 km) E of Clarksdale 🚌 🛈 399 E Main St; www.tupelo.net

Tupelo is the birthplace of Elvis Presley, one of the world's most enduring cultural icons. Elvis lived in Tupelo until age 13, when the family was forced to move to Memphis. Today the **Elvis Presley Birthplace** is a pilgrimage site for fans the world over. An adjacent museum holds a private collection of memorabilia. A chapel overlooking the birthplace displays Elvis's own Bible.

The Tupelo Automobile Museum, the first of its kind in the state, displays more than 150 restored cars and includes a replica of a vintage garage.

Tupelo offers all the basic necessities for lodging and dining, and serves as a pit stop for the famous Natchez Trace Parkway (p353).

Elvis Presley Birthplace

🚲 🏠 306 Elvis Presley Dr 🕐 9am-5pm Mon-Sat, 1-5pm Sun 🚫 Thanksgiving, Dec 25 🌐 elvispresleybirthplace.com

↑ A medley of guitars on display at the Delta Blues Museum in Clarksdale

↑ The Lyceum Building of the University of Mississippi in Oxford

7
Oxford

⏴ 63 miles (101 km) E of Clarksdale 🚌
ℹ 1013 Jackson Ave E; www.visitoxfordms.com

Home to the 1848 University of Mississippi, fondly known as "Ole Miss," Oxford is the state's intellectual and cultural center. The local literary landmark is the secluded 1844 **Rowan Oak**, former home of the pioneer of the Southern Gothic literature movement, William Faulkner.

The University of Mississippi campus houses the **University Museum**, featuring 19th-century scientific instruments.

Rowan Oak
⊛ ⏴ 916 Old Taylor Rd
🕐 10am–4pm Tue–Sat, 1–4pm Sun (Jun & Jul: to 6pm)
🌐 rowanoak.com

University Museum
⊛ ⏴ University Av at 5th St
🕐 10am–6pm Tue–Sat
🌐 olemiss.edu

---

8 ⟨⊘⟩
Vicksburg

⏴ 43 miles (69 km) W of Jackson 🚌
ℹ 52 Old Highway 27; www.visitvicksburg.com

Vicksburg was the site of perhaps the defining battle of the American Civil War, which is commemorated in the **Vicksburg National Military Park**. The remains of an 1861 warship, the USS *Cairo*, can also be seen here. The town itself is picturesque and dates back to the early 1700s. The Old Warren County Courthouse is another key Civil War site.

Vicksburg National Military Park
⏴ 3201 Clay St 🕐 8am–5pm daily 🌐 nps.gov/vick

→ Statue of a Union soldier with musket at Vicksburg National Military Park

↑ The Mississippi State Capitol and grounds, and the plush interior of the Capitol's Senate Chamber *(inset)*

9

Jackson

921 S President St; www.visitjackson.com

Founded on a bluff above the Pearl River, Mississippi's capital city was named after popular national hero General Andrew Jackson. During the Civil War, the city was torched by Union General William Tecumseh Sherman, earning it the nickname "Chimneyville." Of the surviving buildings, the old 1839 Capitol, now serving as the **Old Capitol Museum of Mississippi History**, presents an overview of the state's Civil Rights history, juxtaposing stark video footage of violent clashes between the police and protesters. Upstairs, the museum features exhibits on such topics as author Eudora Welty, a Jackson resident, or "Pride of the Fleet" about the battleship USS *Mississippi*. The **Mississippi Civil Rights Museum** exhibits the history of the American Civil Rights Movement in Mississippi. Its eight interactive galleries document the systematic oppression of black Mississippians and their fight for equality.

From the Old Capitol building, it is a short walk along Capitol Street to the current Mississippi State Capitol, built in 1903, which resembles the US Capitol in Washington, DC. Jackson is also home to the **Mississippi Agriculture and Forestry Museum**, an appealing family attraction that celebrates the state's rural heritage. Among its exhibits are an 1850s homestead, complete with livestock and gardens, and a 1930s small-town Main Street with a general store. The adjacent Sports Hall of Fame honors the state's beloved athletes and college teams.

Other sights in Jackson include Mynelle Gardens, the Mississippi Museum of Natural Science, and the Mississippi Museum of Art. All these, plus the city's growing reputation as a hotbed of blues, make Jackson a pleasant stop for visitors coming through the Natchez Trace Parkway.

Old Capitol Museum of Mississippi History
Old Capitol, 100 S State St
Daily Federal hols
mdah.ms.gov

Today, the Natchez Trace Parkway is a scenic, year-round destination. No commercial traffic is permitted in this haven for hikers, motorists, and cyclists.

Mississippi Agriculture and Forestry Museum

◎ ⌂ 1150 Lakeland Dr
⏰ 9am–5pm Mon–Sat
⎙ Jan 1, Thanksgiving,
Dec 25 ⊞ msagmuseum.org

Mississippi Civil Rights Museum

◎ ⌂ 222 North St, #2205
⏰ 9am–5pm Tue–Sat, 1–5pm
Sun ⎙ Jan 1, Easter, Thanksg.,
Dec 25 ⊞ mcrm.mdah.ms.gov

---

⑩

Natchez Trace Parkway

⌂ Starts near 8-12 Natchez
Trace Pkwy, Natchez;
www.nps.gov/natr

This 450-mile (724-km) highway linking Natchez with Nashville, Tennessee *(p268)*, was originally an animal trail. It evolved into a footpath used by American Indians and later by European settlers, and played a vital role in the development of the country's midsection by linking the Ohio River Valley and the Gulf of Mexico.

Today, the Natchez Trace Parkway is a scenic, year-round destination. No commercial traffic is permitted in this haven for hikers, motorists, and cyclists, and the speed limit is a leisurely 50 mph (80 km/h).

The parkway preserves several historical sites situated near Natchez, such as Emerald Mound, the second-largest American Indian ceremonial mound in the country, dating from around 1400. A detour west, along Highway 552, leads to the "Ruins of Windsor," where a ghostly set of 23 towering Corinthian columns serves as a poignant reminder of a mansion that burned down in 1890.

---

⑪

Natchez

▭▭ ⓘ 640 S Canal St;
www.visitnatchez.com

Best known for its fine antebellum architecture, Natchez is an attractive town on the bluffs above the Mississippi River. The first capital of the state, it is the oldest settlement on the entire river, surrounded by a wealth of natural resources. Many of its historic buildings lie within easy walking distance of the compact downtown district. Some gems include the oldest house in town, the 1798 **House on Ellicott's Hill**; the palatial Stanton Hall (1857); the unfinished Longwood (1860), whose construction was interrupted by the Civil War; and Rosalie, an 1829 mansion atop the bluff that served as Union headquarters during the Civil War.

Many more houses can be seen during the twice-yearly Natchez Pilgrimage, held in the spring and fall. At the south end of town, just off Highway 61, is the Grand Village of the Natchez Indians, a historic village with American Indian ceremonial mounds, replicas of huts, nature trails, and a small museum. A short drive east of downtown is the Melrose Plantation, the USA's most intact antebellum estate.

House on Ellicott's Hill

◎ ⌂ Jefferson & Canal sts
⏰ 10am–3pm Fri and Sat
⎙ Dec 25 ⊞ visitnatchez.com

Natchez Pilgrimage

◎ ◉ ⊞ natchezpilgrimage.com

←

A footbridge passing through a cypress swamp along the Natchez Trace Parkway

ALABAMA

The Mississippi Territory was divided in 1817 and the eastern portion became Alabama. The state developed a hugely profitable cotton plantation economy, based on slavery. Alabama was a part of the Confederacy in the Civil War, and though left financially troubled, cities such as Mobile and Birmingham experienced industrial growth. Alabama was a segregationist stronghold, with the famous Montgomery Bus Boycott (1955–56), Freedom Rides (1961), and Selma to Montgomery marches (1965) taking place here. In 2007, the Alabama Legislature passed a resolution expressing "profound regret" over slavery.

Experience

1. Montgomery
2. Mobile
3. Selma
4. Tuskegee
5. Birmingham
6. Huntsville

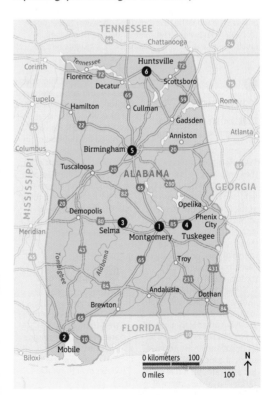

← The poignant National Memorial for Peace and Justice, Montgomery

ALABAMA

Alabama slopes from the Cumberland Plateau in the northeast, across forested ridges and fertile plains to the Gulf of Mexico at Mobile Bay. The state has a contentious history, with cotton and slave labor at the forefront. Today, however, sweet home Alabama is known for its diverse landscape, its antebellum architecture, and, most importantly, its Civil Rights history.

❶ Montgomery

🚌 ℹ️ 300 Water St; www.visitingmontgomery.com

Alabama's capital city since 1846, Montgomery was also the Confederacy's first capital during the Civil War. In 1861, Jefferson Davis was sworn in as the Confederate president on the steps of the Greek Revival State Capitol. Across the street, the **First White House of the Confederacy** is now a museum related to those times.

The city's political and social history, particularly with regard to the Civil Rights Movement (*p359*), is marked in a number of places. The National Memorial for Peace and Justice acknowledges historic racial terrorism and advocates for future social justice. The Dexter Avenue King

Memorial Baptist Church dates back to 1877 and is a National Historic Landmark in memory of Dr. Martin Luther King, Jr., who organized the pivotal Montgomery Bus Boycott in the church's basement. The Civil Rights Memorial Center and the Rosa Parks Museum are also important markers for historic events that took place in the city, as are the Freedom Rides Museum and the Legacy Museum.

Montgomery is also associated with two major figures of 20th-century arts. Local resident Zelda Fitzgerald and her husband, writer F. Scott Fitzgerald, lived here in 1931, while he was writing *Tender is the Night*. Their house now serves as the **Scott and Zelda Fitzgerald Museum**. In 1958, legendary country singer Hank Williams played his final concert in the city three days before his death. Williams is buried in Oakwood Cemetery, and the Hank Williams Museum and a statue of the singer are both located downtown.

First White House of the Confederacy
🏠 644 Washington Av
🕐 9am–4pm Mon–Sat
🌐 firstwhitehouse.org

Scott and Zelda Fitzgerald Museum
♿ 🏠 919 Felder Av 🕐 10am–3pm Wed–Sat 🌐 thefitzgerald museum.org

> **GREAT VIEW**
> **Cooter's Pond**
>
> On the outskirts of Montgomery, you'll find this boating lake, with tree-framed picnic areas and a playground. Walk up to the hilltop park and enjoy scenic views over the water.

Mobile

🏛 50 miles (80 km) W of Montgomery 🚉🚌🚗
🛈 1 S Water St; www.mobile.org

This beautiful port city was founded as a French colony in 1702. Later it served as a strategic Confederate port until the final days of the American Civil War. Today, the city retains both its French and Southern flavors and is best known for its **Mobile Carnival Museum**, which includes memorabilia dating from the early 1800s.

The **History Museum of Mobile** houses 300 years of history and counts thousands of artifacts among its collection. The museum is housed in the Old City Hall, a national historic landmark. The museum also oversees **Fort Condé**, a reconstructed French fort at the head of Mobile Bay. Nearby is the World War II battleship USS *Alabama*. A scenic drive around the bay leads to two other historic forts, Fort Morgan to the east, and Fort Gaines on Dauphin Island. Both are havens for birdlife.

Mobile Carnival Museum
⊗ 🏛 355 Government St
🕑 9am–4pm Mon, Wed, Fri & Sat 🖥 mobilecarnival museum.com

History Museum of Mobile
🏛 111 S Royal St 🕑 9am–5pm Mon–Sat, 1–5pm Sun 🖥 historymuseumof mobile.com

Fort Condé
🏛 150 Royal St 🕑 8am–5pm daily 🔒 Mardi Gras, Federal hols 🖥 colonialmobile.com

Selma

🏛 169 miles (272 km) SW of Montgomery 🚌 🛈 912 Selma Av; www.selma alabama.com

Situated on a bluff high above the Alabama River, Selma was the site of one of the most notorious scenes in US Civil Rights history. On March 7, 1965, a day that would become known as "Bloody Sunday," 600 Civil Rights protesters heading to Montgomery violently clashed with the police at the Edmund Pettus Bridge. A few weeks later, however, Dr. Martin Luther King Jr. led a historic march to the steps of the State Capitol. The **National Voting Rights Museum** encapsulates the story, and an annual reenactment pays tribute to the event.

Before the Civil Rights era, Selma was known as the "Arsenal of the Confederacy." It produced guns, cannons, and ironclad ships. Much of the city was destroyed during the war, but the townscape along the river remained intact. The city's 1891 cherry-red train depot has exhibits on local history.

National Voting Rights Museum
⊗ 🏛 6 US Hwy 80 E 🕑 10am–4pm Mon–Thu, by appt Fri–Sun 🖥 nvrmi.com

> Situated on a bluff high above the Alabama River, Selma was the site of one of the most notorious scenes in US Civil Rights history.

← The Edmund Pettus Bridge crossing the Alabama River into Selma

EAT

Carrigan's Public House

Stylishly presented pub fare, best washed down with a craft beer or cocktail.

⌂ 2430 Morris Av, Birmingham ⊘ Sun
ⓦ carriganspub.com

$$⑤

Continental Bakery

Expect mouthwatering artisan breads and pastries at this French-style café.

⌂ 1909 Cahaba Rd, Birmingham
ⓦ chezlulu.us

$⑤⑤

Paramount Bar

Chow down on bar food while shooting hoops and playing arcade games.

⌂ 200 20th St N, Birmingham ⊘ Mon
ⓦ paramount birmingham.com

$$⑤

Alabama Biscuit Co.

Nourishing breakfasts made with quality ingredients are served up in Scandi interiors.

⌂ 4133 White Oak Dr, Birmingham
ⓦ alabamabiscuit.com

$⑤⑤

Galley & Garden

This sophisticated restaurant dishes up American-French plates in a beautiful setting.

⌂ 2220 Highland Av, Birmingham
ⓦ galleyandgarden.com

$$⑤

→ The Oscar Wells Memorial entrance to the Birmingham Museum of Art, and admiring the artworks inside (inset)

④ Tuskegee

⌂ 128 miles (206 km) SE of Birmingham 🚌 🛈 121 Main St; (334) 727-6619

Born into slavery, Booker T. Washington pursued formal education after the Civil War and became a teacher. He founded the Tuskegee Normal and Industrial Institute, in 1881, which aimed to improve educational opportunities for African Americans. This evolved into **Tuskegee University**, best known for George Washington Carver's innovations that revolutionized agricultural growth in the region. The "Tuskegee Airmen," a group of African American pilots who distinguished themselves in World War II, paving the way for full integration in the US military, also trained at the institute. The **Tuskegee Airmen National Historic Site** interprets their history.

Tuskegee University

⌂ 1200 W Montgomery Rd
ⓦ tuskegee.edu

Tuskegee Airmen National Historic Site

⌂ 1616 Chappie James Av
🕘 9am–4:30pm Mon-Sat
ⓦ nps.gov/tuai

⑤ Birmingham

🚆🚌🚗 🛈 2200 9th Av N; www.birminghamal.gov

The largest city in Alabama, Birmingham was once the region's foremost producer of steel. Celebrating the city's industrial past is the **Sloss Furnaces National Historic Landmark**, a museum housed in an old steel mill, and a colossal iron statue of Vulcan, the Roman god of fire, on the Red Mountain, the source of the iron ore. Today, the city's multitude of attractions include antebellum houses, botanical gardens, and the acclaimed **Birmingham Museum of Art**, with its fine collection of Wedgwood. Yet by far the most moving landmarks in Birmingham are those that relate to the city's African American history. These are all within walking distance of the central downtown district's visitor

> By far the most moving landmarks in Birmingham are those that relate to the city's African American history.

Huntsville

🏛 100 miles (161 km) N of Birmingham 🚌 ℹ 500 Church St; www. huntsville.org

Set in northern Alabama, the cotton market town of Huntsville developed into a space and military R&D and manufacturing center after World War II. Home to NASA's Marshall Space Flight Center, the city's main attractions are the **US Space and Rocket Center** and its daily bus tours. Exhibits here include Apollo capsules and a life-size space shuttle. The hugely popular Space Camp teaches children about space exploration.

Nearby, you'll find the vast **Huntsville Botanical Garden**. Open year-round, highlights include several nature trails and an open-air butterfly house (open April–September).

US Space & Rocket Center

♿ 👶 🍴 🛍 🏛 1 Tranquility Base, I-565 🕐 9am–5pm daily 🌐 rocketcenter.com

Huntsville Botanical Garden

♿ 👶 🍴 🛍 🏛 4747 Bob Wallace Av 🕐 Times vary, check website 🌐 hsvbg.org

---

center, where a variety of maps as well as tours are readily available.

The **Birmingham Civil Rights Institute** uses vintage film footage to explain the city's Civil Rights Movement. Among the exhibits is the door of the cell in which Dr. Martin Luther King, Jr. wrote his famous "Letter from a Birmingham Jail," arguing that individuals have the right to disobey unjust laws. Down the street, the restored 16th Street Baptist Church stands as a memorial to four black girls killed by a Ku Klux Klan bomb in 1963. To its southeast, in the historic Carver Theatre, the Alabama Jazz Hall of Fame hosts live music performances and celebrates the achievements of such artists as Dinah Washington, Nat King Cole, W. C. Handy, and Duke Ellington. At the north end of town, the superb **Alabama Sports Hall of Fame** honors beloved Alabama-born African American athletes such as Joe Louis and Jesse Owens, with over 5,000 sports artifacts.

Sloss Furnaces National Historic Landmark

♿ 🏛 20 32nd St N 🕐 10am–4pm Tue–Fri, noon–4pm Sat & Sun 🕐 Federal hols 🌐 slossfurnaces.com

Birmingham Museum of Art

🏛 2000 Rvd Abraham Woods, Jr. Blvd 🕐 Times vary, check website 🌐 artsbma.org

Birmingham Civil Rights Institute

♿ 🏛 520 16th St N 🕐 10am–5pm Tue–Sat, 1–5pm Sun 🕐 Federal hols 🌐 bcri.org

Alabama Sports Hall of Fame

♿ 🏛 2150 Richard Arrington Jr. Blvd N 🕐 9am–5pm Mon–Fri 🌐 ashof.org

---

CIVIL RIGHTS IN ALABAMA

In the post-World War II era, African American veterans became active in pushing for their constitutional and legal rights in the South: to be allowed to vote, to freely use public places, and to put an end to segregation. The city of Montgomery played a pivotal role during the movement. The segregation of the city's transportation system led to an act of defiance by Rosa Parks, when she refused to surrender her bus seat to a white man. In 1956, Dr. Martin Luther King, Jr. organized the year-long Montgomery Bus Boycott, which led to the desegregation of the public transportation system, strengthening the movement and cementing King as the campaign's leader.

THE GREAT LAKES

Lake Michigan icing over along Chicago's shoreline

EXPLORE
THE GREAT LAKES

This chapter divides the Great Lakes into four
sightseeing areas, as shown on the map
below. Find out more about each area
on the following pages.

Dryden

NORTH DAKOTA

Upper Red Lake

Crookston

Lower Red Lake

**WISCONSIN AND
MINNESOTA**
p398

Virgi

Valley
City

Bismarck   Jamestown

Grand Rapids

Bowman

Fargo   Detroit
Lakes

Duluth

Superior

Fergus Falls

Belle Fourche

Mobridge

MINNESOTA

Rice Lak

SOUTH DAKOTA

Appleton

Saint Paul

Rapid City   Pierre   Redfield

Willmar

Minneapolis

Brookings

Tyler

Red Wing

Winner

Worthington   Owatonna

Rochester

Yankton

Spencer

Alliance

O'Neill   Sioux City

IOWA

Water

NEBRASKA

Norfolk

Ames

North Platte

Des Moines

Iowa City

Ogallala   Grand Island

Omaha

Yuma

Ottumwa

COLORADO

Fairmont   Lincoln

Colby

Saint Joseph

Quincy

Hays

Topeka

MISSOURI

Kansas City

KANSAS   Great Bend   Salina

Columbia

Sedalia

Dodge City

Emporia

Jefferson City

Pratt

Rolla

Liberal

Wichita

Guymon

OKLAHOMA

Springfield

Miami

CANADA

Armstrong

Lake Nipigon

Nipigon

Thunder Bay

Lake Superior

Apostle Islands

Ashland
Ironwood
Houghton
Keweenaw Peninsula
Marquette
Iron Mountain
Escanaba
Rhinelander

ONTARIO

Wawa

Sault Ste.Marie
Espanola
Sudbury
Burk's Falls

Sault Sainte Marie
Saint Ignace
Mackinac Island
Cheboygan
Blind River
Manitoulin Island
Georgian Bay
Parry Sound

WISCONSIN
Wausau
Stevens Point
Appleton
Oshkosh
Tomah
Baraboo
La Crosse
Madison
Milwaukee
Dubuque

Green Bay
Lake Winnebago
Door County

Petoskey
Alpena
Traverse City
MICHIGAN
Ludington
Midland
MICHIGAN
p392
Muskegon
Grand Rapids
Lansing
Kalamazoo
Ann Arbor
Flint
Port Huron

Lake Michigan
Lake Huron
Collingwood
Midland
Clinton
Toronto
Hamilton
London
Leamington

Red

Marquette
Rockford
Chicago
Joliet
Peoria
Bloomington

CHICAGO AND ILLINOIS
p368
Champaign
Springfield
Decatur

ILLINOIS

Saint Louis
East St.Louis
Mount Vernon

Cape Girardeau

Mississippi

Gary
South Bend
Fort Wayne

INDIANA AND OHIO
p382
INDIANA
Anderson
Indianapolis
Terre Haute
Vernon
Vincennes
New Albany
Evansville

Wabash

Detroit
Toledo
Sandusky
Akron
Mansfield
Springfield
Columbus
Dayton
Athens

OHIO

Cleveland
Canton
Cambridge

PENN.

Pittsburgh

Morgantown

Parkersburg

WEST VIRGINIA

Charleston

Lake Erie

Cincinnati
Portsmouth
Huntington

Louisville
Lexington
Elizabethtown

KENTUCKY

Owensboro

Ohio

Mississippi

CANADA

Seattle
San Francisco
Los Angeles

THE GREAT LAKES
Chicago

Boston
New York City
Washington, DC

USA

Atlanta
Houston

Atlantic Ocean

Pacific Ocean

MEXICO

Gulf of Mexico

Miami

NORTH AMERICA

0 kilometers   200
0 miles   200

N

←

1 Chicago's busy pier.

2 University of Chicago.

3 Exhibit in the Field Museum.

4 A musician playing at the city's Buddy Guy's Legends blues club.

This four-day itinerary takes in the best of Chicago, from soaring Willis Tower to Oak Park, the old neighborhood of Frank Lloyd Wright and Ernest Hemingway. The Windy City has good public transportation and plenty of taxis, so there's no need to drive.

4 DAYS
in Chicago

Day 1

Start your visit with an architectural tour to appreciate downtown Chicago's dazzling ensemble of buildings; the most entertaining option is a boat trip *(p370)*, but the Architecture Foundation also offers good walking tours. Eat a pick-up lunch on Navy Pier *(p372)*, then head to the Art Institute of Chicago *(p373)* – don't miss Grant Wood's *American Gothic*. Try to hit the Skydeck Observatory at the Willis Tower *(p374)* before sunset, for gorgeous city views. For dinner, it has to be Chicago's deep-dish pizza at Lou Malnati's *(www.lou malnatis.com)*. If you can still move, Buddy Guy's Legends *(www.buddyguy.com)* is a fun place to experience live Chicago blues.

Day 2

Soak up the city's literary traditions at the American Writers Museum *(p375)*, followed by a musical education at the Chicago Blues Experience *(p372)*. Have a classic German-American lunch at Berghoff *(www.theberghoff.com)*, then stroll around Millennium Park *(p372)* to check out "Cloud Gate." Wander along the Lake Michigan shorefront to the Museum Campus *(p377)* and dip into one of its three excellent museums. Head across the river to the Magnificent Mile *(p370)*, where you can grab a beer and/or "cheezborger" at the infamous Billy Goat Tavern *(www.billygoat tavern.com)*, before cocktails on the 96th floor of the John Hancock Center *(p371)*.

Day 3

Spend the morning exploring Hyde Park, starting with the main campus of the University of Chicago *(p376)*. Grab lunch at no-frills Valois Cafeteria *(www.valois restaurant.com)*, the Obamas' local favorite. Then it's museum time again: Choose between the DuSable Museum of African American History *(p376)* and the family-friendly Museum of Science and Industry *(p376)*. Head up to Old Town, one of Chicago's liveliest neighborhoods. Have dinner and drinks at 1950s throwback Twin Anchors *(www.twinanchorsribs.com)*, then head over to celebrated comedy club Second City *(www.secondcity.com)*.

Day 4

Spend the day in the suburb of Oak Park *(p380)*, starting with a tour of the Wright home and studio, base of celebrated architect Frank Lloyd Wright. You can also tour Wright's Unity Temple, a remarkable Unitarian Universalist church. Grab lunch at Hemmingway's Bistro *(www.hemming waysbistro.com)*, then take an illuminating guided tour of Ernest Hemingway's Birthplace Museum (the author was born nearby in 1899). Head back into the city center to spend the evening in the hip River North district – enjoy Mexican dishes at Frontera Grill *(www.rickbayless.com)* before ending the night in style at Three Dots and a Dash *(www.threedotschicago. com)*, a speakeasy-style take on a tiki bar.

↑ Grand interior of Chicago Cultural Center

LLOYD WRIGHT IN CHICAGO

Frank Lloyd Wright (1867–1959) arrived in Oak Park, then a leafy suburb of Chicago, in 1889. He spent the next 20 years testing his innovative design theories from his small home and studio (*www.flwright.org*). His signature Prairie style – free-flowing, open-plan rooms – is much in evidence, and most of the furniture is also Wright's own design. Prairie-style Robie House (1908–1910), on the University of Chicago campus (*p377*), is just one of Wright's masterpieces, and guided tours are available.

Style and Substance

As buildings grew taller, Chicago's architects embraced an eclectic range of styles to embellish their creations. Louis Sullivan often used Art Nouveau or Celtic Revival decorations, while Daniel Burnham's designs led to a revival of Neo-Classical architecture. Chicago Cultural Center (*p371*) is a great example of the Beaux Arts style, while the Tribune Tower (435 N Michigan Av) is a Neo-Gothic skyscraper inspired by Rouen cathedral.

CHICAGO FOR
ARCHITECTURE

Chicago is world famous as a center of architectural innovation, a city where architects have pushed the boundaries of creativity. It was in Chicago that the world's first skyscraper was built, and here that Frank Lloyd Wright developed his Prairie School of architecture. Here are some standout sights.

Contemporary Chicago

Chicago's architecture is still making waves. Millennium Park (*p372*) became a showcase for the best of contemporary design, involving Kathryn Gustafson, Anish Kapoor, Jaume Plensa, and notably Frank Gehry. He designed the Jay Pritzker Pavilion, an open-air auditorium of swirling steel, and the BP Bridge, a spectacular silvery walkway across Columbus Drive. Aqua Tower (225 N Columbus Dr) by Jeanne Gang is perhaps the current talk of the city. Built in 2010, it has an undulating facade.

A yoga lesson in modern Millennium Park ↑

Birth of the Skyscraper

The Chicago School developed in the 1880s, leading to an engineering and aesthetic revolution. Celebrated architect Daniel Burnham and his partners John Welborn Root and Charles Atwood, designed the revolutionary Montauk Building (1883), Reliance Building (1895), and Masonic Temple Building (1892) using structural steel. Louis Sullivan, the "father of skyscrapers" – and mentor to Frank Lloyd Wright – grasped the possibilities of creating tall, slender buildings with a strong but lightweight steel skeleton. He designed the Auditorium Building (1889) and Sullivan Center (1899).

←

The Masonic Temple
Building, built in 1892

Modernist Monoliths

The 1950s and 1970s saw the arrival of the Modernist International style. This was thanks to the "less is more" approach of German-American architect Mies van der Rohe. His 860-880 Lake Shore Drive apartment building of 1951 became the prototype for steel-and-glass skyscrapers all over the world. Supertall skyscrapers the 1968 John Hancock Center *(p371)* and Willis Tower *(p374)*, by local powerhouse Skidmore, Owings & Merrill, were the pinnacle of this style.

↑ John Hancock Center
and its incredible
observatory *(inset)*

CHICAGO AND ILLINOIS

Illinois was first explored and settled by the French. Although it was granted US statehood in 1818, settlers didn't arrive here in numbers until after the native Sauk were subjugated. Founded in the 1830s, Chicago was virtually destroyed in the Great Chicago Fire of 1871, an event that sparked a skyscraper boom that has never really ended. Al Capone thrived in the 1920s aided by bought politicians. In more recent times, the city plays a prominent role in domestic politics; Barack Obama served as the 44th President of the United States and, in 2019, Lori Lightfoot became the city's first black female and first openly gay mayor.

Experience

1. Chicago
2. Springfield
3. Oak Park
4. Rockford
5. Galena
6. Southern Illinois

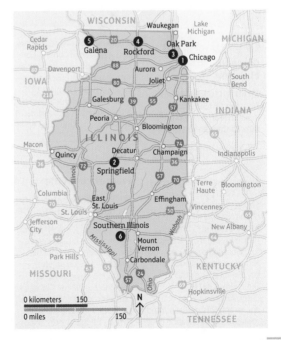

↑ Chicago's downtown skyline, lighting up as dusk begins to fall

1

CHICAGO

Situated at the southwest edge of the vast Lake Michigan, Chicago claims 26 miles (42 km) of lakefront and is the third-largest city in the US. Culturally, it is world-famous for its innovative architecture, vibrant cultural and educational institutions, and its colorful and turbulent political history. It is also home to the 44th US president, Barack Obama.

①

Chicago History Museum

🏛 1601 N Clark St Ⓜ Clark/Division 🚌 🕙 9:30am–4:30pm Mon-Sat, noon–5pm Sun 🌐 chicagohistory.org

The city's oldest cultural institution, the 1856 Chicago Historical Society is a major museum and research center, with a library open to the public. It traces the history of Chicago and Illinois, from the first explorers through the development of the city to major modern-day events. Miniature dioramas depict key events such as the Great Fire of 1871.

The American Wing holds one of only 23 original printed copies of the Declaration of Independence, and a 1789 copy of the American Constitution, first printed in a Philadelphia newspaper. The building has two faces – the original 1932 Neo-Georgian structure, and a 1988 addition with a glass-and-steel atrium entrance.

②

Magnificent Mile

🏛 Michigan Av, between E Walton Pl & E Kinzie St

This stretch of Michigan Avenue north of the Chicago River is the city's most fashionable street. Almost completely destroyed in the 1871 fire, the street grew into Chicago's premier shopping district after the opening of the Michigan Avenue Bridge in 1920. Shops line the wide boulevard, with modern retail outlets and skyscrapers rubbing shoulders with historic buildings.

To the north lies the Fourth Presbyterian Church. Its stone spire and exposed buttresses reflect the influences of medieval European churches. To its right are two historic castellated structures: the Water Tower and the Pumping Station, among the few buildings that survived the 1871 fire. Across the street, Water Tower Place has eight floors of upscale boutiques and restaurants.

Some blocks south, the Gothic-style Tribune Tower, office of the *Chicago Tribune*, holds rock fragments from world-famous sites, such as the Forbidden City in Beijing, and even a 3.3-billion-year-old

---

💬 INSIDER TIP
By Boat

The best way to see Chicago's amazing architecture is from the river. Several companies offer informative boat tours – try Chicago Line Cruises (chicagoline.com), in connection with the Chicago History Museum.

piece of moon rock embedded in its exterior walls.

At the southernmost end of the street is the beloved two-towered Wrigley Building. This white terracotta structure features a giant four-sided clock and a quiet courtyard.

③ 🛹 🍽

John Hancock Center

🏠 875 N Michigan Av
Ⓜ Chicago 🚌 🕐 9am-11pm daily 🌐 jhochicago.com

Affectionately called "Big John" by Chicagoans, the 100-story, cross-braced steel John Hancock Center stands out in the Chicago skyline. The tapering obelisk tower's major attraction is 360 Chicago on the 94th floor, where an open-air (screened) skywalk offers spectacular city views. The elevator ride to the top is one of the fastest in the US.

Designed by architect Bruce Graham and engineer Fazlur R. Khan, the center houses offices, condos, and shops.

④ Ⓜ 💻 🛍

Chicago Cultural Center

🏠 78 E Washington St
📞 (312) 744-6630
Ⓜ Lake, Washington 🚌
🕐 10am-7pm Mon-Fri, 10am-5pm Sat & Sun

Built as the city's first central public library, this downtown landmark was completed in 1897. Carrara marble, mother-of-pearl mosaics, two splendid stained-glass domes and other sumptuous features make it an architectural feast. Today it is a cultural arts venue, with hundreds of free events each year by artists and performers from all around the world. You can join a tour, take in a lunch-time concert, peruse an art exhibit, attend a lecture, or enjoy a family event.

↑ The Chicago Cultural Center's huge Tiffany glass dome

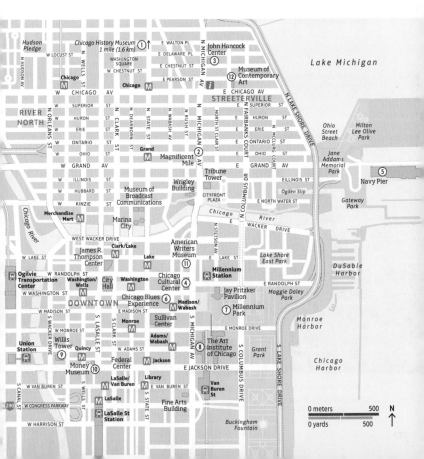

⑤ 🍴 🍵
Navy Pier

🏠 600 E Grand Ave
🚌 🕐 From 10am; closing times vary, check website
🌐 navypier.com

Navy Pier is a bustling recreational and cultural center. Designed by Charles S. Frost, the huge pier was the world's largest when built in 1916. Over 20,000 timber piles were used in its construction.

Originally a municipal wharf, the pier was used for naval training during World War II. After a four-year renovation, Navy Pier opened in its present incarnation in 1995. Navy Pier Park has an old-fashioned carousel, an outdoor amphitheater, ice skating, and an IMAX® 3D

Did You Know?

In 1937, Chicago was the first city in the US to establish a blood bank, thanks to Dr. Bernard Fantus.

theater. A 196-ft (60-m) Ferris wheel with 40 gondolas carries up to 414 passengers.

⑥ 🎨 🍴
Chicago Blues Experience

🏠 25 E Washington St
Ⓜ Washington/Wabash 🚌
🌐 chicagobluesexperience.com

Chicago is famous as the home of the modern blues. Scheduled to open in 2020, this cultural attraction celebrates that musical genre, which has influenced a multitude of American music styles, from jazz to rock 'n' roll. The interactive exhibits, spread over three subterranean levels, will take visitors on a musical journey; from the beginnings of the blues in West Africa and its blossoming in the Delta blues of the South, to its arrival in Chicago in the early 20th century, when African Americans migrated to northern cities. Memorabilia immerses visitors in blues culture and traditions, shining a light on pioneering blues musicians, as well as artists

💬 INSIDER TIP
Visitor Center

Chicago's official visitor information center is located at 111 N State St, inside Macy's department store. Admire the building's landmark features while picking up your maps and brochures.

who have been inspired by them. A live music venue and a restaurant are also on site.

⑦ 🏛 🍴 🍵
Millennium Park

🏠 55 N Michigan Av
Ⓜ Madison 🕐 6am–11pm daily 🌐 millenniumpark.org

The award-winning center for art, music, architecture, and landscape design opened in 2004 on 24.5 acres (10 ha) of former railroad property. The nearby Welcome Center, at 201 East Randolph Street, is a good place to find out about what the park has to offer.

Unusual design elements within the park include Frank

Anish Kapoor's gleaming *Cloud Gate* sculpture, Millennium Park ↑

A painting by Gustave Caillebotte, on display at the Art Institute of Chicago

Gehry's spectacular Jay Pritzker Pavilion, with its roof of huge, curling, stainless-steel ribbons. This outdoor concert venue hosts the Grant Park Music Festival each summer, plus other free concerts and events. Another Gehry-designed ribbon-style, winding bridge connects the park to Daley Bicentennial Plaza.

Video images of the faces of 1,000 local residents rotate over the two towers of glass blocks that make up the interactive Crown Fountain designed by Spanish artist Jaume Plensa. Other unique features within the park are the contemporary Lurie Garden and British artist Anish Kapoor's *Cloud Gate* sculpture, which resembles a giant silver bean and allows visitors to view themselves as a part of the Chicago skyline.

⑧ 🐾 Ⓜ 🍴 🛍

The Art Institute of Chicago

🏛 111 S Michigan Av
🚇 Van Buren St Ⓜ Adams
🚌 🕐 10:30am–5pm daily
(to 8pm Thu) 🌐 artic.edu

The extensive collections at the Art Institute of Chicago represent nearly 5,000 years of creativity. Founded by civic leaders and art patrons in 1879 as the Chicago Academy of Fine Arts, the museum became the Art Institute of Chicago in 1882. Outgrowing two homes as wealthy patrons donated their art collections, it finally settled in this Neo-Classical structure. The addition of the Modern Wing has made this the second-largest museum in the US.

The museum's holdings span from 3rd-millennium-BC Egyptian and Chinese artifacts to contemporary American and European art. Though best known for its world-famous Impressionist and Post-Impressionist collection, the museum represents almost every major artistic movement of the 19th and 20th centuries. The 35,000-strong Asian collection is especially noteworthy.

DRINK

Billy Goat Tavern

This legendary journalist's watering hole is near the Tribune Tower and Wrigley Building (though there are now a number of other locations). Be sure to try one of the juicy "cheezborgers" that inspired comedian John Belushi's famous *Saturday Night Live* sketch.

🏠 430 N Michigan Av, Lower Level
🌐 billygoattavern.com

Goose Island Brewhouse

Enjoy Chicago's own locally brewed beer at the brewpub where it all began. There's a good range of beers, ciders, food, and even tours of Goose Island's state-of-the-art brewery.

🏠 1800 N Clybourn Av
🌐 gooseisland.com

---

⑨ 🛹 🍴 🛍️

Willis Tower

🏠 233 S Wacker Dr 🚇 Quincy
🚌 🕐 Observatory: Mar–Sep: 9am–10pm daily; Oct–Feb: 10am–8pm daily; last adm 30 min before closing
🌐 theskydeck.com

At a height of 1,450 ft (442 m), Willis Tower (formerly, and most famously, known as the Sears Tower) is one of the world's tallest buildings. Boasting the highest occupied floor and the highest height to the rooftop, it was designed by Bruce Graham, of Skidmore Owings & Merrill, and engineer Fazlur Khan, the same team who designed the John Hancock Center (*p371*). Over 110 concrete caissons, anchored in bedrock, support the tower's 222,500 tons.

Today, Willis Tower contains 3.5 million sq ft (0.3 million sq m) of office space, more than 100 elevators, and almost enough telephone cable to circle the earth twice. The elevator to the glass-enclosed 103rd-floor Skydeck travels at 1,600 ft (490 m) per minute, and offers stunning views. Nearby, the 12-story **Rookery** building, which was the tallest in the world when it opened in 1888, is one of the city's most-photographed edifices.

Its dark red-brick facade with terracotta trim gives way to a two-tiered court, remodeled in 1907 by Frank Lloyd Wright, who was nearing the peak of his fame at the time. He covered the iron columns and staircases with white marble, inlaid with gold leaf.

Rookery

🛹 🏠 209 S LaSalle St
📞 (312) 922-3432
🕐 For tours; call ahead
🚫 Federal hols

---

⑩ 🛹

Money Museum

🏠 230 S LaSalle St
🚇 Quincy 🕐 8:30am–5pm Mon–Fri 🌐 chicagofed. org/education/money-museum/index

A fun and fascinating exploration into money, this small museum is housed in the Federal Reserve Bank of Chicago. Exhibits include rare monetary artifacts, such as a pine tree shilling from Colonial times. Games and simulations let you try your hand at saving the economy or detecting counterfeit money. And if you've ever wondered what a million dollars looks like, you can marvel at the million-dollar cube or put your hands on

---

> **GREAT VIEW**
> ## Lakefront Trail
>
> For dramatic views of the skyline, jog, hike, or bike along Chicago's Lakefront Trail, a paved path along the western shore of Lake Michigan. It connects four lakeside parks, and offers countless vistas.

←

Looking out at the city through the glass floor of Willis Tower's Skydeck

↑ A project by Amanda Ross-Ho at the Museum of Contemporary Art

the million-dollar suitcase stuffed with 100-dollar bills. Near the museum on Jackson Boulevard is the landmark Chicago Board of Trade building with its Art Deco tower.

⑪

American Writers Museum

🏠 180 N Michigan Av, 2nd Floor Ⓜ State/Lake, Washington/Wabash
🕐 10am–5pm daily
🌐 americanwriters museum.org

A must-visit for bibliophiles, the American Writers Museum is a delight, casting a light on authors such as Edgar Allan Poe, Edith Wharton, and Jack Kerouac. Permanent galleries feature interactive exhibits that let visitors look more deeply into the history of American writers and their masterpieces, the mind of a writer, and more. There are word-play games, with tips for budding authors, and a delightful, mural-lined gallery of children's literature. Tem-porary exhibits have ranged from a collection of historic typewriters to the lyrics of Bob Dylan, who was awarded the Nobel Prize for Literature in 2016. You can also share your own story when you visit.

⑫

Museum of Contemporary Art

🏠 220 E Chicago Av
Ⓜ Chicago Avenue 🚌
🕐 10am–5pm daily (to 9pm Tue & Fri) 🌐 mcachicago.org

With more than 2,500 artworks that showcase a variety of media and movements from the 1920s to the present, this is one of the largest contemporary art museums in the world. Founded in 1967 as a non-collecting art gallery, the museum expanded rapidly and moved to its current location in 1996. Rather than permanent galleries, the art here is displayed on a rotating basis in curated exhibitions throughout the year. Temporary shows also feature works on loan by famous artists, with previous exhibits having included pieces by Jeff Koons, Cindy Sherman, and Andy Warhol. The galleries are reached via a dramatic, elliptic staircase – itself an architectural masterpiece – which leads to a glass-walled atrium with views over the city and Lake Michigan.

The museum also hosts a series of programs and events, including music, talks and live art, and there is free admission for residents of Illinois on Tuesdays. The well-stocked shop offers an entire floor of housewares, jewelry, and other gift items.

> A must-visit for bibliophiles, the American Writers Museum is a delight, casting a light on authors such as Edgar Allan Poe, Edith Wharton, and Jack Kerouac.

experiences and achievements of African Americans.

The substantial wooden Freedom Now mural depicts the experiences of African Americans throughout 400 years of US history. Other exhibits include memorabilia from the life and political career of Chicago's first black mayor, Harold Washington.

⑮ 🚲 Ⓜ 🏛

Wrigley Field

🏠 1060 W Addison St
Ⓜ Addison 🕐 Mar–Nov
🌐 mlb.com/cubs

The Chicago Cubs baseball team are much-loved local stars, and a behind-the-scenes tour of their home ground at Wrigley Field is a highlight for sports fans. Non-game-day tours include a visit to the seating bowl, press box, Cubs' clubhouse, dugout, and more, along with a chance to step onto the field. Game-day tours visit the indoor batting cage instead of the clubhouse, and capture the excitement of the site before the gates open.

⑯ 🚲 Ⓜ 🏛

University of Chicago

🏠 5801 S Ellis Av 🚲
Ⓜ Garfield 🌐 uchicago.edu

The University of Chicago was founded in 1890 with the endowment of John D. Rockefeller, on land donated by Marshall Field. Today, this outstanding private university has one of the greatest number of Nobel laureates among faculty, alumni, and researchers of any US university. It is particularly lauded in the fields of economics, chemistry, and physics.

The north entrance houses the ornamental Cobb Gate, a gargoyled gateway donated by Henry Cobb in 1900. Across the street, the Regenstein Library holds rare book and

AROUND CHICAGO

⑬ 🚲 Ⓜ 🍴 💻 🏛

Museum of Science & Industry

🏠 5700 S Lake Shore Dr 🚲
Ⓜ Garfield 🚌 🕐 9:30am–4pm daily; extended hours in summer 🌐 msichicago.org

The Museum of Science and Industry celebrates scientific and technological accomplishments, with an emphasis on achievements of the 20th and 21st centuries. With over 800 exhibits and 35,000 artifacts, the museum makes the exploration of science and technology an accessible experience.

The Henry Crown Space Center features the Apollo 8 Command Module, the first manned spacecraft to circle the moon. A 20-minute movie simulates the experience of blasting off in a space shuttle, complete with shaking seats.

Visitors can walk through a 16-ft (5-m) replica of the human heart, or look inside the human body in a detailed exhibit on anatomy. Genetics: Decoding Life explores the ethical, biological, and social issues of this field of research. Other crowd-pleasers include a toy factory staffed by robots, the five-story Omnimax theater, and Colleen Moore's Fairy Castle, an exquisite dollhouse.

⑭ 🚲 Ⓜ 🏛

DuSable Museum of African American History

🏠 740 E 56th Pl Ⓜ Garfield
🚌 🕐 10am–5pm Tue–Sat, noon–5pm Sun 🚫 Federal hols 🌐 dusablemuseum.org

This museum was founded in 1961 to preserve and interpret the diverse historical

manuscript collections, along with millions of other volumes.

At the northern end of the campus is the intimate Smart Museum of Art. It holds more than 10,000 objects spanning five centuries of Western and Eastern civilizations. Outside, sculptor Henry Moore's *Nuclear Energy* marks the spot where, in 1942, a team of scientists led by Enrico Fermi ushered in the atomic age with the first controlled nuclear reaction.

In the southeast of the vast campus lies the Oriental Institute Museum, the highlights of which include a 17-ft (5-m) sculpture of King Tutankhamen, the tallest ancient Egyptian statue in the Western Hemisphere (c 1334–25 BC). Opposite the museum, the massive Rockefeller Memorial Chapel is among the tallest buildings on campus. Two blocks north lies Frank Lloyd Wright's famous Robie House (1908–1910), currently being restored. It is one of Wright's last Prairie School houses, with the exterior perfectly capturing the prairie landscape of flat, open fields.

⑰
Museum Campus

🅰 S Lake Shore Dr
🅡 Roosevelt Ⓜ Roosevelt 🚌

The Museum Campus is a vast lakefront park connecting three world-famous natural science museums. This extension of Burnham Park was created by the relocation of Lake Shore Drive in 1996.

In the southwest part of the campus is the Daniel Burnham-designed structure housing the Field Museum, which holds an encyclopedic collection of zoological, geological, and anthropological objects from around the world. Founded in 1894 to house objects from the 1893 World's Columbian Exposition, the museum now holds over 20 million objects. There is a particularly fine collection of dinosaur fossils, while the permanent "Ancient

↓ The University of Chicago, and Cobb Gate *(inset)*

Americas" exhibit covers Ice Age to Aztec cultures.

A short walk northeast leads to the John G. Shedd Aquarium, housing more than 32,500 saltwater and freshwater animals, representing 1,500 species of fish, birds, reptiles, amphibians, invertebrates, and mammals. The remodeled Oceanarium has a magnificent curved wall of glass facing Lake Michigan, whose water flows into its tank.

Farther east, the Museum Campus houses the Adler Planetarium. Antique astronomical instruments include the world's oldest known window sundial, and it is also home to the world's first virtual-reality theater.

A SHORT WALK
THE LOOP

Distance 1.5 miles (2 km) **Time** 25 minutes
Nearest subway Quincy

The Loop gets its name from the elevated track system
that circles the center of downtown. Screeching trains and
a steady stream of people add to its bustle. In the canyon
vistas, through the historic buildings and modern edifices,
you can catch glimpses of the bridges spanning the
Chicago River. The renovation of warehouses and historic
theaters is helping to enliven the Loop at night.

Marquette Building, an
*early skyscraper (1895), was
designed by William Holabird
and Martin Roche, central
Chicago School figures and
architects of more than 80
buildings in the Loop.*

The Rookery (p374),
*designed in 1888,
typifies the
Richardsonian
Romanesque style.*

**190 South LaSalle
Street** (1987),
*designed by Philip
Johnson, has a
white-marble lobby
with a gold-leafed,
vaulted ceiling.*

↑ The lobby of the
Rookery, remodeled
by Frank Lloyd Wright

Willis Tower
(p374)

STREET

CLARK

ADAMS

START

WACKER

FRANKLIN STREET

DRIVE

Chicago Board of Trade
*occupies a 45-story Art Deco
building, a statue of Ceres atop
its roof. The frenetic action
inside can be observed from a
viewers' gallery.*

0 meters 100 N
0 yards 100

Did You Know?

Jane Addams – from Chicago – was the first woman to win a Nobel Peace Prize, in 1931.

Locator Map
For more detail see p371

The Loop

CHICAGO

Santa Fe Center, *a classic Chicago School building, with an elegant two-story atrium, houses the Chicago Architecture Foundation.*

Art Institute of Chicago (p373)

FINISH

Federal Center *is a three-building office complex designed around a central plaza by Ludwig Mies van der Rohe.*

Auditorium Building, *an 1889 multipurpose skyscraper, features one of Adler and Sullivan's best interiors in its seventh-floor, birch-paneled recital hall.*

MONROE ST

SOUTH

WABASH

STATE

STREET

JACKSON BLVD

MICHIGAN AVENUE

AVENUE

PARKWAY

STREET

BUREN

VAN

CONGRESS

Monadnock Building's *north half is one of the tallest buildings constructed entirely of masonry.*

Fine Arts Building, *designed by Solon S. Beman in 1885, was originally a wagon carriage showroom. It once also housed Frank Lloyd Wright's studio.*

←
Landmark skyscrapers of the Loop, seen from Grant Park

379

ILLINOIS

Except for the densely populated area around Chicago (p370), Illinois is a predominantly rural state. Its farmlands are dotted with scenic byways, historic towns, and wine trails. Known as the "Land of Lincoln," Illinois is chock-full of sites related to the president, mostly found in the heart of the state. Picturesque scenery can be found along the Mississippi.

② Springfield

🚗🏨🚄 🛈 109 N 7th St; www.visit-springfield illinois.com

The state capital since 1837, Springfield gained fame as the adopted hometown of 16th US president, Abraham Lincoln, who lived here before assuming the presidency in 1861. The Abraham Lincoln Presidential Library and Museum is full of artifacts and interactive displays, while the four-block **Lincoln Home National Historic Site** is a pedestrian-only historic district, with restored 19th-century homes surrounding the neat frame house where Lincoln and his wife, Mary, lived for 16 years. The city's other Lincoln-related attractions include his law office, tomb, and the 1853 **Old State Capitol**. It was here that he delivered his famous 1858 "House Divided" speech, outlining the sectional differences that would soon plunge the nation into the Civil War.

Another key attraction is the elegant Dana-Thomas House, a 1904 Prairie-style home designed by Frank Lloyd Wright. It contains much of Wright's original white oak furniture, art-glass doors, windows, and light panels. Many Wright experts consider this to be the best-preserved of the houses designed by the famous architect.

Springfield is also rich in Route 66 lore. The old road follows a clearly marked path through the city, leading to the southside Cozy Dog Drive-in, a legendary Route 66 eatery, which claims to have invented the corn dog. Route 66 Museum is at the site.

Lincoln Home National Historic Site

🚗 413 S 8th St 🕐 8:30am-5pm daily 🌐 nps.gov/liho

Old State Capitol

🚗 5th & Adams sts 🕐 9am-5pm daily 🌐 illinois.gov

↑ The Lincoln Home National Historic Site, a notable attraction in Springfield

③ ⓂⓈ Oak Park

🚗 Bounded by North Av, Roosevelt Rd, Austin Blvd, & Harlem Av 🚇 Oak Park Ⓜ Oak Park, Harlem/Lake 🛈 1010 Lake St; www.visitoakpark.com

Frank Lloyd Wright moved to Oak Park in 1889, at the age of 22. He created many groundbreaking buildings here as his legendary Prairie School style evolved. This tranquil community is now home to 25 Wright buildings – the largest grouping of his work anywhere. Tours of the superbly restored 1889 Frank Lloyd Wright Home and Studio, and of the Unity Temple are given by the Frank Lloyd Wright Trust. The latter was built in 1906–1908, using a then-unusual technique of poured reinforced concrete. Nearby are two private homes: the 1902 Arthur Heurtley House and the 1895 Moore-Dugal House, rich with Tudor-Revival and Gothic elements.

At the southern end of Oak Park is the Pleasant Home, a Prairie-style mansion designed in 1897 by George W. Maher. The house holds extraordinary art glass – designed panels of leaded glass – and includes a display on the area's history.

Oak Park was also the birthplace of US writer Ernest Hemingway (1899–1960), who lived here until the age of 20. Although Hemingway rejected the conservative mind-set of this Chicago suburb, Oak Park prides itself on this literary association, and the Ernest Hemingway Museum features artifacts from his early life.

④ Rockford

🚗🚄 🛈 102 N Main St; www.gorockford.com

Dubbed the Forest City in the late 1800s, Rockford today has beautiful public and private gardens and miles of

↑ The rocky landscape of Shawnee National Forest in Southern Illinois

parkland along the Rock River, which bisects the city. Its most-visited gardens are the Klehm Arboretum and Botanic Garden, the Anderson Japanese Gardens, and the Nicholas Conservatory and Gardens.

On the city's east side, the Midway Village and Museum Center is both a living history center and local history museum. Exhibits tell the story of the communities that flocked to the city's factories.

The growth of Rockford followed the tragic 1830s Blackhawk War between the Sacs of northern Illinois and the US Army, determined to displace the tribes from their farmlands. After the Sacs lost, they were relocated to Iowa.

❺ Galena

🚗 🚌 🛈 123 N Commerce St; www.galena.org

Perched on a bluff above the Galena River, this immaculately preserved town is a relaxing tourist destination with 19th-century homes, historical landmarks, and antique shops. A number of magnificent homes that were built during the Civil War are now open to visitors. The 1857

Belvedere Mansion is a 22-room Italianate structure with a varied collection of period furnishings. Civil War general and US president Ulysses S. Grant lived in Galena before his time in the White House, and his Federal-style 1860 home contains many of the original furnishings.

The Galena/Jo Daviess County History Museum chronicles Galena's lead-mining and Civil War shipping days.

❻ Southern Illinois

🚌 🌐 southernmost illinois.com

In Southern Illinois, flat farmlands give way to rolling hills and forests along the Ohio and Mississippi rivers. This terrain offered vantage points from which American Indian tribes and, later, French traders and missionaries could monitor river traffic. Near the confluence of the Missouri, Illinois, and Mississippi rivers are the remains of the largest prehistoric American Indian city north of Mexico. The Cahokia Mounds State Historic and World Heritage Site contains more than 100 earthen

mounds dating from 1050 to 1250. The site's interpretive center recounts the story of these mounds, which were mysteriously abandoned by around 1500. The Shawnee National Forest can be viewed most dramatically at the Garden of the Gods, an area of sandstone outcroppings.

Indianapolis 500 at Indianapolis Motor Speedway

Experience

INDIANA AND OHIO

The French established trading posts here in the 18th century, and the region was the scene of heavy fighting during the French and Indian War (1754–1763) and Revolutionary War (1775–1783). A series of one-sided treaties, backed by violent military campaigns, subsequently forced out the American Indians and US settlers poured in; Ohio was created in 1803 and Indiana in 1816. The region became heavily industrialized in the 19th century; Hoover was founded in Ohio, with Cleveland the base of oilman John Rockefeller and Dow Chemical, Cincinnati the nation's pork capital and head-quarters of Procter & Gamble, and Dayton the home of the Wright Brothers.

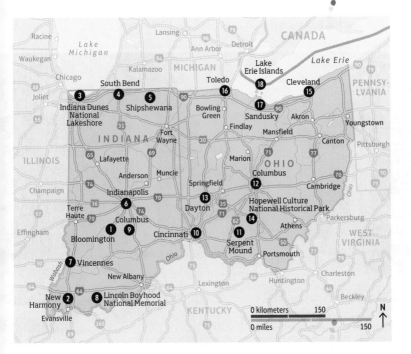

INDIANA

Unlike the other states of the Great Lakes region, Indiana has only a short stretch of shoreline along Lake Michigan. As a result, the state's extensive river systems have proved crucial, along with the development of railroads and highways. Indiana today is an engaging place to explore by car, especially along its hilly Ohio River backroads and Amish-country scenic lanes.

① Bloomington

🚓🚌 ℹ 2855 N Walnut St;
www.visitbloomington.com

Surrounded by limestone outcrops, this city is home to the leafy Indiana University campus. Quarrying of the limestone deposits fueled Bloomington's 19th-century growth, the results of which can still be seen in the city's magnificent public buildings. A prime example is the 1906 Beaux Arts Monroe County Courthouse, at the center of the downtown Courthouse Square Historic District.

On the campus are a variety of historic buildings and outdoor spaces. The 1941 Auditorium displays 20 panels of Thomas Hart Benton's 1933 *Century of Progress* murals, painted for the World's Fair. The Tibetan Cultural Center is the only one in the US and is a haven for meditation. The **Indiana University Art Museum** was designed by architect I.M. Pei, and includes works by Matisse, Monet, Rodin, and Andy Warhol, as well as Picasso's 1934 *L'Atelier (The Studio)*.

Indiana University Art Museum

🏠 1133 E 7th St 🕐 10am–5pm Tue-Sat, noon–5pm Sun 🚪 Federal hols 🌐 artmuseum.indiana.edu

② New Harmony

ℹ 401 N Arthur St; www.newharmony.org

America's two most successful utopian communities flourished in this neat village on the eastern banks of the Wabash River. The tree-lined town is now a State Historic Site with 25 well-preserved Harmonist buildings and many beautiful manicured gardens,

---

UTOPIAN HARMONY

The Harmony Society was founded in 1814 by a German Lutheran sect from Pennsylvania, who followed a doctrine of perfectionism and celibacy, while developing profitable agricultural enterprises. In 1825, the Harmonists sold their lands to Scottish textile magnate Robert Owen. He, too, sought to create an ideal society based on free education and the abolition of social classes. The colony failed after two years, but Owen's two sons later set up the Smithsonian Institution in Washington, DC.

Cycling through the grounds of Indiana University, Bloomington ↑

The Basilica of the Sacred Heart at Notre Dame, South Bend ↑

which include the superb reconstructed Labyrinth, a maze-like set of hedges around a stone temple.

3

Indiana Dunes National Lakeshore

ℹ️ 1215 In-49, Chesterton; www.nps.gov/indu

One of the nation's most diverse groups of ecosystems is contained within the 23-sq-mile (61-sq-km) Indiana Dunes National Lakeshore. Its ecosystems include bogs, swamps, marshes, glacial moraines, prairies, forests, oak savannas, and dunes linked by scenic roads and a network of hiking and biking trails. The Beyond the Beach Discovery Trail leads to the area's natural treasures. The park is also a bird-watcher's paradise.

4

South Bend

🚗🚆🚌 ℹ️ 101 N Michigan St; www.visitsouthbend.com

South Bend is widely known today as the home of the Roman Catholic University of Notre Dame, which was established in 1842. While religion is still important, the students and countless alumni are hugely passionate about the Notre Dame "Fighting Irish" football team, one of the most successful in college football history.

Tours by appointment are available at the **Morris Performing Arts Center**, which was the most modern theater in the US when it first opened as a vaudeville house in 1921. Many celebrities, from Frank Sinatra to Jerry Seinfeld, have performed here.

South of downtown, the Studebaker National Museum contains a collection of horse-drawn carriages and early automobiles, including the carriage in which President Lincoln rode to Ford's Theatre the night he was assassinated.

Morris Performing Arts Center

📍 211 N Michigan St 🎫 Box office: 10am–5pm Tue–Fri 🌐 morriscenter.org

5

Shipshewana

🚌 ℹ️ 780 S Van Buren St; www.visitshipshewana.org

This small village, in northeastern Indiana, has one of the world's largest Amish communities. The town's Menno-Hof Mennonite Anabaptist Interpretive Center provides an informative and detailed background on the European Anabaptist movement, with exhibits that re-create periods from its history as well as examining the sects and their lifestyles as they are today.

Shipshewana and its many surrounding villages of Bristol, Elkhart, Goshen, Middlebury, Nappanee, and Wakarusa are also home to an Amish farming community. Tourists come to the area in search of furniture, baked goods, and quilts.

EAT

Das Dutchman Essenhaus

Located in the heart of Amish country, head here to try tasty, homemade family recipes.

📍 240 Hwy 20, Middlebury 🕐 Sun 🌐 essenhaus.com

$$$ ⓢⓢ

Gasthof Amish Village

This rustic restaurant serves a buffet of traditional Amish dishes.

📍 6659 E Gasthof Rd, Montgomery 🌐 gasthof amishvillage.com

$$$ ⓢⓢ

Blue Gate Restaurant & Bakery

Sample some delicious baked goods, made fresh with produce from the attached farm.

📍 195 N Van Buren St, Shipshewana 🕐 Sun 🌐 bluegatebakery.com

$$$ ⓢⓢ

Indianapolis

⬆🏛🚌 ℹ 200 S Capitol Av; www.visitindy.com

Known as "The Crossroads of America," Indianapolis is much more than a transportation hub. The city's many parks and monuments, and vibrant neighborhoods, make it one of the region's most surprising and satisfying destinations.

Selected as the state capital in 1820, Indianapolis was laid out on the banks of the White River, with a network of boulevards radiating outward from the central Monument Circle.

The city's first-rate museums and lively arts scene are complemented by an active program of sports. Every Memorial Day, the world's largest single-day sporting event – the Indianapolis 500 auto race – fills the **Indianapolis Motor Speedway** with nearly 300,000 fans. Built in 1909 as a test track for the city's then-burgeoning automotive industry, the speedway played host to the first Indy 500 in 1911. The track's Hall of Fame displays more than 75 racing cars and other Indy 500 memorabilia, in addition to examples of the automobiles built in the city. Visitors can also take a guided bus tour around the track.

The Children's Museum of Indianapolis, which opened in 1976, has been consistently rated as one of the country's best, and is the largest in the world. It has around 120,000 artifacts, and its exhibits encourage hands-on exploration of the sciences, history, and the arts.

The Indiana State Museum is among the sites within the downtown **White River State Park**, a 250-acre (101-ha) urban oasis. The museum is constructed of locally sourced materials, and is close to the Indianapolis Zoo. The Eiteljorg Museum of American Indians and Western Art, also in this park, has one of the most impressive collections of American Indian and Western American art in the US. Established in 1989, the museum is housed in a Southwest-inspired adobe building, in deference to its large collection of works from the early 20th-century Taos Society of Artists *(p526)*.

> 💬 INSIDER TIP
> **Brickyard Fun**
>
> As well as the Indy 500, the Indianapolis Motor Speedway hosts NASCAR races, vintage car races, concerts, a half-marathon, and other events *(www.indianapolismotorspeedway.com)*.

→ A racecar displayed at the Indianapolis Motor Speedway

Downtown Indianapolis, with a towering obelisk at its center

Lockerbie Square District is the city's oldest surviving 19th-century immigrant neighborhood, with preserved workers' cottages, cobblestone streets, and period street lights.

Just north of downtown, the **Indianapolis Museum of Art** houses a wide-ranging collection of American, Asian, African, and European art. The house and estate where the museum is sited have been carefully restored to their original 1920s grandeur, and are open for tours. On view are paintings by such celebrated artists as Georgia O'Keeffe, Frederic Remington, and Charles M. Russell.

Indianapolis Motor Speedway

🏛 Hall of Fame, 4790 W 16th St ⏰9am–5pm daily (extended hours in May) 🌐indyracingmuseum.org

White River State Park

⏰Daily; times vary, check website 🌐inwhiteriver.com

Indianapolis Museum of Art

🏛4000 Michigan Rd ⏰11am–5pm Tue–Sat (to 8pm Thu & Sat) 🌐imamuseum.org

❼ Vincennes

ℹ 779 South 6th St; www.vincennescvb.org

Indiana's oldest city is a delight for history buffs. Tour Grouseland, the mansion where President William Henry Harrison lived in the early 1800s, and visit the Vincennes State Historic Site. Check out the strategic Fort Knox II or visit George Rogers Clark National Historical Park. The Indiana Military Museum has one of the largest collections in the US, with artifacts dating back to the Revolutionary War. For contemporary fun, go wine-tasting at Windy Knoll Winery.

❽ Lincoln Boyhood National Memorial

🏛 Indiana Hwy 162, Lincoln City 🌐nps.gov/libo/index

Delve into presidential history and experience pioneer life at the farm site where President Abraham Lincoln lived as a boy. His family moved here from Kentucky in 1816, when Lincoln was seven years old, and it was his home until 1830. His experiences here influenced his character, and he developed the honesty, compassion, and anti-slavery stance that marked his presidency.

The Memorial Visitor Center, built in 1945, features five sculpted limestone panels that depict different periods of Lincoln's life. Inside, a 15-minute film about Lincoln's life in Indiana is screened, and the museum's exhibits make for fascinating insight.

The historical farm site stands nearby, alongside the Pioneer Cemetery. A replica log cabin has been built as part of the Living Historical Farm, and park rangers in period clothing work the farm from mid-April to September, demonstrating daily life in the 1820s.

❾ Columbus

ℹ 506 5th St; www.columbus.in.us

One of the world's most concentrated collections of modern architecture can be found in this small Indiana city. From 1942 on, after the completion of architect Eliel Saarinen's First Christian Church, Columbus garnered international attention for the many churches, schools, banks, and commercial and public buildings constructed here. Today, the city is ranked sixth on the American Institute of Architects' list of cities marked by innovation in architecture and design.

Among those who left their stamp on the city are Robert Trent Jones, Richard Meier, Robert Venturi, Alexander Girard, and I.M. Pei, whose 1969 Cleo Rodgers Memorial Library is at 536 5th Street. The Columbus Architecture Tours allow visitors to glimpse these architectural delights.

OHIO

Ohio is a study in contrasts. As one of the nation's largest agricultural producers, the state is dotted with scenic farmland, historic small towns, and Amish communities that still use horse-drawn buggies. Yet Ohio also contains several of the country's most urbanized industrial centers along the Ohio River, and in port cities along the shores of Lake Erie.

⑩ Cincinnati

▸ ▣ ▨▨ 🛈 525 Vine St; www.cincinnatiusa.com

Built on a series of steep hills overlooking the Ohio River, Cincinnati was once called "the most beautiful of America's inland cities" by British prime minister Winston Churchill. The city is today a vibrant corporate center with a revitalized riverfront entertainment and parks district.

Cincinnati's strategic perch on the border of the slave-holding South and the industrializing North, made it a heterogeneous cultural and commercial crossroads. Many prominent locals, including writer Harriet Beecher Stowe, strongly supported the anti-slavery movement. The National Underground Railroad Freedom Center focuses on the city's one-time heroic past. Cincinnati's most celebrated landmark is the 1867 suspension bridge, built by Brooklyn Bridge engineer

John A. Roebling to link the city with Covington, Kentucky, across the Ohio River. The Cincinnati Bell Connector streetcar opened in 2016, and links key stops downtown.

Another landmark is the 1933 Cincinnati Museum Center at Union Terminal. The refurbished terminal now houses attractions that specialize in city history, children's activities, and natural history/science. On the eastern part of town, the **Cincinnati Art Museum** overlooks Eden Park and contains a specially commissioned portrait by Andy Warhol of the controversial Cincinnati Reds baseball great, Pete Rose.

Cincinnati Art Museum

⊗ 🏠 953 Eden Park Dr
🕐 11am–5pm Tue–Sun (to 8pm Thu) 🚫 Federal hols
🌐 cincinnatiartmuseum.org

⑪ Serpent Mound

🏠 3850 Rte 73, Peebles
📞 (800) 752-2757 🕐 Times vary, call ahead

The Serpent Mound overlooks Brush Creek in the Ohio River Valley. Although its exact age is unknown, research suggests that it was constructed between 800 BC and AD 400 by the ancient Adena people, Ohio's earliest American Indian farming community.

The wide mound appears to represent an uncoiling serpent, with a tightly coiled tail at one end and a mouthlike opening, swallowing an oval-shaped egg, at the other. A museum describes the mound's history and its protection under an

> **Cincinnati's most celebrated landmark is the 1867 suspension bridge, built by Brooklyn Bridge engineer John A. Roebling, to link the city with Covington, Kentucky.**

↑ Reading about huge exhibits on display at the National Museum of the US Air Force in Dayton

1888 law, the first in the US to safeguard important archaeological sites.

12 Columbus

🚗🅿️🚌 ℹ️ 277 W Nationwide Blvd; www.experience columbus.org

Ohio's capital since 1816, Columbus has grown from a sleepy, swampy lowland site to become a bustling cultural, political, and economic center. Downtown's central feature is the Greek-Revival style Ohio Statehouse. Built between 1839 and 1861, the structure is surmounted by a unique drum-shaped cupola marked by a 29-ft- (9-m-) wide skylight. Begin your exploration at the **Ohio History Center**, which has interactive displays tracing Ohio's evolution, with nationally acclaimed attractions such as the COSI (Center of Science and Industry) outdoor science park and 300 interactive indoor exhibits.

Ohio History Center

♿ 📍 1982 Velma Av
🕐 10am–5pm Wed–Sun
📅 Most Federal hols 🌐 ohio history.org/places/ohc

←

Cincinnati's striking steel-and-stone suspension bridge

13 Dayton

🚗🚌 ℹ️ 1 Chamber Plaza, Suite A; www.daytoncvb. com

This pleasant city on the Great Miami River is known as the "Birthplace of Aviation." It was here that the Wright brothers carried out much of the experimentation that led to their 1903 successful flight in Kitty Hawk, North Carolina. The **Carillon Historical Park** holds the Wright *Flyer III* aircraft – the first capable of executing a turn. Other aviation museums in the area include the Dayton Aviation Heritage National Historical Park, the National Museum of the US Air Force, and the National Aviation Hall of Fame.

Carillon Historical Park

♿ 📍 1000 Carillon Blvd
🕐 9:30am–5pm Tue–Sat, noon–5pm Sun & federal hols
🌐 carillonpark.org

14 Hopewell Culture National Historical Park

📍 16062 Rte 104 🕐 Dawn–dusk daily 🌐 nps.gov/hocu

Located in the Scioto River Valley, this 120-acre (48-ha) park preserves 23 American Indian burial mounds built

EAT

Skyline Chili

Tuck into a dish of hearty, meaty chili – made from a special family recipe – at this popular regional chain.

📍 1001 Vine St, Cincinnati
🌐 skylinechili.com

💲💲💲

Lola Bistro

TV chef Michael Symon's upscale eatery has an inventive menu featuring excellent local ingredients.

📍 2058 E 4th St, Cleveland
🌐 lolabistro.com

💲💲💲

Thurman Café

A landmark since its opening in 1942, this cozy café is known for its juicy burgers and authentic Coney Island hot dogs.

📍 183 Thurman Av, Columbus 🌐 the thurmancafe.com

💲💲💲

by the Hopewell people, who lived here from 200 BC to AD 500. The Hopewell culture, which emerged from the Adena culture, covers a broad network of beliefs and practices among different American Indian groups spread over the eastern US. A characteristic of the culture, the mounds are arranged in geometric shapes, ringed by an earthen wall. A visitor center provides an in-depth look at the social and economic life of the long-vanished Hopewell peoples, based on the archaeological work conducted here.

Locals lunching in
Cleveland's buzzing
East 4th Street District ↑

15

Cleveland

🚇🅿🚌 ℹ 334 Euclid Av;
www.thisiscleveland.com

Cleveland is a hard-working, vibrant, and ever-changing community. Founded in 1796 by speculator Moses Cleaveland, the city evolved from a frontier town into a bustling commercial port by 1832. Cleveland's steel industry was born after the Civil War and thrived in the early 1900s, with the city's railroads catering to the Detroit automobile industry's demand for easily transported steel. After World War II, however, the city's fortunes faded as industries moved away, leaving behind polluted landscapes and scores of unemployed workers.

Today, Cleveland's "Rust Belt" image is a thing of the past. The city now encompasses miles of pristine parkland, and the East 4th Street District and historic Warehouse District are the entertainment hubs.

A signature feature since 1927, the 52-story Beaux Arts Terminal Tower, was designed as a "city within a city." The 42nd-floor observation deck offers grand views and, on a clear day, one can see the Canadian shoreline.

The **Rock & Roll Hall of Fame and Museum**, which opened in 1995 on the Lake Erie waterfront, put Cleveland at center stage of the nation's entertainment scene. The massive museum traces the development of the musical genre, beginning with its roots in the Mississippi Delta blues (*p351*) and Appalachian string bands. On display are memorabilia ranging from Chuck Berry's Gibson electric guitar to a Cub Scout shirt worn by Jim Morrison. To its west, the Great Lakes Science Center stimulates public interest in the complex ecosystem of the Great Lakes region.

Cleveland's principal cultural attractions lie around University Circle. Surrounding this expanse of parkland near the Case Western Reserve University campus is a series of fine museums. Among them is the **Cleveland Museum of Art**, with its superb collection of ancient Egyptian relics and pre-Columbian artifacts. Facing this museum, the city's popular Botanical Garden features 10 acres (4 ha) of outdoor gardens, a Japanese garden, and a peace garden.

Did You Know?

In Cleveland, you need a hunting license to catch a mouse.

DRINK

Great Lakes Brewing Co.
This brewery and brewpub plays a big role in Cleveland's identity, and is a must for beer lovers. Tours are available.

🏠 2516 Market Av, Cleveland 🌐 greatlakes brewing.com

Located 25 miles (40 km) west of Cleveland, Oberlin is home to Oberlin College, one of the first to admit female and African American students. The Allen Memorial Art Museum on campus displays American, Asian, and European art.

Rock & Roll Hall of Fame and Museum

⊛ ⌂ 1100 Rock and Roll Blvd 🕙 10am–5:30pm daily (to 9pm Wed) 🌐 rockhall.com

Cleveland Museum of Art

⌂ 11150 East Blvd 🕙 10am–5pm Tue–Sun (to 9pm Wed & Fri) 🚫 Jan 1, Jul 4, Thanksgiving, Dec 25 🌐 clevelandart.org

---

16
Toledo

🚻♿🚌 ℹ 401 Jefferson Av; www.dotoledo.org

One of the world's leading glass manufacturing centers and the third-busiest Great Lakes port, Toledo occupies a Maumee River site steeped in history. Today, the city is famed for the **Toledo Museum of Art**, which was founded by local glass tycoon Edward Drummond Libbey. It features one of the world's largest collections of ornamental glass, housed in the Post-Modern Glass Pavilion. The nearby Fort Meigs State Memorial, a reconstructed fort dating from the War of 1812, features

← A classical bust, on display at the Toledo Museum of Art

a museum and interactive displays, with various outdoor reenactments in summer. Fort Meigs, south of Toledo in Perrysburg, commemorates the stockade that withstood two British and American Indian sieges in 1813.

Toledo Museum of Art

⌂ 2445 Monroe St 🕙 10am–4pm Tue–Sat (to 9pm Fri, 5pm Sat), noon–6pm Sun 🚫 Jan 1, Jul 4, Thanksgiving, Dec 25 🌐 toledomuseum.org

---

17
Sandusky

🚻♿🚌 ℹ 216 E Water St; www.shoreandislands.com

Once one of the Great Lakes' largest coalshipping ports, today Sandusky's ferry terminal provides easy access to many of the Lake Erie Islands. The city is best known, however, for the **Cedar Point Amusement Park**, which claims to have the world's largest collection of roller coasters. They range from rickety old wooden ones to the world's tallest, largest, and fastest divecoaster, Valravn.

Cedar Point Amusement Park

⊛ ⌂ 1 Cedar Point Dr 🕙 Mid-May–Labor Day: 10am–8pm daily; Labor Day–end of Oct: days vary, check website 🌐 cedarpoint.com

---

18
Lake Erie Islands

🚌 ℹ 770 SE Catawba Rd, Port Clinton; www.shoresandislands.com

Located just offshore from the Marblehead Peninsula separating Sandusky Bay

↑ Lighthouse on South Bass Island, Sandusky

from the lake, the Lake Erie Islands are a prime summer tourist destination. They include bucolic Kelleys Island and the rowdier South Bass Island, with the village of Put-in-Bay as its nightlife hub.

Home of the Erie, Ottawa, and Huron tribes until the 19th century, the Lake Erie Islands rose to national prominence during the War of 1812, when the pivotal Battle of Lake Erie was fought off South Bass Island in September 1813. A visitor center and granite column at Put-in-Bay, **Perry's Victory and International Peace Memorial**, commemorates this battle.

Kelleys Island State Park has the fascinating Glacial Grooves, a series of deep limestone grooves caused by the movement of a heavy glacial wall. These grooves have been protected from quarrying since 1923.

Perry's Victory and International Peace Memorial

⊛ ⌂ 93 Delaware Av, S Bass Island 🕙 Mid-May–Oct: 10am–5pm daily, or by appt 🌐 nps.gov/pevi

Kelleys Island State Park

⌂ Kelleys Island 🕙 6am–10pm daily 🌐 ohiostateparks.org

MICHIGAN

Once populated by the Ojibwe (Chippewa), Ontario, Miami, and Potawatomi peoples, Michigan was studded with French fur-trading posts in the 18th century. The US rapidly extended its control after independence, expelling most American Indians, and Michigan became a state in 1837. In the 1840s, copper and iron were discovered on the Upper Peninsula. Car manufacturers set up shop in Detroit in the early 20th century and thousands of African Americans migrated from the South to work here. Times have been hard, especially in Detroit; there were the tragic Detroit race riots of 1967 and, more recently, the city declared bankruptcy in 2013.

Experience

1. Detroit
2. Ann Arbor
3. Lansing
4. Grand Rapids
5. Lake Michigan Shore
6. Mackinac Island
7. Upper Peninsula

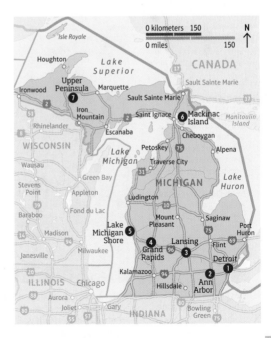

MICHIGAN

Michigan's principal landmass, the so-called Lower Peninsula, is a mitten-shaped area, home to wind-blown dunes and rolling cherry orchards. It is surrounded by three Great Lakes – Michigan, Huron, and Erie. The region contains the state's largest cities, including Detroit, and accounts for most of Michigan's industry. The Upper Peninsula to the northwest is more wild and rugged.

❶
Detroit

🚏🏛🚌 ℹ 211 W Fort St; www.visitdetroit.com

Known today as the "Motor City," Detroit (meaning "the Strait" in French) was founded in 1701 by French fur trader Antoine de la Mothe Cadillac. The city evolved from a ship-building center into a leading manufacturer of railroad equipment, cars, and bicycles. Its massive industrial growth, however, took place after Henry Ford began manufacturing automobiles here in 1896. By the 1920s, most US automobile manufacturers had moved their headquarters and production facilities to Detroit, and by the 1940s, it was the fourth-largest city in the country. However, in the late 20th century, Detroit's population dropped by more than 60 percent. A loss of jobs in the auto and manufacturing

industries, plus an exodus to the growing suburbs, led to the surreal abandonment of half the inner city. In 2013, Detroit filed for bankruptcy.

The automobile industry still dominates Detroit. The city's present focal point is the huge riverfront Renaissance Center, General Motors' current headquarters. Nearby, Hart Plaza hosts year-round riverfront festivals, including the Detroit Jazz Festival during Labor Day weekend. East of downtown is the lively Greektown neighborhood and restaurant district centered on Monroe Avenue. Just north of downtown are Comerica Park and Ford Field sports venues.

The **Charles H. Wright Museum of African American**

History commemorates the contributions made by Detroit's African American population to the city's commercial and cultural progress. A range of exhibits for all age groups depicts milestones in African American history.

The **Detroit Institute of Arts**' centerpiece is a vast 27-panel mural by Mexico City artist Diego Rivera. His controversial *Detroit Industry* reflects the artist's Leftist views of the relationship between management and labor. The museum's outstanding collections range from pre-Columbian, American Indian, and African art to 17th-century Dutch paintings.

The renovated "Streets of Old Detroit" display and an exhibit on Detroit's automotive heritage are the main features of **Detroit Historical Museum**. The society's Historic Fort

> **The Detroit Institute of Arts' centerpiece is a vast 27-panel mural by Mexico City artist Diego Rivera.**

HEIDELBERG PROJECT

In 1986, artist Tyree Guyton created an outdoor art environment on Detroit's east side, painting bright dots on houses along Heidelberg Street, and attaching salvaged items to others. He transformed an area blighted by crime and poverty, but after arson attacks in 2013–14, Guyton began dismantling the project. Go see this unique piece of history before it's gone.

A striking mural by Diego Rivera, one of the Detroit Industry Murals ↑

Wayne and Tuskegee Airmen Museum, on the city's southwest side, incorporates many of the surviving buildings from Fort Wayne, the last military bastion to defend the city.

During the early 1960s, the Motown record label revolutionized American pop music with its trademark blend of pop, soul, and rhythm and blues. Label founder Berry Gordy, Jr. and his stable of talented artists, such as Marvin Gaye, Stevie Wonder, and Diana Ross and the Supremes, are honored at the **Motown Historical Museum**, housed in the original brick building where records were produced. Exhibits comprise photographs, instruments, and recording equipment.

The suburb of Dearborn, 8 miles (13 km) west of Detroit, is home to the Henry Ford Museum, which displays one of the nation's most impressive collections of Americana, including a cot used by George Washington and the Rosa Parks bus. Nearby, open-air Greenfield Village exhibits Ford's eclectic

↑ The picturesque campus of the University of Michigan in Ann Arbor

collection of objects and buildings, such as inventor Thomas Edison's laboratory.

Charles H. Wright Museum of African American History

⊛ ⌂ 315 E Warren Av
🕒 9am–5pm Tue–Sat, 1–5pm Sun 🗓 Federal hols & Feb
🌐 thewright.org

Detroit Institute of Arts

⊛ ⌂ 5200 Woodward Av, Detroit Cultural Center
🕒 9am–4pm Tue–Fri (to 10pm Fri) 🌐 dia.org

Detroit Historical Museum

⊛ ⌂ 5401 Woodward Av
🕒 9:30am–4pm Tue–Fri, 10am–5pm Sat & Sun
🌐 detroithistorical.org

Motown Historical Museum

⊛ ⌂ 2648 W Grand Blvd
🕒 Times vary, check website
🗓 Mon, Federal hols
🌐 motownmuseum.org

❷
Ann Arbor

➕ 🏨🚌 ℹ️ 315 W Huron St; www.visitannarbor.org

A picturesque city, with a vibrant pedestrian-friendly downtown, Ann Arbor is a bastion of laid-back liberalism and environmental activism. The city's independent streak is strongly linked to the presence of the University of Michigan, the city's largest employer. The university's central campus straddles Washtenaw Avenue, southeast of downtown. The city is also known for its arts scene, with one of the nation's largest outdoor art fairs held here every July. A highlight for children is the Hands On Museum, which tackles science, math, and technology in fun, interactive ways.

③

Lansing

🚌🚇🚃 ℹ 500 E Michigan Av; www.lansing.org

A government and industrial center, this city benefits from its proximity to the Michigan State University in adjacent East Lansing. Selected as the state capital in 1847, the subsequent arrival of railroads in 1871 and the completion of the downtown statehouse in 1879 fueled the city's growth. The Michigan Historical Museum recounts the construction of the Revival-style State Capitol, the public areas of which may be toured.

Lansing's status as a major automotive manufacturing center is linked to the business founded by Ransom E. Olds, who began building prototype vehicles here in 1885. He later produced the Curved Dash Olds, widely considered the world's first mass-produced automobile. The **R.E. Olds Transportation Museum** showcases an original 1901

TOP 4 CRAFT BREWERIES IN GRAND RAPIDS

Founders Brewing Company
🖥 foundersbrewing.com
Credited with starting the city's craft beer movement.

Grand Rapids Brewing Company
🖥 grbrewingcompany.com
Try their Silver Foam, first brewed in 1893.

Brewery Vivant
🖥 breweryvivant.com
French- and Belgian-inspired beers.

City Built Brewing Company
🖥 citybuiltbrewing.com
Creative brews with unusual ingredients.

Curved Dash Olds Runabout and a variety of models from the 1930s through to 2004.

R.E. Olds Transportation Museum

♿ 🏠 240 Museum Dr
🕐 10am–5pm Tue–Sat, noon–5pm Sun 🚫 Nov–Mar: Sun
🖥 reoldsmuseum.org

④

Grand Rapids

🚌🚇🚃 ℹ 171 Monroe Av NW, Suite 545; www.experiencegr.com

The Grand River flows through the heart of this city, with water-powered lumber mills that were set up in the 19th century lining its banks.

East of downtown is the historic Heritage Hill neighborhood. **Grand Rapids Public Museum** explores the history of the town and has a planetarium. Affiliates include the 1909 Meyer May House, one of Frank Lloyd Wright's last Prairie-style family homes. A scenic gathering spot is the spacious Frederik Meijer Gardens and Sculpture Park, with 300 sculptures including works by August Rodin, Edgar Degas, Henry Moore, and Alexander Calder.

Also in town is the Gerald R. Ford Museum. It traces the career of the 38th president, who grew up in Grand Rapids. The museum includes a holographic tour of the White House and a replica of the Oval Office.

→

The Porcupine Mountains Wilderness State Park, on the Upper Peninsula

Grand Rapids Public Museum

♿ 🏠 272 Pearl St NW
🕐 Times vary, check website
🖥 grpm.org

⑤

Lake Michigan Shore

🚌🚃 ℹ 741 Kenmoor Av, Grand Rapids; www.wmta.org

A major tourist destination since wealthy Chicagoans first came here in the late 1800s, the Lake Michigan Shore is lined with sandy beaches, working ports, and pretty

lighthouses. The excellent **Michigan Maritime Museum**, 20 miles (30 km) south of the resort town of Saugatuck, narrates the history of fishing, shipping, and shipbuilding on the Great Lakes.

In the north, Sleeping Bear Dunes National Lakeshore incorporates many ecosystems and its signature sand dunes, which tower some 460 ft (140 m) above the lakefront beaches and an inland lake.

Still farther north, Traverse City is a convenient base for visiting the scenic Old Mission Peninsula. Drive north along Route 37 for beautiful views of green rolling hills, the lake, and Old Mission Point Lighthouse, built in 1870.

Michigan Maritime Museum

🧭 📍260 Dyckman Rd, South Haven ⏰May–late Sep: 10am–5pm daily; off-season times vary, check website 🖥michiganmaritime museum.org

←

The American Horse by Nina Akamu, in the Frederik Meijer Gardens and Sculpture Park

6

Mackinac Island

✈️🚌 ℹ️7274 Main St; www. mackinacisland.org

The limestone outcrop of Mackinac Island sits in the middle of the Straits of Mackinac. Ferries departing from Mackinaw City and St. Ignace on the mainland are the only way to reach the island, where no cars are permitted. The principal landmark here is the 1887 Grand Hotel, a classic Gilded Age summer resort that has the world's longest front porch. The restored Fort Mackinac, in Mackinac Island State Park, is also well worth a visit.

7

Upper Peninsula

✈️🚌 ℹ️Iron Mountain; www.uptravel.com

The sparsely populated wilderness of the Upper Peninsula (also known as the "UP") is dotted with old lumber, mining, and fishing towns. Here you'll find Michigan's oldest community – Sault

Sainte Marie, on its north-eastern tip – established by a 17th-century French explorer.

The UP also home to some of Michigan's most striking natural attractions. The popular Pictured Rocks National Lakeshore stretches along Lake Superior. Although accessible by car, this 40-mile (64-km) stretch of beaches and bluffs can be viewed more dramatically on guided cruises, departing from Munising.

For more rugged scenery, head west to Porcupine Mountains Wilderness State Park, known for its forests, lakes, and network of trails.

WISCONSIN AND MINNESOTA

The French arrived here in the 17th century and founded fur-trading posts, leading to the creation of Milwaukee. The US absorbed the region after independence, but settlement of Wisconsin was delayed until the 1830s by a series of short, bloody wars with American Indian tribes. Wisconsin became a state in 1848. By the time Minnesota became a state, in 1858, treaties with local tribes had opened up more land for settlement and the logging industry. Both states became popular with German and Scandinavian immigrants. Wisconsin was the nation's top dairy producer until the 1990s, and remains the largest cheese maker.

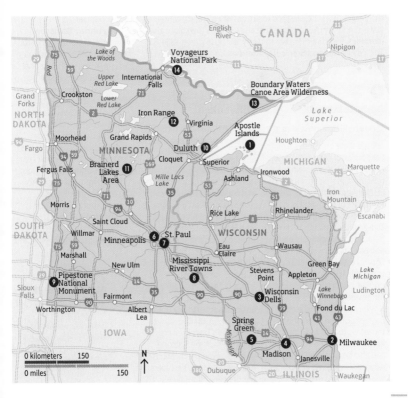

WISCONSIN

This predominantly agricultural state is the Midwest's premier vacation destination. Wisconsin's recreational jewels range from the gorgeous Apostle Islands to dozens of carefully maintained state parks, forests, and trails that allow visitors to explore glacial moraines, lakeside cliffs, broad rivers, and lush green valleys. The Ice Age National Scenic Trail stretches 1,000 miles (1,600 km).

1

Apostle Islands

Bayfield bayfield.org

Off the state's northeastern Lake Superior coast lies a group of 22 islands, the remains of retreating glaciers from the last Ice Age. Today, 21 of these form part of the Apostle Islands National Lakeshore. Old-growth forests provide the habitat for resident bald eagles and black bears, while stretches of sand beaches with sea caves make the Apostle Islands a popular destination for those interested in ecotourism.

A local cruise service from Bayfield, on the mainland, ferries visitors to the islands; kayak rental and guided tours can also be arranged here. Adventurous hikers walk miles to see ice caves in winter.

2

Milwaukee

648 N Plankinton Av; www.visitmilwaukee.org

Like Chicago, its more famous neighbor, this manufacturing and brewing center grew up on a swampy Lake Michigan marshland. Treaties signed with local American Indian tribes opened the area to white settlement in the 1830s. The city's strong German ambience dates to the arrival of "Forty-Eighters," revolutionaries who fled Germany after an aborted attempt to overthrow the monarchy in 1848.

The city's beer brewing tradition took such strong root that even the local baseball team came to be called the Brewers. Milwaukee's spectacular Lake Michigan shoreline hosts many festivals, with Summerfest, an 11-day extravaganza held in late June and early July, being the most popular.

The **Harley-Davidson Museum** celebrates a century of motorcycle manufacturing in Milwaukee and is a global mecca for bikers. Inside are about 140 Harley vehicles and 16,000 smaller artifacts.

The large Milwaukee Public Museum is part science museum, part local and cultural history center. It has interactive, child-centric science exhibits, walk-through villages transporting visitors to old Milwaukee, and a tropical butterfly garden.

The city's Historic Third Ward warehouse district is a hub for upscale shopping and

Did You Know?

The QWERTY typewriter was invented in Milwaukee by Christopher Latham Scholes.

Kayaking around the breathtakingly beautiful Apostle Islands

entertainment, with many performance theaters and art galleries. Eastward, the lakefront Milwaukee Art Museum was established in 1888 and holds a 25,000-piece collection. Its signature pieces include decorative arts holdings.

Pabst Brewing Company closed in 1996, but a microbrewery opened on the campus in 2016 and the 14 German Renaissance-Revival buildings on the historic campus are being renovated.

The **MillerCoors Brewery** is the only longtime brewer still in operation in the city. Opened in 1855, today it is the second-largest brewer in the US, after the St. Louis-based Anheuser-Busch. Tours takes visitors around the brewery and the nearby Caves Museum, where beer was cooled deep inside Milwaukee's bluffs.

Milwaukee's other major sight is the Annunciation Greek Orthodox Church, one of Frank Lloyd Wright's last commissions. Designed in 1956, it was opened in 1961, two years after Wright's death.

Harley-Davidson Museum
◈ ⑦ ⬛ 400 Canal St
🕙 10am–6pm daily (to 8pm Thu) 🅆 harley-davidson.com

MillerCoors Brewery Tour
◈ ⬛ 4251 W State St
🕙 For tours only; times vary, check website 🅇 Federal hols 🅆 millercoors.com

---

③

Wisconsin Dells

🛈 701 Superior St; www. wisdells.com

Wisconsin Dells has one of the most spectacular locations along the Wisconsin River as it winds through an awe-inspiring stretch of deep sandstone

canyons. A prime summer vacation destination, its highlights include the guided Dells Boat Tours, which offer excursions past the storied cliffs, and the highest concentration of water parks in the world.

The region owes much of its popularity to photographer H.H. Bennett, whose late 19th-century photographs of the rugged landscapes became famous throughout the US. The Wisconsin Historical Society operates the H.H. Bennett Studio and History Center.

---

④

Madison

🚗 🚉 🚌 🛈 21 N Park St; www.visitmadison.com

Nestled on a narrow isthmus between Lake Mendota and Lake Monona, Madison is one of the country's most attractively situated capital cities. Established as the territorial capital in 1836, it became the state capital and home of the University of Wisconsin campus when Wisconsin achieved statehood in 1848. The majestic dome of the **Wisconsin State Capitol** rises above the city's beautiful downtown. Madison is considered one of the nation's best places to live and work. The city's liberal

political leanings have drawn scores of artists and environmentalists to the area, and a network of biking and walking trails provides access to the shimmering surrounding lakes.

Wisconsin State Capitol
◈ ◈ ⬛ 2 E Main St 🕙 8am–6pm Mon–Fri, 8am–4pm Sat–Sun 🅆 wisconsin.gov

---

⑤

Spring Green

🚌 🛈 208 N Winsted St; www.springgreen.com

This handsome farming community lies just north of the Wisconsin River. In 1911 Frank Lloyd Wright, who spent his childhood nearby, built Taliesin ("Shining Brow" in Welsh) on a bluff overlooking the river. The estate was Wright's home until his death in 1959, and today the Taliesin Fellowship runs a design school and an architectural firm on the grounds. Just north of Spring Green is the House on the Rock, a sprawling resort complex with a home built atop a 60-ft (18-m) chimney rock. The 1940s house, built by eccentric architect Alex Jordan, is the focal point for a museum exhibiting Jordan's vast collection of Americana.

↑ Leafy Madison's domed Wisconsin State Capitol

MINNESOTA

Seductively nicknamed "The Land of 10,000 Lakes," Minnesota's beautiful lakes certainly add to the state's appeal as an affordable outdoors destination. It was the meandering rivers, however, that shaped Minnesota's history as a key trading and agricultural hub. Many of these waterways have been preserved, and offer a natural splendor in its vast stretches of watery wilderness.

6 Minneapolis

🚗🏛️🚌 ℹ️ 505 Nicollet Mall Suite 100; www.minneapolis.org

Downtown Minneapolis revolves around the pedestrian Nicollet Mall and the Mississippi riverfront, which is home to the Mill City Museum, the acclaimed Guthrie Theater, and historic Stone Arch Bridge. It also offers walking trails near the water. On the southwest, the Uptown neighborhood revolves around the Chain of Lakes, with its lakeside biking and jogging trails. The largest enclosed shopping mall in the US, the Mall of America, is located in the southern suburb of Bloomington.

The performing, visual, and media arts are the focus at the comprehensive **Walker Art Center**. Highlights include the minimalist work of sculptor Donald Judd and realist painter Edward Hopper's *Office at Night* (1940).

Established in 1915, the **Minneapolis Institute of Art (MIA)** is one of the region's largest and most highly regarded museums. Its traditional collection includes a wide range of Greek and Roman statuary, Italian and Dutch Renaissance paintings, as well as American works by Georgia O'Keeffe and regionalist Grant Wood. The Ulrich Architecture and Design Gallery houses an astonishing collection of Prairie School furniture, architectural fragments, art-glass windows, silver, and more.

Housed in a grand 1907 mansion, the **American Swedish Institute** chronicles the contributions of Swedish-Americans to the state's history and culture. Guided tours of the house, built by Swedish newspaper publisher Swan Turnblad, allow visitors to view his quirky collection of Swedish-American artifacts. The striking Nelson Cultural Center was added to the museum in 2012.

Walker Art Center
♿♿ 🚗 725 Vineland Pl
🕐 11am–5pm Tue–Sun (to 9pm Thu, 6pm Fri) 🌐 walkerart.org

Minneapolis Institute of Art (MIA)
🚗 2400 3rd Av S
🕐 Times vary, check website
🌐 artsmia.org

American Swedish Institute
♿ 🚗 2600 Park Av 🕐 10am–5pm Tue–Sat (to 8pm Wed), noon–5pm Sun 🌐 asimn.org

7 St. Paul

🚗🏛️🚌 ℹ️ 175 W Kellogg Blvd; www.visitsaintpaul.com

Founded in 1841 on the site of a notorious French-Canadian trading post, St. Paul flourished as the busiest river port on the Upper Mississippi. By the late 19th century, the new state capital had emerged as a railroad hub, and the stately mansions along Summit Avenue date from those prosperous days. Downtown centers on the Art Deco City Hall and Courthouse on Kellogg Boulevard and St. Peter Street. Designed by Cass Gilbert, architect of the US Supreme Court *(p208)*, the monumental **Minnesota State Capitol** is a stunning domed Beaux Arts structure. After a $310-million restoration, the building reopened in 2017.

A treasure trove of interactive exhibits that chronicles

↑ The modern Walker Art Center, a stunning contemporary art resource

A lookout in the bucolic Great River Bluffs State Park

The strikingly beautiful Great River Bluffs State Park occupies one of the Mississippi's most scenic stretches.

the state's 19th-century history is housed in the **Minnesota History Center**. Exhibits such as a giant grain elevator, lifelike meat-packing plant, and a replica of a 1930s dairy farm help visitors relive history from the point of view of a farmer or factory worker.

EAT

Al's Breakfast
Patrons wait in line for made-to-order classics at this tiny, breakfast-only diner. There are just over a dozen seats, but it's worth the wait for the buttermilk pancakes.

🅿 413 14th Av SE, Minneapolis 🆆 als breakfastmpls.com

Minnesota State Capitol
🅿 🅿 75 Rev Dr. Martin Luther King, Jr. Blvd
🅾 8:30am–5pm Mon–Fri, 10am–3pm Sat, 1–4pm Sun
🆆 mnhs.org/capitol

Minnesota History Center
🅿 🅿 345 Kellogg Blvd W
🅾 Times vary, check website
🆆 minnesotahistory center.org

8
Mississippi River Towns
🅿 🆆 🆆 mnmississippiriver. com

The Mississippi River courses 572 miles (921 km) through Minnesota, originating in the north-central part of the state and continuing until its confluence with the St. Croix River. The Great River Road Scenic Byway, or US 61, hugs the river's west bank, revealing breathtaking views.

Notable sites along the way include Frontenac State

Park, a premier bird-watching spot, and the National Eagle Center in Wabasha houses injured raptors that cannot be returned to the wild. Picturesque Winona, located on an island in the river, is home to the Minnesota Marine Art Museum. The strikingly beautiful Great River Bluffs State Park occupies one of the Mississippi's most scenic stretches.

9
Pipestone National Monument
🅿 36 Reservation Av, Pipestone 🆆 🆆 nps.gov/ pipe

Pipestone sits in the state's southwestern corner. The name derives from Dakota Sioux, who lived here for generations, quarrying the region's soft red quartzite to craft ceremonial pipes. The stone catlinite has been named in honor of artist George Catlin, who depicted this place in his 1838 work, *Pipestone Quarry*.

American Indian craftsmen continue the tradition in the remains of the quarries. The pipes are then sold at the adjoining Cultural Center.

EAT

New Scenic Café

Trek to Lake Superior's northern shore to sample this café's seasonal, local fare. Colorful gardens and local art add to the inviting ambience.

🏠 5461 N Shore Dr, Duluth 🔲 new sceniccafe.com

$ $ $

🔟

Duluth

➕🚌 *i* 225 W Superior St; www.visitduluth.com

Minnesota's third-largest city, Duluth is one of the Midwest's most enjoyable destinations. Clinging to the sides of the 800-ft (240-m) granite slopes that ring its lively downtown, this city successfully juxtaposes nature preserves with operating industries, which fuel its bustling port. Its most striking feature is the Aerial Lift Bridge, a huge steel structure linking the mainland to the mouth of the Duluth harbor, which can be raised to allow hulking freighters to pass into the harbor. The Great Lakes Aquarium, an "all-freshwater" aquarium, provides a close-up view of the bridge in action, while interactive exhibits explain environmental issues.

The centerpiece of Duluth's attractive downtown is the 1892 **Depot**, or **St. Louis County Heritage and Arts Center**. The restored brownstone railroad depot houses the Duluth Art Institute, Lake Superior Railroad Museum, and several performance art companies. Depot Square features the waiting room where US immigration officials processed many of the state's Scandinavian and German immigrants.

The North Shore Scenic Railroad offers sightseeing trips from the depot aboard period trains. The excursions head north along the shore of Lake Superior, with spectacular views of waterfalls and plunging cliffs. Motorists can also experience this magical trip on the North Shore Scenic Drive.

Depot/St. Louis County Heritage and Arts Center

◈ 🏠 506 W Michigan St 🕐 Jun-Aug: 9am-6pm daily (Sep-May: to 5pm) 🔲 duluthdepot.org

---

⓫

Brainerd Lakes Area

➕🚌 *i* 124 N 6th St, Brainerd; www.explore brainerdlakes.com

Founded by the Northern Pacific Railroad in 1871, the city of Brainerd was carved out of a dense forest, felled to meet the demands of the state's lumber boom. The city is the gateway to north-central Minnesota's lake region, where the state's trademark lakeshore lodge-resorts were first developed. Mille Lacs Lake, 40 miles (64 km) southeast of Brainerd, is bordered by beautiful state parks and the Mille Lacs Band of Ojibwe tribal reservation. The Minnesota Historical Society collaborated with the tribe to develop the Mille Lacs Indian Museum, on the lake's southwest shore.

⓬

Iron Range

🚌 *i* 111 Station 44 Rd, Eveleth; www.ironrange. org

When iron ore was discovered in northeastern Minnesota in the 1880s, waves of immigrant workers came to boomtowns that grew up along three ranges that collectively came to be known as the Iron Range district. By the 1960s, many of the mines were shut down, decimating local communities and leaving behind empty pits. But in the past three decades, a growing tourist interest has revitalized the area.

The **Soudan Underground Mine** is Minnesota's oldest and deepest iron mine. It opened in 1882, closed in 1962, and is now part of a state park. Visitors can go a half-mile (1 km) underground into the heart of the mine, which also holds an atomic physics lab.

The city of Chisholm is home to the **Minnesota Discovery Center**, which presents a theme-park version of the Iron Range story, complete with trolley rides.

→

Tranquil beauty at Voyageurs National Park, home to a large beaver population (*inset*)

Soudan Underground Mine
1379 Stuntz Bay Rd, Soudan (218) 753-2245
Times vary, call ahead

Minnesota Discovery Center
1005 Discovery Dr, Chisholm Times vary, check website mndiscovery center.com

13

Boundary Waters Canoe Area Wilderness

116 W Hwy 61, Grand Marais; www.ely.org, www.grandmarais.com

The largest, and also the most visited, wilderness preserve east of the Rocky Mountains, the Boundary Waters Canoe Area Wilderness stretches along the Canadian border in the state's northeastern corner. It attracts many adventurers looking to escape civilization, and is one of the world's largest canoeing and fishing destinations. To preserve the area's unique appeal, there is a limit on the number of campers as well as restrictions on the use of motorized watercraft.

The Dorothy Molter Museum is a memorial to the wilderness area's last human resident, who ran a resort here and died in 1986. The International Wolf Center in Ely promotes the survival of the region's once-threatened wolf population. The North American Bear Center, a research, education, and rehab facility, is nearby.

14

Voyageurs National Park

360 Hwy 11 E, International Falls nps.gov/voya

This water-based national park preserves 218,000 acres (87,200 ha) of Canadian Shield wilderness, with 30 large lakes, beaver ponds, and islands – the habitat of large packs of Eastern timber wolves.

Rainy Lake, the park's finest fishing lake, abounds in pike, walleye, and bass. The Rainy Lake Visitor Center is one of three staffed access points to the park and the only one open year-round. Although most visitors traverse the park's vast area by watercraft, hikers can take advantage of a network of trails. Those keen on boating can stock up on supplies at the border city of International Falls. In winter, the park offers opportunities for snowmobiling, ice fishing, and cross-country skiing.

Did You Know?

Voyageurs National Park is home to one of the largest wolf populations in the US.

THE GREAT PLAINS

Carhenge in Alliance, Nebraska

EXPLORE THE GREAT PLAINS

This chapter divides the Great Plains into four sightseeing areas, as shown on the map below. Find out more about each area on the following pages.

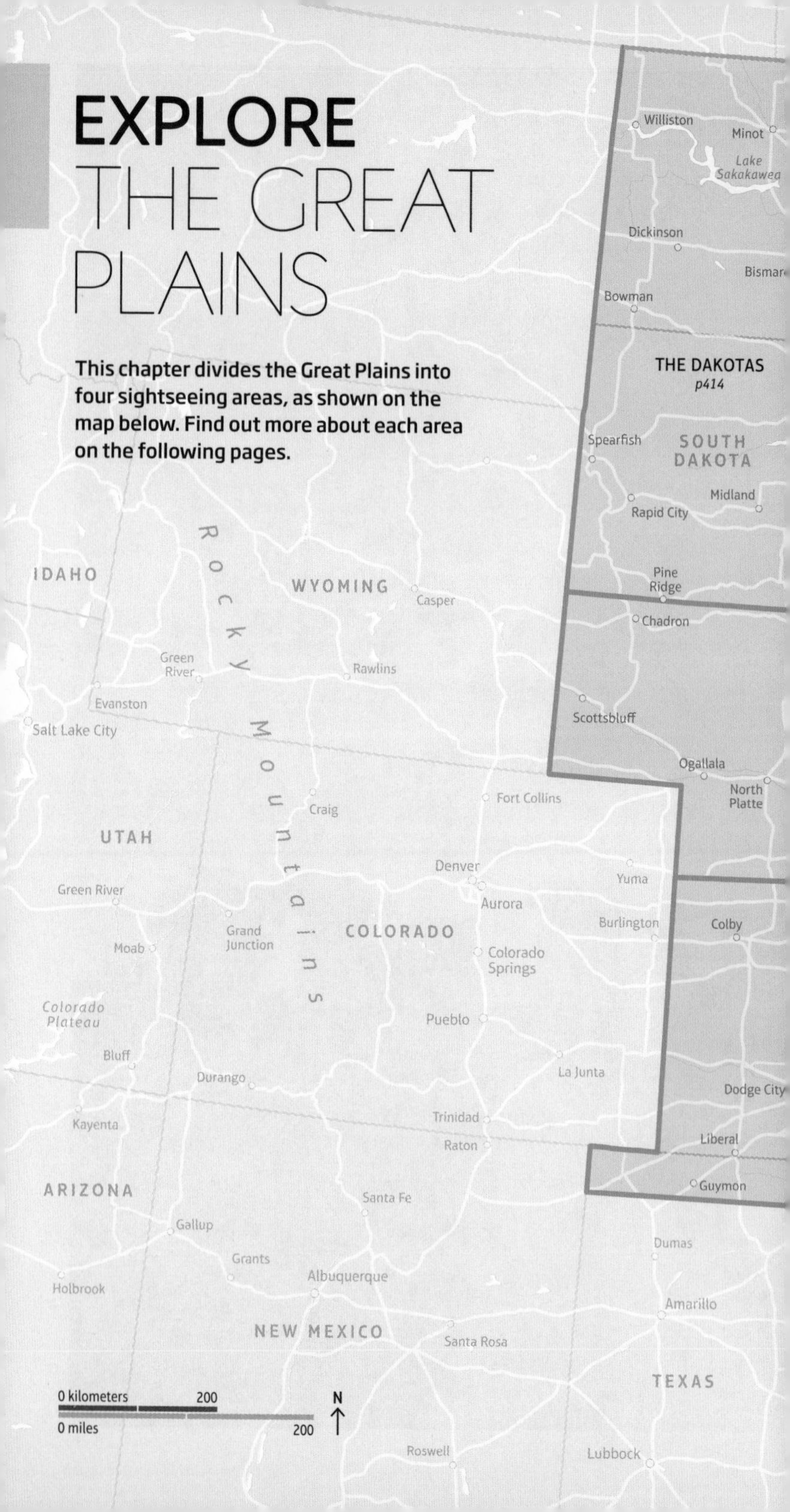

THE DAKOTAS
p414

Williston · Minot · Lake Sakakawea · Dickinson · Bismarc · Bowman

SOUTH DAKOTA · Spearfish · Midland · Rapid City · Pine Ridge · Chadron

IDAHO · ROCKY · WYOMING · Casper · Green River · Rawlins · Evanston · Salt Lake City

Scottsbluff · Ogallala · North Platte

UTAH · Green River · Moab · Craig · Fort Collins · Denver · Aurora · Yuma · Colby · Burlington · Grand Junction · COLORADO · Colorado Springs · Colorado Plateau · Bluff · Durango · Pueblo · La Junta · Dodge City · Trinidad · Liberal · Raton · Guymon · Kayenta · Mountains

ARIZONA · Santa Fe · Dumas · Gallup · Grants · Albuquerque · Amarillo · Holbrook · NEW MEXICO · Santa Rosa · TEXAS

0 kilometers 200
0 miles 200
N

Roswell · Lubbock

Winkler

Rolla

Devils Lake

NORTH
DAKOTA

Grand
Forks

Jamestown

Fargo

Detroit
Lakes

Sheyenne

Lake
Oahe

Redfield

Fergus Falls

Appleton

Lake
Sharpe

Brookings

Tyler

MINNESOTA

White

Mitchell

Worthington

La Crosse

WISCONSIN

Winner

Sioux Falls

Spencer

Mason City

Madison
Marquette

Butte

Niobrara

Yankton

Sioux City

Waterloo

Dubuque

Rockford

O'Neill

Norfolk

Carroll

IOWA

Ames

Cedar Rapids

NEBRASKA
p424

Des Moines

Iowa City

Davenport

Galesburg

NEBRASKA

Omaha

Ottumwa

Grand Island

Platte

Lincoln

Peoria

Fairmont

IOWA AND MISSOURI
p430

Keokuk

Decatur

Saint Joseph

Hannibal

Springfield

ILLINOIS

KANSAS AND OKLAHOMA
p438

Kansas City

Moberly

Saint
Louis

Hays

Topeka

Sedalia

Jefferson City

Salina

Great Bend

Emporia

KANSAS

MISSOURI

Pratt

Wichita

Lake of
the Ozarks

Rolla

Coffeyville

Liberal

Cape Girardeau

Woodward

Ponca
City

Bartlesville

Joplin

Springfield

Sikeston

Enid

Miami

Poplar Bluff

West Plains

ILLINOIS

OKLAHOMA

Tulsa

Fayetteville

Blytheville

Oklahoma City

Muskogee

Canadian

ARKANSAS

Memphis

Snyder

Lawton

McAlester

Holly Springs

Ardmore

Durant

Hugo

Little Rock

Clarksdale

Wichita Falls

Red

Sherman

MISSISSIPPI

NORTH AMERICA

CANADA

Seattle

USA

THE GREAT
PLAINS

Chicago

Boston

San Francisco

New York City
Washington, DC

Los Angeles

Atlanta

Pacific
Ocean

Houston

MEXICO

Gulf of
Mexico

Miami

Atlantic
Ocean

←

① Sun rising over the peaks of the Badlands.

② The gargantuan Crazy Horse Memorial.

③ Bison in Custer State Park.

④ Main Street in Deadwood.

This four-day road trip takes in South Dakota's most iconic landscapes and show-stopping attractions, from the Badlands to Mount Rushmore. Rent a car at Rapid City airport, the region's primary air hub, and hit the road.

4 DAYS

in the Black Hills and the Badlands

Day 1

From Rapid City airport, head to Ben Reifel Visitor Center in Badlands National Park (p422) via Hwy 44. Grab park maps and visit the Fossil Preparation Lab, before taking the Badlands Loop Road into the heart of the park. The road snakes through the best of the Badlands, with plenty of overlooks en route where you can park and drink in the dazzling panoramas. Leave the park at the Pinnacle Entrance and continue on Hwy 240 to Wall (p422), where you can enjoy the goofy charms of Wall Drug Store. Grab some hot beef sandwiches at the café before driving back to Rapid City for the night.

Day 2

First stop today is the infamous Wild West town of Deadwood in the heart of the Black Hills (p418). Visit the Days of '76 Museum to learn about the town's gold-mining origins, then stroll the atmospheric Main Street, where you can watch a daily dramatization of Wild Bill Hickok's murder in Saloon No. 10. Drive on to neighboring Lead, a well-preserved gold-mining town. Start at the Sanford Lab Homestake Visitor Center to learn about the original Homestake gold claim, then take some time to explore the old town. Head back to Deadwood for the night; the town hums with the buzz of its many casinos, but there are plenty of old-school spots for dinner and drinks – try the Oyster Bay & Historic Fairmont (628 Main St) for live bands, ghost tours, and fresh oysters.

Day 3

Drive south to Mount Rushmore National Memorial, aiming to arrive just after it opens at 8am to avoid the crowds and get the best light for photos. Then take a scenic route to Crazy Horse Memorial, through the Black Hills and on the winding Iron Mountain Road – break at Sylvan Lake for lunch along the way. Spend the evening in the small town of Custer, where old-time bars such as the Gold Pan Saloon (508 Mt Rushmore Rd) offer good food and lively entertainment.

Day 4

Set an early alarm and drive to the Custer State Park Visitor Center, to take in the 18-mile (29-km) Wildlife Loop Road. The road rolls through meadows rich with antelope, elk, deer, and the park's main attraction – a herd of 1,350 buffalo. Fuel up with lunch at the rustic Blue Bell Lodge, then drive south to Wind Cave National Park. Here you can take one of the fabulous guided cave tours – try the family-friendly Natural Entrance Cave Tour or the more strenuous Fairgrounds Cave Tour. End your trip in the town of Hot Springs, where the fascinating Mammoth Site preserves mammoth fossils in situ, and Evans Plunge Mineral Springs is a great place to cool off.

Not in Kansas Anymore

The lesser traveled Flint Hills National Scenic Byway runs for around 47 miles (75 km) across the Flint Hills of Kansas *(p440)*, between Council Grove and Cassoday. Yes – there are rolling hills in Kansas, with the tallgrass prairies here especially enticing in spring, when wildflowers blanket the slopes with purples, yellows, and bright reds. Get oriented at the Flint Hills Discovery Center *(www.flinthillsdiscovery.org)*, and spend time at the Tallgrass Prairie National Preserve, just north of Strong City, where there's a visitor center and trails across the hills.

→

A prairie of tallgrasses on the Flint Hills National Scenic Byway, Kansas

THE GREAT PLAINS FOR
ICONIC ROAD TRIPS

With miles of empty highways, peppered with quirky Americana and plenty of 1950s nostalgia, the Great Plains area is perfect for American road trips. And it's not all endlessly flat highways – from the Flint Hills to Mount Rushmore Needles Highway, the region has a surprising array of landscapes.

↑ Route 66 passing through Tulsa, Oklahoma

Get Your Kicks on Route 66

Route 66 once ran from Chicago to LA, but today the longest remaining stretch of the "Mother Road" spans the state of Oklahoma for over 400 miles (644 km). It snakes through Tulsa *(p442)* and Oklahoma City *(p442)*, with entertaining Americana en route. Visit the Route 66 Nut House *(www.66nuts.com)*, a log cabin made from real pecan logs, and Tulsa's 1950s-style Admiral Twin Drive-In *(www.admiraltwindrivein.com)*.

THE ENCHANTED HIGHWAY

North Dakota's Enchanted Highway is one of the most surreal roads in the US. Running from Exit 72 (I-94) at Gladstone to the small town of Regent, the 32-mile (51-km) route is lined with the world's largest scrap metal sculptures, conceived by local artist Gary Greff. Beginning with the giant mobile-like "Geese in Flight," you can view a terrifyingly large grasshopper, and the bizarre "Pheasants on the Prairie."

Negotiating Nebraska

Sandhills Journey Scenic Byway travels across rural Nebraska *(p425)* and takes in undulating sand dunes, native sand grass prairies, and vivid blue lakes. It seems a million miles from urban America. The route follows Nebraska Hwy 2 for 272 miles (438 km) between Grand Island and Alliance. Along the way you'll pass through friendly farming communities like Broken Bow, and tranquil reserves such as Victoria Springs State Recreation Area. Wherever you spend the night, don't forget to look up to the heavens – this route offers some of the best star-gazing in the world.

←
Dramatic skies of lightning over the state of Nebraska

EAT

Classic diners offer sustenance for weary drivers along Route 66. Here are our favorites.

Ann's Chicken Fry House
⌂ 4106 NW 39th St, Oklahoma City
☎ (405) 943-8915

$ $ $

Clanton's Café
⌂ 319 E Illinois, Vinita
🌐 clantonscafe.com

$ $ $

Johnnie's Grill
⌂ 301 S Rock Island Av, El Reno ☎ (405) 262-4721

$ $ $

Ollie's Station Restaurant
⌂ 4070 Southwest Blvd, Tulsa 🌐 olliesstation.com

$ $ $

POPS
⌂ 660 W Hwy 66, Arcadia
🌐 pops66.com

$ $ $

Driving Through South Dakota

The Needles Highway (aka Hwy 87) was an engineering marvel when completed in 1922, cutting through a rugged section of Custer State Park for a winding 14 miles (23 km) of hairpin bends, narrow tunnels, and gasp-inducing views. Continue on the 70-mile (113-km) Peter Norbeck Scenic Byway, and visit Crazy Horse Memorial and Mount Rushmore *(p418)*.

←
Needles Highway, Custer State Park, South Dakota

THE DAKOTAS

Sioux tribes dominated the Dakota plains, though US colonization increased after the Civil War. In 1868, the Treaty of Fort Laramie guaranteed Sioux and Arapaho land rights in Dakota, but settlers poured in following rumors of gold in the Black Hills, and 1876 saw the Great Sioux War. Resistance ended in 1890, when Sioux leader Sitting Bull was murdered and hundreds of Lakota Sioux were massacred by US troops. The states of North and South Dakota were created in 1889. Both agricultural states suffered in the 1930s but, thanks to the lucrative (and controversial) fracking industry, North Dakota is now the second-biggest oil-producing state in the US.

Experience

1. Washburn
2. Grand Forks
3. Devils Lake
4. Theodore Roosevelt National Park
5. Black Hills
6. Fargo
7. Bismarck and Mandan
8. Mitchell
9. Pierre
10. Badlands National Park
11. Wall
12. Pine Ridge Reservation

THE DAKOTAS

North Dakota's vast blue skies, tiny farming communities, and endless fields can lull visitors into a state of quiet contemplation. Rivers, buttes, prairies, and badlands define South Dakota, with the Missouri River bisecting the state. Culturally, it is dominated by the heritage of the Dakota, Lakota, and Sioux tribes, who roamed and hunted here until they were moved onto reservations in the late 1800s.

❶ Washburn

✉🏨 ℹ 907 Main Av; www.washburnnd.com

The key attraction in the area surrounding the sleepy Missouri River town of Washburn is the **Lewis and Clark Interpretive Center**. A stunning view of the Missouri River Valley greets visitors, who can view exhibits tracing the river's shifting course over the past 200 years.

The Center is an ideal starting point for a tour of the sites associated with explorer's Lewis and Clark's historic expedition, who were some of the earliest visitors to North Dakota. About 2 miles (3 km) west of the visitor center is the reconstructed Fort Mandan. It was here that Lewis and Clark's 44-man Corps of Discovery wintered between 1804 and 1805, en route to the Pacific Ocean.

The Knife River Indian Village National Historic Site, 20 miles (32 km) west of Washburn, contains the remains of the largest villages of the interrelated Mandan, Hidatsa, and Arikara tribes. Among these is a massive restored earth lodge. The French trapper Charbonneau, and his American Indian wife, Sacagawea, joined the Lewis and Clark expedition near this spot in 1804.

Lewis and Clark Interpretive Center

⊕ 🚗 US 83 & Rte 200A
🕐 9am–5pm daily 🚫 Oct–Mar: Sun 🌐 fortmandan.com

❷ Grand Forks

✈🏨🚗 ℹ 4251 Gateway Dr; www.visitgrandforks.com

Located at the junction of the Red and Red Lake Rivers, Grand Forks is the third-largest city in North Dakota. Following a devastating flood of the Red River in 1997, which destroyed many historic structures and inflicted huge damage, the city has been largely rebuilt. Today, its lively downtown area brims with restaurants, bars, and shops.

The **Empire Arts Center**, housed in the restored 1919 Empire Theatre, is now downtown's vibrant performing arts center. The University of North Dakota campus, 2 miles (3 km) west of downtown, is home to the North Dakota Museum of Art, with its fine collection of contemporary art.

Empire Arts Center

⊕ 🚗 415 Demers Av
🕐 Times vary, check website
🌐 empireartscenter.org

❸ Devils Lake

🏨🚗 ℹ 208 Hwy 2 W; www.devilslakend.com

The primary recreational attraction in northeastern North Dakota is the glacial Devils Lake, which lies 90 miles (150 km) west of

→ The Painted Canyon in Theodore Roosevelt National Park, North Dakota

↑ Modest living quarters within the Fort Mandan, in Washburn, North Dakota

Grand Forks. With miles of shoreline, the lake is a great spot for fishing and boating.

Fort Totten State Historic Site, 14 miles (22 km) to the south, is one of the best-preserved United States Army bases from the post-Civil War era. Built in 1867, it remained in use as a military reservation until 1890, when it became a boarding school for American Indian children. The restored buildings around the parade ground contain period furniture.

Fort Totten State Historic Site

⊘ ⊙Rte 57 ⊙May–Sep: 9am–5pm daily ⊡history. nd.gov/historicsites/totten

4 ⊗

Theodore Roosevelt National Park

⊙Medora ⊙24 hrs daily
⊙Jan 1, Thanksgiving, Dec 25 ⊡nps.gov/thro

The tiny western North Dakota town of Medora is the gateway to the Theodore Roosevelt National Park and the ruggedly beautiful North Dakota badlands. Roosevelt first came to this area to hunt bison in 1883, but his awareness of vanishing species and habitats provided the basis for many of his conservationist policies as president of the United States. The bill that created this park as a memorial to Roosevelt was signed on April 25, 1947, by President Truman. On November 10, 1978, the area was given national park status by virtue of another bill signed by President Carter.

The Theodore Roosevelt National Park covers a sprawling 110 sq miles (280 sq km) of three areas – the North and South Units and Elkhorn Ranch. The butte-studded South Unit has the phantasmagoric Painted Canyon and can be explored on horseback or seen from an overlook from a 36-mile (58-km) self-guided auto tour. Part of the landscape is dotted with mushroom-shaped stone formations. The North Unit features a dramatic, oxbow bend in the Little Missouri River, and windswept grasslands. Unlike the much-visited South Unit, this pocket lies in very isolated country. However, a 14-mile (22-km) auto route through this rugged landscape provides access to nature trails and numerous scenic overlooks.

INSIDER TIP
Medora Musical

Billing itself as "the greatest show in the Midwest," this live musical performance takes place outside against the backdrop of Theodore Roosevelt National Park.

BLACK HILLS

🏠 Rapid City ✈🚌 ℹ Black Hills Visitor Information Center; (605) 355-3700
🕐 Times vary, check website 📅 Federal hols 🌐 blackhillsbadlands.com

Known to the Lakota Sioux as Paha Sapa, these majestic hills were a mysterious, sacred place where American Indians would retreat to seek guidance from the Great Spirit. Today, the Black Hills harbor some of the state's most visited attractions, including the spectacular Mount Rushmore National Memorial.

In 1874, George Armstrong Custer's expedition from Bismarck (*p420*) led to the discovery of gold deposits in these thickly forested, oddly shaped granite hills. A series of misleading treaties followed, forcing the Sioux to relinquish their land, as miners, speculators, and settlers rushed into these once-sacred hills to stake their claims. The bucolic hills remain a wonderful place to explore, not least for their striking monuments. Mount Rushmore National Memorial is perhaps the most famous. An American icon since its completion in 1941, the giant sculpted heads of presidents George Washington, Thomas Jefferson, Theodore Roosevelt, and Abraham Lincoln took 14 years to create. Sculptor Gutzon Borglum's studio is on site. Another must-see is the Crazy Horse Memorial, which shows the great Sioux warrior. Once completed, it will be the world's largest sculpture. The carving first began in 1948.

> 💬 INSIDER TIP
> ## Historic Deadwood
>
> Fancy trying your luck in a lawless gold-mining town? Head to the restored town of Deadwood, where gunfighter Wild Bill Hickok was shot in 1876, and frontiers-woman Calamity Jane also left her mark. A gaming hall re-creates the action.

1 Sylvan Lake in Custer State Park is one of the region's most pristine natural habitats.

2 Visitors at Wind Cave National Park, which is home to one of the world's longest limestone caverns. You can join a historical candlelight tour and the Natural Entrance tour.

3 The striking Crazy Horse Memorial is not yet finished.

BLACK HILLS' MAMMOTH SITE

Discovered in 1974, this site displays the world's largest concentration of Columbian mammoth fossils. Originally a spring-fed sinkhole where animals were trapped and preserved, a mere 30 percent of the 26,000-year-old site has been explored so far *(www.mammoth site.com).*

↑ Mount Rushmore National Memorial, showing the faces of presidents George Washington, Thomas Jefferson, Theodore Roosevelt, and Abraham Lincoln

Fargo

⊕ ⊞ 🚗 ℹ 2001 44th St S;
www.fargomoorhead.org

The largest city in North Dakota, Fargo lies directly across the Red River from its sister city, Moorhead, Minnesota. Fargo's historic downtown includes the renovated 1926 **Fargo Theatre**, an Art Moderne structure that presents art and period films, plus live performances. Southwest of the theater is the superb Plains Art Museum, which is housed in a restored 1904 International Harvester Company warehouse. This museum has the state's largest public art collection, with works by the region's American Indian and folk artists. The Roger Maris Baseball Museum, in the West Acres Shopping Center, celebrates the achievements of Fargo's native son, who hit 61 home runs in 1961, setting a record for most home runs in a season.

Fargo Theatre
⊗ 🏛 314 Broadway 📞 (701) 239-8385 🕐 Call for schedule

> Fargo's historic downtown includes the renovated 1926 Fargo Theatre, an Art Moderne structure that presents art and period films, plus live performances.

7
Bismarck and Mandan

⊕ 🚗 ℹ 1600 Burnt Boat Dr, Bismarck; www.discover bismarckmandan.com

Riverboat traffic, railroads, and the government were instrumental in the development of the state capital of Bismarck, founded in 1872 on the east bank of the Missouri River. The 19-story, Art Deco North Dakota State Capitol dominates the city's leafy, low-slung skyline. Known as the "Skyscraper of the Prairies," the 1933 structure is visible for miles in every direction, mainly because of its location on top of a small rise in the center of the city. The State Museum at **North Dakota Heritage Center**, on the Capitol grounds, provides a fascinating introduction to the state's American Indian heritage and territorial settlement. It also traces the story of the state's rich historical past to the present age.

Mandan, a gateway to the West, lies just across the Missouri. To the south of downtown is **Fort Abraham Lincoln State Park**, which contains On-a-Slant Indian Village, the excavated remains of a 17th-century Mandan American Indian community, and several other reconstructed buildings. The fort was the last base for reckless George Armstrong Custer, who led the 7th Cavalry from here to their disastrous defeat at the Battle of Little Bighorn in 1876.

North Dakota Heritage Center
🏛 612 E Boulevard Av, Bismarck 📞 (701) 328-2666 🕐 8am–5pm Mon–Fri, 10am–5pm Sat & Sun

→
The striking facade of Fargo Theatre, North Dakota

→
The magnificent domed ceiling of the South Dakota State Capitol, Pierre

Fort Abraham Lincoln State Park

♿ ⌂ 4480 Fort Lincoln Rd ☎ (701) 667-6340 ⊙ Apr - Memorial Day: 9am-5pm daily; Memorial Day-Labor Day: 9am-7pm daily; Labor Day-Sep: 9am-5pm daily

---

8

Mitchell

🚌 🛈 601 N Main St; www.visitmitchell.com

Located in the fertile James River Valley, Mitchell is a combination of agricultural and industrial businesses. The city's main claim to fame is the world's only **Corn Palace**, a Moorish auditorium that was built in 1921 to house the city's Corn Belt Exposition. Colorful domes, minarets, and kiosks are the only permanent design features on the ever-changing façade of the palace. Every year, local artists use more than 3,000 bushels of corn and grasses to create new murals, which depict agricultural and myriad other scenes. This tradition dates back to 1892, when the Corn Real Estate Association constructed the first palace to showcase the area's crops and lure settlers.

Corn Palace

⊙ Apr-May & Sep-Nov: 8am-5pm daily; Jun-Aug: 8am-9pm; Dec-Mar: 8am-5pm Mon-Sat 🌐 cornpalace.com

---

9

Pierre

🚐🚌 🛈 800 W Dakota Av; www.pierre.org

One of the smallest state capitals in the US, Pierre lies in the Missouri River Valley, and forms a leafy oasis in the shortgrass, largely treeless plains of central South Dakota. The 1910 **South Dakota State Capitol** has a grand marble staircase and overlooks a lake visited each spring and fall by thousands of migratory birds.

The **South Dakota Cultural Heritage Center** is built into the side of a Missouri River bluff, covered with shortgrass prairie. Its exhibits trace the history of South Dakota's Sioux tribes and provide information on the diverse ethnic backgrounds of the state's homesteading white settlers. On display is a lead plate that was buried in a nearby river bluff in 1743 by the French-sponsored Verendrye expedition to mark the site as French territory.

The Verendrye Museum, across the river in Fort Pierre, focuses on French trading and exploration activities.

South Dakota State Capitol

⌂ 500 E Capitol Av ☎ (605) 773-3011 ⊙ 8am-7pm Mon-Fri, 8am-5pm Sat & Sun

South Dakota Cultural Heritage Center

♿ ⌂ 900 Governors Dr ☎ (605) 773-3458 ⊙ 9am-6:30pm Mon-Sat, 1-4:30pm Sun 🚫 Jan 1, Easter, Thanksgiving, Dec 25

The otherworldly rock formations of Badlands National Park, South Dakota ↑

Badlands National Park

🕐 24 hrs daily 🛈 Ben Reifel Visitor Center, Rte 240, S of I-90 exit 131; www.nps. gov/badl

The eerie desolation of Badlands National Park is an awe-inspiring sight for travelers unprepared for such a stark, rugged landscape after miles of gentle, rolling South Dakota prairie. Formed over 14 million years ago from sediment deposition and erosion in the Black Hills (p418), the Badlands were sculpted into their present craggy form by harsh sun and powerful winds.

One of the most complete fossil accumulations in North America is contained in this 380-sq-mile (990-sq-km) park. The Ben Reifel Visitor Center is the gateway to several self-guided hiking tours – try the Door Trail – and the 30-mile (48-km) Badlands Loop Road (Route 240). The scenic drive follows the northern rim of the 450-ft (137-m) Badlands Wall escarpment and leads to several overlooks and trails that provide breathtaking vistas of the eroded gullies below.

The road loops back north to I-90 near Sage Creek Wilderness Area, where golden eagles, hawks, and various songbirds gather in a vast expanse of steep grasslands, which burst into color each summer with a proliferation of wildflowers. The park-managed buffalo herd can be seen grazing on large stretches of prairie.

Wall

🚌 🛈 501 Main St; www. wall-badlands.com

Often referred to as the gateway to the Badlands, Wall has been a thriving tourist trade town since 1936, when local pharmacist Ted Hustead put up signs along the highway offering free ice water. This primitive roadside advertising tactic soon grew into a state-wide slew of billboards, which still line I-90 all the way across South Dakota. Hustead's small-town

THE SIOUX NATION

The Great Sioux Nation comprised several tribes who lived mostly in the Dakotas. The name "Sioux" was first attributed to the tribe by French trappers, who adapted a negative Chippewa term (meaning "snake" or "enemy"). The best-known of these multiple tribes is the Lakota Sioux, but there was also a Dakota Sioux tribe. This was subdivided into two groups: the Eastern Dakota Sioux were called the Santee, and lived in Minnesota and northern Iowa. The Western Dakota Sioux were made up of the Yankton and the Yanktonai, and they spread into Montana.

pharmacy, **Wall Drug**, is now a sprawling Wild West shopping and entertainment complex. Along with Western and American Indian souvenirs are interactive exhibits of cowboys, homesteaders, gunfighters, and medicine-show hucksters.

The sprawling **Buffalo Gap National Grassland** lies south, west, and east of Wall. Its comprehensive visitor center describes the ecological and cultural history of the grasslands. Exhibits outline the various habitats and illustrate the astonishing biodiversity of the shortgrass, mixed-grass, and tallgrass prairies, which once covered most of the region.

Wall Drug

📍 510 Main St 🕐 7am–9pm daily 🌐 walldrug.com

Buffalo Gap National Grassland Visitor Center

📍 708 Main St 📞 (605) 279-2125 🕐 Memorial–Labor Day: 8am–5pm daily; Labor Day–Memorial Day: 8am–4:30pm Mon–Fri

12

Pine Ridge Reservation

🏢 Oglala Sioux tribe, Pine Ridge; (605) 867-5821

Home to the Oglala Sioux tribe, the Pine Ridge Reservation is one of the nation's largest American Indian reservations. The reservation lands abut the South Dakota–Nebraska border and extend west into the badlands region. The Oglala and their chief, Red Cloud, were relocated here in 1876. On December 29, 1890, the US Army's 7th Cavalry massacred about 300 Lakota men, women, and children at Wounded Knee. This was the last in a series of misunderstandings concerning the ceremonial Ghost Dance, which the tribe believed would reunite them with their ancestors, bring the buffalo back, and help them regain their lost lands. A lone stone monument, east of the town of Pine Ridge, marks the site.

The **Red Cloud Heritage Center**, on the Red Cloud Indian School campus near Pine Ridge, contains the gravesite of Chief Red Cloud. It also displays a range of American Indian artifacts and contemporary art.

Red Cloud Heritage Center

📍 4.5 miles (7 km) N of Pine Ridge Village on Hwy 18 🕐 Times vary, check website 🌐 redcloudschool.org

←

A traditional hand drum, which can be seen at the Pine Ridge Reservation

NEBRASKA

Nebraska Territory was created in 1854 and was settled rapidly after the Homestead Act of 1862 (which essentially gave away free land), beginning with Omaha, a major transportation crossroads. Much of western Nebraska remained off limits due to conflict with American Indian tribes, such as the Sioux and Pawnee, well into the 1870s. Nebraska became a state in 1867, and a huge railroad boom precipitated the conversion of the prairies into vast farms producing cattle and wheat. Today the state remains primarily rural.

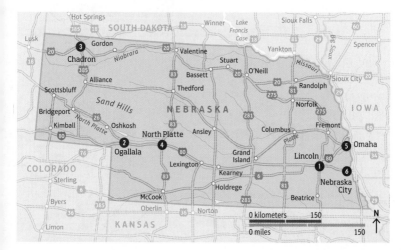

NEBRASKA

Nebraska's vast, grassy expanses of open range, and ruts from old overland wagon routes, epitomize the geography and history of the Great Plains. In the north, the sparsely settled Nebraska Sandhills contain some of the nation's largest expanses of mixed-grass prairie, while the state's two largest cities, Omaha and Lincoln, are in the southeast.

❶ Lincoln

✈ 🚗 🚌 ℹ 201 N 7th St; www.lincoln.org

State capital and Nebraska's second-largest city, Lincoln is also home to the University of Nebraska, whose Cornhuskers football team is so popular that it has sold out every home game at the 85,000-seat Memorial Stadium since 1962. The city's principal landmark is the 400-ft (120-m) Indiana limestone tower of the Nebraska State Capitol. Completed in 1932, the "Tower of the Plains" is visible for miles around. The building houses the nation's only unicameral legislature, a vestige of cost-saving measures introduced by the state during the Great Depression of the 1930s.

The state's political history is related alongside its rich American Indian heritage in the excellent Nebraska History Museum, which covers 12,000 years of the state's history. The University of Nebraska State Museum has a wide-ranging collection of elephant fossils and American Indian artifacts. In the nearby historic Haymarket District, several 19th-century warehouses have been converted into bars and restaurants.

Nebraska History Museum

🏛 131 Centennial Mall N
🕐 10am–5:30pm Mon–Fri, 1–5:30pm Sat 🔒 Federal hols
🌐 history.nebraska.gov

University of Nebraska State Museum

🏛 Morrill Hall, 14th & Vine sts
🕐 9:30am–4:30pm Mon–Sat (to 8pm Thu), 12:30–4:30pm Sun 🌐 museum.unl.edu

Did You Know?

The 911 system of emergency calling was developed and first used in Lincoln.

A football game at Lincoln's Memorial Stadium, and *(inset)* its Husker Legacy Statue ↓

2
Ogallala

🚌 🚏 119 E 2nd St; www.visitogallala.com

Located on the South Platte River, Ogallala is the gateway to the Panhandle part of the Oregon Trail tour (p429). The city gained a rowdy reputation after its founding in 1867, when the arrival of the railroad drew herds of cattle and hordes of Texas cowboys. Today, most visitors come seeking camping, boating, hunting, and fishing supplies for their exploration of **Lake McConaughy State Recreation Area**, about 9 miles (14 km) to the north.

A refreshing oasis in the middle of the dry Panhandle

plains, Lake McConaughy is the state's largest reservoir. Known locally as "Big Mac," its cool waters are a prime breeding ground for fish, while the marshes, woodlands, and grasslands on the lake's western end attract a wide variety of waterfowl. It is also one of the richest birding spots in the Great Plains region.

Lake McConaughy State Recreation Area

♿ 🚏 1475 Hwy 61 N
📞 (308) 284-8800 🕐 Daily

3
Chadron

🚏 🚻 706 W 3rd St; www.chadron.com

Chadron is an ideal base from which to tour this region as well as explore aspects of the state's fascinating past. Just east of town is the Museum of the Fur Trade, which traces the history of the complex North American fur trade and its effect on American Indian communities. It features a reconstructed trading post built into the sides of a low hill.

The area's key historical attraction is **Fort Robinson State Park**, a 30-minute drive west of Chadron. The park occupies the parade grounds, barracks, and officers' quarters of the US Army's Fort Robinson. The fort was built in 1874 to protect the nearby Red Cloud Indian Agency, where Sioux chief Red Cloud and his followers moved to before being relocated at Pine Ridge (p423). In 1877, the great Oglala Sioux chief, Crazy Horse, and 900 of his tribe surrendered and set up camp outside the fort. In a series of tragic events, Crazy Horse was killed while federal troops attempted to imprison him. A blockhouse commemorates the site where he fell.

The Fort Robinson Museum details the fort's other lives as an experimental cattle ranch and a training ground for the army's World War II canine

corps. The fort's restored quarters provide accommodations for visitors, while horseback trails lead through the surrounding lonesome buttes and grassy plains.

Chadron State Park is a quieter, more scenic alternative to Fort Robinson, with ample campgrounds, cabin facilities, and numerous hiking and biking trails.

Fort Robinson State Park

🚏 US 20, 3 miles (5 km) W of Crawford 🕐 Daily 🌐 outdoornebraska.ne.gov/fortrobinson

↑ Bustling shops and bars within Omaha's historic Old Market district

4

North Platte

🚗🚌 ℹ️ **101 Halligan Dr; www.visitnorthplatte.com**

Now one of the country's major railroad centers, North Platte was the late 19th-century home of the famed William "Buffalo Bill" Cody. The comfortable ranch house he built on the outskirts of town was the base of operations for his spectacular traveling Wild West show until 1902, when he founded Cody in Wyoming. Cody's home is now part of

↑ Buffalo Bill Ranch State Historical Park in North Platte

the **Buffalo Bill Ranch State Historical Park and State Recreation Area**. The nearby **Lincoln County Historical Museum** exhibits a replica of the famous North Platte Canteen, which served countless pots of coffee and numerous snacks to the troops who passed through the town during World War II.

Buffalo Bill Ranch Historical Park and State Recreation Area

♿ 📍2921 Scouts Rest Ranch Rd 🕐May–Sep: times vary, check website 🌐outdoor nebraska.ne.gov

Lincoln County Historical Museum

♿ 📍2403 Buffalo Bill Av 🕐Summer: 9am–5pm Mon–Sat, 1–5pm Sun; winter: by appt 🌐lincolncounty museum.org

---

5

Omaha

🚗🚆🚌 ℹ️ **1001 Farnam St, Ste 200; www.visitomaha. com**

Omaha evolved from a rough-and-tumble Missouri River town and outfitting post into

a major railroad terminus with the construction of the transcontinental railroad in 1868. The restored Old Market warehouse district just south of downtown preserves the city's historical roots. Its old commercial buildings and cobblestone streets are now home to some of the region's best restaurants, bookstores, and antique shops. A few blocks south, the city's landmark 1931 Art Deco Union Station now houses the **Durham Western Heritage Museum**. This splendid local history museum features displays on Omaha's railroad and transportation heritage.

Just west of downtown is the pink marble **Joslyn Art Museum**, a Smithsonian affiliate and the crown jewel of Omaha's cultural attractions. It features 19th- and 20th-century European and American art, and is also a treasure trove of Western American art, with paintings, sculpture, and photographs by George Catlin, Frederic Remington, George Caleb Bingham, and Edward S. Curtis. The centerpiece of its Western collection are the watercolors and prints by Swiss artist Karl Bodmer, who documented life on the upper

Plains when he traveled across North America with German naturalist Prince Maximilian of Wied in 1833.

North of downtown, the Great Plains Black History Museum relates the rarely told story of African American migration and settlement on the Great Plains. The Mormon Trail Center, farther north still, commemorates the 1846-48 migration of Mormons from the Midwest to Utah. Located on the pioneers' late 19th-century Winter Quarters campsite, a visitor center explains the religious persecution that led to the migration.

Durham Western Heritage Museum

◈ ⚑ 801 S 10th St
🕒 Times vary, check website
🌐 durhammuseum.org

Joslyn Art Museum

◈ ⚑ 2200 Dodge St
🕒 10am-4pm Tue-Sun (to 8pm Thu) 🌐 joslyn.org

> Just west of downtown is the pink marble Joslyn Art Museum, a Smithsonian affiliate and the crown jewel of Omaha's cultural attractions.

❻
Nebraska City

🛈 806 1st Av; www. nebraskacity.com

Sedate, tree-lined Nebraska City's origins were as a rowdy Missouri River way station, where families and adventurers bound for the Oregon Trail mingled with trappers, traders, and riverboat employees. Today, the city is best known as the birthplace of Arbor Day, established by Nebraska politician Julius Sterling Morton (1832–1902), who introduced a resolution to make April 10 a state holiday to encourage farmers in Nebraska to plant trees as protection from high plains

winds and soil erosion. Later, the date was changed to April 22, Morton's birthday. It is still commemorated throughout the US, although the date varies from state to state. The Arbor Lodge State Historical Park contains Morton's mansion, greenhouse, and grounds.

The city is also well known as the home of **Arbor Day Farm**, an experimental farm, conference center, and forestry research center. Scenic hiking trails and guided tours of the site are on offer.

Arbor Day Farm

⚑ 2611 Arbor Av 🕒 Summer: 9am-5pm Mon-Sat, 10am-5pm Sun; winter: 10am-5pm Mon-Sat, 11am-5pm Sun
🌐 arbordayfarm.org

THE OREGON TRAIL

Founded by trader William Sublette in 1830, this formidable 2,000-mile (3,200-km) trail was the main wagon route between Independence, Missouri, in the east and Oregon to the west. The original route curved northwest after crossing the Missouri River near present-day Kansas City, passing through northeastern Kansas and southeastern Nebraska on the way to the Platte River. Between 1841 and 1866, a staggering 500,000 settlers bound for Oregon and the goldfields of northern California passed through Nebraska, following the northern banks of the Platte. As the trail veered northwest, away from the flat landscape of the Platte River Valley and up into the craggy Panhandle plateau along the North Platte River, pioneers were awestruck by the massive rock formations that signaled the Rockies to the west.

IOWA AND MISSOURI

The French settled the region in the 18th century. The US took over in 1803 and Missouri subsequently boomed as a hub for cattle heading east, and settlers heading west. Missouri became a free state in 1821, though it remained in the Union during the Civil War. Iowa was settled after the defeat of the Sauk in 1832, and the Sioux ceded their last Iowa land in 1851. Iowa became a non-slave state in 1846, and thrived as an agricultural powerhouse. The state gets considerable media attention every four years thanks to the Iowa caucuses, the country's first presidential primary vote.

Experience

1. Des Moines
2. Sioux City
3. Amana Colonies
4. Cedar Rapids
5. Dubuque
6. Iowa City
7. St. Louis
8. Kansas City
9. Branson
10. St. Joseph
11. Jefferson City

IOWA

Stretching from the Mississippi on its eastern border to the Missouri River on the west, Iowa offers seemingly endless vistas of rolling hills, lush cornfields, tidy farming communities, and clapboard country churches. These are the images that make the state a perfect setting for Hollywood movies seeking to capture a nearly vanished rural America.

❶ Des Moines

🚗 🚌 ℹ️ 400 Locust St, Suite 265; www.catchdesmoines.com

The state capital draws its name from French *voyageurs* who named the Des Moines River Valley "*La Rivière des Moines*" (River of the Monks). The city is now an important agricultural and entertainment center and home of the Iowa State Fair, which draws over a million visitors every August.

Dominating the area east of downtown is the gold-leafed central dome of the Iowa State Capitol. Nearby is the Iowa Historical Building, with displays on the state's American Indian, geological, and cultural history. West of the Capitol, the **Des Moines Art Center** exhibits an impressive collection of paintings by Henri Matisse, Andy Warhol, and Georgia O'Keeffe.

Winterset, located about 35 miles (56 km) to the south, is the quaint and attractive seat of Madison County and birthplace of Hollywood Western star John Wayne. The house where the actor grew up is a much-visited museum today. The local Chamber of Commerce provides a map of the six covered bridges that inspired author Robert Waller's famous 1992 novel, *The Bridges of Madison County*.

Des Moines Art Center

📍 4700 Grand Av 🕐 11am–4pm Tue–Fri (to 9pm Thu), 10am–4pm Sat, noon–4pm Sun 🌐 desmoines artcenter.org

❷ Sioux City

🚗 🚌 ℹ️ 401 Gordon Dr; www.visitsiouxcity.org

Sioux City sits on the northern cusp of Iowa's green, shaggy Loess Hills. This unique ecosystem is explained at the **Dorothy Pecaut Nature Center** in Stone State Park, just north of the city. The northern tip of the Loess Hills National Scenic Byway, which traverses the hills, can be accessed from the park. The park also has one of the state's few surviving stands of tallgrass prairie and a network of bike and hiking trails.

Just south of downtown, the Sergeant Floyd Monument,

The gilded Iowa State Capitol in Des Moines, and *(inset)* one of its impressive chambers

the first ever designated national monument, marks the 1804 burial of Sergeant Charles Floyd, who was a member of Lewis and Clark's Corps of Discovery. Floyd was the first and only member to die on the transcontinental journey of the expedition. Exhibits from the voyage can be seen in the Sergeant Floyd River Museum and Welcome Center on the riverfront.

Dorothy Pecaut Nature Center

📍 4500 Sioux River Rd
📞 (712) 258-0838 🕐 9am-4:30pm Tue-Sat, 1-4:30pm Sun 🚫 Jan 1, Thanksgiving, Dec 24 & 25

EAT

The Class Act
This delightful gourmet restaurant is also a teaching venue for culinary arts students.

📍 7725 Kirkwood Blvd SW, Cedar Rapids 🌐 the hotelatkirkwood.com

💲💲💲

Iowa River Power Restaurant
A local favorite, housed in an old power station with superb river views. Seafood and steak are the main draws.

📍 501 1st Av, Coralville 🌐 iowariverpower.net

💲💲💲

Flying Mango
A casual eatery with inventive cocktails, live music, and innovative takes on barbecue.

📍 4345 Hickman Rd, Des Moines 🌐 flying mango.com

💲💲💲

❸
Amana Colonies

ℹ️ 622 46th Av, Amana; www.amanacolonies.com

The seven Amana Colonies along the Iowa River were settled in the 1850s by the Inspirationists, a mainly German religious sect. The colonists prospered, but in 1932 residents voted to end their communal lifestyle, setting up a profit-sharing society instead. The **Amana Heritage Museum** commemorates the success of the colonies' enterprises and their history in seven museums and preserved historical sites.

Amana Heritage Museum
♽ 📍 4310 220th Trail
🕐 Apr-Oct: 10am-5pm Mon-Sat (Jun-Aug: from 9am), 11am-4pm Sun 🌐 amana heritage.org

❹
Cedar Rapids

✈️🚗 ℹ️ 370 1st Av NE; www. cedar-rapids.com

The Iowa artist Grant Wood lived in this town for much of his adult life and developed a Regionalist style that celebrated the people and landscapes of his home state. The Cedar Rapids Museum of Art has one of the country's largest collections of Wood's paintings.

The Carl and Mary Koehler History Center details the area's early history, while the National Czech and Slovak Museum and Library celebrates the city's large Czech and Slovak immigrant population.

❺
Dubuque

✈️🚗 ℹ️ 280 Main St; www. traveldubuque.com

Iowa's oldest city was established in 1788 by a French *voyageur*, Julian Dubuque.

↑ The Fenelon Place Elevator in Dubuque, emerging from the trees

During the 19th century, the city's nouveau riche constructed luxurious homes atop the bluffs ringing the city. These citizens rode to and from downtown, 296 ft (90 m) below, via the Fenelon Place Elevator, an incline railway that is now a major tourist attraction.

The city's main draw is the National Mississippi River Museum and Aquarium, a riverfront complex with exhibits on the mighty river's history and ecology. Aquariums replicate the habitat and ecosystem of the country's different rivers.

❻
Iowa City

🚗 ℹ️ 900 1st Av, Coralville; www.iowacitycoralville.org

Easygoing Iowa City is home to the University of Iowa campus and the school's noteworthy Iowa Writers' Workshop. The city served as the territorial and state capital until 1857, and the Old Capitol, now the Old Capitol Museum, is on campus.

Just east of Iowa City is the Herbert Hoover National Historic Site, where the president's boyhood home has been restored.

MISSOURI

The Missouri River and the I-70 Interstate Highway bisect the state of Missouri, linking its two largest cities – St. Louis and Kansas City – and providing quick access to the centrally located state capital of Jefferson City. In southern Missouri, the rugged Ozark Mountain region is veined with beautiful streams and rivers, making the area a popular camping and canoeing destination.

INSIDER TIP
Busch Stadium

If you can't get a match ticket to see the St. Louis Cardinals, the city's revered baseball team, you can still tour the stadium, visit the dugout, see the radio broadcast booth, and the museum too.

⑦
St. Louis

⊞ 🅿 🚌 *i* Gateway Arch; www.explorestlouis.com

Located just south of the point where the Missouri empties into the Mississippi River, St. Louis has been one of the country's most active crossroads. Founded by a French fur trader in 1764, this frontier city became a part of the US as a result of the Louisiana Purchase in 1803. It soon established itself as the "Gateway to the West," as steamboats chugged up the Missouri River into territories opened up by the Lewis and Clark expedition.

Completed in 1965 on the site of fur trader Pierre Laclede's original 1764 settlement, Eero Saarinen's 630-ft- (192-m-) tall **Gateway Arch** symbolizes the city's role as a commercial and cultural gateway between the settled eastern US and the wide-open lands to the west. Elevator-like tram rides transport visitors to the top of the arch, where picturesque views of the surrounding city and Illinois farmlands make the cramped quarters well worth the 1-hour round trip.

The domed **Old Courthouse** (1839–62) is one of the oldest buildings in the city. This Greek Revival structure was the site of two of the initial trials in the landmark Dred Scott case, which resulted in an 1857 decision by the US Supreme Court stating that African Americans were not citizens of the country and had no rights under US law. The decision overturned an earlier suit by Scott, an enslaved man, and deepened the sectional and racial differences that finally erupted in the American Civil War that lasted from 1861 to 1865. A museum within the Old Courthouse recounts the events of that famous trial and depicts what life must have been like for ordinary people living in 18th-century St. Louis under the yoke of French and Spanish rule.

The vibrant restaurant and entertainment district of **Laclede's Landing** consists of several blocks of restored 19th-century cotton, tobacco, and food warehouses along the riverfront. The popular restaurants and blues clubs attract large crowds, especially during the annual Big Muddy Blues Festival, held over Labor Day weekend. The 1874 Eads Bridge defines the Landing's southern boundary.

Designed in 1876, the 2-sq-mile (5-sq-km) Forest Park is one of the nation's largest urban green spaces. The 1904 World's Fair, known officially as the Louisiana Purchase Exposition, was held on the grounds, drawing nearly 20 million visitors. After the fair, nearly all the grand Beaux Arts structures designed by

2019
The year that Gateway Arch and its surroundings was made into a National Park.

Cass Gilbert were demolished. The only exception, the Palace of Fine Arts, is now home to the **St. Louis Art Museum**. Its vast collection of American art includes paintings by Missourians and artists Georgia O'Keeffe, Winslow Homer, and Andy Warhol.

The **Missouri History Museum**, originally the Jefferson Memorial Building, sits on the site of the main entrance to the 1904 fair. It houses exhibits depicting the multicultural history of St. Louis, with items including an original Louisiana Purchase transfer document, a replica of aviator Charles Lindbergh's 1927 *Spirit of St. Louis* airplane, and extensive displays on the World's Fair.

Anheuser-Busch Brewery was founded in 1860 by entrepreneurial German immigrants. Its famous trademark Budweiser lager brand is still very popular. The complex contains the company's 19th-century brick structures. Tours include a visit to the famous Clydesdale stables.

The **Missouri Botanical Garden** was created in 1859 by a wealthy St. Louis businessman. The grounds contain an English woodland garden, a Japanese garden, a Turkish-style Ottoman garden, and a scented garden for the visually impaired. The domed Climatron® conservatory has exotic birds and over 1,200 species of tropical plants, including banana trees and orchids.

Gateway Arch

🏛 Memorial Dr & Market St 🕐 Times vary, check website 🔳 gatewayarch.com

Old Courthouse

♿ 🏛 11 N 4th St 📞 (314) 655-1700 🕐 8am–4:30pm daily (winter: 10am–6pm)

Laclede's Landing

🏛 Morgan St & Lucas St between I-70 & the Mississippi River 🔳 lacledeslanding.org

St. Louis Art Museum

🏛 1 Fine Arts Dr 🕐 10am–5pm Tue–Sun 🔳 slam.org

Missouri History Museum

🏛 Jefferson Memorial Building, 5700 Lindell Blvd 🕐 10am–5pm daily (to 8pm Tue) 🔳 mohistory.org

Anheuser-Busch Brewery

🏛 1127 Pestalozzi St 🕐 Times vary, check website 🔳 budweisertours.com

Missouri Botanical Garden

♿ 🏛 4344 Shaw Blvd 🕐 9am–5pm daily (Jun-Aug: to 8pm Wed) 🔳 mobot.org

---

LOCAL CUISINES

There are plenty of Missouri dishes to try, many of them very localized. For the sweet-toothed there's Missouri corn, while butter cake is for those who don't find regular cakes rich enough. Toasted ravioli is regular ravioli deep-fried, and St. Louis-style pizza has a thin crust, local Provel cheese, and is cut into squares. The ice-cream cone was also first popularized here at the 1904 World's Fair in St. Louis.

↑ Downtown St. Louis, dominated by its sweeping Gateway Arch

↑ Dusk over downtown Kansas City, with Union Station in the foreground

STAY

21C Museum Hotel
This historic hotel features stained-glass windows and elegant rooms with claw-footed bath tubs.

🏠 219 W 9th St, Kansas City 🌐 21cmuseum hotels.com

$ $ $

Chateau on the Lake
Most rooms have private balconies, to make the most of lakeside views.

🏠 415 N Hwy 265, Branson 🌐 chateau onthelake.com

$ $ $

Moonrise Hotel
A quirky hotel with lunar-themed art and a rooftop bar.

🏠 6177 Delmar Blvd, St. Louis 🌐 moonrise hotel.com

$ $ $

❽ Kansas City

🚆🅿️🚌 ℹ️ 4010 Blue Ridge Cutoff; www.visitkc.com

Kansas City is rife with imagery associated with the Wild West but this vibrant city has so much more on offer; beautiful parks, sophisticated museums, fine public architecture, and high-end urban retail districts.

On the bluffs overlooking the Missouri River, the City Market sits on the site of the town's 19th-century Westport Landing business district. Today, the 1930s City Market building houses an eclectic collection of shops, farmers' markets, retail outlets, and the Arabia Steamboat Museum.

Northeast of here, the **Kansas City Museum** is housed in a 50-room mansion, with collections that trace the city's evolution from a fur trading post into a railroad and agricultural center. Currently closed for renovation, it is expected to reopen in late 2020.

The city's two most prominent architectural landmarks are located in the "Crossroads Arts District". The Beaux Arts Union Station, built in 1914, was one of the country's busiest railroad terminals. Renovated after years of neglect, the station is now a planetarium, children's science museum, and restaurant complex. The 217-ft (66-m) Liberty Memorial overlooks the old train depot on the grassy bluffs of Penn Valley Park. It houses the nation's only World War I museum, and the "Torch of Liberty" observation tower offers a sweeping view of the city.

Southeast of downtown, the 18th & Vine Historic Jazz District commemorates the city's rich African American heritage. The neighborhood's premier attractions include the American Jazz Museum and the Baseball Museum, which honors talented African American baseball players who toiled in low-paid obscurity for all-black teams in the

> Kansas City is rife with imagery associated with the Wild West but this vibrant city has so much more on offer.

US, Canada, and Latin America. In 1945, Kansas City Monarchs shortstop Jackie Robinson broke the color barrier by signing with the all-white Brooklyn Dodgers in the National League.

Once an outfitting post for travelers on the Santa Fe and Oregon Trails, the village of Westport became part of Kansas City in 1899, and is home to some of the city's oldest buildings. To its east, the **Nelson-Atkins Museum of Art** has a stellar collection of paintings by Missouri's George Caleb Bingham and Thomas Hart Benton, as well as an outdoor sculpture garden.

Kansas City Museum

◎ 🏠 3218 Gladstone Blvd 📞 (816) 483-8300 🕙 For renovation

Nelson-Atkins Museum of Art

🏠 45th St & Oak St 🕙 10am-5pm Wed-Mon (to 9pm Thu & Fri) 🕙 Federal hols 🌐 nelson-atkins.org

---

9

Branson

🛈 269 State Hwy 248; www.explorebranson.com

This once-sleepy Ozark Mountain resort has transformed thanks to the success of several family-oriented tourist attractions. A pageant revolving around the Ozarks-based novel *The*

Shepherd of the Hills was one of the area's first big hits. It is still staged in an outdoor arena attached to a working, mountain farm, at **Shepherd of the Hills Homestead**.

The biggest draws are Branson's nightly music programs, presented at over 30 alcohol-free performance venues crowded together on "The Strip" (Route 76 W). Star performers are as varied as the Acrobats of China, country legends like Buck Trent and the Oak Ridge Boys, and Russian-born American comedian Yakov Smirnoff. The **Silver Dollar City** theme park, just west of town, features high-tech roller coasters and water rides.

Shepherd of the Hills Homestead

◎ 🏠 5586 W Hwy 76, 2 miles W of Branson 🕙 May-Oct: 9am-4pm daily 🌐 oldmatt.com

Silver Dollar City

🏠 399 Silver Dollar City Rd 🕙 Open daily, closed Feb 🌐 silverdollarcity.com

---

10

St. Joseph

🚆 🛈 502 N Woodbine Rd; www.stjomo.com

Like many Missouri River communities, St. Joseph grew from a fur-trading post into a wagon-train outfitting center. Its position as the nation's westernmost railroad terminal instigated

← A Pony Express memorial in St. Joseph

local entrepreneurs to launch the Pony Express in the mid-1800s. This service sought to deliver mail from St. Joseph to Sacramento – a 1,966-mile (3,214-km) trip – in less than ten days. Informative displays in the **Pony Express National Museum** relate the story of this short-lived enterprise.

Pony Express National Museum

◎ 🏠 914 Penn St 🕙 9am-5pm Mon-Sat, 11am-4pm Sun 🕙 Jan 1, Thanksg., Dec 24, 25 & 31 🌐 ponyexpress.org

---

11

Jefferson City

🚗🚆🚌 🛈 700 E Capitol Av; www.visitjeffersoncity.com

Soon after its founding as the state capital in 1821, Jefferson City grew into a busy Missouri River port. The **Jefferson Landing State Historic Site** preserves many structures from its original waterfront, including the 1839 Lohman Building. The Classical Revival Missouri State Capitol, completed in 1917, now houses the Missouri State Museum and a provocative mural by Thomas Hart Benton. His 1935 *A Social History of the State of Missouri* depicts the state's widespread poverty and seamier underclass.

Jefferson Landing State Historic Site

🏠 Jefferson St 📞 (573) 751-2854 🕙 Mar-Nov: 10am-4pm Tue-Sat

KANSAS AND OKLAHOMA

American Indian tribes – such as the Choctaw, Chickasaw, Seminole, Creek, and Cherokee – and bison herds roamed here for thousands of years. In 1854 the establishment of the Kansas Territory led to fierce "Bleeding Kansas" clashes between anti- and pro-slavery forces, the former aided by abolitionist John Brown. Kansas eventually joined the Union as a free state in 1861. Indian Territory was opened up for settlement in 1889; though native leaders sought to create their own state, Oklahoma absorbed the territory as a state in 1907. The region suffered in the Depression, though agriculture, oil, and gas are all booming today.

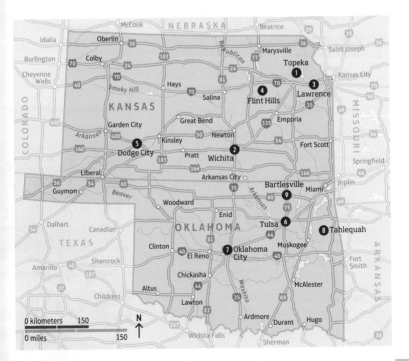

KANSAS

For most Americans, Kansas conjures up images of rolling wheat fields, sunflowers, and scenes from the 1939 movie *The Wizard of Oz*. The real Kansas, however, is infinitely more interesting. Reminders of the state's history can be frequently glimpsed, and Kansas is also home to the largest continuous area of natural tallgrass prairie left in North America, preserved in the Flint Hills.

① Topeka

🚲🚌 ℹ️ 719 S Kansas Av; www.visittopeka.com

Topeka's most significant historical attraction is Kansas Regionalist painter John Steuart Curry's mural in the Kansas State Capitol, *The Settlement of Kansas*. It depicts abolitionist John Brown in a dramatic confrontation with pro-slavery forces that threatened to make Kansas a slave state in the 1850s. More background on this tense period can be found at the Kansas Museum of History.

DRINK

Free State Brewing Company

The headquarters of the beer producer as well as an eatery, Free State is a great choice for craft beer fans.

🏠 636 Massachusetts St, Lawrence 🌐 freestate brewing.com

Blind Tiger Brewery & Restaurant

The brewpub here offers six flagship beers plus seasonal specialties, served up in a rustic, Alpine-style setting.

🏠 417 SW 37th St, Topeka 🌐 blindtiger.com

② Wichita

🚲🚗🚌 ℹ️ 515 S Main St; www.visitwichita.com

Wichita developed in 1865 as a lawless railhead town, where Texan cowboys driving north on the Chisholm Trail would stop to let off steam in the saloons and brothels. Those early cattle hands would not recognize today's Wichita, which has grown into a busy aircraft manufacturing and oil-refining center. The town's past is recreated at the **Old Cowtown Museum**, which has the original jail and period houses on display. To its southeast is the **Mid-America All-Indian Center**, which depicts the 19th-century lifestyles of the Kiowa, Cheyenne, and Lakota tribes. Its main feature is a reconstructed village.

Old Cowtown Museum

♿ 🏠 1865 Museum Blvd 🕐 10am–5pm Tue–Sat, noon–5pm Sun 🌐 oldcowtown.org

Mid-America All-Indian Center

♿ 🏠 650 N Seneca St 🕐 10am–4pm Tue–Sat 🌐 theindiancenter.org

③ Lawrence

🚌 ℹ️ 402 N 2nd St; www.explorelawrence.com

Founded in 1854, Lawrence's strong "free state" leanings made it a target for Missouri's pro-slavery "border ruffians." The downtown retail district is lined with 19th-century

---

commercial buildings, reminders of the city's reconstruction drive after a destructive 1863 guerrilla raid by Confederates.

The Lawrence Visitor Information Center relates key episodes in the city's history and provides information about the University of Kansas campus, which includes the University of Kansas Natural History Museum and the Spencer Museum of Art.

---

④ Flint Hills

🚲🚌 🌐 kansasflinthills.travel

The shaggy Flint Hills are among Kansas's most spectacular natural features.

The best way to explore the area is to drive along the scenic Route 177, running south from the university town of Manhattan to Cassody. About 6 miles (10 km) southeast of Manhattan is **Konza Prairie**, the country's largest remaining parcel of virgin tallgrass prairie. The 13-sq-mile (35-sq-km) preserve contains a variety of superb hiking trails, while the Flint Hills Discovery Center in Manhattan explores the biology, geology, and cultural history of the prairie.

The **Tallgrass Prairie National Preserve**, 20 miles (32 km) south of the town of Council Grove, protects what remains of a 19th-century cattle ranch. Nearby, the ranching community of Cottonwood Falls is home to the 1873 Chase County Courthouse, which is is the oldest still in use in Kansas.

Konza Prairie

🏠 McDowell Creek Rd
🕐 Dawn-dusk daily 🌐 kpbs.konza.k-state.edu

Tallgrass Prairie National Preserve

🏠 Hwy 177, 2 miles (3 km) N of Strong City 🕐 8:30am-4:30pm daily (winter: from 9am) 🌐 nps.gov/tapr

↑ A faded wagon standing outside the Boot Hill Museum in Dodge City

5

Dodge City

🚗 🚌 ℹ 400 W Wyatt Earp Blvd; www.visitdodgecity.org

Between 1872 and 1884, this town flourished as a High Plains buffalo-hunting, cattle-driving, and railroad center. The **Boot Hill Museum** re-creates the infamous Front Street strip of saloons and burlesque houses that earned Dodge City the sobriquet of "Hell on the Plains."

Before hordes of cowboys and buffalo hunters came to town, Dodge City was just another stop on the Santa Fe Trail. Ruts from the old wagon trail can still be seen along US 50 and at the Fort Larned National Historic Site, which contains several restored sandstone structures from the US Army fort that protected travelers along the Santa Fe Trail from 1859 to 1878.

Boot Hill Museum

♿ 🏠 500 W Wyatt Earp Blvd
🕐 Times vary, check website
🌐 boothill.org

Did You Know?

It was once against the law to serve ice cream on cherry pie in Kansas.

↑ Students relaxing on the University of Kansas campus, Lawrence

The serene Oklahoma City National Memorial, and the interior of the museum (inset) ↑

OKLAHOMA

Bordered by six states, Oklahoma is a cultural, geographical, and historical crossroads. The state has the nation's largest American Indian population – with 39 sovereign tribes – but is perhaps most famous for the Americana-rich Route 66. Oklahoma epitomizes the open range, with great arid plains punctuated by canyons and historic towns.

6
Tulsa

🚉🚌🚐 *i* **1 W 3rd St, Suite 100; www.visittulsa.com**

Originally a railroad town, Tulsa prospered after the discovery of oil in 1901. Fortunes were made literally overnight, leading to the construction of Art Deco commercial buildings, roads, and bridges across the Arkansas River. Although Tulsa is still a major oil center,

it also contains numerous man-made lakes, parks, and Arkansas River bike trails. Its top attraction is the **Thomas Gilcrease Institute**, an art museum founded by a wealthy local oilman. Its collection includes a wide range of Western American and American Indian works by such artists as George Catlin and Frederic Remington. The city's most popular roadside sight is the Prayer Tower Visitor Center and the huge bronze statue of a pair of hands folded in prayer at the entrance to Tulsa's Oral Roberts University.

Thomas Gilcrease Institute

♿ 🏠 **1400 N Gilcrease Museum Rd** ⏱ **10am–5pm Tue–Sun** 🌐 **gilcrease.org**

←
A statue of praying hands, which stands outside Oral Roberts University in Tulsa

7
Oklahoma City

🚉🚌 *i* **123 Park Av; www.visitokc.com**

Oklahoma City was built and founded in a single day – April 22, 1889 – as part of the first Oklahoma Territory land rush. Over 10,000 land claims were filed on that day, creating a city out of thin air. The city became the state capital in 1910 and saw its first oil strike in 1928. Today, there are more than 2,000 still-active oil wells, including one on the grounds of the Oklahoma State Capitol, within the city limits.

The **Oklahoma History Center** chronicles the state's intimate relationship with oil, as well as its pre-settlement history. The **National Cowboy and Western Heritage Museum** contains one of the country's most comprehensive collections of Western-related art. Among its exhibits is a giant statue of the famed Wild West figure Buffalo Bill, and a collection of Western actor John Wayne memorabilia. On a more somber note, the city has paid homage to the 168 people killed in the tragic 1995 Federal Building bombing with the dignified Oklahoma City National Memorial. The 3.3-acre

ORAL ROBERTS UNIVERSITY

home since 1839. Of primary interest here is the **Cherokee Heritage Center**. Its attractions include a village dating from the 1875–90 American Indian Territory era and a re-creation of a 17th-century settlement from the tribe's ancestral lands in the Appalachian Mountains. Exhibits at the Cherokee National Museum chronicle the tribe's forced march along the "Trail of Tears" from North Carolina to Oklahoma in the 1830s (*p53*). This tragic event is also dramatized every year in June.

Cherokee Heritage Center

⊘ 🏠 21192 S Keeler Dr
🕙 9am–5pm Mon–Sat (winter: Tue–Sat)
🌐 cherokeeheritage.org

9
Bartlesville

🚉🚌 ℹ️ 201 SW Keeler Av; www.bartlesville.com

The state's first commercial oil well was drilled here in 1897, kicking off a large-scale oil boom. A replica of the original well, the Nellie Johnstone #1, now stands as a memorial in a downtown park. Today, the city's largest employer is still the ConocoPhillips company, founded in 1917 as Phillips Petroleum, by two speculators from Iowa.

EAT

Cattlemen's Steakhouse

Specializing in steak dinners since 1945, this spot caters to cowboys and celebrities alike.

🏠 1309 S Agnew Av, Oklahoma City 🌐 cattlemensrestaurant.com

$$$

Frank Phillips' extensive rural estate, **Woolaroc Museum and Wildlife Preserve**, is located to the southwest of Bartlesville. The picturesque ranch includes a superb Western art collection, an American Indian heritage center, and a wildlife preserve. About 45 miles (72 km) northwest of Bartlesville is the Nature Conservancy's Tallgrass Prairie Preserve. In this vast expanse of rolling prairie, a herd of bison graze among stands of big bluestem grasses and blazing star wildflowers.

Woolaroc Museum and Wildlife Preserve

⊘ 🏠 Rte 123, 12 miles (19 km) SW of Bartlesville 🕙 10am–5pm Wed–Sun (Memorial Day to Labor Day: also Tue)
🌐 woolaroc.org

(1.3-ha) downtown memorial includes a museum, reflecting pool, and the elm tree that survived the blast and symbolizes strength.

Oklahoma History Center

🏠 2401 N Laird Av 🕙 10am–5pm Mon–Sat 🌐 okhistorycenter.org

National Cowboy and Western Heritage Museum

⊘ 🏠 1700 NE 63rd St
🕙 10am–5pm Mon–Sat, noon–5pm Sun 🌐 nationalcowboymuseum.org

8
Tahlequah

🚌 ℹ️ 123 E Delaware St; www.tourtahlequah.com

The capital of the Cherokee Nation, Tahlequah lies in the eastern Oklahoma Ozark Mountain foothills, the tribe's

OLD ROUTE 66

Immortalized as the "mother road" in author John Steinbeck's 1939 novel *The Grapes of Wrath*, this historic highway, charted in 1926, was the first to link Chicago to Los Angeles. Old Route 66 heads southwest from Oklahoma state's northeastern corner to its western border with Texas. West of Oklahoma City, the route runs alongside I-40, with several sections of old road veering off the Interstate. The Oklahoma Route 66 Museum in Clinton and the National Route 66 and Transport Museum in Elk City offer two of the most engaging Route 66 collections in the country. Other sights along the route include the Totem Pole Park and the Will Rogers Memorial Museum at Claremore. The latter relates the life story of Oklahoma's favorite son - humorist Will Rogers, who was born in a log cabin in nearby Oologah.

TEXAS

Fort Davis Drug Store, Texas

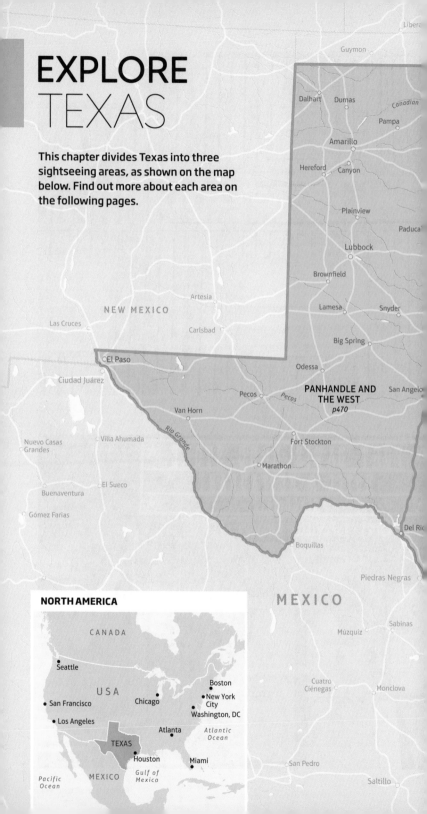

EXPLORE
TEXAS

This chapter divides Texas into three
sightseeing areas, as shown on the map
below. Find out more about each area on
the following pages.

Libera

Guymon

Dalhart   Dumas   Canadian

Pampa

Amarillo

Hereford   Canyon

Plainview

Paducah

Lubbock

Brownfield

Artesia

NEW MEXICO

Lamesa   Snyder

Las Cruces

Carlsbad

Big Spring

El Paso

Odessa

Ciudad Juárez

Pecos   Pecos

**PANHANDLE AND
THE WEST**
p470

San Angelo

Van Horn

Nuevo Casas
Grandes

Villa Ahumada

Rio Grande

Fort Stockton

Marathon

El Sueco

Buenaventura

Gómez Farias

Del Rio

Boquillas

Piedras Negras

MEXICO

NORTH AMERICA

CANADA

Seattle

USA

San Francisco   Chicago

Boston

New York
City

Washington, DC

Los Angeles

Atlanta   *Atlantic
Ocean*

TEXAS

Houston   Miami

*Pacific
Ocean*   MEXICO   *Gulf of
Mexico*

Sabinas

Múzquiz

Cuatro
Ciénegas   Monclova

San Pedro

Saltillo

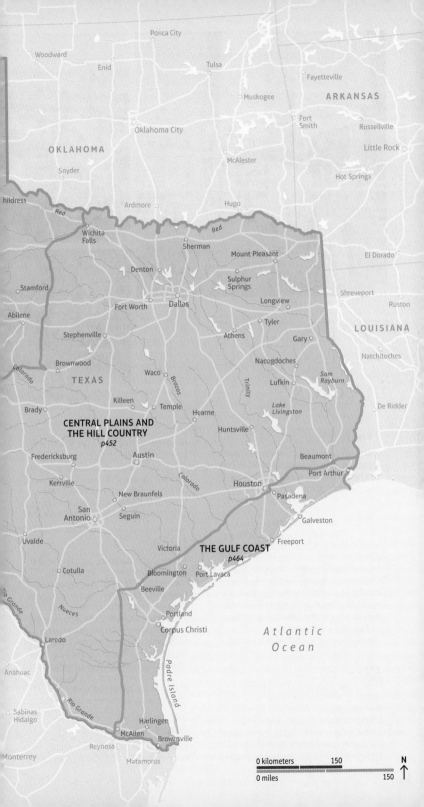

CENTRAL PLAINS AND
THE HILL COUNTRY
p452

THE GULF COAST
p464

OKLAHOMA

ARKANSAS

LOUISIANA

TEXAS

Atlantic
Ocean

Woodward
Ponca City
Enid
Tulsa
Fayetteville
Muskogee
Fort Smith
Russellville
Oklahoma City
Little Rock
Snyder
McAlester
Hot Springs
hildress
Red
Ardmore
Hugo
Red
Wichita Falls
Sherman
Mount Pleasant
El Dorado
Stamford
Denton
Sulphur Springs
Longview
Shreveport
Ruston
Fort Worth
Dallas
Abilene
Tyler
Gary
Natchitoches
Stephenville
Athens
Colorado
Brownwood
Nacogdoches
Waco
Lufkin
Sam Rayburn
De Ridder
Brady
Killeen
Brazos
Trinity
Lake Livingston
Temple
Hearne
Fredericksburg
Austin
Huntsville
Kerrville
Colorado
Beaumont
New Braunfels
Houston
Port Arthur
San Antonio
Seguin
Pasadena
Uvalde
Galveston
Victoria
Freeport
Cotulla
Bloomington
Port Lavaca
Rio Grande
Beeville
Nueces
Portland
Laredo
Corpus Christi
Anáhuac
Padre Island
Sabinas Hidalgo
Rio Grande
Harlingen
McAllen
Brownsville
Monterrey
Reynosa
Matamoros

0 kilometers   150
0 miles   150

N

1

2

3

7 DAYS

in Texas

Day 1

Start your road trip in the beating heart of Texas: Houston *(p462)*. The state's largest and wealthiest city is a fascinating mix of boot-scootin' country charm and high-brow culture. Its top draw is the globally revered, architecturally marvelous Menil Collection, which has works by Jasper Johns, Cy Twombly, Jackson Pollock, and more. Spend a couple of hours here, then explore Montrose – one of Houston's few walkable boroughs – on foot. The hipster enclave is stacked with galleries, boutiques, and cute cafés. Tex Mex is a must-try in Houston; sup on fajitas and pork *tamales* at the famous Ninfa's *(www. ninfas.com)*. Wash them down with signature house "ninfarita" margaritas.

Day 2

Head toward the Third Coast beaches, swinging by the Space Center on the way. Marvel at mission control for all manned US explorations of space since 1965, before driving out to sultry barrier island Galveston *(p466)* on the Gulf of Mexico for some beach time. Saunter through this

late 19th-century port city's Strand and East End Historic Districts for a glimpse of old-world charm. East Beach or Appfel Park are the top picks here for live music, parties, and sunbathing. After a swim, feast on Gulf seafood on the deck at waterfront Porch Cafe *(www.porchcafe.com)*.

Day 3

With an early start, you can be in Austin *(p458)* for a barbecue lunch from pit master Aaron Franklin at his eponymous Franklin Barbecue *(www.franklinbbq.com)*. A hot spot for all things music, Austin is a vinyl lover's dream. Browse the crates at Waterloo Records downtown *(www. waterloorecords.com)* before cooling off at Barton Springs Pool, a natural limestone pool, fed by underground springs. Cap the day with live music and cocktails at the iconic Continental Club *(www. continentalclub.com)*, founded in 1955.

Day 4

After the state capital's hot nightlife, roll out into the Old West towns, vineyards,

1 Sundance Square, Fort Worth.

2 Barton Springs Pool, backed by Austin's skyline.

3 Interior of the Dallas Museum of Art.

4 A picnic basket within one of Texas Hill Country's pastures.

5 A performer at Austin's Continental Club.

and wildflower-filled pastures of nearby Hill Country (p453). Break at Blue Hole, one of the loveliest swimming holes in Texas, with clear water and a canopy of ancient cypress trees. Fredericksburg (p459) lies at the epicenter of this region's vineyards; taste the *terroir* at Lost Draw Vineyards (www.lostdrawcellars.com) before settling in for a luxurious evening at the award-winning Barons Creek Vineyards (www.baronscreekvineyards.com). Reserve a pizza-wine tasting and sample their reds, cavas, chardonnays and rosés with dinner.

Day 5

Drive north through Hill Country, picking up picnic lunch supplies on the way to Wild West Fort Worth (p456), famous for the cattle market and Chisholm Cattle Drive trail. Visit the Cowgirl Hall of Fame and take in a cattle drive at the Stockyards. Grab some Tex Mex snacks near Sundance Square, then make your way to an extraordinary barbecue experience at Woodshed Smokehouse (www.woodshedsmoke house. com). They wood-fire everything from classic beef ribs to local veg.

Day 6

Finish your week with a splash at Fort Worth's glitzy neighbor, Dallas (p455). The rich city, with its glittering glass skyline, is home to the largest contiguous urban arts district in the nation; take your time in the vast Dallas Museum of Art. Nearby, Klyde Warren Park is a lively green space with daily events and food trucks. Head to the city's hippest hood, Deep Ellum, in the evening, for artful tacos at Revolver Taco Lounge (www.revolvertacolounge.com) followed by skyline views with cocktails at Vidorra rooftop bar (www.vidorradallas.com).

Day 7

No trip to Dallas is complete without paying homage to John F. Kennedy and the world-altering events of November 22, 1963 (p454). The JFK Memorial (1970) and Sixth Floor museum at Dealy Plaza commemorate the dramatic event – one symbolically and the other in bone-chilling detail. Get in line early for a memorable last meal at Cattleack Barbeque (www. cattleack bbq.com); free beer is served to patient diners in the line.

Hiking the state's utterly spectacular Guadalupe Peak Trail ↑

TEXAS FOR
OUTDOOR ADVENTURES

Everything is larger than life in Texas – including nature – and adventurers are spoiled for choice when it comes to big thrills. The country's second-largest state beckons with its turquoise waters, wide beaches, shimmering deserts, and rocky canyons. Where will you begin?

Around the River Bend

Slicing through sun-warmed rock under cobalt skies, the primal Rio Grande river functions as a liquid border between Texas and Mexico. Vast Big Bend National Park *(p472)* is named for a curve in the river. Nature buffs and adrenaline junkies flock here to canoe or raft through five magnificent river canyons, on the Rio Grande. Each canyon is a distinct playground. Santa Elena has the most dramatic beauty, while Mariscal is more remote and also boasts soaring cliff heights.

←

Canoeing along awesome Big Bend River

Moving Mountains

Every outdoor enthusiast should trek around Guadalupe Mountains National Park (p474), a visceral reminder of the untamed West. This craggy, arid mountain desert borders New Mexico (p525), home to 8,750-ft- (2,670-m-) high Guadalupe Peak. To the south of Guadalupe, you'll discover Davis Mountains, the most extensive mountain range in Texas. Popular with hikers, Fort Davis (p472) can also be found here in the mountains and is a good spot to refuel. During rainy years, the region is carpeted with wildflowers.

INSIDER TIP
Palo Duro Canyon

Head to Canyon (p474) and its Palo Duro Canyon State Park – it has amazing vistas, hiking, and horseback-riding opportunities, with very few crowds.

Into the Wild

Texas has a menagerie of astonishing wildlife. Aransas National Wildlife Refuge (p467) on the coast is a great spot to witness all manner of creatures, including rare whooping cranes. Dolphin boat safaris run off the coast of Port Aransas, while protected Kemp's ridley sea turtles hatch on Padre Island National Seashore (p469). In Big Bend National Park (p472) you could spy bobcats or mule deer.

$\rightarrow$

Kemp's ridley sea turtles on Padre Island National Seashore

Life's a Beach

Texas has some 600 miles (1,000 km) of inviting coastline along the Gulf Coast (p465), which is often nicknamed the USA's "third coast." Here you'll discover pristine nature preserves, excellent surf spots, and even party destinations. In Galveston (p466) gorgeous beaches call out to surfers, including Surfside Beach, famous for its clear waters. At Padre Island National Seashore (p469), a virtually untouched barrier reef island, wild beaches await.

Railroad vine ↑
on Padre Island
National Seashore

Hotel Valencia Riverwalk, San Antonio

CENTRAL PLAINS AND THE HILL COUNTRY

The Spanish established Catholic missions here in 1716, and San Antonio was founded two years later. In 1821, Texas became part of newly independent Mexico, but Anglo-Americans rebelled, and General Sam Houston overpowered the Mexican president in 1836. The independent Republic of Texas was created before it was annexed by the US in 1845, confirmed after the Mexican-American War. Texas became a slave state and joined the Confederacy in the Civil War, and segregation remained until the 1960s. Since the discovery of oil in the early 1900s, the state has become the nation's top oil producer.

Experience

1. Dallas
2. Fort Worth
3. Austin
4. Fredericksburg
5. New Braunfels
6. San Antonio
7. Houston

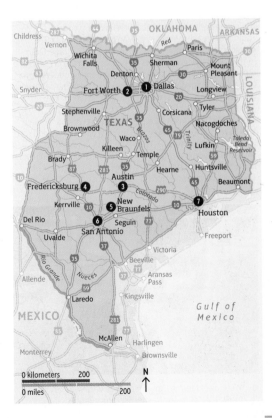

CENTRAL PLAINS AND THE HILL COUNTRY

This is a brilliant region to start exploring the USA's second largest state (after Alaska). The Hill Country is exquisite, its rolling landscape, punctuated with lakes and valleys, calls out for exploration. Here you'll also find Texas's most famous cities – creative Austin, cosmopolitan Houston, cultural San Antonio, and celebrity Dallas.

①

Dallas

✈ 🚌 🚇 ℹ **100 S Houston St; www.visitdallas.com**

When most people think of Texas, they think of Dallas, even though it is not the state capital. Located in the north-eastern corner of the state, this is where the cotton fields and oil wells of East Texas meet the wide-open West Texas rangelands. With a forest of glass office towers dominating the downtown area, Dallas is the commercial and financial center of the "Lone Star" state.

This fast-growing metropolis is using its wealth and status to regenerate, splashing out on cool art spaces and – in doing so – shaking off an outdated reputation. Infamous as the city where President Kennedy was shot, Dallas is nonetheless an energetic, enjoyable city. The lively West End and hip Deep Ellum districts lie at the edges of downtown, both brimming with top dining and shopping destinations. Walking in Dallas is an option, but a car, a cab, or the DART trams can help make the most of your time. Just outside town, the George W. Bush Presidential Library and Museum is dedicated to the presidency of this prominent Texan.

The 50-story **Reunion Tower** is topped by a geodesic sphere containing a rotating restaurant, a cocktail bar, and an observation area. The tower offers unforgettable panoramic views of Dallas and its surrounding suburbs, and remains one of the city's most distinctive landmarks.

Those interested in the city's most famous moment in history should head to the **Sixth Floor Museum**, which meticulously re-creates the controversial events of November 22, 1963, when

↑ Light reflecting off office towers in downtown Dallas at sunset

President Kennedy was assassinated. Located in the former warehouse from which Lee Harvey Oswald shot and killed Kennedy, the exhibition concentrates on the life and times of Kennedy. The window from which the shots were fired has been rebuilt to look as it did on the day of the assassination. One exhibit

---

EAT

Revolver Taco Lounge
A Deep Ellum hot spot for inventive tacos.
🏠 2701 Main St, Suite 120
📅 Mon 🌐 revolvertaco lounge.com

$ ⑤ ⑤

Cattleack Barbeque
The darling of Dallas barbecue - expect a line, but it's well worth it.
🏠 13628 Gamma Rd
🕐 10:30am-2pm Thu-Fri
🌐 cattleackbbq.com

$ $ ⑤

↑ *Working Model for Three Piece No.3: Vertebrae* by Henry Moore, the Nasher Sculpture Center

The compact **West End Historic District** comprises century-old warehouses that have been revitalized as the city's prime recreation center, with sidewalk cafés, bars, and shops. Dallas World Aquarium features marine life, while Old Red Museum showcases Dallas history.

Housed in a large modern building, the wide-ranging collection of the **Dallas Museum of Art** gives a fine overview of art history. The main galleries are arranged by continent; particularly noteworthy is the Art of the Americas gallery, which displays ancient Maya and Inca treasures through to Texas-made art of the Wild West. The world's most extensive collection of works by Dutch artist Piet Mondrian (1872–1944) is also on display.

A peaceful and quiet oasis in bustling downtown, the pocket-sized **Thanks-Giving Square** is packed with waterfalls, gardens, a bell tower, and an all-faiths chapel. A small museum traces the history of the American custom of Thanksgiving.

Fair Park is an exhibition center and site of the annual Texas State Fair. It also hosts the famous annual Cotton Bowl football game and many concerts. A highlight is the Hall of State, an Art Deco repository of exhibits tracing all things Texan.

The **Nasher Sculpture Center** is a collection of over 300 sculptures, acquired by the late Raymond and Patsy Nasher, who were avid art collectors. The collection is of international importance, with works by such artists as Joan Miró, Henri Matisse and Jeff Koons displayed throughout a glass-roofed building and in a garden-like setting.

Reunion Tower
🕸 🏠 300 Reunion Blvd E
🕐 Times vary, check website
🎫 Special events 🖥 reunion tower.com

Sixth Floor Museum
🕸 🏠 411 Elm St 🕐 Noon-6pm Mon, 10am-6pm Tue-Sun 🖥 jfk.org

West End Historic District
💬🕸 🖥 dallaswestend.com

Dallas Museum of Art
🕸 🏠 1717 N Harwood St
🕐 11am-5pm Tue-Sun (to 9pm Thu) 🖥 dma.org

Thanks-Giving Square
🏠 1627 Pacific Av
🖥 thanksgiving.org

Fair Park
🏠 1211 First Av
🖥 fairpark.org

Nasher Sculpture Center
🕸 🏠 2001 Flora St 🕐 11am-5pm Tue-Sun 🖥 nasher sculpturecenter.org

---

THE ASSASSINATION OF JFK

The 35th president, John Fitzgerald Kennedy, was fatally wounded as he rode in a motorcade with his wife Jackie in Dallas, on November 22, 1963. Their car was passing the Texas School Book Depository – now the JFK Memorial Museum - when shots rang out and hit their target in the roofless limo. Lee Harvey Oswald, an employee at the Depository, was arrested for the murder. Two days later, local club owner Jack Ruby shot Oswald on live TV.

↑ An elaborate fountain in Fort Worth's Water Gardens

2 Fort Worth

508 Main St; www.fortworth.com

Unlike its flashy neighbor, Dallas *(p454)*, Fort Worth is small, calm, and down-to-earth. Founded in 1849 as a US Army outpost, Fort Worth boomed after the Civil War, when Chisholm Trail cattle drives made the city one of the country's largest livestock markets. Although cowboy culture still thrives in the Stockyards District, Fort Worth is also a capital of "high" culture, with some of the nation's finest performing arts spaces and organizations.

The city has three main areas of interest. Downtown Fort Worth revolves around Sundance Square. To the north is the Stockyards District, where the Wild West culture is alive and well. About 2.5 miles (4 km) to the west, the Fort Worth Cultural District has some of the country's best museums. The Modern Art Museum is a stunning space with a 3,000-strong collection, and the National Cowgirl Museum and Hall of Fame honors extraordinary women of the American West. Other museums include the Kimbell Art Museum and the Museum of Science and History, which also houses a planetarium. While walking is enjoyable in and around downtown, a car is essential to get around the rest of the city.

Located on the site of Fort Worth's historic red-light district of Wild West saloons, the **Water Gardens** have a variety of waterfalls, cascades, streams, and fountains. Designed by architect Philip Johnson, the park provides welcome relief on hot days.

The heart of downtown, **Sundance Square**'s name is a reminder of the city's Wild West past, when Chisholm Trail cattle drives used to through town, and cowboys and outlaws such as Butch Cassidy and the Sundance Kid frequented the city's many saloons. Filled with well-restored commercial buildings dating from the turn of the 20th century, the square's streets are now lined with theaters, shops, and restaurants, which buzz with dining and drinking culture. The city's symphony orchestra, ballet, and opera companies are all housed here. An important museum is the Sid Richardson Museum on Main Street, which exhibits 60 paintings by artists Frederic Remington and Charles M. Russell. The crown jewel of this area is the Bass Performance Hall – an old-world opera house and home to the city's symphony orchestra, opera, and ballet.

With its cobblestoned streets, raised wooden sidewalks, and period-looking street lights, the engaging ten-block **Forth Worth Stockyards National Historic District** is located 2 miles (3 km) north of downtown. Known as the Stockyards District, it developed alongside the sprawling Fort Worth Stockyards, though these ceased to be commercially viable many years ago. Today,

Did You Know?

Around 60 percent of America's paper money is printed in Fort Worth.

EAT

Woodshed Smokehouse

This rambling, riverside barbecue joint is a deserved local favorite.

🏠 3201 Riverfront Dr
🌐 woodshedsmoke house.com

$$$

Joe T. Garcia's

An iconic Tex Mex joint serving up classic – and delicious – border fare.

🏠 2201 N Commerce St
🌐 joetgarcias.com

$$$

One of the most unforgettable museums and art collections in the US, the **Kimbell Art Museum** is an architectural masterpiece, designed by Louis Kahn in 1971 as a series of vaulted roofs that seem to hover in mid-air. The gallery spaces are bathed in natural light, showing off the diverse collections, which include pre-Columbian Mayan pottery, and jewelry, as well as rare ancient Asian bronzes. Paintings on display range from Baroque and Renaissance masterpieces by Rubens, Rembrandt, Tiepolo, and Tintoretto to a collection of Post-Impressionist and early Modernist works.

Along with the Kimbell Art Museum across the street, the **Amon Carter Museum of American Art** anchors Fort Worth's much-vaunted Cultural District, located 2.5 miles (4 km) west of downtown. The museum concentrates entirely on American art of the Wild West, housing seminal paintings, drawings, and sculptures by Thomas Moran, Frederic Remington, Charlie Russell, and Georgia O'Keeffe, among others. Said to be one of the foremost collections of cowboy art, the museum has over 150,000 pieces, including 66,000 microfilm reels. It also has more than 300,000 photographs documenting the discovery, exploration, and settlement of the country's western frontier.

the neighborhood offers a glimpse of what life in Texas was like a century ago. A number of lively cowboy-themed saloons and honky-tonk nightclubs, many with live music, are also located here. The oldest and most atmospheric of these is the White Elephant Saloon. Also nearby is Billy Bob's Texas. Said to be the largest honky-tonk in the world, it has 42 bar areas, and live bull-riding demonstrations also take place here on weekend nights. Other attractions include a daily parade of longhorn cattle down Exchange Avenue.

↑ Wandering the wide, bright galleries of the Kimbell Art Museum

Sundance Square

📞 (817) 255-5700
🌐 sundancesquare.com

Fort Worth Stockyards National Historic District

📞 (817) 624-4741
🌐 fortworthstockyards.org

Kimbell Art Museum

♿ 🏠 3333 Camp Bowie Blvd 🕐 10am-5pm Tue-Thu & Sat, noon-8pm Fri, noon-5pm Sun 🌐 kimbellart.org

Amon Carter Museum of American Art

🏠 3501 Camp Bowie Blvd 🕐 10am-5pm Tue-Sat (to 8pm Thu), noon-5pm Sun 🌐 cartermuseum.org

Water Gardens

🏠 Houston & Commerce sts
📞 (817) 392-7111

🔍 HIDDEN GEM
National Cowgirl Museum

From sharpshooter Annie Oakley to authors like Laura Ingalls Wilder, this museum tips its hat to courageous pioneer women who shaped the Wild West (www.cowgirl.net).

← A cowgirl statue at Fort Worth's wonderful National Cowgirl Museum

❸

Austin

✈🚌🚍 ℹ️209 E 6th St;
www.austintexas.org

The capital city of Texas, Austin is also renowned as the "Live Music Capital of the World." The singer-songwriter scene has thrived since the 1960s, and musicians as diverse as Janis Joplin and Willie Nelson achieved prominence in Austin. Two music festivals, South by Southwest (SXSW) and the Austin City Limits Festival, are world-famous, hosting an eclectic mix of recognised and emerging artists. The **Austin City Limits at Moody Theater** also hosts around 100 concerts a year.

Although urban, Austin excels at outdoor opportunities and enjoys some 300 days of sunshine every year. Residents think of it as one big playground, making use of 300 parks and miles

> The capital city of Texas, Austin is also renowned as the "Live Music Capital of the World."

of urban trails. Nightly, from April through October, bat colonies take to the skies and spectators flock to Ann W. Richards Congress Avenue Bridge at dusk to watch.

Showcasing the Texan love of all things large, the downtown **Texas State Capitol** has a soaring pink granite dome and is taller than the US Capitol in Washington (p209). Built in 1888, it has 500 rooms covering some 8.5 acres (3.5 ha) of floor space.

Austin is also noteworthy as the home of the state's main university, which gives it a youthful, sociable vibe. North of the Capitol complex, the expansive campus of the **University of Texas** spreads east from Guadalupe Street and encompasses a number of museums and libraries. The **Blanton Museum of Art** has over 17,000 works of art, many of which were donated by novelist James Michener. The **Lyndon Baines Johnson Presidential Library** is a repository for all official documents of the Texas-born Johnson (1908–73), who served as US senator, vice-president, and US president following the assassination of John F. Kennedy (p455).

TOP 4 AUSTIN MUSIC VENUES

Continental Club
🌐continentalclub.com
Nightly live rockabilly, country, rock, jazz and soul since 1955.

Antone's Nightclub
🌐antonesnightclub.com
The home of the blues.

Hole in the Wall
🌐holeinthewallaustin.com
Emerging songwriters.

Broken Spoke
🌐brokenspoke austintx.net
Boot-scootin' line dancing galore.

Austin City Limits at Moody Theater
🏠310 Willie Nelson Blvd
🌐acltv.com

Texas State Capitol
🏠11th St & Congress Av
🕐9am–5pm Mon–Sat (from noon Sun) 🌐tspb.state.tx.us

University of Texas
ℹ️405 W 25th St; www.utexas.edu

The striking Texas State Capitol, with its 300-ft (92-m) pink domed roof ↑

Blanton Museum of Art

♦ ◎ ♿ 🎫 200 E MLK at Congress ⏰ 10am–5pm Tue–Fri (to 9pm every third Thu), 11am–5pm Sat, 1–5pm Sun 🌐 blantonmuseum.org

Lyndon Baines Johnson Presidential Library

🎫 2313 Red River St ⏰ 9am–5pm Mon–Fri 🌐 lbjlibrary.org

4

Fredericksburg

ℹ️ 302 E Austin St; www.visitfredericksburgtx.com

One of the loveliest small towns in Texas, and centerpiece of the rolling Hill Country west of Austin, Fredericksburg was first settled by German immigrants in 1846. This region is home to over 50 wineries and vineyards, with Fredericksburg as its epicenter.

The town is also home to the **National Museum of the Pacific War**, which traces the history of US military activities in the South Pacific during World War II. The museum includes the steamboat-shaped Nimitz Hotel, which was built in the 1850s by the family of US Admiral Chester

↑ Tubing on the Guadalupe River, through New Braunfels

Nimitz, the commander-in-chief of US forces.

Located midway between Fredericksburg and Austin, the boyhood home of the 36th US president has been preserved as the **Lyndon B. Johnson National Historical Park**. Other features of the park are Johnson's one-room rural school and his grave.

National Museum of the Pacific War

♦ ♿ 🎫 340 E Main St ⏰ 9am–5pm daily 🌐 pacificwarmuseum.org

Lyndon B. Johnson National Historical Park

♿ 🎫 US 290 in Johnson City ⏰ 9am–5pm daily 🌐 nps.gov/lyjo

5

New Braunfels

ℹ️ 237 I-35 N; www.nbcham.org

A popular daytrip from San Antonio (*p460*), New Braunfels was one of many towns settled by German immigrants in the tumultuous 1840s, when Texas was an independent republic offering land grants to Anglo-Saxon settlers. The German heritage

still thrives in local architecture, cuisine, language, and festivals – including sausage and beer festivals. New Braunfels is also popular for outdoor activities, chiefly tubing on the Guadalupe.

Built on the site that the town's founder, Prince Carl of Solms-Braunfels, chose for his castle (it was never built), the **Sophienburg Museum and Archives** documents the town's history. Exhibits include local artifacts and re-creations of pioneers' homes and shops.

Sophienburg Museum and Archives

♦ ♿ 🎫 401 W Coll St ⏰ 10am–4pm Tue–Sat 🌐 sophienburg.com

> **Did You Know?**
>
> Austin has celebrated the birthday of A. A. Milne's fictional Eeyore character since 1963.

6

SAN ANTONIO

✈🚃🚌 ℹ 317 Alamo Plaza; (210) 207-6700 🕐 The Alamo: Sep-May:
9am-5:30pm daily; Jun-Aug: 9am-5:30pm Sun-Thu, 9am-7pm Fri & Sat
🌐 visitsanantonio.com

This dynamic city reflects the best of Texas. With its diverse mix
of residents, charming network of waterways and restaurant-
lined streets, and gentle pace of life, you'd be hard-
pressed not to fall in love with this city.

The most historic city in Texas, San Antonio is also the most
popular, both for its pivotal historic role and its natural beauty.
Once home to the Comanche, the riverside site drew the
attention of Spanish missionaries, who founded Mission San
Antonio de Valero in 1718. Later converted into a military outpost and renamed the Alamo, it was the site of the most heroic
episode of the Texan revolution. Predominantly Hispanic and
Mexican in character, San Antonio balances a thriving economy
with a careful preservation of its past. Most of the historic sites
lie within a block of the pedestrian-friendly Riverwalk in the
downtown core, and there are a number of wonderful art
galleries, too, such as the McNay Art Museum.

💬 INSIDER TIP
Blue Star

When you've had your
fill of history, head to
the non-profit Blue Star
Contemporary Art
Center. For just $5 entry
you can take in exhibi-
tions displaying works
by local artists. Note the
center is open only Thu-
Sun (www.bluestar
contemporary.org).

1 In 1836, Mexicans and Texans battled here at the Alamo, as Texas fought for independence. The Texas Republic was born.

2 The bar at the Buckhorn Saloon and Museum is jam-packed with taxidermy.

3 San Antonio's McNay Art Museum has a lovely garden.

MISSIONS NATIONAL HISTORICAL PARK

This 819-acre (331-ha) historical park and UNESCO World Heritage Site preserves four Spanish frontier missions, which, along with the Alamo, formed the northern edge of Spain's North American colonies in the 18th century. Still in use as Catholic parish churches, the former Missions San José, San Juan, Espada, and Concepción spread south from downtown San Antonio along the 9-mile (14-km) "Mission Trail." The finest, Mission San José, is known for its intricately carved Rose Window.

Did You Know?

San Antonio dyes its river green – with eco-friendly dye – on St. Patrick's Day.

←

San Antonio's scenic Riverwalk, with a tour boat on the canal

←

Modern skyscrapers towering above the illuminated streets of downtown Houston

display here is of Surrealist paintings, notably by René Magritte and Max Ernst. The museum also has a world-class collection of Cubist painting by Picasso and Braque in particular, as well as a full survey of 20th-century American paintings. Ancient and medieval art of the Mediterranean, and works by Native peoples of Africa, the South Pacific, and the Pacific Northwest region of North America are also represented. Modern and contemporary works on paper form the fastest growing part of the Menil Collection. These are housed in the Menil Drawing Institute, which opened in late 2018.

The **Museum of Fine Arts** is the oldest art museum in Texas, and one of the largest in the US. Its collections range from Greek and Roman antiquities to Wild West sculptures by Frederic Remington. The striking Beck Building has European art of the late 19th and early 20th century, while other galleries are devoted to works by artists from Africa, the South Pacific, and the Northwest US and Canada.

The largest public gardens, **Bayou Bend**, surround the pink stucco mansion of oil heiress Ima Hogg (1882–1975), who became one of Houston's greatest benefactors. Now run by the Museum of Fine Arts, her home displays a collection

⑦ Houston

✈ 🚗 🚌 ℹ 901 Bagby St; www.visithoustontexas.com

The story of Houston, a city of constant change and great diversity, is a typical Texas success story. Founded in 1836 in what was then a swamp, the city was named in honor of Texas hero General Samuel Houston and served as capital of the Texas Republic until 1839. A center for shipping cotton, Houston's fortunes faded after the Civil War, but it developed into a major port following the construction of a shipping channel to the Gulf of Mexico. The discovery of oil turned the city into a major petrochemical producer, and it has grown into the biggest city in Texas and the fourth-largest in the US. It also has some of the world's finest art museums.

Covering over 600 sq miles (1,554 sq km), Houston is a thoroughly confusing place. The frequent changes in street names and directions, and often heavy road traffic, can make getting around difficult for a first-time visitor. The light-rail system is useful as it links downtown to the museum district. Be prepared to drive – and to get lost more than once. The main visitor attractions lie on and around the Rice University campus.

One of the world's better assemblies of painting and sculpture, the **Menil Collection** was endowed by the family of Houston philanthropist Dominique de Menil, who died in 1997. The most extensive

---

🔍 HIDDEN GEM
Rothko Chapel

This ecumenical chapel, near the Menil Collection, was designed around a series of abstract paintings by artist Mark Rothko, in 1971. It's wonderfully calm inside (*www.rothkochapel.org*).

> **Montrose District is one of the few walkable neighborhoods in Houston, and is especially popular on weekend nights.**

of decorative arts, highlighted by a sugar bowl crafted by Colonial hero Paul Revere.

Montrose is a catch name for the lively collection of galleries, shops, nightclubs, cafés, and restaurants that can be found along Montrose Street and its intersection with Westheimer Road. **Montrose District** is one of the few walkable neighborhoods in Houston and is especially popular on weekend nights.

The mission control for all manned US explorations of space since 1965, the visitor-friendly **Space Center Houston** traces the full story of the Space Race. Visitors can try on space helmets, touch moon rocks, or peer into actual space-ships. Computer simulations let visitors fly the space shuttle or land on the moon. The major attraction of the Space Center is the tour of the still-in-use mission control facilities.

The vast plains of Texas can be seen for miles from the foot of the 605-ft (184-m) San Jacinto Monument in the **San Jacinto Battleground State Historic Site**, claimed to be the world's tallest freestanding masonry monument. It marks the site of the final battle for the independence of the Texas Republic in 1836. The shaft is topped by a huge "Lone Star" of Cordova limestone, while a museum at the base traces the history of the state.

Menil Collection
🏠 1533 Sul Ross St 🕐 11am-7pm Wed-Sun 🌐 menil.org

Museum of Fine Arts
♿ 🏠 1001 Bissonnet St 🕐 10am-5pm Tue & Wed, 10am-9pm Thu, 10am-7pm Fri & Sat, 12:15pm-7pm Sun 🌐 mfah.org

Bayou Bend
♿ 🅿 🏠 6003 Memorial Dr at Wescott St 🕐 10am-5pm Tue-Sat, 1-5pm Sun 🌐 mfah.org

Montrose District
🏠 1409 Sul Ross St 📞 (713) 524-9839

EAT

BB's Tex Orleans
Texas flair meets Cajun cuisine at this popular 24-hr Houston chain.
🏠 2701 White Oak Dr
🌐 bbstexorleans.com
💲💲💲

The Original Ninfa's on Navigation
Specializing in Tejano classics, this joint is famed for its margarita.
🏠 2704 Navigation Blvd
🌐 ninfas.com
💲💲💲

Space Center Houston
♿ 🅿 🏠 1601 NASA Pkwy
🕐 10am-6pm Mon-Fri, 9am-7pm Sat & Sun
🌐 spacecenter.org

San Jacinto Battleground State Historic Site
♿ 🏠 Independence Pkwy 📞 (281) 479-2421 🕐 9am-6pm daily

↑ A painting and sculpture gallery in the city's Museum of Fine Arts

THE GULF COAST

The history of the Gulf Coast is inextricably tied to Central Texas *(p453)*, with Spanish and Mexican rule giving way to independence in 1836 and American statehood in 1845. Mexico established Galveston in 1825 – a major port of entry for immigrants – while Corpus Christi began as a trading post in the 1840s. Malaria, yellow fever, and cholera epidemics were common in the 19th century, with pesticides only bringing mosquitos under control in the 1950s. In 1900 a hurricane devastated Galveston and a storm similarly destroyed much of Corpus Christi in 1919. The region remains vulnerable to hurricanes.

Experience

1. Big Thicket National Preserve
2. Galveston
3. Aransas National Wildlife Refuge
4. Corpus Christi
5. Padre Island National Seashore

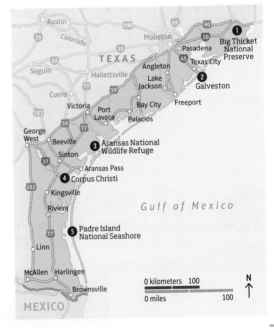

THE GULF COAST

Affectionately dubbed America's "third coast," the bucolic Gulf Coast is a far cry from the great metropolises of northern Texas. The state's coastline is loved for its nostalgic seaside towns and stunning natural beauty. This is the place for being in the great outdoors, spotting local wildlife, and enjoying walks along the never-ending beaches.

❶
Big Thicket National Preserve

🅰 Junction of US 69 & Hwy 420, 8 miles (11 km) N of Kountze Ⓦ nps.gov/bith

A unique mixture of mountains, plains, swamps, and forests, the Big Thicket National Preserve protects 15 distinct biologically diverse areas (9 land units and 6 water corridors) spread over 152 sq miles (393 sq km) along the Texas/Louisiana border.

Did You Know?

Leading out of Big Thicket, Bragg Road is said to be haunted – look for a mysterious floating light.

Although much of the preserve is relatively inaccessible, the area once served as a hideout for runaway slaves and outlaws. Today, it is best known as home to a wide range of plants and animals. A series of short hiking trails offer close-up views of dense groves of resident oaks, cactus, carnivorous "pitcher plants," and millions of mosquitoes.

❷
Galveston

✈ 🚌 ℹ 2328 Broadway; www.galveston.com

Perched on a barrier island on the north of the long Texas coastline, Galveston has a sun-burned character. Originally a notorious hideout for slave-trading Gulf Coast pirate Jean Lafitte, by the 1890s the port had grown to be the largest and wealthiest city in Texas. The economy soon declined following a devastating hurricane in 1900. The subsequent rise of Houston also contributed to Galveston's fading fortunes, and the city was again whipped by a hurricane in 2008.

Many of the city's grand Victorian mansions – such as Ashton Villa, now the site of Galveston Island Visitor Center – and 19th-century storefronts have been restored to their original glory. Strand National Historic Landmark District, near the waterfront, has the greatest concentration of exuberant architecture. This area is also home to a charming pleasure pier, which opened in 2012. It was built on the site of the city's original pleasure pier, which dated from the 1940s but was destroyed by Hurricane Carla in 1961. The Texas Seaport Museum relates the city's history as a port, with an 1873 triple-mast ship moored out front that is open for tours.

Often hailed as one of the state's best resorts on the Gulf of Mexico, the charming island city features more than 30 miles (48 km) of pristine, sandy beaches. East Beach or Appfel Park is

Galveston's pleasure pier, punctuated with thrill rides ↑

→ Two white-tailed deer in Aransas National Wildlife Refuge

the top pick for live music, parties, and sunbathing. Visitors can also indulge in the family-friendly fun of **Moody Gardens**, with its waterpark, a ten-story tropical Rainforest Pyramid, and a series of massive aquariums showcasing life from the world's oceans. Galveston Island State Park protects over 2,000 acres (809 ha) of Gulf Coast barrier island ecosystem, which is home to hundreds of bird species.

Moody Gardens

🔗 🏠 1 Hope Blvd
🕐 10am–6pm daily (Apr-Oct: to 8pm) 🌐 moody gardens.com

3 ✒️

Aransas National Wildlife Refuge

🏠 Hwy 239, 65 miles (105 km) NE of Corpus Christi 🕐 Dawn–dusk 🌐 fws.gov/refuge/aransas

While sun-worshipers flock to the Gulf Coast beaches in winter, birds and bird-watchers congregate slightly inland at the 109-sq-mile (283-sq-km) Aransas National Wildlife Refuge. Established in 1937 to protect the vanishing wildlife of coastal Texas, Aransas is today home to alligators, armadillo, boars, coyotes, white-tailed deer, and many other species of wildlife. The most famous visitors here are the endangered whooping cranes, the tallest birds native to North America. Standing 5 ft (1.5 m) tall, with white bodies, black-tipped wings, and red crowns, the cranes migrate here from Canada between November and March, feeding in the marshes.

Ringed by tidal marshes and broken by long, narrow ponds, Aransas is an ever-changing land that is still being shaped by the turquoise waters of San Antonio Bay and the storms of the Gulf of Mexico. Grasslands, live oaks, and red bay thickets that cover deep, sandy soils provide spectacular background scenery.

4

Corpus Christi

1590 N Shoreline Blvd; www.visitcorpus christitx.org

Corpus Christi is defined by having the deepest commercial port in Texas and an extensive US military presence. Its military importance is marked by the famous 910-ft (277-m) aircraft carrier, the USS *Lexington*, moored along the 2-mile (3-km) downtown waterfront. To its south, the **Texas State Aquarium** explores the sea life of the Gulf of Mexico with whales, rays, and sharks, and re-creations of reefs similar to those that have grown around the Gulf's many offshore oil rigs. Texas river otters and the critically endangered Kemp's ridley sea turtle are also found here.

West of downtown, the **Selena Museum** is another of the city's biggest draws. It pays homage to the singer Selena Quintanilla-Pérez, and is housed in her former studio. Part of the museum is also still a working music and production house, but can be toured on days when the studio is not in use. Inside, displays are dedicated to Selena's life, with memorabilia including her red Porsche.

"Corpus," as locals call the city, looks out across the harbor to Mustang Island State Park, where over 5 miles (8 km) of sandy beach stretch along the Gulf of Mexico. At the park's north end, modern resorts detract from the pleasant natural scenery, overshadowing the historic community of Port Aransas at the island's northern tip.

Texas State Aquarium

2710 N Shoreline Blvd

9am–5pm daily (Memorial Day–Labor Day: to 6pm)

Thanksgiving, Dec 25

texasstateaquarium.org

SELENA QUINTANILLA-PÉREZ

Queen of Tejano Texas and often referred to as "Mexican Madonna," Selena (1971-1995) was an American singer, songwriter, model, and actress. She achieved status as one of the most-revered Mexican-American performers of the 20th century, before being tragically shot by the president of her fan club, aged only 23. Selena's cult-like following still honors her with the Fiesta de la Flor, a two-day festival dedicated to her legacy, held every April in her hometown of Corpus Christi. Her fourth album, *Amor Prohibido*, sold 1,246,000 copies and is the perfect place to start listening.

Padre Island's scenic shoreline, home to white pelicans *(inset)* and many other species of wildlife

EAT

Pop's Tavern & Café

"Pop's Place" is a beloved local seafood spot, perched on the edge of the Rockport bridge. Must-tries include oysters (in season) and blackened gator.

🏠 202 Park Rd 13, Rockport 🕐 Tue 🌐 pops tavernandcafe.com

Wanna Wanna Beach Bar & Grill

This blissful thatched-roof tiki hut pairs icy beers with sizzling seafood fry-ups and boiled shrimp. It's located directly on the sand for unbeatable beach access.

🏠 5100 Gulf Blvd, South Padre Island 🌐 wanna wanna.com

💲💲💲

Selena Museum

⊘ 🏠 5410 Leopard St
🕐 10am–4pm Mon–Fri
🌐 q-productions.com

5

Padre Island National Seashore

📍 20420 Park Road 22, Corpus Christi; www.nps.gov/pais

Bordered by a pair of tourist resorts at its north and south ends, Padre Island is a slender sandbar that stretches for more than 110 miles (177 km) between Corpus Christi and the Mexican border. The central 65 miles (105 km) have been preserved as the Padre Island National Seashore, which, with few roads and no commercial development, is among the longest wild stretches of coastline in the country. The park is open throughout the year for camping, surfing, swimming, hiking, fishing, and various other activities. Coyotes and other native wild animals still roam the heart of the island.

The Padre Island National Seashore is also known as a nesting habitat for endangered Kemp's ridley sea turtles. The turtles are closely protected, and visitors who arrive in the area in late summer (typically from mid-June through August) may be able to participate in a turtle release. The hatchlings can take up to 45 minutes to make their way to the water, so there's time to get a good look.

This is one of the South's most popular vacation spots. The area receives an average of 800,000 visitors per year, especially during the Spring Break, when university students from colder climes flock here to unwind and party. South Padre Island marks the southern end of the Gulf Coast of Texas.

> **The Padre Island National Seashore is also known for its lovely bathing spots, and as a nesting habitat for endangered Kemp's ridley sea turtles.**

PANHANDLE AND THE WEST

The Spanish were unable to establish permanent rule in West Texas. From the 1750s to the 1860s, the Comanche controlled a large area dubbed Comancheria, but their hegemony was destroyed by smallpox, cholera epidemics, and conflict with Anglo-American settlers in the 1840s. The Panhandle first saw American farmers settling in the 1870s, with Amarillo founded in 1887, booming as a cattle depot; Abilene and Lubbock also emerged in the 1880s. The region was hard hit by the Depression and a devastating drought in the 1950s.

Experience

1 Fort Davis
2 Big Bend National Park
3 Terlingua
4 Marfa
5 El Paso
6 Guadalupe Mountains National Park
7 Canyon
8 Amarillo
9 Lubbock
10 Abilene

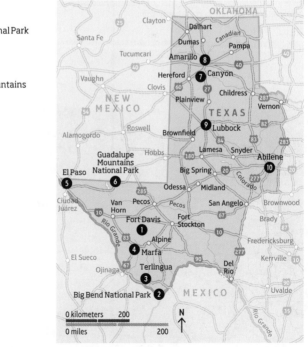

PANHANDLE AND THE WEST

This is the Texas of popular imagination. Great expanses of arid land, punctuated only by a lone turbine or spinning tumbleweed, the landscape between New Mexico and Oklahoma is eerie and otherworldly. Incredible national parks and characterful small towns provide respite and a change of pace from the open road.

❶ Fort Davis

🛈 4 Memorial Square; www.fortdavis.com

Situated in the scenic Davis Mountains, Fort Davis is a popular destination for visitors seeking relief from a typical Texas summer. A key site during the Indian Wars of the 19th century, it was originally established in 1854 as a US Army fort along the main road between El Paso and San Antonio (p460). Today, it has been preserved as the **Fort Davis National Historic Site**. In summer, costumed interpreters help visitors on self-guided tours through the site's restored structures.

The area's high altitude and isolation from large cities has also made it a fine location for astronomical research. Located atop Mount Locke, 17 miles (27 km) northwest of town, the **McDonald Observatory** gives visitors the opportunity to see stars and planets. The Hobby-Eberle spectroscope here has a 430-inch (1,092-cm) mirror, the world's largest.

Fort Davis National Historic Site

⌖ 🅐 Hwy 17 🕒 8am–5pm daily 🚫 Federal hols 🅦 nps.gov/foda

McDonald Observatory

🅐 Hwy 118 🕒 10am–5:30pm daily (check website for evening schedule) 🚫 Jan 1, Thanksgiving, Dec 25 🅦 mcdonaldobservatory.or

❷ Big Bend National Park

🛈 Panther Junction; www.visitbigbend.com

One of the wildest and most isolated corners of the US, this diverse park sprawls across southwest Texas. The name "Big Bend" comes from the 90-degree turn made by the Rio Grande as it carves its way toward the Gulf of Mexico

450

The number of bird species in Big Bend National Park.

through the volcanic rock of the San Vicente and Sierra del Carmen Mountains. From river canyons along the Rio Grande to the pine-forested Chisos Mountains, Big Bend offers a complete experience of the landscapes that define the American Southwest. These contrasts in topography have created a unique diversity of plant and animal habitats.

❸ Terlingua

🌐 ghosttowntexas.com/ terlingua

Although it resembles an abandoned movie set, Terlingua was a real mining town that went bust. The thriving cinnabar mining operation fell apart in 1911, when the market for mercury crashed, and the miners abandoned the town and their homes. Today, visitors will find a ghost town with little beyond crumpling buildings and empty mine shafts – although the town has been slightly revitalized with rustic Texas lodgings

and a fully operational saloon. You can pick up a brochures for self-guided walking tours from the preservation society.

❹ Marfa

🌐 visitmarfa.com

A seven-hour drive from Austin (p458), avant-garde artists mingle with cowboy culture in this tiny but thriving art community, whose celebrity visitors have included Beyoncé and Solange.

Although the town was first established in 1883 to service the railroad, it was popularized as an arts centre by artist Donald Judd. Arriving in the 1970s from New York, the sculptor transformed many buildings into art galleries and studios, and erected outdoor installations – many of which are still on display at the Chinati Foundation Museum, a former army barracks.

Ballroom Marfa is another must-visit; it's an edgy art space located in an Art Deco dance hall. Instagram favorite

Prada Marfa – the fake Prada store installation by artists Elmgreen & Dragset – is about 30 minutes outside town. Marfa has less than 2,000 residents, but it's stacked with fine hotels and trendy restaurants.

❺ El Paso

✈🏠🚌 ℹ 1 Civic Center Plaza; www.visitelpaso.com

Located on the northern bank of the Rio Grande, El Paso has long been part of the largest and liveliest international community along the US/ Mexico border. In 1598, Spanish explorer Juan de Onate crossed the river from Mexico and named the place "El Paso del Rio del Norte." It took another 80 years before the city was established with a trio of Catholic missions at Ysleta, Socorro, and San Elizario. Still in operation, the missions are among the oldest communities in Texas. A museum at the **Chamizal National Memorial** details the story of Rio Grande and its international border. The memorial is a 55-acre (22-ha) park on the US side.

Chamizal National Memorial
🏠 800 S San Marcial St
🕐 Exhibits: 10am–5pm daily; grounds: 7am–10pm daily
🌐 nps.gov/cham

↑ Rio Grande sweeping through the dramatic landscape of Big Bend National Park

6

Guadalupe Mountains National Park

🛈 US 62/180; www.nps.gov/gumo

This national park covers 85,000 acres (34,398 ha) of rugged landscape and is a virtually road-free region on the Texas/New Mexico border. The mountains also make up portions of the world's most extensive Permian limestone fossil reef, El Capitan, while Guadalupe Peak is the highest point in Texas. Formed as part of the same prehistoric limestone that makes up the nearby Carlsbad Caverns National Park (p534), the Guadalupe Mountains reward visitors with lofty peaks, spectacular views, unusual flora and fauna, and a colorful record of the past.

Although named for the notorious Wild West town in Kansas, Abilene evolved from a frontier settlement to a solid, stable community.

A short trail from the visitor center leads to the remains of a stone wall and foundations of a former frontier stagecoach station. This was built as part of the Butterfield Trail, which first linked St. Louis and California in 1858.

A few miles northeast of the visitor center, a forest of hardwood trees lines the trail of McKittrick Canyon. Here lies the site's most famous attraction, the spectacular red-and-orange foliage in October and November. The hiking trails between the canyon walls that shelter a perennial stream are also very popular.

7

Canyon

🛈 1518 5th Av; www.visitcanyontx.com

Taking its name from the beautifully sculpted geology of nearby Palo Duro Canyon, this tiny Texas town is also home to the largest and best-known historical museum in the state. The **Panhandle-Plains Historical Museum**, housed in a stately 1930s complex on the campus of West Texas A&M University, holds over three million exhibits tracing the history of north-central Texas. Flint arrowheads from the Alibates quarry, north of Amarillo, highlight the culture of the region's prehistoric people, while geology and paleontology come together in exhibits exploring prehistoric dinosaurs and their relation to the region's petroleum industry. Cattle ranching is explored through the life of Wild West rancher Charles Goodnight, who led the fight to save native bison from extinction. His home is now preserved in the enjoyable "Pioneer Town," located behind the museum.

East of town, **Palo Duro Canyon State Park** protects the massive, deep red and yellow sandstone gorge also known as the "Grand Canyon of Texas." A number of scenic drives and hiking routes run between the rim and the canyon floor. Palo Duro is home to a wide variety of flora and fauna, including spring wildflowers, mule deer,

← Admiring the striking fall colors within Guadalupe Mountains National Park

↑ The eye-catching *Cadillac Ranch*, an art installation outside downtown Amarillo

and wild turkeys. In summer, one of the canyon's 600-ft (183-m) cliffs forms the backdrop for the pageantry of *Texas*, a popular play on the history of the state.

Panhandle-Plains Historical Museum
2503 4th Av Jun-Aug: 9am-6pm Mon-Sat; Sep-May: 9am-5pm Tue-Sat panhandleplains.org

Palo Duro Canyon State Park
Hwy 217 8am-6pm daily (Mar-Nov: later closing) palodurocanyon.com

8

Amarillo

1000 S Polk St; www.visitamarillotx.com

The commercial heart of the sprawling Texas Panhandle region, Amarillo was first settled in 1887 along the Santa Fe Railroad. The city later thrived thanks to its location along the legendary Route 66. The route is now immortalized by **Cadillac Ranch**, a Pop Art work created from ten classic Cadillac cars planted nose-down in a pasture west of downtown. Another more typically Texas experience is the Amarillo Livestock Auction, where modern-day cowboys buy and sell their cattle.

Cadillac Ranch
S side of I-40 between Hope Rd & Arnot Rd exits 24 hrs

9

Lubbock

1500 Broadway; www.visitlubbock.org

Home to 30,000 sports-crazy students at Texas Tech University, this cattle-ranching and cotton-growing city is perhaps best known for its musical progeny. Local musicians including Roy Orbison, Joe Ely, Waylon Jennings, and Tanya Tucker are all honored in Lubbock's guitar-shaped **Buddy Holly Center**, a musical Hall of Fame named for the city's favorite son, Charles Hardin Holley.

Other aspects of Lubbock history are covered in the Texas Tech University's **Ranching Heritage Center**, an outdoor assembly of historic structures from all over Texas. Over 30 original ranch buildings are on display, from cowboy huts to stately overseers' mansions.

Buddy Holly Center
1801 Crickets Av 10am-5pm Tue-Sat, 1-5pm Sun buddyhollycenter.org

Ranching Heritage Center
3121 4th St 10am-5pm Mon-Sat, 1-5pm Sun Federal & university hols nrhc.ttu.edu

10

Abilene

1101 N 1st St; www.abilenevisitors.com

Although named for the notorious Wild West town in Kansas, Abilene evolved from a frontier settlement to a solid, stable community. Also known as the "Buckle of the Bible Belt," thanks to its predominantly Christian colleges, Abilene's past is kept alive at **Buffalo Gap Historical Village**, 14 miles (23 km) southwest of downtown. Founded in 1878, Buffalo Gap maintains over a dozen old buildings, and exhibits include Paleo-Indian artifacts and a frontier weapons collection.

Buffalo Gap Historical Village
133 William St Times vary, check website buffalogap.com

EAT

Cochineal
This is the most in-demand spot in Marfa, with a wine list as long as your arm and a modern American menu.

107 W San Antonio St, Marfa Lunch, Tue, Wed cochinealmarfa.com

$$$

Cagle Steaks & BBQ
This family-run steakhouse is hard to beat. All meat is cooked traditionally on an open grill, best enjoyed with a Texan sunset.

8732 4th St, Lubbock Lunch, Sun, Mon caglesteaks.com

$$$

THE SOUTHWEST

Spectacular Monument Valley, Arizona

EXPLORE
THE SOUTHWEST

This chapter divides the Southwest into four sightseeing areas, as shown on the map below. Find out more about each area on the following pages.

NORTH AMERICA

CANADA

USA

THE SOUTHWEST

MEXICO

Pacific Ocean

Gulf of Mexico

Atlantic Ocean

Seattle
San Francisco
Los Angeles
Chicago
Boston
New York City
Washington, DC
Atlanta
Houston
Miami

WYOMING

NEBRASKA

KANSAS

COLORADO

OKLAHOMA

TEXAS

NEW MEXICO

NEW MEXICO
p524

Colorado Plateau

Sheridan
Thermopolis
Rawlins
Rock Springs
Green River
Vernal
Laramie
Cheyenne
Ogallala
Craig
Fort Collins
Glenwood Springs
Denver
Yuma
Limon
Burlington
Colby
Aspen
Grand Junction
Colorado Springs
Moab
Pueblo
Arkansas
La Junta
Cortez
Durango
Trinidad
Bluff
Raton
Kayenta
Shiprock
Taos
Canadian
Dalhart
Santa Fe
Gallup
Albuquerque
Canadian
Grants
Pecos
Tucumcari
Canyon
Holbrook
Santa Rosa
Clovis
Saint Johns
Socorro
Pecos
Lubbock
San Antonio
Roswell
Brownfield
Silver City
Tularosa
Artesia
Hobbs
Safford
Alamogordo
Duncan
Las Cruces
Carlsbad
Odessa
Deming
La Mesa
Bisbee
El Paso
Pecos
Ciudad Juárez
Van Horn

Green River
White
Green
Colorado
Rio Grande

←

1 Hiking in the Narrows gorge, Zion National Park.

2 Indian teepees at Capitol Reef Resort, Torrey.

3 Scenic Drive in Capitol Reef National Park.

4 Thor's Hammer in Bryce Canyon National Park, seen from the Navajo Loop Trail.

The Southwest is a vast region, but the stunning scenery makes the miles fly by. These itineraries offer options that take in some of the top national parks, cities, and historical sights.

2 WEEKS

touring the Southwest

Day 1

Get an early start from Las Vegas *(p490)* on I-15 North. After 119 miles (192 km), stretch your legs in St. George. The Bear Paw Cafe *(75 N Main Street)* is a good place for coffee or a late breakfast. Continue 42 miles (68 km) to reach your lodgings at Zion National Park *(p508)* by lunchtime. If you're not staying at historic Zion National Park Lodge *(www.zion lodge.com)*, there are several options at Springdale. Ride the park shuttle buses the full length of the canyon, then follow the short River Walk to see the Virgin River emerge from the mouth of the Narrows.

Day 2

Tunnel your way east out of Zion via the extraordinary Zion–Mount Carmel Highway, then head north 75 miles (121 km) to spend the night near the fiery red-rock hoodoos of Bryce Canyon National Park *(p506)*. Hiking the Navajo Loop takes you into the heart of this labyrinth of towering pinnacles, while Sunset Point offers an evening vista of the vast desert ahead. The Lodge at Bryce Canyon *(www.bryce canyonforever.com)* has vintage rooms and cabins and a good restaurant.

Day 3

Continue east along Highway 12, a lovely route through the wilderness of Grand Staircase-Escalante National Monument *(p504)*. Hike to the iridescent waters of Calf Creek Falls; then, back on the road, cross the Hogsback, a knife-edge ridge of

rock with guardrails, to reach Torrey (116 miles/186 km), just west of the forbidding 100-mile (160-km) wall of rock at Capitol Reef National Park *(p509)*. The Capitol Reef Resort *(www.capitolreefresort.com)* has atmospheric accommodations in luxury cabins, teepees, and Conestoga wagons.

Day 4

Drive through the clay badlands that lie east of Capitol Reef on Highway 24 for 80 miles (129 km) to reach Goblin Valley State Park. The bizarre rock formations here resemble fairy-tale monsters. Another 50 miles (80 km) north, visit the museum dedicated to pioneer river-rafter John Wesley Powell in the town of Green River *(p503)*. Moab *(p508)*, 52 miles (84 km) southeast, makes a lively overnight base. The Gonzo Inn *(www.gonzoinn.com)* is a fun choice, with eclectic, colorful rooms and a relaxing pool and hot tub. Moab is on the doorstep of Arches National Park *(p502)*, which holds the world's largest array of naturally formed stone arches. Hike to Delicate Arch for an unforgettable sunset.

Day 5

Stay another night in Moab, and visit the Island in the Sky district of Canyonlands National Park *(p504)*, about a half-hour's drive away. Hike the short trail to Mesa Arch, and take in sweeping views over the mighty canyons carved by the Green and Colorado rivers. Stop off on your way back at the dramatic viewpoints at Dead Horse Point State Park.

→

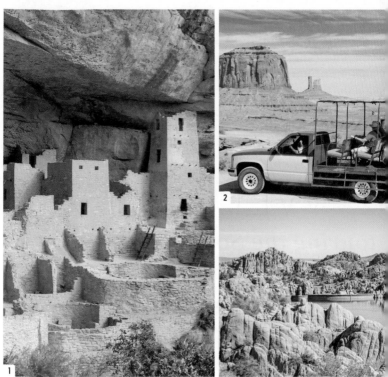

Day 6

Drive east into Colorado from La Sal Junction, south of Moab, to the Rocky Mountains. After 132 miles (212 km), stop at Telluride for lunch at Floradora Saloon (www.floradorasaloon.com), a local favorite. Follow the San Juan Skyway north, which leads up amid the snow-crested peaks to the former mining town of Ouray. Then continue on the Million Dollar Highway over the 11,000-ft (3,350-m) Red Mountain Pass and drop back down to the Wild West outpost of Silverton. Drive 48 miles (77 km) to Durango for an overnight stay at the historic Strater Hotel (www.strater.com).

Day 7

Spend the morning exploring the Victorian frontier town of Durango. Then head west for 56 miles (90 km), climbing into the forested tablelands above the Montezuma Valley to reach Mesa Verde National Park. Take a ranger-led tour to explore inside the fascinating ancient dwellings of Cliff Palace and Balcony House. Spend the night at Cortez, 31 miles (50 km) farther

west. Kelly Place (www.kellyplace.com) is a lovely B&B with prehistoric sites and ruins on its grounds.

Day 8

Southwest of Cortez, 121 miles (195 km) away, Monument Valley Navajo Tribal Park (p520) represents the Wild West at its most majestic. Drive the scenic loop and take a Navajo-guided tour into the backcountry. The View Hotel (www.monumentvalleyview.com) makes an unforgettable stay.

Day 9

About an hour's drive southwest, take a tiny detour to see Navajo National Monument (p523), where the ancient Betatakin pueblo can be visited on guided hikes. Then press on for 118 miles (190 km) to the South Rim of the Grand Canyon (p514), where you'll enter the national park at Desert View. Visit sites along Desert View Drive, including Grandview Point overlook, then check into your hotel in Grand Canyon Village.

1 Cliff Palace, Mesa Verde National Park.

2 Jeep tour around Monument Valley Navajo Tribal Park.

3 A weaver in a hogan, Navajo National Monument.

4 Watson Lake, Prescott.

5 African display in the Musical Instrument Museum, Phoenix.

Day 10

To make the most of a day on the South Rim, set off early to hike part of the Bright Angel Trail down into the canyon; don't try to reach the Colorado River, and turn back well before you're tired. Spend the after-noon touring the Hermit Road, and try to catch the sunset at Hopi Point.

Day 11

Head 80 miles (129 km) southeast to the lively university town of Flagstaff (p513). Visit the Museum of Northern Arizona, explore the historic downtown and venture 9 miles (15 km) east to see ancient ruins in Walnut Canyon National Monument. Stay overnight at the historic Weatherford Hotel (www.weatherfordhotel.com).

Day 12

Drive 30 miles (49 km) on Highway 89A through Oak Creek Canyon to Sedona (p513), cooling off en route with a dip at Slide Rock State Park. Explore Sedona's galleries, tour the Red Rock Country, and relax in Amara Resort and Spa (www.amararesort.com).

Day 13

Head 27 miles (44 km) southwest to the old mining town of Jerome; stop off on the way to see the pueblo ruins at the Tuzigoot National Monument. In Jerome, browse the numerous art galleries and have lunch at the Haunted Hamburger (www.thehauntedhamburger.com). Less than an hour's drive south and set among the cool woodlands of the Prescott National Forest, the charming town of Prescott is the site of beautiful Watson Lake, where you can take a hike before seeing American Western art at the Phippen Museum. Stay overnight at the landmark Hassayampa Inn (www.hassayampainn.com).

Day 14

Drive to Phoenix, about 100 miles (160 km) away. En route, make a short detour to visit the experimental town of Arcosanti to see its ecological landscape-inspired architecture. In Phoenix (p512), visit the Heard Museum to see American Indian art, and the Musical Instrument Museum (www.mim.org), the largest museum of its type in the world.

A DRIVING TOUR
NORTHERN PUEBLOS

Length 45 miles (70 km) **Starting point** Tesuque Pueblo, N of Santa Fe on Hwy 84

The fertile valley of the Rio Grande between Santa Fe and Taos is home to eight pueblos of the 19 American Indian pueblos in New Mexico. Although geographically close, each pueblo has its own government and traditions, and many offer attractions to visitors. Nambe gives stunning views of the surrounding mountains, mesas, and high desert. San Idefonso is famous for its fine pottery, while other villages produce handcrafted jewelry or rugs. Visitors are welcome, but must respect the local laws and etiquette.

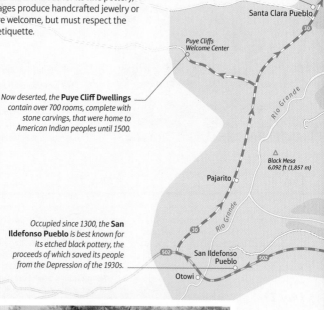

*This small **Santa Clara Pueblo** is known for its artisans and their work. As in many pueblos, it contains a number of craft shops and small studios, often run by the artisans themselves.*

El Guacho

Español

Guachupangue

Santa Clara Pueblo

Puye Cliffs Welcome Center

*Now deserted, the **Puye Cliff Dwellings** contain over 700 rooms, complete with stone carvings, that were home to American Indian peoples until 1500.*

△ Black Mesa 6,092 ft (1,857 m)

Pajarito

*Occupied since 1300, the **San Ildefonso Pueblo** is best known for its etched black pottery, the proceeds of which saved its people from the Depression of the 1930s.*

San Ildefonso Pueblo

Otowi

← Characteristic adobe buildings found in San Ildefonso Pueblo

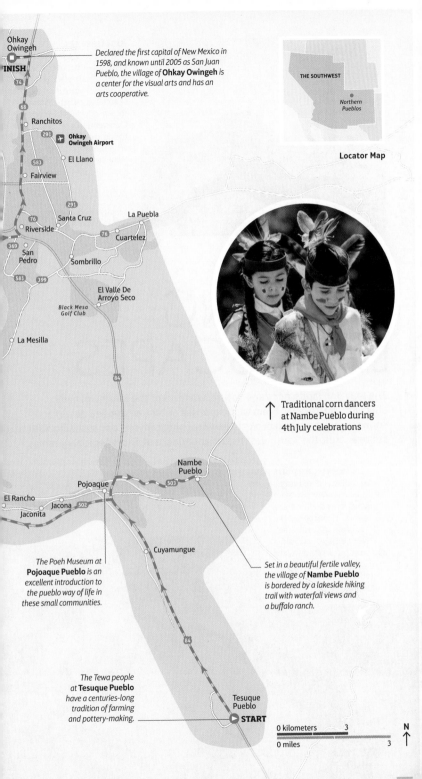

Ohkay
Owingeh
INISH

Declared the first capital of New Mexico in 1598, and known until 2005 as San Juan Pueblo, the village of **Ohkay Owingeh** *is a center for the visual arts and has an arts cooperative.*

THE SOUTHWEST

Northern
Pueblos

Locator Map

Ranchitos

291

Ohkay Owingeh Airport

583

El Llano

Fairview

291

Santa Cruz   La Puebla

76   76   Cuartelez

Riverside

369
San
Pedro   Sombrillo

581   399

El Valle De
Arroyo Seco

*Black Mesa
Golf Club*

La Mesilla

84

↑ Traditional corn dancers
at Nambe Pueblo during
4th July celebrations

Nambe
Pueblo

Pojoaque   503

El Rancho   Jacona   502

Jaconita

Cuyamungue

The Poeh Museum at
Pojoaque Pueblo *is an
excellent introduction to
the pueblo way of life in
these small communities.*

*Set in a beautiful fertile valley,
the village of* **Nambe Pueblo**
*is bordered by a lakeside hiking
trail with waterfall views and
a buffalo ranch.*

84

*The Tewa people
at* **Tesuque Pueblo**
*have a centuries-long
tradition of farming
and pottery-making.*

Tesuque
Pueblo
⏺ **START**

0 kilometers   3

0 miles   3

N
↑

Just Deserts

Each desert in the Southwest has its own distinctive features. The Sonoran Desert is home to the multiarmed saguaro cactus; the Mojave to unique Joshua Trees. In the Chihuahuan Desert you'll find the dunes of New Mexico's White Sands National Monument, the world's largest gypsum dune field *(p534)*.

←

A multiarmed saguaro cactus, native to the Sonoran desert

THE SOUTHWEST'S
AMAZING
LANDSCAPES

The amazing landscapes and natural wonders of the Southwest will stay with you forever. From vast expanses of cactus-studded desert and snowcapped mountain peaks to jaw-dropping canyons and stunning natural stone arches, the Southwest has an abundance of photogenic panoramas.

Craggy Canyons

The Grand Canyon *(p514)* may be the best known, but there are many other breathtaking ravines in the region. The Horseshoe Canyon's Green River creates its awesome curved gorge, while the walls of Arizona's Canyon de Chelly *(p523)* shelter centuries of American Indian heritage.

Did You Know?

The saguaro cactus can take 10 years to grow an inch (2.5 cm) in height.

Ancient Rock

The Southwest is home to some of the most incredible natural arches in the world. Red-tinged Utah is particularly photogenic. There are more than 2,000 of them in Arches National Park *(p502)* alone, while Bryce Canyon *(p506)* holds an army of fascinating formations called hoodoos.

→

Turret Arch, in Arches National Park

Below Ground

Awesome subterranean landscapes mirror the beauty of the Southwest above ground. Carlsbad Caverns *(p534)* is a magical kingdom of soda straws, stalactites, stalagmites, and other magnificent cave formations. In Kartchner Caverns in Arizona, you can walk amid huge mineral columns of a living cave.

←

Stalactites hang from the roof of one of the region's many caves

Montane Vistas

The Rocky Mountains of Colorado and northern New Mexico make a breathtaking backdrop for scenic road trips. Drive the San Juan Skyway for some spectacular panoramas, or chug through the mountains on the historic Durango and Silverton Narrow Gauge Railroad to take in fabulous views from the gondola cars.

↑ Horseshoe Bend, carved out by the winding Green River

→

The tree-lined Durango and Silverton rail route

LAS VEGAS AND NEVADA

American Indian tribes such as the Paiute and Shoshone inhabited the deserts of Nevada long before the arrival of settlers in the 19th century. Spain and Mexico never established real control here, and it wasn't until the silver-mining boom of the late 1850s that Virginia City and Carson City were established. Nevada became a state in 1864, but development was confined to the mining areas on its western border. Nevada legalized gambling in 1931, a decision that saw Reno (founded 1868), then Las Vegas (founded 1905) mushroom as casino boomtowns in the 1940s. Las Vegas is now the "gambling capital of the world."

Experience

1 Las Vegas
2 Valley of Fire State Park
3 Discovery Children's Museum
4 Las Vegas Natural History Museum
5 Boulder City and Hoover Dam
6 Red Rock Canyon
7 Fremont Street Experience
8 Great Basin National Park
9 Virginia City
10 Reno
11 Carson City

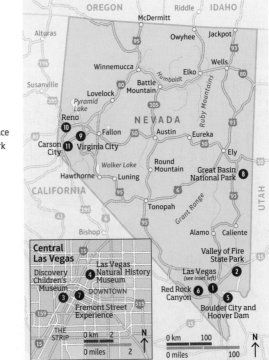

❶

LAS VEGAS

🏠 The Strip ✈️🚌 🌐 visitlasvegas.com

This is fabulous Las Vegas, the country's entertainment capital. The main sights of Nevada's most famous city lie along Las Vegas Boulevard, a sparkling vista of neon known simply as "the Strip." It's here that you'll find lavishly themed hotels, with their own shops, restaurants, and gaming casinos.

The city's famous hotels attract more than 40 million visitors every year. When the lights come on in the evening, these new megaresorts become a fantasyland with riotous design and architecture. Las Vegas's ability to constantly reinvent itself is epitomized by the ever-expanding CityCenter complex, which opened in 2009.

The legalization of gambling in Nevada paved the way for Las Vegas's casino-based growth. The first casino resort, the El Rancho Vegas Hotel-Casino, opened in 1941 and was located on the northern section of the Strip. A building boom followed in the 1950s, resulting in a plethora of resorts. The Sands, Desert Inn, Sahara, and Stardust hotels began the process that transformed the Strip into a high-rise adult theme park. Million-dollar rebuilding programs have replaced all the legendary North Strip resorts and casinos. The facades of the new casinos are designed now to encourage people to walk up and enter to enjoy the casinos, shops, shows, and restaurants inside.

💬 INSIDER TIP
Casino Culture

It's worth tipping when you first sit down at a table, and it is etiquette to tip the dealer if you are winning. Dealers can stop gamblers from making silly mistakes, explaining the finer points of the game.

1941–46

Hotel magnate Thomas Hull builds the luxury El Rancho Vegas, the first resort on the Strip. Mobster Bugsy Siegel builds The Flamingo, a high-class casino, with mafia money increasingly fueling the development of new casinos.

1966–70

Billionaire Howard Hughes arrives and begins investing in Las Vegas properties, bringing legitimate business to the city and ending mob investment. He moves into a luxurious suite on the ninth floor of the Desert Inn hotel.

1931–35

△ Gambling is legalized in Nevada and Las Vegas sees an influx of licensed casinos on Fremont Street. The construction of Hoover Dam spurs the building of casinos and theaters, making the city a hedonistic escape from the Depression.

1950s

▷ The city becomes an entertainment hub. The most famous performers included Peter Lawford, Sammy Davis, Jr., Frank Sinatra, Joey Bishop, and Dean Martin, collectively called the Rat Pack.

1989

△ The opening of Steve Wynn's Mirage ushers in the era of megaresorts; MGM Grand, Luxor, New York-New York, and others open on the Strip.

The Strip at dusk, with the Eiffel Tower of Paris Las Vegas and Bellagio Fountains

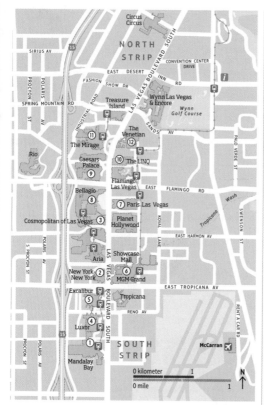

④ Ⓜ Ⓨ
Luxor

🏠 3900 Las Vegas Blvd S
Ⓦ luxor.com

The Luxor's 30-story pyramid opened in 1993. Despite the fact that the resort is named for the Egyptian city of Luxor, which has no pyramid, there is impressive attention to detail in the Ancient Egyptian features. The strongest beam of light in the world is projected from the pyramid nightly.

⑤ Ⓨ Ⓐ
Excalibur

🏠 3850 Las Vegas Blvd S
Ⓦ excalibur.com

The medieval world of King Arthur is the inspiration at this family-friendly resort, with its turrets, moat, and drawbridge. The second floor houses the Medieval Village, where quaint alleyways are lined with shops and restaurants.

⑥ Ⓜ Ⓨ
MGM Grand

🏠 3799 Las Vegas Blvd S
Ⓦ mgmgrand.com

The MGM Grand building is fronted by the famous Leo, a 45-ft- (14-m-) tall bronze lion that serves as the symbol of the MGM film studio. The first MGM hotel was built in the 1970s farther down the Strip, and reopened here in 1993. The MGM Grand is known for its entertainment, and has hosted Barbra Streisand, Andrea Bocelli, and Kanye West.

⑦ Ⓜ Ⓨ Ⓐ
Paris Las Vegas

🏠 3655 Las Vegas Blvd S
Ⓦ parislv.com

Be transported to Paris at this hotel and casino. The facade is composed of replicas of land-

① Ⓜ Ⓨ
Mandalay Bay

🏠 3950 Las Vegas Blvd S
Ⓦ mandalaybay.com

This resort aims to re-create the tropics with an old-world feel. At the south end of the Strip, it has 3,000 rooms and a lagoon-style swimming pool with a sandy beach and water ride. More subtle than other Strip resorts, Mandalay Bay has more than 20 restaurants and the House of Blues Music Hall.

② Ⓨ ▢ Ⓐ
New York-New York

🏠 3790 Las Vegas Blvd S
Ⓦ newyorknewyork.com

This hotel's re-creation of the Manhattan skyline is striking, with a replica of the Statue of

Liberty and some of Manhattan's most famous landmark buildings. Adding to the flavor are many popular New York-style eateries and the Greenwich Village-style brownstones have a wide variety of bars, restaurants, and live music venues, featuring swing, jazz, and rock.

③ Ⓨ
Cosmopolitan

🏠 3708 Las Vegas Blvd S
Ⓦ cosmopolitanlas vegas.com

Situated within two high-rise towers on the Strip, the Cosmopolitan offers a huge casino, an oasis-inspired spa, and three pools. Guests will find a wide variety of cuisines among the two-dozen restaurants here.

↑ Rich interior, including Classical statues, of Caesars Palace

marks such as the Louvre, the Hotel de Ville, and the Arc de Triomphe. A 50-story, half-scale Eiffel Tower dominates the complex, and visitors can ride an elevator to the observation deck at the top or dine in its gourmet restaurant.

⑧ Ⓜ Ⓨ
Bellagio

🏠 3600 Las Vegas Blvd S
Ⓦ bellagio.com

This $1.6 billion luxury resort opened in 1998. Its design is based on the northern Italian town of Bellagio, with terra-cotta-colored Mediterranean buildings set back from the Strip behind a lake modeled on Italy's Lake Como. One of the hotel's many attractions is the sublime fountain display on the lake that springs into action at regular intervals.

⑨ Ⓨ 🏛
Caesars Palace

🏠 3570 Las Vegas Blvd S
Ⓦ caesars.com

Roman statues, Greek columns, and cocktail waitresses in togas can all be found here. This was the first themed hotel on the Strip and quickly established a reputation for attracting top artists to its 4,000-seat Colosseum. Today the hotel houses a lavish casino, four

lounges, a health spa, and the Garden of the Gods – an oasis with seven pools.

⑩ Ⓨ 🖥 🏛
The LINQ

🏠 3535 Las Vegas Blvd S
Ⓦ caesars.com/linq

The LINQ hotel and casino is a relative newcomer to the Strip. It originated in 1959 as the Flamingo Capri, and became the LINQ in 2014. Here you can expect modern rooms, casual eateries, and a pool for day parties. The hotel contains its own shopping district, the LINQ Promenade, plus the mind-boggling High Roller ferris wheel and Fly LINQ zipline.

⑪ Ⓜ Ⓨ 🏛
The Mirage

🏠 3400 Las Vegas Blvd S
Ⓦ mirage.com

The Mirage opened in the fall of 1989, when it was the largest hotel in the US. The Mirage revolutionized the Strip, setting out to draw visitors with attractions other than just the casino. A volcano stands outside the main entrance and erupts, daily at 8pm and 9pm, and at 10pm on Friday and Saturday.

⑫ Ⓜ Ⓨ 🏛
The Venetian

🏠 3355 Las Vegas Blvd S
Ⓦ venetian.com

This was once the home of the "Rat Pack." The facade has copies of the Doge's Palace and Campanile, which overlook the waters of the Grand Canal.

↑ The famous dancing fountains of the Italian-themed Bellagio

AROUND LAS VEGAS

It's not all star-studded performances and gaudy hotels in Las Vegas. Beyond the Strip are the glittering malls and museums in the downtown area. Those who can tear themselves away from Sin City have a wealth of natural beauty and outdoor pleasures on their doorstep, with surrounding canyons, mountains, deserts, and parks on offer.

2

Valley of Fire State Park

🏠 29450 Valley of Fire Rd
🚌 Las Vegas 🌐 parks.nv.gov/parks/valley-of-fire

This spectacularly scenic state park lies some 65 miles (105 km) northeast of the Strip. It derives its name from the red sandstone formations that began as huge, shifting sand dunes about 150 million years ago. The extreme summer temperatures mean that spring or fall are the best times to explore the wilderness. Of the four well-maintained trails, the Petroglyph Canyon Trail is a gentle loop that takes in several prehistoric Ancestral Puebloan rock carvings. One of the most famous depicts an *atlatl*, a notched stick used to add speed and distance to a thrown spear. Ancestral Puebloan people settled in the nearby town of Overton, along Muddy River, around 300 BC. They left some 1,500 years later, perhaps because of a long drought. Archaeologists have discovered hundreds of prehistoric artifacts in the area, many of which are housed in Overton's **Lost City Museum of Archaeology**. Its large collection includes beads, pottery, woven baskets, and delicate turquoise jewelry.

Lost City Museum of Archaeology

 🏠 721 S Moapa Valley Blvd, Overton 📞 (702) 397-2193 🕗 8:30am–4:30pm daily

TOP 5 **VEGAS WEDDING CHAPELS**

Graceland Wedding Chapel
🌐 gracelandchapel.com

The Little Vegas Chapel
🌐 thelittlevegaschapel.com

Chapel of the Flowers
🌐 littlechapel.com

Little Church of the West
🌐 littlechurchofthewest.com

Viva Las Vegas Wedding Chapel
🌐 vivalasvegasweddings.com

3

Discovery Children's Museum

🏠 360 Promenade Place
🕗 Times vary, check website
📅 Jan 1, Easter, Thanksgiving, Dec 24 & 25
🌐 discoverykidslv.org

Nine interactive galleries provide fun hands-on learning activities in science, arts, culture, and early childhood development. There is also a gallery for temporary exhibitions from leading museums.

4

Las Vegas Natural History Museum

🏠 900 Las Vegas Blvd N
🕗 9am–4pm daily
🌐 lvnhm.org

A popular choice with families who need a break from the Strip resorts, this museum has an appealing range of exhibits. Dioramas re-create the African savanna, while the marine exhibit offers a chance to view live sharks and eels at close quarters. Kids will love the animatronic dinosaurs and the hands-on discovery room,

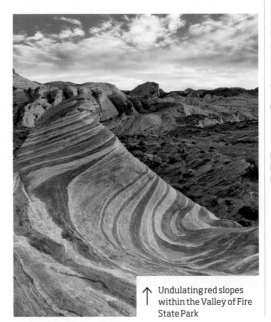

↑ Undulating red slopes within the Valley of Fire State Park

↑ Casinos on Fremont Street, lit up by neon

where visitors can dig for fossils and operate a robotic baby dinosaur.

5 ♿ 🅿

Hoover Dam and Boulder City

📍 30 miles (48 km) E of city center 🚍 🅿 ⏰ 5am–9pm daily 🌐 usbr.gov/lc/hooverdam

The historic Hoover Dam is named after Herbert Hoover, the 31st president. Before its construction between 1931 and 1935, the Colorado River often flooded acres of farmland in Mexico and southern California. Hailed as an engineering marvel, the dam gave this desert region a reliable water supply and provided

Did You Know?

Standing 726 ft (221 m) high, Hoover Dam is the USA's highest concrete arch dam.

inexpensive electricity to Nevada, Arizona, and California. This colossus of concrete is today a huge attraction, offering guided tours into its depths and superb views from the top.

Just 8 miles (13 km) west, Boulder City was built to house the dam's construction workers. Several 1930s buildings remain, such as the historic Boulder Dam Hotel, housing the Hoover Dam Museum.

6 ♿

Red Rock Canyon

📍 10 miles (16 km) W of city center 🅿 ⏰ 6am–dusk daily 🚫 Federal hols 🌐 redrockcanyonlv.org

From downtown Las Vegas it is a short drive west to the low hills and steep gullies of the Red Rock Canyon National Conservation Area. Here, baked by the summer sun, a gnarled escarpment rises out of the desert, its gray limestone and red sandstone the geological residue of an ancient ocean and the huge sand dunes that succeeded it. The canyon is easily glimpsed along a scenic road that loops off Hwy 159,

but the best way to explore is on foot. Watch for the bighorn sheep when hiking.

7

Fremont Street Experience

⏰ Light Shows: 6pm–midnight daily 🌐 vegasexperience.com

Known as "Glitter Gulch," Fremont Street was where the first casinos with neon signs and illuminated icons were located. Following a period of decline during the 1980s and 1990s, a $70-million project was initiated by the city in 1994 to revitalize the area. The street is now a colorful pedestrian mall, covered by a vast steel canopy, from which spectacular sound-and-light shows are projected every night.

Historic casinos along the street include the landmark Binion's, with its old-style Vegas atmosphere, and Four Queens, which claims to have the world's largest slot machine.

NEVADA

Nevada is perhaps most synonymous with adult fun, thanks to the presence of the world's largest gambling and entertainment mecca at Las Vegas *(p490)*. Away from the state's handful of cities, Nevada is mostly uninhabited and eerie desert, with ridge after ridge of rugged mountains dividing the endless sagebrush plains.

8

Great Basin National Park

🏠 5 miles (8 km) W of Baker
ℹ 100 Great Basin Hwy, Baker; www.nps.gov/grba

Travelers driving along the "Loneliest Road in America" are beckoned by the towering silhouette of Wheeler Peak, which stands at the center of this national Park. Below the peak lies the park's centerpiece: the Lehman Caves, discovered by homesteader Absalom Lehman in 1885. Their fantastic limestone formations can be seen on various guided tours of the site. Tours start from the park visitor center, which offers hiking and camping details, along with exhibits on Great Basin's wildlife. The Wheeler Peak Scenic Drive begins near the center and passes through all

the major Great Basin climate zones while climbing steeply over 12 miles (19 km). Great Basin National Park's remote location has made it one of the least-visited national parks in the US, so hikers and campers can find immense solitude amid the landscape.

9

Virginia City

ℹ 86 S C St; www.visit virginiacitynv.com

Prospectors following the gold deposits up the slopes of Mount Davidson discovered one of the world's richest strikes, the Comstock Lode, in 1859. Almost overnight, the bustling camp of Virginia City grew into the largest settlement between Chicago and San Francisco, with over 25,000 residents.

Over the next 20 years, tons of gold and silver were mined here, but by the turn of the 20th century the town had begun to fade. A National Historic Landmark, the city's steep streets offer fine views of the surrounding mountains. Along B Street, the elegant castle is the state's best-preserved mansion. Built in 1863–68, it was once considered to be one of the finest mansions in the west.

The city's main historical museum fills the old **Fourth Ward School** at the south end of C Street. It showcases the city's lively history with topics

BURNING MAN

This annual, nine-day gathering takes place in the Black Rock Desert, northeast of Reno. Tens of thousands of participants construct a temporary city, dedicated to community, art, and self-expression. Known as "Burners," they join in activities including art and musical performances, as well as the ritual burning of a male effigy *(www. burningman.org)*.

← A glassy lake surrounded by mountains within Great Basin National Park

dogsled tours, sleigh rides, and snowshoeing. The **Truckee River Whitewater Park** in downtown Reno is one of the premier white-water parks in the country. Kayaking, tubing, and rafting can be enjoyed, with all equipment available for rent at the park.

The city's **National Automobile Museum** has one of the country's most extensive car collections, showcased against stage-set "streets."

West of Reno, the beauty of Lake Tahoe (*p685*), one of the most popular sites in the western US, greets visitors at the Nevada/California border.

Truckee River Whitewater Park
🏠 Wingfield Park (off W 1st St) 📞 (775) 334-2270

National Automobile Museum
🌐 🏠 10 S Lake St 🕐 9:30am-5:30pm Mon-Sat, 10am-4pm Sun 🌐 automuseum.org

---

11
Carson City
📧 ℹ️ 716 N Carson St, Suite 100; www.visitcarsoncity.com

The state capital and third-largest city in Nevada, Carson City was named after Wild West explorer Kit Carson. Nestled at the base of the eastern escarpment of the Sierra Nevada, the city was founded in 1858, and still retains a few old-fashioned

ranging from mining tools to Mark Twain, who began his career at the city's newspaper.

Fourth Ward School
🌐 🏠 537 South C St 🕐 May-Oct: 10am-5pm daily 🌐 fourthwardschool.org

---

10
Reno
🔀 🏠 📧 ℹ️ 135 N Sierra St; www.visitrenotahoe.com

Reno was Nevada's main gambling destination until it was surpassed by Las Vegas in the 1950s. Although smaller than Vegas, Reno has a similar array of 24-hour casino-fueled fun. It also offers a huge variety of winter and outdoor activities, including ski resorts,

← A red motorcar at Reno's National Automobile Museum

West of Reno, the beauty of Lake Tahoe (*p685*)

---

casinos in its downtown core. The **Nevada State Museum** is housed inside the 1870 US Mint building, where coins were made from Comstock silver. The museum holds a full-scale replica of a working mine, as well as displays on the region's natural history.

On the south side of the city, the **Nevada State Railroad Museum** preserves steam engines from the old Virginia & Truckee Railroad, which carried ore from the Comstock Lode until the 1930s.

Nevada State Museum
🌐 🏠 600 N Carson St 🕐 8:30am-4:30pm Tue-Sun 🌐 nvculture.org

Nevada State Railroad Museum
🌐 🏠 2180 S Carson St 🕐 9am-4:30pm Thu-Mon 🌐 nvculture.org

UTAH

The history of Utah is indelibly linked to the Mormons, who arrived here in 1847 and founded Salt Lake City. The region was originally inhabited by the Shoshone, Ute, Paiute, and Navajo, and formally transferred to US rule in 1848. The Mormons remained virtually autonomous despite conflict with the US over their polygamous practices in the Utah War (1857–58). Disputes continued until Utah was made a state in 1896. With five national parks, several ski resorts, the Sundance Film Festival, and Salt Lake City hosting the 2002 Winter Olympics, tourism has blossomed here.

Experience

1. Great Salt Lake
2. Timpanogos Cave National Monument
3. Salt Lake City
4. Arches National Park
5. Lake Powell and Glen Canyon National Recreation Area
6. Green River
7. Park City
8. Grand Staircase-Escalante National Monument
9. Hovenweep National Monument
10. Canyonlands National Park
11. Bryce Canyon National Park
12. Zion National Park
13. Moab
14. Cedar City
15. Capitol Reef National Park

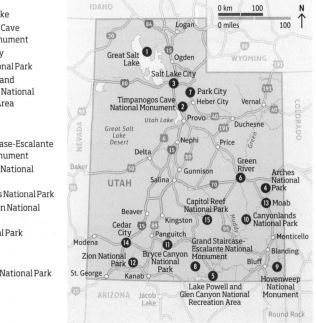

UTAH

Best known as the world headquarters of the Mormon Church, Utah is also home to some of the USA's most remarkable landscapes. The sandstone canyons of the Colorado Plateau are preserved within a series of stunning national parks, while the snowcapped Wasatch Mountains loom in the north. West of these is the state capital, Salt Lake City, Utah's only major city.

❶
Great Salt Lake

🅰 Great Salt Lake State Park, I-80 exit 104 📞 (801) 828-0787 🕐 Apr-Sep: dawn-dusk daily; Oct-Mar: 7am-5pm daily

The largest salt lake in North America, the Great Salt Lake is a shallow remnant of the prehistoric Lake Bonneville. Depending on the weather, the lake covers an area ranging from 1,000 sq miles (2,590 sq km) to 2,500 sq miles (6,477 sq km). The salt flats stretching west from the lake to the Nevada border are so hard and expansive that they have long been used as a proving ground for automobile racers.

Apart from some algae and microscopic brine shrimp, the lake itself supports almost no life. However, the **Antelope Island State Park**, located in the middle of the lake, is home to resident herds of bighorn sheep, mule deer, bison, and its namesake, the pronghorn antelope. Access to the island, which lies about 40 miles (64 km) northwest of Salt Lake City, is by way of a 7-mile- (11-km-) long causeway. Visitors can camp or swim along the shore or take guided lake cruises. You'll also find excellent picnic spots.

West from Salt Lake City, toward the lake's south shore, the Great Salt Lake State Park offers a broad, sandy beach with a marina and observation deck, which provides plenty of stunning views.

Antelope Island State Park

♿ 🅰 I-15 exit 335 📞 (801) 773-2941 🕐 Oct-Apr: 6am-6pm daily; May-Sep: 6am-10pm daily

❷ ♿
Timpanogos Cave National Monument

🅰 Hwy 92, American Fork 🕐 Mid-May-mid-Oct: times vary, check website 🚫 Mid-Oct-mid-May 🌐 nps.gov/tica

One of the most popular destinations around Salt Lake City, the Timpanogos Cave National Monument lies deep beneath the 11,750-ft (3,581-m) summit of Mount Timpanogos. The site preserves a trio of massive limestone caverns stretching nearly 1,800 ft (549 m) into the mountain. Reached by way of a steep, 1.5-mile (2-km) uphill hike from the visitor center, and linked by man-made tunnels, the three caves are very cool (43° F/ 6° C), very damp, and full of spectacular

Did You Know?

The town of Levan – which is "navel" spelled backward – is found at the supposed "belly-button" of Utah.

↓ The vast, calm waters of Great Salt Lake in Utah

DRINK

High West Distillery & Saloon

This Old Town saloon features a bar made from the Trestle Bridge of 1804. The food is Western-inspired, and cocktails are prepared using spirits made at the on-site distillery.

🏠 703 Park Av, Park City
🌐 highwest.com

---

limestone formations. Electric lights showcase the sundry stalactites, stalagmites, crystalline helictites, and other water-sculpted formations, all of which are still being formed. Only a limited number of people are allowed inside, so visitors should come early in the day or during the week, or call ahead for reservations.

Timpanogos Cave is one of the many highlights of the drive along the 40-mile (64-km) Alpine Loop, which follows Highway 92 around the landmark mountain. Many campgrounds, picnic spots, scenic views, and hiking trails can be enjoyed by trekkers along the way.

---

❸ Salt Lake City

🚂🏠🚌 ℹ️ 90 South West Temple St; www.visit saltlake.com

Pleasant and friendly Salt Lake City makes a great stopover for weary travelers between Denver (p566) and San Francisco (p648). Although its name derives from the undrinkable alkaline Great Salt Lake that spreads to the west, the city actually has abundant fresh water, thanks to the rain and snowmelt of the Wasatch Range, which rises to the east. Founded and controlled by the Mormons since 1847, the city spreads for miles and miles along the base of the snowcapped peaks.

Apart from its spectacular natural setting, Salt Lake City is also known as the spiritual base of the Mormon church, which has its worldwide headquarters in Temple Square downtown. Here, the six spires of the main Mormon temple and the famous oblong auditorium of the **Mormon Tabernacle**, built in 1867, stand side by side. The Mormon Tabernacle choir rehearsals are open to the public.

To the west of Temple Square, the amazing **Family History Library** holds records of Mormon family trees dating back to the mid-16th century. Eastward, the 1850 Beehive House has been preserved as it was when Mormon leader Brigham Young, the second president of the Mormon church, lived here. At its entrance stands the stately 76-ft (23-m) Eagle Gate, which is capped by a 4,000-pound (1,800 kg) eagle with an impressive wingspan of 20 ft (6 m). To the north stands the domed Utah State Capitol,

↑ The soaring spires of Salt Lake Temple, downtown Salt Lake City

modeled after the US Capitol, which features a series of exhibits on Utah's history.

Mormon Tabernacle
🏠 Temple Square
🕐 9am–9pm daily
🌐 templesquare.com

Family History Library
🏠 35 NW Temple St 📞 (866) 406-1830 🕐 8am–5pm Mon, 8am–9pm Tue–Fri, 9am–5pm Sat; always call in advance 🚫 Jan 1, Jul 4, Thanksgiving, Dec 24–26

THE MORMONS

The Church of Jesus Christ of Latter Day Saints, believed to be "another revelation of Jesus Christ" by its leaders, was founded by Joseph Smith (1805–44), a farm worker from New York State. In 1820 Smith claimed to have seen visions of the Angel Moroni, who led him to a set of golden tablets that he translated and later published as the Book of Mormon, thus establishing the Mormon Church. Although this new faith grew rapidly, it attracted hostility because of its political and economic beliefs, and the practice of polygamy. Seeking refuge, the Mormons moved to Illinois in 1839, where Smith was killed by an angry mob. Leadership passed to Brigham Young, who led the members west in the hope of escaping persecution and setting up a safe haven in Salt Lake Valley. The pioneers traveled across bleak prairies and mountains in primitive wagons, and finally established successful farming communities across Utah's wilderness. Today, Mormons form 60 percent of Utah's population.

EAT

Milt's Stop & Eat
Stop here for old-fashioned malts at the 1950s-style counter.

🏠 356 Millcreek Dr, Moab 🕐 Mon
🌐 miltsstopandeat.com

$$$

Moab Diner
This sparsely decorated diner is popular with locals and tourists alike.

🏠 189 S Main St, Moab
🕐 Sun 🌐 moabdiner.com

$$$

Sunset Grill
The big draws here are the views and the chocolate mousse pie.

🏠 900 N Route 191 on Main St, Moab 🕐 Sun
🌐 moabsunsetgrill.com

$$$

4

Arches National Park

🏠 Hwy 191, 5 miles (8 km) N of Moab 🌐 nps.gov/arch

Arches National Park has the the highest concentration of natural sandstone arches in the world. More than 2,000 of these red rock natural wonders have formed over millions of years. The park "floats" on a salt bed, which once liquefied under the pressure exerted by the rock above it. About 300 million years ago, this salt layer bulged upward, cracking the sandstone above. Over time the cracks eroded, leaving long "fins" of rock. As these fins in turn eroded from the ground up, the remaining sections of overhead rock formed arches, which range today from the solid-looking Turret Arch to the graceful Delicate and Landscape arches. The latter is a slender curve of sandstone stretching more than 300 ft (91 m) in length, which is the longest natural arch in the US.

↑ The famous Delicate Arch and *(inset)* the Fiery Furnace, two of the most spectacular sights within Arches National Park

5

Lake Powell & Glen Canyon National Recreation Area

🏠 2 miles (3 km) N of Page on Hwy 98, off Hwy 160
🏠 ℹ Carl Hayden Visitor Center; www.nps.gov/glca, lakepowell.com

The Glen Canyon National Recreation Area (NRA), established in 1972, covers more than one million acres (400,000 ha) of dramatic desert and canyon country around the 185-mile- (298-km-) long Lake Powell, which is named after John Wesley Powell. The massive lake was created by damming the Colorado River and its tributaries to supply electricity to the region's growing population.

Park. Within the area is the Antelope Canyon, a famously deep "slot" canyon. Other highlights include Lees Ferry, a 19th-century Mormon settlement that now offers tourist facilities, and the Rainbow Bridge National Monument. Rising 309 ft (94 m) high, this is the largest natural bridge in the world.

Today, the lake is busy with water-sports enthusiasts and houseboat parties, exploring the myriad sandstone side canyons. Glen Canyon is also one of the most popular hiking, biking, and 4WD destinations in the country.

---

❻

Green River

ℹ️ 460 E Main St; www. greenriverutah.com

Located in a broad, bowl-shaped valley, the town here grew around a ford of the wild Green River in the 19th and early 20th centuries. Today, it is a launching spot for white-water rafting on the Green and Colorado rivers. It was from here that the explorer and ethnologist John Wesley Powell (1834–1902) began his intrepid exploration of the Colorado River and Grand Canyon in 1871. The **John Wesley Powell River History Museum** has 20,000 sq ft (1,860 sq m) of displays tracing the history of the area's exploration. Principally these displays examine the surveying and fascinating discoveries made by Powell on his expedition.

John Wesley Powell River History Museum

♿ 🅿️ 🏠 1765 E Main St
🕐 Apr–Oct: 9am–7pm Mon–Sat, noon–5pm Sun; Nov–Mar: 9am–5pm Tue–Sat
🚫 Federal hols 🌐 johnwesleypowell.com

The construction of the Glen Canyon Dam, completed in 1963, was controversial from the beginning. The spirited campaign, led by the environmentalist Sierra Club, continues to argue for the restoration of Glen Canyon, believing that ancient ecosystems are being ruined. Pro-dam advocates, however, firmly believe in its ability to store water, generate power, and provide recreation.

The "Y"-shaped recreation area follows the San Juan River east almost to the town of Mexican Hat, and heads northeast along the Colorado toward Canyonlands National

---

❼

Park City

ℹ️ 1794 Olympic Parkway & 528 Main St; www.visitparkcity.com

An hour's drive east from downtown Salt Lake City, through the Wasatch Mountains, leads to this popular resort. The city started life in the 1860s as a silver-mining camp and still retains several turn-of-the-20th-century buildings along its photogenic Main Street.

Park City has become world-famous as the home of the prestigious Sundance Film Festival. Founded by actor and director Robert Redford in 1981, the 10-day festival focuses on independent and documentary films, and has become America's foremost venue for innovative cinema, with film stars and fans alike flocking to the city every January. The festival's popularity is linked to Park City's excellent skiing facilities, which were showcased in the 2002 Winter Olympics. Around 350 ski runs criss-cross 7,300 acres (2,950 ha), catering to all abilities. A sense of the city's history can be obtained at **Park City Museum** in the old City Hall.

Park City Museum

🏠 528 Main St 🕐 10am–6pm Mon–Sat (May & Nov: 11am–5pm), noon–6pm Sun 🚫 Jan 1, Thnksg., Dec 25 🌐 parkcityhistory.org

---

💬 INSIDER TIP
Sundance Film Festival

If you're interested in attending Sundance, tickets go on sale in fall but register early to avoid disappointment. You can also try your luck at the box office around 8am on the morning of a showing (www.sundance.org).

⑧
Grand Staircase-Escalante National Monument

🛈 745 E Hwy 89, Kanab; www.ut.blm.gov/monument

Established by President Clinton in 1996, the Grand Staircase-Escalante National Monument encompasses 3,000 sq miles (7,700 sq km) of pristine rock canyons, mountains, and high desert plateaus. It was named for its four 12-million-year-old cliff faces that rise in tiered steps across the Colorado Plateau. To preserve its wild state, no new roads, facilities, or campgrounds are being built here. The spectacular beauty of this vast untamed area is best explored on scenic drives combined with day-long hikes. Just south of Highway 12 stands **Kodachrome Basin State Park**, a distinctive landscape noted for its 67 freestanding sand pipes or rock chimneys, formed millions of years ago as geyser vents.

Kodachrome Basin State Park
 📞 (435) 679-8562
🕐 Dawn-dusk daily

⑨
Hovenweep National Monument

🅰 E of Hwy 191 🔲 nps.gov/hove

The six separate sets of ruins at this Ancestral Puebloan site were discovered by W.D. Huntington, leader of a Mormon expedition, in 1854. The culture at Hovenweep, a Ute word meaning "Deserted Valley," reached its peak between 1200 and 1275. Very little is known of the site's builders beyond the clues found in the round, square, and D-shaped towers, and pottery and tools that they left behind.

Many researchers have speculated that the towers may have been built as defensive fortifications, astronomical observatories, storage silos, or as religious structures for the community.

> INSIDER TIP
> **State Park Fees and Passes**
>
> Like the national parks, most state parks charge a day-entry fee. If you are planning to visit several parks, check to see if they offer passes for unlimited admission. Camping fees are extra.

⑩
Canyonlands National Park

🛈 Grand Viewpoint Rd, Moab; www.nps.gov/cany

Millions of years ago, the Colorado and Green rivers cut winding paths deep into rock, creating a labyrinth of rocky canyons that forms the heart of this stunning wilderness. The rivers' confluence divides the park into three districts – the Maze, the Needles, and the grassy plateau of the Island in the Sky. Established as a national park in 1964, most wilderness travel here requires a permit.

↑ Jacob Hamblin Arch, Grand Staircase-Escalante National Monument

EXPLORING CANYONLANDS NATIONAL PARK

The park has many good hiking trails. At Island in the Sky, Mesa Arch is reached by a short, easy trail that starts halfway along the main road. The views through the arch make it a great spot for photos, especially at sunrise. At Grand View Point, you can walk a mile along the edge of the canyon to a second awesome overlook at the end of the mesa. In the Needles, easy-to-moderate hikes include the Cave Springs trail, which leads to a historic cowboy camp and prehistoric petroglyphs, and the Pothole Point trail. Both districts contain more strenuous and overnight hikes. The Maze area is best tackled by hardy back-country veterans. You'll need a permit to visit the more remote areas; check the website for permit info.

Locator Map

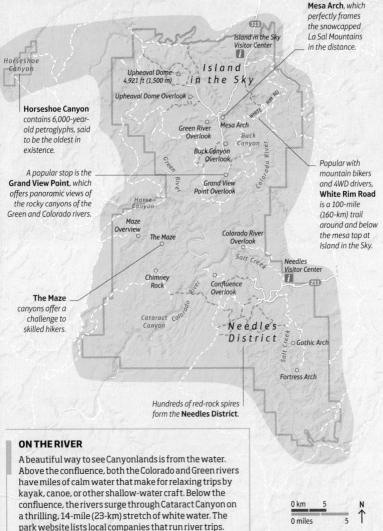

An easy and rewarding 500-yard (457-m) trail leads to **Mesa Arch**, which perfectly frames the snowcapped La Sal Mountains in the distance.

Horseshoe Canyon contains 6,000-year-old petroglyphs, said to be the oldest in existence.

A popular stop is the **Grand View Point**, which offers panoramic views of the rocky canyons of the Green and Colorado rivers.

The Maze canyons offer a challenge to skilled hikers.

Popular with mountain bikers and 4WD drivers, **White Rim Road** is a 100-mile (160-km) trail around and below the mesa top at Island in the Sky.

Hundreds of red-rock spires form the **Needles District**.

Island in the Sky Visitor Center

Upheaval Dome 4,921 ft (1,500 m)

Upheaval Dome Overlook

Island in the Sky

Green River Overlook

Mesa Arch

Buck Canyon

Buck Canyon Overlook

Grand View Point Overlook

Horse Canyon

Maze Overview

The Maze

Colorado River Overlook

Chimney Rock

Confluence Overlook

Cataract Canyon

Needles Visitor Center

Needles District

Gothic Arch

Fortress Arch

Horseshoe Canyon

ON THE RIVER

A beautiful way to see Canyonlands is from the water. Above the confluence, both the Colorado and Green rivers have miles of calm water that make for relaxing trips by kayak, canoe, or other shallow-water craft. Below the confluence, the rivers surge through Cataract Canyon on a thrilling, 14-mile (23-km) stretch of white water. The park website lists local companies that run river trips.

0 km 5
0 miles 5

N

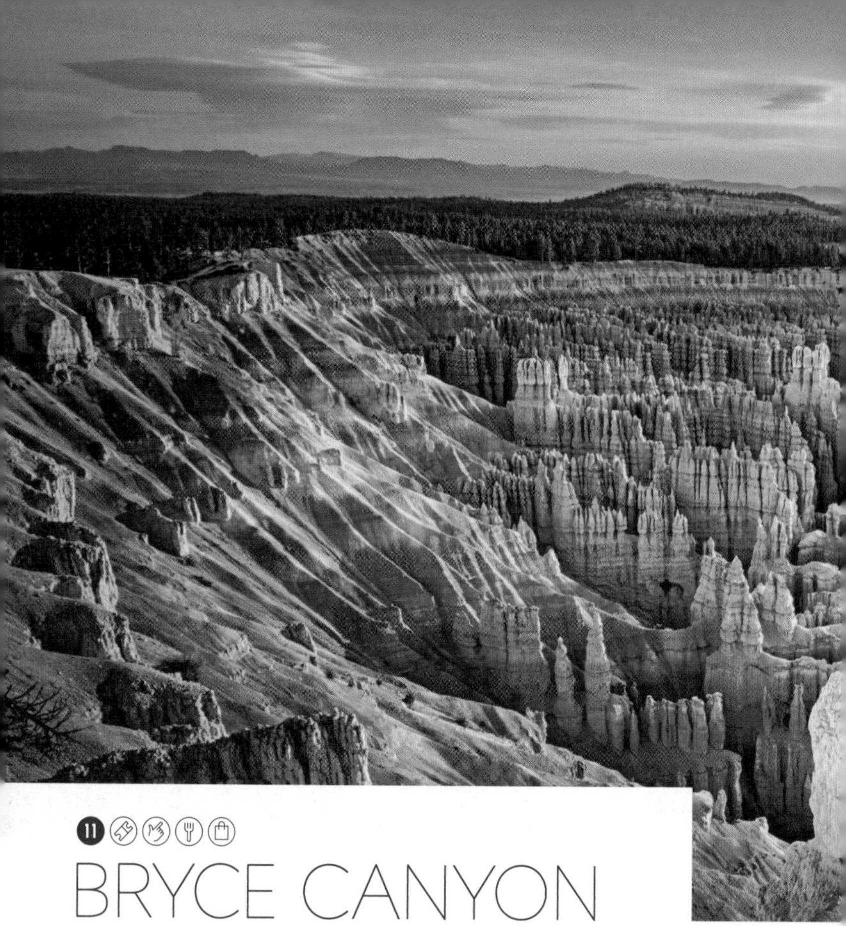

BRYCE CANYON NATIONAL PARK

⌂ Hwy 63, off Hwy 12 ⏏🚌 ⓦnps.gov/brca

Despite its name, this spectacular landmark is not a solitary canyon, but a series of deep amphitheaters. The largest of these, Bryce Amphitheater, is filled with flame-colored pinnacle rock formations called hoodoos, the hallmark of this national park. Bryce Canyon contains more hoodoos than any other place on earth.

The Paiute Indians, once hunters here, described these vast mesmerizing fields of irregular pink, orange, and red spires as "red rocks standing like men in a bowl-shaped recess."

Bryce is high in altitude, reaching elevations of 8,000–9,000 ft (2,400–2,700 m). A scenic road runs for 18-miles (30-km) along the rim of Paunsaugunt Plateau, from the park's only entrance in the north to its highest elevation in the south. From April to October, a free shuttle bus operates from the visitor center to the four main viewpoints at Sunrise, Sunset, Bryce, and Inspiration Points. There is also a free three-and-a-half-hour bus tour that stops at many more viewpoints and goes all the way to the end at Rainbow Point. From Bryce Point and Sunset Point you can look down over the tight maze of hoodoos and fins known as the Silent City. Nearby is the Bryce Canyon Lodge, a National Historic Landmark built in 1923.

GREAT VIEW
Pretty Peaks

Bryce Canyon is famous for its clear skies. Most days, you can see Navajo Mountain, 80 miles (129 km) south on the Utah-Arizona border. On very clear days you can see across the Grand Canyon to Humphrey's Peak, which is 150 miles (242 km) away.

The hoodoos of Bryce
Amphitheater viewed from
Inspiration Point at dawn

→

A hiker setting out on
one of the park's many
trails that start along
the canyon rim

←

A Utah prairie dog in the park, which
is home to one of the largest groups
of this threatened species

⑫
Zion National Park

📍 Hwy 9, near Springdale
🌐 nps.gov/zion

At the heart of this beautiful national park lies Zion Canyon, perhaps the most popular of all of Utah's natural wonders. It was carved by the powerful waters of the Virgin River and then widened, sculpted, and reshaped by wind, rain, and ice. Its majestic walls rise up to 2,000 ft (600 m) and are shaped into jagged peaks and formations in shades of red and white.

The Virgin River meanders quietly through banks of wildflowers, cottonwood, oak, and willow trees, which grow beneath the sloping walls of the canyon. These wild meadows and luxuriant foliage along the river account for the area's abundant wildlife. In summer, the park shuttle is the only way into the canyon. A number of hiking trails of varying length and difficulty start at the shuttle stops along the way. The Zion Narrows Trek, which entails a tough 16-mile (26-km) hike wading through the river, is the most challenging of all.

---

⑬
Moab

ℹ️ 25 E Center St; www.discovermoab.com

A town of dramatic ups and downs, Moab is currently riding its second great boom since the 1950s. Once a quiet Mormon settlement, the discovery in 1952 of several major uranium deposits outside town made Moab one of America's wealthiest communities. When the uranium market declined in the 1970s, the town was saved by tourism and its proximity to Arches and Canyonlands national parks. Many Western movies, including some John Wayne Westerns and the Indiana Jones classics, were also shot here.

Today, Moab is a top destination for lovers of the outdoors. Mountain bikers come here for the challenging ride from Moab Rim, reached by Moab Skyway, a scenic tram ride offering panoramic views of the area. Numerous hiking trails and 4WD routes take in some of this region's fabulous landscapes. Moab is also a major center for white-water rafting on the Colorado River. **Matheson Wetlands Preserve** off Kane Creek Boulevard has 2 miles (3 km) of hiking trails along a riverside wetland, home to birds and indigenous wildlife.

Matheson Wetlands Preserve
♿ 📍 Off Kane Creek Blvd
📞 (435) 259-4629 🕐 Dawn–dusk daily

---

⑭
Cedar City

🚗🚌 ℹ️ 581 N Main St; www.visitcedarcity.com

Founded by Mormons in 1851, Cedar City developed as a center for mining and smelting iron. The Frontier Homestead

↑ The Virgin River winding through Zion Canyon, bordered by lush foliage

Sunset over snow-dusted cliffs at Cedar Breaks National Monument ↑

State Park Museum offers a glimpse of this pioneering spirit and features a large collection of early vehicles. The town is within an hour's drive of Zion National Park, and is also popular for its Shakespeare Festival, staged in a replica of London's neo-Elizabethan Globe Theatre and held annually from late June to mid-October. East of town, the spectacular **Cedar Breaks National Monument** features limestone cliffs and a lake topped by a deep green forest. In winter, the area is a popular skiing resort.

Cedar Breaks National Monument

⊕ 🅐 Off Hwy 14 🆆 nps.gov/cebr

🕒 ⊗ ⊗

Capitol Reef National Park

🅐 10 miles (16 km) E of Torrey, Hwy 24 🆆 nps.gov/care

Covering 378 sq miles (980 sq km), this spectacular park encloses a 100-mile- (160-km-) long colorful wall of rock that was thrust up by the earth 65 million years ago. The strata buckled upward then folded back on itself, trapping water in the process. Around 100 years ago, prospectors crossing the desert were forced to stop at this wind-carved Waterpocket Fold. They likened the rock barrier to an ocean reef and thought its round white domes looked just like the US Capitol building, hence the park's name. As the light changes through the day, the multicolored cliffs, buttes, and rock formations do indeed resemble a tropical reef.

An adventurous drive along the partly unpaved Notom-Bullfrog Road provides a good overview of the area. Cars can negotiate the road in dry weather, but extra gas and water are essential. Capitol Gorge, to the north,

Did You Know?

Capitol Reef National Park is home to around 22 orchards planted by Mormon settlers in the 1880s.

💬 INSIDER TIP
Park Programs

There are many free, ranger-led activities in Capitol Reef National Park. These include hikes and bird walks, Ride with a Ranger shuttle tours, nature center youth programs, and evening talks on stargazing and wildlife.

can be reached via a scenic route that extends for approximately 10 miles (16 km) into the heart of the park. Guided walking tours are available during summer, but only experienced hikers should attempt to explore the backcountry here.

To the north of the park lies the 1908 Gifford Farmhouse. Now a cultural center, this building is dedicated to the 1880s Mormon settlement that once flourished here. Fremont Canyon, on its right, features the famous Fremont Petroglyphs, created by the Ancestral Puebloans between AD 700 and 1250. Farther north is the Cathedral Valley, named for the rock monoliths that tower over the desert.

ARIZONA

The Spanish founded Catholic missions in Arizona from 1700, though attacks by the Apaches kept development to a minimum. In 1848 the US acquired Arizona above the Gila River – and the Gadsden Purchase of 1854 added territory to the south. Phoenix was settled in 1867, and gold, silver, and copper were discovered, transforming mining camps such as Tombstone into Wild West boom-towns. In 1901 the railroad reached Grand Canyon's South Rim, initiating large-scale tourism. Arizona became a state in 1912 but remained primarily rural until the 1950s, when retirees began arriving from the northeast and the population grew rapidly.

Experience

1 Phoenix

2 Sedona

3 Montezuma Castle National Monument

4 Flagstaff

5 Grand Canyon National Park

6 Amerind Foundation

7 Saguaro National Park

8 Tucson

9 Tombstone

10 Monument Valley Navajo Tribal Park

11 Hopi Cultural Center

12 Petrified Forest National Park

13 Pima Air and Space Museum

14 Navajo National Monument

15 Window Rock

16 Canyon de Chelly National Monument

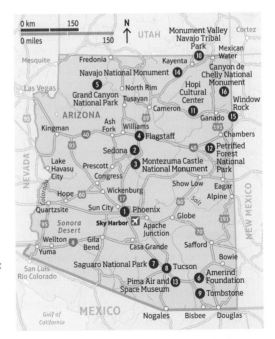

ARIZONA

Arizona offers a range of stunning natural beauty, from the eerily mesmerizing Sonoran Desert in its southwest corner to the high desert plateaus, canyons, and mountains of the north; the romanticized "Wild West" of cowboy films. Over 25 percent of Arizona is American Indian reservation land, and the state also houses several Ancestral Puebloan ruins.

> **Did You Know?**
>
> Lake Havasu City in Arizona is home to London Bridge, transported from the UK in the 1960s.

1 Phoenix

⊠ 🚍 *i* Suite 120, 125 North 2nd St; www.visitphoenix.com

Stretching across the entire Salt River Valley, Arizona's capital, Phoenix, started out as a farming town in the 1860s and soon developed into the economic hub of the state. There are now over 1.5 million people within the city and almost twice that in Metropolitan Phoenix.

Downtown's Washington Street houses the copper-domed Arizona Capitol Museum, originally the state legislature. The museum documents the state's political history. More glimpses of the city's history can be seen in the restored Victorian houses on Heritage Square, some of which have been converted into tearooms and museums. Nearby stands the modern Arizona Science Center, with over 300 interactive science exhibits offering virtual reality trips through the human body.

North of downtown is the highly acclaimed Phoenix Art Museum, renowned for its stimulating temporary exhibitions. The second floor houses works by 18th- and 19th-century American artists, particularly those painters connected with the Southwest.

The **Heard Museum**, farther north, was founded in 1929 by Dwight Heard, a wealthy rancher and newspaper tycoon, whose wife, Maie, amassed an extraordinary collection of Southwestern American Indian art. The museum exhibits over 40,000 works, but its star attraction is the display of more than 500 *kachina* dolls, which are small, vibrantly painted wooden dolls.

About 7 miles (11 km) east of downtown is Papago Park with its distinctive red rock formations, museums, and Desert Botanical Garden. Immediately south of the park, the Hall of Flame Fire Museum houses a large collection of firefighting equipment dating from the early 1700s, while a few miles to the north lies the city of Scottsdale, founded in the late 19th century and now famous for its world-class golf courses. Scottsdale's quiet, tree-lined streets attracted the visionary architect Frank Lloyd Wright to establish his winter studio Taliesin West here in 1937. The huge complex is now an architecture school

→

The wraparound veranda of a hotel in downtown Flagstaff

Heard Museum

 2301 North Central Av 🕘9:30am–5pm Mon–Sat, 11am–5pm Sun 🌐heard.org

---

➋
Sedona

ℹ️331 Forest Rd; www.visitsedona.com

Sedona sits amid magnificent red-rock cliffs and canyons south of Flagstaff. Its awesome scenery has formed the backdrop for dozens of Hollywood Westerns, but the town shot to fame in the 1980s when psychics identified "vortexes" in the area, and it became a spiritual destination for upscale New Agers.

➌
Montezuma Castle National Monument

📍Hwy I-17, exit 289 🕘8am–5pm daily 🌐nps.gov/moca

Dating from the 1100s, the pueblo remains that make up Montezuma Castle occupy an idyllic location, built into the limestone cliffs high above Beaver Creek. Declared a National Monument in 1906, this cliff dwelling was once home to the Sinagua people, and the visitor center today has a display on Sinaguan life.

The National Monument also incorporates Montezuma Well, a natural sinkhole to the northeast that had great religious significance for the American Indians, with several tribes believing it was the site of the Creation.

➍
Flagstaff

🚉🚌ℹ️Amtrak depot, 1 E Rte 66; www.flagstaffarizona.org

Nestling among the pine forests of northern Arizona's San Francisco Peaks, Flagstaff is one of the region's most attractive cities. Its historic downtown dates from the 1890s, when the city developed as a lumber center.

Flagstaff's Northern Arizona University is home to two campus art galleries. The Beasley Gallery holds temporary exhibitions and student work, while the Northern Arizona University Art Museum has the permanent Weiss collection, with works by the Mexican artist Diego Rivera.

Situated on Mars Hill is the 1894 Lowell Observatory, named for its wealthy benefactor Percival Lowell, who wanted to look for life on Mars. Although he did not succeed, the observatory earned repute with its documented evidence of an expanding universe, along with the discovery of Pluto by astronomer Clyde Tombaugh.

Northwest of downtown is the **Museum of Northern Arizona**. It holds a vast collection of Southwestern archaeological artifacts, and also presents an excellent overview of Ancestral Puebloan history and contemporary Navajo, Hopi, and Pai cultures. The award-winning anthropology exhibition in the Ethnology Gallery documents 12,000 years of American Indian cultures on the Colorado Plateau.

Museum of Northern Arizona

 3101 N Fort Valley Rd 🕘10am–5pm Mon–Sat, noon–5pm Sun 🌐musnaz.org

↑ Vibrant skyline of Phoenix, backed by an imposing mountain range

and a working design studio. The Cosanti Foundation, west of Taliesin West, was established by the Italian architect Paolo Soleri (1919–2013), to further his study of "arcology": a combination of architecture and ecology to create new urban habitats. South of here is the Camelback Mountain, one of Phoenix's most distinctive landmarks, which was named for its humped shape.

More glimpses of the area's American Indian past can be found at the Pueblo Grande Museum, which is dedicated to the study of the people who lived there from the 8th to the 14th centuries. Reproductions of adobe Hohokam homes can be viewed, and the museum offers workshops and activities to promote an understanding of the Hohokam culture.

5 ⚒ 🏞 🍴 🖥

GRAND CANYON NATIONAL PARK

✕ 🅿 🚌 🕐 South Rim: year-round daily; North Rim: mid-May–mid-Oct: daily
ℹ Mather Point; www.nps.gov/grca

One of the world's great natural wonders, the Grand Canyon offers awe-inspiring beauty on a vast scale and is an instantly recognizable symbol of the Southwest. Its beauty is revealed in the ever-shifting patterns of light and shadow and the colors of the rock, bleached white at midday, but bathed in red and ocher at sunset.

An iconic World Heritage Site, the Grand Canyon National Park covers 1,904 sq miles (4,930 sq km) and is made up of the canyon itself, which starts where the Paria river empties into the Colorado, and surrounding lands that stretch from Lees Ferry to Lake Mead. The area gained national park status in 1919. The park has two main entrances, on the North and South rims of the canyon. The southern section of the park receives the most visitors and can become very congested during the summer season. Visitors can park in nearby Tusayan and take a free shuttle bus to the South Rim.

The canyon is 277 miles (446 km) long, an average of 10 miles (16 km) wide, and around 5,000 ft (1,500 m) deep. It was formed over a period of six million years by the Colorado River, whose

GREAT VIEW
Hopi Point

Projecting far into the canyon, the tip of Hopi Point offers one of the best spots for viewing sunsets along Hermit Road. As the sun sets, it highlights the canyon's numerous beautiful sculpted peaks.

Did You Know?

The temperature at the Grand Canyon varies by 20° F (11° C) from top to bottom. It is hotter at the bottom.

↑ A ranger leading tourists on a mule ride along the narrow trails of the South Rim

fast-flowing waters sliced their way through the Colorado Plateau, which includes the gorge and most of northern Arizona and the Four Corners region. The plateau's geological vagaries have defined the river's twisted course and exposed vast cliffs and pinnacles that are ringed by rocks of different color, variegated hues of limestone, sandstone, and shale. The magnificent rock formations, with towers, cliffs, steep walls, and buttes, recede as far as the eye can see, their bands of rock varying in shade, as light changes through the day. The park's main roads, Hermit Road and Desert's View Drive, start at Grand Canyon Village and encompass a selection of the choicest views of the gorge. Walking trails along the North and South rims offer staggering views, but to experience the canyon at its most fascinating, explore the more challenging trails that lead to the canyon floor.

HERMIT ROAD

Running from Grand Canyon Village west to Hermits Rest, this 7-mile (11-km) road follows the canyon rim and provides some of the best canyon views from anywhere. It is closed to all private vehicles from March through November, when a free shuttle bus takes visitors between eight stunning overlooks along the way, including Trailview Overlook, Maricopa Point, and Hopi Point. You can also walk between the viewpoints on the Rim Trail, and catch the shuttle at any time. Hermit Road is also a great cycle route. At Hermits Rest there is a rustic-looking gift shop.

↑ The south rim of the utterly breathtaking Grand Canyon

The South Rim

Most of the Grand Canyon's 6.3 million annual visitors come to the South Rim, since, unlike the North Rim, it is open year-round and is easily accessible along Highway 180/64 from Flagstaff *(p513)* or Williams. Hermit Road *(p515)* is closed to private vehicles March through November, but there are free shuttle buses. The longer Desert View Drive (Highway 64) is open all year, winter snows permitting, and leads 60 miles (97 km) in the opposite direction to Cameron. After winding for 12 miles (20 km) from Grand Canyon Village it reaches Grandview Point, where the Spaniards may have had their first glimpse of the canyon in 1540. Ten miles (16 km) farther on lie the pueblo remains of Tusayan Ruin, where a small museum has exhibits on the Ancestral Puebloans. After a few miles, the road leads to Desert View, with a fanciful Watchtower, its upper floor decorated with early 20th-century Hopi murals. It was designed by ex-schoolteacher and architect Mary E. J. Colter, who drew on American Indian and Hispanic styles and is responsible for many of the historic structures that grace the South Rim, including the 1914 Lookout Studio and Hermits Rest, and the rustic 1922 Phantom Ranch on the canyon floor.

Did You Know?

The final scene from *Thelma & Louise* (1991) was filmed in Utah, not the Grand Canyon.

The North Rim

Sited at about 8,000 ft (2,400 m), the North Rim is higher, cooler, and greener than the South Rim, with dense forests of ponderosa pine, aspen, and Douglas fir. Visitors are likely to spot wildlife, such as mule deer, Kaibab squirrel, and wild turkey. The North Rim is reached via Highway 67, off Highway 89A, ending at Grand Canyon Lodge, where there is a campground, gas station, restaurant, and a general store.

STAY

El Tovar

With a perfect location right on the canyon rim, this luxurious landmark lodge, built in 1905, incorporates natural stone and Douglas fir. The restaurant serves excellent Southwestern cuisine.

🏠 1 El Tovar Rd
🌐 grandcanyon lodges.com

$ $ $

Bright Angel Lodge

The famed architect Mary Elizabeth Jane Colter designed this rustic, log-and-stone lodge and cabins in 1935. Accommodations range from basic lodge rooms to historic cabins with fireplace and TV.

🏠 9 North Village Loop Dr
🌐 grandcanyon lodges.com

$ $ $

← A tour group gathered at Mather Point on the canyon's South Rim

↑ Wotans Throne, seen from Cape Royal on the North Rim

The North Rim is twice as far from the river as the South Rim, and the canyon really stretches out from the overlooks, giving a sense of its massive width. There are about 30 miles (48 km) of scenic roads, as well as hiking trails to high viewpoints or down to the canyon floor (of particular note is the North Kaibab Trail that links to the South Rim's Bright Angel Trail). The picturesque Cape Royal Drive starts north of Grand Canyon Lodge and travels 23 miles (37 km) to Cape Royal on the Walhalla Plateau. From here, several famous buttes and peaks can be seen, including Wotans Throne and Vishnu Temple. There are also several short, easy walking trails around Cape Royal. A 3-mile (5-km) detour leads to Point Imperial, the highest point on the canyon rim, while along the way the Vista Encantada has delightful views and picnic tables overlooking the gorge.

The Bright Angel Trail

The most popular of all Grand Canyon hiking trails, the Bright Angel trail begins near the Kolb Studio at the western end of Grand Canyon Village on the South Rim. It then continues via a series of switchbacks down the side of the canyon for 9 miles (14 km). The trail crosses the river over a suspension bridge, ending a little farther on at Phantom Ranch. Do not attempt to walk all the way to the river and back in one day. Temperatures at the bottom of the canyon can reach 110° F (43° C) or higher during the summer. It is essential for day hikers to carry plenty of water and salty snacks in summer.

CALIFORNIA CONDORS

The California Condor is America's largest bird, with a wingspan of over 9 ft (2.7 m). The species was on the edge of extinction in the 1980s, when the last 22 condors were captured for breeding in captivity. In 1996 the first captive-bred birds were released in Northern Arizona. Today, over 80 condors fly the skies over Northern Arizona. They are frequent visitors to the South Rim, though visitors should not approach or feed them.

Sited at about 8,000 ft (2,400 m), the North Rim is higher, cooler, and greener than the South Rim, with dense forests of ponderosa pine, aspen, and Douglas fir.

6

Amerind Foundation

🏛 Dragoon Rd, off I-10
exit 318 🕐 10am-4pm
Tue-Sun 🗓 Federal hols
🌐 amerind.org

The Amerind Foundation is one of the country's most important private archaeological and ethnological museums. The name Amerind is a contraction of "American Indian," and this collection depicts all aspects of American Indian life through thousands of artifacts from different cultures. The displays include Inuit masks, Cree tools, and sculpted effigy figures from Mexico's Casas Grandes.

The adjacent Amerind Art Gallery has a fine collection of Western art by such artists as William Leigh and Frederic Remington. The delightful Spanish Colonial Revival-style buildings are also interesting.

7

Saguaro National Park

🏛 3693 S Old Spanish Trail
🕐 Tucson Mountain District:
dawn-dusk daily; Rincon
Mountain District: 7am-
dusk daily 🌐 nps.gov/sagu

Perhaps the most famous symbol of the American Southwest, the saguaro (pronounced sa-wah-ro) cactus grows only in the Sonoran Desert. The park, which was set up in 1994 to protect this unique species, comprises two tracts of land on the eastern and western flanks of Tucson. Together they cover more than 142 sq miles (368 sq km).

Both sections of the park are equally rewarding. In the west, the 9-mile (14.5-km) Bajada Loop Drive runs deep

→

Saguaro Cacti peppering
the landscape of Saguaro
National Park

Did You Know?

The Saguaro is the largest species of cactus in the US, and can grow up to 5 ft (15 m) tall.

into the park on a dirt road. The Signal Hill Trail leads to ancient Hohokam petroglyphs carved into the volcanic rock. The eastern park has the oldest saguaros, which can be seen along the Cactus Forest Drive. There are also over 100 miles (160 km) of hiking trails here. You'll see an intriguing array of other cacti and desert plants; watch for desert wildlife, including roadrunners, coyotes, and Gambel's quail.

8

Tucson

❌🏠🚌 ℹ 811 N Euclid Av;
www.visittucson.org

The second-largest city in Arizona, Tucson (pronounced too-sahn) is located on the northern boundary of the Sonoran Desert, in a basin surrounded by five mountain ranges. The town's Colonial past dates to the 1770s, when strong resistance from the local Tohono O'odham and Pima tribes forced the Spanish to move their regional fortress from nearby Tubac to Tucson.

The city's major sights are clustered around the University of Arizona campus and the historic downtown area. The El Presidio district occupies the area where the original Spanish fortress was built, with many of the historic buildings there converted into restaurants, offices, and shops. Five of El Presidio's oldest dwellings form a part of the Tucson Museum of Art, with its excellent collections of pre-Columbian artifacts, and contemporary American and European work. Southeast of the museum, the Pima County Courthouse is a fine example of Spanish Colonial Revival style.

The St. Augustine Cathedral is southwest of El Presidio. Begun in 1896, the cathedral is modeled after the Spanish Colonial style of the Cathedral of Querétaro in central Mexico. The Barrio Historic District,

↑ The pink and elegant Pima County Courthouse in Tucson

farther south, was once a business district. Today, its quiet streets are lined with brightly painted adobe houses.

The University of Arizona campus houses several museums. The most notable is the Arizona State Museum, renowned for its collections of artifacts covering 2,000 years of American Indian history. The Museum of Art is also excellent, focusing on European and American fine art.

Metropolitan Tucson extends into the surrounding mountain ranges. Mount Lemmon, the highest peak, is to the north, while to the west is one part of the Saguaro National Park.

About 14 miles (22 km) west of the university lies the fascinating Arizona-Sonora

Desert Museum, which includes a botanical garden, zoo, and a natural history museum.

Nearby is the Old Tucson Studios, a Wild West theme park originally built as a set for a Western movie in 1939. Some of Hollywood's most famous Westerns, such as *Gunfight at the OK Corral* (1957), were filmed here.

The Southwest's oldest and best preserved Mission church lies south of Tucson. The 1797 **San Xavier del Bac Mission** is built of adobe brick and is considered the finest example of Spanish Colonial architecture in the US. Its highlights include a Baroque facade and a spectacular main altar.

San Xavier del Bac Mission

🕐 🚹 1950 W San Xavier Rd, on I-19 🕐 7am–5pm daily
🌐 sanxaviermission.org

9

Tombstone

🚹 109 S 4th St; www. tombstonechamber.com

The site of the 1881 gunfight between the Earp brothers, Doc Holliday, and the Clanton gang at the **OK Corral**, Tombstone was founded by Ed Schieffelin, who went prospecting on Apache land in 1877 despite a warning that "all you'll find out there is your

---

---

tombstone." He found a silver mountain instead, and his sardonically named shanty town boomed with the ensuing silver rush.

In 1962 the town became a National Historic Landmark. The OK Corral is preserved as a museum, and regular re-enactments of the infamous gunfight are staged daily.

Tombstone Courthouse, the county's seat of justice from 1882 to 1929, is now a State Historic Site. It contains a museum featuring the restored courtroom and historical artifacts.

OK Corral

♿ 🚹 326 E Allen St 🕐 9am–5pm daily 🌐 ok-corral.com

Tombstone Courthouse

♿ 🕐 🚹 223 Toughnut St 🕐 9am–5pm daily 🌐 azstateparks.com

⑩ 🚴 🥾 🍴 🏕

MONUMENT VALLEY NAVAJO TRIBAL PARK

🏠 Hwy 163 🕐 Dawn–dusk daily 🌐 navajonationparks.org/tribal-parks/monument-valley

Located within the Navajo Reservation on the border of Arizona and Utah, Monument Valley is full of awe-inspiring sandstone buttes and mesas that soar upward from a seemingly boundless desert.

These ancient, towering rocks have come to symbolize the American West, largely because Hollywood has used these breathtaking vistas as a backdrop for hundreds of movies, TV shows, and commercials since the 1920s.

Centuries ago, Monument Valley was a lowland basin. Over time, eroded material from the Rocky Mountains built up layers of sediment, and pressure from below the surface uplifted the basin into a high plateau. Forces of erosion then chiseled through the layers of hard and soft rock, creating the spectacular formations that rise above the valley floor. The Three Sisters are among the most distinctive pinnacle rock formations at Monument Valley. Others include the Totem Pole and the "fingers" of the Mittens.

The valley was home to the Ancestral Puebloan people until AD 1300. Over 100 sites and ruins have been found dating from these ancient people, including petroglyphs.

Today, these lands are sacred to the Navajo. Apart from a designated scenic drive and hiking trail, other areas within the tribal park are accessible only with a licensed guide. The park is spectacular at night too, with dark skies that reveal billions of stars and the timeless wonder of the landscape.

↑ The Three Sisters and other formations reflected in a car mirror

↑ The Milky Way sparkling over the alien-looking terrain of Monument Valley

HOLLYWOOD IN MONUMENT VALLEY

Director George B. Seitz first used the area's spectacular buttes as a backdrop in his 1924 film, *The Vanishing American*. A young John Wayne – and the Western movie genre itself – shot to stardom with John Ford's first film here, *Stagecoach* (1939). Ford shot nine more movies in Monument Valley, including *The Searchers* (1956), hailed as one of the finest Westerns ever made. Sergio Leone paid homage to Ford with his 1968 film, *Once Upon a Time in the West*. Monument Valley has also starred in such classics as *2001: A Space Odyssey* (1968), *Easy Rider* (1969), *Thelma & Louise* (1991), and *Forrest Gump* (1994).

The iconic Left Mitten, Right Mitten, and Merrick Butte in the glow of the sunset ↑

Landscape of striped red-rock boulders in the Hopi Indian Reservation ↑

11 🏍️ 🍴 🛍️

Hopi Cultural Center

🏠 Hwy 264, Second Mesa 🕐 9am–5pm daily (extended hours in summer) 🌐 hopiculturalcenter.com

Believed to be direct descendants of the Ancestral Puebloans, the Hopi have lived in and cultivated this barren reservation area for almost a thousand years. They worship through the *kachina*, the living spirits of plants and animals, believed to visit the tribe during the growing season. Most Hopi villages are located on or near one of three mesas (flat-topped elevations), named First, Second, and Third Mesa. Artisans of each mesa specialize in particular crafts.

Visitors can take a guided walking tour of the impressive pueblo, **Walpi**, on the First Mesa. Inhabited since the 12th century, it was built to be easily defended against possible Spanish or Navajo attacks. It straddles a dramatic knife-edge of rock, extending from the tip of the First Mesa. In places, Walpi is less than 100 ft (33m) wide, with a drop of several hundred feet on both sides. The tour includes stops

where visitors can purchase *kachina* dolls, handcrafted pottery, rugs, and baskets, or sample the Hopi *piki* bread. A wider range of Hopi arts and crafts are available in the galleries and stores of the Second Mesa. The Hopi Cultural Center here has a restaurant and the only hotel for miles around, as well as a museum that has an excellent collection of photographs depicting various aspects of Hopi life.

On the Third Mesa, Old Oraibi pueblo, thought to have been founded in the 12th century, is fascinating because of claims that it is the oldest continually occupied human settlement in North America.

Walpi

🏍️ �“ 🕐 Tours: 9:30am–3pm daily 🌐 experiencehopi.com

🔍 HIDDEN GEM
Tuba City

Northwest of the Hopi Cultural Center, Tuba City is home to 65-million-year-old dinosaur tracks. Visit the Explore Navajo Interactive Museum to learn about the city's history.

---

12 🏍️

Petrified Forest National Park

🏠 Hwy 180, off I-40 🕐 Park road hours vary, check website 🌐 nps.gov/pefo

This fossilized prehistoric forest is one of Arizona's most unusual attractions. Millions of years ago, rivers swept trees downstream into a vast swamp that once covered this whole area. Groundwater transported silica dioxide into downed timber, eventually turning it into the quartz stone logs seen today, with colored crystals preserving the shape and structure of the trees.

Running the entire length of the forest is the famous Painted Desert. This is an area of colored bands of sand and rock that change from blues to reds throughout the day as the shifting light catches the different mineral deposits.

A scenic road starting at the visitor center travels the length of the park. There are nine overlooks along the way, including Kachina Point, where the Painted Wilderness trailhead is located. Near the south end of the road is the fine Rainbow Forest Museum.

13

Pima Air and Space Museum

📍 6000 E Valencia Rd
🕐 9am-5pm daily (last adm 3pm) 🌐 pimaair.org

The Pima Air and Space Museum contains one of the largest collections of aircraft in the world. Visitors are met with the astonishing sight of more than 300 vintage aircraft set out in ranks across the desert. The VC-118 "Air Force 1" planes used by presidents Kennedy and Johnson are on display here, alongside a replica of the Wright brothers' famous 1903 aircraft and bombers from World War II. Exhibits in five aircraft hangars show military and aviation memorabilia, including a replica World War II barracks. The adjacent Davis-Monthan Air Force Base displays more than 2,000 planes, including B-29s and supersonic bombers.

14

Navajo National Monument

🕐 9am-5pm daily (extended hours in summer) 🌐 nps.gov/nava

Although named because of its location on the Navajo Reservation, this monument is actually known for its Ancestral Puebloan ruins. The most accessible ruin here is the well-preserved 135-room pueblo of Betatakin, which fills a vast, curved niche in the cliffs of Tsegi Canyon. A short trail from the visitor center leads to an overlook, which provides a captivating view of Betatakin. For a closer look at these ancient houses, visitors can take the five-hour hiking tours held daily from late May to early September.

A demanding 17-mile (27-km) hike leads to Keet Seel, a more impressive ruin. Only a limited number of permits to visit it are issued each day, and the hike requires overnight camping at a site with the most basic facilities. Keet Seel was a larger and more successful community than Betatakin. Construction began here in about 1250, but the site is thought to have been abandoned by 1300.

15

Window Rock

📞 ℹ️ Hwy 264; (928) 871-6436

Window Rock is the capital of the Navajo Nation, the largest American Indian reservation in the Southwest. The town is named for the natural arch found in the sandstone cliffs located about a mile north of the main strip on Highway 12.

The **Navajo Nation Museum** in Window Rock is one of the largest American Indian museums in the country. The

huge hogan-shaped building houses displays that cover the history of the Ancestral Puebloans and the Navajo.

Navajo Nation Museum
📍 Hwy 264 & Post Office Loop Rd 🕐 8am-5pm Mon, 8am-6pm Tue-Fri, 9am-5pm Sat 🚫 Federal hols
🌐 navajopeople.org/nnm

16

Canyon de Chelly National Monument

📍 2 miles (3.5 km) E of Chinle & Hwy 191 🕐 8am-5pm daily 🌐 nps.gov/cach

The thousand-foot (305-m) cliffs of the Canyon de Chelly boast of a long and eventful history of human habitation. Archaeologists have found evidence of four periods of American Indian culture, starting with the Basketmaker people around AD 300, followed by the Ancestral Puebloans in the 12th century. They were succeeded by the Hopi, who lived here seasonally for around 300 years, taking advantage of the canyon's fertile soil. Today, the canyon is the cultural and geographic heart of the Navajo Nation, where Navajo farmers still tend sheep and women weave rugs at outdoor looms. Pronounced "d'Shay," de Chelly is a Spanish corruption of the Navajo word *tsegi*, meaning rock canyon.

←

Exhibits at the Pima Air and Space Museum

NEW MEXICO

New Mexico has a rich indigenous culture that dates back thousands of years. The Ancestral Puebloans (Anasazi) constructed large cities here but, in the 12th and 13th centuries, they were mysteriously abandoned. The Spanish established Santa Fe in 1610 and Albuquerque in 1706, though they never gained dominance over the American Indians. New Mexico became American in 1848 and a state in 1912; the Navajo were defeated in 1864. Georgia O'Keeffe's landscape paintings of the 1940s made the area around Santa Fe popular with other artists. The first atomic bomb was tested here in 1945, making it a hub for the military (and UFO hunters).

Experience

1. Taos
2. Chaco Culture National Historical Park
3. Very Large Array
4. Santa Fe
5. Albuquerque
6. Acoma Pueblo
7. El Morro National Monument
8. Bandelier National Monument
9. Lincoln Historic Site
10. Roswell
11. White Sands National Monument
12. Gila Cliff Dwellings National Monument
13. Carlsbad Caverns National Park
14. Los Alamos

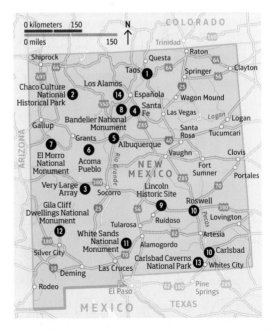

NEW MEXICO

New Mexico's rich heritage and unique mix of American Indian, Hispanic, and Anglo American people make it a fascinating place to visit. The Rocky Mountains offer ski resorts in winter and cool retreats in summer, while northern New Mexico is known for its creative centers of Santa Fe and Taos. In the south, visitors can explore ancient ruins and the cave systems of Carlsbad Caverns.

①

Taos

🚌 Taos Bus Center, Hwy 68
ℹ️ 1139 Paseo del Pueblo Sur;
www.taoschamber.com

The town of Taos, home to Pueblo peoples for around 1,000 years, is now a vibrant artistic center. In 1898, artists Ernest Blumenschein and Bert Phillips stopped here to repair a wagon wheel and never left. In 1915 they established the Taos Society of Artists, which continues to promote the work of local artists. Some of these are exhibited at the Harwood Museum of Art, located in a 19th-century adobe compound. More works by the society's artists are housed in the Blumenschein Home and Museum, nearby.

The tree-lined Spanish Plaza at the heart of Taos makes for a pleasant stroll. East of it is the Kit Carson Home and Museum, which looks at the remarkable life of Carson (1809–68), a fur trapper and soldier.

A few miles north of the town center, Taos' main highway, Paseo del Pueblo Norte, leads to the Millicent Rogers Museum, with its brilliant collection of American Indian arts and crafts, and black-on-black pottery of Puebloan artist Maria Martinez. This road leads to the dramatic Rio Grande Gorge Bridge, the country's second-highest suspension bridge, built in 1965. It offers awesome views of the gorge and the surrounding stark, sweeping plateau.

Taos Pueblo is north of the town. It features two multi-story communal adobe houses still inhabited by villagers, making it one of the oldest communities in the country.

The Hacienda Martinez at Ranchos de Taos, south of the city, is a Spanish Colonial house with thick adobe walls and heavy gates. The 18th-century church of San Francisco de Asis was often painted by

A massive radio telescope, one of the Karl G. Jansky Very Large Array

Georgia O'Keeffe, one of the state's favorite artists.

②

Chaco Culture National Historical Park

🚗 25 miles (40 km) SE of Nageezi off US 550 🕖 7am–dusk daily 🚫 Federal hols
🌐 nps.gov/chcu

One of the Southwest's most impressive cultural sites, Chaco Canyon reflects the

↑ The Kit Carson Home and Museum, a fascinating institution in Taos

One of the Southwest's most impressive cultural sites, Chaco Canyon reflects the sophistication of the Ancestral Puebloan civilization that existed here.

sophistication of the Ancestral Puebloan civilization that existed here. With its six "great houses" (pueblos that contained hundreds of rooms) and many lesser sites, the canyon was once the political, religious, and cultural center for settlements across much of the Four Corners.

Visitors can access the site via a 16-mile (26-km) dirt road that is affected by flash floods in wet weather. A paved loop road in the site passes several of Chaco's highlights. The major stop is Pueblo Bonito, the largest of the "great houses," a D-shaped, four-story structure with more than 600 rooms, and 40 kivas – round, pit-like rooms used for religious ceremonies. Begun around AD 850, it was built in stages over the course of 300 years. Casa Riconada,

which holds the largest religious chamber at Chaco, measuring 62 ft (19 m) in diameter, lies to the southeast.

A short trail from Pueblo Bonito leads to another great house, Chetro Ketl, covering 3 acres (2 ha). The masonry used to build the later portions of this structure is among the most sophisticated found in any Ancestral Puebloan site. A two-hour hike northward leads to Pueblo Alto, built on top of the mesa at the junction of many ancient Chacoan roads.

Very Large Array

🏠 **The Plains of San Agustin, Hwy 60** 🕐 **8:30am–dusk daily** 🌐 **public.nrao.edu/ visit/-very-large-array**

West of Socorro on US Hwy 60 is the surreal sight of 27 enormous radio telescopes rising up from the plains of San Agustin. The Karl G. Jansky Very Large Array (VLA) is part of the National Radio Astronomy Observatory. The giant telescopes are mounted on railroad tracks, which allows them to be adjusted to the necessary

angle. Astronomers use the VLA to observe young stars, black holes, and other deep space phenomena. You can visit the VLA on a self-guided walking tour and stand at the base of one of the huge dish antennas. In-depth tours are offered on the first and third Saturdays of the month.

Wilder Nightingale Fine Art
🏠 119 Kit Carson Rd
🌐 wnightingale.com

Michael Gorman Gallery
🏠 103 East Plaza, Site B
🌐 michaelgormangallery. com

Crookedman Studio
🏠 417 Camina de la Placita
🌐 crookedmanstudio.com

Charles Collins Gallery
🏠 1 McCarthy plaza
🌐 charlescollinsgallery.com

Pat Woodall Fine Art
🏠 207 Paseo del Pueblo Sur, Site D 🌐 patwoodall.com

4

SANTA FE

⊠🏛🚌 *i* Old Santa Fe Trail; www.santefe.org

The artist colony of Santa Fe has a rich history and beautiful architecture, and is a key draw to the state of New Mexico. The blending of Hispanic, American Indian, and Anglo cultures contribute to the city's vibrancy.

The oldest state capital in North America, Santa Fe was founded by the Spanish conquistador Don Pedro de Peralta, who established a colony here in 1610. This colony was abandoned in 1680 after the Pueblo Revolt, but was later recaptured. When Mexico gained independence in 1821, traders and settlers from Missouri poured into the area via the Santa Fe Trail. Perched on a high plateau, this beautiful city is surrounded by mountains. Its heart, since its founding, is the central Plaza, and there is no better place to begin exploring the city. Today, it houses an American Indian market under the portal of the Palace of the Governors, and the square is lined with shops, cafés, and several galleries.

Did You Know?

Sited at an altitude of 7,199 ft (2,194 m), Santa Fe is the highest state capital in the US.

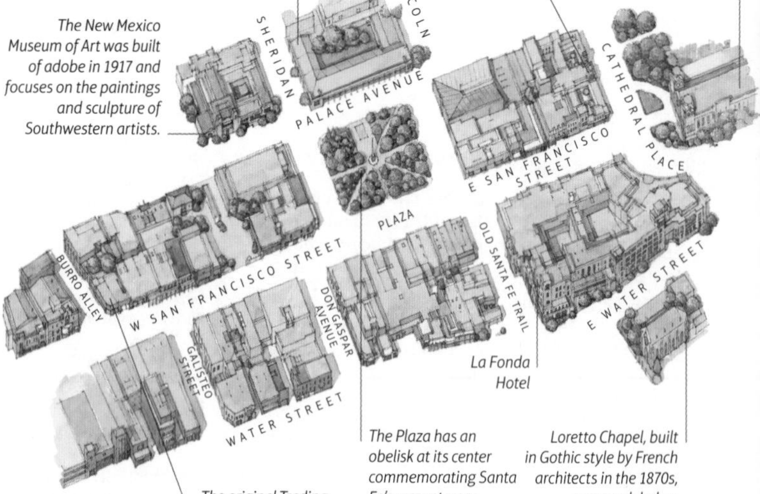

The Palace of the Governors, a single-story adobe building from 1600, was the seat of regional government for 300 years and is now part of the New Mexico History Museum.

Museum of Contemporary Native Arts

St. Francis Cathedral was built in 1869 on the site of a 17th-century church.

The New Mexico Museum of Art was built of adobe in 1917 and focuses on the paintings and sculpture of Southwestern artists.

La Fonda Hotel

Santa Fe, built around the central Plaza

The original Trading Post sells Hispanic art, antiques, and American Indian crafts.

The Plaza has an obelisk at its center commemorating Santa Fe's war veterans.

Loretto Chapel, built in Gothic style by French architects in the 1870s, was modeled on the Sainte-Chappelle in Paris.

↑ The quiet streets of Santa Fe at nighttime

← Interior of the chapel at St. Francis Cathedral, which has an impressive spiral staircase

The obelisk of Santa Fe, which towers above
↓ the city's Plaza

STAY

Hotel Santa Fe
Owned by the Picuris Pueblo peoples, this is a stylishly decorated and welcoming spot. There is also a fine restaurant on site.

🏠 1501 Paseo de Peralta
🌐 hotelsantafe.com

$$$

La Fonda on the Plaza
Located on the site of a 1610 adobe inn, this luxurious hotel is full of original local artworks and features a seasonal outdoor cocktail bar.

🏠 100 E San Francisco St
🌐 lafondasantafe.com

$$$

5

Albuquerque

⊠🚌🚏 *i* 303 Romero St;
www.itsatrip.org

American Indians lived on the site of Albuquerque from 1100 to 1300. They were followed by a small group of Colonial pioneers who settled by the Rio Grande in the wake of late 16th-century Spanish explorers. In 1706, a band of 18 families won formal approval for their town from the Spanish crown by naming the city after the Spanish Duke of Alburquerque, (the first "r" in the name was later dropped). Today Albuquerque's Old Town still has many original adobe buildings dating from the 1790s, while downtown is much more contemporary.

Dominating the historic Old Town is the Plaza, which was the center of Albuquerque for over 200 years. Today, this charming square is a pleasant open space where both locals and visitors relax on benches, surrounded by lovely adobe buildings. Opposite is the imposing San Felipe de Neri Church. Completed in 1793, this was the city's first civic structure and still retains its original adobe walls. The nearby streets are lined with museums, colorful craft shops, and restaurants, such as the Church Street Café. Said to occupy the oldest house in the city, this café serves great New Mexican cuisine. Beyond is a craft store, the Agape Pueblo Pottery, which stocks handcrafted pueblo pottery.

Encompassed within **ABQ BioPark**, the Rio Grande Botanic Garden occupies 10 acres (4 ha) of woodland along the Rio Grande and has a variety of rare plants and gardens. The city's aquarium is also here and focuses on the marine life of the Rio Grande, one of America's great rivers, and features a fascinating walk-through eel cave containing moray eels. There is also an impressive floor-to-ceiling shark tank.

Housed in a castle with beautiful grounds, the **Turquoise Museum** contains an unsurpassed collection of rare and varied turquoise specimens and jewelry from around the world. Exhibits include 400 pieces of American Indian

EAT

Church Street Café
Housed in an early 1700s adobe building, this spot serves superb regional dishes.

🏠 2111 Church St NW
Ⓦ churchstreetcafe.com

⑂⑂⑂

Antiquity
Consistently voted one of the city's best restaurants, this gem serves clever takes on American classics.

🏠 112 Romero St NW
🕐 Lunch Ⓦ antiquity restaurant.com

⑂⑂⑂

> **Today Albuquerque's Old Town still has many original adobe buildings dating from the 1790s, while downtown is much more contemporary.**

←
Gift and craft stores
on Albuquerque's
Old Town Plaza

turquoise art, and displays relating to science, turquoise mining, and the mystical qualities of the stones.

The **New Mexico Museum of Natural History and Science** has a series of inter-active exhibits. Visitors can stand inside a simulated live volcano or explore an ice cave. The "Evolator" is a ride through 38 million years of the region's evolution using the latest video technology. Replica dinosaurs, a state-of-the-art planetarium, and a large-screen film theater are all highly popular with children.

The **Albuquerque Museum** depicts four centuries of history in the middle of Rio Grande Valley, with artifacts expertly arranged for maximum impact. Exhibits focus on the Spanish Colonial period (1598–1821) and include a reconstructed 18th-century house and chapel. From March to mid-December, the museum organizes informative walking tours of the Old Town.

The **American International Rattlesnake Museum** explains the life cycles and ecological importance of some of Earth's most misunderstood creatures. It contains the world's largest collection of different species of live rattlesnakes; the snakes are displayed in glass tanks that simulate their natural habitat as closely as possible. The museum also features other venomous animals such as tarantulas and the Gila monster lizard.

Built in 1927, the **KiMo Theatre** was one of many entertainment venues con-structed in the city during the 1920s and 30s. The build-ing's distinctive design was inspired by that of the nearby American Indian pueblos and created a fusion of Pueblo Revival and Art Deco styles. Today, the theater presents

an eclectic range of musical and theatrical shows.

The **Rio Grande Zoological Park** is noted for its imagina-tive layout, with enclosures that mimic the animals' natural habitats, including the African savanna. Among the most popular species are lowland gorillas and white Bengal tigers.

ABQ BioPark
⊛ ⌂ 2601 Central Av NW
🕘 9am–5pm daily 🗓 Jan 1,
Thanksgiving, Dec 25
ⓦ cabq.gov/biopark

Turquoise Museum
⊛ⓐ ⌂ 400 2nd St SW 📞 (505)
433-3684 🕘 10am–5pm
Mon–Sat 🗓 Thanksg., Dec 25

New Mexico Museum of Natural History and Science
⊛ ⌂ 1801 Mountain Rd NW
🕘 9am–5pm daily 🗓 Federal
hols ⓦ nmnaturalhistory.org

Albuquerque Museum
⌂ 2000 Mountain Rd NW
🕘 9am–5pm Tue–Sun
🗓 Federal hols
ⓦ cabq.gov/museum

American International Rattlesnake Museum
⊛ ⌂ 202 San Felipe Av
NW 🕘 Times vary, check
website 🗓 Federal hols
ⓦ rattlesnakes.com

KiMo Theatre
⊛ ⌂ 423 Central Av NW
🕘 Box office: noon–6pm
Wed–Sat, noon–3pm Sun)
ⓦ cabq.gov/kimo

Rio Grande Zoological Park
⊛ ⌂ 903 10th St SW
📞 (505) 768-7200
🕘 9am–5pm daily
(summer: to 6pm Sat-Sun) 🗓 Thanksgiving,
Dec 25

↑ The KiMo Theatre, a landmark building
that still puts on a varied program

6
Acoma Pueblo

◪ Rte 23, off I-40

The incredible beauty of Acoma Pueblo's setting on the top of a 357-ft- (107-m-) high mesa has earned it the sobriquet "Sky City." Looking out over a stunning panorama of distant mountains, mesas, and plains, it gave the Puebloans a natural defense against enemies. Acoma is one of the oldest continuously inhabited towns in the US, occupied since before the 12th century. Today, fewer than 30 people live on the mesa top year round; 6,000 others from local towns return to their ancestral home for festivals and celebrations.

As well as original pueblo buildings, the village has a 1629 mission church, San Esteben del Rey. There are also seven ceremonial kivas. Acoma can be visited only on a guided tour (arranged at

Did You Know?

With ranches covering over 60 percent of the state, New Mexico has more cows than human beings.

the **Sky City Cultural Center and Haak'u Museum**), where experts explain its rich history.

Sky City Cultural Center and Haak'u Museum

◪ Base of the mesa ◎ Mid-Mar-Oct: 9am-5pm daily; Nov-mid-Mar: 9am-4pm Fri-Sun
ⓦ acomaskycity.org

7
El Morro National Monument

◪ Off Hwy 53 ◎ 9am-5pm daily (summer: to 6pm); trails shut 1 hour before close ⓦ nps.gov/elmo

Rising dramatically from the surrounding plain, El Morro is a long sandstone cliff that slopes gently upward to a high bluff, where it suddenly drops off. Its centerpiece is the 200-ft- (61-m-) tall Inscription Rock, which is covered with more than 300 petroglyphs and pictographs from early Pueblo people, as well as the thousands of inscriptions left by Spanish and Anglo travelers.

For centuries people were drawn to this remote spot by a pool of fresh water, formed by runoff and snowmelt. Here they carved their initials into the rock. Among the signatures is that of the Spanish colonizer Juan

HIDDEN GEM
Pie Town

The rustic little community of Pie Town lies 83 miles (134 km) west of Socorro on US Hwy 60. Here, three restaurants specialize in serving delicious, homemade pies. Hours vary, so arrive early.

de Oñate, who wrote in 1605 "pasó por aquí," meaning "I passed by here."

The people of Zuni Pueblo, 32 miles (51 km) west of El Morro, are the descendants of the early mesa dwellers of the region. Today, Zuni artists are known for their fine pottery and jewelry. Murals depicting Zuni history can be seen in the pueblo's 17th-century mission church.

8
Bandelier National Monument

◪ Off Hwy 4 ⓦ nps.gov/band

Set in the rugged cliffs and canyons of the Pajarito Plateau, Bandelier National Monument has over 3,000 archaeological sites that are the remains of an Ancestral Pueblo culture. The site is thought to have

been occupied by ancestors of the Puebloan peoples for around 500 years from the 12th to the 16th centuries, when successive communities grew crops of corn and squash. The earliest occupants are thought to have carved the soft volcanic rock of the towering cliffs to make cave dwellings; some time later, people built houses and pueblos from rock debris.

One of the most fascinating sights here is the ruin of the 400-room Tyuonyi pueblo. The settlement is laid out in semicircular lines of houses on the floor of Frijoles Canyon.

From the visitor center, the Main Loop Trail leads past the Tyuonyi village to some of the cave dwellings and the Long House – multistoried dwellings built into a stretch of the cliff. Petroglyphs can be spotted above the holes that once held the roof beams. Another trail leads to the Alcove House, reached by four wooden ladders and some stone stairs.

9

Lincoln Historic Site

🏠 Hwy 380 🕑 9am–5pm daily 🌐 nmhistoricsites. org/lincoln

The peacefulness of this small town, surrounded by the beautiful Capitan

↑ A reenactment of Billy the Kid's legendary escape from Lincoln County Jail

Mountains, belies its violent past. It was at the center of the 1878 Lincoln County War, a battle between rival ranchers involving the legendary Billy the Kid. It is now a State Historic Site, with 11 buildings preserved as they were in the late 1800s. At the Lincoln County Courthouse visitors can see the room where Billy the Kid was held, and the bullet hole made in the wall during his escape. The Tunstall Store is stocked with original 19th-century merchandise. The Historic Lincoln Visitor Center and Museum has displays on the Apache people, the early Hispanic settlers, and the Buffalo Soldiers all-black regiment from Fort Stanton, along with the Lincoln County War.

10

Roswell

🏠 426 N Main St; www. seeroswell.com

The small ranching town of Roswell has been a byword for aliens and UFOs since the night of July 4, 1947, when an unidentified airborne object crashlanded here. Jim Ragsdale, camping nearby, later claimed (in 1995) to have seen a flash, a craft hurtling through the trees, and the bodies of four "little people," with snake-like skin. The US Air Force issued a statement at the time that a flying saucer had been recovered, and despite a denial later on, "the Roswell Incident" caught people's imagination.

Witnesses were allegedly sworn to secrecy, fueling rumors of a cover-up and alien conspiracy theories to this day. The International UFO Museum and Research Center features an extensive collection of newspaper clippings and photographs of the crash site, and a 70-minute film with over 400 interviews of various people connected to the incident.

Roswell's Museum and Art Center houses a large collection of artifacts on the history of the American West. The fascinating Robert H. Goddard Collection details 11 years of experiments by the famous rocket scientist.

← Acoma Pueblo, or Sky City, perched on top of the mesa

11

White Sands National Monument

📍 Hwy 70 🕐 9am–5pm daily (Memorial Day–mid-Sep: extended hours) 🌐 nps.gov/whsa

The White Sands National Monument rises up from the Tularosa Basin at the northern end of the Chihuahuan Desert. It is the world's largest gypsum dune field, covering around 300 sq miles (800 sq km). Gypsum is a water-soluble mineral, rarely found as sand. But here, with no drainage outlet to the sea, the sediment washed by the rain into the basin becomes trapped. As the rain evaporates, dry lakes form and strong winds blow the gypsum up into the vast fields of rippling dunes.

Visitors can explore White Sands by car on the 16-mile (26-km) Dunes Drive. Four trails lead from points along it, including the wheelchair-accessible Interdune Boardwalk. Year-round ranger-led

> **The White Sands National Monument rises up from the Tularosa Basin at the northern end of the Chihuahuan Desert.**

walks introduce visitors to the dunes' flora and fauna. Only plants that grow quickly enough not to be buried survive, such as the hardy soaptree yucca.

The park is surrounded by the White Sands Missile Range, a military testing site. For safety, the park and the road leading to it may close for up to three hours when testing is underway. The White Sands Missile Range Museum displays many of the missiles tested here, as well as the V-2 rockets used in World War II.

12

Gila Cliff Dwellings National Monument

📍 Off Hwy 15 🕐 8am–5pm daily 🌐 nps.gov/gicl

The Gila (pronounced hee-la) Cliff Dwellings are one of the most remote archaeological sites in the Southwest, situated among the Gila National Forest. The dwellings occupy five natural caves in the side of a sandstone bluff high above the Gila River.

Hunter-gatherers and farmers called the Tularosa Mogollon established their 40-room village here in the late 13th century. The Mimbres Mogollon people

also lived in this area. The ruins are accessed by a hike from the footbridge crossing the Gila River's West Fork. Allow 2 hours to navigate the 40-mile (64-km) road to the site from Silver City as it climbs through the mountains and canyons of the forest.

13

Carlsbad Caverns National Park

📍 3225 National Parks Hwy, Carlsbad 🚗🚌 🕐 May–Aug: 8am–7pm daily (last hiking entrance 3:30pm); Sep–Apr: 8am–5pm (last hiking entrance 2:30pm) 🌐 nps. gov/cave

Located in the state's remote southeastern corner, this park protects one of the world's largest cave systems. Geological forces carved out this complex of chambers, and their decorations began to be formed around 500,000 years ago when dripping water deposited drops of the crystalized mineral calcite. Pictographs near the Natural Entrance indicate that they had been visited by American

↑ A lone figure strolling across the glinting dunes at White Sands National Monument

Indians, but it was cowboy Jim White who brought them to national attention in 1901.

A self-guided tour leads to the 25-story Big Room, festooned with stalactites, stalagmites, and flowstone formations. The ranger-led King's Palace Tour takes in the deepest cave open to the public, 830 ft (250 m) below ground. To its right, a paved section serves as a lunchroom, a diner and gift shop.

The caverns' recesses are the summer abode of almost a million free-tailed bats. They emerge at dusk to cross the desert in search of food.

↑ Marveling at Carlsbad Caverns, and *(inset)* the zigzag path to the entrance

🄯 Los Alamos

🛈 109 Central Park Sq; www.visitlosalamos.org

Los Alamos is famous as the location of the Manhattan Project, the top-secret research program that developed the atomic bomb during World War II.

Today, the town is home to scientists from the Los Alamos National Laboratory, a leading defense facility. The **Bradbury Science Museum** showcases its current and historic research and includes replicas of the bombs dropped on Hiroshima and Nagasaki in 1945. The **Los Alamos History Museum** covers the geology of the region.

Bradbury Science Museum
♿ 🏛 1350 Central Av
🕐 10am–5pm Tue–Sat, 1–5pm Sun & Mon 🚫 Federal hols
🅦 lanl.gov/museum

Los Alamos History Museum
♿🅟🛍 🏛 1050 Bathtub Row 🕐 10am–4pm daily (summer: from 9am)
🅦 losalamoshistory.org

THE MANHATTAN PROJECT

In 1943 a former boys' school, the Los Alamos Ranch School set high on New Mexico's remote Pajarito Plateau, was chosen as the research site for the top-secret Manhattan Project, which resulted in the world's first nuclear explosion. Work began under the direction of physicist J. Robert Oppenheimer and General Leslie R. Groves, and in just over two years they had developed the first atomic bomb. It was detonated at the secluded Trinity Test Site, now the White Sands Missile Range, on July 16, 1945. The decision to explode the bomb in warfare was highly controversial, and some of the scientists who developed the bomb signed a petition against its use. Displays on the project can be seen at the Bradbury Science Museum in Los Alamos and the Los Alamos History Museum.

THE ROCKIES

Reflections of Sawtooth Range, Idaho

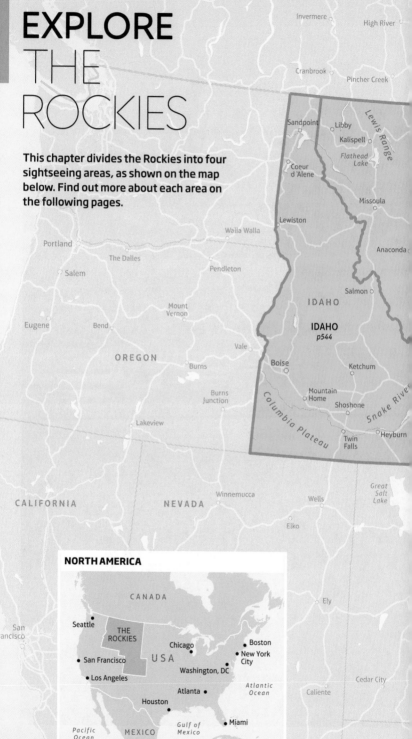

EXPLORE
THE
ROCKIES

This chapter divides the Rockies into four
sightseeing areas, as shown on the map
below. Find out more about each area on
the following pages.

IDAHO
p544

NORTH AMERICA

7 DAYS
in Colorado

This mammoth seven-day road trip covers the best of Colorado's Rocky Mountain hinterland, taking in ancient pueblos and dizzying canyons. The route makes a loop from Denver International Airport.

Day 1

Aim for an early start – it takes around 1.5 hrs to reach Estes Park, the eastern gateway of Rocky Mountain National Park *(p568)*, but you'll need a full day to make the most of this exceptional, high alpine playground. Get oriented at the Beaver Meadows Visitor Center before driving Trail Ridge Road. This road crests at 12,183 ft (3,713 m), with the whole sweep of the snowcapped Rockies before it. Grab a snack lunch at the dizzying Alpine Visitor Center, and then cruise on to Grand Lake to spend the night. Dine at the World's End Brewpub *(www.theworldsendgrandlake.com)* for tasty bar food and local craft beers.

Day 2

Your next stop is Leadville, an atmospheric Old West mining town. Ringed by snow-capped mountains at an elevation of more than 10,000 ft (3,048 m), Leadville is rich in character and history. The National Mining Hall of Fame and Museum chronicles the town's goldmining past, while the majestic Tabor Opera House was once posh enough to attract a

performance by Oscar Wilde. Relax with dinner and a beer or two at the Legendary Silver Dollar Saloon *(www.legendarysilver dollarsaloon.com)*, Leadville's oldest bar.

Day 3

Drive over spectacular Independence Pass via the Top of the Rockies National Scenic Byway (aka Hwy 82) between Leadville and Aspen. Assuming it's summer, there's plenty of non-skiing action in Aspen – stroll the town's leafy streets, browse its chic stores and galleries, or drive out to Ashcroft Ghost Town, a long-abandoned 1880s mining settlement. If you'd prefer some exercise, cycling is the main summer pursuit around here; various outlets offer mountain bikes to rent. Reward yourself with a burger in Aspen's oldest pub, the Red Onion *(www.redonionaspen.com)*.

Day 4

From Aspen, it's a fairly fast 137 miles (220 km) to the entrance of Colorado National Monument *(p573)*, on the western edge of the Rockies. Here multicolored rocks,

1 A family taking in the view in Rocky Mountain National Park.

2 A mountain biker riding through forest in Aspen.

3 The Red Onion, Aspen's oldest pub.

4 Colorado National Monument.

5 A lone hiker in Great Sand Dunes National Park.

dusty pinnacles, and great red canyons replace snowy peaks. Explore the 22-mile (35-km) Rim Rock Drive, and the park's many trails. Aim to spend most of the day here before bunking down in nearby Grand Junction (p573). Small-plates gourmet restaurant 626 On Rood (www.626onrood. com) is the place to splurge, while for those in search of comfort food, Pablo's Pizza (www.pablospizza.com) is hard to beat.

Day 5

The sensational (but surprisingly under-visited) Black Canyon of the Gunnison (p570) lies 73 miles (117 km) southeast of Grand Junction, about a 90-minute drive. Take your time exploring the 7-mile (11-km) South Rim Road, which twists and turns along the canyon past several overlooks and trails. When you've had your fill of the spectacular views, drive another 147 miles (237 km) to Cortez, to save time tomorrow. Stop for dinner at the Smuggler's Brewpub (www.smugglers brew pub.com) in Telluride, or hold off for the excellent Loungin' Lizard (www. lounginlizard cortez.com) in Cortez itself.

Day 6

Drive up to Mesa Verde National Park (p572), and aim to spend the best part of a day at this exceptional American Indian site. Tour the intriguing cliff dwellings that were inhabited by the indigenous Puebloan people some 800 years ago, and check out illuminating artifacts in the Archaeological Museum. It's a long drive to the next destination, so spend the night en route in pleasant Pagosa Springs. Here you'll find the Alley House Grille (www. alleyhousegrille.com), a fine New American restaurant set in a restored 1912 cottage.

Day 7

Great Sand Dunes National Park (p570), some 110 miles (177 km) on from Pagosa Springs, is an utterly surreal sight. North America's tallest sand dunes are framed by the Sangre de Cristo Mountains, gargantuan piles of the Sahara in the middle of the Rockies. Scale the dunes and peruse the exhibits in the visitor center. It's a 4-hr drive back to Denver airport from here, though Colorado Springs (p571) makes an enticing pit stop.

◁ "There's gold in them thar hills"
Mines once littered the Rocky Mountains. Gold, silver, and copper made Butte *(left)* rich in the 19th century, commemorated today at various museums *(p554)*. Leadville was another mining boomtown, remembered at the National Mining Hall of Fame and Museum *(www.mininghalloffame.org)*.

▷ Forts and Trading Posts
In the 19th century a network of forts and trading posts stretched across the West, manned by US Army troops and groups of hardy traders. The Fort Laramie National Historic Site *(p563)* in Wyoming is incredibly evocative of those times, with the wind howling across the plains and the buildings left as if just abandoned by their former inhabitants *(right)*. Also in Wyoming, restored Fort Caspar Museum *(p563)* contains exhibits on the frontier army and the Oregon Trail.

THE ROCKIES AND THE
WILD WEST

Cowboys, ghost towns, old gold mines, and American Indian villages – the Rockies are littered with icons of the American West. Though the golden age of the frontier ended over a century ago, its legacy lives on through countless ranches, rodeos, wildlife refuges, and Wild West towns.

◁ Mostly Ghostly
When the gold ran out, so did the people. The Rockies are home to many abandoned settlements, in various states of ruin. In Colorado *(p565)* there's Independence Ghost Town and Ashcroft Ghost Town. Eerie old buildings have been preserved in Virginia City *(p554)*, and Garnet Ghost Town *(www.garnetghost town.org)* in Montana is another lonely ensemble of empty, wood-framed saloons and cabins *(left)*.

◁ Wildlife in the Rockies

The great herds of buffalo that once roamed the American West are long gone, but the National Bison Range in Montana *(p552)* contains a small herd of American bison. In Wyoming, the National Elk Refuge *(p559)* offers a safe haven for large migrating elk herds in winter *(below)*. Elk also roam the Rocky Mountain National Park *(p568)*, Colorado, with moose, deer, and pronghorn.

▷ American Chieftains

Sacagawea *(p40)* grew up in Idaho *(p545)* and helped guide European settlers *(right)*. Lakota Sioux legends Crazy Horse and Sitting Bull defeated General Custer's 7th Cavalry in 1876 at the Battle of the Little Bighorn, today a national park *(p554)*. The Big Hole National Battlefield *(p553)*, Montana, preserves the site of an 1877 confrontation between the US Army and the Nez Perce.

△ Cody Cowboys

"Buffalo Bill" Cody was once the most famous cowboy in the world. The town of Cody *(above)* was founded by the man himself in 1896 and is now home to the Buffalo Bill Center of the West *(p559)*. Modern cowboy culture is celebrated at rodeos. One of the biggest is the July Cheyenne Frontier Days festival *(p562)*.

BUFFALO BILL

William Frederick "Buffalo Bill" Cody, born in Iowa in 1846, began a life of adventure at the age of just eleven, when the murder of his father forced him to take a job on a wagon train. He became a Pony Express rider, then a Union soldier, and chief army scout. His Buffalo Bill's Wild West show, first staged in 1883, was a spectacular carnival. The show spent ten of its 30 years in Europe, yet Cody was penniless when he died in 1915.

IDAHO

Idaho was the last of the Western states to be settled by Anglo-Americans. The Nez Perce lived here for hundreds of years until gold was discovered in 1860, and they were gradually forced out – the "Flight of the Nez Perce" ended with the surrender of Chief Joseph in 1877. Boise, the capital, was established in 1862, and Idaho became a state in 1890 after much political wrangling. Coeur d'Alene was founded in 1878 – like most of the towns in the Idaho Panhandle, it began life as a silver- and gold-mining camp, though tourism and farming dominate today. Idaho was one of the first states to give women the vote, in 1896.

Experience

1. Sawtooth National Recreation Area
2. Hells Canyon National Recreation Area
3. Three Island Crossing State Park
4. Coeur d'Alene
5. Boise
6. Craters of the Moon National Monument
7. Sun Valley
8. Twin Falls
9. Idaho Falls
10. Bruneau Dunes State Park

IDAHO

Idaho has vast tracts of unexplored wilderness, offering abundant opportunities for hiking, mountain biking, and white-water rafting. To the north lie resorts such as Coeur d'Alene; the center has the majestic Sawtooth Mountains; while the cultivated fields of the south have inspired automobile license plates in the state to declare Idaho's pride in its "Famous Potatoes."

INSIDER TIP
Jet Boat Rides

Experience the rugged scenery of Hells Canyon on an exciting jet boat ride. Operators offer day trips from several different starting points that include thrilling rapids, calm swimming holes, lunch, and some wildlife spotting.

①

Sawtooth National Recreation Area

🏠 Hwy 75, 8 miles (13 km) N of Ketchum 🌐 fs.usda.gov/recarea/sawtooth

This superb destination for hiking and camping encompasses 1,195 sq miles (3,096 sq km) of rivers, meadows, forests, and the jagged peaks of the Sawtooth Range. For visitors driving up Hwy 75 from Sun Valley, the best introduction to the area is at Galena Summit, where a spectacular panorama looks north over the Salmon River.

Surrounded by the Sawtooth Mountains, the tiny hamlet of Stanley (population 67), has one of the most awe-inspiring settings of any town in the US. The unpaved streets and wood-fronted frontier-style buildings make visitors feel like they have, at last, arrived in the Wild West, despite the fact that the glitzy resort of Sun Valley is barely an hour away to the south. Another attraction is Little Redfish Lake, 10 miles (16 km) south of Stanley, where rustic Redfish Lake Lodge is found near the foot of Mount Heyburn.

②

Hells Canyon National Recreation Area

🏠 US 95, 155 miles (249 km) N of Boise 🏢 1550 Dewey Av, Baker City 🌐 fs.usda.gov/detail/wallowa-whitman

The deepest river gorge in North America, Hells Canyon was carved from the craggy granite of the Seven Devils Mountains by the Snake River. Over a mile (1.6 km) deep and straddling the three-state border where Idaho, Washington, and Oregon meet, the area includes some 336 sq miles (870 sq km) of wilderness where no motor vehicles are permitted. Nearly 100 miles (161 km) of undeveloped and turbulent white water draws kayakers, rafters, and other thrill-seekers. Hells Canyon lies downstream from Hells Canyon Dam. The main visitor center is on the Oregon side of the dam, while in Idaho, the best introduction to the area is from Riggins, where you will find plenty of outfitters who provide rental gear.

→ Ready for a day on the stunning lake at the Coeur d'Alene Resort

❸
Three Island Crossing State Park

🅰 Off I-84, Glenns Ferry Exit, 72 miles (116 km) SE of Boise Ⓦ parksand recreation.idaho.gov

Now one of the most evocative sights along the Oregon Trail, the famous Three Islands Crossing provided one of the few safe places for emigrants to cross the dangerous Snake River. Not all attempts at crossing were successful, however, and some pioneers instead continued along the barren south bank before rejoining the main trail west of Boise.

Today, the park offers a campground and picnic areas. At the Oregon Trail History and Education Center, visitors can learn about the life of early pioneers and American Indians in this area. Displays include replicas of the wagons used by pioneers and the original ruts.

❹
Coeur d'Alene

🅰 Off I-90, 33 miles (53 km) E of Spokane 🚗🚌 ⓘ 105 N 1st St; www.coeurdalene. org

A major vacation destination, Coeur d'Alene was founded in the 1870s as a US Army outpost. Located along the shore of a beautiful Lake, the exclusive Coeur d'Alene Resort is world famous. On the resort's east side, **Tubbs Hill Park** is a nature preserve with hiking trails, pine forests, and great views. Lake Coeur d'Alene is also home to one of the largest populations of ospreys and bald eagles in the US.

A number of Victorian-era towns still stand in the former mining districts, and museums and mine tours offer a glimpse into this lost world. The town of Wallace, 52 miles (84 km) east, offers the **Sierra Silver Mine Tour**, which guides visitors through an 1890s silver mine.

Tubbs Hill Park

🅰 Main entrance at 3rd St S Ⓞ 5am–11pm daily Ⓦ tubbshill.org

Sierra Silver Mine Tour

♿ 🅰 420 5th St, Wallace Ⓞ May & Sep–Oct: 10am–2pm daily; Jun–Aug: 10am–4pm daily Ⓦ silverminetour.org

↑ Majestic beauty of Little Redfish Lake, Sawtooth National Recreation Area

⑤ Boise

🏠 154 miles (247 km) W of Sun Valley 🚌 🚐 ℹ 250 S 5th St; www.boise.org

French trappers in the 19th century named this outpost Boise, meaning "wooded." Even today, this homespun, relaxed city presents a picture-postcard image of America. Locals and visitors walk, ride bicycles, or picnic in the vast Greenbelt parkland adjoining the Boise River downtown.

Boise is also the state capital and the largest city in rural Idaho. Its focal point is the 1920 State Capitol. The building's main distinction is that it is the only US capitol to be naturally heated by geothermal water. It was built of sandstone blocks quarried by inmates at the Old Idaho Penitentiary, 2 miles (3 km) east of the capitol.

Three blocks south of the capitol is the city's historic center, where a dozen late-Victorian commercial buildings have been restored and house a lively set of cafés, bars, restaurants, and boutiques. Boise's oldest building, completed in 1864, now houses the Basque Museum and Cultural Center, which traces the presence of Basque sheep-herders in Boise and across western US. An excellent cluster of museums and cultural centers lies in Julia Davis Park, which straddles the Boise River. A highlight of these is the Idaho State Museum, with entertaining exhibits that explore Idaho's history and its unique landscape.

A 15-minute drive by car from the city is the **Peregrine Fund World Center for Birds of Prey**, where visitors also have the rare opportunity to see a variety of birds while enjoying a hilltop view of the surrounding sagebrush plains.

Peregrine Fund World Center for Birds of Prey

✈ 🏠 5668 W Flying Hawk Ln 🕐 Times vary, check website 🌐 peregrinefund.org/visit

⑥ Craters of the Moon National Monument

🏠 US 20, 170 miles (274 km) W of Boise 🌐 nps.gov/crmo

Sprawled across 83 sq miles (215 sq km) in central Idaho, Craters of the Moon National Monument showcases one of the most extraordinary landscapes in the country. The most accessible section can be explored via the numerous short trails that lead through rippling, jagged lava fields, strewn with cones and craters. They range from 15,000 to 2,000 years of age. Despite their forbidding, blackened appearance, the lava fields harbor more than 50 species of mammals, 170 species of birds, and millions of resplendent wildflowers, which bloom in summer each year. Numerous caves and lava tubes also run beneath the surface.

Camping is also available in the park during the summer, and the main loop road draws crowds of cross-country skiers during winter.

⑦ Sun Valley

🏠 155 miles (249 km) W of Boise 🚌 ℹ 491 Sun Valley Rd, Ketchum; www.visitsunvalley.com

Developed in the late 1930s, Sun Valley is one of the oldest and highest-profile winter resorts in the US, and once served as the playground of celebrities such as Errol Flynn, Gary Cooper, Clark Gable, and Ernest Hemingway. Since then, the Olympic-quality skiing on Bald Mountain has continued to draw an exclusive clientele between November and April.

Before the 1930s, the area was a center for mining and sheep-ranching, based in the adjacent town of Ketchum. This town still retains much of its rugged frontier character, despite the influx of multi-million-dollar vacation homes. The region's history is on view

Did You Know?

Ernest Hemingway lived in Ketchum, Sun Valley, and finished *For Whom the Bell Tolls* here.

←

Exploring tunnel caves at the otherworldly Craters of the Moon National Monument

← Shoshone Falls, the mighty "Niagara of the West," near the city of Twin Falls

Temple, the city has a vast Greenbelt area. The **Museum of Idaho** showcases the state's history and hosts traveling exhibits. The **Idaho National Laboratory** (INL), 50 miles (80 km) west of the city, was established in 1949 to design, build, and test nuclear reactors.

Museum of Idaho

♿ 🏛 200 N Eastern Av
🕐 10am-8pm Mon, 10am-6pm Tue-Sat, 1-5pm Sun
🚫 Mid-Apr-early May; early Dec 🌐 museumofidaho.org

Idaho National Laboratory

🏛 Hwy 20/26, 2525 Fremont Av 🕐 Memorial Day–Labor Day: 9am-5pm daily 🚫 Jul 4 🌐 inl.gov

---

in the **Sun Valley Museum of History**. The surrounding landscape is filled with other recreational options. Bicyclists can follow the 20-mile (32-km) Wood River Trail, along the old Union Pacific Railroad right-of-way. The Wood River is also a prime trout-fishing stream.

Sun Valley Museum of History

🏛 180 1st St E 🕐 1-5pm Tue-Sat 🌐 comlib.org/museum

8

Twin Falls

🏛 128 miles (206 km) SW of Boise 🚌 ℹ️ 2015 Nielsen Point Pl; www.twinfalls chamber.com

The falls for which the city was named have been diminished by dams and irrigation, but Twin Falls is still home to the splendid Shoshone Falls, the "Niagara of the West," whose water flows peak in spring.

Located 5 miles (8 km) north-east of the city, the falls are framed by the deep Snake River Gorge, famous for the ill-fated attempt by motorcycle daredevil Evel Knievel to leap across it in 1974. He survived, but with many injuries.

9

Idaho Falls

🏛 Hwy 15, 160 miles (267 km) SW of Twin Falls 🚐🚌 ℹ️ 355 River Pwy; www.visitidahofalls.com

Set along the banks of the Snake River, Idaho Falls is a charming and mainly agricultural city with a large Mormon population. Dominated by the towering Mormon Idaho Falls

10

Bruneau Dunes State Park

🏛 Hwy 78 (off Hwy 51), 62 miles (100 km) SW of Boise 🌐 parksand recreation.idaho.gov

Immediately south of the Snake River, at the foot of the Owyhee Mountains, are some of the largest sand dunes in North America: the Bruneau Dunes. Their location within one of Idaho's largest state parks protects them from the destructive impacts of motor vehicles. The visitor center explains how the dunes were formed, and there are specimens of local wildlife on show. A small astronomical observatory is often open to the public. The park comprises a variety of habitats such as marsh, prairie, and desert. A few small lakes lie at the foot of the dunes, suitable for fishing. Other activities offered are camping, sandboarding, and horseback riding.

> **Immediately south of the Snake River, at the foot of the Owyhee Mountains, are some of the largest sand dunes in North America: the Bruneau Dunes.**

MONTANA

The Blackfeet, Sioux, and Shoshone roamed Montana long before Fort Benton was established as a fur-trading post in 1847. American Indians fought hard to keep their land; Custer's 7th Cavalry was defeated at the Battle of Little Bighorn in 1876. Yet white hunters had nearly wiped out the buffalo by the 1870s, and by 1890 all native resistance had been crushed. Montana Territory became a state in 1889, with copper, silver, and gold mining initially driving development. Cattle ranching also became important, with Billings founded in 1882. In 1916, Montana resident Jeannette Rankin became the first woman ever elected to Congress. Today, the state's fastest-growing sector is tourism.

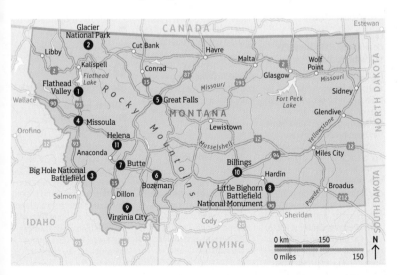

MONTANA

The northernmost Rocky Mountain state, Montana abounds in rugged mountains, snowcapped peaks, lush valleys, and vast plains stretching beneath its trademark "big sky." The sheer scale and majesty of its wide open spaces inspired novelist John Steinbeck to write, "For other states I have admiration, respect, recognition, even some affection. But with Montana it is love."

❶ Flathead Valley

🛈 Bigfork Chamber of Commerce, 8155 Hwy 35; www.bigfork.org

Most of the valley's land, which stretches between Flathead Lake and Missoula, constitutes part of the Flathead Indian Reservation. Since 1855 this has been home to descendants of the region's Salish, Kootenai, and Pend d'Oreille tribes. In summer, communities such as Elmo and Arlee celebrate their traditions in traditional gatherings with rodeos, crafts, and sales.

The **People's Center** in Pablo traces a comprehensive history of the Flathead region from an American Indian perspective.

The largest natural freshwater lake west of the Mississippi, Flathead Lake is a deep-blue jewel at the western foot of the Rockies. Cherry orchards and towns like Bigfork line Hwy 35 on the eastern shore. Take Hwy 93 to Dayton for a kayak or boat ride to Wild Horse Island, home to mule deer, big-horn sheep, and wild horses.

> 💬 INSIDER TIP
> **Seeing Bison**
>
> Along with Yellowstone National Park, the best place to see bison in their natural habitat is at Flat-head Valley's National Bison Range. The visitor center is about 9 miles (14 km) from Charlo.

People's Center
⊘ 🏠 56633 Hwy 93, Pablo
🕐 9am–5pm Mon–Fri; Jun–Aug: also 9am–5pm Sat
🔡 peoplescenter.org

❷ Glacier National Park

🏠 North of W Glacier
🕐 Late May–mid-Sep
🔡 nps.gov/glac

The seemingly boundless Glacier National Park holds some of the world's most sublime scenery. Alongside four-dozen glaciers and ancient limestone cliffs, there are lakes, waterfalls, and abundant wild-life, including moose, wolves, and bears. The flora ranges from high grassy plains to alpine tundra.

↑ A hiker admiring the breathtaking scenery of Glacier National Park, home to the American black bear *(inset)*

❸
Big Hole National Battlefield

🏠 Hwy 43 near Wisdom
🕐 9am–5pm daily (Nov–Apr: from 10am–5pm)
🚫 Most federal hols
🌐 nps.gov/biho

Located near the Idaho border in the Bitterroot Mountains, this battlefield site sits at the head of the lush Big Hole Valley. This pastoral scene is far removed from the terrible suffering experienced here on August 9, 1877, when the flight north by 750 Nez Perce people, mostly women and children, was cut short by an attack by the US Army, leading to the death of nearly 100 American Indians. The tribe continued another 1,500 miles (2,414 km) before finally surrendering in October, just 30 miles (48 km) short of the Canadian border.

❹
Missoula

✈️ 🚌 ℹ️ 101 East Main St; www.destination missoula.org

Nestling in the mountains of western Montana, Missoula is still dependent on traditional industries, such as timber and transportation, and is home to the University of Montana. The Montana Museum of Art and Culture, which largely deals with the art of the contemporary American West, is on the university campus, off I-90.

Surrounded by wilderness, this picturesque city formed the backdrop of the book and subsequent movie *A River Runs Through It*. The city also houses the **Smokejumpers Base**, a center for fighting forest fires in the Rockies. Exhibits explore fire-fighting techniques and equipment, and guests are able to tour the airplanes.

To the south, the Bitterroot Valley has ranches and small towns, hemmed in by a pair of towering mountain ranges.

Smokejumpers Base Visitor Center

🏠 Aerial Fire Depot, W of Missoula Int'l Airport, Hwy 93
🕐 Summer: 8:30am–5pm daily; rest of year: by appt
🌐 smokejumpers.com

❺
Great Falls

✈️ 🚌 ℹ️ 100 1st Av N
🌐 greatfalls mt.net

Huddled between the majestic Rocky Mountains to the west and Little Belt Mountains to the east, this rural city owes its

→ Wild West-inspired art at the C. M. Russell Museum, Great Falls

name to its location along the Missouri River.

As the river cuts through the city, it drops over 500 ft (152 m) in a series of rapids and breathtaking waterfalls, first noted by the intrepid explorers Meriwether Lewis and William Clark in 1805.

The city is best known for its excellent museums. One, the **C. M. Russell Museum**, traces the history of the American West, focusing on the life and work of cowboy and prolific artist "Charlie" Russell.

On a bluff overlooking the Missouri River, 2 miles (3 km) northeast of downtown, is the **Lewis and Clark National Historic Trail Interpretive Center**, which details the epic explorations of the Corps of Discovery, the cross-country expedition led by Lewis and Clark from 1803 to 1806.

For 45 miles (72 km) downstream from the center, the Missouri River runs as a "Wild and Scenic" river on one of its virgin stretches, paralleled by a bike trail and driving tour along US 87. The route ends at the historic Fort Benton, the oldest settlement in Montana.

C. M. Russell Museum

♿ 🎫 🏠 400 13th St N
🕐 Times vary, check website
🚫 Jan 1, Easter, Thanksg., Dec 25
🌐 cmrussell.org

Lewis & Clark Nat'l Historic Trail Interpretive Center

♿ 🏠 4201 Giant Springs Rd
🕐 Times vary, check website
🚫 Mon, Jan 1, Thanksg., Dec 25
🌐 fs.usda.gov/lcnf

6
Bozeman

i 2000 Commerce Way; www.bozemancvb.com

Situated in the heart of the Gallatin Valley, Bozeman lies in the middle of a sacred Sioux hunting ground, now the state's most productive agricultural region. Founded in the 1860s, the city is one of the few towns in Montana where the economy and history are not based on mining or railroads. Its present prominence is due mainly to the Montana State University. Established in 1893, it is the state's largest university and houses the **Museum of the Rockies**, which takes visitors through earth's history, delving into everything from dinosaur fossils to pioneer history, American Indian artifacts, and Western art. Join a tour through the cosmos at the Taylor Planetarium. Downtown's tree-lined streets make for a pleasant stroll, and you can learn about local history at the **Gallatin History Museum**, housed in the former jail.

Museum of the Rockies
♦ 600 W Kagy Blvd May–Sep: 8am–6pm daily; Oct–Apr: 9am–5pm daily (from noon Sun) Federal hols museumoftherockies.org

Gallatin History Museum
♦ 317 W Main St 11am–4pm Tue–Sat (summer: to 5pm) Federal hols gallatinhistory museum.org

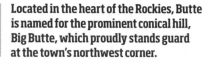

Located in the heart of the Rockies, Butte is named for the prominent conical hill, Big Butte, which proudly stands guard at the town's northwest corner.

7
Butte

i 1000 George St; www.butteelevated.com

Located in the heart of the Rockies, Butte is named for the prominent conical hill, Big Butte, which proudly stands guard at the town's northwest corner. That Butte has some of the world's richest mineral reserves is evident by the extensive signs of the mining industry that thrived here from the 1870s into the 20th century. Glimpses of Butte's multiethnic, immigrant culture are also visible in such events as the St. Patrick's Day celebration. One of many fine museums, the **World Museum of Mining** occupies the site of an early gold mine. Its collection of mineral specimens, mining machinery, and mementos of the town's industrial heritage also includes displays on its leading role in the development of unions. Outside, some 30 historic buildings dating from 1880 to 1910 re-create an early mining camp.

Downtown, the 1888 Copper King Mansion was the residence of W. A. Clark, one of Montana's Copper Kings. Now a B&B, the owners give tours of the mansion, which boasts fine frescoes, ornate stairways, and stained-glass windows.

World Museum of Mining
♦ 155 Mining Museum Way, off Park St Apr–Oct: 9am–6pm daily miningmuseum.org

←
The huge skull of a *Tyrannosaurus rex* at the Museum of the Rockies, Bozeman

8
Little Bighorn Battlefield National Monument

Exit 510 off I-90, Hwy 212, Crow Agency 8am–4:30pm daily (Apr, May & Sep: to 6pm; Jun–Aug: to 7:30pm) nps.gov/libi

Located on the Crow Indian Reservation, this battlefield preserves the site of a key moment in American history, known as "Custer's Last Stand." In June 1876, the impetuous US Army Lieutenant Colonel George Armstrong Custer led his troop of 210 soldiers of the 7th Cavalry in an attack on a large American Indian encampment along the Little Bighorn River. They were quickly surrounded by more than 2,000 combined Lakota, Sioux, Arapahoe, and Cheyenne warriors under the leadership of legendary Chief Sitting Bull and war leader Crazy Horse. Custer's soldiers were wiped out. A sandstone marker stands above the soldiers' mass grave, and a museum describes the battle.

9
Virginia City

i 300 Wallace St; www.virginiacity.com

Gold was first discovered in Virginia City in 1863 and the ensuing stampede created a boomtown. More than 100 historic buildings have been preserved, and visitors can enjoy stagecoach tours and panning for gold. On the Alder Gulch Short Line Railroad, a 1910 steam train makes the 30-minute trip to Nevada City, where the entire town is a state museum.

↑ The ritzy interior of the Montana State Capitol, centerpiece of Helena

10

Billings

🚗🚌 ℹ️ 815 S 27th St; www.visitbillings.com

Founded by the Northern Pacific Railroad in 1882, and now Montana's largest city, Billings was named after the railroad company's president. In just a few months, Billings grew into a bustling community of 2,000 people. Visitors can get a feel of the city's frontier days, and of Montana's cowboy traditions, from the Wild West paintings and sculptures displayed in the **Yellowstone Art Museum**, located in the old county jail. However, by far the most striking feature of Billings is the Rimrocks, a 400-ft- (122-m-) high sandstone wall that runs the length of the city along the Yellowstone River. Outside the city the scenery is even more spectacular, especially along the Beartooth Highway that runs southwest to Yellowstone National Park (p560). The 65-mile (105-km) section between Red Lodge and the Wyoming border is stunning.

Yellowstone Art Museum

🌐🕐♿ 🏠 401 N 27th St 🕐 10am–5pm Tue–Sun (to 8pm Thu & Fri, 4pm Sun); summer: also Mon 🔒 Federal hols 🌐 artmuseum.org

11

Helena

🚗🚌 ℹ️ 225 Cruse Av; www.helenamt.com

The state capital, Helena makes the perfect base for exploring Montana. Originally known as "Last Chance Gulch," Helena was founded as a gold-mining camp in the 1860s. Fortunately much of the wealth generated here remained, as is evident from the number of mansions built by mining millionaires. Many of these exuberantly designed Victorian-era homes have been converted into B&B inns. The centerpiece of Helena is the copper-domed Montana State Capitol, decorated with several fine historical murals. A statue in the grounds portrays Jeanette Rankin, who in 1917 was the first woman to be elected to the US Congress.

Nearby, Montana's museum collects fine art and historical and archaeological artifacts from the region.

Experience

WYOMING

The least populous state in the union, Wyoming remains classic cowboy country. Fort Laramie was established by fur traders in the 1830s, though conflict with American Indian tribes continued into the 1870s. By the 1880s railroad and cattle- farm development had engulfed much of the state. Tourism also developed early; Yellowstone became the world's first national park in 1872. This state was the first to grant women the right to vote in 1869 – 50 years before the federal government. The "Equality State" also elected the first female US governor, Nellie Tayloe Ross, in 1924.

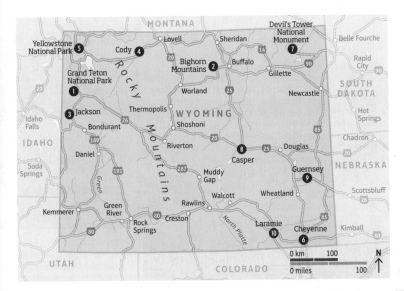

WYOMING

The Wyoming state insignia, an image of a cowboy waving his Stetson hat while riding on the back of a bucking horse, says it all. This is classic cowboy country, a land of wide-open grasslands stretching for miles in every direction. For visitors, the main draws lie in the northwestern corner, with the twin spectacles of Yellowstone and Grand Teton national parks.

Grand Teton National Park

⌂ Moose *i* Grand Teton National Park Headquarters; www.nps.gov/grte

The youngest peaks in the Rockies, the Grand Tetons are among the most dramatic mountains in the world. Their silver granite peaks rise over a mile above the lush Snake River Valley of Jackson Hole, all of which is within the boundaries of Grand Teton National Park. There are miles of hiking trails that lead to numerous glaciers and lakes. In summer, kayakers and rafters float the Snake River, while powerboats and canoes leisurely cruise on Jackson and Jenny lakes. In winter, hiking trails are open for cross-country skiers to make their way through the snowy wilderness.

The Craig Thomas Discovery and Visitor Center, off Teton Park Road in Moose, provides an introduction to the National Park's natural wonders, with an emphasis on preservation. A short walk away is Menor's Ferry Historic District, where 19th-century entrepreneur Bill Menor established a home-stead, a general store, and a ferry to safely cross the river.

Bighorn Mountains

⌂ Bighorn National Forest ⓦ fs.usda.gov/bighorn

Standing at the western edge of the historic plains of the Powder River Basin, the Bighorn Mountains were named for the bighorn sheep that were once abundant here. Crowned by the 13,175-ft (4,016-m) Cloud Peak, the mountains are crossed by a pair of scenic highways, US-16 in the south (the old Yellowstone Trail) and US-14 in the north, which divides into two forks. The northernmost section of US-14 climbs past one of the country's most enigmatic archaeological sites, the Medicine Wheel, an 80-ft (24-m) diameter stone circle, located 27 miles (43 km) east of Lovell. This ancient circle is held sacred by the Sioux and Cheyenne peoples, and offers a vast panorama from its 10,000-ft (3,048-m) elevation.

---

③ Jackson

✈ 🚌 *i* 260 W Broadway; www.jacksonhole chamber.com

A popular stop since the days of the fur-trapping mountain men, Jackson may well be

← Hiking along the Snake River beneath the dramatic peaks of Grand Teton National Park

Wyoming's most visited city. Located at the southern entrance to Grand Teton and Yellowstone national parks, much of its natural beauty is giving way to ski resorts. But despite the boutiques and art galleries that surround its tree-lined central square, Jackson retains its Wild West vibe.

Alongside the national parks, dude ranches, and Wild West reenactments, the main attraction is wildlife. Stretching from Jackson to Grand Teton National Park, the **National Elk Refuge** is home to some 7,500 native elk that congregate here in winter. Its entrance is a short walk northeast of Jackson. Guided tours on horse-drawn sleighs are available between mid-December and early April. Built into a hillside overlooking the elk refuge, the National Museum of Wildlife Art holds over 5,000 artworks depicting wild animals, including works by Georgia O'Keeffe, Andy Warhol, and Robert Kuhn. In summer, the Aerial Tram at Jackson Hole Ski Area lifts sightseers over the top of Rendezvous Peak for a grand panorama.

National Elk Refuge
♿ 🛈 532 N Cache St
🕐 9am–5pm daily (Mem. Day–Lab. Day: 8am–7pm)
🚫 Thanksg., Dec 25
🌐 fws.gov/refuge/national_elk_refuge

↑ Bull elk braving the elements at the National Elk Refuge near Jackson

4
Cody
🛈 836 Sheridan Av; www.codyyellowstone.org

Cody was founded by Wild West impresario "Buffalo Bill" Cody in 1896. Long the symbol of the American West, the city maintains its frontier look and is home to two museums that document this unique era. The smaller of these is Trail Town, a homespun collection of artifacts and buildings assembled on the original site of Cody. One highlight here is a log cabin reputedly used as a hideout by outlaws Butch Cassidy and the Sundance Kid. Cody's main attraction, however, is the **Buffalo Bill Center of the West**, a vast complex of galleries that traces the

← *Buffalo Bill – Plainsman* by Bob Scriver, Buffalo Bill Center, Cody

STAY

Inn on the Creek
Spacious rooms, warm hospitality, and delicious food in a picturesque setting by Flat Creek.
🏠 295 N Millward St, Jackson 🌐 innonthecreek.com

$$$

Bill Cody Ranch
Secluded cabins in a canyon near Yellowstone. Offers trail rides and outdoor activities.
🏠 2604 Yellowstone Hwy, Cody 🕐 Oct–May 🌐 billcodyranch.com

$$$

Old Faithful Inn
Built in 1903–04 from local logs and stone, a historic landmark close to Old Faithful.
🏠 Yellowstone National Park 🕐 Oct–Apr 🌐 yellowstonenationalparklodges.com

$$$

natural, cultural, and military history of the Wild West. It holds more than 500 weapons, a superb collection of Western art, and American Indian artifacts, as well as a museum on Buffalo Bill himself.

In keeping with Buffalo Bill's pursuit of public spectacle, Cody's other great attraction is the Cody Nite Rodeo, the nation's longest-running rodeo, held daily between late June and August.

Buffalo Bill Center of the West
♿ 🏠 720 Sheridan Av
🕐 Times vary, check website
🚫 Jan 1, Thanksg., Dec 25
🌐 centerofthewest.org

5 (icons)

YELLOWSTONE NATIONAL PARK

US 26 in Moose YNP Headquarters, Mammoth Hot Springs; www.nps.gov/yell

One of the marvels of the world, and the country's oldest national park, this wild wonderland in fact spreads across the three states of Wyoming, Montana, and Idaho. Its heart is a volcanic plateau at an average elevation of 8,000 ft (2,438 m), housing over 10,000 hot springs and geysers – more than half of the world's total.

Alongside the spectacular shows of geothermal activity, the national park has dense forests, towering peaks, deep river canyons, and enough outdoor recreation to last a lifetime. The 175-mile (282-km) Grand Loop Road does a full circuit of the main sights.

Lodging is often booked solid, so visitors should reserve in advance. Also note that facilities and roads are often closed from October to May due to winter snows, so be sure to check ahead. The only open road is US 212, along the northern edge.

↑ Lower Falls tumbling into Yellowstone's impressive Grand Canyon

↑ A black bear and her cubs wandering through Yellowstone National Park

TOP 3 GEOTHERMAL WONDERS

Old Faithful Geyser
Named for its precise 90-minute eruption cycle, Old Faithful is the park's icon. Its steaming plume shoots as high as 120–180 ft (36–55 m).

Grand Prismatic Spring
The 370-ft-(113-m-) wide Grand Prismatic Spring lies close to Old Faithful. The rainbow-colored hot spring is one of the world's largest.

Mammoth Hot Springs
These mineral-rich springs result in curtains of marble-like travertine cascading over the terraces of stone.

↑ The USA's largest hot spring, Grand Prismatic Spring, and a hiker exploring Yellowstone National Park *(inset)*

6

Cheyenne

🚗🏨🚌 ℹ️ 121 W 15 St, #202;
www.cheyenne.org

Founded in 1867 as a US Army fort along the newly constructed Union Pacific Railroad, Cheyenne later matured from a typical Wild West town into Wyoming's state capital and the largest city in the area.

Visitors can get a sense of Cheyenne's heritage at the **Cheyenne Frontier Days Old West Museum**. Among the hundreds of antique saddles and wagons on display is the historic Deadwood Stage, which traveled from Cheyenne to the gold mines at Deadwood in South Dakota in the 1870s and 1880s. Downtown Cheyenne features two landmark buildings – the 1917 State Capitol and the Cheyenne Depot Museum, an elaborate Romanesque-style structure that has been restored to its 1886 splendor. The Historic Governors' Mansion, sitting on the corner of 21st Street and House Avenue, was home to 19 of Wyoming's governors and their families. The Wyoming State Museum on Central Avenue houses artifacts that showcase Wyoming's natural and human history.

> 💬 INSIDER TIP
> ## Cheyenne Frontier Days
>
> The 10-day Cheyenne Frontier Days festival (July) brings the old days to life with parades, American Indian pow-wows, and the world's largest outdoor rodeo (www.cfdrodeo.com).

Cheyenne Frontier Days Old West Museum

◈ 🏠 Frontier Park on N Carey Av 🕐 10am–4pm daily 🚫 Federal hols Ⓦ oldwestmuseum.org

7

Devil's Tower National Monument

🏠 US 24 Ⓦ nps gov/deto

Rising over 1,200 ft (366 m) above the surrounding plains, Devil's Tower is a flat-topped volcanic plug that looks like a giant tree stump. Featured in the Steven Spielberg movie *Close Encounters of the Third Kind* (1977), this geological wonder is located in Wyoming's northeastern corner, looming over the banks of the Belle Fourche River. Set aside as the first national monument by President Theodore Roosevelt in 1906, Devil's Tower is a sacred site of worship for many American Indians. The rolling hills of the park are covered with pine forests, deciduous woodlands, and prairie grasslands, and abound in wildlife. The site's vertical walls and scenic trails are a magnet for rock climbers and hikers.

8

Casper

🚗 ℹ️ 139 W 2 St, #1B; www.visitcasper.com

In the heart of Wyoming, surrounded by miles of broad, flat plains, this city grew up around the 1860s Fort Caspar, now the **Fort Caspar Museum**. Many of the buildings have been reconstructed at the point where the Oregon Trail crossed the North Platte River, west of downtown. The museum features a variety of cultural and natural exhibits pertaining to central Wyoming.

North and west of Casper lie miles of arid badlands, including such sites as the legendary "Hole in the Wall,"

↑ Arapahoe dancer performing at the Cheyenne Frontier Days festival

← Prairie grass and pine trees surrounding Devil's Tower National Monument, a magnet for rock climbers *(inset)*

the outlaw hideout of Jesse James and Butch Cassidy. More accessible is the eroded forest of figures known as "Hell's Half Acre," 35 miles (56 km) west of town on US 20. Northwest on I-25 is the National Historic Trails Interpretive Center, which shares the stories of the many thousands of people who braved the Oregon, Mormon, California, and Pony Express trails in the 19th century.

Fort Caspar Museum

⚘ 🏠 4001 Fort Caspar Rd ⏰ 8am–5pm Tue–Sat (May–Sep: daily) 🌐 fortcaspar wyoming.com

9
Guernsey

🏠 US 26 ℹ️ 90 S Wyoming St (summer only); www. townofguernseywy.us

Set along the banks of the North Platte River, this is a small town whose size belies a wealth of historical interest. Just south of town are two of the most palpable reminders of the pioneer migrations westward along the Oregon Trail. The Oregon Trail Ruts State Historic Site preserves a set of deep gouges carved by wagon wheels into the soft riverside sandstone. A mile south, the Register Cliff has been inscribed with the names of hundreds of pioneers who crossed here in the mid-1800s.

The invaluable **Fort Laramie National Historic Site** is a reconstructed fur-trapping and US cavalry outpost. Between the 1830s and 1890s, the fort was a point of contact between Europeans, Americans, and American Indians. Many of the buildings have been restored, and costumed interpreters act out roles from the fort's history.

Fort Laramie National Historic Site

⚘ 🏠 US 26 ⏰ Dawn–dusk daily 🚫 Jan 1, Thanksgiving, Dec 25 🌐 nps.gov/fola

10
Laramie

🚉 🚌 ℹ️ 210 E Custer St; www.visitlaramie.org

This small city exudes youthful vitality. Located east of downtown at 7,200 ft (2,195 m), the University of Wyoming is the highest college in the US. The campus is dominated by the **UW Art Museum**. West of downtown, the city's old prison is now the centerpiece of the **Wyoming Territorial Prison State Historic Site**.

The 50-mile (80-km) stretch of highway between Laramie and Cheyenne preserves part of the first transcontinental road in the US. To the west, Hwy 130 follows the Snowy Range Scenic Byway through the Medicine Bow Mountains.

UW Art Museum

🏠 2111 E Willett Dr ⏰ 10am–5pm Tue–Sat (to 7pm Thu) 🚫 Federal hols & Jan 🌐 uwyo.edu/artmuseum

Wyoming Territorial Prison State Historic Site

⚘ 🏠 975 Snowy Range Rd ⏰ May–Oct: 8am–7pm daily 🌐 wyomingterritorial prison.com

> **North and west of Casper lie miles of arid badlands, including such sites as the legendary "Hole in the Wall," the outlaw hideout of Jesse James and Butch Cassidy.**

Busy Larimer Square, Denver

COLORADO

Colorado was still part of Kansas Territory when gold was discovered near Denver in 1858, initiating a mini gold rush – Colorado became a territory in 1861, and a state in 1876. From then until the end of the century, Colorado expanded; American Indian tribes were largely destroyed by military campaigns in the 1860s. Women won the right to vote in Colorado in 1893, but a coal strike in 1913 resulted in the notorious 1914 Ludlow Massacre, which saw 21 killed. The 1930s saw the beginning of the ski industry, and tourism is now a major part of the state's economy.

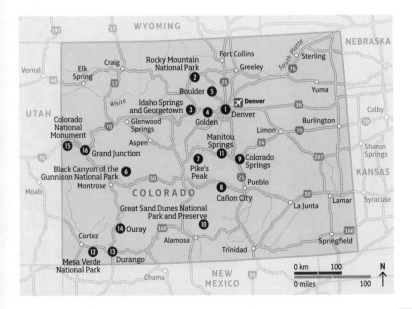

COLORADO

The name "Colorado" refers to the red rock formations that skirt the Front Range of the Rockies. As the most mountainous state in the US, Colorado is synonymous with majestic peaks and snow-clad ski slopes. During the past century Colorado has evolved from sparsely inhabited mining and trapping country to become the most populous business center in the Rockies.

HIDDEN GEM
Red Rocks Amphitheatre

In Red Rocks Park, 15 miles (24 km) from Denver, you'll find this stunning venue. Wedged between two sandstone rocks, it has hosted concerts since 1941 (www.redrocks online.com).

① Denver

🚗🚌🚊 ℹ 1575 California St; www.denver.org

Founded at the junction of the Platte River and Cherry Creek as a supply base for miners in 1858, Denver's mild climate attracted settlers. Soon after, it emerged as the region's primary trade and population center, and eventually became the state capital in 1876. Today, abundant parklands, a vibrant downtown, and a number of excellent museums define this growing city.

The geographical, cultural, and political heart of Denver, Civic Center Park is dominated by the gold-domed Colorado State Capitol, housing the state legislature and governor's office. To the south of the park stands the **History Colorado Center**, where exhibits focus on varied aspects of Colorado's rich heritage. Continue clockwise around the park to reach the tiled, seven-story-high **Denver Art Museum**. This is one of the city's most impressive museums, with collections of both Western and American Indian objects. Right next door is the Clyfford Still Museum, which showcases a rotating collection of the giant, swirling canvases of this abstract painting pioneer.

The restored **Molly Brown House**, now a museum, was the home of "The Unsinkable Molly Brown," so-called for her survival of the Titanic disaster in 1912. Margaret Tobin Brown was a flamboyant and persistent woman whose life story exemplifies the boom-and-bust backdrop of Colorado history. Having made and lost a fortune in silver only to regain their wealth in gold mining, she and her husband J.J. Brown moved to Denver and lived in luxury. Her courageous rescue efforts during the sinking of the Titanic then made her a celebrity. However, she died in New York in 1932, penniless and alone. She was later immortalized on stage and screen.

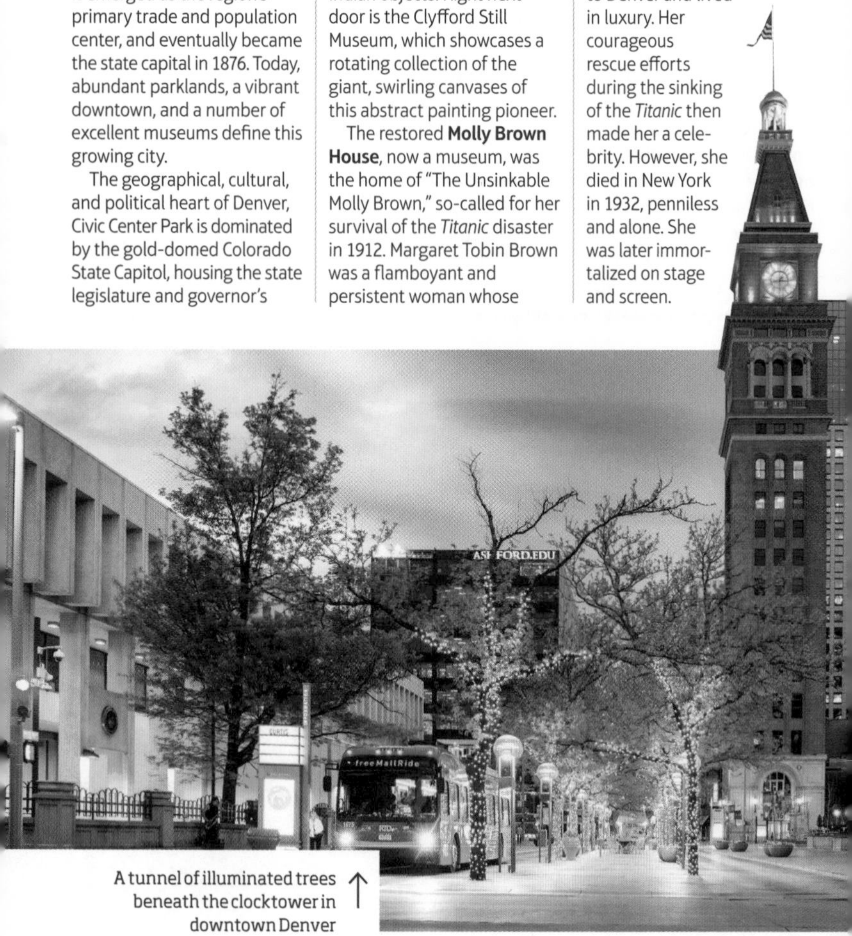

A tunnel of illuminated trees beneath the clocktower in downtown Denver

→ Fossilized dinosaurs at the Denver Museum of Nature and Science

The birthplace of Denver, Larimer Square remains a commercial and cultural hub for the city. Lying adjacent to Confluence Park, where the Platte River and Cherry Creek meet, this was the site where settlers first set up camp. The square bustles with activity day and night, mainly due to the many boutiques, galleries, bars, and restaurants.

Red-brick Victorian architecture dominates the square and the Lower Downtown area (nicknamed "LoDo"). Centered on Union Station, LoDo is a favorite club-hopping district, known for its jazz joints, dance clubs, and microbreweries.

About 2 miles (3 km) east of downtown is City Park, which offers a wide range of activities. It has a fishing lake, picnic areas, running trails, and sports fields. On the eastern edge of the park, the **Denver Museum of Nature and Science** has a broad spectrum of exhibits.

A hidden gem in the Five Points neighborhood, the fascinating **Black American West Museum and Heritage Center** is housed in a Victorian home, previously the abode of Justina Ford. In 1902 she became Denver's first female African American doctor. The collection includes letters, photographs, and memorabilia that effectively re-create the incredible stories of African Americans in pioneer times.

Founded in the early 1990s, the **Museo de las Americas** offers a fascinating glimpse of the artistic and cultural traditions of Mexicans and Latin Americans.

History Colorado Center
⊛ ⌂ 1200 Broadway
🕙 10am-5pm daily
🌐 historycolorado.org

Denver Art Museum
⌂ 100 W 14th Av Pkwy
🕙 10am-5pm daily (to 8pm Fri)
🚫 Thanksgiving, Dec 25
🌐 denverartmuseum.org

Molly Brown House
⊛⊛ ⌂ 1340 Pennsylvania St
🕙 10am-4pm Tue-Sat, noon-4pm Sun 🚫 Federal hols
🌐 mollybrown.org

Denver Museum of Nature and Science
⌂ 2001 Colorado Blvd
🕙 9am-5pm daily 🚫 Dec 25
🌐 dmns.org

Black American West Museum & Cultural Center
⊛ ⌂ 3091 California St
🕙 10am-2pm Fri & Sat 🚫 Jan 1, Easter, Thanksgiving, Dec 25
🌐 bawmhc.org

Museo de las Americas
⊛ ⌂ 861 Santa Fe Dr
🕙 Noon-5pm Tue-Sat
🚫 Federal hols 🌐 museo.org

TOP
4 **DENVER MICRO-BREWERIES**

Wynkoop Brewing Co.
⌂ 1634 18th St
🌐 wynkoop.com
Colorado's first brewpub and still a winner.

Great Divide Brewing Co.
⌂ 2201 Arapahoe St
🌐 greatdivide.com
Longstanding downtown brewery with award-winning beers.

Odell Brewing Co.
⌂ 2945 Larimer St
🌐 odellbrewing.com
Taste small-batch brews round the fire pit on a rooftop patio.

Denver Beer Co.
⌂ 1695 Platte St
🌐 denverbeerco.com
Unique brews and a Bavarian beer garden.

2

Rocky Mountain National Park

🏠 1000 US 36 ⏰ Park: 24 hrs daily; Trail Ridge Rd: May-Oct 🌐 nps.gov/romo

Rocky Mountain National Park offers some of the most spectacular mountain views in the US. Snaking through the alpine scenery is the Continental Divide, which separates the western US from the east, and where snowmelt flows into the Atlantic or Pacific. Almost 150 lakes begin here, some occupying forested settings, while others are perched high in the wilderness.

Most visitors drive 50 miles (80 km) on Trail Ridge Road, which showcases the park's brilliant panoramas. After leaving Estes Park, the road climbs to its highest point near the center of the park, before descending into a valley north of Grand Lake. Wildlife here include elk, moose, black bear, and bighorn sheep.

Popular summer activities within the park include hiking, biking, backpacking, and fishing, while winter attracts snowshoers and skiers. Although there are no hotels inside the park, there are five fee-based campgrounds and numerous accommodations in both Estes Park and Grand Lake.

3

Idaho Springs and Georgetown

🚌 ℹ️ 2060 Miner St; www.visitidahosprings colorado.com

Situated within an hour's drive from downtown Denver, the 1860s mining towns of Idaho Springs and Georgetown are best known for their pristine Victorian architecture, stunning mountains, and fine museums.

Idaho Springs was founded in 1859 and quickly emerged as a gold-mining center. The town's mining history is traced at the **Argo Mill and Tunnel**.

Georgetown, similarly set up during the mid-19th-century gold rush, is tucked into an alpine valley 15 miles (24 km) west of Idaho Springs and is a vision of Victorian elegance.

↑ St Malo's church, sitting on a quiet outcrop in Rocky Mountain National Park

The **Hamill House Museum**, built in 1867, re-creates the opulent lifestyle of a mining magnate. The historic 3-mile (4-km) Georgetown Loop Railroad winds up the spectacular Clear Creek Canyon.

South from Idaho Springs, summer drivers can climb up the highest road in the country. The Mount Evans Scenic Byway follows Highways 103 and 5 through the Pike National Forest toward the 14,264-ft-(4,347-m-) high summit of Mount Evans.

Argo Mill and Tunnel

🎫 🕐 🏠 S of I-70, exit from 241 A (2350 Riverside Dr) ⏰ 10am-6pm daily (winter: hours subject to weather) 🌐 argomilltour.com

Hamill House Museum

🎫 🕐 🏠 305 Argentine St ⏰ Times vary, check website 🌐 historicgeorgetown.org

❹ Golden

🔁🚌 ℹ️ 1010 Washington Av; www.visitgolden.com

This city's history as an early nexus of trade and politics remains visible today. Golden's origins date to the early 1840s, when hunter Rufus Sage, one of the first Anglos to camp in this area, spotted flakes of gold in the waters of Clear Creek. By the 1860s the city emerged as a regional railroad hub and was declared the capital of the Colorado Territory. The original Territorial Capitol in the Loveland Building, which forms the center of downtown, dates from that period.

The Old Armory nearby is the largest standing cobblestone building west of the Mississippi River. The **Clear Creek History Park** houses many historic structures such as an 1876 schoolhouse. The town is also home to Coors Brewery, which offers tours.

The **Buffalo Bill Museum and Grave** on Lookout Mountain collects artifacts associated with Wild West impresario William F. Cody.

Clear Creek History Park

🏠 11th St between Arapahoe & Cheyenne St ⏰ Dawn-dusk daily 🌐 goldenhistory.org

Buffalo Bill Museum and Grave

🏠 987 1/2 Lookout Mountain Rd ⏰ May-Oct: 9am-5pm daily; Nov-Apr: 10am-5pm Tue-Sun 🚫 Dec 25 🌐 buffalobill.org

---

🏔️ **GREAT VIEW**
Lookout Mountain

There are wonderful views over Golden, Denver, and the Front Range from the observation deck on Lookout Mountain, near Buffalo Bill's gravesite.

---

❺ Boulder

🔁🚃🚌 ℹ️ 2440 Pearl St; www.bouldercoloradousa.com

An idyllic college town at the foot of the Rockies, Boulder is best known for its bohemian culture, liberal politics, and thriving hi-tech industry. The city was founded in 1858 as a commercial hub for miners and farmers. Since then, the attractive Victorian-era campus of the University of Colorado and its vibrant culture have defined Boulder, attracting intellectuals, radicals, and individualists.

Northwest of the campus, Pearl Street Mall is the stage for street performers. Nearby, the Hill District is the center of Boulder's nightlife scene.

Housed in a red-brick building in the northeast corner of the city, the **Boulder Museum of Contemporary Art** is dedicated to presenting work by today's most innovative artists.

West of Boulder, the forested crags of the Rockies provide a scenic backdrop to the city below. The nearby Flatiron Range, Eldorado Canyon, and **Indian Peaks Wilderness Area** are popular with climbers, hikers, and backpackers.

Boulder Museum of Contemporary Art

♿ 🏠 1750 13th St ⏰ 11am-5pm Tue-Sun 🌐 bmoca.org

Indian Peaks Wilderness Area

♿ 🏠 20 miles (32 km) W of Boulder, US Forest Service 🌐 indianpeakswilderness.org

---

EAT

Boulder Dushanbe Teahouse
Charming international teahouse decorated by Tajik artisans.

🏠 1770 13th St, Boulder 🌐 boulderteahouse.com

💲💲💲

Flagstaff House
Award-winning New American cuisine and an impressive wine list.

🏠 1138 Flagstaff Rd, Boulder 🌐 flagstaffhouse.com

💲💲💲

↑ The exquisite artisanal decoration at Boulder Dushanbe Teahouse

DRINK

Phantom Canyon Brewing Co.

As well as craft beer and billiards, this microbrewery offers award-winning food.

🅰 2 E Pikes Peak Av, Colorado Springs
🆆 phantomcanyon.com

$$$

6

Black Canyon of the Gunnison National Park

🅰 E of Montrose via US 50
🅽 North Rim Rd: late Nov-mid-Apr 🆆 nps.gov/blca

Black Canyon was created by the Gunnison River as it slowly sliced through solid stone for two million years. Its north and south rims have completely different ecosystems and are separated by a deep crevice.

The South Rim Road meanders for about 7 miles (11 km) past several overlooks, including a fantastic vista of a multihued rock face known as Painted Wall, which is twice the height of New York's Empire State Building (p91). Although the park's northern edge is more isolated, it has a nice campground and offers magnificent sunset views.

7

Pike's Peak

🅰 W of Colorado Springs, via US 24 🆆 pikes-peak.com

Ever since 1859, when it was the focus of a major gold rush, Pike's Peak has been one of America's most famous mountains. Rising majestically along Colorado's Front Range to a height of 14,110 ft (4,300m), it was named after the explorer Zebulon Pike, who led an expedition in 1806 but failed to reach the top. The stupendous view from the summit inspired an early visitor, Katharine Lee Bates, to write the patriotic song "America the Beautiful" in 1893. Today you can drive to the top along the Pike's Peak Highway, a 19-mile (31-km) toll road. There are two visitor centers along the way, as well as one at the summit. The Pikes Peak Cog Railway is a historic train that climbs to the summit from its depot in Manitou Springs; it is closed for refurbishment until 2021. Hikers can make the strenuous, 13-mile (21-km) one-way trip up along the Barr Trail.

8

Cañon City

🅸 403 Royal Gorge Blvd; www.canoncity.com

Blessed with sunshine, clear skies, and spectacular scenery, Cañon City, surprisingly, is also the "Prison Capital of Colorado," a title it acquired in 1876, after it chose to house the state prison instead of the state university. Today, prisons remain a key component of the economy. The **Museum of Colorado Prisons** is housed in a former women's prison built in 1935. Just 12 miles (19 km) west of the city stands the breathtaking **Royal Gorge Bridge and Park**. Traversed by the world's highest suspension bridge and the **Royal Gorge Route Railroad**, the park also attracts white-water rafters.

Museum of Colorado Prisons

⊘ 🅰 201 N 1st St 🅾 May-Sep: 10am-6pm daily; Oct-Apr: 10am-5pm Wed-Sun 🆆 prisonmuseum.org

Royal Gorge Bridge & Park

⊘ 🅰 Country Rd 3A, US-50 🅾 Times vary, check website 🆆 royalgorgebridge.com

Royal Gorge Route Railroad

⊘ 🅾 Late May-Oct: daily; rest of year: check website 🆆 royalgorgeroute.com

→ Taking on the mighty white waters of the Arkansas River near Cañon City

9 Colorado Springs

515 S Cascade Av; www.visitcos.com

The beautiful scenery and hot springs here attracted scores of tourists in the 19th century, making it the first resort town in the western US. The Italian Renaissance-style **Broadmoor** resort on Lake Cheyenne epitomizes this era.

The **Garden of the Gods** on the west side of town lures hikers and climbers with its awe-inspiring red sandstone rock formations. The spirit of the Wild West remains alive and well at the **Pro Rodeo Hall of Fame**. The Colorado Springs Pioneers Museum presents the area's history in the restored 1903 courthouse. Old Colorado City is now a neighborhood with cafés, shops, and galleries. Other attractions include the World Figure Skating Museum and the US Olympic Training Center.

INSIDER TIP
White-water Rafting

Enjoy the state's pristine wilderness on the Arkansas River. There are dozens of rafting companies but the Colorado River Outfitters Association *(www.croa.org)* is one of the best sources of information.

Broadmoor
1 Lake Dr Daily
broadmoor.com

Garden of the Gods
1805 North 30th St
Seasonal: check website
gardenofgods.com

Pro Rodeo Hall of Fame
101 Pro Rodeo Dr
9am-5pm daily (Sep-Apr: Wed-Sun) Federal hols
prorodeohalloffame.com

10 Great Sand Dunes National Park and Preserve

11500 Colorado Hwy 150, NE of Alamosa nps.gov/grsa

North America's tallest sand dunes sit at the foot of the Sangre de Cristo Mountains. This unusual ecosystem is home to some equally unusual animals, such as a species of kangaroo rat that never drinks water, and the Great Sand Dunes tiger beetle, found nowhere else in the world.

The park has a campground, which fills up quickly on weekends in summer, and a mix of long and short trails.

← Enjoying the views at the Black Canyon of the Gunnison National Park

11 Manitou Springs

354 Manitou Av; www.manitousprings.org

This charming former Victorian community attracts weekend visitors who come to explore its art galleries, restaurants, and shops. A product of the Gold Rush of the 1850s, it later became a popular spa town because of the natural springs found here. Manitou (meaning "Full of Spirit" in Native Algonquian) is one of the largest national historic districts in the country. It is famous for two attractions that predate it by centuries: the **Cave of the Winds**, an impressive limestone cavern (now with light shows and tours) dating from AD 1100–1300, and the Manitou Springs Cliff Dwellings, reconstructed using original bricks.

Cave of the Winds
100 Cave of the Winds Rd (US 24, exit 141)
10am-5pm daily (Jun-Aug: 9am-9pm) caveofthewinds.com

12

Mesa Verde National Park

🏠 E of Cortez via US Hwy 160 🕐 Park: 8am-5pm daily (summer: to 7pm); cliff dwellings: early Apr-Oct 🌐 nps.gov/meve

In 1906, Mesa Verde became the first archaeological site in the US to receive national park status. Tucked into the recesses of the canyon walls, the park's defining features are the hundreds of cliff dwellings last inhabited by the indigenous Puebloan people around AD 1300. The dwellings range from small houses to the 150-room Cliff Palace.

Park rangers lead tours between April and November to some of the most impressive dwellings, or you can explore some structures on your own. Square Tower House, the park's tallest ruin, can be viewed from an overlook. The **Chapin Mesa Archaeological Museum** has a fascinating collection of items used by the Puebloan people.

There are also 18 miles (29 km) of hiking trails within the park. The Petroglyph Point Trail will take you past ancient rock art. In winter, cross-country skiing and snowshoeing are popular.

Chapin Mesa Archaeological Museum

📞 (970) 529-4631 🕐 Mar & Oct: 9am-5pm daily; Apr-Sep: 8am-6:30pm daily; Nov-Feb: 9am-4:30pm daily

---

13

Durango

✈ 🚌 ℹ 802 Main Av; www.durango.org

Described as "out of the way and glad of it," Durango is a model of historic preservation, with 19th-century saloons and hotels lining Main Avenue, and elegant mansions from the same era on Third Street. Now, however, mountain bikers, entrepreneurs, and artists have replaced the miners.

Many visitors take a day trip on the **Durango & Silverton Narrow Gauge Railroad**, a fully functional 1882 steam engine that travels from the valley floor to rock ledges en route to Silverton. Durango's other prime attraction is the **San Juan National Forest**, popular with mountain bikers.

Durango & Silverton Narrow Gauge Railroad

🎟 🏠 479 Main Av 🕐 Early May-late Oct: daily; rest of the year: check website 🌐 durangotrain.com

San Juan National Forest

🏠 15 Burnett Ct 🌐 fs.usda.gov/sanjuan

> Durango is a model of historic preservation, with 19th-century saloons and hotels lining Main Avenue, and elegant mansions from the same era on Third Street.

Cliff Palace tucked into the recesses of the canyon in Mesa Verde National Park, and visitors exploring the cliff dwellings *(inset)*

down a natural cliff-side chute, – are easily accessible from the town.

Ouray is also on the San Juan Skyway, a 236-mile (380-km) loop that includes the "Million Dollar Highway" to Silverton. Its surrounding wildlands lure rock- and ice-climbers, four-wheel-drive enthusiasts, and other outdoors adventurers.

Ouray Hot Springs Pool

⊗ ⌂ 1220 Main St
⏲ Mem. Day-Labor Day: 10am–10pm daily; rest of year: noon–9pm Mon–Fri, 11am–9pm Sat & Sun ⏲ Major federal hols
ⓦ ourayhot springs.com

Box Canyon Falls

⊗ ⌂ S of Ouray via County Rd 361 & US Hwy 550

14

Ouray

ℹ 1230 Main St; www. ouraycolorado.com

Nicknamed the "Switzerland of America" for its resemblance to an alpine village, Ouray lies 80 miles (128 km) north of Durango. It was named for the Ute chief whose people hunted in the area before prospectors established the town in 1876. Today it is listed on the National Register of Historic Places, a testament to the number of well-maintained 19th-century structures here. Two natural wonders – the massive geothermal-powered **Ouray Hot Springs Pool** and the stunning **Box Canyon Falls**, which cascades 285 ft (87 m)

---

15 ⊗

Colorado National Monument

⌂ W of Grand Junction via I-70 or 7 miles (11 km) S of Fruita on US Hwy 340
⏲ Dec 25 ⓦ nps.gov/colm

Carved by wind and water over the last 225 million years, this immense 32-sq-mile (83-sq-km) national monument has been molded into an eerie high desert landscape of spectacular canyons, and red sandstone arches. A driving tour on the 22-mile (35-km) Rim Rock Drive offers splendid panoramas, while several trails lead into the heart of the landscape. The park's geological highlights are the incredible sandstone arches of Rattlesnake Canyon,

---

TOP 5 **SKI RESORTS**

Aspen, Pitkin
ⓦ aspensnowmass.com
Favorite resort of the rich and famous.

Leadville, Lake
ⓦ skicooper.com
Small resort near the highest city in the US.

Breckenridge, Summit
ⓦ breckenridge.com
Lively, family friendly, with varied terrain.

Vail, Eagle
ⓦ vail.com
Large, chic single-mountain resort.

Crested Butte, Gunnison
ⓦ skicb.com
Expert terrain above a former mining town.

---

and Miracle Rock, thought to be the largest balanced rock in the world.

16

Grand Junction

ℹ 740 Horizon Dr; www. visitgrandjunction.com

Named for its location at the confluence of the Colorado and Gunnison rivers, Grand Junction is the largest city on Colorado's Western Slope. In recent years the surrounding Grand Valley has become the state's leading wine region, and you can visit dozens of vineyards. Outdoor activities abound, including the Colorado Riverfront Trail. You can also visit the **Museum of the West**.

Museum of the West

⌂ 462 Ute Av ⏲ May–Sep: 9am–5pm Mon–Sat; Oct–Apr: 10am–4pm Tue–Sat
ⓦ museumofwesternco.com/ museum-of-the-west

THE PACIFIC NORTHWEST

Astoria-Megler Bridge disappearing in the fog, Oregon

EXPLORE
THE PACIFIC
NORTHWEST

This chapter divides the Pacific Northwest into two sightseeing areas, as shown on the map below. Find out more about each area on the following pages.

Courtenay

Vancouver Island

Nanaimo

Cape Flattery

Olympic Peninsula

Port Angele

Aberdeen

Long Beach

Astoria

Cannon Beach

Pacific Ocean

McMinnville

Lincoln City

Salem

Newport

Albany

Corvallis

Eugene

Springfield

Coos Bay

Coast Ranges

Roseburg

Cape Blanco

Grants Pass

Medford

Brookings

NORTH AMERICA

CANADA

Seattle

THE PACIFIC NORTHWEST

Chicago

Boston

New York City

San Francisco

USA

Washington, DC

Los Angeles

Atlanta

Atlantic Ocean

Houston

Pacific Ocean

MEXICO

Gulf of Mexico

Miami

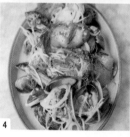

→

1 A fish seller at Pike Place Market.

2 Olympic Mountains.

3 General Porpoise café.

4 Dish from the Walrus and the Carpenter.

5 Bainbridge Island ferry.

Sandwiched between Puget Sound and the Cascade mountain range, Seattle is the ideal getaway for city goers and outdoor lovers alike. This itinerary covers Seattle's highlights, taking in both hip urban culture and bucolic delights farther afield.

4 DAYS

in Seattle

Day 1

Start the day with a caffeine fix with a twist: Enjoy it at the original Starbucks in Pike Place Market (p584). Browse local delicacies throughout the market, snacking as you go. Next, wander toward the waterfront and the Seattle Great Wheel; a spin on this goliath offers unparalleled panoramas over Elliot Bay. Catch a harbor boat tour with Argosy Cruises (www.argosy cruises.com), before feasting on succulent shellfish at Ivar's Acres of Clams (www.ivars. com). Stroll toward Pioneer Square, where you can browse independent shops and galleries before finishing your day with cocktails and a lofty view from the bar at Smith Tower (www.smithtower.com).

Day 2

Breakfast on filled doughnuts and fancy coffee at General Porpoise (www.gpdough nuts.com) before heading to the light-filled galleries of Seattle Art Museum (p585). Pass through Belltown for lunch – try sustainable eatery Local 360 (www. local360.org). At its base, explore the flamboyant art of Chihuly Garden and Glass. Then head eastward to Capitol Hill, Seattle's hippest neighborhood: an LGBT+ epicenter packed with independent shops and fun bars along parallel Pike and Pine streets. Capitol Cider (www.capitol cider.com) – with over 200 ciders and live music – makes for a great night.

Day 3

Start today in historic-meets-hipster Ballard. Breakfast at Hattie's Hat (www. hatties-hat.com), an institution since 1904 that specializes in stacks of hotcakes. Then browse the smattering of independent retailers around NW Market Street – don't miss September boutique. Pick up one of the city's dockless bikes and take the Burke-Gilman Trail to Golden Gardens Park for beach strolls, forest trails, and views of the Olympic Mountains. Sip suds in the brewery district at Peddler Brewing (www.peddlerbrewing.com), before dinner at in-demand The Walrus and the Carpenter (www.thewalrusbar.com).

Day 4

A 35-minute ferry ride will get you from downtown Seattle to Bainbridge Island, a postcard-perfect day trip. Head to the downtown area on Winslow Way and grab coffee and a cream scone at Blackbird Bakery (www.blackbirdbakery.com) before exploring the quaint town. Rent bikes from Bike Barn and cycle north to Fay Bainbridge Park at the tip of the island. Dip into one of the tasting rooms along Winslow – the standout is boutique vineyard Fletcher Bay (www.fletcherbay winery.com). Proper Fish (www.properfish. com) – voted Seattle's best fish and chips – is a must for dinner, and then soak up sunset on your return ferry to town.

THE PACIFIC NORTHWEST FOR
NATURAL WONDERS

The Pacific Northwest is rich with achingly beautiful natural wonders. From rugged coastlines punctuated with postcard-perfect coves and beaches, to lush rainforest and towering volcanoes, this region is littered with indisputably dramatic sights.

Breathtaking Beaches

Emerald forests and craggy cliffs kiss swaths of golden sands along Oregon's 362-mile- (580-km-) long coastline *(p603)*. Oregon's Highway 101 snakes between towns and wild beaches, offering a less-traveled route with vistas to rival California's Highway 1. From north to south, the staggering beauty begins in Astoria *(p602)* and threads through to lovely Cannon Beach. Nearby Devils Punchbowl State Natural Area has caves, seals, and whales.

←

Sun setting over the coastline near Cannon Beach, Oregon

Kingly Volcanoes

The Pacific Northwest is a hot spot for volcaones thanks to the movement of tectonic plates here (and in neighboring Alaska). Mount St. Helens in Washington erupted in 1980 *(p597)*, and a hike through the National Volcanic Monument *(p597)* shows the fiery effects first-hand, including a gaping crater. Mount Rainier National Park *(p592)* is home to an active volcano, which is also the seventh tallest peak in the US. Over in Oregon, Mount Hood *(p602)* is still active. It's also worth visiting the massive Newberry National Volcanic Monument *(p606)* to see and understand how lava shaped the magnificent landscape here. Wizard Island, on hauntingly beautiful Crater Lake *(p611),* is a 764-ft (233-m) cinder cone born 7,700 years ago when a volcano erupted to form its watery home.

←

Majestic Mount Rainier, and *(inset)* hiking around Mount St. Helens, both in Washington state

PICTURE PERFECT
Multnomah Falls

You can't visit Oregon without stopping by Multnomah Falls, along the Columbia River Gorge *(p602).* The best spot to capture the waterfall is on Benson Bridge, which crosses the creek below.

Unforgettable Forests

Lush, misty, and primeval, the Pacific Northwest's temperate rainforests are the ultimate way to disconnect from modern life. Washington's Olympic National Park *(p586)* has the best spots to hike through and discover untouched, almost cathedral-like nature. Here you'll discover the spectacular Hoh Rainforest, ranked a World Heritage Site. It has two easy trails to follow. In Oregon, Drift Creek Wilderness gets 120 in (305 cm) of rainfall every year, and it's one of the largest remaining groves of old growth in the Coast Range.

→

Admiring the beauty of Olympic National Park, Washington

Frank Gehry's Museum of Pop Culture, Seattle

Experience

WASHINGTON

Though Europeans had been charting the Pacific Northwest coast since the 18th century, the Lewis and Clark expedition arrived as US emissaries in 1805. The region was disputed territory with British Canada until 1846. Following the Walla Walla Treaty of 1855, the US bought land from indigenous tribes, but these agreements were soon voided by the flood of settlers coming in, prompting a series of wars through the 1870s. In 1872 the border with Canada was fixed, and in 1889 Washington became a state. The 1890s Klondike Gold Rush created a boom in Seattle; in 1991, grunge rock again brought the city fame. Giants such as Boeing, Microsoft, Starbucks, and Amazon were founded here.

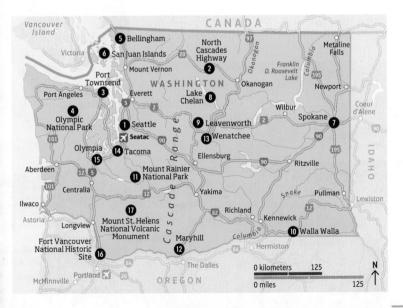

WASHINGTON

The only US state named for a president, Washington offers an extraordinary geographical diversity. Of its three distinct regions, the coastal Olympic Peninsula is dominated by great tracts of forest. Most of the state's largest cities are in the damp, green western region, while a drive through the spectacular peaks of the North Cascades takes visitors to the dry eastern part of the state.

① Seattle

🛫🚉🚌 ℹ 800 Convention Pl; www.visitseattle.org

Nestled between Puget Sound and Lake Washington, with Mount Rainier in the background, Seattle has a stunning setting. The home of Microsoft, Starbucks, and Amazon, the city's growth since the Klondike Gold Rush of 1897–98 has been vigorous. Its prime location and enviable lifestyle make Seattle one of America's coolest cities.

Seattle's first downtown, **Pioneer Square** is now a thriving business neighborhood and National Historic District. Many of its buildings were constructed between the two pivotal events in Seattle's past: the Great Fire of 1889 and the Klondike Gold Rush of 1897–98. The story of Seattle's role in the Gold Rush is told in the Klondike Gold Rush National Historical Park. Opened in 1914, Seattle's first skyscraper, the nearby Smith Tower, offers superb views from its wrap-around observation deck.

Seattle Aquarium showcases over 400 species of animals and plants indigenous to the Pacific Northwest. Highlights include the huge underwater glass dome, filled with sharks, octopus, and other Puget Sound creatures and the world's first aquarium-based salmon ladder.

Trendy Belltown is Seattle's answer to Manhattan's Upper West Side. Once filled with sailors' taverns, the area's identity transformed in the 1970s, when artists, attracted by cheap rents and studio space, moved in. The **Virginia Inn**, on the southern boundary, is a stand-out historic building. A popular watering hole for more than a century, it became a hip art bar in 1981 and hosts regional exhibits.

Pike Place Market is known as much for its colorful personality as for its abundant local produce. Established in 1907, the country's oldest continuously operating farmers' market is now a historic district bustling with stalls and street performers. Rachel, an enormous piggy bank, stands at the main entrance to the market, where counters display fresh fruit, vegetables, herbs, and flowers. Attractions include

> 🔍 HIDDEN GEM
> **Gum Wall**
>
> One of Seattle's more unusual sights is the Gum Wall beside Pike Place Market. It's dotted with thousands of colorful pieces of gum; head down to snap a quirky photo or leave your own sticky souvenir.

↓ Seattle's downtown skyline, best known for its iconic Space Needle (inset) the first ever Starbucks and Pike Place Fish, the site's best-known seafood vendor.

At the entrance of the **Seattle Art Museum** stands the giant *Hammering Man*, an animated steel sculpture created as a tribute to workers. The permanent collection comprises over 23,000 objects, ranging from ancient Egyptian reliefs to Old Master paintings and contemporary American art. Also part of the museum are the Seattle Asian Art Museum in Capitol Hill and the Olympic Sculpture Park.

Home of the Seattle Symphony, **Benaroya Hall** occupies an entire city block and houses two performing halls. The multilevel Grand Lobby, dramatic at night when lit, offers stunning views of the city skyline.

A lovely mash-up of seafood restaurants, tourist traps, and spectacular views, **Seattle Waterfront** runs along Elliott Bay. At **Miner's Landing** on Pier 57, stores stock weird and wonderful souvenirs, while standout seafood spots include Crab's Pot, Ivar's Acres of Clams, and the upscale AQUA. Harbor cruises are the ultimate way to soak up the beauty of this area.

Seattle Center is the proud legacy of the city's 1962 World's Fair. The urban park contains several innovative structures and excellent museums. Among the most striking is the Space Needle, with its observation deck and revolving restaurant. At its base is the exuberant Frank Gehry-designed Experience Music Project (EMP), as well as the world's first museum devoted to science fiction. The Pacific Science Center has hands-on science and math exhibits that are especially appealing to kids.

Beyond downtown you'll find the lively, colorful district of Capitol Hill. Broadway, the neighborhood's major avenue, is lined with shops and ethnic restaurants. The hill is also home to St. Mark's Episcopal Cathedral, known for its

↑ The bustling hub of Seattle's Pike Place Market chockfull of stalls selling fish and produce

magnificent Flentrop organ, consisting of 3,944 pipes.

Having declared itself an "artists' republic" in the 1960s, the district of Fremont began to change by the late 1990s. However, some cherished traditions remain, such as the Summer Solstice Parade and an outdoor film series. Public art is also still a fixture in Fremont; perhaps the best-known example is the 15-ft (4.5-m) troll that lurks beneath the Aurora Bridge.

Pioneer Square
🏠 Bounded by Alaskan & Yesler Ways, 4th Av & S King St Ⓜ🚇 Ⓦ nps.gov/klse

Seattle Aquarium
♿ 🏠 Pier 59, 1483 Alaskan Way 🚌🚇 Ⓞ 9:30am–5pm daily Ⓒ Jun 3 Ⓦ seattle aquarium.org

Virginia Inn
🏠 1937 1st Av Ⓒ (206) 728-1937 Ⓞ 11am–2am daily

Pike Place Market
♿👶 🏠 1st & Pike St 🚇 Ⓞ 9am–6pm daily (from 7am for fish and produce) Ⓦ pikeplacemarket.org

Seattle Art Museum
♿👶🚌🚇 🏠 100 University St 🚇 Ⓞ 10am–5pm Wed–Sun (to 9pm Thu); free 1st Thu of month, and 1st Fri of month for seniors Ⓦ seattleart museum.org

Benaroya Hall
♿🚌🚇 🏠 200 University St 🚌🚇 Ⓞ 10am–6pm Mon–Fri, 1–6pm Sat (box office) Ⓦ seattlesymphony.org

Seattle Waterfront and Miner's Landing
🏠 Pier 57, 1001 Alaskan Way Ⓦ minerslanding.com

Seattle Center
🏠 305 Harrison St Ⓦ seattlecenter.com

EAT

Matt's at the Market

Well located and offering a seasonal menu of American favorites, Matt's suits all occasions.

🏠 94 Pike St, #32 Ⓒ Sun Ⓦ mattsinthe market.com

💲💲💲

The Walrus and the Carpenter

A city hot spot, this 40-seat oyster bar also has a great drinks list.

🏠 4743 Ballard Av NW Ⓦ thewalrusbar.com

💲💲💲

② North Cascades Highway

🅰 State Rte 20

The scenic North Cascades Highway is the northernmost mountain pass route in the state of Washington. It is the 132-mile (213-km) section of Highway 20 between Winthrop in the east and I-5 to the west. Bisecting the **North Cascades National Park**, it offers access to the many wonders of this breathtakingly beautiful ecosystem of jagged snow-capped peaks, forested valleys, and cascading waterfalls. The entire route is open from mid-April to mid-October.

The road follows the Skagit River, passing Gorge Creek Falls, Lake Diablo, and Ruby Creek. At 5,477 ft (1,669 m), Washington Pass Overlook provides heart-pounding vistas of the steep pass up Liberty Bell Mountain. A dominant feature of the park, Mount Shuksan is one of the state's highest mountains. The heavily glaciated park is also home to a variety of animals – bald eagles, gray wolves, and bears.

North Cascades National Park

🄸 SR 20, near milepost 120 & Newhalem 🅆 nps.gov/noca

---

③ Port Townsend

🚍 🄸 2409 Jefferson St; www.enjoypt.com

This seaport, a National Historic Landmark, is one of only three seaports on the National Registry. A building boom in the late 1800s left the town with several grand Victorian mansions, which now form the cornerstone of its thriving tourism industry.

Downtown's Romanesque Jefferson County Courthouse is claimed to be the jewel of Port Townsend's Victorian architecture. The old City Hall is now the Jefferson County Historical Society, home to the city council, as well as an excellent museum.

The Fire Bell Tower, on the bluff overlooking downtown, was built to summon the town's voluntary firefighters. Point Wilson Lighthouse, in Fort Worden State Park, was first lit in 1879 and is still in operation. The fort is dotted with dozens of historic

buildings and the grounds make a delightful stroll.

Port Townsend is also an excellent base from which to make whale-watching, kayaking, and cycling day trips.

---

④ Olympic National Park

🄸 3002 Mt Angeles Rd, 1 mile S of Port Angeles; www.nps.gov/olym

Bordered by the Pacific Ocean, the Strait of Juan de Fuca, and Puget Sound, Washington's Olympic Peninsula is an extraordinary piece of land. Its coastline, etched with bays and inlets, is peppered with majestic sea stacks – portions of wave-eroded headlands that remain as offshore mounds. Some of the most pristine mountains, beaches, and forestlands in the US can be found in this remote region.

The centerpiece of the peninsula is the sprawling Olympic National Park, a UNESCO biosphere reserve and World Heritage Site.

← Cycling through the mountains along the North Cascades Highway

↑ Wandering the lush greenery of the Hoh Rainforest, on the Olympic Peninsula

DRINK

Aslan Brewing Company

An organic downtown brewery, offering modern takes on classic pub fare.

🅰 1330 N Forest St, Bellingham
Ⓦ aslanbrewing.com

McMenamins Spar Café

This homey 1935 café brews its own ales on site, and serves them up alongside American classics.

🅰 114 4th Av E, Olympia
Ⓦ mcmenamins.com

Encompassing 923,000 acres (373,540 ha), this biologically diverse park is a treasure-trove of snowcapped mountain peaks, lakes, waterfalls, rivers, and rainforests. Running through the center of the park are the jagged, glacier-covered Olympic Mountains. With its West Peak rising to a height of 7,965 ft (2,428 m), the three-peaked Mount Olympus is the highest mountain in the range.

The park headquarters are located in Port Angeles, a working port town. Sitting in the rain shadow of the Olympic Mountains, Sequim (pronounced "Squim") features an elk viewing site and the Olympic Game Farm, home to endangered animals.

To the west is the pretty Lake Crescent area and the 4-mile (6.5-km) Rialto Beach, which offers superb views of the Pacific Coast. The coastline receives the highest rainfall in the state, and as a result, rain-forests carpet much of the region. The Hoh Rainforest, with its annual rainfall of 14 ft (4 m), is a magical place, lush with Sitka spruce, Douglas fir, yew, and red cedar, draped with moss. Ancient trees here tower to nearly 300 ft (91 m) in height, and even the ferns grow taller than the hikers.

---

❺ Bellingham

☒ 🚹 904 Potter St; www.bellingham.org

Overlooking Bellingham Bay and many of the San Juan Islands (p588), this town consists of four original towns – Whatcom, Sehome, Bellingham, and Fairhaven – consolidated into a single entity in 1904. The town's historic architecture includes the majestic City Hall; built in 1892 in the Victorian Second Empire style, it is now part of the **Whatcom Museum**, with historical displays from Bellingham's past. The museum's main building, the Lightcatcher, opened in 2009 and features an iconic translucent wall and a kid-friendly gallery. The downtown Art District has numerous restaurants, galleries, and specialty shops.

Just up the hill from downtown sits the campus of **Western Washington University**, with its famous collection of outdoor sculp-tures, including artworks by noted American artists Richard Serra, Mark di Suvero, and Richard Beyer.

From Bellingham's ports, passenger ferries leave for whale-watching cruises and tours to Vancouver Island and the San Juan Islands. Some 55 miles (88.5 km) east of Bellingham is Mount Baker, which is a popular location for skiing and snowboarding.

Whatcom Museum
♿ 🅿 🅰 250 Flora St
🕐 Noon–5pm Wed–Sun (to 8pm Thu, from 10am Sat)
Ⓦ whatcommuseum.org

Western Washington University
🚹 S College Dr & College Way; www.wwu.edu

From Bellingham's ports, passenger ferries leave for whale-watching cruises and tours to Vancouver Island and the San Juan Islands.

SAN JUAN ISLANDS

San Juan Islands From Anacortes to Lopez, Shaw, Orcas, and San Juan islands
 visitsanjuans.com

Unspoiled and remote, this is the arcadian San Juan archipelago. Scattered between the Washington mainland and Vancouver Island there are more than 700 islands, and just 176 of them are named. The most visited are also the largest – San Juan, Orcas, Shaw, and Lopez islands – all of which are served by Washington State Ferries.

The San Juan Islands make for a wonderful expedition after visiting one of Washington's cities, with each of the archipelago's key islands having its own character. Affectionately referred to as "Slow-pez" because of its laid-back nature, Lopez's gently rolling roads, numerous stopping points, and friendly drivers make it a popular destination for cycling. Primarily residential, meanwhile, Shaw Island has limited visitor facilities.

The main two islands, however, are Orcas and San Juan. Horseshoe-shaped Orcas is the hilliest island in the chain and offers breathtaking views from atop 2,409-ft (734-m) Mount Constitution, which falls in Moran State Park. Here visitors will find a wealth of wildlife, gorgeously craggy beaches, and a number of great hiking trails. San Juan Island is the archipelago's unofficial capital, and lends its name to the region as a whole. Friday Harbor is the largest town in the archipelago, home to restaurants, shops, and the nationally renowned Whale Museum, which conveys everything there is to know about the mammals.

Summer is a particularly popular time to visit the islands, especially Orcas and San Juan. As a result, it's sensible to reserve your accommodations and transportation from Anacortes well in advance. You can also catch services to Sidney from Anacortes.

Overlooking bucolic Orcas, one of the archipelago's main islands ↑

TOP 3 SAN JUAN POINTS OF INTEREST

Roche Harbor, San Juan Island
A charming seaside village, Roche Harbor features a marina, Victorian gardens, a chapel, and the historic Hotel de Haro.

Lime Kiln Point State Park, San Juan Island
This state park, with its picturesque lighthouse, is the only park in the country dedicated to whale-watching.

Deer Harbor, Orcas Island
Sea kayakers flock to Deer Harbor and the waters of the islands of Orcas, Lopez, and San Juan.

↑ Morning fog over boats in Friday Harbor, on the island of San Juan

→ A killer whale breaching the waters around Orcas Island, in the San Juan archipelago

7 Spokane

 808 W Main Av; www.visitspokane.com

Washington's largest inland city, this is the Inland Northwest's commercial and cultural center. The city was rebuilt in brick and terra-cotta after a disastrous fire in 1889; its many handsome buildings are reminders of that construction boom.

Of the city's two museums, the **Northwest Museum of Arts and Culture** showcases regional history, while nearby Campbell House (1898) is an interactive museum. Other attractions include Riverfront Park, a 100-acre (40-ha) expanse in the heart of the city; an IMAX® Theater; and a 1909 carousel.

Did You Know?

Spokane was the hometown of *White Christmas* singer Bing Crosby.

Northwest Museum of Arts and Culture

2316 W 1st Av 10am–5pm Wed–Sat Federal hols northwestmuseum.org

8 Lake Chelan

216 E Woodin Ave; www.lakechelan.com

Magnificent Lake Chelan, in the remote northwest end of the Cascades, claims the distinction of being the country's third-deepest lake, reaching 1,500 ft (457 m) at its deepest point. Fed by 27 glaciers and 59 streams, the lake stretches for 55 miles (89 km). In summer, it buzzes with water-sports enthusiasts. The resort town of Chelan at the southeastern end of the lake has long been a popular summer vacation destination for generations of Western Washingtonians seeking the sunny, dry weather on the eastern side of the state. Basking in the rain shadow of the Cascade Mountains, the town enjoys 300 days of sunshine each year. The town's vintage Ruby Theatre on East Woodin Avenue is one of the oldest continuously running movie theaters in the Northwest. Chelan's other highlights are the murals on buildings, which depict the history of the Lake Chelan Valley.

About 9 miles (14 km) from downtown Chelan is the town of Manson, whose Scenic Loop offers easy exploration of the surrounding countryside.

 GREAT VIEW
Grand Coulee Dam

Continue on from Lake Chelan to Grand Coulee Dam, one of the world's largest concrete dams. At 350 ft (107 m) above the Columbia River and 5,223 ft (1,590 m) long, everything about this hydro powerhouse is impressive.

9 Leavenworth

220 9th St; www.leavenworth.org

Once a logging town, Leavenworth, at the foot of the Cascade Mountains in

↑ Scrambling across the rocky shore of Lake Chelan

central Washington, is now a quaint little Bavarian-style town seemingly straight out of a fairy tale. This theme was consciously developed in the 1960s to help revitalize the town and, today, every commercial building, Starbucks and McDonald's included, looks as if it belongs in the Alps.

The town bustles with art shows, festivals, and summer theater productions, attracting more than a million visitors each year. Among its popular festivals are a classic Bavarian carnival held in February; Maifest, with its 16th-century costumes, maypole dances, and jousting; and Oktoberfest, the traditional celebration of German food, beer, and music. Teeming with Bavarian specialty shops and restaurants, the town also has the fascinating **Leavenworth Nutcracker Museum**, which showcases 5,000 nutcrackers from 38 countries, some dating back 500 years.

Leavenworth Nutcracker Museum

🎨🌐 🏠735 Front St 📞(509) 548-4573 🕐May-Dec: 1-5pm daily; winter: times vary

---

❿ Walla Walla

ℹ 29 E Sumach St; www. wwvchamber.com

Located in the southeast corner of the state, Walla Walla is a green oasis in the midst of an arid landscape. The town features several National Register buildings and a wealth of public art. The attractive campus of Whitman College, one of the nation's top-rated liberal arts colleges, is three blocks from downtown.

A popular destination for wine connoisseurs, the Walla Walla Valley has more than 35 wineries. Among the town's other claims to fame are its delicious sweet Walla Walla onions and its annual Hot Air Balloon Stampede, a rally of some 35 pilots.

Fort Walla Walla Museum, consisting of original and replica pioneer buildings, gives a historical perspective of the area. The **Whitman Mission National Historic Site**, just west of town, is a memorial to pioneer missionaries Marcus and Narcissa Whitman, who were massacred by the Cayuse tribe.

Fort Walla Walla Museum

🎨🌐 🏠755 Myra Rd 🕐10am-5pm daily (Nov & Dec: to 4pm; Jan-Mar: to 4pm Mon-Fri) 🌐fortwalla wallamuseum.org

Whitman Mission National Historic Site

🌐 🏠Hwy 12 🕐Jun-Sep: 8am-6pm daily; Oct-May: 8am-4:30pm daily 🌐nps. gov/whmi

---

EAT

Wild Sage American Bistro

An intimate spot with regional ingredients and inventive preparation.

🏠916 W 2nd Av, Spokane 📞(509) 456-757 🕐Lunch

💲💲💲

Whitehouse Crawford

Expect seasonal fine-dining at this converted 1904 sawmill.

🏠55 Cherry St, Walla Walla 🕐Lunch, Tue 🌐whitehousecrawford. com

💲💲💲

Local Myth Pizza

This pizzeria is popular with locals thanks to its thorough menu.

🏠122 S Emerson St, Chelan 🕐Mon 🌐localmythpizza.com

💲💲💲

↑ The Hot Air Balloon Stampede, held in Walla Walla every May

11 🚵 🏔

MOUNT RAINIER NATIONAL PARK

🏠 Hwy 706 near Ashford ℹ️ Jackson Visitor Center, Paradise;
www.visitrainier.com

Mount Rainier is the seventh highest mountain in the US, an active volcano, and an icon of Washington state. Set in its own national park, the mountain is decked in snow and ice for much of the year, with animals and flowers appearing on its slopes in the short summer months. Whatever the time of year, outdoor activities and stunning views await.

Established in 1899, Mount Rainier National Park encompasses 337 sq miles (872 sq km), of which 97 percent is designated wilderness. Its centerpiece is Mount Rainier, an active volcano towering 14,410 ft (4,392 m) above sea level. Surrounded by old-growth forest and wildflower meadows, Mount Rainier was named in 1792 by Captain George Vancouver for fellow British naval officer Peter Rainier. Designated a National Historic Landmark District in 1997, the park, which features 1920s and 1930s National Park Service rustic architecture, attracts two million visitors a year. The summer draws hikers, mountain climbers, and campers; the winter lures snowshoers and cross-country skiers.

Note that the national park has several entrances, with the Nisqually Entrance open year-round. For all other entrances, it's worth checking in advance as these tend to be open seasonally.

> 💬 INSIDER TIP
> **Be Road Safe**
>
> You'll need a car to visit Mount Rainier. Carry chains in the trunk in winter. Check the status of the roads before setting out, as conditions can change quickly and closures may be made at short notice.

Did You Know?

Mount Rainier is considered one of the most dangerous volcanoes in the world.

← Hiking the Mount Fremont Lookout Trail, Mount Rainier National Park

TOP 3 MOUNT RAINIER HIKES

Mount Fremont Lookout Trail
This day-long, 6 mile (10-km) trail starts at the Sunrise visitor center. It's best enjoyed in Jun–Sep when you can view the park's wildflowers.

Northern Loop Trail
Lasting for 40 miles (64 km), this trail takes in the park's most pristine wilderness, including forests, meadows, and mountain lakes.

Wonderland Trail
This is the most difficult of the trails, circum-navigating Mount Rainier. Traveling for 93 miles (150 km), it takes 10 to 12 days to complete.

1 Narada Falls, along Paradise River, is a short, steep hike from Route 706. The falls plummet 168 ft (51 m).

2 A cozy inn, located in Longmire, which makes for a lovely spot from which to enjoy stunning views of Mount Rainier.

3 Paradise, on the south slope of Mount Rainier, has marked trails and bursts with wildflowers in summer.

12

Maryhill

🛈 Klickitat County Visitor Information Center; (509) 773-4395

A remote sagebrush bluff overlooking the Columbia River is where entrepreneur Sam Hill chose to build his palatial residence. In 1907, he purchased 7,000 acres (2,833 ha) here, with the vision of creating a utopian colony for Quaker farmers. He called the community Maryhill, in honor of his daughter, Mary. The ideal community did not materialize, and Hill turned his unfinished mansion into a

museum. The treasures of the **Maryhill Museum of Art** include the throne and gold coronation gown of his friend Queen Marie of Romania, 87 sculptures and drawings by Auguste Rodin, and an impressive collection of American Indian art. The beautifully landscaped grounds include a picnic area.

Maryhill Museum of Art
🎨😊📷 **⌂** 35 Maryhill Museum Dr, Goldendale 🕐 Mar 15–Nov 15: 10am–5pm daily 🌐 maryhillmuseum.org

13

Wenatchee

🛈 2900 Euclid Av; www.visitwenatchee.org

The "apple capital of the world" sits in a sweet spot on the banks of the Columbia River. While the small town and suburbs lack charm, the apple orchards and opportunities for outdoor activities more than compensate. Around 1,700 fruit growers

in the region produce over half of America's apples, from braeburn and golden delicious to sweet honey crisp and refined pink ladies. The Washington Apple Commission Visitor Center is a fun and informative way to get the stats, which have been ever more fruitful since the first apple orchard in 1826.

Pybus Public Market is a bustling spot to scoop up local produce from a farm stand or sit and dine on comfort food. In addition to apples – and all the pie and cider sampling that

---

Exploring the vast wilderness around the town of Wenatchee

EAT & DRINK

Southern Kitchen
The made-from-scratch soul food at this spot has been satisfying diners since 1981.

⌂ 1716 6th Av, Tacoma 🌐 southernkitchen-tacoma.com

$$$

Engine House No. 9
A brewpub housed in a 1907 fire station, this popular spot serves up its own brews and tasty pub grub.

⌂ 611 N Pine St, Tacoma 🌐 ehouse9.com

$$$

The Lobster Shop
Head here for sweeping views of Puget Sound, a killer cocktail list, and heaps of local seafood.

⌂ 4015 Ruston Way 🌐 wp.lobstershop.com

$$$

Martin Blank's *Fluent Steps* (2009) at the Museum of Glass in Tacoma entails – Wenatchee serves as a handy gateway and supply stop for exploring Central Washington's wilderness. Don't miss the Apple Capital Loop Trail, which runs next to Pybus Market.

14

Tacoma

☒ ℹ **1516 Pacific Av; www. traveltacoma.com**

Washington's third-largest city, located south of Seattle (p584), Tacoma was founded as a sawmill town in the 1860s. It prospered with the arrival of the railroad in the late 1880s, becoming a major shipping port for important commodities such as lumber, coal, and grain. Many of the Pacific Northwest's railroad, timber, and shipping barons settled in Tacoma's Stadium District. This historic area, with its stately turn-of-the-20th-century mansions, is named for the French château-style Stadium High School, also known as the "Castle."

The undisputed star of the city's revitalized waterfront is the striking **Museum of Glass**. The 75,000-sq-ft (6,968-sq-m) landmark building showcases contemporary art, with a focus on glass. A dramatic 90-ft (37-m), metal-encased cone houses a spacious glass-blowing studio.

Continuing the city's glass theme, the stunning Chihuly Bridge of Glass serves as a pedestrian walkway linking the museum to downtown Tacoma and the innovative **Washington State History Museum**. The museum features interactive exhibits, high-tech displays, and theatrical storytelling by actors in period costume, who relate stories of the state's past history. The 50,000-sq-ft (4,645-sq-m), stainless-steel-wrapped Tacoma Art Museum was designed to be a dynamic cultural center and a show-piece for the city. Its growing collection of works, from the 18th century to the present day, include a large assembly of Pacific Northwest art, European Impressionist pieces, Japanese woodblock prints, and Tacoma artist Dale Chihuly's glassworks. In keeping with its vision of creating a place that "builds community through art," the museum's facilities include the Bill and Melinda Gates Resource Center, providing visitors with access to a range of state-of-the-art research equipment. Children of all ages can also make use of the in-house interactive art-making studio, ArtWORKS.

Tacoma's most popular attraction is Point Defiance Park, ranked among the 20 largest urban parks in the US. Encompassing 700 acres (285 ha), its grounds include Fort Nisqually, the first European settlement on Puget Sound, and a major fur-trading establishment. Also in the park are seven specialty gardens, a scenic drive, hiking and biking trails, beaches, a boat marina, and a picnic area.

Highlighting a Pacific Rim theme, the Point Defiance Zoo and Aquarium on Pearl Street features more than 5,000 animals. A vantage point at the park's west end offers fine views of Mount Rainier (p592), Puget Sound, and the Tacoma Narrows Bridge, famous as one of the longest suspension bridges in the world.

The fishing village of Gig Harbor, 11 miles (17 km) south of Tacoma, has shops and restaurants that reflect the Scandinavian and Croatian heritage of its inhabitants.

Museum of Glass
♿🅿🔊🅿 🏛 **1801 E Dock St**
🕐 10am–5pm Wed–Sat (Jun–Aug: also Mon & Tue), noon–5pm Sun 🕐 Jan 1, Thanks-giving, Dec 25 🌐 museumofglass.org

Washington State History Museum
♿🅿 🏛 **1911 Pacific Av**
🕐 10am–5pm Wed–Sun
🕐 Federal hols 🌐 wshs.org

> **Did You Know?**
>
> Teen movie *Ten Things I Hate About You* (1999) was filmed in Tacoma.

← Fruit stalls and shoppers at the bustling Olympia Farmers Market

SHOP

Olympia Farmers Market

Giving Seattle's Pike Place stiff competition, this buzzing market has 100 vendors selling local goods, from eggs and flowers to fresh fruit and cured meats.

🏠 700 Capitol Way N, Olympia 🕐 Mon 🌐 olympiafarmers market.com

---

15

Olympia

🏠 103 Sid Snyder Av, SW; www.visitolympia.com

Named for its magnificent view of the Olympic Mountains, Washington's state capital is located at the southern tip of Puget Sound. The city's **State Capitol Campus** is dominated by the 28-story Legislative Building (the Capitol), whose 287-ft (87-m), brick-and-sandstone dome is one of the tallest masonry domes in the world. One of the most impressive in the nation, the campus encompasses superb buildings, several fountains, and monuments. Its landscaped grounds were designed in 1928 by the Olmsted Brothers, sons of Frederick Olmsted, one of the creators of New York City's Central Park (p96).

The **State Capital Museum** provides a historical perspective of Washington's early pioneer settlements,
through its collections of early photographs and documents. The **State Archives**, with its historical records and artifacts, is another institution related to the state's past. Visitors can access such unique treasures as documents from the Canwell Committee, which blacklisted suspected Communists during the 1950s.

Tree-lined streets, old homes, a picturesque waterfront, and a thriving cultural community all contribute to Olympia's charm. Tucked among downtown's historic buildings are several shops, restaurants, and galleries. Within walking distance are attractions such as the lively Olympia Farmers Market, offering local produce, seafood, and crafts, along with dining and entertainment.

Percival Landing, a 1.5-mile (2.5-km) boardwalk along Budd Inlet, offers views of the Olympic Mountains, the Capitol dome, Puget Sound, and ships in port.

State Capitol Campus

🕐 🏠 409 13th Av SW 🕐 Legislative Building: Memorial Day–Labor Day: 7am–5pm Mon–Fri, 11am–4pm Sat & Sun; Labor Day–Memorial Day: 8am–5pm Mon–Fri 🕐 Federal hols 🌐 ga.wa.gov/visitor

State Capital Museum

🏠 211 21st Av SW 🕐 10am–4pm Sat 🕐 Federal hols 🌐 washingtonhistory.org

State Archives

🏠 1129 Washington St SE 📞 (360) 586-1492

16

Fort Vancouver National Historic Site

🏠 1501 E Evergreen Blvd 🕐 Apr–Oct: 9am–5pm Mon–Sat, 10am–5pm Sun; Nov–Mar: 9am–4pm Mon–Sat, noon–4pm Sun 🕐 Jan 1, Thanksg., Dec 24, 25, & 31 🌐 nps.gov/fova

Between 1825 and 1849, Fort Vancouver was a major trading outpost for the

---

INDIE ROCK IN OLYMPIA

A musical powerhouse, Olympia is the birthplace of the underground feminist punk genre known as riot-grrrl, as well as being a hotbed for indie and grunge. Thanks to liberal Evergreen College and record labels such as K Records, Olympia's live music scene is brimming with punk hipsters and indie rockers. K Records famously put out records by Moldy Peaches, Built To Spill, and Modest Mouse, and other Olympia greats include The Gossip, Courtney Love and Sleater Kinney. Catch a show on 4th Avenue or on campus.

Hudson's Bay Company, the British-based fur-trading organization. Located close to major tributaries and natural resources, the fort was the center of political and commercial activities in the Pacific Northwest during these years. In the 1830s and 1840s, it also provided essential supplies to settlers.

Fort Vancouver burned down in 1866, but today the site features reconstructions of nine original buildings, including the jail, carpenter shop, and the blacksmith's store, which stand on their original lots. Guided tours and reenactments offer a window into the fort's past. Over a million artifacts have been excavated from this site.

> On the morning of May 18, 1980, Mount St. Helens exploded. Triggered by a powerful earthquake, the peak erupted, spewing 1 cubic mile (4.2 cubic km) of rock into the air.

⑰ Mount St. Helens National Volcanic Monument

📍 3029 Spirit Lake Hwy, Castle Rock 🌐 fs.fed.us/gpnf/mshnvm

On the morning of May 18, 1980, Mount St. Helens exploded. Triggered by a powerful earthquake, the peak erupted, spewing 1 cubic mile (4.2 cubic km) of rock into the air and causing the largest recorded avalanche in history. In the blink of an eye, the mountain lost 1,314 ft (400 m), and 234 sq miles (606 sq km) of forestlands were destroyed. The eruption also claimed 57 human lives and those of millions of animals and fish. The 170-sq-mile (445-sq-km) monument was created in 1982 to allow the environment to recover naturally while encouraging research, recreation, and education. Roads and trails allow visitors to explore this fascinating region by car and foot. On the west side of the mountain, Highway 504 leads to three visitor centers that document the disaster and recovery efforts. Mount St. Helens National Volcanic Monument Visitor Center, at milepost 5, features interpretive exhibits of the mountain's history.

The visitor center at Hoffstadt Bluffs, at milepost 27, gives visitors their first full view of Mount St. Helens and offers helicopter tours into the blast zone from May to September.

↑ Wildflowers surrounding Mount St. Helens, and *(inset)* a visitor center

A dry lakebed in Malheur National Wildlife Refuge

Experience

OREGON

The home of American Indians, such as the Chinook, Bannock, Klamath, Nez Perce, and Killamuk, Oregon was contested territory well into the 1800s. The Americans pressed their claim to what was now being called Oregon Territory (the origin of the name remains a mystery), after the expedition of Lewis and Clark in 1805. Great Britain and the US initially shared control, but the large numbers of American settlers arriving from the 1830s made Britain's claims unrealistic, and in 1846 the country gave up its claim. Oregon became a state in 1859 and began its economic ascent in the 1880s when the transcontinental railroad reached Portland.

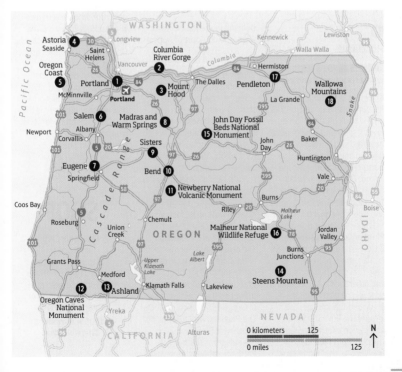

Sunset over downtown Portland's waterfront, on the banks of the Willamette River

OREGON

Oregon is best known for its scenic wonders: Verdant forests, snowcapped mountains, and desert vistas are just some of the diverse attractions. This rugged landscape was first settled by pioneers who migrated along the Oregon Trail. Today, the state is also known for its cosmopolitan pleasures, with locals eager to claim their city as one of America's most sophisticated.

❶ Portland

🚻🏠🚹🚻 ℹ 701 SW 6th Av; www.travelportland.com

Known as the City of Roses, Portland was founded in 1843, on the bank of the Willamette River. It grew into a major port, but later, with the arrival of the railroad and decline in river trade, the city center moved inland. This area is now the city's downtown, while Old Town includes the former port and riverfront quarter.

The one-block, brick-paved **Pioneer Courthouse Square** is the heart of Portland, where locals gather for free lunchtime concerts, flower shows, and other events. Underground spaces next to the square accommodate offices that include the Portland Visitors Association Information Center.

Opposite is the Pioneer Courthouse, the first federal building in the Pacific Northwest. The US Court of Appeals and a US post office branch are housed here. Its octagonal tower has been a fixture of the Portland skyline since 1873.

A green ribbon of elm-shaded lawns, the so-called **South Park Blocks** is a 12-block stretch running through the central city. It is the venue for a colorful Saturday market, where farmers sell their wares to locals and visitors alike. The Oregon Historical Society to the south of the park has huge murals on its facades that depict scenes from the Lewis and Clark expedition and other significant moments in the state's history. On display in the galleries are photographs and documents that make this the largest archive of Oregon's historical artifacts. The Portland Art Museum, on Southwest Park Avenue, is the oldest museum in the Pacific Northwest. Its sizable European collection includes paintings by Picasso, van Gogh, and Monet. Its Grand Ronde Center for American Indian Art displays masks, jewelry, totem poles, and more.

Governor Tom McCall Waterfront Park is named after Tom McCall, Oregon's environmentally minded governor, who served from 1967 to 1975. Today it is the venue for many local festivals. One of its most popular attractions is Salmon Street Springs, a fountain whose 100 jets splash water onto the pavement, providing relief on a hot day. Another highlight is the Battleship Oregon Memorial, which honors an 1893 US Navy ship and has a time capsule sealed in its base.

SHOP

Powell's City of Books
Taking up almost an entire city block, this is the world's largest independent bookstore for new and used books.

🏠 1005 W Burnside St
Ⓦ powells.com

of interactive exhibits is the earthquake simulator, in which visitors are shaken and rattled while learning about the tectonic plates that still shift beneath Portland.

Nearby, Eastbank Esplanade is a pedestrian and bicycle path following the east bank of the Willamette River.

Pioneer Courthouse Square

📍 SW Broadway & Yamhill St
🌐 thesquarepdx.com

South Park Blocks

♿ 😐 👜 📍 Bounded by SW Salmon St & I-405, SW Park & SW 9th Avs

Governor Tom McCall Waterfront Park

📍 Bounded by SW Harrison & NW Glisan sts, SW Naito Pkwy & Willamette River

Pearl District

W Burnside to NW Lovejoy sts, from NW 8th to NW 15th Avs 🌐 shopthepearl.com

Washington Park

♿ 👜 📍 SW Park Pl ⏰ Dawn-dusk daily 🌐 portlandonline.com/parks

Oregon Museum of Science and Industry

♿ ♿ 😐 👜 📍 1945 SE Water Av ⏰ Times vary, check website 🌐 omsi.edu

Elegant brick facades and quiet streets belie **Old Town**'s raucous, 19th-century frontier-town past. A National Historic Landmark today, this riverfront district once drew dockworkers, shipbuilders, and traders from all over the world during its heyday as a major port and the city's commercial center. Old Town is now a trendy, colorful neighborhood, especially during weekends, when vendors gather for the popular Portland Saturday Market, America's largest handicrafts bazaar. Chinatown Gate, a five-tiered, dragon-festooned gateway, located at the intersection of NW 4th Avenue and West Burnside Street, leads to **Chinatown**, formerly home to the city's many Asian immigrants, who first arrived here more than 135 years ago. It is home to the tranquil Lan Su Chinese Garden, a beautiful Ming-style walled enclave with waterways and pavilions.

Pearl District occupies an old industrial area on the north side of Burnside Street. Many former warehouses have been refurbished to house chic galleries, designer shops, and eateries. A good time to visit is on the first Thursday of every month, when the area's many art galleries remain open until late. A quaint way to travel between Pearl District and Nob Hill, a gracious, late 19th-century neighborhood, is to take the Portland Streetcar.

Washington Park, a popular outdoor playground, is surrounded by the city on all its sides. Its attractions include the Hoyt Arboretum, which has more than 8,000 trees and shrubs, and a Japanese Garden.

The **Oregon Museum of Science and Industry** (OMSI) is a top US science museum. A favorite among the hundreds

SNACKING IN PORTLAND

Famous for its dining scene, Portland has a huge array of snack choices, from food carts to cafés and doughnut shops. Standout carts include Stretch the Noodle, for hand-pulled noodles and salty shrimp dumplings, or Little Conejo's tacos. Voodoo Doughnuts is the iconic Portland doughnut shop, while Pip's fries custom doughnuts to order.

← Multnomah Falls, Columbia River Gorge

②
Columbia River Gorge

📍 402 W 2nd St, The Dalles; www.crgva.org

This magnificent fir- and maple-covered river canyon cuts through the Cascade Mountains, forming a boundary between the states of Oregon and Washington. The best way to explore the area is to

80

The number of ghost towns in Oregon, more than any other state.

take the Historic Columbia River Highway. Blasted out of narrow cliffs, this road was designed to maximize viewing pleasure while minimizing environmental damage as much as possible. Along the route you can glimpse the picturesque Multnomah Falls.

③
Mount Hood

📍 24403 E Welches Rd, Welches; www.mthood.org

The spectacular snow-covered peak of Mount Hood, the tallest of Oregon's Cascade peaks, rises south of the Columbia River Gorge. Home to year-round skiing and snowboarding, the valleys below are famous for their

produce of apples, apricots, pears, and peaches.

The Mount Hood Loop is a good way to explore the area; its highest point, known as Barlow Pass, is so steep that at one time wagons had to be lowered down the hillsides with ropes. The Hood River Valley offers blossoming fruit trees in season and lovely views of the majestic Mount Hood throughout the year.

④
Astoria

📍 111 W Marine Dr; www. travelastoria.com

The oldest American settlement west of the Rocky Mountains, Astoria was established when John Jacob Astor sent fur traders around Cape Horn to establish a trading post at the mouth of the Columbia River in 1811. Earlier, explorers Lewis and Clark spent the winter of 1805–06 at a crude stockade near Astoria, making moccasins, preserving fish, and recording in their journals accounts of bear attacks and the almost continual rain. The stockade has since been rebuilt at Fort Clatsop National Memorial. These days, the town is a bustling port dotted with old Victorian homes. One such home, the stately **Captain George Flavel**

 HIDDEN GEM
The Goonies

The white hilltop house from 1985 cult movie *The Goonies* can attract as many as 1,000 fans per day in summer. Its current owner doesn't mind visitors taking a peek, provided they approach by foot only.

House Museum, retains the cupola from which the captain and his wife once watched river traffic. An even better view can be enjoyed from atop the 164-step spiral staircase of the Astoria Column.

The town honors its seafaring past at the **Columbia River Maritime Museum**, where riverside galleries house fishing dories, American Indian dugout canoes, and other river-related artifacts. The lightship *Columbia*, berthed in front, once guided ships across the treacherous area at the mouth of the river.

Captain George Flavel House Museum

⊛ 🅐 441 8th St 🄲 (503) 325-2203 🄾 10am–5pm daily 🄲 Jan 1, Thanksgiving, Dec 24–25

Columbia River Maritime Museum

⊛ 🄐 🅐 1792 Marine Dr 🄾 9:30am–5pm daily 🅦 crmm.org

5

Oregon Coast

🄵 137 NE 1st St, Newport; www.visittheoregoncoast.com

Hundreds of miles of pristine beaches make the Oregon Coast one of the state's best-loved tourist destinations. Head north for some of Oregon's most popular resorts, while the southern part is wilder and more rugged. The coast is ideal for a range of recreational activities such as driving, hiking, shell-fishing, and whale- or bird-watching.

Oregon's favorite beach town, Cannon Beach, retains a quiet charm. Haystack Rock, one of the tallest coastal monoliths in the world, towers 235 ft (72 m) above a long beach and tidal pools. Ecola State Park, at the beach's north end, carpets Tillamook Head, a basalt headland, with verdant forests. Viewpoints

---

DRINK

Eem

A tropical cocktail bar meets Thai pit BBQ, with drinks served in quirky clamshells.

🄐 3808 N Williams Av, Portland 🅦 eempdx.com

Buoy Beer Company

Housed in a former canning factory, Buoy serves up the state's best microbrews.

🄐 18th St, Astoria 🅦 buoybeer.com

---

look across a spirited scene of West Coast surfers to Tillamook Rock Lighthouse, which was built in 1880. Nature is the main attraction along the **Three Capes Scenic Route**, farther south. The rocks below Cape Meares State Scenic Viewpoint and Cape Meares Lighthouse are home to one of the largest colonies of nesting seabirds in North America. The Cape Lookout State Park is a good place to spot migrating gray whales.

The **Cape Perpetua Scenic Area** has the highest viewpoint on the coast. An easy hike along the Giant Spruce

---

Trail leads to a majestic, 500-year-old Sitka spruce. From Cape Perpetua, Highway 101 leads to Heceta Head State Park, with its glorious ocean views. Steller's sea lions inhabit the Sea Lion Caves, the only wild sea-lion rookery on the North American mainland.

The massive sand dunes of the **Oregon Dunes National Recreation Area** stretch south from Florence for 40 miles (64 km). Lakes, pine forests, grasslands, and open beaches attract a variety of recreation enthusiasts, and boardwalks make it easy to enjoy stunning vistas from Oregon Dunes Overlook.

Bandon, near the mouth of the Coquille River, is so small and weathered that it is hard to imagine that it was once a major port. Rock formations rise from the ocean just off the beach, including Face Rock, allegedly an American Indian girl who was turned to stone by an evil spirit.

Three Capes Scenic Route

🄐 Oregon State Parks 🅦 oregon.gov/oprd

Cape Perpetua Scenic Area

⊛ 🅢 🄲 (541) 547-3289 🄾 From 10am daily (Nov–mid-Mar: Thu–Mon); closing times vary 🄲 Federal hols

Oregon Dunes National Recreation Area

⊛ 🄵 855 Highway Av, Reedsport; www.fs.fed.us/r6/siuslaw/recreation

↑ Beachgoers enjoying the shallow surf around Haystack Rock, Oregon Coast

---

EXPERIENCE Oregon

❻ Salem

🛈 1313 Mill St SE; www.
travelsalem.com

Once a thriving trading
and lumber port on the
Willamette River, Salem
became the capital of the
Oregon Territory in 1851.

At the edge of Bush's
Pasture Park stand Asahel
Bush House, an 1878 home
with a conservatory said to be
the first greenhouse west of
the Mississippi River, and the
historic Deepwood Estate. The
**Willamette Heritage Center
at the Mill** preserves some of
the state's earliest structures,
including the 1841 home of
Jason Lee, who helped found
Salem, and the Kay Woolen Mill.

The state's history is also in
evidence around the Oregon
State Capitol. A gilded pioneer
stands atop the rotunda,
marble sculptures of Lewis
and Clark flank the entrance,
and murals inside depict
Captain Robert Gray's
discovery of the Columbia
River. Across the street is the
Hallie Ford Museum of Art, with
its outstanding collection of
American Indian crafts.

Willamette Heritage Center at the Mill
🛈 1313 Mill St SE
🕙 10am–5pm Mon-Sat
🌐 willametteheritage.org

❼ Eugene

🛈 754 Olive St; www.
eugene-or.gov

The University of Oregon
brings culture and distinction to the city of Eugene,

Salem's Oregon
State Capitol in
spring, and the
interior of its
chambers *(inset)*

> Eugene's cool
> neighborhood
> of Whiteaker is
> overflowing with
> specialty coffee
> shops and craft
> beer pubs.

which straddles the banks
of the Willamette River. The
glass-and-timber Hult Center
for the Performing Arts is
regarded as one of the best-
designed performing arts
complexes in the world.
The University of Oregon
Museum of Natural and
Cultural History counts
among its holdings some
ancient shoes – a pair of
sagebrush sandals dating
from as early as 9500 BC.

Local artisans sell their
wares at the Saturday Market,
in downtown Park Blocks.
The Fifth Street Public Market,
an assemblage of shops and
restaurants in a converted
feed mill, bustles with locals
and university students, while
Eugene's cool neighborhood
of Whiteaker is overflowing
with specialty coffee shops
and craft beer pubs.

604

↑ Hiking along the cliffs above the Deschutes River, near Madras

❽ Madras & Warm Springs

🛈 Madras: 274 SW 4th St, www.ci.madras.or.us; Warm Springs: 1233 Veterans St, www.warmsprings.com

Madras is a desert ranching town surrounded by vast tracts of wilderness recreation lands. Crooked River National Grassland provides endless vistas as well as fishing and rafting opportunities on two US National Wild and Scenic Rivers – the Deschutes and the Crooked. Cove Palisades State Park surrounds the deep waters of Lake Billy Chinook, a popular spot for boaters.

The Treaty of 1855 between the US government and the Wasco, Walla Walla, and Paiute tribes established lands for the tribes located on the Warm Springs Reservation in central Oregon. Today, these Confederated Tribes preserve their cultural heritage at the **Museum at Warm Springs** with a stunning collection of basketry and beadwork, historic photographs, and tapes of tribal ceremonies.

Museum at Warm Springs

♿🅿 🏛 2189 Hwy 26, Warm Springs 🕐 9am–5pm daily 🚫 Dec–Feb: Sun & Mon, Jan 1, Thanksg., Dec 25 🖥 museumatwarmsprings.org

❾ Sisters

🛈 291 E Main Av; www.sisterschamber.com

This Wild-West-style ranching town is surrounded by pine forests, alpine meadows, and rushing streams. The peaks of the Three Sisters, each above 10,000 ft (3,000 m), rise majestically in the background.

The McKenzie Pass climbs from Sisters to a 1-mile (1.5-km) summit amid a massive lava flow. The **Dee Wright Observatory** provides panoramic views of over a dozen Cascade Mountain peaks, buttes, and lava fields.

Dee Wright Observatory

🏛 Hwy 242, 15 miles (24 km) W of Sisters 🕐 Mid-Jun–Oct: dawn–dusk daily 🚫 Nov–mid-Jun, depending on snow conditions

❿ Bend

🛈 750 NW Lava Rd; www.visitbend.com

Busy Bend, once a sleepy lumber town, is alluringly close to ski slopes, lakes, streams, and many other natural attractions. It is famous for having the most breweries per capita in the Pacific Northwest.

Drake Park is a grassy downtown retreat on both banks of the Deschutes River, and Pilot Butte State Scenic Viewpoint overlooks the High Desert and snowcapped Cascade peaks.

The **High Desert Museum** celebrates life in the rugged terrain that covers much of central and eastern Oregon. Walk-through dioramas use lighting and sound effects in authentic re-creations of American Indian dwellings. A trail leads to replicas of a settler's cabin and a sawmill, and to natural habitats, including an aviary full of hawks and other raptors.

The best way to explore the magnificent South Cascades Mountains is to take the Cascade Lakes Highway, a 95-mile (153-km) loop starting from Bend. The route passes Lava Butte, which offers fine mountain views. Another interesting sight is Mount Bachelor, 12 miles (20 km) west of Bend, which offers some of the best skiing and snowboarding in the region.

High Desert Museum

♿😊🅿 🏛 59800 S Hwy 97 🕐 May–Oct: 9am–5pm daily; Nov–Apr: 10am–4pm daily 🖥 highdesertmuseum.org

> ### OREGON WINE COUNTRY
>
> Just outside of Salem is Willamette Valley. Its rolling, peaceful farmland is home to around 500 boutique vineyards and the region is sometimes nicknamed "anti-Napa." Here, small-scale wineries are dedicated to producing wine that's often difficult to buy out of state. Willamette's Pinot Noirs have won awards thanks to the local terroir, and anyone passing through must try. Find a vineyard at www.willamettewines.com.

↑ Musicians performing at the iconic Oregon Shakespeare Festival

Newberry National Volcanic Monument

🏠 Hwy 97 🕐 Apr–Oct: dawn–dusk daily ℹ️ Lava Lands Visitor Center, 11 miles S of Bend on US 97; www.fs.fed.us/r6/central oregon/newberry nvm

Newberry National Volcanic Monument encompasses eerily bleak landscapes of black lava, plus sparkling mountain lakes, waterfalls, and snowcapped peaks. The area occupies a whopping 86 sq miles (220 sq km). Exhibits at the Lava Lands Visitor Center explain how the volcano has been built by thousands of eruptions that, seismic activity suggests, may begin again. Other exhibits here highlight central Oregon's cultural history.

At Lava River Cave, a passage extends for almost 1 mile (1.6 km) into a lava tube, through which molten lava once flowed. The Lava Cast Forest has a trail through a forest of hollow molds, formed by molten lava that created casts around the tree trunks.

Oregon Caves National Monument

🏠 20000 Caves Hwy 🕐 Late Apr–early Nov; for tours only ℹ️ 19000 Caves Hwy; www.nps.gov/orca

Visitors on the compulsory 70-minute guided tours of these vast underground caverns follow lit trails past strange, otherworldly formations. They cross underground rivers, squeeze through giant ribs of marble, and clamber up and down staircases into huge chambers hung with stalactites. Various tours are available; check online for details.

Although archaeologists believe nomadic hunters and gatherers lived here, the caves were discovered in 1874 by a hunter chasing his dog into a hole in the side of Elijah Mountain. The caves have been formed by the steady trickling of water over hundreds of thousands of years.

13 Ashland

ℹ️ 110 E Main St; www. ashlandchamber.com

Amiable Ashland promises fine dining, craft beer, and walkable shopping but the town is most famous for the Oregon Shakespeare Festival, which welcomes 400,000 theatergoers every year. The schedule includes plays by Shakespeare as well as by classical and contemporary playwrights. Theater buffs can also see props and costumes and take backstage tours of the festival's three venues. Beyond the plays, the festival also offers talks on dramatic arts.

> **Newberry National Volcanic Monument encompasses eerily bleak landscapes of black lava, plus sparkling mountain lakes, waterfalls, and snowcapped peaks.**

⑭

Steens Mountain

📍 Steens Mountain Loop Rd, starting at North Loop Rd in Frenchglen 🏷️ 484 N Broadway, Burns; www. blm.gov/programs/national-conservation-lands/oregon-washington/steens-mountain

Scenery does not get much grander than here on this impressive 9,700-ft (2,910-m) mountain in southeastern Oregon. The west slope rises gradually from sagebrush country, while the eastern slope drops more steeply. Antelope, bighorn sheep, and wild horses roam glacier-carved gorges and alpine tundra carpeted with lovely

Did You Know?

The highest point in Oregon, Steens Mountain, is excellent for stargazing.

wildflowers, while eagles and falcons soar overhead.

There is plenty of hiking in the area, as well as camping and opportunities for exploring the area on horseback. In winter, people come here for cross-country skiing or snowshoeing. The 58-mile (94-km) Steens Mountain Loop Road traverses this remarkable landscape. Lovely, marsh-fringed Lily Lake, on the west side of the Warner Mountains, is slowly silting up. However, it is still popular with anglers because of its trout-fishing opportunities. The nearby Donner and Blitzen River was named "Thunder and Lightning" by an army officer attempting to cross it during a thunderstorm in 1864. Kiger Gorge to the east affords views of four immense gorges scooped out from the mountainside by massive glaciers. East Rim Viewpoint is a full mile (1.6 km) above the alkali flats of the Alvord Desert. Sitting in the mountain's rain shadow, this desert receives a mere 6 inches (15 cm) of rain a year.

DRINK

Ninkasi Brewing Co. Tasting Room

Innovative microbrewery established in the noughties.

📍 272 Van Buren St, Eugene 🌐 ninkasi brewing.com

Deschutes Brewery Public Brewhouse

A local favorite, with 19 of its own beers on tap.

📍 1044 NW Bond St, Bend 🌐 deschutesbrewery.com/pubs/bend

EAT

Celilo Restaurant

Refined locavore interpretations of Mediterranean dishes.

📍 16 Oak St, Hood River 🌐 celilorestaurant.com

$$$

↑ Spring lupine blooming among the sagebrush at the base of Steens Mountain

↑ The Painted Hills and a walking trail *(inset)*, John Day Fossil Beds National Monument

15
John Day Fossil Beds National Monument

🕐 Dawn–dusk daily
🛈 32651 Hwy 19; www.nps.gov/joda

Prehistoric fossil beds litter the John Day Fossil Beds National Monument, where sedimentary rocks preserve the plants and animals that flourished in jungles and savannas for 40 million years, between the extinction of the dinosaurs and the start of the most recent Ice Age. The monument's 22 sq miles (57 sq km) comprise three units: Sheep Rock, Painted Hills, and Clarno. At all three, trails provide opportunities for the close-up observation of the fossil beds. Painted Hills presents the most dramatic landscapes – volcanic rock formations in vivid hues of red, pink, bronze, tan, and black. Clarno contains some of the oldest formations, dating back 54 million years and including some of the finest fossil plant remains on earth. At Sheep Rock, the excellent visitor center displays many important finds from the beds.

16
Malheur National Wildlife Refuge

🚗 36391 Sodhouse Ln, Princeton 🕐 Times vary, check website 🖥 fws.gov/malheur

One of the nation's largest wildlife refuges, Malheur spreads across 290 sq miles (760 sq km) of the Blitzen Valley floor. More than 320 species of birds and 58 species of mammals are found here. Sandhill cranes, tundra swans, snowy white egrets, white-faced ibis, pronghorn antelope, mule deer, and red-band trout are among the most common inhabitants.

Spring and fall are the best times to view birds, which alight in the refuge on their annual migrations up and down the Pacific Flyway, a major north–south route for migrating North American waterfowl. A small museum houses specimens of birds commonly seen in the refuge.

From the refuge, the 69-mile (111-km) **Diamond Loop National Back Country Byway** heads into sage-covered hills and red rimrock canyons. Along the route are Diamond Craters, a volcanic landscape; the Round Barn, which is a distinctive 19th-century structure; and Diamond, a small, poplar-shaded ranch town.

Diamond Loop National Back Country Byway
🛈 28910 Hwy 20 W, Hines
🖥 blm.gov/or

💬 HIDDEN GEM
Round-Up Hall of Fame

The Pendleton Round-Up and Happy Canyon Hall of Fame honors cowboys, cowgirls, and rodeo stars of Oregon's Wild West (*www.pendletonhall offame.com*).

17 Pendleton

🛈 501 S Main St; www.
pendletonchamber.com

Pendleton's reputation for raucous cowboys and lawless cattle rustlers is matched by the fact that it is eastern Oregon's largest town. Although these colorful days belong to the past, cowboy lore comes alive during the Pendleton Round-Up each September, when rodeo stunt performers and some 50,000 spectators crowd into town.

The town's biggest business, the Pendleton Woolen Mills, is known for its warm clothing and blankets, particularly its "legendary" blankets, whose designs are a tribute to American Indian tribes. The mill wove its first American Indian trade blanket in 1895.

The Pendleton Underground Tours begin in a subterranean labyrinth of opium dens, gaming rooms, and Prohibition-era drinking establishments and include stops at a bordello and the cramped 19th-century living quarters of Chinese laborers.

The Tamástslikt Cultural Institute commemorates local history by re-creating historic structures, exhibits of war bonnets, and other artifacts.

18 Wallowa Mountains

⛰ Elkhorn Drive National Scenic Byway Ⓦ fs.usda.gov/wallowa-whitman

The Wallowa Mountains form a 10,000-ft- (3,050-m-) high, 40-mile- (64-km-) long wall of granite in northeastern Oregon. Driving through the region takes in some of the finest scenery in the state.

The best way to explore the Wallowa Mountains is to take the Elkhorn Drive National Scenic Byway, a two-lane paved road that begins from Baker City. Nestled between the Wallowa Mountains and the Elkhorn Range, Baker City has some lovely downtown blocks and fine Victorian houses. Farther north, the National Historic Oregon Trail Interpretive Center displays replicas of pioneer scenes.

The sleepy town of Joseph lies to the east of the Wallowa Mountains. Named after Chief Joseph, leader of the Nez Perce peoples, Joseph is a popular destination for recreation enthusiasts and artisans. One of Joseph's main attractions is the **Wallowa County Museum**, which is devoted to Chief Joseph's famous retreat, and to the history of both American Indians and settlers of the area. Joseph is also home to the famous Stein Distillery.

The crystal waters of Wallowa Lake sparkle at the foot of the Wallowa Mountains. The Wallowa Lake Lodge, a log building dating from the 1920s, is still in operation. The popular Wallowa Lake Tramway whisks riders up to the summit of Mount Howard, to enjoy spectacular views of the sparkling lake below and majestic peaks rising up.

Wallowa County Museum
🏛 110 S Main St, Joseph
🕐 Memorial Day–late Sep: 10am–4pm daily
Ⓦ co.wallowa.or.us

Wizard Island and
the caldera rim of
Oregon's Crater Lake

A DRIVING TOUR
CRATER LAKE

THE PACIFIC NORTHWEST

Crater Lake

Locator Map

Length 35 miles (55 km) **Stopping-off points** Meals are offered at Crater Lake Lodge; snacks are sold in Rim Village. Two-hour boat trips (Jun–Sep) depart from Cleetwood Cove.

Oregon's only national park surrounds Crater Lake. At 1,943 ft (592 m), this lake is the deepest in the country and the seventh deepest in the world. Its creation began about 7,700 years ago, when Mount Mazama erupted and then collapsed, forming the caldera in which the lake now sits. The rim of the crater rises to an average of 1,000 ft (300 m) above the lake. On the drive encircling the lake, 90 miles (144 km) of trails, various overlooks, and a beautiful lodge offer magnificent views.

0 kilometers 4
0 miles 4

N

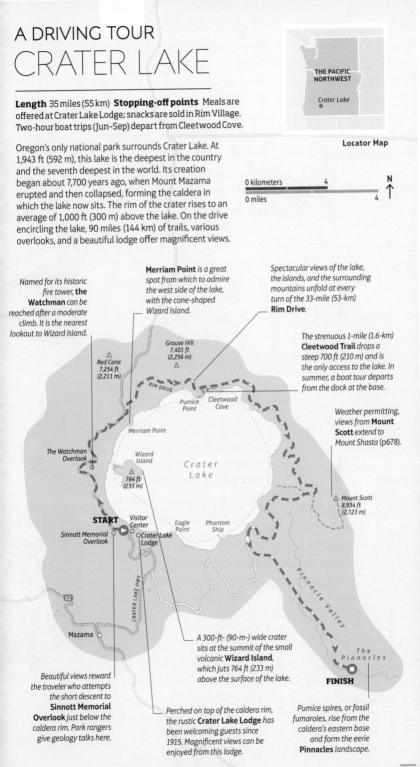

Named for its historic fire tower, **the Watchman** can be reached after a moderate climb. It is the nearest lookout to Wizard Island.

Merriam Point is a great spot from which to admire the west side of the lake, with the cone-shaped Wizard Island.

Spectacular views of the lake, the islands, and the surrounding mountains unfold at every turn of the 33-mile (53-km) **Rim Drive**.

The strenuous 1-mile (1.6-km) **Cleetwood Trail** drops a steep 700 ft (210 m) and is the only access to the lake. In summer, a boat tour departs from the dock at the base.

Weather permitting, views from **Mount Scott** extend to Mount Shasta (p678).

Grouse Hill
7,401 ft
(2,256 m)

Red Cone
7,254 ft
(2,211 m)

RIM DRIVE

Pumice Point

Cleetwood Cove

Merriam Point

Crater Lake

Wizard Island
764 ft
(233 m)

Mount Scott
8,934 ft
(2,723 m)

The Watchman Overlook

START

Visitor Center

Sinnott Memorial Overlook

Crater Lake Lodge

Eagle Point

Phantom Ship

CRATER LAKE HWY

62

Mazama

Pinnacle Valley

The Pinnacles

FINISH

Beautiful views reward the traveler who attempts the short descent to **Sinnott Memorial Overlook** just below the caldera rim. Park rangers give geology talks here.

A 300-ft- (90-m-) wide crater sits at the summit of the small volcanic **Wizard Island**, which juts 764 ft (233 m) above the surface of the lake.

Perched on top of the caldera rim, the rustic **Crater Lake Lodge** has been welcoming guests since 1915. Magnificent views can be enjoyed from this lodge.

Pumice spires, or fossil fumaroles, rise from the caldera's eastern base and form the eerie **Pinnacles** landscape.

CALIFORNIA

A skate park in Venice Beach, Los Angeles

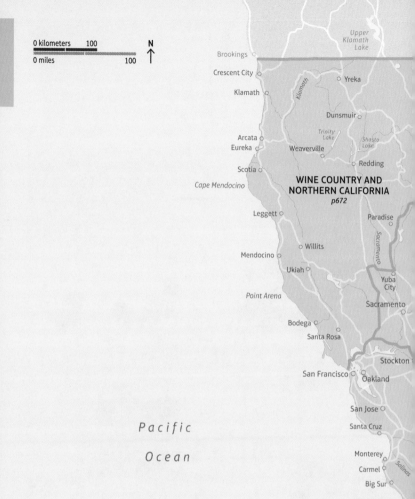

0 kilometers 100

0 miles 100

N

Upper Klamath Lake

Brookings

Crescent City

Klamath

Klamath

Yreka

Dunsmuir

Trinity Lake

Shasta Lake

Arcata

Eureka

Weaverville

Redding

Scotia

WINE COUNTRY AND NORTHERN CALIFORNIA
p672

Cape Mendocino

Paradise

Leggett

Sacramento

Mendocino

Willits

Ukiah

Yuba City

Point Arena

Sacramento

Bodega

Santa Rosa

Stockton

San Francisco

Oakland

Pacific

San Jose

Santa Cruz

Ocean

Monterey

Salinas

Carmel

Big Sur

SAN FRANCISCO AND THE CENTRAL COAST
p644

EXPLORE
CALIFORNIA

This chapter divides California into four sightseeing
areas, as shown on the map above. Find out more
about each area on the following pages.

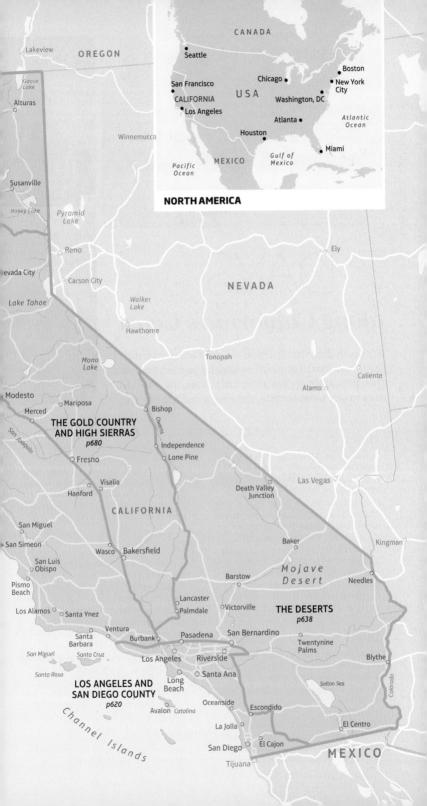

CANADA

Seattle

Chicago

Boston

New York
City

San Francisco

USA

Washington, DC

CALIFORNIA

Los Angeles

Atlanta

Atlantic
Ocean

Houston

Pacific
Ocean

MEXICO

Gulf of
Mexico

Miami

NORTH AMERICA

Lakeview

OREGON

Goose
Lake

Alturas

Winnemucca

Susanville

Honey Lake

Pyramid
Lake

Reno

Ely

Nevada City

Carson City

Lake Tahoe

NEVADA

Walker
Lake

Hawthorne

Mono
Lake

Tonopah

Caliente

Alamo

Modesto

Mariposa

Bishop

Merced

**THE GOLD COUNTRY
AND HIGH SIERRAS**
p680

Owens

Las Vegas

San Joaquin

Fresno

Independence

Lone Pine

Death Valley
Junction

Visalia

Hanford

CALIFORNIA

San Miguel

Baker

Kingman

San Simeon

Wasco

Bakersfield

Barstow

*Mojave
Desert*

Needles

Pismo
Beach

Lancaster

Los Alamos

Santa Ynez

Palmdale

Victorville

THE DESERTS
p638

Ventura

Burbank

Pasadena

San Bernardino

Twentynine
Palms

Blythe

Santa
Barbara

San Miguel

Santa Cruz

Los Angeles

Riverside

Colorado

Santa Rosa

Long
Beach

Santa Ana

Salton Sea

**LOS ANGELES AND
SAN DIEGO COUNTY**
p620

Avalon

Catalina

Oceanside

Escondido

Channel Islands

La Jolla

El Cajon

El Centro

San Diego

Tijuana

MEXICO

1

2

7 DAYS
along California's Coast

This seven-day road trip covers the most enticing stretch of California's coast, between Los Angeles and San Francisco. Though beaches are the prime attractions, there are also seals to see, wines to taste, and even a castle to explore.

3

Day 1

Santa Barbara *(p666)* is just over two hours from LAX by car, though allow time for LA's notoriously heavy traffic (even if you leave early). Happily, there are a few stops en route to help alleviate the stresses of Hwy 101. Ventura has an attractive downtown, with Spanish Revival buildings converted to restaurants. Farther up the road in Carpinteria, French emporium Chocolats du CaliBressan (www.chococalibressan.com) offers tasty sweet treats. Once in Santa Barbara, take in the sunset along the boardwalk and feast on seafood at Brophy Bros Clam Bar (www.brophybros.com).

Day 2

Spend the day soaking up the Spanish Revival charms of Santa Barbara. The city's Colonial heritage is preserved within El Presidio de Santa Bárbara State Historic Park, the excellent Santa Barbara Historical Museum, and at 19th-century Santa Barbara Mission. Have lunch at Three Pickles (www.threepickles.com), which knocks out huge sandwiches. If the weather is good, spend the afternoon on Santa

Barbara's beaches – rent kayaks, bikes, and paddleboards, or just laze on the golden sands. In the evening, sample the local wines on the Santa Barbara Urban Wine Trail (www.urbanwinetrailsb.com), before an indulgent dinner at Bouchon (www.bouchonsantabarbara.com).

Day 3

Cut inland today to explore the Santa Ynez Valley *(p670)* wine region (popularized by 2004 movie *Sideways*). The Carr Winery (www.thecarrwinery.com) is a good place to start, while Sunstone Vineyards (www.sunstonewinery.com) could have been plucked straight from Spain's Rioja. Be sure to visit the kitsch but endearing Danish-themed town of Solvang, not least for its bakeries. Spend the night at the Sideways Inn (114 E, CA-246) in Buellton, and dine at local favorite Pea Soup Andersen's (www.peasoupandersens.com).

Day 4

Reserve a late afternoon or evening tour of Hearst Castle *(p666)* in advance for

1 Santa Barbara beach at sunset.
2 Monterey Bay Aquarium.
3 17-Mile Drive along the coast.
4 Cannery Row, Monterey.
5 Hikers in Limekiln State Park.

today. It's 76 miles (122 km) from Buellton to the low-key seaside town of Morro Bay, which is dominated by the giant massif of Morro Rock in the harbor. Trawl up and down the Embarcadero, grabbing a famed dipped beef sandwich at Hofbrau *(www. ofbraumorro bay.com)*. From here, it's a 45-minute drive to the fabulous Piedras Blancas elephant seal rookery, and then just 6 miles (10 km) to Hearst Castle itself. Tour the extravagant memorial to tycoon William Randolph Hearst before spending a quiet night in nearby San Simeon.

Day 5

Set an early alarm and head along the coast to Carmel; it's a 90-mile (145-km) drive, but this section is worth lingering over. With soaring cliffs and dense redwood forests, Big Sur *(p670)* is the most enchanting section of Californian coast. Take it slow and stop often – good spots include Sand Dollar Beach and the scenic Limekiln State Park. Have a leisurely lunch at Nepenthe *(www.nepenthe.com)* before going on a mini-hike at Pfeiffer Big Sur State Park. End the day in Carmel *(p669)*.

Day 6

Spend the morning enjoying the charms of Carmel's central district. The beach here is among the most beautiful in California, but don't skip Carmel Mission, the most romantic Spanish edifice in the state. Grab lunch or afternoon tea at the fun Tuck Box *(tuckbox.com)*, a mock-Tudor cottage. Then it's worth paying the toll to drive 17-Mile Drive between Carmel and Pacific Grove, which skirts the coastline here. Reserve a Caribbean-California fusion dinner at Fishwife *(1996 Sunset Dr)*.

Day 7

It's possible to get a decent taster of Monterey *(p670)* in one day, provided you start early. Hit Cannery Row first, since this tends to get busy as the day goes on – head straight for the excellent aquarium. Afterward, stroll the main strip of converted sardine warehouses and grab a bite at one of the many family-friendly restaurants. Later, explore Old Monterey, taking in Fisherman's Wharf and Monterey State Historic Park. San Francisco Airport is about 100 miles (160 km) on fast roads from here.

▷ Californian Cult Classics

Many of cinema's favorite movies are set here. Quentin Tarantino's *Pulp Fiction* (1994) is an LA cult classic, and 2000's *Erin Brockovich (right)* is revered for dramatizing the contamination of a local water supply. Further classics include James Dean's *Rebel Without a Cause* (1955) and Cuba Gooding Jr.'s *Boyz N the Hood* (1991).

◁ Around the Golden State

Movie backdrops can be found wherever you turn. From a shabby diner in the Mojave Desert in *Bagdad Café* (1988), to state capital Sacramento *(p682)* in Greta Gerwig's 2017 *Lady Bird (left)*, to Monterey *(p670)* in HBO's blockbuster *Big Little Lies* (2017-).

CALIFORNIA
ON SCREEN

Parts of California – especially Los Angeles – can feel surprisingly familiar, even for first-time visitors. The state has served as a backdrop for thousands of movies and TV shows since the early 20th century, and it continues to play a starring role on screen. Here are a handful of memorable scenes.

◁ San Franciscan Scenery

San Fran *(p644)* has long been used as a movie set. In *Dirty Harry* (1971) Clint Eastwood patrols a virtually lawless city. Eastwood also stars in *Escape from Alcatraz* (1979), one of the best movies about the prison *(p650)*. Hitchcock's *Vertigo* (1958) is a classic, with the Golden Gate Bridge centre stage before Madeleine takes to the water *(left)*.

◁ Hooray for Hollywood

It's not surprising that a popular subject on screen is Tinseltown itself. *A Star Is Born* (1937) was one of the original "making it big" movies, since re-made three times. TV series and movie *Entourage* (2015) was shot across LA *(p622)* and 2016's *La La Land (left)* is known for the dance scene in Griffith Park *(p631)*.

◁ City of Angels?

The dark side of Los Angeles *(p622)* has long been shown on screen. Roman Polanski's *Chinatown* (1974) highlights the corruption that dogged LA in the early 20th century, with locations ranging from Echo Park to Santa Catalina Island. The dark side of the city is also shown in *LA Confidential* (1997), and in 1973's *The Long Goodbye (left)*. *Mulholland Drive* (2001) is forever associated with the highway.

TOP 4 CALIFORNIA-BASED MOVIES

Die Hard (1988)
LA's Fox Tower served as the setting for Nakatomi Plaza.

Easy A (2010)
The entire movie was shot on location in Ojai.

The Big Lebowski (1998)
Filmed in and around LA.

Drive (2011)
Locations were picked by director Nicolas Winding Refn while Ryan Gosling drove him around LA at night.

△ Diversity on the Small Screen

There has been a spate of incisive, inclusive TV series. *Looking* (2014–2016) is a comedy about a group of gay friends in San Francisco *(p644)*, while 2019's *Tales of the City (above)* miniseries highlighted the lives of San Franciscans, including transgender characters. Ground-breaking comedy-drama *Insecure* (2016–) portrays African American women living in Los Angeles *(p622)*.

Sunbathers on Santa Monica Beach, Los Angeles

Experience

1 Los Angeles
2 San Diego
3 Balboa Park
4 Huntington Beach
5 La Jolla

LOS ANGELES AND SAN DIEGO COUNTY

Home to the Kumeyaay, Chumash, and Tongva peoples, southern California was first colonized by the Spanish. San Diego was established in 1769 and Los Angeles in 1781, though the region remained insignificant until it was acquired by the US in 1848. LA's population surged after the arrival of the transcontinental railroad in 1876 and, by 1912, the movie industry had arrived in Hollywood. The population exploded again, and LA eclipsed Chicago as the nation's second-largest metropolis in 1980. Ethnic tensions increased, too: in the 1965 Watts Riots and 1992 LA riots. LA is now the third-largest economic metropolitan area in the world.

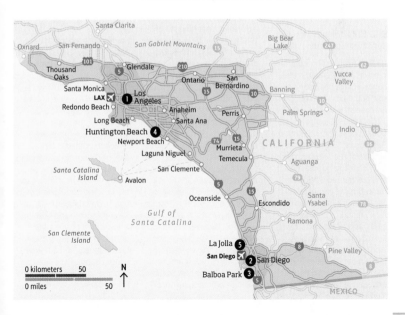

The bright lights of Santa Monica's popular pier at sunset ↑

❶

LOS ANGELES

Sitting in a broad basin, surrounded by beaches, deserts, and mountains, the sprawling city of Los Angeles has a population of 3.8 million. The city's celluloid self-image, with its palm trees, malls, and opulent lifestyles, has been idealized as the ultimate "American Dream." Families similarly love the City of Angels for its proximity to Disneyland® and Universal Studios Hollywood.

① Santa Monica

✕ ☎ 🛈 2427 Main St; www.santamonica.com

With its fresh sea breezes, mild climate, and friendly streets, Santa Monica has been the star of the Los Angeles coastline since the 1890s. In the 1920s and 1930s, movie stars bought land here, creating the "Gold Coast." Following the success of the television series *Baywatch*, the popular beach and pier gained worldwide fame. But the city, overlooking Santa Monica Bay, is also noted for its restaurants, shopping areas, and vibrant arts scene. Lush parks dot the city's landscape, with none quite as beautiful as Palisades Park. For the quintessential California experience, take a walk or jog along the ocean-facing paths.

Inland, between Wilshire Boulevard and Broadway, is Third Street Promenade. Once a decaying shopping street, this boulevard has undergone a major face-lift and is now lined with shops and theaters, and at night lively street performers appear. Santa Monica's other important shopping area is Main Street. Many examples of public art are displayed along the street, such as Paul Conrad's *Chain Reaction*, a stainless-steel and copper-link chain statement against nuclear war. The Frank Gehry-designed Binoculars Building dominates the street, which also features the California Heritage Museum. Northeast of the beach, the 1908 Santa Monica Pier is the West Coast's oldest amusement pier. **Bergamot Station** is a huge arts complex that stands on the site of an abandoned trolley station. More than 20 galleries display the latest in contemporary, as well as radical, art.

Bergamot Station
⌂ 2525 Michigan Av
🕐 11am–6pm Tue–Sat
Ⓦ bergamotstation.com

②
Venice

🛈 313 Grand Av, #202; www.venicechamber.net

Founded by tobacco tycoon Abbot Kinney, as a US version of Venice (Italy), this lively beach town was a swampland little more than 100 years ago. Kinney built a system of canals and imported gondolas to punt along the waterways. The best place to see the remaining canals is on Dell Avenue, where old bridges and boats grace the waterways.

The town is best known for the bustling atmosphere of its beach. On the boardwalk on weekends, men and women whiz past on bicycles and skates, while an array of acrobats, jugglers, and one-man bands captivate the crowds. Muscle Beach, where Arnold Schwarzenegger used to work out, still attracts bodybuilders.

③ 🛡️ 🏛️

Museum of Tolerance

🏠 9786 W Pico Blvd
🕐 10am-5pm Mon-Fri & Sun
(Nov-Mar: to 3:30pm Fri)
🌐 museumoftolerance.com

This museum focuses on the history of racism and prejudice in the US, and on the European Holocaust experience. The museum tour begins in the Tolerancenter, where visitors are challenged to confront racism and bigotry. The Holocaust section has a re-creation of the Wannsee Conference, in which Third Reich leaders decided on "The Final Solution of the Jewish Question." Some exhibits are not suitable for under-tens.

④ 🍴 🖥️ 🏛️

The Getty Center

🏠 1200 Getty Center Dr
🕐 10am-5:30pm Tue-Fri & Sun, 10am-9pm Sat
🌐 getty.edu

The Getty Center holds a commanding physical and cultural position. Opened in 1997, the complex houses not only the Getty Museum but also the center's research, conservation, and grant programs, dedicated to art and cultural heritage.

J. Paul Getty (1892–1976) made his fortune in the oil business and became an ardent collector of art. He amassed a remarkable collection of European art works, focusing on pre-20th-century artistic movements. Since Getty's death, the Trust has purchased works to complement the existing collection, and created new departments. From below, the center may look like a fortress, but once inside, the scale is intimate. Highlights of the collection include Vincent van Gogh's *Irises* (1889), statues by Joseph Nollekens, and photographic works by pioneers such as Louis-Jacques-Mandé Daguerre. The museum also holds a superb collection of decorative arts and illuminated manuscripts.

↑ The Getty Center, which stands amid the Santa Monica Mountains and overlooks the city

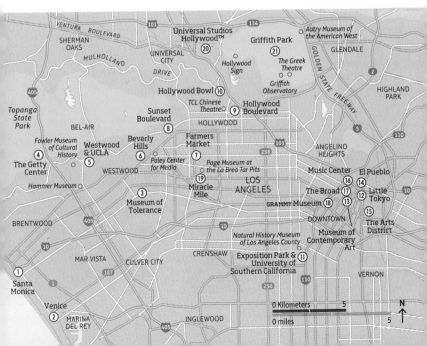

⑤
Westwood & UCLA

📧 🌐 ucla.edu

With its many academic departments and professional schools, and a student body of over 35,000, the University of California Los Angeles (UCLA) is a city within a city. The original campus was designed in 1925 to resemble the Romanesque towns of Europe. But as the university expanded, more modern architecture was favored. The disappointing mix of structures that resulted is redeemed by beautiful landscaped grounds. The four red-brick buildings that make up the Royce Quadrangle are the oldest on UCLA's campus, and far surpass the other buildings in beauty.

Since it was first developed in 1928, Westwood Village, with its pedestrian-friendly streets, has been one of the most successful shopping districts in Southern California. South of here, the **Hammer Museum** holds the varied art collection of oil industry businessman Armand Hammer (1899–1990). Southeast of the museum, the tranquil Westwood Memorial Park marks the final resting place of several celebrities such as Dean Martin, Natalie Wood, and Marilyn Monroe.

Farther north, UCLA's **Fowler Museum of Cultural History** is home to 750,000 artifacts that focus on the prehistoric, historic, and contemporary societies of Africa, Asia, the Americas, and Oceania.

Hammer Museum

🕐 💲 📍10899 Wilshire Blvd 🕐11am–8pm Tue–Fri, 11am–5pm Sat & Sun 🌐hammer.ucla.edu

Fowler Museum of Cultural History

📍308 Charles E. Young Dr 🕐Noon–5pm Wed–Sun (to 8pm Wed) 🌐fowler.ucla.edu

---

MULHOLLAND DRIVE

Mulholland Drive, one of the most famous roads in Los Angeles, runs for nearly 50 miles (80 km) from north of Beverly Hills to the Malibu Coast. It winds along the ridge of the Santa Monica Mountains, offering stunning views of Los Angeles and the San Fernando Valley. The road was named for William Mulholland (1855–1935), who designed a series of aqueducts to channel water into Los Angeles. He oversaw the completion of Mulholland Drive in 1924.

---

⑥ 🍴 💻 🏛
Beverly Hills

The area bordered by Santa Monica Boulevard, Wilshire Boulevard, and North Crescent Drive is the business district of Beverly Hills, known as the "Golden Triangle." The shops, restaurants, and art galleries here are some of the most luxurious in the world. Cutting through the middle is the celebrated Rodeo Drive. Its tree-lined sidewalks house Italian designer boutiques and the best names in fashion, and the place is also a prime area for celebrity-spotting.

To the north are the beautifully manicured Beverly Gardens and the elegant Beverly Hills Civic Center, with its landmark Spanish Colonial

↑ Stalls at the historic Farmers Market

City Hall. Designed in 1932 by local firm Koerner and Gage, the hall's majestic tower, capped by a tiled cupola, has become a symbol of the European-inspired city of Beverly Hills. Billboards are banned in this area, and a height restriction of three stories is imposed on any new buildings, leaving City Hall to dominate the skyline.

The latest addition to the Golden Triangle, the **Paley Center for Media**, holds a collection of more than 140,000 television and radio shows and offers a comprehensive history of broadcasting. Pop music fans can see footage of the early Beatles or of a young Elvis Presley making his television debut, while sports enthusiasts can relive classic Olympic competitions.

North of Golden Triangle, above Sunset Boulevard, lie the famed Hollywood Actors' Homes that have made Beverly Hills the symbol of success for those in the entertainment industry. Houses come in almost every architectural style, and can be toured along a 5-mile (8-km) drive, maps for which are available from

←
Elegant storefronts at Two Rodeo Drive, Beverly Hills

street vendors. Visitors must remember that film stars' homes are private residences.

Paley Center for Media
🏠 465 N Beverly Dr ⏰ Noon-5pm Wed-Sun 🚫 Federal hols
🌐 paleycenter.org

---

⑦ 🍴 💻 🛍️

Farmers Market
🏠 6333 W 3rd St ⏰ 9am-9pm Mon-Fri, 9am-8pm Sat, 10am-7pm Sun
🌐 farmersmarketla.com

During the Great Depression in 1934, a group of farmers began selling their produce directly to the public in a field at the edge of town. Ever since, Farmers Market has been a favorite meeting place for Angelenos. Bustling with stalls and shops selling everything from fresh produce to antiques, the market also has some of the best cafés and restaurants in the city.

---

⑧ 🍴 💻 🛍️

Sunset Boulevard
Sunset Boulevard has been associated with the movies since the 1920s, when it was a dirt track linking burgeoning Hollywood studios with the hillside homes of the screen stars. Its liveliest and most historically rich stretch, Sunset Strip, is filled with restaurants, luxury hotels, and nightclubs.

EAT

Father's Office
A casual gastropub serving healthy options alongside an impressive craft beer menu.
🏠 1018 Montan Av, Santa Monica
🌐 fathersoffice.com

$⑤$⑤

Broken Spanish
Whether tacos, tamales, or more elaborate dishes, the Mexican food here bursts with flavor.
🏠 1050 S Flower St
🌐 brokenspanish.com

$$⑤

Spago
One of the city's sublime dining experiences at chef Wolfgang Puck's flagship restaurant.
🏠 176 N Canyon Dr, Beverly Hills
🌐 wolfgangpuck.com

$$$

Diddy Riese Cookies
Build your own ice-cream sandwich, or go for a chocolate brownie at this local favorite.
🏠 926 Broxton Av, Westwood
🌐 diddyriese.com

$⑤⑤

Once a magnet for gamblers and bootleggers, this 1.5-mile (2.5-km) stretch held famous nightclubs such as Ciro's and Mocambo – where legend says Margarita Cansino met studio boss Harry Cohen, who renamed her Rita Hayworth. While the Strip continues to be the center of LA's nightlife, old "Hollywood" has become newly hip, especially at the Hollywood & Highland Center.

⑨ Hollywood Boulevard

One of the most famous streets in the world, Hollywood Boulevard's name is still redolent with glamor. Despite its recent run-down appearance, many of its landmark sights retain their original appeal.

Perhaps the only sidewalk in the city to be cleaned six times a week, the **Walk of Fame** is set with over 2,500 polished marble stars. Since 1960, luminaries from the worlds of film, radio, television, theater, and music have been immortalized here. Stardom does not come easily, however: Each personality is sponsored and approved by the Chamber of Commerce, and must pay a $30,000 installation fee. Nearby, the **TCL Chinese Theatre** has changed little since opening in 1927 as Grauman's Chinese Theatre. The theater's creator, Sid Grauman, is credited with one of Hollywood's longest-running publicity stunts: its famed autograph patio with hand- and footprints of stars. Legend has it that the custom began when silent screen star Norma Talmadge accidentally stepped on the wet cement. Grauman then invited her to legitimately leave her imprints. Across the road is the Hollywood Roosevelt Hotel, the locale of the first Academy Awards ceremony in 1929. Nearby, the neon lights of the restored El Capitan Theatre draw visitors to premieres of Disney animations. The Hollywood Museum features thousands of items, from the Moulin Rouge windmill to clothing worn by stars.

Walk of Fame
ℹ 6801 Hollywood Blvd; (323) 469-8311

TCL Chinese Theatre
♿ 🏠 6925 Hollywood Blvd
⏰ Daily 🌐 manntheatres.com

⑩ Hollywood Bowl

🏠 2301 N Highland Av
⏰ Late Jun–late Sep
🌐 hollywoodbowl.com

Set in a natural amphitheater, the Hollywood Bowl is practically sacred to Angelenos. The summer home of the LA Philharmonic since 1922, the site attracts thousands of people on warm evenings to listen to the orchestra. Much altered over the years, the shell-shaped stage was first designed in 1929 by Lloyd Wright, son of architect Frank

---

THE RISE OF HOLLYWOOD

In 1887, prohibitionist Harvey Henderson Wilcox and his wife set up a sober, Christian community in an LA suburb and called it Hollywood. Ironically, in the following decades the decadent movie business came to replace their utopia. Silent film stars were succeeded by icons of a more glamorous Hollywood, such as Errol Flynn and Mae West. Wall Street bankers realized their potential and invested heavily in the film industry.

Hollywood Boulevard, flanked by palm trees and roadside stores

Lloyd Wright. The Edmund D. Edelman Hollywood Bowl Museum explores the site's rich history through videos, old programs, and memorabilia of past performers.

⑪ 🏍

Exposition Park & University of Southern California

 4.5 miles (7 km) from city center 🚌

Southwest of downtown, Exposition Park began life in the 1880s as an area of open-air markets, carnivals, and horseracing. By the end of the century, the district was rife with drinking, gambling, and prostitution. In the early 1900s, Judge William Miller Bowen pushed for the transformation of the area into a cultural landmark that today includes three museums. The **Natural History Museum of Los Angeles County** displays a variety of specimens and artifacts, alongside an insect zoo and a hands-on Discovery Center. A short drive southeast

leads to the California Museum of Science and Industry, with its interactive exhibits aiming to make science accessible to all. Farther east lies the California African American Museum, which is a record of African American achievements in various fields. The park is also home to the Los Angeles Memorial Coliseum, which was the site of the 1932 and 1984 Olympics, and was home to the University's Trojan football team. Across the street stands the University of Southern California, which houses about 28,000 students.

Natural History Museum of Los Angeles County

🏛 900 Exposition Blvd 🕐 9:30am–5pm daily 🌐 nhm.org

⑫

Little Tokyo

📍 244 S San Pedro St; www. jaccc.org

Little Tokyo attracts more than 200,000 visitors to its Japanese markets and temples. The first Japanese settled here in 1884. Today, the heart of the area is the Japanese American Cultural and Community Center, from which cultural activities are organized. Nearby, the Japanese Village Plaza is a lively place to shop. Housed in a former Buddhist Temple, the **Japanese American National Museum** traces the history of Japanese-American life in the US.

Japanese American National Museum

♿ 🚌 🏛 369 E 1st St 🕐 11am–5pm Tue, Wed & Fri–Sun, noon–8pm Thu 🌐 janm.org

⑬ 🏍

Museum of Contemporary Art

🏛 250 S Grand Av 🕐 11am–6pm Mon, Wed & Fri, 11am–8pm Thu, 11am–5pm Sat & Sun 🌐 moca.org

Rated as one of the ten best works of architecture in the US, the Museum of Contemporary Art (MOCA) presents an intriguing combination of cubes, pyramids, and cylinders. It holds a selection of post-1940 art, including Pop Art and Abstract Expressionist works by artists as diverse as Mark Rothko and Claes Oldenburg. On North Central Avenue the Geffen Contemporary at MOCA, once an old police garage, hosts exhibition highlights.

↑ Cyclists and students milling across the pleasant campus of the University of Southern California

DRINK

NoMAD

The rooftop bar in LA's NoMAD hotel is worth it for the views (and the pool!). Try the fun tiki cocktails.

📍649 S Olive St
🌐thenomadhotel.com

The Wolves

Featuring stained glass and pew-like wooden booths, this spot has a huge wow factor.

📍519 S Spring St
🌐thewolvesdtla.com

Esters Wine Shop and Bar

This friendly, café-like bar offers an array of delicious California wines by the glass.

📍1314 7th St, Santa Monica 🌐esterswineshop.com

Clayton's Public House

A high-ceilinged vintage bar in downtown, with dozens of draft beers and good pub grub.

📍541 S Spring St
🌐claytonspub.com

High Rooftop Lounge

The perfect place to watch the sun set over the Pacific. There are great live DJs some nights, too.

📍Hotel Erwin, 1697 Pacific Av
🌐hotelerwin.com

The Daily Pint

An archetypal bar offering pool, good craft beers and an exceptional whiskey menu.

📍2310 Pico Blvd, Santa Monica 🌐thedailypint.net

↑ Interior of the grand Union Station, in historic El Pueblo

⑭ El Pueblo

📍Between N Main St & Olvera St & N Alamenda St

The oldest part of the city, El Pueblo de la Reina de Los Angeles was founded in 1781 by Felipe de Neve, the Spanish governor of California. Today, El Pueblo is a State Historic Monument, housing some of the city's oldest buildings, such as the Avila Adobe, the city's oldest existing house, furnished as it would have been in the 1840s. Olvera Street, preserved as a Mexican marketplace from the 1920s, abounds in shops selling colorful Mexican dresses, leather sandals, *piñatas* (clay or papier-mâché animals), and snacks like *churros*, a Spanish-Mexican fried bread. During festivals, the neighborhood is ablaze with color and sound.

Nearby, the 1939 passenger terminal, Union Station, is a blend of Spanish Mission, Moorish, and Streamline Moderne architectural styles. It has been the location for several movies, such as Sydney Pollack's *The Way We Were* (1973).

15

The Arts District

East of Little Toyko (*p627*), this industrial area of old factories and warehouses has become the city's latest arts district. Long home to artists' studios, a wave of colorful street murals, along with trendy restaurants and galleries, have given the area a new cachet. The A+D Museum of Architecture and Design, with changing exhibitions and programs on LA's architecture, has relocated here, as did the Institute of Contemporary Art, Los Angeles in 2016.

16 ⌖

Music Center

⌂ 135 N Grand Av
🌐 musiccenter.org

This performing arts complex is situated at the northern end of Bunker Hill. The Dorothy Chandler Pavilion is

💬 INSIDER TIP
Grand Central Market

This market, a few blocks south of the Music Center, is a great place to sample LA's varied cuisines. It gets busy around lunchtime – go for breakfast instead.

home to the Center Theatre Group, the Los Angeles Opera, the Los Angeles Master Chorale, and, from fall to spring, the Los Angeles Philharmonic. The Ahmanson Theatre stages Broadway plays while the Mark Taper Forum has won almost every theatrical prize in the US. The Walt Disney Concert Hall is the home of one of the world's leading choirs, the LA Philharmonic Master Chorale.

17

The Broad

The striking honeycomb "veil" that filters light into the block-long building beneath is a fitting home for this contemporary art museum. Founded by philanthropists Eli and Edythe Broad, it contains some 2,000 pieces in one of the world's leading collections of postwar and contemporary art, displayed in rotating exhibitions. Viewing windows into "the vault" let you see the extent of this fine collection.

18 ⌖

GRAMMY Museum

⌂ 800 W Olympic Blvd
🕐 10:30am–6:30pm Mon, Wed, Thu & Sun, 10am–8pm Fri & Sat 🌐 grammy museum.org

This modern, interactive museum is dedicated to the prestigious Grammy Awards. It opened in 2008 to coincide with the awards' 50th anniversary and is packed with memorabilia and modcons, including touch-screen exhibits and recording booths. Theres also a number of outfits worn by the biggest artists of the day, and changing exhibitions.

← Striking exterior of Walt Disney Concert Hall, designed by Frank Gehry

⑲ Miracle Mile

🏛 Wilshire Blvd between La Brea & Fairfax avs ℹ 6801 Hollywood Blvd; (323) 467-6412

Built by developer A.W. Ross in 1920, today "Miracle Mile" is dotted with grocery stores – a shadow of the upscale shopping district it once was. The western end has fared the best. With its five museums, including the **Los Angeles County Museum of Art (LACMA)**, the area is now known as Museum Row. The largest encyclopedic art museum west of Chicago, LACMA offers a comprehensive survey of the history of world art, with a collection of over 100,000 objects dating from the prehistoric to contemporary times. Especially impressive are its collection of scrolls and ceramics from Asia.

Nearby, the **Page Museum at the La Brea Tar Pits** has over one million fossils discovered at the La Brea Tar Pits, the largest collection from the Pleistocene Epoch ever found in one place. The only human skeleton found in the pits is that of the "La Brea Woman." A hologram changes her from a skeleton to a fully fleshed person and back again.

The Peterson Automative Museum traces the evolution of the nation's car culture, while farther along, the Craft and Folk Art Museum, houses more than 3,000 folk art and craft objects from all around the world.

LACMA

🏛 5905 Wilshire Blvd ⏱ 11am–5pm Mon, Tue & Thu; 11am–8pm Fri; 10am–7pm Sat & Sun 🌐 lacma.org

Page Museum at the La Brea Tar Pits

🏛 5801 Wilshire Blvd ⏱ 9:30am–5pm daily 🌐 tarpits.org

⑳ Universal Studios Hollywood™

🏛 100 Universal City Plaza, Universal City ⏱ Times vary, check website 🌐 universalstudios hollywood.com

Universal Studios Hollywood™, the world's largest working movie and television studio, opened in 1915. The theme park followed in 1964. To celebrate its 50th anniversary, the owners spent $1.6 billion on upgrades and new attractions.

HOLLYWOOD SIGN

Up in the Hollywood Hills, on the edge of Griffith Park, is the famous Hollywood sign, a protected historic site. Though visible for miles, there is no legitimate trail leading to the 45-ft (13-m) letters. First erected in 1923, it first advertised the Hollywoodland housing development of the former *Los Angeles Times* publisher Harry Chandler. The "LAND" was removed in 1949. It has been the scene of one suicide and numerous prank spellings.

↑ The exterior and interior *(inset)* of the Peterson Automative Museum, Miracle Mile

The famous Studio Tour takes guests through movie sets in trams. Passengers can experience an earthquake, encounter King Kong and Jaws, and survive a collapsing bridge, a flash flood, and an avalanche.

Other areas of the park and rides are based on movies; visitors can explore the magical world of Hogwarts and neighboring Hogsmeade at the Harry Potter and "Wizarding World"™, while the TV show *The Simpsons* was the inspiration for one of the most popular motion simulator rides, and has its own themed village. CityWalk® Promenade has an assortment of shops, bars, theaters, and restaurants, and is a prime area for visitors to buy Hollywood memorabilia.

 🤟 🍴 🖥 🛍

Griffith Park

🚍 ⏰ 5am-10:30pm daily
🛈 4730 Crystal Springs Dr; www.laparks.org

Griffith Park is a 6-sq-mile (16-sq-km) wilderness of rugged hills, forested valleys, and green meadows in the center of LA. Today, people come here to escape the city crowds, visit the sights, picnic, hike, or go horseback riding. The **Griffith Observatory** is located on the southern slope of Mount Hollywood, and commands stunning views of the LA basin below. Inside, the Hall of Science demonstrates important scientific concepts such as the earth's rotation, while on the roof, the Zeiss Telescope is open to the public on clear nights.

Northeast of here lies the Greek Theatre, an open-air music venue with excellent acoustics. On summer nights, more than 6,000 people sit under the stars and enjoy musical performances.

A short drive north leads to the hilly compound of Los Angeles Zoo, housing more than 1,200 mammals, reptiles, and birds living in simulations of their natural habitats. Many newborn creatures can be seen in the Animal Nursery, including some from the zoo's respected breeding program for rare and endangered species.

Opposite the zoo, the **Autry Museum of the American West** explores the many cultures of the American West, shedding light on both the American Indian and the Western perspectives. Exhibits include a replica of a 19th-century Mexican-American ranch, pueblo pottery, and American Indian beadwork. The Autry also includes the collection of the Southwest Museum of the American Indian, which displays tribal artifacts from prehistoric times to the present day.

Griffith Observatory
♿ 🛈 2800 Observatory Rd
⏰ Noon-10pm Wed-Fri,
10am-10pm Sat & Sun
(reservations required)
🌐 griffithobs.org

Autry Museum of the American West
♿ 🛈 4700 Western Heritage Way ⏰ 10am-4pm Tue-Fri, 10am-5pm Sat & Sun 🌐 theautry.org

> ### INSIDER TIP
> **LA Dodgers**
>
> If you're a baseball fan, don't just aim to take in a game but do the stadium tour too. The site, southeast of Griffith Park, is the third-oldest stadium in the US.

→ *De L'Esprie*, David L. Spellerberg, Autry Museum of the American West

Greater Los Angeles

Santa Gabriel Mountains
Pasadena
BURBANK
CALABASAS
GLENDORA
Area of map on p623
Santa Monica
Mountains
LOS
ANGELES
COUNTY
EL MONTE
LOS ANGELES
Malibu
Santa
Monica
Bay
Lax
Watts
Towers
FULLERTON
Pacific
Ocean
TORRANCE
Disneyland®
Resort
ORANGE
COUNTY
SANTA
ANA
Long Beach
San
Pedro
Bay
IRVINE

0 km   20
0 miles   20
N

AROUND LOS ANGELES

㉒
Malibu

🏠 25825 Stuart Ranch Rd; www.malibucity.org

The Rancho Topanga Malibu Sequit was bought in 1887 by Frederick and May Rindge, who fought with the state for many years to keep their property secluded. Eventually failing, they had to sell much of Malibu to film stars such as Bing Crosby and Gary Cooper. Today the Malibu Colony is a private, gated compound still favored by people from the entertainment industry.

A few miles east, the Malibu Lagoon State Beach is a natural preserve and bird refuge. To its east, Surfrider County Beach is considered by many to be the surfing capital of the world. Nearby, the Spanish Colonial **Adamson House** is home to a museum showcasing the history of Malibu.

To the north, **Malibu Creek State Park** features forests, meadows, waterfalls, picnic areas, and hiking trails. Much of the park was owned by

20th Century Fox until 1974. *M*A*S*H*, *Butch Cassidy and the Sundance Kid*, and *Tarzan* were all filmed here.

Adamson House
📞 (310) 456-8432
🕐 11am-3pm Wed-Sat

Malibu Creek State Park
♿ 🕐 Dawn-dusk 🌐 parks.ca.gov

㉓
Long Beach
Ⓜ

With palm trees and ocean as a backdrop, downtown Long Beach is a mixture of carefully restored buildings and modern glass high-rises. At its heart, Pine Avenue, lined with stores, cafés, and restaurants, retains the early Midwestern charm that gave the city its nickname, "Iowa by the Sea."

Along the ocean, Shoreline Village offers views of the ocean liner **Queen Mary**. The Cunard flagship from the 1930s to the 1960s, this luxury liner was converted into a troopship during World War II, carrying more than 80,000 soldiers during its wartime career. It was permanently docked for use as a hotel and tourist attraction in 1967. Visitors can view part of the original Engine Room, examples of accommodations, and an exhibition on the war years.

Nearby, the **Aquarium of the Pacific** is one of the largest aquariums in the US. It holds 550 species in 17 habitats, offering a fascinating exploration of marine life from the Pacific Ocean's three distinct regions: Southern California Baja, the Tropical Pacific, and the Northern Pacific.

↑ Discovering underwater worlds at the Aquarium of the Pacific in Long Beach

Looking up at striking and sculptural Watts Towers ↑

Queen Mary
🚹 Pier J, 1126 Queens Hwy 🕐 Daily 🅦 queenmary.com

Aquarium of the Pacific
🚹 100 Aquarium Way 🕐 9am-6pm daily 🕐 Dec 25, weekend of the Toyota Grand Prix (Apr) 🅦 aquariumofpacific.org

---

㉔
Watts Towers
🚹 1761-1765 E 107th St, Watts 🕐 10am-4pm Wed-Sat, noon-4pm Sun 🅦 wattstowers.us

Watts Towers embodies the perseverance and vision of Italian folk artist Simon Rodia. Between 1921 and 1954, the tile-worker sculpted steel rods and pipes into a huge skeletal framework, adorning it with shells, tiles, and broken glass. He never gave a reason for the towers and, upon finishing, deeded the land to a neighbor. The towers are now a State Historic Site. Next door, the Watts Towers Arts Center holds exhibitions by African American artists. The towers are undergoing restoration, but tours are running outside the fence.

㉕
Pasadena
🚌 🛈 300 E Green St; www.visitpasadena.com

With the completion of the Santa Fe Railroad in 1887, wealthy people from the East Coast, along with artists and bohemians, settled in Pasadena to savor the warm winters of Southern California. This mix of creativity and wealth has resulted in a city with a splendid cultural legacy.

The historic district of Old Town Pasadena, at the heart of the city, underwent a recent face-lift ushering in a spate of upscale shops, restaurants, and cafés in restored historic buildings. The highlights of the area include the Norton Simon Museum, which features one of the finest collections of Old Masters and Impressionist paintings in the country. To the north, local architects Charles and Henry Greene's sprawling Gamble House is considered a consummate craftsman bungalow by many.

A few miles east of Old Town, opulent San Marino is home to the **Huntington Library, Art Collections, and Botanical Gardens**. Once the estate of railroad tycoon Henry E.

Huntington (1850–1927), the mansion holds an important collection of rare books, including a Chaucer manuscript and Benjamin Franklin's handwritten autobiography.

Huntington Library, Art Collections, and Botanical Gardens
🚹 1151 Oxford Rd 🕐 10am-5pm Wed-Mon 🅦 huntington.org

㉖
Disneyland® Resort
🚹 1313 Harbor Blvd, Anaheim 🚌🕐 9am-10pm daily (Jun-Aug: 8am-midnight) 🅦 disneyland.disney.go.co

Visitors to "The Happiest Place on Earth" will discover thrill rides, glittering shows, and shopping in a brightly orchestrated land of fireworks and Mickey Mouse. The original Disneyland® Park is divided into nine theme areas or "lands." Disney California Adventure® Park is smaller, with seven theme areas. At the heart of the Resort, Downtown Disney® is a lively area full of restaurants, shops, and entertainment venues.

SAN DIEGO COUNTY

San Diego's character has always been determined by the sea. Its magnificent natural harbor attracted the Spanish as well as gold prospectors and whalers. The US Navy arrived in 1904, and today San Diego is one of the largest military establishments in the world. Its coastline has miles of stunning beaches, rocky cliffs, and seaside resorts, with many opportunities for leisure activities.

❷
San Diego

🚫🅿️🚐 *i* 996B N Harbor Dr; www.sandiegovisit.org

The museums and art venues of Balboa Park (*p636*) are the prime cultural attractions of San Diego, California's second-largest city. San Diego's growth as a modern city began with the waterfront development initiated by San Francisco businessman Alonzo Horton in the 1870s. He also designed the plan of the Gaslamp Quarter, which is now the centerpiece of downtown, and the best place to shop and dine. The district is particularly attractive at night, when it is illuminated by graceful gas lamps. Close by is Horton Plaza, an innovatively designed shopping center that was built in 1985.

At the western end of Broadway is the Santa Fe Depot, a Spanish-Colonial-style railroad station dating from 1915. The towering America Plaza houses the Museum of Contemporary Art, whose galleries display work by new artists and selections from its permanent collection.

The promenades and piers of the Embarcadero waterfront pathway lead to the Maritime Museum and its three historic ships. Of these, the highlight is the *Star of India*, an 1863 merchantman. To the south is Broadway Pier, where visitors can take a harbor excursion.

North of downtown is Old Town, site of the original Spanish settlement near the San Diego River. Today, more than 20 historic buildings have been restored to form the Old Town San Diego State Historic Park. The Plaza, at its center, was where parades and fiestas once took place. The old Spanish presidio and mission is now part of Presidio Park. Crowning the hill, the **Junípero Serra Museum** is named after the founder of California's missions. On display are archaeological finds plus exhibits on San Diego's successive American Indian, Spanish, Mexican, and American communities.

To the west of Old Town is the Point Loma Peninsula, at the southern tip of which

CRAFT BEER

San Diego vies with Denver, Portland (Oregon), Chicago, and other cities as the craft beer capital of the US. With over 150 craft breweries in San Diego County, there are plenty of places to try the local brews, from trendy tasting rooms to craft beer tours to innumerable beer bars. The city's signature beer style is the very hoppy and flavorsome West Coast-Style IPA.

Boats moored in San Diego's harbor, against a backdrop of the downtown cityscape ↑

↑ The lush poolside of the Hotel del Coronado in San Diego

is the Cabrillo National Monument, named after the city's discoverer, Juan Rodríguez Cabrillo; his statue overlooks the bay. Between December and March, the nearby Whale Overlook is a popular spot to watch gray whales in the water.

The peninsula of Coronado has the city's most exclusive boutiques and hotels. The Hotel del Coronado, or "Del," opened in 1888 and is a lovely Victorian seaside hotel. Its guest list reads like a Who's Who of 20th-century US history, including Presidents Franklin D. Roosevelt and Bill Clinton, and film star Marilyn Monroe. It has been the setting for several films, including *Some Like It Hot* (1959). The Coronado Ferry ride is enchanting at dusk, when the sun's last rays illuminate the skyscrapers of downtown.

On the site of the former Naval Training Center San Diego (NTC) is **Liberty Station**. This mixed-use development on the Point Loma Peninsula styles itself as the city's new Town Square. It features shopping, restaurants, galleries, and a variety of arts and events venues, alongside residential, hotel, and office districts. Many of these are set inside the historic buildings of the NTC, preserving their Spanish Colonial Revival style. You can admire them from the promenade, with its broad lawns, parks, and plazas, or stroll along the waterfront and boat channel. The arts district offers First Friday concerts (a popular free program), art walks, installations, and a variety of events.

For good old-fashioned fun, visit the landmark **Belmont Park**, set along the ocean in the Mission Bay district. It features rides such as the Giant Dipper, an iconic wooden roller coaster that dates to the park's opening in 1925, and the recently renovated pool known as The Plunge. There are also a number of vintage rides such as the Liberty Carousel, Tilt-a-Whirl, and Bumper Cars, as well as a zip line and other newer attractions. There are full-service restaurants and quick-bite eateries throughout the park.

Junípero Serra Museum
♿ 🏠 2727 Presidio Dr
📞 (619) 232-6203
🕐 10am–5pm Sat & Sun

Liberty Station
🌐 libertystation.com

Belmont Park
♿ 👶 😊 🅿️ 🏠 3146 Mission Blvd 🕐 11am–11pm Sun-Thu, 11am–midnight Fri & Sat 🌐 belmontpark.com

③ ⓜ ⌨ 🖐

Balboa Park

📍 **Park Blvd, Laurel & 6th sts** 🚌 ℹ️ **Plaza de Panama; www.balboapark.org**

Located in the heart of San Diego (*p634*), Balboa Park is one of the city's most popular attractions. Founded in 1868, its lush beauty owes much to the horticulturalist Kate Sessions, who planted trees throughout its 2 sq miles (5 sq km). In 1915, the park was the site of the Panama-California International Exposition, which celebrated the opening of the Panama Canal. Many of the Spanish-Colonial-style pavilions built in that year survive along El Prado (the park's main street), while the animals gathered for the exhibition formed the nucleus of the renowned San Diego Zoo. Today, Balboa Park has one of the country's richest concentrations of museums, dedicated to photography, automobiles, model railroads, and precious gems.

Most of the park's museums lie along the central El Prado, while some are located to the south. The pleasant grounds, shady picnic groves, and traffic-free promenades are usually crowded with joggers, cyclists, and street artists. The San Diego Museum of Man, which is found at the western

end of El Prado, is an anthropological museum about the early history of mankind. Exhibits cover the cultures of ancient Egypt and the Mayans, and American Indian crafts. The Mingei International Museum is dedicated to "art of the people" from all over the world. It is currently closed for major renovations, however, and is due to reopen in late 2020. Close by, the San Diego Museum of Art's large and varied collection is boosted by special exhibitions. It displays

a vast range of European and American art from 1300 to the 20th century, as well as some fine exhibits from South Asia, Japan, and China.

The Timken Museum of Art, lying to the east of the Museum of Art, displays a world-class collection of European masters such as Frans Hals, Rembrandt, and Paul Cézanne. It also has a collection of Russian icons.

Farther east along El Prado, the Natural History Museum features a giant-screen 3-D

An attractive plaza fountain in Balboa Park ↑

← The sun sinking towards the waves beyond the pier at Huntington Beach

program where accompanied little ones can visit exhibits before the site officially opens. The zoo is open in summer for nocturnal exploration.

4

Huntington Beach

🛈 325 Pacific Coast Hwy; www.surfcityusa.com

Known as Surf City USA, this sunny town is a beach-lover's paradise, whether or not you want to ride the waves. Its miles of continuous, sandy shoreline have consistently scooped national "best beach" awards. The strand is split into five distinct public beaches, catering for couples, families and pets, and of course for surfers. The romantic pier, which juts out into the ocean and is one of the longest on the West Coast, is a perfect place to watch the sun set.

Downtown, there's a lively shopping and dining district, while other local attractions include the International Surfing Museum and the Surfing Walk of Fame. Whale-watching excursions run regularly here, and the nearby Bolsa Chica Ecological Reserve is a great place for bird-watching. Huntington Beach hosts a number of temporary events each year, including the US Open of Surfing, the world's largest surf competition.

1967

The first recorded year that La Jolla experienced snow.

theater showing five screenings of films that focus on the biodiversity of Southern California and the natural world. The main attraction at the Reuben H. Fleet Science Center, just across the plaza, is the IMAX® cinema in the Space Theater, where films are projected onto an enormous domed screen. Laser and planetarium shows are also staged here. Also well worth a visit is the San Diego Air and Space Museum. An affiliate of the Smithsonian Institution, over 60 aircraft are on display here, along with hundreds of flight-related artifacts.

Just north of the museums, the San Diego Zoo is one of the best in the world and is famous for its conservation programs. Spread over 100 acres (40 ha), it houses more than 650 animal species in enclosures designed to closely resemble their natural habitat. A 35-minute narrated bus tour covers most of the zoo, while the aerial Skyfari ride offers an exciting trip across the south of the park in gondola cars that run 180 ft (55 m) up. There is also a Children's Zoo, as well as a "Kinderzoo"

┌─────────────────────────────┐

TOP 5

SAN DIEGO COUNTY BEACHES

Santa Monica Beach
Popular sandy beach with volleyball nets and an awesome pier.

Carmel City Beach
This well-located, dog-friendly beach has lovely white sand.

Venice Beach
This is undoubtedly the best strand for people-watching.

La Jolla Shores
Stretching for over a mile (1.5 km), this popular beach is busy.

Huntington City Beach
Head here for a 3.5-mile (6-km) strand that is often voted California's best beach.

└─────────────────────────────┘

5

La Jolla

🚌 🛈 7590 Fay Av, Ste 404; www.lajollabythesea.com

Set amid cliffs and coves, La Jolla is an elegant coastal resort. Its streets are lined with gourmet chocolatiers and jewelers, and visitors come to enjoy the art galleries and the restaurants that promise a "Mediterranean" view. The town is home to the University of California at San Diego and the Salk Institute for Biological Studies, which was founded by Dr. Jonas Salk, who developed the polio vaccine. The Scripps Institution of Oceanography is one of the oldest and largest marine research centers in the world. The San Diego Museum of Contemporary Art occupies a prime oceanfront location. A companion to the gallery in San Diego, it displays works of post-1950 art.

THE DESERTS

The arid deserts of California were once the domain of indigenous tribes such as the Serrano, the Chemehuevi, and the Cahuilla. Anglo-American cattle farmers arrived in the 1850s, while low-key mining operations continued until the 1940s. Palm Springs was established in the 1880s, attracting "health tourists" thanks to its dry climate and hot springs. The Cahuilla still own much of the town as part of the Agua Caliente Indian Reservation. In the 1940s and 1950s Palm Springs' "Desert Modern" architecture became the model for mass-produced suburban housing in the US, and tourism blossomed.

Experience

1 Death Valley National Park

2 Joshua Tree National Park

3 Anza-Borrego Desert State Park

4 Coachella Valley

5 Salton Sea State Recreation Area

6 Palm Springs

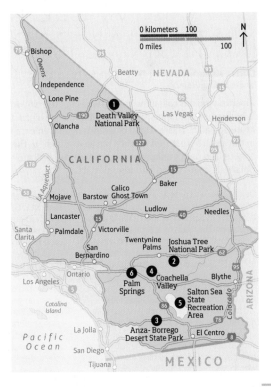

1913

The year that the valley broke temperature records; 134°F (57°C) in the shade.

DEATH VALLEY NATIONAL PARK

⌂ Rte 190, Furnace Creek 🛈 Death Valley Museum and Visitor Center; www.nps.gov/deva

American Indians called the valley Tomesha, "the land where the ground is on fire," an apt name for a valley that has the highest mean temperature on earth. This is a land of wrenching extremes, a sunken trough in the earth's crust that reaches the lowest point in the western hemisphere. The park's unique landscape includes delicate rock formations, polished canyons, and burning salt flats.

Death Valley was once an insurmountable barrier to miners and emigrants. Today, it is accessible by car, and visitors can take short walks from the roads to spectacular viewpoints. The best time to visit is between October and April, when temperatures average 65° F (18° C). Avoid May to September, when the ground temperatures can exceed a searing 100° F (38° C). Whatever the time of year, be sure to bring plenty of water and maps.

There is a surprising amount of plant life, and for a few weeks each year wildflowers appear amid the rocks. An array of animals such as foxes and tortoises have also evolved to survive in this harsh climate. Furnace Creek, with its visitors' complex, is located in the heart of Death Valley. The springs here are some of the desert's few freshwater sources and are thought to have saved the lives of hundreds of gold prospectors crossing the desert. Today, the same springs make Furnace Creek a desert oasis shaded by date palms. There are a variety of restaurants and motels, and the Death Valley Museum and Visitor Center has exhibits explaining the area's history. In winter, ranger programs and guided walks are available. Some of the valley's most breathtaking natural features lie south of Furnace Creek. About 3 miles (5 km) south, on Hwy 178, a short hike leads into Golden Canyon. The mustard-colored walls, after which the canyon was named, are best seen in the afternoon sun.

THE DESERTS

The searing deserts of Southern California have a haunting beauty all their own. Palm Springs, in the Low Desert, is the region's most sought-after resort. The stark Joshua Tree National Park lies to the east. Farther north, the Mojave Desert is the state's greatest secret. Its main draw, Death Valley National Park, has some of the highest temperatures in the western hemisphere.

←

Looking out at Death Valley's eroded foothill formations

WHAT MAKES DEATH VALLEY HOT AND DRY?

The valley's location, lack of rainfall, and composition together make it so deathly hot and dry. The park generally gets just 2 in (5 cm) of rain every year - less than many other deserts. The lack of water means few plants grow, and expanses of sand in turn heat up. On top of this, heat from the valley floor can't escape. It is so frequently the hottest spot in the US that many tables of the country's highest daily temperatures omit Death Valley.

2

Joshua Tree National Park

🛈 **Oasis Visitor Center: 74485 National Park Dr; (760) 367-5500**

California's Joshua Tree National Park takes its name from the storybook Joshua trees that thrive here. The tree was named by early Mormon travelers, who saw the knarled, upraised arms of the biblical Joshua in its twisted branches. The species can grow up to 30 ft (9 m) and live for about 1,000 years.

The magical 1,240-sq-mile (3,200-sq-km) park, with its formations of pink and gray rocks, abandoned mines, and oases, is a climber's and hiker's paradise. A popular trail begins close to the Oasis Visitor Center. South of here, the gigantic boulders in Hidden Valley form corrals, which were hideouts for cattle rustlers. Farther south, Keys View offers sweeping vistas of the valley, desert, and

🔍 HIDDEN GEM
Keys Ranch

It's worth seeking out this ranch in the national park and joining a ranger-guided tour. You'll hear the story of William F. Keys and his family, who embodied the hard work it took to settle and prosper here.

mountains. Close to Keys View, the Lost Horse Mine was the historic mine where over $270,000 in gold was extracted in its first decade of operation.

A variety of animals, which have specially adapted to this environment, thrive in the national park. The kangaroo rat gets its food and water from seeds alone, and the jackrabbit has a coat of muted fur to camouflage it from local predators such as the coyote, bobcat, and eagle.

Note that you really need a car to visit the park, and there are three visitor centers.

A rock climber scaling a mountainous wall in Joshua Tree National Park ↑

❸
Anza-Borrego Desert State Park

🚌 ⏰ Dawn-dusk daily
🌐 parks.ca.gov

During the Gold Rush of 1849, tens of thousands of miners passed through the Anza-Borrego Desert. Today, this former gateway to San Diego County is a remote and pristine park, offering an insight into the unique desert environment, with its steep ravines and rocky badlands. The visitor center is in Borrego Springs, the park's only significant town. Nearby, the Palm Canyon Nature Trail leads to an oasis where endangered bighorn sheep can often be seen. From the Box Canyon Historical Monument there are views of the old road once used by miners en route to the gold fields, which lay 500 miles (800 km) to the north.

The desert bursts into bloom between March and May. Cacti and desert flowers such as desert poppies and dune primroses produce a riot of – weather-dependent – color.

Much of the park, including its campgrounds, can be accessed via the 100 miles (160 km) of roads. Four-wheel drive vehicles are still recommended, however, as there are also over 500 miles (800 km) of unsurfaced tracks.

❹
Coachella Valley

South of the San Bernardino Mountains, this desert valley runs for some 45 miles (72 km), but is only about 15 miles (24 km) wide. It contains the upscale resorts of Palm Springs and Palm Desert, as well as Rancho Mirage, La Quinta, Indian Wells and Cathedral City. In the 1950s and 1960s, Hollywood movie stars built lavish homes and exclusive communities here, and it was known as the "playground of celebrities." Today, more than 100 luxury golf courses and other attractions make the valley a popular destination, not forgetting the fashionable Coachella Festival.

> **INSIDER TIP**
> **Coachella Music Festival**
> If you're heading to this April music festival, it's worth downloading the app. This includes maps, alerts for upcoming acts, and you can even sync and share your schedule with friends.

Wildflowers in bloom across Anza-Borrego Desert State Park, and enjoying the view from a tent *(inset)*

⑤ Salton Sea State Recreation Area

🅿️ 🚍 🕐 Winter: daily; summer: Fri–Sun 📞100-225 State Park Rd, Mecca; www.parks.ca.gov

The Salton Sea was created by accident in 1905, when the Colorado River flooded and flowed into a newly dug irrigation canal leading to the Imperial Valley. By the time the flow was stemmed two years later, an inland sea had formed in the Salton Sink.

Despite the high salinity, saltwater game fish live here, with orangemouth corvina being caught regularly. Waterskiing, windsurfing, and boating are other popular activities, and the area off Mecca Beach has the best spots for swimming. The adjoining marshlands are a refuge for migrating birds.

---

⑥ Palm Springs

🚡 🅿️ 🚍 📞2901 N Palm Canyon Drive; www.visitpalmsprings.com

The largest of the desert cities, Palm Springs was first sighted in 1853 when a survey party came across a grove of palm trees surrounding a fresh-water spring pool in the Coachella Valley. The first hotel was constructed in 1886, and by the turn of the century Palm Springs was a thriving health spa. Today, its popula-tion doubles each winter, when visitors come to enjoy the relaxing, outdoor lifestyle.

Downtown's two main shopping streets are Palm Canyon and Indian Canyon drives; both are lined with restaurants, boutiques, and art galleries. The Village Green Heritage Center has a few historic buildings, including Ruddy's 1930s General Store Museum, a replica of the origi-nal. The Agua Caliente Cultural Museum displays the heritage of the area's Cahuilla people.

The Oasis Water Resort has 13 waterslides, including a 70-ft (20-m) free-fall slide. An enormous wave-action pool creates waves suitable for surfing and boogie boarding. The **Palm Springs Aerial Tramway** covers a 2.5-mile (4-km) trip via cable car, which ascends 5,900 ft (1,790 m) over spectacular scenery to the Mountain Station in the

↑ Popular shopping spot Palm Canyon Drive, downtown Palm Springs

Mount San Jacinto Wilderness State Park. Visitors travel through five distinct eco-systems, ranging from desert to forest. At the top, which is 30–40° F cooler than the desert floor, there are miles of hiking trails, a ski center, campgrounds, and observation decks offering terrific views.

The Palm Springs Art Museum focuses on art, natural science, and the performing arts. The galleries contain pain-tings from the 19th century to the present day, as well as American Indian artifacts and natural history exhibits.

Just south of Palm Springs are the Indian Canyons, four spectacular natural palm oases, set in rocky gorges. Clustered along streams fed by mountain springs, Murray, Tahquitz, Andreas, and Palm canyons are located on the land of the Agua Caliente Band of the Cahuilla. Rock art and other traces of these early inhabitants can still be seen.

Palm Springs Aerial Tramway
♿ 🏠 Tramway Rd 🕐 Daily 🌐 pstramway.com

> **Just south of Palm Springs are the Indian Canyons, four spectacular natural palm oases, set in rocky gorges.**

SAN FRANCISCO AND THE CENTRAL COAST

The Spanish established Catholic missions all along the Central Coast and harsh mission life, combined with the spread of European diseases, killed off most of the indigenous peoples. The region came under American rule in 1848 – San Francisco's population exploded thanks to the California Gold Rush that same year. In 1906 a massive earthquake devastated San Francisco and further earthquakes leveled Santa Barbara in 1925. Since the 1950s San Francisco has been a counterculture hub, from the Beats and hippies, to an LGBT+ capital, while nearby Silicon Valley also developed in the 1950s and is now home to Apple, Facebook, and Google.

Experience

1. San Francisco
2. Santa Barbara
3. Hearst Castle
4. Pinnacles National Park
5. Santa Cruz
6. Channel Islands National Park
7. San Luis Obispo
8. Carmel
9. Santa Ynez Valley
10. Big Sur
11. Monterey

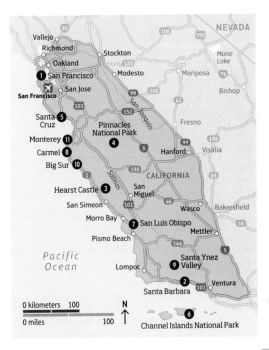

San Francisco's pretty "Painted Ladies," with the modern city beyond ↑

❶ SAN FRANCISCO

After New York, San Francisco is the second most densely populated city in the US. Known for vibrant neighborhoods, major museums, and waterfront esplanades, this is the crowning city of the Bay Area. Visitors get around the seven steep hills by cable car and streetcar, but braving the city on foot can lead to hidden stairways that turn up pocket parks and stunning views.

① SOMA

🚇 3rd St, between Mission & Howard Sts 🚊🚋

SoMa (South of Market) is an area that has become the city's "artists' quarter," with its warehouses-turned-studios, bars, avant-garde theaters, and museums. At its heart is the **Yerba Buena Center for the Arts**, after the construction of the underground Moscone Center, San Francisco's largest venue for conventions, heralded the beginning of ambitious plans for this site. New housing, hotels, museums, and shops have sprung up. The Esplanade Gardens give visitors a chance to wander the paths or relax on benches. Close by, the Martin Luther King, Jr. Memorial has words of peace in several languages.

The adjacent Center for the Arts Galleries and Forum have visual arts galleries and a screening room featuring contemporary art and films. The Center for the Arts Theater presents performing arts that reflect the cultural diversity of the city. The Children's Creativity Museum, located at the Yerba Buena Rooftop, has an ongoing program of events involving design. The Contemporary Jewish Museum showcases scholarly and artistic work relating to the Jewish experience. It includes film, music, and literature. The Museum of the African Diaspora is also excellent, with exhibits and public events celebrating black culture.

Yerba Buena Center for the Arts

🕐 11am–6pm daily (to 8pm Thu) 🌐 ybca.org

② Union Square

🚊🚋🚌

Union Square, lined with palm trees, is at the heart of the city's main shopping district and is home to numerous fine department stores. It was named after the pro-Union

0 kilometers   1   N ↑
0 miles   1

Pacific Ocean

Lincoln Park
Legion of Honor ⑬
CLEMENT ST
GEARY BOULEVARD
32ND AV
34TH AV
43RD AV
3RD AV
GREAT HIGHWAY
FULTON ST
Golden Gate Park ⑯
LINCOLN WAY
SUNSET BOULEVARD

LEVI STRAUSS & CO.

In 1853 Levi Strauss left New York to set up a branch of his family's cloth firm in San Francisco. In the 1860s he pioneered the use of durable blue canvas to make workpants for miners. In the 1870s his company began to use metal rivets to strengthen stress points in the garments, and demand increased. Levi's jeans are now made and worn worldwide. The company is still owned by Strauss's descendants.

rallies held here during the Civil War of 1861–65. The original churches, gentlemen's clubs, and a synagogue were eventually overtaken by shops and offices. Some of the main stores include Macy's, Gump's, and Saks. The area also houses many antiquarian bookshops and smaller boutiques.

Union Square marks the edge of the Theater District and is bordered on the west side by the luxurious Westin St. Francis Hotel. At the center of the square there is a bronze statue of the Goddess of Victory, sculpted by Robert Aitken in 1903 to commemorate Admiral Dewey's victory during the Spanish–American War (1898). The former Circle Gallery at 140 Maiden Lane was designed by Frank Lloyd Wright as a precursor to his Guggenheim Museum in New York (p94).

③ Ⓜ 🛍

SFMOMA

🏛 151 3rd St 🚍🚇
🕐 10am–5pm Tue–Thu
(to 9pm Thu; summer:
also 10am–9pm Sat)
🅆 sfmoma.org

The dramatic San Francisco Museum of Modern Art forms the nucleus of San Francisco's reputation as a leading center of modern art. Created in 1935 with the aim of displaying works by 20th-century artists, it moved into new quarters in 1995, and in spring 2016 reopened after a three-year, $365-million expansion that doubled its capacity. The focus of Swiss architect Mario Botta's Modernist building is the 125-ft (38-m) cylindrical skylight, which channels light down to the first-floor atrium court. More than 17,000 works of art are housed in its 50,000 sq ft (4,600 sq m) of gallery space, and it offers a dynamic schedule of changing exhibits from around the world.

The galleries display design, paintings, sculptures, architecture, photography, and media art, and include art of the Bay Area and California. Among the highlights are works by Dalí, Matisse, and Picasso; Diego Rivera's mural *The Flower Carrier*, a powerful irony on the human cost of luxury, painted in oil and tempera on Masonite in 1935; and the Pritzker Center for Photography, the largest such space dedicated to this art form in the US.

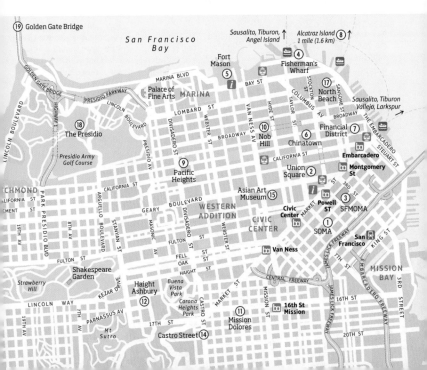

④ 🍽 🛍

Fisherman's Wharf

📍 Between the coastline & Beach St 🚃🚋

Italian seafood restaurants have replaced fishing as the primary focus of Fisherman's Wharf. Fishermen from Genoa and Sicily first arrived here in the late 19th century and founded San Francisco's fishing industry. Since the 1950s, the area has given way to tourism, although brightly colored boats still set out to sea early each morning.

Pier 39 is the Wharf's hub, with restaurants, shops, basking sea lions, and stunning bay views. Docked at Pier 45 is the World War II submarine USS *Pampanito*, which fought several battles in the Pacific and is open for tours. To its south on Jefferson Street is The Cannery, a former fruit processing factory that now houses a mall. The San Francisco Maritime National Historical Park incorporates a museum on Beach Street, which displays various nautical objects. The park also includes a large collection of old ships moored at the nearby Hyde Street Pier. Among the finest is the *C.A. Thayer*, an 1895 three-masted schooner.

⑤ 🍽 🖼 🛍

Fort Mason

📍 2 Marina Blvd
🕐 9am–5pm Mon–Fri
🌐 fortmason.org

The original 1850s buildings here were private houses, which were confiscated by the US government when the site was taken over by the US army during the American Civil War (*p54*). Fort Mason remained an army command post until the 1890s, and also housed those left homeless by the 1906 earthquake. During World War II, Fort Mason Army Base was the point of embarkation for around 1.6 million soldiers. The fort was converted to peaceful use in 1972, and its original barracks and the old hospital are open to the public. Part of the fort is now occupied by one of the city's prime art complexes, with highlights including the SFMOMA Artists Gallery and the Mexican Museum.

⑥

Chinatown

🚃🚋

An estimated 25,000 Chinese migrants settled in the plaza on Stockton Street during the Gold Rush era of the 1850s (*p54*). Today, the district evokes the atmosphere of a bustling southern Chinese town, although the architecture and customs are distinctly American hybrids on a Cantonese theme. The sweatshops, laundries, and cramped apartment buildings that once earned this area the nickname "Golden Ghetto" have been replaced with tidy shops and refurbished residential areas.

The ornate Chinatown Gateway, marking the district's southern entrance, was designed by Clayton Lee as an arch over the main tourist street, Grant Avenue. The three-arched structure was inspired by the entrances of traditional Chinese villages, and is capped with green roof tiles.

Dragon lampposts and stores selling everything from cooking utensils to silks line Grant Avenue. In the 1830s and 1840s it was the main thoroughfare of Yerba Buena, the village that preceded San Francisco. A plaque at No. 823 marks the site of the first dwelling, a canvas tent that was built in 1835.

To the east of Grant Avenue is Portsmouth Plaza, the city's original town square, which was laid out in 1839. In 1846, marines raised the American flag above the plaza, officially

↑ Crimson lanterns strung up in San Francisco's Chinatown

seizing the port as part of the United States. It soon became the hub of the new booming city in the 1850s, and today is the social hub of Chinatown.

Running parallel to Grant Avenue, Stockton Street is where locals shop. China-town's busy alleys echo with authentic sights and sounds of East Asia. The largest of the four narrow lanes is Waverly Place, also known as the "Street of Painted Balconies." Watch for the

Tin How Temple, which is brightly decorated with gold and red lanterns, and the nearby Fortune Cookie Factory, the city's last hold-out of handmade cookie makers, where visitors can watch how they are made. The alleys have many old buildings as well as old-fashioned herbalist shops, and numerous small restaurants serving cheap and delicious food. The **Chinese Historical Society** has a range of fascinating exhibits and artifacts that illuminate the daily life of Chinese immigrants in San Francisco from the 1600s to the present day.

Chinese Historical Society
🏛 🏠 965 Clay St 🚃🚋
🕐 11am–4pm Wed–Sun
🌐 chsa.org

---

⑦
Financial District
🏠 Between Washington & Market sts 🚃🚋🚋

Lying at the heart of downtown, this district stretches from the skyscrapers and plazas of the Embarcadero Center to staid Montgomery Street, called the "Wall Street of the West." All the main banks, brokers, and law offices are located here.

North of Washington Street, the Jackson Square Historical

←
An enormous crab sculpture standing at the entrance to Pier 39

EAT

In Chinatown you can find family-run bakeries as well as upscale spots – here are our favorites.

Sam Wo
🏠 713 Clay St
🕐 Tue 🌐 samwo restaurant.com

💲💲💲

Good Mong Kok Bakery
🏠 1039 Stockton St
🌐 goodmongkok.com

💲💲💲

Mister Jiu's
🏠 28 Waverly Pl 🕐 Sun & Mon 🌐 misterjius.com

💲💲💲

District was once the heart of the business community. Renovated in the early 1950s, this area contains brick, cast-iron, and granite facades dating from Gold Rush days. Today, these buildings are used as showrooms, law offices, and antique shops.

Standing adjacent is a San Francisco landmark, the Transamerica Pyramid. Capped with a spire, it reaches 853 ft (260 m) and is the tallest building in the city. It stands on what was earlier the site of the historic Montgomery Block, which many writers, including Mark Twain, once frequented. At the district's northeastern corner lies the Ferry Building, built in 1903. In the early 1930s, over 50 million passengers a year passed through here, to and from the transcontinental railroad in Oakland or homes across the bay. With the opening of the Bay Bridge in 1936, its usage declined, but a few ferries still cross to Tiburon, Sausalito, and Oakland.

⑧ ⊛ ⊗ 🖰

ALCATRAZ ISLAND

📍 Alcatraz Island 🚢 Pier 33 🕐 Times vary, check website
🌐 nps.gov/alcatraz; www.alcatrazcruises.com

Even on the crowded shores of San Francisco, gazing out at this bleak, rocky island and abandoned prison can send a chill down anyone's spine.

Alcatraz means "pelican" in Spanish, reference to the first inhabitants of this rocky, steep-sided island. Lying 3 miles (5 km) east of the Golden Gate Bridge (p660), its location is both strategic and exposed to harsh ocean winds. In 1859, the US military established a fort here that guarded San Francisco Bay until 1907, when it became a military prison. From 1934 to 1963 it served as a maximum-security federal Penitentiary. Abandoned until 1969, the island was occupied by Indians of All Tribes laying claim to the island as their land. The group was expelled in 1971, and Alcatraz is now part of the Golden Gate National Recreation Area.

Did You Know?

There were 14 escape attempts during the 29 years Alcatraz Federal Penitentiary was in operation.

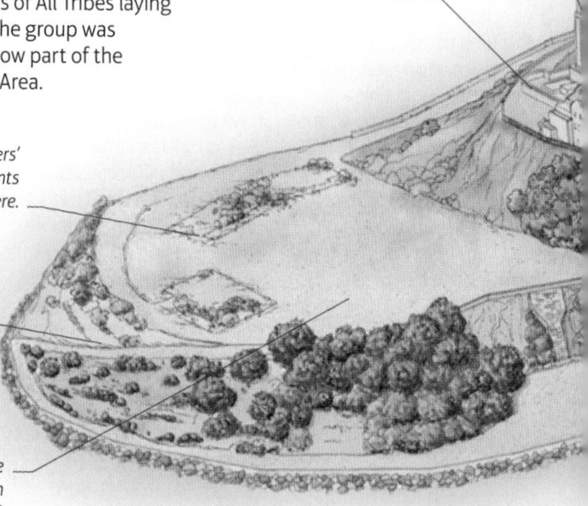

Lighthouse

Warden's house

The officers' apartments stood here.

Agave Trail (open seasonally)

Military parade ground (open seasonally)

Timeline

1775
△ Spanish explorer Juan Manuel de Ayala names Alcatraz after the "strange birds" that inhabit it.

1848
△ Military Governor of California, John Frémont, buys Alcatraz.

1850
Alcatraz is declared a military reservation by President Fillmore.

1854
▽ First Pacific Coast lighthouse activated on Alcatraz.

1859
△ Fort Alcatraz completed; equipped with 100 cannon and 300 troops.

↑ The former prison and its lighthouse standing atop Alcatraz Island

Metal detectors checked prisoners on their way to and from the dining hall and exercise yards.

Water tower

Cell block

The Officer's Club, also known as the Enlisted Men's Club.

The Military Dorm was built in 1933 for the military prison guards.

Equipped with drawbridge and dry moat, the Sally Port guardhouse defended the approach to Fort Alcatraz.

The Exhibit Area is in the barracks building. It houses displays, bookstore, a multimedia show and an information center. .

Alcatraz Pier

↑ Alcatraz Island and the old prison complex

1909
▽ Army prisoners begin construction on the cell house.

1962
▽ Frank Morris and the Anglin brothers escape.

1963
Prison closed.

1934
△ Federal Bureau of Prisons turns Alcatraz into a civilian prison.

1972
△ Alcatraz becomes a national park.

Inside Alcatraz

The maximum-security prison on Alcatraz, dubbed "The Rock" by the US Army, housed an average of 264 of the country's most incorrigible criminals, who were transferred here for disobedience while serving time in prisons elsewhere in the US. The strict discipline at Alcatraz was enforced by the threat of a stint in the isolation cells and by loss of privileges, including the chance at special jobs, time for recreation, use of the prison library, and visitation rights.

> 💬 **INSIDER TIP**
> **Plan Ahead**
>
> Tickets for Alcatraz go on sale 90 days in advance, and sell out particularly fast in summer months. Make sure you bring a jacket or sweater, as the weather can be far wilder and colder out here than it is in the city.

↑ The corridor that separates C and B blocks, nicknamed Broadway by the prisoners

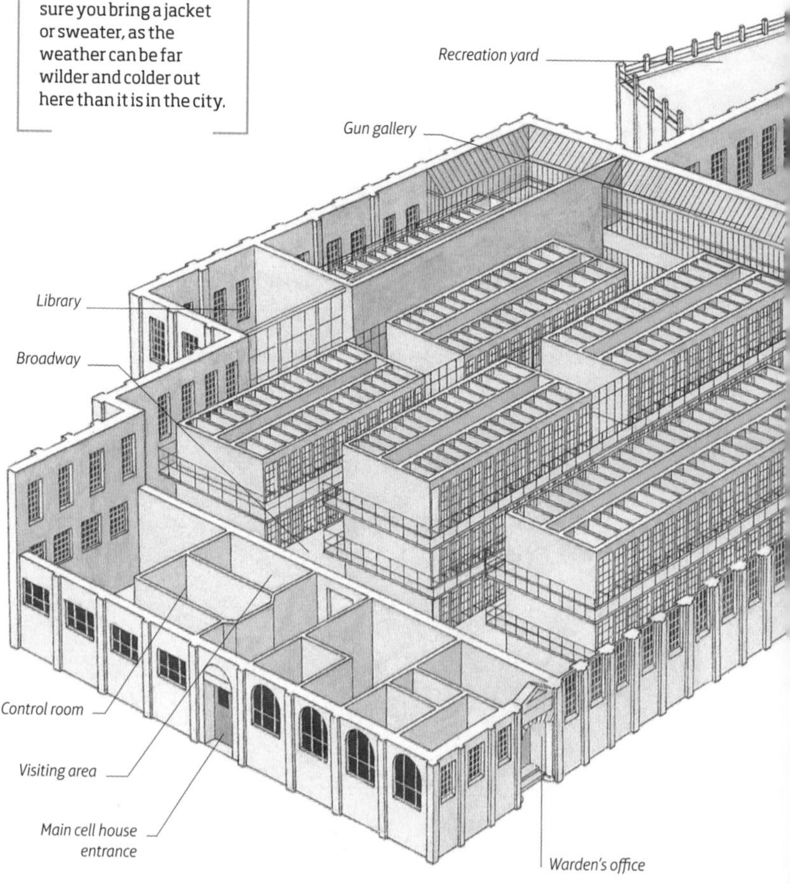

Recreation yard

Gun gallery

Library

Broadway

Control room

Visiting area

Main cell house entrance

Warden's office

↑ Cross-section of the interior of Alcatraz Federal Penitentiary

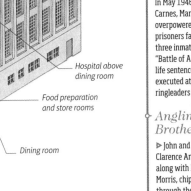

Kitchen

Hospital above dining room

Food preparation and store rooms

Dining room

↑ The prison kitchen, off the dining room where inmates were well fed to help quell rebellion

Infamous Inmates

Al Capone

▷ The notorious Prohibition-era gangster "Scarface" Capone was actually convicted, in 1934, for income tax evasion! He spent much of his 10-year sentence on Alcatraz in a hospital isolation cell, and finally left the prison mentally unbalanced after contracting syphilis.

Robert Stroud

◁ Stroud spent all of his 17 years on The Rock in solitary confinement. Despite assertions to the contrary in the film *The Birdman of Alcatraz* (1962), Stroud was in fact prohibited from keeping birds in his prison cell.

Carnes, Thompson, and Shockley

In May 1946, a group of prisoners led by Clarence Carnes, Marion Thompson, and Sam Shockley overpowered guards and captured their guns. The prisoners failed to break out of the cell house, but three inmates and two officers were killed in the "Battle of Alcatraz." Carnes received an additional life sentence, and Shockley and Thompson were executed at San Quentin prison, for their part as ringleaders of the insurrection.

Anglin Brothers

▷ John and Clarence Anglin, along with Frank Morris, chipped through the back walls of their cells, hiding the holes with cardboard grates. They left dummy heads in their beds and made a raft to enable their escape. They were never caught. Their story was dramatized in the film *Escape from Alcatraz* (1979).

George Kelly

▷ "Machine Gun Kelly" served 17 years on The Rock for kidnapping and extortion. He was then sent to a Kansas jail, where he later died.

DRINK

Cityscape Bar & Lounge

Craft cocktails and a vast selection of wines are served up with views of the Golden Gate Bridge at this chic rooftop bar.

📍333 O'Farrell St
🌐cityscapesf.com

The View Lounge

Those in the know head to this rooftop bar before sunset to grab a seat for one of the best views over the city's skyscrapers and toward the Bay.

📍780 Mission St
🌐sfviewlounge.com

Press Club

This underground bar is an excellent spot for happy hour, offering generous discounts on local craft brews and wine by the glass.

📍20 Yerba Buena Lane
🌐pressclubsf.com

↑ The stunning central rotunda at the Palace of Fine Arts, Pacific Heights

⑨ Pacific Heights

The steep blocks between Alta Plaza and Lafayette Park are set in the heart of the exclusive Pacific Heights district. After cable cars linked it with the downtown area in the 1880s, this quickly became a desirable place to live, and many palatial Victorian houses line its quiet streets. Some date from the late 19th century, while others were built after the devastating earthquake and fire of 1906.

The **Haas-Lilienthal House**, an elaborate Queen Anne-style mansion, was built in 1886 for the merchant William Haas. Furnished in Victorian style, it is the only intact private home of the period that opens regularly as a museum. It houses the head-quarters of the Architectural Heritage Foundation. The impressive Spreckels Mansion on Washington Street, constructed on the lines of a French Baroque palace, is now home to best-selling novelist Danielle Steel. Close by, Lafayette Park is one of San Francisco's loveliest hilltop gardens, lined with pine and eucalyptus trees. It offers excellent views of the nume-rous Victorian houses in the surrounding streets. Located across the street from the park, 2151 Sacramento Street is an ornate French-style mansion, which has a plaque commemorating a visit by Sherlock Holmes author Sir Arthur Conan Doyle in 1923.

At the center of Pacific Heights is Alta Plaza, a land-scaped urban park, where the San Franciscan elite come to relax. Set up in the 1850s, this hilltop green has tennis courts and a playground. The stone steps rising from Clay Street on the south side offer views of Haight Ashbury.

North of Pacific Heights, the streets drop steeply down to the Marina District, which was created from reclaimed land for the 1915 Panama–Pacific Exposition. The Expo's only surviving monument is the grand Palace of Fine Arts. This Neo-Classical building has a large rotunda with alle-gorical paintings on its dome. It houses the entertaining Exploratorium Science Museum and hosts events such as the May Film Festival.

Haas-Lilienthal House

♿🏠 📍2007 Franklin St
🕐Noon–3pm Wed & Sat, 11am–4pm Sun 🌐haas-lilienthalhouse.org

⑩ Nob Hill

Nob Hill is the highest summit of the city itself, rising 338 ft (103 m) above the bay. It is San Francisco's most

Nob Hill is the highest summit of the city itself, rising 338 ft (103 m) above the bay. It is San Francisco's most celebrated hilltop, famous for its cable cars, plush hotels, and views.

celebrated hilltop, famous for its cable cars, plush hotels, and views. The steep slopes kept prominent citizens away until the opening of the California Street cable car line in 1878 (p649). The rich then flocked to build homes here, including the "Big Four" railroad barons, who were among its richest tenants. The name "Nob Hill" is thought to come from the Indian word *nabob*, meaning "chieftain". Sadly, all the grand mansions were leveled in the great earthquake and fire of 1906. The only building that survived was the home of James C. Flood, which is now the Pacific Union Club. Nob Hill still attracts the affluent to its hotels, which recall the opulence of the Victorian era and offer fine views of the city.

Grace Cathedral is the main Episcopal church in San Francisco. Designed by Lewis P. Hobart, this building was inspired by Notre Dame in Paris. Preparatory work began in 1928, but the cathedral was not completed until 1964. Its entrance doors are cast from molds of Ghiberti's "Doors of Paradise," made for the Baptistry in Florence. Inside, it is replete with marble and beautiful stained glass, with leaded windows that were designed by Charles Connick.

A short distance north of Nob Hill is the **Cable Car Museum**. Housed in a 1909 barn that garages cable cars at night, it is a repair shop, museum, and powerhouse of the cable car system. Anchored to the ground floor are the engines and wheels that wind the cables through the system of channels and pulleys beneath the city's streets. Visitors can observe them from the mezzanine, then walk down to look under the street. The museum also houses an early cable car and the mechanisms that control individual cars.

Grace Cathedral
🏠 1100 California St
Ⓦ gracecathedral.org

Cable Car Museum
🕐 🏠 1201 Mason St
🕐 Summer: 10am–6pm daily; winter: 10am–5pm daily
🗓 Jan 1, Thanksgiving, Dec 25
Ⓦ cablecarmuseum.com

The labyrinth laid across the floor of Grace Cathedral, and its imposing exterior (inset)

⑪ 〔⬦〕〔🏛〕

Mission Dolores

🏠 3321 16th St 🚌🚊
🕐 9:30am–4pm daily
🌐 missiondolores.org

Preserved intact since it was built in 1791, Mission Dolores is the oldest building in the city and an embodiment of San Francisco's Spanish Colonial roots. Founded by Father Junípero Serra, it is formally known as the Mission of San Francisco de Asis. The name Dolores reflects its proximity to Laguna de los Dolores (Lake of Our Lady of Sorrows), an ancient swamp. Paintings by American Indians adorn the restored ceiling of the modest building, and there is a display of historical documents in the small museum. The cemetery contains graves of San Franciscan pioneers, as well as a mass grave of 5,000 American Indians who died in the measles epidemics of 1804 and 1826.

⑫

Haight Ashbury

🚌🚊

Haight Ashbury was the center of the hippie world in the 1960s. Originally a quiet,

middle-class suburb – hence the dozens of elaborate Queen Anne-style houses – it changed dramatically into the mecca of a bohemian community that defied social norms and conventions. In 1967, the "Summer of Love" brought some 75,000 young people in search of free love, music, and drugs, and it became the focus of a worldwide youth culture. Thousands lived here, and there was even a free clinic to treat hippies without medical insurance.

Today, "the Haight" retains its radical atmosphere and has settled into one of the liveliest and most unconventional places in San Francisco, with an eclectic mix of people, second-hand clothing shops, and music and bookstores.

Buena Vista Park on its eastern fringe has a mass of knotted trees and offers magnificent views of the city. The grand (Richard) Spreckels Mansion on Buena Vista Avenue (not to be confused with the one on Washington Street) is a typical late Victorian home. It was once a guesthouse, and its visitors

→

Leafy Dolores Park, with the cityscape in the distance

included writer Jack London and journalist Ambrose Bierce. The Red Victorian B&B, affectionately dubbed the "Jeffrey Haight" in 1967, was a favorite among hippies. It now caters to a New Age clientele and offers rooms with transcendental themes.

Halfway between City Hall and Haight Ashbury, the Lower Haight marks the border of the predominantly African American Fillmore District. Unusual art galleries, boutiques, inexpensive cafés, and bars serve a largely bohemian clientele. It also has dozens of houses known as "Victorians," built from the 1850s to the 1900s. Although safe during the day, visitors should take care after dark.

⑬ 〔⬦〕〔🅼〕〔💻〕〔🏛〕

Legion of Honor

🏠 100 34th Av at Clement, Lincoln Park 🚌 🕐 9:30am–5:15pm Tue–Sun 🌐 famsf.org

Inspired by the Palais de la Légion d'Honneur in Paris, Alma de Bretteville Spreckels built this museum in the

---

SOUNDS OF 1960S SAN FRANCISCO

During the late 1960s, and especially during the "Summer of Love," young people from all over the country flocked to the Haight Ashbury district. They came to listen to rock musicians, from Janis Joplin to the Grateful Dead, all of whom emerged out of the thriving music scene. Impresario Bill Graham linked unlikely pairings and brought big-name performers to Fillmore Auditorium, making "the Haight" the focus of the rock world.

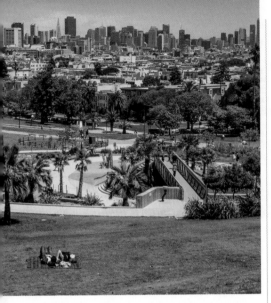

GREAT VIEW
Painted Ladies

The row of Victorian houses on Steiner Street, just north of Haight Ashbury, is a must for first-timers to the city. If possible, visit at sunset when the crowds have thinned and the light is particularly beautiful.

⑮ 🔌 🚫 🖥 🏛

Asian Art Museum

🏠 200 Larkin St 🚌🚋
🕐 10am-5pm Tue-Sun (mid-Feb-Aug: to 9pm Thu)
🌐 asianart.org

The Asian Art Museum is located on Civic Center Plaza in a building that was the crown jewel of the Beaux Arts movement. The former Main Library, built in 1917, is now the largest museum outside Asia devoted exclusively to Asian art. The museum's exhibits include 12,000 art objects spanning 6,000 years of history and representing over 40 Asian nations. There are also performance venues, education programs, a hands-on discovery center, and a pleasant terrace café.

1920s to promote French art in California. Designed by the architect George Applegarth, it displays European art from the last eight centuries, with paintings by Rembrandt and Monet, and over 70 sculptures by Rodin. The Achenbach Foundation, a well-known collection of graphic works, occupies a part of the gallery.

The museum's collection of European art is displayed on the first floor. Claude Monet's beautiful *Waterlilies* (1914–17) is one of a series depicting the lily pond in his gardens near Paris. The original bronze casting of Rodin's *Le Penseur* (1904), better known as *The Thinker*, is located at the center of the colonnaded Court of Honor. It is one of the 11 castings of the statue in collections around the world. Admission here includes a visit to the nearby de Young Museum on the same day.

⑭ 🍴 🖥 🏛

Castro Street

🚌🚋

Focused on the intersection of Castro Street and 18th Street,

the self-proclaimed "Gayest Four Corners of the World" emerged as an LGBT+ nexus during the 1970s. Gay people of the Flower Power generation moved into this predominantly working-class district and began restoring Victorian houses and setting up businesses. They also opened gay bars, including Mary Ellen Cunha and Peggy Forster's Twin Peaks Tavern on the corner of Castro Street and 17th Street. Unlike earlier bars, where gay people had to hide in dark corners out of public view, the Twin Peaks Tavern had large windows that made it the first gay bar where passersby could see inside. Though the many shops and restaurants attract all kinds of people, the Castro's openly queer identity has made it a place of pilgrimage for members of the LGBT+ community. It symbolizes for this minority group a freedom not generally found in cities elsewhere.

→

An ornate sculpture on display in the Asian Art Museum

↑ The lush Japanese Tea Garden, part of San Francisco's Golden Gate Park

📷 PICTURE PERFECT
Lombard Street

With its eight hairpin turns, this is the most photographed street in San Francisco. It's also incredibly steep – so you'll be pleased to know that the best perspective is from the bottom looking up.

⑯
Golden Gate Park

🌐 goldengatepark.com

Though it's often compared to New York's Central Park, San Francisco's vast urban green space is 20 percent larger. It was created in the 1870s from a rugged stretch of sand dunes on the western edge of the city, and today covers 1,017 acres (412 ha), stretching east from the beach to Haight Ashbury (p656). It has a verdant landscape of gardens, lawns, lakes, woodlands, and trails, with playgrounds and picnic areas. There's even a meadow that serves as a paddock for the resident herd of bison, established here in 1892.

Within the park there are numerous attractions. These include the Botanical Garden, the Conservatory of Flowers, the Japanese Tea Garden, the Queen Wilhelmina Tulip Garden, the Garden of Shakespeare's Flowers, and the Golden Gate Park Carousel. Strawberry Hill, an island in the middle of Stow Lake, is the highest point in the park and offers great views of the city. Hippie Hill was a gathering place for the counterculture movement during San Francisco's "Summer of Love" in 1967. Also located in the park are the California Academy of Sciences and the de Young Museum.

---

⑰
North Beach

South of Fisherman's Wharf is North Beach, also known as "Little Italy." Settlers from Chile, China, and Italy brought their enthusiasm for nightlife to the area, earning North Beach its vibrant reputation and attracting bohemians and writers, including the leading chronicler of the "Beat generation," Jack Kerouac. At the junction of Broadway and Columbus Avenue, the City Lights Bookstore – once owned by the Beat poet Lawrence Ferlinghetti – was the first bookshop in the US to sell only paperbacks. Vesuvio, south of City Lights, was one of the most popular Beat bars. Welsh poet Dylan Thomas was a patron here, and it is still a favorite with poets and artists. The Condor Club is located on a stretch of Broadway known as The Strip, noted for its "adult entertainment." This landmark establishment was where the area's first topless show was staged in June 1964. Caffè Trieste, on the corner of Vallejo Street, is the oldest coffeehouse in San Francisco and has been a genuine Beat rendezvous since 1956. Very much a part of Italian-American culture, it offers live opera on Saturday afternoons.

Lombard Street, a little to the north, is renowned as "the crookedest street in the world." Banked at a natural incline of 27 degrees, this hill proved too steep for vehicles to climb. In the 1920s the section close to the summit of Russian Hill was revamped, and eight tight curves were added. There are spectacular views of San Francisco from the summit, especially at night. Close by, the San Francisco Art Institute is famous for its Diego Rivera Gallery, which contains an outstanding mural by the famous Mexican muralist, created in 1931.

The 210-ft (64-m) Coit Tower, built in 1933, stands at the top of Telegraph Hill. The

100

The estimated number of cayotes living in Golden Gate Park.

→

A car driving down the winding ribbon of Lombard Street

lobby has a number of absorbing murals, which were sponsored by a government-funded program in 1934 that was designed to keep artists employed during the Great Depression.

---

⑱

The Presidio

🏛 Federal hols 🛈 105 Montgomery St; www. nps.gov/prsf

To the north of Golden Gate Park, overlooking San Francisco Bay, the Presidio was established as an outpost of Spain's New World empire in 1776. For many years it was a military base, but in 1994 it became a national park, with acres of woodland full of wildlife. There are also many hiking trails, bike paths, and beaches. The coastal path is particularly popular.

The Presidio Museum is part of the Mott Visitor Center in the Main Post area. It houses artifacts relating to the Presidio's long history. Close by, the Officers' Club was built over the adobe remains of the original 18th-century Spanish fort, still preserved inside the building. A 19th-century cannon from the Spanish–American War lies across the adjoining parade ground.

To the north, close to the bay, is the large, grassy Crissy Field, which was reclaimed from marshland for the 1915 Panama-Pacific Exposition. The Military Cemetery, east of the visitor center, holds the remains of 15,000 US soldiers killed during various wars.

The northwestern tip of the Presidio, Fort Point is an impressive brick fortress that once guarded the Golden Gate during the Civil War and also survived the 1906 earthquake. The fort was built in

↑ A civil war memorial, standing guard over the cemetery in the Presidio

1861 to protect the bay from attack, and to defend ships carrying gold from mines in California. It is a good place from which to view Golden Gate Bridge (p660) and there is also a museum displaying military uniforms and arms.

The Golden Gate
Bridge against the
San Francisco skyline

Timeline

Aug 11, 1930
△ After decades of
debate and deliberation,
a construction permit is
finally issued for a
suspension bridge over
the Golden Gate strait.

Feb 26, 1933
The official ground-
breaking ceremony
takes places – a festive
event with over
100,000 attendees
eager to celebrate
the long-awaited
bridge project.

Jun 1934
The north tower
(near the Marin
County end of the
Bridge) is completed,
although some
records claim it was
finished in November.

Jun 1936
▽ With the last
suspender rope in
place since March,
work begins on the
roadway that will
connect San Francisco
and Marin County.

May 27, 1937
△ Opening day. Every
siren and church bell in
San Francisco and Marin
sounds in unison as part
of a huge celebration. The
following day, President
Roosevelt holds a dedication
ceremony via telegraph.

INSIDER TIP
Cyclists

Check the bridge's website for a few top tips so you don't get caught out on your visit (*www.goldengate bridge.org/bikesbridge/bikes.php*).

⑲ 🖥 🛍

THE GOLDEN GATE BRIDGE

🚌 🕐 Times vary, check website 🌐 goldengatebridge.org

Whether you journey across the Golden Gate Bridge, or you just view it from the shore, this icon is sure to capture your imagination and get your fingers itching for a stunning photo of your own.

Named for the entrance to the Strait of San Francisco Bay, called "Golden Gate" by John Fremont in 1846, the bridge opened in 1937, connecting San Francisco with Marin County. Breathtaking views are offered from this world-famous landmark, which has six lanes for vehicles, plus a pedestrian and bicycle path. It is the world's ninth-largest suspension bridge but it was the world's longest one when it was built.

The bridge that most people said could never be built was completed on time and under budget in the midst of the Great Depression, under chief engineer Joseph Strauss. On May 27, 1937, Golden Gate Bridge opened only for pedestrians and an estimated 200,000 people came to be the first to walk across.

Cars driving southbound from Marin County must pay a toll. Pedestrians and cyclists are only allowed on the eastern sidewalk.

TOP 3 VIEWS OF THE BRIDGE

Baker Beach
The city's biggest beach isn't ideal for swimming, but it makes up for it with stunning views.

Fort Point
The northernmost point of San Francisco offers angles that really highlight the incredible scale of the bridge.

Vista Point
Head to this popular spot on Marin County side to get a photo of Golden Gate Bridge with a San Francisco backdrop (*p220*).

AROUND SAN FRANCISCO

✕🚇🚋 🛈2030 Addison St;
www.visitberkeley.com

Berkeley began to boom after the earthquake of 1906, when many San Franciscans fled their city and settled on the East Bay. Many stores still hark back to its 1960s hippie era, but Berkeley has begun to change its profile, with an emerging reputation for fine food.

Berkeley is essentially a university town. The **University of California at Berkeley** has a reputation for counter-cultural movements which sometimes eclipses its academic reputation, but it is one of the country's most prestigious institutions, with at least ten Nobel laureates among its professors.

University of California at Berkeley
🌐berkeley.edu

㉒

Oakland

✕🚆 🌐www.visitoakland.org

At one time a small, working-class suburb of San Francisco, Oakland grew into a flourishing city when it became the West Coast terminus of the transcontinental railroad. Many of the African Americans who worked on the railroad settled here, later followed by the Hispanics, giving Oakland a multicultural atmosphere.

🔍 HIDDEN GEM
Head to Heinold's

Heinold's First and Last Chance Saloon, in Oakland, opened in 1883. Largely unchanged, it's a reminder that the Wild West came to California, too (*www.heinoldsfirst andlastchance.com*).

㉕

San Jose

✕📷🚌 🛈408 Almaden Blvd; www.sanjose.org

The only other original Spanish Colonial town in California apart from Los Angeles, San Jose was founded in 1777 by Felipe de Neve and is now the state's third-largest city.

The Mission Santa Clara de Asis, on the campus of the Jesuit University of Santa Clara, is a modern replica of the adobe original, first built in 1777. The large Rosicrucian Egyptian Museum and Planetarium has an extensive collection of ancient Egyptian artifacts, including a replica of the sarcophagus in which Tutankhamen was discovered.

At the heart of San Jose, the Tech Museum of Innovation is crowded with hands-on exhibits, encouraging visitors to discover how technological inventions, particularly computer hard- and software, work.

The **Winchester Mystery House**, on the edge of town, has a remarkable history. Sarah Winchester, heiress of the Winchester Rifle fortune, was told by a medium that the expansion of her farmhouse would exorcise the spirits of those killed by the rifle. She kept builders working 24 hours a day, daily, for 38 years, until her death in 1922. The result is a bizarre complex of 160 rooms, and the cost amounted to $5.5 million.

Winchester Mystery House

◈◈◈◈ 🔒525 S Winchester Blvd 🕘9am-7pm daily (Labor Day-Memorial Day: to 5pm daily) 🌐win chestermysteryhouse.com

The city's Jack London Square was named after author Jack London, who grew up here in the 1880s. Today, it is a bright promenade with shops, restaurants, and a museum. To the east is the **Oakland Museum of California**, which is dedicated to documenting the state's art, history, and ecology, and is known for its early oil paintings of San Francisco and Yosemite. To the north, Old Oakland, or "Victorian Row," attracts crowds of shoppers.

Oakland Museum of California

⊗ ⊛ ⊜ ⊕ 🅿 📍1000 Oak St ⏰11am–5pm Wed–Fri (to 9pm Fri), 10am–6pm Sat & Sun 🆆 museumca.org

↑ The Romanesque-style arches of the Memorial Church, Stanford University

㉓
Muir Woods

🚌 ℹ️ Hwy 1, Mill Valley; www.nps.gov/muwo

At the foot of Mount Tamalpais is Muir Woods National Monument, one of the few remaining stands of old-growth coastal redwoods. Before the 19th-century lumber industry boom, these tall trees covered the Californian coastline. The woods were named in honor of John Muir, the naturalist who turned Yosemite into a national park (*p684*).

㉔
Palo Alto and Silicon Valley

ℹ️ Stanford University: 295 Galvez St, (650) 723-2560; Palo Alto Visitor Center: 355 Alma St, (650) 324-3121

Among the most pleasant of the Bay Area suburbs, Palo Alto grew up to serve the renowned Stanford University. It was founded in 1891 by the railroad tycoon Leland Stanford in honor of his son. Today the campus covers 8,200 acres (3,320 ha) and is larger than the downtown district of San Francisco. The Stanford Museum of Art holds one of the largest collections of sculptures by Auguste Rodin, including the *Gates of Hell*.

The center of the computer industry, Silicon Valley stretches from Palo Alto to San Jose. The name refers to myriad businesses rather than a specific location. The seeds of the hardware and software industries were sown in the 1980s at Stanford University, at the Xerox Palo Alto Research Center, and in the garages of pioneers William Hewlett, David Packard, and later Steve Jobs and Stephen Wozniak, who invented the Apple personal computer.

A sun-dappled trail ↑ through the towering redwoods of Muir Woods

A DRIVING TOUR
49-MILE DRIVE

Length 49 miles (79 km) **Stopping-off points** Hop out of the car at Fort Point for some fresh air and lovely Bay views **Signs** Follow the blue signs for the "49 Mile Scenic Drive"

Linking the city's most intriguing neighborhoods, fascinating sights, and spectacular views, the 49-Mile Scenic Drive is an official route that provides a splendid overview of San Francisco for the determined motorist. Keeping to the well-marked route is simple enough – just follow the blue-and-white seagull signs. Some of these are hidden by overhanging vegetation or buildings, so you need to be alert. You should set aside a whole day for this trip; there are plenty of places to stop to take photographs or admire the views, and you may encounter slow city traffic.

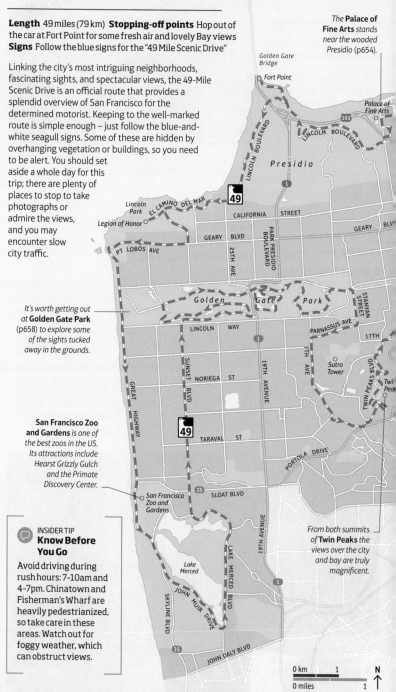

The **Palace of Fine Arts** stands near the wooded Presidio (p654).

It's worth getting out at **Golden Gate Park** (p658) to explore some of the sights tucked away in the grounds.

San Francisco Zoo and Gardens is one of the best zoos in the US. Its attractions include Hearst Grizzly Gulch and the Primate Discovery Center.

From both summits of **Twin Peaks** the views over the city and bay are truly magnificent.

💬 INSIDER TIP
Know Before You Go

Avoid driving during rush hours: 7–10am and 4–7pm. Chinatown and Fisherman's Wharf are heavily pedestrianized, so take care in these areas. Watch out for foggy weather, which can obstruct views.

0 km   1
0 miles   1

N ↑

Marina Green *is an excellent vantage point from which to view the Golden Gate Bridge (p660).*

The **Maritime Museum** *has a fine collection of model ships. Real historic ships are moored nearby at Hyde Street Pier.*

Overlooking North Beach, Telegraph Hill is topped by the **Coit Tower**, *which has stunning murals and a viewing terrace.*

The **Ferry Building** *is a great place to stop for lunch or dinner during your drive.*

The triple-arched portal of the **Chinatown Gateway** *(p650) marks the southern entrance to San Francisco's famous Chinatown district.*

The **Civic Center** *is the stately heart of San Francisco, where imposing Beaux Arts buildings surround a central plaza.*

Mission Dolores *(p656) is one of the city's few remaining buildings from San Francisco's early Mission era (1776–1823).*

Marina Green

Maritime Museum

BAY ST

LOMBARD STREET

BROADWAY

VAN NESS AVENUE

DIVISADERO

COLUMBUS AVE

MASON STREET

WASHINGTON ST

Coit Tower

THE EMBARCADERO

GRANT AVE

Ferry Building

CALIFORNIA STREET

POST STREET

GEARY STREET

Chinatown Gateway

Civic Center

MARKET STREET

HOWARD STREET

80

THE EMBARCADERO

FELL STREET

OAK STREET

101

49

280

14TH ST

CENTRAL FREEWAY

16TH STREET

SOUTH VAN NESS AVE

EMBARCADERO FREEWAY

3RD STREET

STREET

Mission Dolores

DOLORES STREET

JAMES LICK FREEWAY

CASTRO STREET

ARMY ST

ARMY STREET

DOLORES ST

MISSION ST

101

280

SOUTHERN FREEWAY

→ A view of downtown San Francisco from the summit of Twin Peaks

THE CENTRAL COAST

California's Spanish heritage is highly visible in this coastal area. Franciscan friars, resident here in the 18th and early 19th centuries, established 21 missions in the state, with several in this region. These, as well as the capital at Monterey, preserve vestiges of the state's rich Colonial past. Besides historic sights, the shoreline along the Pacific Ocean harbors large areas of natural beauty.

2 Santa Barbara

🏞🏛🚗🚉 ℹ 1 Garden St; www.santabarbaraca.com

Santa Barbara is a Southern Californian rarity: a city with a single architectural style. After a devastating earthquake in 1925, the entire center was rebuilt according to strict rules that dictated Mediterranean-style architecture. Today Santa Barbara is a quiet administrative center with a sizable student population.

Often called the "Queen of the Missions," **Santa Barbara Mission** is the most visited in the state. The tenth mission built by the Spanish, it was founded in 1786 on the feast day of St. Barbara – four years after the colonists established a garrison here. The present structure took shape after the third adobe church on the site was destroyed by an earthquake in 1812. Its twin towers and the blend of Roman, Moorish, and Spanish styles were the inspiration for what

came to be known as Mission Style. Santa Barbara is the only California mission that has been in continuous use since it was founded.

The beautifully landscaped Sacred Gardens were once a working area for American Indians. The surrounding living quarters now display a rich collection of mission artifacts. The church's Classical facade was designed by Padre Antonio Ripoll, who was influenced by the Roman architect Vitruvius Pollio (around 27 BC). Its Neo-Classical interior has imitation marble columns, while the reredos has a painted canvas backdrop and carved wooden statues. The County Court-house on Figueroa Street is still in use. In the Assembly Room are murals depicting California history. The nearby **Museum of Art**, close by, has an outstanding collection that includes Asian and American art, antiquities, and photographs. To its south is the Lobero Theatre. This graceful 1924 structure stands on the site of the city's original

INSIDER TIP
Santa Barbara Urban Wine Trail

Forget the car and hit the wine trail. Walk to 28 tasting rooms in down-town Santa Barbara on this self-guided tour and sample superb US wines (www.urbanwine trailsb.com).

theater. Farther east is the Presidio. Built in 1782, this was the last in a chain of four Spanish forts erected along the coast. Other sights include the Paseo Nuevo, a colorful outdoor shopping center, and the Historical Museum. Among the many artifacts on display here is a statue of the 4th-century martyr St. Barbara.

Santa Barbara Mission

♿♨ 🏛 2201 Laguna St
🚌 🕐 9am–4:30pm daily
🌐 sbmission.org

Museum of Art

♿ 🏛 1130 State St 🕐 11am–5pm Tue–Sun (free 5–8pm Thu) 🌐 sbma.net

3

Hearst Castle

🏛 750 Hearst Castle Rd 🚌
🕐 From 9am daily; closing times vary, check website
🌐 hearstcastle.com

Perched on a hill above the village of San Simeon and set in extensive grounds, Hearst Castle was the private playground and estate of media tycoon William Randolph Hearst. One of California's top tourist attractions, the highlight of the tour is the twin-towered Casa Grande ("Main House"). Designed by architect Julia Morgan and built in stages from 1919 to 1947, its 165 rooms hold many artworks and epitomize the glamor of the 1930s and 1940s. Visitors must take one of the six

↑ Standing outside the tranquil Santa Barbara Mission

The Theater, the walls of which are lined with damask, has 50 seats. The lamps inside are held by gilded caryatids.

Casa Grande®'s façade is in the Mediterranean Revival style.

Hearst ran his media empire from the study. His most prized books were kept behind griles.

↑ Hearst Castle, William Randolph Hearst's impressive home

The Billiard Room features an early 16th-century millefleurs tapestry of a stag hunt.

Refectory Tapestries and choir stalls cover the walls of the dining hall.

Main entrance

The Assembly Room features a 16th-century French fireplace, Italian choir stalls, and Flemish tapestries.

guided tours. The Grand Rooms Tour is best for first-timers. In spring and fall, evening tours feature docents or "guests" in period costume.

Casa Grande was built from reinforced concrete to withstand California's earthquakes. This gilded playhouse for Hearst's many famous guests has 38 bedrooms, an assembly room, a billiards room, two pools, and a theater, where up to 50 guests could watch film premieres. Hearst himself lived in the sumptuous, third-floor Gothic Suite, and ran his media empire from a study here. His most prized books and manuscripts were kept behind grilles. The exquisite heated indoor Roman Pool is entirely covered with mosaics made of colored and fused-gold glass tiles.

Outside, Hearst created a veritable Garden of Eden, laying 127 acres (51 ha) of gardens. Fan palms, Italian cypresses, and huge oaks were hauled up at great expense. Four greenhouses

and thousands of fruit trees supplied plants and fruit. Ancient and modern statues were collected to adorn the terraces. Among the finest are four statues of Sekhmet, the Egyptian goddess of war, dating from 1560 to 1200 BC. The 104-ft (32-m), light-veined marble Neptune Pool is flanked by colonnades and the facade of a Greek temple.

A great lover of the outdoors, Hearst had a covered bridle path built, so that he could ride in all weathers. There was also a private zoo on Camp Hill that once had lions, bears, leopards, and pumas. Zebras, giraffes, ostriches, and even a baby elephant were free to wander the grounds. The three guesthouses – Casa del Mar, Casa del Sol, and Casa del Monte – are luxurious mansions in their own right.

Hearst and his mistress – the actress and producer Marion Davies – lived royally at this estate for 30 years, but

moved to Beverly Hills when Hearst suffered heart problems in 1947.

Pinnacles National Park

🏠 5000 Hwy 146, Paicines
🌐 nps.gov/pinn

Formed millions of years ago by erupting volcanoes, the landscape of this wilderness park ranges from rare talus caves to soaring rock spires. The pinnacles are a draw for rock climbers, and the park has a number of hiking trails of varying difficulties. The caves are home to breeding bat colonies, and close periodically to protect the young. Over a dozen bat species live within the park, which also harbors California condors. The park facilities on the east side are a lot more developed.

Skyline of the Santa Cruz Beach Boardwalk, dominated by the Giant Dipper ↑

5

Santa Cruz

📍🚃 *i* 303 Water St, Ste 100; www.santacruzca.org

Perched at the northern tip of Monterey Bay, Santa Cruz is a lively beach town, backed by forested mountains. Surrounded by farmland, it evokes an agricultural rather than suburban feel. The town's cosmopolitan character is due to the presence of the large University of California campus, with its students and professors from all over the world.

The town's highlight is the waterfront, particularly the **Santa Cruz Beach Boardwalk**, the last surviving old-style amusement park on the West Coast. Its main attraction is the Giant Dipper roller coaster, built by Arthur Looff in 1924 and now a National Historic

Landmark. The nearby carousel has horses hand-carved by Looff's father, craftsman Charles Looff, in 1911. The park also has 27 other modern rides and an Art Deco dance hall.

The Museum of Art and History at the McPherson Center is a huge cultural center that opened in 1993. The Art Gallery shows works primarily by local north-central artists, while the History Gallery displays various aspects of Santa Cruz County's past.

To the northeast of town is a replica of the Mission Santa Cruz, founded in 1791. The original was obliterated by frequent earthquakes, and the present structure was built in 1931. It now houses a small museum. The scenic Cliff Drive along the coast takes in the Natural Bridges State Beach, named for the archways that were carved into the cliffs by ocean waves. The park also preserves a eucalyptus grove and a nature trail, which shows the stages in the life cycle of the monarch butterfly. Also along the coast is the Surfing Museum, housed in a lighthouse and featuring artifacts from every era of Santa Cruz surfing history.

East of downtown, Mystery Spot is a redwood grove that

> **Perched at the northern tip of Monterey Bay, Santa Cruz is a lively beach town.**

has been drawing visitors for decades due to various strange events here. Balls roll uphill, parallel lines converge, and the laws of physics seem to be suspended. Part tourist trap, part genuine oddity, this attraction has to be seen to be believed.

Santa Cruz Beach Boardwalk

🏠 400 Beach St 📞 (831) 423-5590 ⏰ Times vary, call ahead

6

Channel Islands National Park

🏠🚃 *i* 1901 Spinnaker Dr; www.nps.gov/chis

The unpopulated volcanic islands of Santa Barbara, Anacapa, San Miguel, Santa Cruz, and Santa Rosa together comprise the Channel Islands National Park. Access is strictly monitored by park rangers, who issue landing permits

Did You Know?

Much of the 1987 comic horror movie *The Lost Boys* was filmed in Santa Cruz.

San Luis Obispo Mission de Tolosa

🏠 751 Palm St 🕐 9am–4pm daily (summer: to 5pm) 🌐 missionsanluisobispo.org

---

8

Carmel

🚌 🚹 San Carlos between 5th & 6th; www.carmel california.org

This wealthy resort, with its art galleries and shops, has one of the area's most spectacular beaches. A short drive from town is the **Carmel Mission**, founded in 1770 by Father Junípero Serra. The most important of the 21 missions, it served as the administrative center for the state's northern missions. Father Serra, who lived here until his death in 1784, is buried at the foot of the altar. Carmel Mission was abandoned in 1834, and restoration work began in 1924, following the original plans. It now functions as a Catholic church, while recon-structed living quarters evoke 18th-century mission life.

Carmel Mission

♿ 🏠 3080 Rio Rd, Carmel 📞 (831) 624-1271 🕐 9:30am–5pm Mon–Sat, 10:30am–5pm Sun

---

from the visitor center, and those who wish to camp must book two weeks in advance. They must also bring their own food and water, since none is available on any of the five islands. All the rock pools across this unique coastal ecosystem are rich in marine life, and the surrounding kelp forests provide shelter for more than 1,000 plant and animal species. The snorkeling and scuba diving here are considered to be among the best on the Pacific Coast, while sea caves make sea kayaking an exciting experience.

Wildlife on these islands is plentiful and includes sea lions, elephant seals, gulls, cormorants, and – seasonally – gray whales, dolphins, and California brown pelicans on the passage across the Santa Barbara Channel.

7

San Luis Obispo

✈️ 🚉 🚌 🚹 895 Monterey St; www.slocal.com

This small city, situated in a valley in the Santa Lucia Mountains, developed around the **San Luis Obispo Mission de Tolosa**, founded on September 1, 1772, by Father Junípero Serra. Fifth in the chain of 21 missions, and also one of the wealthiest, it is still in use as a parish church. Beside the church, the mission's museum displays artifacts of the Chumash tribe and the mission's original altar.

In front of the church is Mission Plaza, a landscaped public square bisected by the tree-lined San Luis Creek. During the 1860s, bullfights and bearbaiting took place here; today it hosts many of the city's less bloody events.

SURFING IN CALIFORNIA

Surfing was originally practiced by the Hawaiian nobility as a religious ceremony; it was introduced to California by Hawaiian George Freeth in 1907. The sport evolved into a truly Californian pursuit in the 1960s, with films such as *Ride the Wild Surf* (1964) and *Beach Blanket Bingo* (1965) helping to establish its cultural allure. Today, surf culture influences fashion as well as language.

⑨ Santa Ynez Valley

🖳 Ⓦ visitsyv.com

Northwest of Santa Barbara, the Santa Ynez Valley is one of California's leading wine-producing regions. With more than 120 wineries, the area's many wine trails and tasting rooms are a big attraction, made famous by the hit film *Sideways* (2004), which was shot here. The valley is also a big ranching and farming area, and there's a Western atmosphere in many towns that are popular getaway destinations. Los Olivos, Santa Ynez, and Los Alamos offer country-town charm, with art galleries, boutiques, wine-tasting rooms, and restaurants tucked among historic or Western-style buildings. Solvang, meanwhile, has delightful Danish architecture, windmills, and flower-lined streets, and provides a pleasant haven from which to experience old-world traditions, from cuisine to festivals with music and folk dancing.

> **The Santa Ynez Valley is one of California's leading wine-producing regions. With more than 120 wineries, the area's many wine trails and tasting rooms are a big attraction.**

⑩ Big Sur

🖳 🎫 47555 CA-1; www. bigsurcalifornia.org

California's wildest length of coastline was named El Pais Grande del Sur, "The Big Country to the South," by Spanish colonists at Carmel (*p669*) in the late 18th century, and ever since, Big Sur has been attracting hyperbole.

The novelist Robert Louis Stevenson called Point Lobos "the greatest meeting of land and sea in the world," and the 100 miles (160 km) of breathtaking mountains, cliffs, and rocky coves still leave visitors groping for adjectives.

The scenic Highway 1 was constructed along this rugged landscape during the 1930s, but otherwise Big Sur has been preserved in its natural state. There are no large towns and very few signs of civilization in the area. Much of the shore is protected in a series of state parks that offer dense forests, scenic rivers, and crashing surf, all easily accessible within a short distance of the road. Drive carefully when taking the snaking Pacific Coast route, as it has many switchbacks and is often fog-bound, especially in summer. Be sure to stop to photograph Bixby Bridge, a classic landmark and single-arch engineering marvel with a stunning setting.

⑪ Monterey

🖳 🎫 401 Camino El Estero; www.montereyinfo.org

The navigator Sebastián Vizcaíno landed here in 1602 and named the bay after his patron, the Count of Monterrey. But it was not until the Spanish captain Gaspar de

Bixby Bridge, part of the stunning Pacific Coast Highway near Big Sur ↑

Portolá and Father Serra arrived in 1770, establishing a church and presidio, that Monterey properly began to develop. It served as the Spanish Colonial capital of California until the Gold Rush of 1849, when it lost its status to San Francisco. Monterey still retains its unique character as a fishing port and market town. Today, visitors come to tour its carefully restored historic sites and attend the famous annual jazz festival in September.

In the center of town, a cluster of old buildings form the Monterey State Historic Park. The stately Colton Hall was where the California State Constitution was first signed in 1849. It now houses a museum commemorating the event. Northeast of here, Stevenson House is where Robert Louis Stevenson lived in 1879, and is now a museum. The Royal Presidio Chapel on Church Street was built in 1794 and is the town's oldest building. To the north are the Old Whaling Station, where mementos of the whaling

↑ Monterey's historic Cannery Row aglow at twilight

industry are displayed, and the Custom House, preserved as it was in the 1830s and 1840s. Close by, Fisherman's Wharf, once the center of the fishing and whaling industries, is now well known for its seafood restaurants.

Located on Custom House Plaza, the Dalí Expo is another intriguing Monterey museum. Exhibits recount local links to the renowned Surrealist Salvador Dalí, who spent the wartime 1940s in Pebble Beach, California, while the main collection contains 570 of his artworks.

Cannery Row, a six-block harborfront street celebrated by John Steinbeck in his ribald novels *Cannery Row* and *Sweet Thursday*, was once the site of more than 20 fish-packing plants that processed fresh sardines. The canneries thrived in the early 20th century. In 1945 the sardines disappeared, and the canneries were abandoned. The buildings that remain house a collection of electic restaurants and shops. One notable building, at No. 800, is the old laboratory of "Doc" Ricketts, noted marine biologist, beer drinker, and Steinbeck's best friend. It is now a private club.

At the end of Cannery Row, the **Monterey Bay Aquarium** is the largest in the US. More than 570 species and 350,000 specimens portray Monterey

Bay's rich marine environment. Among the exhibits are an enclosed kelp forest, a rock pool, and a display of live jellyfish. The Outer Bay Wing has a 1-million-gallon (4.5-million-liter) tank that re-creates the conditions of the ocean. It contains yellow-fin tuna, ocean sunfish, and barracuda. The Research Institute offers visitors a chance to watch marine scientists at work, while the Splash Zone is a hands-on aquarium for kids.

The wealthy resort of Pacific Grove, at the end of the peninsula, was originally founded in 1889 as a religious retreat. Today, it is best known for its quaint wooden houses, many now converted into inns, its coastal parks, and the beautiful migratory monarch butterflies that arrive between October and April.

Monterey Bay Aquarium
♿ 🏠886 Cannery Row
🕐Daily 🌐montereybay aquarium.org

1958

The year of the first Monterey Jazz Festival, now the longest-running jazz festival in the world.

WINE COUNTRY AND NORTHERN CALIFORNIA

Northern Californian tribes such as the Wiyot, Shasta, and Miwok remained independent until the mid-19th century, when American settlers began to arrive. Eureka and Mendocino were founded in the 1850s, soon becoming "timber capitals," as well as hubs for fishing, shipping, and boating. Pioneers began making wine in Napa and Sonoma in the 19th century, with Russian-born winemaker André Tchelistcheff credited with reestablishing the industry after Prohibition. The remaining forests of the "Redwood Empire" were protected in the 1920s, with Redwood National Park established in 1968.

Experience

1. Napa Valley
2. Mendocino
3. Fort Ross State Historic Park
4. Sonoma Valley
5. Eureka
6. Russian River Valley
7. Redwood National Park
8. Humboldt Redwoods State Park
9. Weaverville
10. Mount Shasta
11. Lava Beds National Monument
12. Lassen Volcanic National Park

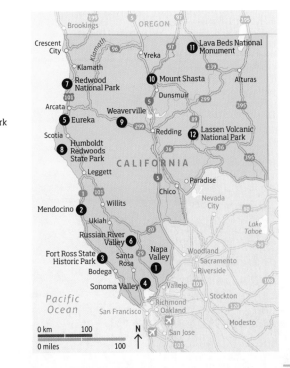

WINE COUNTRY

The clue is in the title; Wine Country is synonymous with the grape, and the region famously produces the country's finest. Visitors are spoiled for choice when it comes to local vintages and vineyard tours, but Wine Country is also known for its mild climate, rocky landscapes, secluded beaches, redwood groves, and impressive architecture.

① Napa Valley

🔼 🚹 600 Main St, Napa; www.napavalley.com

Lying at the heart of California's wine industry, the 35-mile (56-km) sliver of land known as Napa Valley encompasses the towns of Yountville, Oakville, St. Helena, Calistoga, and Rutherford. Over 250 wineries are scattered across its hillsides and valleys, some dating from the early 19th century. Prominent among these is the Mumm Napa Valley Winery, partly owned by French champagne producer G.H. Mumm, where wines are made in the classic tradition. To its north, the Rutherford Hill Winery features caves dug into the hillsides, for aging wines. Farther north, the modern Clos Pegase Winery is famed for its distinctive art collection and superior wines.

For a bird's-eye view of the valley, visitors can take hot-air balloon trips or a 3-hour luxury tour in the Napa Valley Wine Train, enjoying gourmet cuisine. But the best way to explore the valley is along a scenic 40-mile (64-km) drive, breaking at B&B inns in the towns of St. Helena and Calistoga. The latter is popular for its spa treatments and good Wine Country cuisine. A few miles north of here, the Old Faithful Geyser spouts jets of boiling mineral water into the sky once every 40 minutes. To the west lies the **Petrified Forest**, home of the largest petrified trees in the world – huge redwoods which were turned to stone by a volcanic eruption that took place more than three million years ago.

Petrified Forest

🌐 🏠 4100 Petrified Forest Rd ⏰ Daily 🅦 petrifiedforest.org

TOP 3 WINERY VISITS

Francis Ford Coppola Winery
🅦 francisfordcoppola winery.com
Set up using earnings from *The Godfather*, which Coppola directed. The tours here are great.

Robert Mondavi Winery
🅦 robertmondaviwinery.com
This leading winery offers twilight walking tours, art tours, and tours by bicycle.

Justin Vineyards
🅦 justinwine.com
A standout vineyard in the underrated Paso Robles wine area.

② Mendocino

🚌 🚹 217 S Main St, Fort Bragg; www.mendocino coast.com

The founders of this fishing village came to California from New England in 1852, building

their new homes to resemble those they had left behind. The Mendocino coastline is thus often referred to as "California's New England Coast." The community retains the charm of its days as a fishing center, with heather-covered bluffs, migrating gray whales, and stunning ocean vistas. It is a thriving arts center, and has many exclusive boutiques, art galleries, bookshops, and cafés.

CALIFORNIAN WINES

With over 327,000 acres (132,000 ha) of land under viticulture, California produces 90 percent of the nation's wine. Its latitude, proximity to the ocean, and sheltered valleys create a mild climate ideal for growing grapes. The north coast accounts for less than a quarter of California's wine-growing acreage, but produces many of the country's best Sauvignon Blanc, Cabernet Sauvignon, Merlot, and Chardonnay grapes. Chardonnay and Pinot Noir grapes are the mainstays of the central coast region.

3

Fort Ross State Historic Park

🚌 🕙 10am–4:30pm daily
ℹ️ 19005 Coast Hwy, Jenner; www.fortross.org

This well-restored Russian trading outpost was founded in 1812 ("Ross" is a derivative of the Russian word *Rossyia*, meaning "Russia"). The Russians were the first Europeans to visit the region, but they never tried to expand their territory in California and abandoned the fort after 30 years of peaceful trading.

Built in 1836, the house of the fort's last manager is still intact. Within the wooden palisade are several other reconstructed buildings. The most impressive is the 1824 Russian Orthodox chapel. Every July, a living history day is held with costumed actors.

4

Sonoma Valley

➕🚌 🚐 ℹ️ 453 1st St E; www. sonomavalley.com

The crescent-shaped Sonoma Valley is home to 6,000 acres (2,400 ha) of beautiful vineyards. At the foot of the valley lies the tiny town of Sonoma. It was here, on June 14, 1846, that about 30 American farmers captured Mexican General Mariano Vallejo and his men, to protest the fact that land ownership was reserved for Mexican citizens. They seized control of Sonoma, declared California an independent republic, and flew their own flag, with a crude bear drawing. Although the republic was annulled 25 days later, when the United States annexed California, the Bear Flag design was adopted as the official state flag in 1911.

Sonoma's main attractions are its world-famous wineries and well-preserved historical sites lining the Spanish-style plaza. East of the plaza is the restored Mission San Francisco Solano de Sonoma, founded by Father José Altimira of Spain in 1823. Today, all that survives of the original building is the corridor of his quarters.

Just north of here is the **Jack London State Historic Park**. In the early 1900s, London, a famous author, abandoned his hectic lifestyle to live in this tranquil expanse of oaks, madrones, and redwoods. The park retains eerie ruins of London's dream home, the Wolf House, mysteriously destroyed by fire just before completion. After London's death, his widow, Charmian Kittredge, built a magnificent home on the ranch, which has since been made into a museum with displays of London memorabilia.

Jack London State Historic Park

♿🅿️ 🏠 2400 London Ranch Rd, Glen Ellen 🕙 9am–5pm daily (museum: from 10am)
🌐 jacklondonpark.com

← Sunrise over a Napa Valley vineyard, where many of the region's grapes *(inset)* are grown

← Exterior of the Gothic-style Carson Mansion in Eureka

NORTHERN CALIFORNIA

Rugged and sparsely populated, Northern California has a diverse landscape of dense forests, volcanic mountains, and arid plains. It also has the world's largest concentration of giant redwood trees, now protected by national parks. Scenic routes in the parks offer visitors a chance to view their awesome beauty.

⑤ Eureka

✈🚌 *i* 322 1st St; (800) 346-3482

Founded by gold miners in 1850, Eureka was named after the state's ancient Greek motto, meaning "I have found it." Today, it is the northern coast's largest industrial center, with extensive logging and fishing operations surrounding the state-protected natural harbor. Its Old Town's many restored 19th-century buildings are now fashionable cafés, bars, and restaurants. Eureka also houses the 1885 Carson Mansion, once home of the millionaire lumber baron William Carson, and now a private club. Its Gothic design is enhanced by its redwood construction, painted to resemble stone.

⑥ Russian River Valley

🚌 *i* 16200 1st St, Guerneville; www.russianriver.com

Bisected by the Russian River and its tributaries, this valley contains many smaller valleys, dotted with vineyards, apple orchards, redwood groves, family farms, and sandy river beaches. At its hub is the town of Healdsburg, with a Spanish-style town square lined with shops, restaurants, and cafés.

Southwest of Healdsburg lies Guerneville, a summer haven for San Francisco's gay population. Every September, the town hosts the famous Russian River Jazz Festival at Johnson's Beach, where visitors can take a canoe or raft down the gentle Russian River. Otters and blue herons can often be seen here.

Hikers and equestrians also flock to Guerneville to visit the 805-acre (330-ha) **Armstrong Redwoods State Natural Reserve**, one of the few remaining old-growth redwood forests in California. The park was established in the 1870s by Colonel James Armstrong, a local landowner. Among its redwoods is a towering 308-ft (94-m) giant – a 1,400-year-old tree named after the Colonel.

Armstrong Redwoods State Natural Reserve

🏠 17020 Armstrong Woods Rd, Guerneville ◯ Daily
🌐 parks.ca.gov

Did You Know?

The earliest redwoods arrived in California around 20 million years ago.

→ Hiking beneath a mammoth tree trunk in Redwood National Park

❼ Redwood National Park

🏛 1111 Second St, Crescent City; www.nps.gov/redw

Some of the largest original redwood forests in the world are preserved in this national park. Stretching along the coastline, the 58,000-acre (23,500-ha) park includes many smaller state parks and can be explored on a day-long drive. A two-day trip, however, allows time to walk away from the roads and experience the tranquility of the stately groves, or spot one of the world's last remaining herds of Roosevelt elk.

The park's headquarters are in Crescent City, a few miles north of which lies the 9,200-acre (3,720-ha) Jedediah Smith Redwoods State Park, with the most awe-inspiring coastal redwoods. Named after the fur trapper Jedediah Smith, the first white man who walked across the US, it has excellent campground facilities. South from Crescent City, the Trees of Mystery grove features unusual-looking fiberglass statues of the mythical lumberjack Paul Bunyan and his faithful ox, Babe. The park's main attraction is the world's tallest tree, a 368-ft (112-m) giant, standing in the Tall Trees Grove. Farther south is Big Lagoon, a freshwater lake that stretches for 3 miles (5 km) and two other estuaries. Together, they form the Humboldt Lagoons State Park. The headlands at Patrick's Point State Park, at the southern end, are a good place to watch for migrating gray whales in winter.

---

❽ Humboldt Redwoods State Park

🚗 US Hwy 101 🚌 ⏰ Daily 🌐 humboldtredwoods.org

This park has the world's tallest redwood trees and the most extensive primeval redwood groves. The tallest individual specimen, the 364-ft (110-m) Dyersville Giant, was blown over by a storm in 1991. Now seen lying on its side, its size appears even more astounding. The serpentine Avenue of the Giants runs through the park, with the visitor center, in Weott, located halfway along the road.

To the north is the town of Scotia, built in 1887 to house the workers of the Pacific Lumber Company's massive redwood mill. Scotia is the only complete lumber community still in existence in California. Its small museum traces the history of the town, and of the lumber industry, and offers self-guided tours.

BIGFOOT SIGHTING

In 1967, video footage supposedly showing Bigfoot walking through Bluff Creek, northeast of Redwood National Park, materialized. There have been other "sightings" in the state. A 2014 poll revealed more citizens believe in Bigfoot than in the Big Bang.

9

Weaverville

📍 ℹ 509 Main St; www.
trinitycounty.com

This small rural town has changed little since it was founded by gold prospectors 150 years ago. The Jake Jackson Museum, which stands in the heart of the small commercial district, traces the history of the town and its surrounding gold-mining and lumber region. Next door, the Joss House State Historic Site is the country's oldest and best-preserved Chinese temple. Built in 1874, it is a reminder of the thousands of Chinese immigrants who came to the US to mine gold, and stayed on as cheap labor to build the California railroads.

North of Weaverville, the chiseled Trinity Alps rise up at the center of beautiful mountain wilderness. The mountains are popular with hikers and backpackers in summer, offering a range of trails of varying difficulty, and with cross-country skiers during the winter months.

> Mount Shasta is considered sacred by American Indians, and attempts have been made to place the entire mountain on the National List of Historic Places.

10

Mount Shasta

🏨 🚌 Siskiyou, Shasta
ℹ 300 Pine St; www.
mtshastachamber.com

At a height of 14,162 ft (4,316 m), Mount Shasta is the second highest of the Cascade Mountains, after Mount Rainier in Washington (p592).

Mount Shasta is considered sacred by American Indians, and attempts have been made to place the entire mountain on the National List of Historic Places. Visible from more than 100 miles (160 km) away on a clear day and usually covered with snow, the summit is a popular destination for adventure sports enthusiasts such as mountaineers. There are gentle, looping trails on offer too, however, and in winter there is usually skiing offered on the mountain's western slope. At its foothills lies the picturesque town of Shasta, which was once one of the state's largest gold-mining camps. Today, Shasta makes a welcome base, with plenty of good places to stay.

Mount Shasta city is also nearby, and offers all sorts of accommodations, from luxury retreats to wilderness camping.

The looming peak of Mount Shasta, a draw for intrepid mountaineers (inset) ↑

↑ Celebrating the incredible formations of
Lava Beds National Monument

11

Lava Beds National Monument

📷 🌐 nps.gov/labe

Spreading over 46,500 acres (18,800 ha) of the Modoc Plateau, this eerie landscape of lava flows has over 200 caves and lava tubes – those cylindrical tunnels created by exposed lava turning to stone. Most of the volcanic caves, through which visitors can take ranger-led or self-guided tours, are scattered near the visitor center. Anyone interested in a cave tour should wear sturdy shoes, carry a flashlight, and inquire first at the visitor center (which is open daily).

The park is also notable as the site of the 1872–73 Modoc War, one of the many conflicts between the US and the American Indians. For six months a group of the Modoc tribe, under the command of "Captain Jack," evaded the US Cavalry from a natural fortress of passageways along the park's northern border. The captain was eventually captured and hanged, and the rest of the band were forced into a reservation in what is now Oklahoma.

12

Lassen Volcanic National Park

📷 🌐 nps.gov/labo

Before the eruption of Mount St. Helens in 1980 (p597), the 10,457-ft- (3,187-m-) high Lassen Peak was the last volcano to erupt on mainland US. In nearly 300 eruptions between 1914 and 1917, it laid 100,000 acres (40,500 ha) of the surrounding land to waste.

Lassen Peak is considered to be still active, with areas on its flanks showing clear signs of the geological processes. The boardwalk trail of Bumpass Hell (named for a guide who lost his leg in a boiling mudpot in 1865) leads past a series of sulfurous pools of boiling water, heated by molten rock deep underground. In summer, visitors can take the winding road through the park, climbing to Summit Lake. The road continues through the so-called Devastated Area, a bleak landscape that terminates at the Manzanita Lake, and the **Loomis Museum**.

Loomis Museum

🏠 Lassen Park Rd, N entrance ☎ (530) 595-6140 🕐 May 27–Oct: 9am–5pm daily

EAT

Lost Coast Brewery Restaurant

Located separately from the brewery, this spot serves up pub staples along with its own excellent ales.

🏠 617 4th St, Eureka
🌐 lostcoast.com

$$$

Samoa Cookhouse

Opened in 1893, this is the last surviving cookhouse where food is dished up lumber-camp style.

🏠 908 Vince Av, Samoa
🌐 samoacookhouse.net

$$$

Restaurant 301

This award-winning restaurant is set in an elegant Victorian building and offers a daily changing menu.

🏠 Carter House Inn, 301 L St, Eureka
🌐 carterhouse.com

$$$

Trillium Café & Inn

Upscale dining at this farm-to-table restaurant, which also offers on-site rooms.

🏠 10390 Kasten St, Mendocino 🌐 trillium mendocino.com

$$$

Ravens Restaurant

This vegan restaurant has elegant, healthful dishes, served in a beautiful dining room.

🏠 The Stanford Inn by the Sea, Mendocino
🌐 ravensrestaurant.com

$$$

A grove of giant sequoias in Kings Canyon National Park

THE GOLD COUNTRY AND HIGH SIERRAS

The California Gold Rush began in 1848 and Sacramento was developed the same year; by 1854 it had become the de facto capital of California. Thousands poured into the region, though most of the gold was gone within 15 years. Once tranquil Lake Tahoe became a transportation hub as logging and mining boomed in the late 19th century, and Tahoe City was founded in 1864. Tourists began arriving in Yosemite Valley from 1855. The valley has been protected since 1864 and, in 1890, Yosemite became the third US national park, thanks in part to Scottish-American naturalist John Muir.

Experience

1. Nevada City
2. Sacramento
3. Grass Valley
4. Columbia State Historic Park
5. Highway 49
6. Marshall Gold Discovery State Park
7. Yosemite National Park
8. Lake Tahoe
9. Eastern Sierras
10. Sequoia and Kings Canyon National Parks

↑ A locomotive at the California State Railroad Museum, Sacramento

THE GOLD COUNTRY

The Gold Country was once a real-life El Dorado, with a thick vein of gold waiting to be found. Miners have long left but the name has stuck, and today the Gold Country is rich in national parks, sleepy towns, and fertile vineyards. The jewel in the region's crown is Sacramento, the dynamic capital city of the state of California.

① Nevada City

📧 **ⓘ** 132 Main St; www.nevadacitychamber.com

Located at the northern end of the Mother Lode gold fields, this picturesque city deserves its reputation as the "Queen of the Northern Mines." But the once-thriving city faded into oblivion after the Gold Rush subsided. It was resurrected as a tourist destination a century later with galleries, restaurants, and inns recreating Gold Rush themes.

Did You Know?

The only city in the world with more trees than Sacramento is Paris.

The city boasts one of the region's most-photographed facades in the Firehouse #1 Museum, with its white cupola and dainty balconies. It is now a local history museum. Other historic buildings include the Nevada Theatre, a performance venue since 1865, and the National Hotel. One of California's oldest hotels, it first opened in the mid-1850s.

② Sacramento

❌🚆📧 30, 31, 32 **ⓘ** 1002 2nd St; www.visitsacramento.com

Founded by John Sutter in 1839, California's capital city preserves many historic buildings along the waterfront in Old Sacramento. Most of the structures date from the 1860s, when it became the supply point for miners. Both the transcontinental railroad

and Pony Express had their western terminus here, with riverboats providing passage to San Francisco. The **California State Railroad Museum**, at the northern edge of the old town, houses some restored locomotives. A little away from the old town, the State Capitol stands in a landscaped park. To its east, Sutter's Fort is a re-creation of the city's original settlement.

California State Railroad Museum

📍 125 I St 📞 (916) 323-9280 🕙 10am–5pm daily 🚫 Jan 1, Thanksgiving, Dec 25

③ Grass Valley

📧 **ⓘ** 128 E Main St; www.grassvalleychamber.com

One of the largest and busiest gold-mining towns, Grass Valley employed workers from the tin mines of Cornwall in England. It was their expertise that enabled local mines to stay in business. At the entrance to the **Northstar Mine Powerhouse and Pelton Wheel Museum** is the giant Pelton wheel that increased production in underground mines. Also on view are a stamp mill and a Cornish pump.

Grass Valley also served the nearby **Empire Mine**, the state's richest and longest-surviving gold mine. Now a state park, the mine had recovered almost six million ounces of gold when it closed in 1956. Mining equipment and artifacts can be seen in the park and in the museum.

Northstar Mine Powerhouse and Pelton Wheel Museum

10933 Alison Ranch Rd
(530) 273-4255 May-Oct: 11am-5pm Tue-Sun

Empire Mine Historic State Park

10791 E Empire St
10am-4pm daily
empiremine.org

4

Columbia State Historic Park

Hwy 49 11255 Jackson St; (209) 588-9128

At the height of the Gold Rush, Columbia was one of the most important towns in the Gold Country. Most of the state's mining camps disintegrated once the gold ran out in the late 1850s, but Columbia was kept intact by its residents until 1945, when it was turned into a state historic park. Many of the town's buildings are preserved in their original state, like the Wells Fargo Express Office, and the restored Columbia Schoolhouse. Visitors can buy pans of sand to try panning gold.

5

Highway 49

542 Main St, Placerville; (530) 621-5885

The Gold Country offers one of California's best scenic drives along Highway 49. Many of the towns it passes through, such as Sutter Creek, have survived unchanged since the Gold Rush. Leland Stanford, the railroad baron, made his fortune in Sutter Creek, by investing in the town's Lincoln Mine. He used the money to become a railroad magnate and then the governor of California. A short drive southeast leads to Jackson, a bustling gold-mining community that has continued to thrive as a lumber mill town since 1850.

Northward, Highway 49 passes through Placerville. Once a busy supply center for the area's mining camps, the town is still a major transportation center. Of interest here are the Placerville History Museum

CALIFORNIA GOLD RUSH

The discovery of gold in Coloma in 1848 sparked the most famous gold rush in US history. An estimated 300,000 people, called "forty-niners" after the peak year of migration, came from all over the world, seeking their fortune. Within two years, California had grown so much it was officially made it a state. Supply points like San Francisco became boom towns and the US economy prospered. By 1855, it was all over.

and the El Dorado County Historical Museum, which displays a replica of a 19th-century store, artifacts from the Chinese settlement and other local historical exhibits.

6

Marshall Gold Discovery State Park

(530) 622-3470
8am-dusk daily
Jan 1, Thanksgiving, Dec 25

This peaceful park protects the site where gold was first discovered in 1848. James Marshall spotted shiny flakes in the water channel of a sawmill that he and other workers were building for the Swiss entrepreneur John Sutter in Coloma. Gold miners soon took over Sutter's land, leaving him penniless. Within a year, Coloma had turned into a thriving city but then declined, with news of richer deposits elsewhere.

A replica of Sutter's Mill stands on the original site. The park's Gold Country Museum features American Indian artifacts, films, and other exhibits on the discovery of gold.

↑ Wandering around the exhibits at Marshall Gold Discovery State Park

Taking in the spectacle of Yosemite National Park from Glacier Point ↑

HIGH SIERRAS

Forming a towering wall at the eastern side of central California, the densely forested, 14,000-ft- (4,270-m-) high Sierra Nevada Mountains were formed 3 million years ago. Known as the High Sierras, these rugged mountains make up one of the state's most popular recreation areas, preserved by a series of national parks.

Yosemite National Park

🏛🚌 Ⓦ nps.gov/yose

A wilderness of evergreen forests, high meadows, and sheer granite walls, the Yosemite National Park (established in 1890) protects some of the world's most beautiful mountain terrain. Soaring cliffs, rugged canyons, valleys, gigantic trees, and waterfalls all combine to lend Yosemite its incomparable beauty. Each season offers a different experience, from the swelling waterfalls of spring to the russet colors of fall, with numerous roads, bus tours, bike paths, and hiking trails linking the spectacular views.

Yosemite Valley is a good base from which to explore the park. Yosemite Museum, in the village, displays the history of the Native Miwok and Paiute people, along with works by local artists. Just to the south of the Valley Visitor Center, the tiny wooden Yosemite Chapel (1879) is the sole reminder of the park's Old Village, dating from the 19th century.

Standing nearly 1 mile (1.5 km) above the valley floor, the silhouette of the Half Dome cliff has become the symbol of Yosemite. Geologists believe that it is now three-quarters of its original size, rather than a true half. A formidable trail leads to the summit, offering panoramic views of the valley. The other major cliff, El Capitan, at the valley's western entrance, attracts rockclimbers, who spend days on its sheer face to reach the top. But the great Yosemite panorama is best experienced from the 3,215-ft- (980-m-) high Glacier Point. It can be reached only in summer, because snow blocks the road during winter.

Among the park's most recognizable features are the cascading Yosemite waterfalls, the highest in North America. Tumbling in two great leaps, Upper and Lower Yosemite Falls are at their peak in May and June, when the snow melts. By September, however, the falls often dry up. In summer, when the wildflowers are in full bloom, the park's striking landscape is best explored in the subalpine Tuolumne Meadows at Yosemite's eastern edge.

A few miles past Yosemite's southern entrance, Mariposa Grove features over 500 giant sequoia trees (*Sequoiadendron gigantea*), some more than 3,000 years old.

> **Standing nearly 1 mile (1.6 km) above the valley floor, the silhouette of the Half Dome cliff has become the symbol of Yosemite.**

8
Lake Tahoe

ℹ️ 3066 Lake Tahoe Blvd; www.visitinglaketahoe.com

The deep, emerald waters of this beautiful lake are set within an alpine valley at the highest point of the High Sierras. For over a century, Lake Tahoe has been a year-round recreational haven, offering water sports, hiking, and camping. South Lake Tahoe, the largest town here, caters to visitors headed for Nevada's casinos. To its west, the inlet of Emerald Bay State Park is the most photographed part of the lake. The surrounding peaks are also famous for their ski resorts.

9
Eastern Sierras

🚌 ℹ️ End of Hwy 270; www.monolake.org

High up in the foothills of the eastern Sierras lies **Bodie State Historic Park**, the largest ghost town in California. The town thrived in the mid-1870s but declined when the gold ran out in 1882. Now protected as a state historic park, Bodie's

170 buildings have been maintained in a state of "arrested decay."

Nearby **Mono Lake** lies at the eastern foot of the Sierra Nevada Mountains and presents an eerie sight of limestone towers rising from the water. Set between two volcanic islands, the lake has no natural outlet, but evaporation and water diversion to Los Angeles, through aqueducts, have caused it to shrink to one-fifth of its size. The lake's water has turned brackish and alkaline, putting the local wildlife and ecosystem in grave danger.

Bodie State Historic Park
🚌 ℹ️ End of Hwy 270; www.parks.ca.gov/bodie

Mono Lake
🚌 🌐 monolake.org

10
Sequoia and Kings Canyon National Parks

📍 47050 Generals Hwy
🌐 nps.gov/seki

These twin national parks preserve lush green forests, glacier-carved canyons, and granite peaks. America's deepest canyon, the south fork of the Kings River, cuts a depth of 8,200 ft (2,500 m) through Kings Canyon. Roads serve the western side of the parks; the rest is accessible only to hikers or rented pack-trains of horses or mules.

The parks embrace 34 groves of the sequoia tree, the earth's largest living species. Giant Forest, at the southern end of Sequoia National Park, is one of the world's largest groves of living sequoias. A trail leads to Moro Rock, a granite monolith affording a 360-degree view of the High Sierras and the Central Valley. North of the Giant Forest is the world's largest living thing, the 275-ft (84-m) General Sherman Tree. It still grows 0.4 inches (1 cm) every ten years.

Along the eastern boundary of Sequoia is Mount Whitney, the highest peak on the US mainland. A steep trail leads to the summit, offering a panorama over the High Sierras. The mountain was first climbed in 1873.

> 💬 INSIDER TIP
> **Hiking Mount Whitney**
>
> Hiking Mount Whitney requires advance planning, as permits are required and these are doled out in a limited annual lottery. You should also acclimatize to the higher altitude before starting out.

↑ A car lying within the abandoned Bodie State Historic Park, Eastern Sierras

ALASKA

Kayaking out of an ice cave in Valdez

EXPLORE
ALASKA

This chapter divides Alaska into two sightseeing areas, as shown on the map below. Find out more about each area on the following pages.

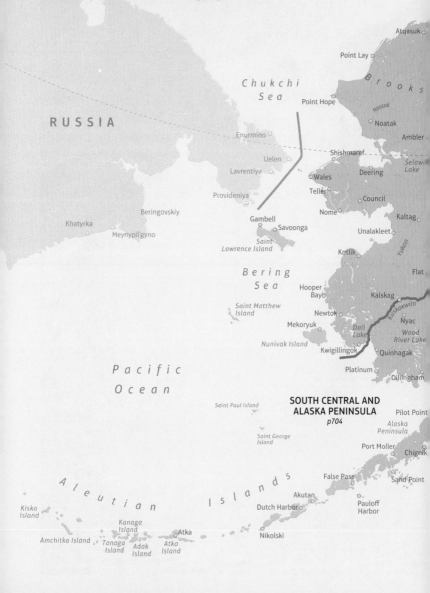

Atqasuk

Point Lay

Chukchi Sea

B r o o k s

Point Hope

Nootok

RUSSIA

Noatak

Ambler

Enurmino

Shishmaref

Selawik Lake

Uelen

Deering

Lavrentiya

Wales

Council

Teller

Providenya

Nome

Kaltag

Beringovskiy

Gambell

Savoonga

Unalakleet

Yukon

Khatyrka

Meynypil'gyno

Saint Lawrence Island

Kotlik

Flat

Bering Sea

Hooper Bay

Kalskag

Saint Matthew Island

Newtok

Kuskokwim

Nyac

Mekoryuk

Dall Lake

Wood River Lake

Pacific Ocean

Nunivak Island

Kwigillingok

Quinhagak

Platinum

Dillingham

Saint Paul Island

SOUTH CENTRAL AND ALASKA PENINSULA
p704

Pilot Point

Alaska Peninsula

Saint George Island

Port Moller

Chignik

A l e u t i a n

I s l a n d s

False Pass

Sand Point

Akutan

Kiska Island

Kanaga Island

Atka

Dutch Harbor

Pauloff Harbor

Amchitka Island

Tanaga Island

Adak Island

Atka Island

Nikolski

Arctic
Ocean

Beaufort
Sea

Barrow

Teshekpuk
Lake

Deadhorse

Kaktovik

Colville   Umiat

Range

Anaktuvuk Pass

Wiseman   Chandalar

Bettles

THE INTERIOR
AND SOUTHEAST
p694

Hughes

ALASKA

Livengood

Ruby

Anderson

McKinley
Park   Cantwell

Farewell   Delta
                Junction

Curry   Gakona

Lime
Village   Port Nikiski

Newhalen

Akhiok   Old Harbor

Naknek

Kodiak

Kodiak Island

English Bay

Homer

Seward

Anchorage

Palmer

Valdez

Cordova

Katalla

Yakutat

Gulf of
Alaska

Shingle
Point

Fort McPherson

Old Crow

Arctic Village

Eagle Plain

Circle

Eagle

Tok

Nabesna

McCarthy

Beaver Creek

Burwash
Landing

Haines
Junction

Skagway

Haines

Pelican

Sitka

Petersburg

Port
Alexander

Hydaburg

Wrangell

Ketchikan

Arctic Circle

Great Bear
Lake

Deline

Fort Good Hope
(Rádeyilikóe)

Norman
Wells

CANADA

Wrigley

Ogilvie

Glenboyle   Elsa

Stewart
Crossing

Faro

Ross River

Carmacks

Whitehorse

Johnsons
Crossing

Atlin

Tungsten

Upper Liard   Watson Lake

Lower
Post

Dease
Lake

Glenora

Meziadin
Junction

Graham
Island

Hecate Strait

Moresby
Island

Pacific
Ocean

Fairbanks
North Pole

Yukon

Susitna

Talkeetna

Paxson

Tazlina
Lake

Pacific
Ocean

Seattle

San Francisco

Los Angeles

CANADA

ALASKA

New York
City

Chicago

Washington, DC

USA

Miami

THE FAR NORTH

0 kilometers   100

0 miles   100

N

7 DAYS
in Alaska

Alaska is vast, but this seven-day road trip covers some of the state's most enticing attractions without spending too many hours behind the wheel.

Day 1

Spend your day exploring Anchorage (*p707*), Alaska's largest city. Tour local attractions such as the Alaska Native Heritage Center and the Anchorage Museum to learn more about Alaskan history and culture. Anchorage is a city, but the natural world is never far away – it's actually possible to fish for salmon in the middle of downtown, at Ship Creek. Enjoy a fine seafood dinner at Simon & Seafort's (*www.simonandseaforts.com*) with panoramic views of Cook Inlet.

Day 2

It's a 1-hr drive from Anchorage to the tranquil Eklutna Lake (42 miles/68 km). The reservoir lies inside Chugach State Park, and there are numerous trails that can be followed through the dense forest – you can also rent kayaks and bikes. It's 10 miles (16 km) back to the main highway and Eklutna Historical Park. This fascinating site comprises an old log-built Russian Orthodox Church, the "new" St. Nicholas Church (built in 1962), and brightly painted Spirit Houses of the local

Tanaina Athabaskan people. In the late afternoon, drive on to the quaint town of Talkeetna, which is a farther 87 miles (140 km) along the Susitna River. Spend the evening exploring the independent gift shops and art galleries in the Talkeetna Historic District.

Day 3

Take the morning in Talkeetna and reserve a scenic fishing trip, rafting trip, or jet boat excursion. If there's time, squeeze in another trip to the historic core. The best sites to visit include the Talkeetna Museum, the Talkeetna Roadhouse, an original log house built in 1917, and Nagley's Store, which has been in business since the early 1900s. In the afternoon, drive the 155 miles (250 km) north to Denali National Park (*p698*). If the weather is cooperating, Hwy 3 offers some of the best views of Denali peak along the way. There's not much choice for dinner in the vicinity, but the Denali Park Salmon Bake (*www.denaliparksalmonbake.com*) offers good Alaskan food and a lively atmosphere.

1 Cook Inlet, Anchorage.

2 Nagley's Store, Talkeetna.

3 Hikers in Denali National Park.

4 Alaskan salmon baking on an outdoor grill.

5 Steamer boat on the Chena River.

Day 4

Get up early for a shuttle or narrated tour-bus ride along the 92-mile (148-km) park road into Denali National Park – buses are the only vehicles allowed on this route (private vehicles can only go as far as Savage River). The full round trip can take 12 hours to Wonder Lake and Kantishna, but shorter routes are available. Soak up the gorgeous scenery, wildlife, and views of Denali along the way.

Day 5

Denali is one of the highlights of Alaska, so it's worth staying another day. Make the 15-mile (24-km) drive to Savage River, stopping at viewpoints and trails en route, or take another guided tour. Popular options include white-water rafting, horseback rides, and tours of the National Park dog kennels. It's also worth checking out the park events schedule, which frequently includes talks and sled dog demonstrations. The Overlook Restaurant – a fine-dining, farm-to-table spot with superb views – is a good place to end the day.

Day 6

Drive the 120 miles (193 km) to Fairbanks (p696), Alaska's second-largest city. Start at the Morris Thompson Cultural and Visitor Center, before hitting the University of Alaska Museum of the North to learn about Arctic Alaska. Pioneer Park contains several historic attractions, including a Gold-Rush-era town and the Alaska Salmon Bake restaurant (www.akvisit.com), a fun place to have dinner. The park's Palace Theatre stages the nightly musical-comedy "Golden Heart Review" about frontier life.

Day 7

Start the day with a cruise along the Chena or larger Tanana River, followed by lunch at Chena's Alaskan Grill (4200 Boat St), which has a lovely deck overlooking the Chena River. Mix things up in the afternoon by taking one of the city's many gold-panning tours; the tour at Gold Dredge 8 (www.golddredge8.com) includes a close-up view of the Trans-Alaska oil pipeline. End your trip with Cuban food and live music at upscale Jazz Bistro On 4th (www.jazzbistroon4th.com).

Above the clouds on the high, snowcapped Denali mountain ↑

ALASKA AND
WILDERNESS ADVENTURES

Alaska is America's great outdoor playground. Here you'll discover towering mountains, vast tracts of wilderness, epic glaciers, and countless lakes. In spite of its subarctic location, much of the state remains accessible and is the ideal territory for adventure seekers.

The Chilkoot Trail

In the late 1890s, hiking the 33-mile (53-km) Chilkoot Trail through Skagway *(p703)*, was fraught with danger for miners heading to Klondike, but today, it's a captivating recreational trail where you can embark on short one-day hikes, or longer backpacking expeditions. The trail crosses churning mountain rivers, cuts through banks of pink fireweed, passes through dense forest, and across vast ponds. The most dramatic (and challenging) section is the scramble up the "Scales" to the top of Chilkoot Pass itself.

↑ Hikers walking the Chilkoot Trail near Crater Lake

Magical Mountaineering

Alaska offers serious mountaineering opportunities, with snowcapped Denali *(p698)* North America's highest peak at 20,320 ft (6,194 m). Expeditions take at least two weeks and guides are crucial – it's one of the world's most dangerous mountains. Equally rugged Wrangell-St. Elias National Park and Preserve *(p697)* contains nine of the 16 highest mountains in the US.

INSIDER TIP
Dog Sledding

There are various operators that provide a half-day "mushing" lesson, such as the Alaska Mushing School, Anchorage *(www. alaskamushing school. com)*. Be sure to check animal welfare standards before you book.

Wild for White-water Rafting

On the edge of Denali National Park *(p698)*, the pristine Nenana River offers white-water rafting thrills, with especially tumultuous waters through Nenana Gorge. If you're wild about white-water rafting, consider an overnight trip and camp in the wilderness. Multi-day expeditions are available on the state's Tana, Chulitna, Talkeetna, and Copper rivers. Closer to Anchorage, the Chugach Outdoor Center *(www.chugachout doorcenter.com)* runs trips along Six Mile Creek.

← Rafting Six Mile Creek in Chugach National Forest

Glorious Glaciers

Alaska's glaciers are spectacular, and it's worth getting up close to them – while you can. Mendenhall Glacier, near Juneau *(p702)*, is accessible via hiking trails, while the six glaciers that form Glacier Bay National Park and Preserve *(p702)* can be reached by a bus and boat from Juneau. Like most glaciers today, Portage Glacier near Anchorage *(p707)* is steadily retreating, but can be visited by boat. Valdez is the gateway to the massive Columbia Glacier *(p706)*.

↑ Inside an ice cave within the mammoth Mendenhall Glacier

THE INTERIOR AND SOUTHEAST

Alaska has been home to indigenous peoples for thousands of years – groups such as the Iñupiat, Yupik, Aleut, and Tlingit comprise 15 percent of the population today. Russians hunting sea-otters established Sitka in 1799 and it became capital of Russian America after the local Tlingit were crushed in 1804. Russia sold Alaska to the US in 1867. Juneau was founded as a gold-mining camp in 1880, Ketchikan followed in 1885, and Fairbanks in 1901. Alaska became a state in 1959, while the discovery of oil at Prudhoe Bay and the completion of the Trans-Alaska Pipeline led to an oil boom.

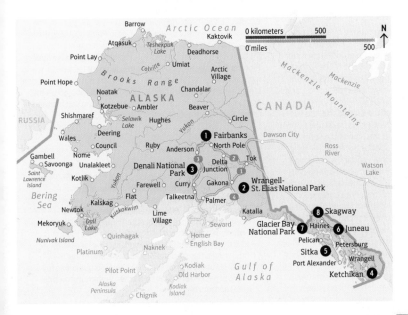

↑ The dazzling lights of the aurora borealis over a cabin in the Fairbanks hills

THE INTERIOR

The Alaska of popular imagination, the interior is largely wilderness. Here in the central region, visitors will discover the likes of Denali, the highest mountain in Northern America, and the one lone city of the interior, Fairbanks. The climate here is much like Scandinavia; expect midnight sun and – if you're lucky – the Northern Lights.

Did You Know?

On the shortest day of the year, Fairbanks has 3 hours and 43 minutes of daylight.

❶

Fairbanks

🔌 ✉ ℹ 101 Dunkel St; www.explorefairbanks.com

Surrounded by subarctic wilderness, Fairbanks is Alaska's second-largest city and has one of the largest populations at this latitude anywhere in the world. Located just 150 miles (241 km) south of the Arctic Circle, the sun barely dips below the horizon at the time of the summer solstice (June 21). The long hours of darkness through winter make it a good place to view the dazzling displays of the aurora borealis, or Northern Lights. This unique phenomenon is produced by electron and proton particles from the solar wind colliding with the earth's atmosphere. Fairbanks is also known for its extremes in temperature, which have been known to soar well above 90° F (32° C)

in summer, but can dip below –60° F (–15° C) in winter.

The downtown **Morris Thompson Cultural and Visitor Center** has information and excellent exhibits on regional history. The University of Alaska Museum of the North focuses on natural history and art. At **Pioneer Park**, historic buildings collected from around the state re-create a Gold Rush-era town on the banks of the Chena River. Each evening

during the summer, Pioneer Park plays host to a musical revue, with dancers dressed in period costume. Situated on the second floor of the Co-op Plaza building, the Fairbanks Community and Dog Mushing Museum is a superb resource for local history, and one room is now a permanent installation focused on the history of dog mushing and the indigenous culture behind it.

THE DALTON HIGHWAY

One of the most isolated highways in the world, the Dalton Highway (Alaska Route 11) is a 414-mile (666-km) road that begins just north of Fairbanks and ends at Deadhorse on the northern coast, passing through beautiful remote wilderness on the way. Originally built in the 1970s to support the Trans-Alaska Pipeline (which at times is your only roadside companion), this mostly gravel road is usually only used by large long-haul trucks. Gas stations, restaurants, and other facilities are few and far between, so it is advisable to be fully packed and prepared when embarking on this epic road journey.

Sixty miles (96 km) northeast of Fairbanks, the **Chena Hot Springs Resort** offers year-round access to natural geothermal springs. These were discovered in 1905 by long-suffering prospectors and within a few years had become the go-to spot in Interior Alaska for a luxury soak. Chena also boasts the Aurora Ice Museum – featuring an ice sculpture and an ice bar – and is a great spot for aurora viewing in winter.

Morris Thompson Cultural and Visitor Center

◨ 101 Dunkel St ◷ Daily
ⓦ morristhompsoncenter.org

Pioneer Park

◨ 2300 Airport Way ◷ 7am–midnight daily ⓦ alaska.org/detail/pioneer-park

Chena Hot Springs Resort

🌀🚶🍴🍽 ◨ 56 Chena Hot Springs Rd ◷ Year-round
ⓦ chenahotsprings.com

Wrangell-St. Elias National Park and Preserve

🚗🚌 ⓘ Mile 106.5, Richardson Hwy; Ranger stations at Chitina and Slana; www.nps.gov/wrst

This is the largest national park in the United States – roughly six times the size of Yellowstone. Wrangell-St. Elias National Park is a 20,000-sq-mile (52,500-sq-km) wilderness sprawling across the southeast corner of the Alaskan mainland. Dominated by the volcanic Wrangell Mountains and the glaciated St. Elias Range, the park has nine of the 16 highest mountains in the country. Designated a UNESCO World Heritage Site in 1992, the park contains historic mining sites, such as the town of McCarthy.

←
Ice-climbing the glacier *(inset)*, Wrangell-St. Elias National Park and Preserve

3

DENALI NATIONAL PARK

🏠 125 miles (200 km) S of Fairbanks 🕐 Year-round 🌐 nps.gov/dena

Alaska's top attraction, Denali National Park encompasses a whopping 9,375 sq miles (24,281 sq km), making it larger than the entire state of New Hampshire. The jewel in its crown is the 20,320-ft- (6,194-m-) high Mount Denali, North America's highest peak, which dominates the beautiful landscape.

The park is home to abundant wildlife, including grizzly bears, moose, and caribou, and wildflowers explode with color across the tundra in July. In winter, the park transforms into Narnia, with glittering snowy scenes and – if you're lucky – the Northern Lights dancing overhead. Vehicles are also banned, and locals get about by skis and dogsleds instead.

Only one road penetrates Denali, traversing varied landscapes that include lowlands and high mountain passes. Several hiking trails can be enjoyed in the vicinity of the visitor center. It's sensible to make reservations for the park campsite at least six months in advance in summer, and three months ahead for accommodations outside the park.

> 💬 INSIDER TIP
> **Shuttle Bus**
>
> Reserve seats for the park shuttle in advance. Some buses come from the Eielson Visitor Center, which has great views of Mount Denali; others continue on to Wonder Lake.

1913

The year of the first successful ascent to Denali's summit.

↑ A mountaineer climbing Mount Denali in snowy conditions

WILDLIFE VIEWING

One of the major attractions in Alaska is wildlife, and Denali National Park provides great opportunities to see a wide variety of the state's largest and most impressive wild animals. Grizzly bears, moose, Dall sheep, and caribou *(below)* are routinely sighted by visitors from the park shuttle buses, with drivers stopping to allow passengers to take photographs. The park is also home to wolves, and while they are not as commonly sighted as many other mammals, spotting these magnificent creatures in the wild is undoubtedly a memorable experience when visiting the Denali National Park.

↑ A brown bear with her cubs in Denali National Park

↑ Wonder Lake backed by Mount Denali, Denali National Park

SOUTHEAST

The Southeast, or the Alaska Panhandle, is milder in climate than the interior, and more populated as a result. Peppered with a number of charming towns, the region has similarities to the Pacific Northwest, with cities such as Sitka and Juneau having the feel of a compact Seattle. Rugged, snow-topped mountains and Sitka spruce trees offer a stunning backdrop.

❹
Ketchikan

🚶 🚆 ℹ 50 Front St; www. visit-ketchikan.com

Strung out along the waters of the Tongass Narrows and backed by steep forested hills, Ketchikan is the first stop along the Inside Passage for Alaska-bound cruise ships and ferries. All kinds of watercraft, floatplanes, and kayakers jostle for space along the crowded waterfront. Cruise ships dock outside downtown, providing passengers with easy access to local attractions such as the Creek Street precinct. Formerly the heart of a red-light district, the street is lined with colorfully restored wooden houses built on pilings over the water and linked by a boardwalk.

One of the most striking such houses is **Dolly's House Museum**, named for Dolly Arthur, Ketchikan's most famous madam. The interior has been preserved much as it was in the 1920s.

Even for those who do not plan to venture out into the wilderness, the **Southeast Alaska Discovery Center** is definitely worth a visit. Exhibits here relate the human and natural history of the Southeast region of Alaska, and also include a fabulous re-creation of a rainforest. Ketchikan's Totem Heritage Center displays an incredible collection

MISTY FJORDS NATIONAL MONUMENT

Grizzly bears grazing on the edge of deep waterfall-filled glacial lakes crowned by snowy peaks - an iconic image of Alaska, and easily seen at the Misty Fjords National Monument, about 22 miles (35 km) east of Ketchikan. Sightseeing flights, boat cruises, and kayaking are fun ways to explore this extraordinary wilderness area.

10,000

Sitka's approximate age in years.

← Mountains and pine forests encircling Sitka's lovely harbor

of more than 30 original poles, many well over a century old.

Lying to the north of the city, Tongass Avenue runs along the waterfront all the way to the Totem Bight State Historical Park. From here, a trail leads past huge totem poles to a reconstruction of an American Indian clan house.

Just 2.5 miles (4 km) south of Ketchikan on the South Tongass Highway, **Saxman Totem Park** holds dozens of totem poles from around the Southeast. Some are restored originals, some replicas. Cape Fox Tours (*www.capefoxtours. com*) operate several times a day in summer, taking in expert carving demonstrations and traditional dances.

Dolly's House Museum
🚹 24 Creek St ☎ (907) 225-2279 ⏰ Call for hours

Southeast Alaska Discovery Center
♿ 🚹 50 Main St ⏰ May-Sep: 8am-4pm daily; Oct-Apr: 10am-7pm Fri 🌐 alaska centers.gov

Saxman Totem Park
♿ 🚹 2660 Killer Whale Ave, Saxman

5

Sitka

🚹 104 Lake St; www. visitsitka.org

Founded by Russian entrepreneur Alexander Baranof in 1799, Sitka, formely Novo-Arkhangelsk (New Archangel), was the capital of Russian America until Alaska was sold to the United States in 1867 – at a meagre 2 cents an acre. Even now, a strong Russian influence survives here. The city is dominated by St. Michael's Cathedral, a Russian Orthodox cathedral that was rebuilt after the 1848 original burned down in 1966. It preserves many Russian artifacts, including the Sitka Madonna, supposedly blessed with healing powers. Beyond St. Michael's is **Sitka National Historical Park**, site of a fierce week-long battle between the Russians and local Tlingit tribe in 1804. The area is sprinkled with totem poles, and its shores are gently lapped by the waters of Sitka Sound. American Indian workers display their craft skills at a cultural center throughout the warm summer. The park is

also a good place to view the city's natural setting. Islands dot the Sound, and the snow-capped Mount Edgecumbe – often compared to Japan's Mount Fuji – sits majestically on the horizon.

The **Alaska Raptor Center**, across Indian River from the park, rehabilitates bald eagles, owls, and falcons. Visitors can learn about raptor habitats and join a guided tour. Sitka also has a network of hiking and biking trails. The Sheldon Jackson Museum was set up in 1895 by missionary Sheldon Jackson, who had traveled much of the region gathering valuable ethnographic materials. It is the oldest museum collection of indigenous culture in Alaska.

Sitka National Historical Park
🚹 Lincoln St ⏰ Trails: May-Sep: 6am-10pm daily; Oct-Apr: 7am-8pm 🌐 nps.gov/sitk

Alaska Raptor Center
♿ ♿ ♿ 🚹 1000 Raptor Way ⏰ May-Sep: 8am-4pm daily; Oct-Apr: 10am-3pm Mon-Fri (by appt) 🌐 alaska raptor.org

→ A towering Tlingit totem, Sitka National Historical Park

⑥

Juneau

🚏🚌 Auke Bay, 14 miles (22 km) NW of downtown
🛈 800 Glacier Av, #201; www.traveljuneau.com

Juneau is possibly the most spectacularly located state capital in the US. It is also the most remote, with no road access to the outside world or even to the rest of Alaska. Sandwiched between steep-sided forested peaks and the Gastineau Channel, the heart of the city is an intriguing mix of modern high-rise buildings and historic gems such as the Red Dog Saloon and the Alaskan Hotel. The best way to appreciate the city's location is by taking the tramway up Mount Roberts, from where the panorama extends across the Gastineau Channel. The downtown **Alaska State Museum** holds a fine collection of Russian artifacts and Inuit crafts. Nearby, the Juneau-Douglas City Museum provides a good introduction to the region's history, with exhibits on Tlingit life, pioneer relics, and walking tours of the area.

The diminutive, wood-framed St. Nicholas Russian Orthodox Church in the northeast corner of town was built in 1894. The building plans, construction funds, and interior furnishings were all imported from Russia.

Located at the northern end of the city, 13 miles (21 km) from downtown, **Mendenhall Glacier** is one of the most impressive – and accessible – glaciers in the world. A part of the massive Juneau Icefield, this slowly retreating half-mile-(1-km-) wide glacier continually calves bright blue icebergs into Mendenhall Lake. The lakeside visitor center offers interpretive panels describing glacial movement, and is the starting point for hiking trails to the glacier. Guided canoe tours are also on offer.

Alaska State Museum

◈ 🏛 395 Whittier St
🕐 May-Sep: 9am-5pm daily; Oct-Apr: 10am-4pm Tue-Sat
🌐 museums.alaska.gov

Mendenhall Glacier

◈ 🏛 Off Mendenhall Loop Rd
🕐 May-Sep: 8am- 7:30pm daily; Oct-Apr: 10am-4pm Fri-Sun

> Juneau is possibly the most spectacularly located state capital in the US. It is also the most remote, with no road access to the outside world.

⑦

Glacier Bay National Park and Preserve

🚏🚌 From Juneau
🌐 nps.gov/glba

Glacier Bay has changed somewhat since the British explorer Captain George Vancouver found his way through the Icy Strait in 1794. Over the ensuing 200 years, the glaciers have retreated 100 miles (160 km) or so, creating a magnificent waterway indented by long bays and protected by the park. Four glaciers reach the sea and break up into icebergs, which float into a bay inhabited by whales, dolphins, and seals.

Most visitors arrive aboard cruise ships. Travelers can also come by way of the hamlet of Gustavus from Juneau, making

A train chugging through the White Pass, Skagway

the short trip to Bartlett Cove and **Glacier Bay Lodge** by bus. From Bartlett Cove, it is 40 miles (64 km) to the nearest glacier in a high-speed catamaran. An onboard park naturalist relates the bay's natural history.

Glacier Bay Lodge & Tours
⊕ ⌂179 Bartlett Cove Rd, Gustavus ⏰Late May-early Sep; tours depart 7am daily
ⓦvisitglacierbay.com

⑧

Skagway

🚉🚌⛴SW Broadway
ⓘ245 Broadway; www.skagway.com

The final northbound stop for travelers on the Inside Passage is this tiny town surrounded by towering peaks. In 1897, thousands of fortune seekers arrived here only to be faced with the almost insurmountable 33-mile (53 km) Chilkoot Trail, traversing a harrowingly steep slope nicknamed the "Golden Staircase" over the White Pass to the Yukon River. Today, Skagway's fortunes rely largely on promoting its colorful history. The downtown district is protected as the Klondike Gold Rush National Historic Park, with false-fronted buildings, old-time saloons, and Arctic Brotherhood Hall, whose distinctive facade is covered with driftwood. The White Pass & Yukon Route Railroad, originally built as an alternative to the Chilkoot Trail, now operates as a 3-hour scenic trip to the pass and back.

EAT

Tracy's King Crab Shack
Feast on freshly caught crab in all its delicious forms at this iconic outdoor dining spot.

⌂432 S Franklin St, Juneau
ⓦkingcrabshack.com

$$⑤

Red Onion Saloon
Gobble up nachos and beer, then tour the on-site former brothel.

⌂205 Bdwy, Skagway
ⓦredonion1898.com

$$⑤

← Kayaking amid the peaks and glaciers around Mendenhall Lake, near Juneau

SOUTH CENTRAL AND ALASKA PENINSULA

Russians established fur-trading posts on Kodiak Island in 1784 and at Seward in 1793. Relations with the local Aleuts were often violent; by the mid-19th century, 85 percent of the indigenous population had died. After the US purchased Alaska in 1867, Kodiak emerged as a commercial fishing hub, while Homer was a coal depot in the 1890s. Anchorage developed from an American settlement, and became a city in 1920 and overtook Juneau as Alaska's biggest. In 1964, a magnitude 9.2 earthquake devastated Anchorage, while the 1989 *Exxon Valdez* oil spill killed wildlife and polluted local waters. Today tourism and commercial fishing are the dominant industries.

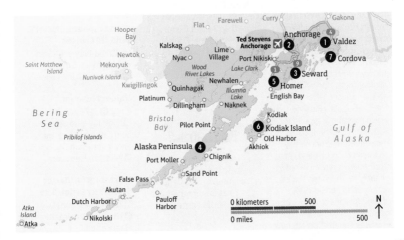

Clouds creeping over
the mountains above
Valdez harbor ↑

SOUTH CENTRAL AND ALASKA PENINSULA

This is a land of stellar seascapes. Comprising the shorelines of the central Gulf of Alaska and the 497-mile (800-km) peninsula that separates the Pacific Ocean from Bristol Bay, the region's climate is subarctic. Wildlife thrives here in spite of the cold temperatures – brown bears, caribou, moose, and wolves. Anchorage, meanwhile, provides a buzzing metropolis for visitors.

❶ Valdez

🚶🚌 Downtown
🏛 309 Fairbanks Dr;
www.valdezalaska.org

The picturesque town of Valdez nestles below snowcapped peaks along an arm of Prince William Sound, a vast bay encompassing islands, glaciers, and icy waters teeming with wildlife. This is North America's northernmost ice-free port. The Trans-Alaska Pipeline, which runs above ground for 800 miles (1,288 km) across the state from Prudhoe Bay on the Arctic Ocean, ends here, from where it is transferred to oil tankers. The *Exxon Valdez* ran aground here in 1989, spilling millions of gallons of oil into the environment. The ensuing cleanup effort attempted to restore the Sound, and there are no obvious signs of the spill today, but its adverse effect on birds, fish, and marine mammals persists.

Stan Stephens Glacier & Wildlife Cruises pass the Columbia Glacier, which is more than 3 miles (5 km) wide at its 250-ft- (75-m-) high face, and continuously calves icebergs into the sea. Check with the vistor center for summer tours. The town's

Did You Know?

Moose are common in Anchorage, with a population of 250 that rises to more than 1,500 in winter.

Valdez Museum explores the American Indian culture, the importance of oil for the local economy, the *Exxon Valdez* oil spill, and the 1964 Good Friday earthquake, whose epicenter lay close to Valdez.

The **Worthington Glacier State Recreation Site** on the Thompson Pass has a paved trail to an observation platform at the glacier's edge. The more challenging Glacier Ridge Trail affords sweeping vistas of the surrounding mountains.

Stan Stephens Glacier & Wildlife Cruises
⊘ 🕐 Mid-May–mid-Sep: departures 10am daily
🌐 stephenscruises.com

Valdez Museum
⊘ 🏛 217 Egan Dr
🕐 Mid-May–mid-Sep: 9am–5pm daily; mid-Sep–mid-May: noon–5pm Tue–Sun
🌐 valdezmuseum.org

Worthington Glacier State Recreation Site
🏛 28.7 Richardson Hwy
❄ Winter 🌐 valdezadventure alliance.com

2 Anchorage

4th Av at F St; www.anchorage.net

Lying between Cook Inlet and the Chugach Mountains, Anchorage is Alaska's largest city. Although this coastal urban sprawl is often described as being un-Alaskan, it is still worth spending a little time in this northern metropolis. It serves as Alaska's financial and transportation hub. Most of downtown was destroyed by the 1964 Good Friday earthquake, when the north side of 4th Avenue sank 10 ft (3 m). Interpretive displays at Earthquake Park, west of downtown, tell the story of the Big One.

One of Alaska's finest museums, the **Anchorage Museum** houses exhibits on Alaskan history, science, and indigenous culture, along with some of the state's finest art. Complementing the exhibits and installations at the **Alaska Native Heritage Center**, staff provide visitors with a glimpse of indigenous culture through art, dance, and games.

Fifty miles (80 km) southeast of the city, Portage Glacier is steadily retreating and is now out of sight from the visitor center. A tour boat cruises the lake close to the glacier.

Anchorage Museum

625 C St
May-Sep: 9am-6pm daily; Oct-Apr: 10am-6pm Tue-Sat, noon-6pm Sun anchoragemuseum.org

INSIDER TIP
Immersive Cinema

Why not head to the movies? Watch Alaska-themed films on the big screen at Anchorage's Alaska Experience Theatre (4th Avenue). There's a documentary on the 1964 earthquake, rattling floor and all.

ALASKA MARINE HIGHWAY

See Alaska by boat via the Alaska Marine Highway, operating all along the south-central coast of the state, the Aleutian Islands, the Inside Passage, and as far south as Bellingham, WA. There are over 30 terminals, all ferries can take vehicles, and some voyages can last many days. Whales can be spotted along the way, cabins and camping can be arranged for overnight travel, and there is ample opportunity to explore interesting villages that would otherwise be inaccessible.

Alaska Native Heritage Center

8800 Heritage Center Dr Mid-May-mid-Sep: 9am-5pm daily alaskanative.net

3 Seward

Downtown
2001 Seward Hwy; www.seward.com

One of the only large towns on the Kenai Peninsula, Seward is a charming fishing port sitting at the head of Resurrection Bay, surrounded by the snowcapped Kenai Mountains. One of its main attractions is the **Alaska SeaLife Center**, which exhibits the marine life of the neighboring ocean. The centerpiece is a string of huge aquariums holding colorful puffins, seals, and sea lions. Smaller tanks provide a home for crabs and octopuses, while the "touch tank" encourages a hands-on approach to exploring sessile life along the tidal zone.

Seward is bordered by the impressive **Kenai Fjords National Park**, a 906-sq-mile (2,347-sq-km) glaciated coastal wilderness. From the vast Hardy Icefield, glaciers radiate in all directions, eight of which are "tidewater glaciers" extending to sea level. Seward's downtown dock is the departure point for boat trips along the park's coastline. These day cruises also provide excellent opportunities for viewing whales, seals, sea lions, porpoises, and large concentrations of photogenic puffins perched on rocky outcrops. The park's most accessible glacier is Exit Glacier, just off the highway, 4 miles (6.5 km) north of Seward. From the end of the access road, a short trail leads through a forest of stunted trees, emerging at a deep-blue river of ice within the valley it carved.

Alaska SeaLife Center

301 Railway Av
Daily (times vary, check website) Thanksg., Dec 25
alaskasealife.org

Kenai Fjords National Park

126 miles (202 km) S of Anchorage 1212 4th Avenue, Seward; www.nps.gov/kefj

↑ Face to face with the residents of the Alaska SeaLife Center, Seward

4

Alaska Peninsula

➤ ℹ️ King Salmon Airport; (907) 246-4250

Dominated by the Alaska Range, this remote part of the state attracts visitors for its intriguing wilderness and wildlife-viewing opportunities. In 1912, the peninsula's Mount Novarupta erupted, covering the area with ash and pumice.

Katmai National Park and Preserve is where the volcano was most active. A remnant is the Valley of 10,000 Smokes, where gases and ash continue to spew across the landscape.

Adjacent to Katmai is **McNeil River State Game Sanctuary and Refuge**, where bears go to catch salmon at McNeil River Falls. Access the falls by air taxi from King Salmon or Homer.

Katmai National Park and Preserve

🏛️ King Salmon 📞 (907) 246-3305 🌐 nps.gov/katm

McNeil River State Game Sanctuary and Refuge

♿ 🕐 Best viewing: Jul-mid-Aug (permit required from Department of Fish and Game) 🌐 adfg.alaska.gov

5

Homer

➤ 🚌 Homer Spit
ℹ️ 201 Sterling Hwy; www.homeralaska.org

At the end of the Sterling Highway lies Homer, a delightful little hamlet by the water. It was discovered by Homer Pennock, a gold prospector who arrived in 1896. Today, the town's main focus is Homer Spit, a 4.5-mile (7-km) finger of land that juts into Kachemak Bay, with the Kenai Mountains glistening across the water. A busy road traverses the entire Spit, passing beaches, fishing boats, fishing-supply stores, and lively restaurants. Known as the "Halibut Capital of the World," fishing is its main attraction. Charter operators and their boats line the Spit.

Those who manage to hook a halibut or salmon can arrange to have it frozen and shipped home. The Fishing Hole is a man-made water hole stocked with salmon for an easy catch.

The **Alaska Islands and Ocean Visitor Center** explores Alaska's natural history and its native coastal inhabitants. As well as fun exhibits, there is a replica seabird rookery and guided beach trails.

The magnificent wilderness of Kachemak Bay State Park, on the bay's opposite shore, can be explored through a number of trails, one of which leads to the Grewingk Glacier.

Alaska Islands and Ocean Visitor Center

🏛️ 95 Sterling Hwy
🕐 Summer: 9am-5pm daily; rest of year: noon-5pm Tue-Sat 🌐 homeralaska.org

> At the end of the Sterling Highway lies Homer, a delightful little hamlet by the water. It was discovered by Homer Pennock, a gold prospector who arrived in 1896.

Did You Know?

In 2012, Walmart in Kodiak won a contest to receive a visit from rapper, Pitbull.

❻ Kodiak Island

🚗🚌 Downtown
ℹ️ 100 E Marine Way;
www.kodiak.org

The second-largest island in the US, most of Kodiak is inaccessible wilderness protected by the Kodiak National Wildlife Refuge. The island is famous as the habitat of Kodiak bears. The visitor center has details on charter flights to the best viewing spots.

Most residents live in the town of Kodiak, home to the country's largest Coast Guard station. North America's oldest Russian building, a storehouse dating to 1808, is now the **Kodiak History Museum**. To explore the local fishing industry, follow Shelikof Street past the harbor to the canneries.

Kodiak History Museum
♿ 🏠 101 E Marine Way
🕐 10am–4pm Tue–Thu & Sat, noon–7pm Fri 🚫 Sun & Mon
🌐 kodiakhistorymuseum.org

❼ Cordova

✈️🚌 ℹ️ 404 1st St; (907) 424-7260

Named after a Spanish admiral from the 18th century, this rural town at the head of the Orca Inlet is accessible only via plane or ferry. Copper was mined here in the early 1900s, leading to the development of the community. Later, the razor clam industry boomed, but sank after the 1964 earthquake. Today, Cordova is popular with bird-watchers and hikers. The Cordova Historical Museum illustrates the town's history.

EAT

Orso
Sea-to-table dining with wild Alaskan salmon, halibut, and king crab.

🏠 737 W 5th Av, Anchorage
🌐 orsoalaska.com

$$$

Moose's Tooth Pub and Pizzeria
Locals and visitors alike line up for tasty pies, paired with craft beer brewed on site.

🏠 3300 Old Seward Hwy, Anchorage
🌐 moosestooth.net

$$$

Nat Shack
For lunch, try this fun food truck right on the harbor, serving Mexican takeout with a twist.

🏠 239 N Harbor Dr, Valdez
📞 (907) 461-0336

$$$

Resurrect Art Coffee House
Grab a morning coffee and pastry at this renovated church. Local art is featured inside.

🏠 320 3rd Av, Seward
🌐 resurrectart.com

$$$

Little Mermaid
Harborfront shack with delicious fish tacos, chowder, pizzas, and house-baked treats.

🏠 4246 Homer Spit Rd, Homer 🌐 littlemermaidhomer.com

$$$

← Camping amid blossoms beneath the Kenai Mountains, near Homer

HAWAII

Lush Waimea Canyon, on the island of Kaua'i

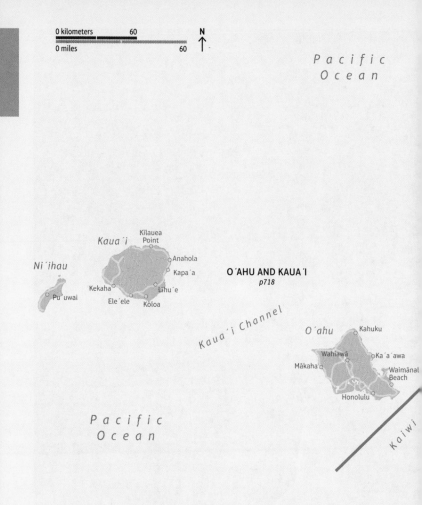

0 kilometers 60

0 miles 60

N

Pacific Ocean

Kaua´i

Kīlauea Point

Ni´ihau

Anahola

Kapa´a

O´AHU AND KAUA´I
p718

Kekaha

Lihu´e

Pu´uwai

Ele´ele

Kōloa

Kaua´i Channel

O´ahu

Kahuku

Wahiawā

Ka´a´awa

Mākaha

Waimānal Beach

Pacific Ocean

Honolulu

Kaiwi

EXPLORE
HAWAII

This chapter divides Hawaii into two sightseeing areas, as shown on the map above.
Find out more about each area on the
following pages.

ACROSS THE PACIFIC

Seattle

USA

San Francisco

Los Angeles

*Pacific
Ocean*

MEXICO

HAWAII

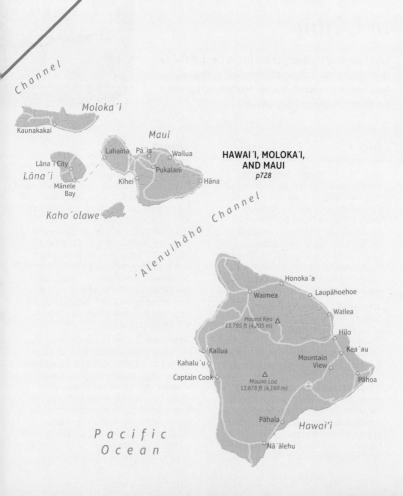

Channel

Moloka'i

Kaunakakai

Maui

Lahaina Pā'ia Wailua

Lāna'i City

Lāna'i

Pukalani

Mānele
Bay

Kīhei

Hāna

Kaho'olawe

**HAWAI'I, MOLOKA'I,
AND MAUI**
p728

'Alenuihāhā Channel

Honoka'a

Waimea Laupāhoehoe

Wailea

*Mauna Kea
13,795 ft (4,205 m)*

Hilo

Kailua

Kea'au

Kahalu'u

Mountain
View

Captain Cook

*Mauna Loa
13,678 ft (4,169 m)*

Pāhoa

Hawai'i

Pāhala

*Pacific
Ocean*

Nā'ālehu

4 DAYS
in O'ahu

This four-day itinerary takes in the best of O'ahu, from the historic heart of Honolulu to the wild surf beaches of the North Shore. You'll need to rent a car from the second day onward.

Day 1

Morning Visit Honolulu's Capitol District *(p720)* this morning to soak up some Hawaiian history (it's a quick bus or taxi ride from Waikīkī). Start at the absorbing Hawaiian Mission Houses Historic Site, which preserves the oldest houses in Hawaii. Across the street is Kawaiaha'o Church, built out of coral blocks for American missionaries in 1842. Next, stroll across to the lavish Iolani Palace, home to Queen Lili'uokalani before the monarchy was overthrown in 1893.

Afternoon It's a short walk from the palace along King Street into the heart of Honolulu's Chinatown. Here you can browse the gift shops and grab lunch – sample Cantonese dishes at Little Village Noodle House *(www.littlevillagehawaii. com)*, or try The Pig and The Lady *(www. thepigandthelady.com)*, a Vietnamese restaurant. After lunch, wander over to the Izumo Taisha Shrine, an authentic Japanese Shinto shrine. Spend the rest of your afternoon in the Hawaii State Art Museum, which has a superb collection of local contemporary and Polynesian art.

Day 2

Morning Dedicate at least half a day to Pearl Harbor National Memorial *(p721)*, one of America's most venerated military sites. Arrive early to avoid the crowds, and take the tour of the USS *Arizona* Memorial first (make reservations in advance). This floats above the ship of the same name that was sunk during the 1941 Japanese raid – 1,177 sailors remain entombed below, making this a very moving experience. Spend some time perusing the exhibits in the Pearl Harbor Visitor Center and take an absorbing tour of the USS *Missouri*, on which the Japanese surrendered in 1945.

Afternoon The best place for lunch is Restaurant 604 *(www.restaurant604.com)*, a short walk from the Pearl Harbor Visitor Center and right on the water. It serves burgers, sandwiches, and Hawaiian favorites such as tuna cakes, Kalua pork, and "Loco Moco." In the afternoon, drive over to the stunning Bishop Museum. You'll need a couple of hours to do justice to this huge collection of rare Polynesian art and artifacts.

1 Banzai Pipeline, North Shore.

2 Honolulu's Chinatown.

3 USS *Arizona* Memorial in Oahu.

4 Performers at the Polynesian Cultural Center.

5 A tunnel of trees over the Pali Highway.

Day 3

Morning Today involves the most driving, so get an early start and head up the Kamehameha Highway to O'ahu's North Shore *(p722)*. Beaches are the main attraction here – family-friendly Hale'iwa Beach Park makes a good introduction. Have a kitsch but tasty Hawaiian lunch at Haleiwa Joe's *(www.haleiwajoes.com)* in Hale'iwa itself – a dessert at Anahulu Shave Ice *(62–620 Kamehameha Hwy)* afterward is a must.

Afternoon Drive farther along the coast to Waimea Valley *(p722)*, a lush botanical garden just inland, with a short, blossom-draped trail to a plunging jungle waterfall. Afterward, you can swim or snorkel at nearby Waimea Bay Beach Park, or drive up to watch daredevil surfers tackle world-famous Banzai Pipeline *(p722)*.

Evening It's around 14 miles (23 km) to the Polynesian Cultural Center from Waimea. Aim to get here in time for dinner (you can reserve the Alli'i Luau Buffet) and their spectacular evening cultural show, which features over 100 Polynesian performers.

Day 4

Morning Start by driving the spectacular Pali Highway, or Hawaii Route 61 from Honolulu, which snakes up the Nu'uanu Valley and over the dizzying Ko'olau Range. En route, make time for several scenic viewpoints and Queen Emma Summer Palace, which has a small museum dedicated to the Hawaiian royal family. On the other side of the mountains, travel up the northeast coast to the Byodo-In Temple *(p723)*. From here, head south to Kailua Beach Park, and have lunch at tiki-style Buzz's Original Steakhouse *(www.buzzsoriginalsteakhouse.com)*.

Afternoon Spend the rest of the day making a loop on Route 72 around the eastern Makapu'u region, which bulges out into the Pacific. Highlights include family-friendly Kaupō Beach Park, and the dazzling views at Makapu'u Lookout (where you can hike to historic Makapu'u Point Lighthouse). Finish up at beautiful Hanauma Bay Nature Preserve *(p722)*, a protected cove renowned for its snorkeling. It's a short trip back to Waikīkī Beach from here.

Vehemently Volcanic

As the destructive eruptions of Kīlauea proved in 2018, the Hawaiian chain is very much an active volcanic region. Huge volcanoes loom over the whole archipelago, with bubbling lava, cinder cones, and blasted rocks offering a totally different experience to the beaches below. Drive to the top of Pu'u 'Ula'ula Summit in Haleakalā National Park *(p736)* on Maui, for mind-bending views, or explore Hawaii Volcanoes National Park *(p731)*, which includes the spectacular 13,677-ft (4,169-m) summit of Mauna Loa.

→

Lava glowing at Hawaii Volcanoes National Park

HAWAII FOR
NATURAL BEAUTY

Cast in the Pacific Ocean, this clutch of islands is paradise. Surrounded by cobalt-blue waters, the islands are rich in reef and marine life, while their mountainous interiors feature enormous volcanoes, gushing waterfalls, and dense forests burgeoning with blossoms.

Sand Between Your Toes

Waikīkī at Honolulu *(p720)*, O'ahu, remains for many the classic Hawaiian beach, but there are far prettier, less visited strands sprinkled throughout the islands. It's not just for surfers either – on the North Shore of O'ahu *(p722)* Ali'i Beach is known for big waves but Hale'iwa Beach Park is much safer for swimmers. Maui's long white beaches are legendary, with Kā'anapali and Kapalua in Lahaina *(p734)* the most popular resorts. On Kaua'i, Kalapakī Beach *(p724)* in Līhu'e is a gem, with chalk-white sands and calm waters.

→

Stunning Kā'anapali Beach on the island of Maui

Dive in the Unknown

Thanks to protected marine areas around the Hawaiian islands, snorkeling and diving are exceptional here. The longest fringing reef in Hawaii lies off Moloka'i, and it's a magnet for whales, hawksbill turtles, spotted eagle rays, and thousands of tropical fish. The calm waters off Maluaka Beach on Maui are home to "Turtle Town", a popular feeding ground for green sea turtles. On the Big Island's Kona Coast (p732), Kealakekua Bay has resident spinner dolphins. Night snorkeling among giant manta rays is also popular down here. Hanauma Bay Nature Preserve (p722) on O'ahu is also teeming with beautiful fish and a favorite spot for swimming.

← Turtles in the waters around Maui

FLOWERS AND GARDENS

Hawaii is known for its spectacular blossoms. You'll see them everywhere you turn, from bright yellow hibiscus (the official state flower) to heavily scented jasmine and plumeria, and the Hawaiian orchids used in purple and white *leis*. The Waimea Valley (p722) on O'ahu is a giant botanical garden smothered with thousands of rare tropical plants. On the Big Island, Lili'uokalani Gardens in Hilo (p730) is primarily a Japanese-style enclave, with a Japanese teahouse.

↑ Stopping to admire the scenery on the Kalalau Trail

Hawaiian Hiking Trails

Lush jungles speckled with exotic birds, jagged peaks, and soaring ocean cliffs make the Hawaiian islands spectacular hiking terrain. One of the world's most dazzling, heart-stopping treks is along the Kalalau Trail (p726) on Kaua'i's Nā Pali Coast. The Kukui Trail is another dramatic route, this time dropping steeply into the Waimea Canyon (p726). For a change of scene, the Sliding Sands Trail drops into the crater of the Haleakalā volcano, in Haleakalā National Park (p736).

O'AHU AND KAUA'I

O'ahu is the political and economic heart of Hawaii, but it wasn't always this way. Polynesians settled the Hawaiian islands from the 4th to 10th centuries, but written records begin with the arrival of Captain Cook off Kaua'i in 1778. Hawai'i Island initially dominated, with Kamehameha I conquering O'ahu in 1795 and Kaua'i in 1810. However, foreign merchant ships favored Honolulu harbor, and in 1845 the capital moved here. Sugar plantations arrived on Kaua'i in 1835 and soon came to dominate the economy. Queen Lili'uokalani was the last monarch of Hawaii – she was overthrown by pro-American forces in 1893 (Hawaii was annexed by the US in 1898).

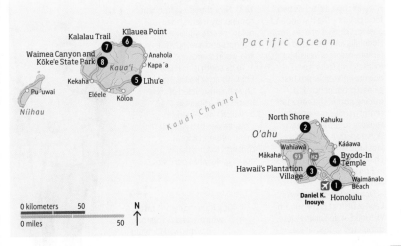

O'AHU

The third-largest island in the archipelago, O'ahu is Hawaii's most visited and most populous island. Three-quarters of the state's 1.4 million residents live here, most of them in the Greater Honolulu area. Outside the urban areas, with their cultural attractions, O'ahu offers spectacular scenery, with lush plantations, tropical beaches, and a surfers' paradise on the North Shore.

① Honolulu

🛈 2270 Kalakaua Av; www.gohawaii.com

Hawaii's capital city has two focal points – the historic and business district of downtown Honolulu, and the world famous resort of Waikīkī, 3 miles (5 km) to its east. The downtown area, which first gained prominence as a trading port in the early 19th century, today manages to squeeze together towering skyscrapers, a royal palace, Japanese shrines, a bustling Chinatown, and fish markets in a relatively small and compact area.

Dominating downtown's Capitol District is the superb Victorian-style 'Iolani Palace, completed in 1882. It was designed and first lived in by King David Kalākaua, followed by his sister Queen Lili'uokalani, who reigned for only two years before the monarchy was overthrown in 1893. Now the site of frequent community events, the palace has truly luxurious interiors and a wonderful koa-wood staircase.

To its south is the New England-style Kawaiaha'o Church, constructed of coral blocks. It was built in 1842, by which time American missionaries had gained many influential local converts to Christianity. The upper gallery has portraits of Hawaiian monarchs, most of whom were baptized, married, and crowned here. Adjacent to the church is the Mission Houses Museum, which contains the oldest timber-frame house in Hawaii, built in 1821 by the New England missionary Reverend Hiram Bingham. Housed in three buildings, the museum has a printing house.

Nearby is the bronze statue of King Kamehameha, Hawaii's most revered monarch, who ruled from 1795 to 1819.

→

King Kamehameha Statue, which stands in historic downtown Honolulu

↑ The skyline of Honolulu at nighttime, backed by Diamond Head volcano

The statue, with its feathered cloak and an arm extended in welcome, is one of Hawaii's most famous sights.

Also near here is the Honolulu Museum of Art, which was founded in 1927 and now houses a collection of over 50,000 works. These span a period of over 5,000 years, with one of the finest Asian art collections in the US, through to modern paintings by artists such as Diego Rivera and Georgia O'Keeffe.

North of the Capitol District is Chinatown, with two marble lions guarding its entrance. The area is an exotic neighborhood of open-air markets, *lei* (flower garland) stands, eateries, and herbal medicine shops. Hawaii's first Chinese arrived on merchant ships in 1789, followed in 1852 by larger numbers who came to work on O'ahu's sugar plantations. Chinatown's buildings include the Art Deco Hawaii Theatre and the state's oldest Japanese Shinto shrine, the 1923 Izumo Taisha Shrine. Moored close to the Honolulu Harbor is the *Hōkūle'a*, a modern replica of an ancient Polynesian canoe with sails.

Waikīkī, originally a place of taro patches and fish ponds, now has one of the world's most famous beaches – a sliver of sand against the backdrop of Diamond Head crater. Waikīkī bustles with thousands of tourists a day, who flock here to sunbathe on the golden sand, swim in the sheltered water, and surf the gentle waves. The sandy beach stretches for 2.5 miles (4 km), from the Hilton Hawaiian Village to Diamond Head. Conspicuous amid the glass and concrete sky-scrapers here are two stately old hotels – the coral pink Royal Hawaiian Hotel and the Colonial-style Moana Surfrider Hotel, Waikīkī's oldest.

Several interesting sights are also located in Greater Honolulu. Considered the world's finest museum of Polynesian culture, **Bishop Museum** was created by American businessman Charles Bishop to preserve royal heirlooms left by his wife, a Hawaiian princess. Its priceless exhibits include fabulous ceremonial feather standards, rare *tamate* costumes made of shredded fiber, sacred images, and a *hale* (traditional house) thatched with *pili* grass.

Pearl Harbor, a place of pilgrimage for a large majority of visitors, houses a great variety of warships, military museums, and memorials. Most significant among these is the USS *Arizona* Memorial, which stands perched above the ship of the same name that was sunk during the Japanese bombing on December 7, 1941. This fateful attack sadly killed more than 2,400 US officers and civilians, and destroyed 18 battleships. It consquently resulted in bringing the United States into World War II.

Bishop Museum

🏛 1525 Bernice St
🚌 ⏱ 9am–5pm daily
🌐 bishopmuseum.org

Pearl Harbor

🏛 7 miles (11 km) NW of downtown Honolulu
🚌 ⏱ Visitor center: 7am–5pm daily 🌐 nps.gov/valr

↑ The beautiful beach of Waikīkī, packed with sun-worshipers

❷
North Shore

🚌 ℹ️ HVCB, O'ahu; www.
gohawaii.com

The hub for the North Shore surfing community is Hale'iwa. The town's picturesque harbor is flanked by well-appointed public beaches. Ali'i Beach is famous for big waves and surfing contests. The adjacent Hale'iwa Beach Park is one of the few North Shore spots where it is usually quite safe to swim in winter. At the enchanting annual O-Bon Festival, thousands of floating lanterns are released into the ocean here. Ehukai Beach is famous for the Banzai Pipeline – perhaps the world's best-known surfing break, it's a challenging spot with perfect barreling waves. Once considered unrideable, the Pipeline was first surfed by Phil Edwards in 2016.

Another popular North Shore spot is **Waimea Valley**. The valley is a botanical paradise, with 41 gardens, thousands of rare tropical plants, a waterfall, and 30 species of birds. There are no longer the commercial shows that Waimea Valley was once famous for, such as hula and cliff-diving. Instead, the center provides an important educational resource and is a beautiful and unspoiled environment. Visitors can tour the valley, but bring binoculars as the park has great opportunities for bird-watchers. Afterward, swim or snorkel at the Waimea Beach Park across the street from the center.

Waimea Valley

⊗ ⊙ 🅿️ 🛍️ 🚗 59-864 Kamehameha Hwy (Hwy 83), Waimea ⏰ 9am–5pm daily 🚫 Jan 1, Thanksgiving, Dec 25

HANAUMA BAY NATURE PRESERVE

It's worth joining the Pali Highway (Route 61) northeast through the Nu'uanu Valley, passing by beautiful old ruins, scenic lookouts, and through long tunnels, all along ancient Hawaiian footpaths. Continue southeast along the coastal Route 72 down to the gorgeous Hanauma Bay Nature Preserve. This is one of O'ahu's most popular snorkeling spots; you can rent gear on-site to explore the lovely fish-dotted reefs *(www. hanaumabaystatepark.com).*

❸
Hawaii's Plantation Village

🚗 94-695 Waipahu St, Waipahu 🚌 ⏰ 10am–3pm Mon–Sat 🚫 Federal hols 🌐 hawaiiplantation village.org

This restored village portrays a hundred years of sugar plantation culture, from 1840 to 1943. It also contains various re-created buildings from the major ethnic groups that worked in the plantations – with Korean, Puerto Rican, and Japanese homes – as well as a Shinto shrine. Personal objects placed in the houses give the impression that the occupants have just left, soon to return. The small on-site

↑ The beautiful Byodo-In Temple, reflected in the glassy lake at its front

museum runs informative walking tours for visitors, and there is also a gift shop.

4

Byodo-In Temple

🏠 47-200 Kahekili Hwy (Hwy 83) 🚌 🕐 8:30am–5pm daily 🌐 byodo-in.com

This replica of a 900-year-old Japanese temple in a tranquil and secluded spot is O'ahu's hidden treasure, its bright red walls framed against the backdrop of fluted green cliffs. A curved vermilion footbridge and a three-ton bell lead to the Byodo-In Temple, which houses a beautiful 9-ft (3-m) Buddha. At sunset the cliffs give off pink and mauve hues and create a truly magical experience. The temple was established in 1968, to celebrate the centenary of the arrival of Hawaii's first Japanese immigrants.

> Another popular North Shore spot is Waimea Valley. The valley is a botanical paradise, with 41 gardens, thousands of rare tropical plants, a waterfall, and 30 species of birds.

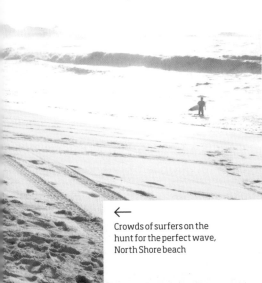

← Crowds of surfers on the hunt for the perfect wave, North Shore beach

EAT

Helena's Hawaiian Food
Traditional Hawaiian home-cooking at its best, in a relaxed setting.

🏠 1240 N School St, Honolulu 🕐 Mon, Sat, Sun 🌐 helenashawaiianfood.com

$ $ $

Duke's Waikiki
Savor fresh fish tacos and classic cocktails at this iconic beach bar.

🏠 116-2335 Kalakaua Av, Honolulu 🌐 dukeswaikiki.com

$ $ $

Lucky Belly
A modern eatery in Chinatown with great Asian-fusion tapas.

🏠 50 N Hotel St, Honolulu 🌐 luckybelly.com

$ $ $

Koko Head Café
Expect lines at this popular and inventive brunch spot.

🏠 1145c 12th Av, Honolulu ☎ (808) 732-8920

$ $ $

Giovanni's Shrimp Truck
This graffiti-clad food truck is a familiar face on Hawaii's snacking scene, serving up plates of piping-hot sautéed garlic shrimp.

🏠 66-472 Kamehameha Hwy, Haleiwa 🌐 giovannisshrimptruck.com

$ $ $

KAUA'I

The oldest of the major Hawaiian islands, Kaua'i is a stunning array of pleated cliffs and yawning chasms, cloaked with a mantle of emerald-green vegetation. Also known as the "Garden Island," it is Hawai'i's most beautiful destination, with highlights including Kīlauea Point's glorious beaches, the dramatic Waimea Canyon, and the soaring cliffs of the Kalalau Trail on the Nā Pali Coast.

5
Līhu'e

🚏🚌 ℹ️ KVB, 4334 Rice St, Suite 101; www.gohawaii.com

Although Līhu'e happens to be the administrative and business center of Kaua'i, it is actually little more than a plantation village. It was built in the 19th century to serve the Līhu'e Sugar Mill, whose rusting machinery still dominates the downtown area. Līhu'e's oceanfront district, with the beautiful Kalapakī Beach, is especially appealing, and the outskirts of town offer such delights as grand plantation mansions and a stunning waterfall.

Within the town, **Kaua'i Museum** displays a splendid collection of traditional artifacts, including huge koa-wood bowls, royal feather standards, and old weapons. It also has exhibits on the island's history and geology. The imposing **Grove Farm Homestead** on Nāwiliwili Road was founded in 1864 and is one of Hawaii's earliest sugar plantations. The historic mansion is paneled in dark, heavy koa wood. A guided tour, which lasts for two hours and must be reserved in advance, covers the rather formal house, the cramped servants' quarters, and the beautifully scented orchard.

Kalapakī Beach, with its beautiful, gently sloping white sands and sheltered inshore waters, is the safest beach in the area and is especially suitable for families with small children. Water sports are popular at the site, with plenty of opportunities for swimming and surfing. On the far side of the beach, the scenic, palm-fringed Nāwiliwili Beach County Park is ideal for picnics.

The grand 1930s house known as **Kilohana Plantation**, 1.5 miles (2.5 km) west of Līhu'e, is surrounded by carefully manicured green lawns and resembles an English country estate. At the time at which it was built, the plantation was the most expensive home ever constructed on Kaua'i. Visitors can tour the house, which has a restaurant and some shops, and explore the cane fields by train. The mansion also commands superb views of the Kilohana mountain inland.

Just north of Līhu'e, a road winds through cane fields to the twin cascades of the Wailua Falls. They are best viewed from the roadside parking lot, as the path down the hillside can be slippery. Menehune Fish Pond, 1.5 miles (2.5 km) south, is located in idyllic pastoral landscape. With its ancient stonemasonry, the pond was used to fatten mullet for the royal table.

Kaua'i Museum
⊗ 📍 4428 Rice St
🕐 9am–4pm Mon–Sat
🌐 kauaimuseum.org

Kilohana Plantation
🍽️🛍️ 📍 3-2087 Kaumualii Hwy 🕐 9am–5pm Mon–Fri, 9:30am–3pm Sat & Sun
🌐 kilohanakauai.com

Grove Farm Homestead
⊗🛍️🍽️ 📍 4050 Nāwiliwili Rd 🕐 For tours only, reserve ahead 🌐 grovefarm.org

Tourists admiring the 80-ft (24-m) Wailua Falls from the pool at the base

6
Kīlauea Point

🏠 Kīlauea Rd, off Kūhiō Hwy (Hwy 56), 10 miles (16 km) NW of Anahola
🚌 *ℹ* KVB, Līhu'e; (808) 245-3971

The northernmost spot on the Hawaiian archipelago, Kīlauea Point is a rocky promontory pounded by mighty waves. The windswept clifftop has been set aside since 1985 as the **Kīlauea Point National Wildlife Refuge**, where bird-watchers can spot frigate-birds, Laysan albatrosses, and many other species. A short walk beyond the visitor center leads to the red-and-white Kīlauea Lighthouse, which was erected in 1913. Approaching

↑ Kīlauea Point National Wildlife Refuge, with Kīlauea Lighthouse *(inset),* crowning the tip

the tip of the headland, there are splendid views westward to the fabled emerald-hued Nā Pali cliffs, which are widely thought to be one of the most beautiful places on earth. Half a mile (800 m) west of the Kīlauea turnoff on Kalihiwai Road, a red dirt track leads to the vast but little-visited shelf of glorious yellow sand known as Secret Beach. The ocean can be rough for swimming here, but this secluded spot is a beautiful place to walk, with its dramatic views of the

lighthouse and a glorious waterfall at the far end.

Kīlauea Point National Wildlife Refuge

⊗ 🏠 Kīlauea Point
🕙 10am–4pm Tue–Sat 🗓 Jan 1, Thanksg., Dec 25 🌐 fws.gov/refuge/kilauea_point

> 💬 INSIDER TIP
> **Hanalei**
>
> This sleepy village is close to Kīlauea Point National Wildlife Refuge. It's home to out-of-this-world beaches, a picture-perfect pier, and a great food-truck scene. It's the place to just sit back and relax, Hawaiian style.

The windswept clifftop has been set aside since 1985 as the Kīlauea Point National Wildlife Refuge, where bird-watchers can spot frigate-birds, Laysan albatrosses, and many other species.

7

Kalalau Trail

🌐 kalalautrail.com

The precipitous cliffs of the Nā Pali Coast make it impossible for the road to continue west of Kē'ē Beach on Kaua'i's north shore. But hardy hikers can follow the narrow Kalalau Trail for another 11 miles (18 km) to isolated Kalalau Valley. One of the most dramatic hikes in the world, it covers a landscape of almost primeval vastness and splendor. While this is not an expedition to undertake lightly, a half-day round-trip to Hanakāpī'ai Valley is within most capabilities and is an unforgettable experience. However, if you plan to proceed past Hanakāpī'ai Valley, you must obtain a camping permit from the Na Pali Coast State Parks office at 3060 'Eīwa Street, Līhu'e.

Before setting out, check the weather forecast to make sure that rain and flash flooding are not expected, as this route can often become unstable or entirely over-whelmed in bad weather. The trail begins at the end of Kūhiō Highway, climbing steeply to Makana Peak and

Did You Know?

By law, no building on Kaua'i is allowed to be built taller than a palm tree.

affording spectacular views of the rugged coastline. It continues on to Ke Ahu A Laka, which was once Hawaii's most celebrated school for hula dancing. The next stop is Hanakāpī'ai Valley, where in summer a pristine sandy beach replaces the pebbles found at the valley mouth in winter. Wading and swimming here are unsafe, due to dangerous rip currents.

The more challenging part of the trail continues through an abandoned coffee plantation to the Hanakāpī'ai Falls, and then to Pā Ma Wa'a, an 800-ft (240-m) cliff, which is the highest point on the trail. The trail then dips into

several hanging valleys where the streams have still to cut their way down to sea level, before reaching the beautiful campsite at Hanakoa Valley, set amid the ruins of ancient taro terraces. For the last 5 miles (8 km), the trail clings perilously to a sandstone cliff. The magical view of Kalalau Valley is the trail's reward. Note that there is no food or safe drinking water en route, so hikers must carry enough supplies for the journey.

8

Waimea Canyon & Kōke'e State Park

📍 Kōke'e Rd (Hwy 550)
📞 (808) 587-0400 🌐 dlnr. hawaii.gov

No visitor should leave Kaua'i without taking in the rugged grandeur of Waimea Canyon and the breathtaking views from Kōke'e State Park. Waimea Canyon, known as the "Grand Canyon of the Pacific," was created by an earthquake

↑ A tiny yellow *'anianiau* bird in gorgeous Kōke'e State Park

that almost split Kaua'i in two. The gorge, now 3,000 ft (915 m) deep, is still eroding as landslides and the Waimea River continue to carry away tons of soil. Of the several lookouts dotted along the rim, the Waimea Canyon Lookout, despite being the lowest of the lookouts, offers the best canyon views. The more adventurous can take hiking trails to explore the area in greater depth. The Kukui Trail heads sharply down into the canyon as far as the Waimea River – a relatively easy and rewarding trip. At the North End of Waimea Canyon is Kōke'e State Park, laced through with more hiking trails. From the park's Pu'u O Kila Lookout, the majestic amphitheater of the Kalalau Valley opens out; another view is from the nearby Kalalau Lookout. In the middle of the park is the **Kōke'e Museum**, which provides an overview of the cultural and natural history of this region. There is an emphasis on wood from the surrounding forests, which are home to many trees found only in Hawaii. Also in the heart of the park is Kōke'e Lodge, where visitors can dine or stay overnight. Another highlight is the Alaka'i Swamp, a bowl-like depression drenched by nearly 42 ft (13 m) of rain every year. Part rainforest, part bog, the area boasts some of Hawaii's rarest birds, such as the *'i'iwi* or honeycreeper, and the tiny yellow *'anianiau*. Information, hiking advice, and maps are all available at the Kōke'e State Park headquarters.

Kōke'e Museum
🕐 9am–4:30pm daily
🌐 kokee.org

← Camping on the breathtaking Kalalau Trail at sunset

EAT

Hamura Saimin
A local hot spot for no-frills ramen.
🏠 2956 Kress St, Līhu'e
📞 (808) 245-3271

$ $ $

Tip Top
This retro diner serves up hearty portions of Hawaiian favorites.
🏠 3173 Akahi St, Līhu'e
📞 (808) 245-2333

$ $ $

Duane's Ono Char-Burger
A cult classic burger joint, perfect after a long day on the waves.
🏠 4-4350 Kuhio Hwy, Anahola
📞 (808) 822-9181

$ $ $

Eat Healthy Café
Head here for tasty and locally sourced vegan options.
🏠 4-369 Kuhio Hwy, Kapaa 🕐 Mon
🌐 eathealthykauai.com

$ $ $

Hanalei Gourmet
A laid-back spot offering American favorites and pre-prepared picnics.
🏠 5-5161 Kuhio Hwy, Hanalei 🌐 hanalei gourmet.com

$ $ $

Beach House Restaurant
A romantic, oceanfront restaurant, perfect for sunset dining.
🏠 5022 Lawai Rd, Poipu
🌐 the-beach-house.com

$ $ $

A car loaded with surfboards in Honolua Bay, Maui

HAWAI'I, MOLOKA'I, AND MAUI

Hawai'i Island became the political center of the archipelago in the 18th century. In the 1780s Kamehameha I consolidated power, aided by his savvy wife Ka'ahumanu. In 1795 he conquered Maui and Moloka'i, and by 1810 he was paramount ruler. Missionaries began arriving in the 1820s, suppressing traditional Hawaiian culture. Lahaina on Maui became a major whaling center and the national capital from 1820 to 1845, while sugar plantations dominated the land and epidemics decimated the native population. From the 1960s, a renaissance has fostered interest in local culture, and though tourism remains dominant, residents of Moloka'i have resisted private developers.

HAWAI'I

The island of Hawai'i, also known as the Big Island, is more than twice the size of all the other islands combined. Its natural wonders include the world's most massive mountain, Mauna Loa, and Kīlauea, the most active volcano on earth, both of which form part of the Hawai'i Volcanoes National Park. Equally fascinating are the island's well-preserved cultural sites within the Pu'uhonua O Hōnaunau National Historical Park.

① Hilo

🚗🚌 𝒊 BIVB, 250 Keawe St; www.gohawaii.com/ bigisland

Although it is the state's second city, "rainy old Hilo" is a contrast to sunny, urban Honolulu. The city's progress has been checked by nature; rain falls 278 days of the year, and two destructive tsunamis pounded Hilo in 1946 and 1960. The city has since retreated from the sea, turning the waterfront area into enormous parks, while the rain has made it a natural garden, full of orchids and anthuriums. Hilo's population is largely Japanese and Filipino in ancestry.

The downtown business district, with its restored buildings, is worth exploring on foot. The Lyman Museum and Mission House vividly evokes a bygone era – it is preserved as it was in the 1830s, with Victorian furnishings and artifacts. Also of note is the **Pacific Tsunami Museum**. Given the area's tragic history of devastating tsunamis, the exhibits at this museum offer some much-needed educational programs. It also serves as a living memorial to those who have died in past tsunami events.

On the Waiākea Peninsula, jutting into Hilo Bay, is the 25-acre (10-ha) Lili'uokalani Gardens, landscaped in Japanese style, while east of downtown are the 80-ft-

---

KING KAMEHAMEHA I

Conqueror, diplomat, and leader, King Kamehameha I is best known for uniting the Hawaiian Islands into one royal kingdom. Born around 1758 into Hawaiian royalty, Kamehameha was hidden away on the island of Hawai'i for many years to protect him from warring clans that saw him as a potential threat. Kamehameha trained as a warrior, even fighting with British explorer James Cook in 1779, and led many successful campaigns throughout the islands. This eventually led him to the throne and he became the first king to rule all the Hawaiian islands in 1810.

↑ A rainbow curving beneath the Rainbow Falls in Hilo

(24-m-) high Rainbow Falls. The morning sun, filtering through the mist of the waterfall, often creates beautiful rainbows.

The east side of Hilo Bay offers fine snorkeling and swimming at the James Kealoha Beach Park; and at the Richardson Ocean Park.

Pacific Tsunami Museum
🅰 📱 🏠 130 Kamehameha Av
🕐 10am–4pm Tue–Sat
🆆 tsunami.org

2 🖊

Hawai'i Volcanoes National Park

🏠 Hawai'i Belt Rd (Hwy 11)
🆆 nps.gov/havo

Encompassing about a quarter of a million acres, this national park includes the 13,677-ft (4,169-m) summit of Mauna Loa, 150 miles (240 km) of hiking trails, and vast tracts of wilderness that preserve some of the world's rarest species of flora and fauna. But it is Kīlauea Cald

and the lava flows of its furious East Rift Zone, often bisected by lava flows, that draw most visitors. Two roads – Crater Rim Drive, which loops around the caldera (although it is currently closed due to an eruption in May 2018), and Chain of Craters Road, which descends through the recent outpourings – form a gigantic drive-through museum. The 2018 eruption started in 1983 and produced slow-moving lava and eruption episodes, but posed no threat to visitors. The lava did, however, cause damage to dwellings. The eruption was officially declared to be over in December 2018, following three months of inactivity.

East of the park, the Kīlauea Iki Overlook gives a view of the crater, which in 1959 filled with bubbling lava, shooting fire fountains 1,900 ft (580 m) into the air. Across the road from the crater, at the eastern edge of the park, lies the Thurston Lava Tube. This huge tunnel was left behind when a subterranean river of lava drained away. An easy trail runs through the tube and a grove of giant ferns, although it is currently closed to the public. Nearby, the short Devastation Trail features ghostly remains of a rainforest, wiped out by ash

falling from Kīlauea Iki's 1959 eruption. Farther west, the Halema'uma'u Overlook affords views of the once boiling lake of lava. The crater below still steams with sulfurous fumes. This is the home of Pele, the fiery-tempered volcano goddess, who migrated from Kahiki (Tahiti) seeking a dry place for her eternal fires.

TOP 5 HAWAIIAN FOODS

Shave Ice
Bowl of finely shaved ice with fruit syrups.

Poke
Raw-fish salad seasoned with Hawaiian sea salt, roasted kukui nuts and local seaweed.

Kalua pig
Roasted pig, slow-cooked in an underground oven.

Loco Moco
Rice topped with burger patties and fried eggs, smothered in gravy.

Manapua
Hawaiian version of traditional Chinese bao.

↑ Walking across cooled lava flows in the Hawai'i Volcanoes National Park

DRINK

Beach Tree Bar and Lounge

Located just steps from the beach, this chic yet casual outdoor lounge is the ideal place to sip tropical cocktails.

⌂ 72-100 Kaupulehu Dr, Kailua-Kona ⓦ four seasons.com/hualalai

Rays on the Bay

This unusual spot combines cocktails, tapas, and live manta ray feedings in the ocean below to give one spectacular evening. Try booking at sunset to make the most of the superb ocean views.

⌂ 78-128 Ehukai St, Kailua-Kona ⓦ rayson thebaykona.com

---

③

Kona Coast

On the western side of the island, the Kona coast is lush and green, sprinkled with powdery soft beaches, luxury resorts, and coffee farms (this is the home of Kona coffee). The water here is usually calm and clear, ideal for snorkeling, diving, kayaking, and spotting marine life – most commonly beautiful dolphins and green sea turtles.

Kailua-Kona town features the **Kamakahonu National Historic Landmark**, with reconstructions of the final home of Kamehameha I (who lived here 1813–1819) and 'Ahu'ena Heiau, the king's temple. Nearby is **Hulihe'e Palace**, a royal residence built in 1838, and now a museum, and Mokuaikaua Church, Hawaii's oldest, founded by missionaries in 1820. To the south, **Kealakekua Bay State Historical Park** is a popular spot for snorkelers and kayakers. Kealakekua Bay also marks the site where Captain James Cook was killed in 1779.

> The Kona coast is lush and green, sprinkled with powdery soft beaches, luxury resorts, and coffee farms.

Kamakahonu National Historic Landmark

⌂ Kaahumanu Place, Kailua-Kona ⓒ 24 hours

Hulihe'e Palace

⌂ 75-5718 Ali'I Drive, Kailua-Kona ⓒ 9am-4pm Mon-Sat, 10am-3pm Sun ⓦ daughters ofhawaii.org

Kealakekua Bay State Historical Park

⌂ 82-6099 Pu'uhonua Beach Rd, Kealakekua ⓒ Dawn-dusk ⓦ dlnr.hawaii.gov

---

④

Kohala Coast

The Kohala coast, on the northwestern tip of the island, is sun-drenched, dry and barren, punctuated with endless black and rust-red rocky lava fields. Some of the island's finest resorts

DEATH OF CAPTAIN COOK

British explorer Captain James Cook is well known for having sailed thousands of miles across uncharted waters in the 18th century. He was possibly the first European to visit the Hawaiian Islands, with a landfall at Kauai in January 1778. Cook returned to Hawai'i in 1779 and was initially welcomed and even treated as an honoured guest. Trades turned sour, however, and Cook and his men attempted to kidnap the local ruler for ransom. This led to Cook being stabbed to death by the perturbed local villagers, who nevertheless gave him a proper Hawaiian burial.

tions, such as stepping on a chief's shadow, were punished by violent death. Lawbreakers could, however, escape punishment by reaching a *pu'uhonua* (place of refuge). The greatest of these was at Hōnaunau, a 6-acre (2-ha) temple compound dating from the 16th century, which offered absolution to all those who could swim or run past the chief's warriors. The sanctuary was stripped of power in 1819, after the fall of the *kapu* system. Now partly restored, it provides a glimpse into precontact Hawai'i.

Located on a peninsula of black lava, whose jagged shoreline made it difficult for *kapu*-breakers to approach from the sea, the *pu'uhonua's* focal point is the 1650 Hale O Keawe Heiau, the temple that once held the bones and therefore the *mana* (sacred power) of great chiefs. Outside it stand Ki'i – wooden images of gods. As impressive is the great drystone wall, 10 ft (3 m) high and 17 ft (5 m) wide. Built around 1550, it separated the *pu'uhonua* from the palace area inland.

are located here, oases of green, as well as Hawaii's best golf courses. For the best chance of seclusion (and to see turtles) take the dirt road and hike down to the gorgeous lagoons of Kiholo Bay. Ravishing beaches line the coast here. Historic sites are found in the region too, including the **Puukohola Heiau National Historic Site**, with its beautifully restored Hawaiian temple, which was constructed by Kamehameha I from 1790 to 1791.

Puukohola Heiau National Historic Site

🏠 62-3601 Kawaihae Rd, Kawaihae 📞 (808) 882-7218 🕐 Dawn–dusk daily

---

5
Hamakua Coast

The Hamakua Coast runs along the northeastern side of the island, north of Hilo, taking in stunning stretches of tropical rainforest, waterfalls, and lush valleys. The scenic Hamakua

←

Hapuna Beach, a stunning stretch of sand between the Kona and Kohala coasts

Heritage Corridor Drive (Hwy 19) runs for 45 miles (72 km) from Hilo to the Waipi'o Valley Lookout. **Botanical World Adventures** features ziplines and Segway trips through the jungle, as well as a series of botanical gardens and Kamae'e Falls. A short detour inland is the 442-ft- (135-m-) high Akaka Falls, one of the island's most spectacular sights, plus the cascading Kahūnā Falls. The drive ends at the jaw-dropping lookout over the fertile Waipi'o Valley.

Botanical World Adventures

🏠 31-240 Old Mamalahoa Hwy, Hakalau 🕐 8am–5:30pm daily 🌐 botanical world.com

---

6
Pu'uhonua O Hōnaunau National Historical Park

🏠 Hwy 160, off Hawai'i Belt Rd (Hwy 11) 🕐 7am–dusk daily 🌐 nps.gov/puho

From the 11th century on, social interactions were regulated by the *kapu* (taboo) system; even minor infrac-

↑ Huge wooden Ki'i, which stand outside Hale O Keawe Heiau temple

MOLOKA'I AND MAUI

The small island of Moloka'i, between O'ahu and Maui, is much less developed for tourism than its neighbors and the gentle pace of life and spectacular scenery found here enchant most visitors. Maui, Hawai'i's second-largest island, offers lively resorts with a range of water sports, as well as lush plantations and the awesome grandeur of the Haleakalā Volcano.

7
Kaunakakai

Ala Malama St & Kamehameha V Hwy (Hwy 450); www.gohawaii.com

Moloka'i's main town, Kaunakakai, was built in the 19th century as a port for the local sugar and pineapple plantations. Today, commercial agriculture has all but disappeared from the island, and Kaunakakai looks its age. The main street, with its wooden boardwalk, is lined with false-fronted stores. A short distance from the town center, local fishermen throng Kaunakakai Harbor, its long stone jetty jutting out into the ocean. About 2 miles (3 km) west of town is the Kapuāiwa Coconut Grove, whose 1,000 soaring trees are a majestic sight silhouetted against the setting sun.

East of Kaunakakai the Kamehameha V Highway begins, which is among the most beautiful coastal drives in Hawaii. The 27-mile (44-km) highway takes in ancient sites, picturesque churches, pristine beaches, and sleepy villages tucked away amid tropical flowers and luxuriant rainforests. The road finally twists to a halt at the stunningly beautiful Hālawa Valley which, with its soaring walls, lush vegetation, idyllic beaches, and shimmering waterfalls, is Moloka'i's most scenic spot.

8
Lahaina

Lahaina Harbor
648 Wharf St; www.visitlahaina.com

One of Maui's most popular attractions, the small harbor town of Lahaina was the capital of the Kingdom of Hawaii until 1845, and a major center of the whaling trade. The area around Front Street has a wealth of well-restored historic sites that are evocative of Lahaina's past. Among them is the Baldwin Home, Maui's oldest Western-style dwelling, dating from the 1830s, with original furnishings and artifacts. Nearby is the Chinese Wo Hing Temple, which was built in 1912.

> **The stunningly beautiful Halawa Valley... with its soaring walls, lush vegetation, idyllic beaches, and shimmering waterfalls, is Moloka'i's most scenic spot.**

←

A pink-streaked sky at sunset on one of Maui's beautiful beaches

Another favorite landmark is Lahaina's first hotel, the charming 1901 Pioneer Inn, still a tourist mecca and hotel.

One of the harbor's main attractions lies beneath the surface of the water: the *Carthaginian II*, a 1920s German schooner that was transformed to look like the kind of small freighter that brought cargo and people to the islands in the 1800s. For years it held a fascinating museum in the hold, which was devoted to whales and the whale trade, until the costs of repairs to the aging ship grew too high. The ship was then deliberately sunk in 2005, to create an artificial reef for marine life and divers. Today visitors can dive to the sunken vessel, which sits at a depth of 97 ft (30 m), and explore the colorful and unusual habitat.

Just 6 miles (10 km) north of Lahaina is Maui's biggest resort, Kāʻanapali, its long white beach lined with hotels. Puʻu Kekaʻa, better known as Black Rock, towers above the beach and overlooks one of Maui's best snorkeling spots. Vintage steam locomotives make the short and scenic trip here from Lahaina. A 20-minute drive north of Kāʻanapali is Maui's other major resort, Kapalua, with its exquisite crescent bays, luxury hotels, golf courses, and pineapple plantations.

---

9 🏛️ 🏝️

Kalaupapa National Historical Park

⏱️📍 **For tours only**
🌐 **nps.gov/kala**

The isolated Kalaupapa Peninsula, sealed off from the rest of Molokaʻi by a mighty wall of cliffs, is home to the Kalaupapa National Historical Park. In 1865, when the imported disease of leprosy seemed to threaten the survival of the Hawaiian people, the peninsula was designated a leper colony, and those afflicted were exiled here. The park now serves as a memorial. The main settlement was at the village of Kalaupapa, on the western side of the peninsula. The last patients arrived in 1969, when the policy of enforced isolation ended. Kalaupapa's small population today includes a few aging patients who chose to live out the remainder of their lives here.

South of the village is the Kalaupapa Trail, once a favorite with hikers and mule riders for its stupendous views. Due to a landslide the trail is currently closed, with no estimate date of reopening.

On the peninsula's eastern shore is St. Philomena Church, in the original leprosy settlement of Kalawao. Shipped out from Honolulu in 1872, the church was later modified by the Belgian priest Father Damien (1840–89), who dedicated his life to caring for the leprosy patients. Father Damien succumbed to leprosy in 1889 and has been beatified by the Pope. From the peninsula's eastern side, small islands poke out of the waters of the ocean, next to staggering 2,000-ft (600-m) cliffs – the tallest sea cliffs in the world.

Reserve tours in advance and note that all visitors must be 16 years or older.

↑ Browsing shop windows within the popular harbor town of Lahaina, Maui

EAT

Kanemitsu Bakery

Having opened its doors back in the 1920s, this bakery is known for its late-night "hot bread," which is served with your choice of sweet or savory fillings.

📍79 Ala Malama St, Kaunakakai, Moloka'i
🕐Tue 📞(808) 553-5855

$$$

Feast at Lele

No visit to Hawaii is complete without indulging in a *luau* – a traditional Hawaiian food feast with live entertainment. At Lele, it's a 5-course oceanfront dining experience.

📍505 Front St, Lahaina, Maui 🕐Lunch
🌐feastatlele.com

$$$

A Saigon Café

This friendly Vietnamese eatery has a Hawaiian twist. The pho, spring rolls, and "Vietnamese burritos" are all excellent.

📍1792 Main St, Wailuku, Maui 🌐asaigon
cafe.com

$$$

Kojima's Sushi Bar

An authentic Japanese spot for fresh sushi. The chef incorporates local flavors, and as an added bonus it's BYOB.

📍81 Makawao Av, Pukalani, Maui 🕐Sun
🌐kojimassushi.com

$$$

↑ The rare Haleakalā Silversword plant growing in Haleakalā National Park, Maui

Haleakalā National Park

📍Haleakalā Crater Rd (Hwy 378) 🌐nps.gov/hale

The landmass of East Maui is really the top of an enormous volcano that begins more than 3 miles (5 km) below sea level. Haleakalā last spewed molten lava some 200 years ago and is still considered to be active, although not currently erupting. Its summit depression is 7.5 miles (12 km) long and 2.5 miles (4 km) wide. This incredible natural wonder is preserved as part of the national park. The 2-hour drive to the 10,023-ft (3,055-m) Pu'u 'Ula'ula Summit, which is the highest point in Maui, is worth it for the truly breathtaking view of the volcano in its entirety, with its cinder cones and brightly colored ashes.

The best way to appreciate Haleakalā's vast scale and varied terrain is to descend 3,000 ft (900 m) into the volcano. The 10-mile (16-km) Sliding Sands Trail takes you from the visitor center through scenery that ranges from barren cinder desert to alpine shrubland. Also worth exploring is the Silversword Loop where you can see one of the world's rarest plants, the Haleakalā Silversword, thriving. This plant takes up to 50 years to flower, when it raises a spectacular spike of purplish flowers.

On the eastern side of the park, not far from Hāna, is the 'Ohe'o Gulch. This beautiful spot is in fact known by many other names, such as the Seven Sacred Pools, although there are more than seven pools at the site, along with a number of lovely waterfalls. When water levels are safe, many of the pools are open for swimming, although you should obey all signs in the area for your own safety.

⓫

Hāna

🔹 ℹ MVB, Wailuku; www.hanamaui.com

Often called Hawaii's "most Hawaiian town," Hāna continues to lag lazily behind modernity. Its perfect round bay and dreamy climate have made it a prized settlement since ancient times. Ka'uiki Head, the large cinder cone found on the right flank of the bay, once served as a natural fortification.

The Hāna Cultural Center presents a *kauhale* (residential compound) in the precontact style once unique to this area and exhibits artifacts that give a sense of local history. Wānanalua Church,

which was constructed from blocks of coral in 1838, was built by missionaries on top of an existing *heiau* (temple), thus symbolizing the triumph of Christianity over paganism.

The scenic Hāna Belt Road twists along the coast to Pā'ia, with views of waterfalls, gulches choked with vegetation, taro fields, botanical gardens, rocky cliffs, and the dramatic Honomanū Bay, with its black-sand beach.

WHALE WATCHING

Although humpback whales can be spotted throughout the Hawaiian Islands, the shallow and protected 'Au'au Channel between Maui, Lanai, and Moloka'i is one of the best whale-watching destinations in the world. Whales migrate here from Alaskan waters from about December through to May, to breed, calve, and nurse their young. Visit www.gohawaii.com for more information on tours.

⓬

Molokini

Around 3 miles (5 km) off the coast of Maui in the 'Alalākeiki Channel, the tiny crescent-shaped islet of Molokini offers some of the best snorkeling and diving in all Hawaii. The island (which is off-limits as a state seabird sanctuary) is all that's left of a large volcanic crater, its shallow inner cove serving as a haven for marine life. Patches of coral reef here attract a huge variety of tropical fish, reef sharks, and even the occasional humpback whale (Dec–May).

🔍 HIDDEN GEM
Palauea Beach

The long, sandy beaches around Wailea in South Maui are some of the best in Hawaii, but Palauea Beach (opposite Molokini) is one of the most pristine and less visited. There's good snorkeling, boogie boarding, and sunbathing to be had here.

↑ Looking down at the waterfalls along the winding Hāna Belt Road

NEED TO KNOW

O'ahu's Ko'olau mountain range, Hawaii

BEFORE
YOU GO

Forward planning is essential to any successful trip. Be prepared for all eventualities by considering the following points before you travel.

AT A GLANCE

CURRENCY
US Dollar
(USD)

AVERAGE DAILY SPEND

SAVE	SPEND	SPLURGE
$100	$250	$500+

BOTTLED WATER	COFFEE	BEER	DINNER FOR TWO
$1.50	$2	$7	$75

TIPPING

Bar staff	$1 per drink
Concierge	$5–10
Housekeeping	$1–5 per night
Hotel Porter	$1–2 per bag
Taxi Driver	10–15%
Wait staff	15–20%

ELECTRICITY SUPPLY

Standard voltage is 110 volts. Power sockets are type A and B, fitting two- or three-pronged plugs.

Passports and Visas

Citizens of the UK, Australia, New Zealand, and EU countries do not require visas for stays of up to 90 days (Canadians can stay for up to six months). These citizens must complete an **ESTA** form online at least 72 hours before travel. For up-to-date visa information specific to your home country, visit the Travel section of the **US Customs and Border Protection** website, or the **US Department of State**.
ESTA
w esta.cbp.dhs.gov/esta
US Customs and Border Protection
w cbp.gov
US Department of State
w travel.state.gov

Travel Safety Information

Visitors can get up-to-date travel safety information from the **UK Foreign and Commonwealth Office** and the **Australian Department of Foreign Affairs and Trade**.
Australia
w smartraveller.gov.au
UK
w gov.uk/foreign-travel-advice

Customs Information

An individual is permitted to carry the following into the US for personal use:
Alcohol One liter of alcohol for each person over 21 (the US Virgin Islands and other Caribbean countries are entitled to more). Additional quantities must be declared.
Cannabis Though some US states have legalized the use of cannabis/marijuana, it is strictly illegal to take any amount across the US border.
Cash If entering or leaving the US with more than $10,000 in cash (or the equivalent in other currencies) it must be declared to the customs authorities.
Tobacco products 200 cigarettes or 100 cigars. No meat products, Cuban cigars, plants, seeds, fruits, or firearms may be taken into the US.

Insurance

It is important to take out insurance covering health problems, accidents, trip cancellation and interruption, as well as theft and loss of valuable possessions.

Vaccinations

No inoculations are required to visit the US.

Money

Major credit and debit cards are accepted almost everywhere, while prepaid currency cards, Apple Pay, and American Express are accepted in many shops and restaurants. ATM machines are widely available, though most charge a fee of $1 to $3 per transaction. Changing foreign currency can be tough outside the big cities and major banks – the best strategy is to bring a small amount of US dollars with you, and then use local ATMs to withdraw cash.

Reserving Accommodations

The US offers a variety of lodgings, from luxury five-star hotels to budget hostels. Camping, motorhomes or RVs, and Airbnb are popular alternatives. In the summer months (June through September), accommodations tend to be snapped up quickly, and prices are often inflated. Sales tax is paid on accommodations (and on goods and other services), though it varies from state to state, and some cities and counties levy additional taxes. When added to "resort fees" imposed by some larger hotels, these can sometimes raise the actual rate by up to 25 percent. These taxes are usually paid on top of the advertised rates.

Hostelling International USA
w hiusa.org
Kampgrounds of America
w koa.com

Travelers with Specific Needs

Nearly all Federal and most public buildings provide wheelchair facilities with ramps and wide doors. However, some lodgings in older buildings may not have these facilities, so always check in advance.

Trains, buses, and taxis are designed to allow for wheelchairs. Amtrak offers a ten percent discount to adult passengers with a disability, plus wheeled mobility device space, transfer accessible seats (for when you travel in a seat and stow your wheelchair), and accessible room accommodations. All Greyhound buses are equipped with a wheelchair lift and can fit two passengers sitting in a wheelchair or mobility scooter. Car rental agencies offer hand-controlled vehicles and vans with wheelchair lifts. A number of organizations that will help disabled visitors plan and enjoy their trips include **The Guided Tour**, **The Lighthouse Guild**, **Scootaround**, and **Traveler's Aid**.

The Guided Tour
w guidedtour.com
The Lighthouse Guild
w lighthouseguild.org
Scootaround
w scootaround.com
Traveler's Aid
w travelersaid.org

Closures

Mondays Some museums and tourist attractions are closed for the day.
Sundays Most shops and businesses are open for limited hours; banks are closed.
Federal holidays Banks, schools, and government offices close all day. A handful of shops and attractions close early or all day.

FEDERAL HOLIDAYS

New Year's Day	Jan 1
Martin Luther King, Jr. Day	Jan 18 (2021) Jan 17 (2022))
Presidents' Day	Feb 15 (2021) Feb 21 (2022)
Memorial Day	May 31 (2021) May 30 (2022)
Independence Day	Jul 1
Labor Day	Sep 6 (2021) Sep 5 (2022)
Columbus Day	Oct 11 (2021) Oct 10 (2022)
Veterans Day	Nov 11
Thanksgiving Day	Nov 25 (2021) Nov 24 (2022)
Christmas Day	25 Dec

GETTING AROUND

Whether you are visiting for a short city break or rural country retreat, discover how best to reach your destination and travel the US like a pro.

TRANSPORTATION COSTS

BOSTON

$2

Single bus journey
[subway $2.90]

CHICAGO

$2.25

Single bus journey
["L" train $2.50]

NEW YORK

$3

Single bus and subway journey

LOS ANGELES

$1.75

Single bus and metro journey

SAN FRANCISCO

$3

Single bus, light rail, and streetcar journey

WASHINGTON, DC

$2

Single bus journey
[Metrorail $2-6]

Arriving by Air

The USA's largest international airports are at Atlanta, Chicago (O'Hare), Dallas/Fort Worth, Denver, Houston, Las Vegas, Los Angeles, Miami, New York (JFK and Newark), Orlando, Seattle, and San Francisco. The country's major carriers are American Airlines, Delta Airlines, and United Airlines, though budget airlines such as JetBlue Airways and Southwest Airlines are now major international as well as domestic competitors. If reserved far enough in advance, prices on the busiest domestic routes can be relatively cheap (and generally less expensive over long distances than bus or train).

All of the USA's international airports are well served by bus and taxi services, and rented cars, while smaller airports depend more on taxis. The table opposite lists popular transportation options to and from the USA's main city airports.

Train Travel

The use of passenger trains in the US is dwindling, though East Coast (between Boston, New York, and Washington, DC) and California (Los Angeles to San Diego) services remain fast and frequent. All long-distance passenger train routes are operated by **Amtrak**, the national rail system, and tickets should be reserved well in advance to avoid pricey fares. Amtrak runs three international routes to Canada (with VIA Rail): New York to Montreal and Toronto, and Seattle to Vancouver. There are no train services to Mexico.
Amtrak
w amtrak.com

Discounts and passes
Amtrak gives one child (2–12) per adult traveling a 50 percent discount (one child under the age of two, not occupying a seat, may ride free with each adult). Travelers aged 65 or over can usually get a 10 percent discount. Amtrak Rail Passes are good value if you intend to travel a lot by train; for each pass type you

GETTING TO AND FROM THE AIRPORT

Airport	Distance to city	Taxi fare	Transportation	Journey time
Atlanta (ATL)	7 miles (11 km)	$30	Light rail	18-20 min
Boston (BOS)	2.5 miles (4 km)	$30-45	Bus/subway	20-40 mins
Chicago (O'Hare)	17 miles (27 km)	$30-45	"L" train	40 mins
Dallas (DFW)	18 miles (29 km)	$45	Light rail	50 mins
Denver	25 miles (40 km)	$56	Train	37 mins
Houston (IAH)	23 miles (37 km)	$57	Bus	50-90 mins
Las Vegas (LAS)	5 miles (8 km)	$15-25	Bus	25-30 mins
Los Angeles (LAX)	15 miles (24 km)	$50-65	Bus/light rail	60-90 mins
Miami (MIA)	10 miles (16 km)	$35-55	Bus	30-40 mins
Newark Liberty (EWR)	9 miles (14 km)	$60-90	Bus/train	40-60 mins
New York (JFK)	15 miles (24 km)	$52	Bus/subway	40-60 mins
Orlando (MCO)	6 miles (10 km)	$38-45	Bus	40-50 mins
San Diego (MCO)	3 miles (5 km)	$15-22	Bus	15-30 mins
San Francisco (SFO)	14 miles (22 km)	$40-50	BART	20-40 mins
Seattle (SEA)	14 miles (22 km)	$40-50	Bus/light rail	40-45 mins
Washington, DC (IUD)	26 miles (42 km)	$65-75	Bus/light rail	40-60 mins

are allowed a limited number of travel segments within a set period. The California Rail Pass allows up to seven days of travel in California over a 21-day period for $159.

Long-Distance Bus Travel

Buses are typically the most economical way to get around the US, but often not the most convenient, especially over huge distances. **Greyhound Lines** runs across the whole country, sometimes in conjunction with regional operators, while budget lines such as **Bolt Bus** (owned by Greyhound) and **Megabus** operate on the busy East Coast corridor and other primary routes. Greyhound also runs routes across the borders with Mexico and Canada; Megabus runs between New York and Toronto in 11–12 hours. Discounts are available on Greyhound for children (2–16), students, and seniors (aged 62 and older).

Bolt Bus
🌐 boltbus.com
Greyhound Lines
🌐 greyhound.com
Megabus
🌐 us.megabus.com

Boats and Ferries

A number of boat trips link the US and Canada, and these can make for a lovely way to sightsee. This includes the tiny car ferries between Deer Island, New Brunswick, and Eastport in Maine. From 2020, the Yarmouth (Nova Scotia, Canada) to Maine car ferry should be running from Bar Harbor, via **Bay Ferries**. On the West Coast, the **Victoria Clipper** catamaran runs between Seattle and Victoria on Vancouver Island, Canada. Washington State Ferries runs from Anacortes to Sidney, Vancouver Island. Further north, Alaska Marine Highway ferries also offer enjoyable experiences, and links several Alaskan towns with Bellingham, in Washington state. Currently the only ferry operating in the Hawaii archipelago is the **Maui-Lanai Expeditions** service. This leaves from Lahaina, on Maui, and sails to Manele Bay, on Lanai, in around 45 minutes .

Bay Ferries
🌐 ferries.ca
Maui-Lanai Expeditions
🌐 go-lanai.com
Victoria Clipper
🌐 clippervacations.com/clipper-experience

SPEED LIMITS

Speed limits in the US vary depending on road type, state, and even by county in Texas. The following are maximum speeds permitted on multi-lane freeways (highways).

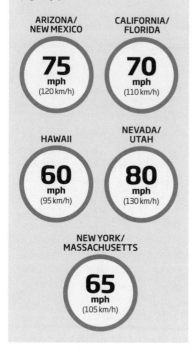

ARIZONA/ NEW MEXICO
75 mph (120 km/h)

CALIFORNIA/ FLORIDA
70 mph (110 km/h)

HAWAII
60 mph (95 km/h)

NEVADA/ UTAH
80 mph (130 km/h)

NEW YORK/ MASSACHUSETTS
65 mph (105 km/h)

Driving in the US

A great way to explore the US is by car, especially when visiting a remote rural area or national park. The USA's highway network is excellent and generally well maintained. However, city-center traffic congestion means that visitors to the major cities of New York, LA, Boston, Chicago, and San Francisco may find that public transportation is quicker and cheaper than driving.

Car rental

Many car rental companies have offices at city airports and towns across the country, and rentals are easily arranged before arriving in the US. When picking up your rental car, you may be asked to show your passport and return airline ticket; you will also need a credit card (debit cards may be refused). Most rental companies offer GPS (SatNav) for an additional daily fee, and child seats with advance notice. Free unlimited mileage is usually included (check ahead), but leaving the car in a different city to the one in which you rent it may incur a substantial drop-off fee. Standard rental cars in the US have automatic transmission.

Drivers' Licenses

Foreign drivers' licenses are valid in the US, but if your license is not in English, you must get an International Driver's License. Drivers need to have held their licenses for at least one year, and visitors under 25 may encounter restrictions when renting, usually having to pay an extra $20–30 a day (confirm ahead). If you're under 21, you will usually not be able to rent a car at all (there are some exemptions, but usually only for US license holders, and then with a hefty surcharge). Most companies also charge a daily fee for additional drivers ($10+), but there are some exceptions, notably in California, where all additional drivers are free (although they must still be listed on the contract). In ten other states (including New York, Illinois, Texas, and Utah), the fee is waived if the additional driver is a spouse.

Insurance

When you rent a car in the US you will be asked to add on a bewildering array of insurance extras. The insurance rules differ by state, but all require at least some type of liability insurance .

In brief, loss-damage waiver (LDW) or collision-damage waiver (CDW) allows you to avoid paying for any damage to the rental vehicle or theft of the car. However, there are sometimes "minimums" as opposed to "full" coverage, which can mean you are liable for the first $1,000 of damage, for example. Punctured tires and windshield damage are often not covered. Supplemental liability protection (SLP) will pay for damage you cause to other drivers' vehicles or property – again, check how much this actually covers. Personal accident insurance covers medical costs if the car is involved in an accident. In general it's a good idea to take at least LDW and SLP, as even a minor accident can result in astronomical costs. Check to see if your own car insurance will cover rentals (most likely if you own a car in the US or Canada), or whether your credit card provides coverage for rental cars (you must use the card to pay, and the rental must be in the cardholder's name).

Rules of the Road

Everywhere in the US you drive on the right-hand side of the road, and all distances are measured in miles. Seat belts are compulsory. Right turns on red (unless otherwise indicated) are allowed after coming to a complete stop. All vehicles must give way to emergency service vehicles, and traffic in both directions must stop for a school bus when signals are flashing. Most states prohibit use of cell phones while driving, with the exception of a "hands-free" system.

Speeding will usually result in a fine that should be paid in person if possible – the rental company will otherwise charge hefty additional admin fees. "Driving under the influence" (DUI) of alcohol is a very serious offence, likely leading to arrest.

Toll roads

There are a number of toll roads in the US. Most still have cash toll booths, but many states are introducing electronic systems. If you drive on one of these roads without an electronic pass, you face a hefty fine and admin fees from your rental company. Your car may be fitted with an electronic pass, subject to a daily fee from the rental company (regardless of usage), plus tolls incurred. Make sure you understand the billing structure before you drive off. If you expect to drive on a high number of toll roads, it may be worth buying a transponder yourself (the **E-ZPass** system is the largest).
E-ZPass
w e-zpassiag.com

Parking

The majority of cities and towns have paid on- and off-street parking with parking meters and designated parking lots. Parking in the down-town core of major cities is usually very expensive, and should be factored into your daily costs. Hotels in major cities charge $25–60 per day for on-site parking. Even the cheapest parking lots in downtown New York, for example, charge $8 per hour, and parking meters cost $4.50–7.50 per hour, with a range of rules that vary by street. Illegally parked drivers run the risk of getting their vehicle towed, with a substantial fine.

Cycling

Cycling is a great way to get around the more rural parts of the country during warmer months, and its popularity is on the rise. Most urban centers have miles of dedicated bike lanes, and almost all cities allow bikes to be taken on public transportation. In some states "trail to rail" projects have created long-distance cycle ways, notably the Suncoast Trail and Fred Marquis Pinellas Trail in Florida, the Burlington Greenway Bike Path (Vermont), Route of the Hiawatha mountain bike trail in Idaho and many others. For more on the US Bicycle Route System, contact the **Adventure Cycling Association**.
Adventure Cycling Association
w adventurecycling.org

Bicycle rental

All major cities have shops that rent bikes, and some have tour guides available too. Specialty bike shops also rent electric and mountain bikes. Most large cities now have bike-share programs with docking stations that allow cyclists to make one-way trips for a nominal fee. **Jump** is a GPS-powered dock-less system that offers e-bikes and scooters via the Uber app in several cities. **Lime** and **Lyft** offer similar services.
Jump
w jump.com
Lime
w li.me
Lyft
w lyft.com

RAIL JOURNEY PLANNER

Chicago to Denver	15–16 hrs
DC to Savannah	9–10 hrs
Denver to Las Vegas	12 hrs
LA to Las Vegas	4–4.5 hrs
LA to San Diego	3 hrs
LA to San Francisco	7 hrs
New York to Boston	3.5–4 hrs
New York to DC	4 hrs
New York to Chicago	13–14 hrs
San Francisco to Seattle	15 hrs
Savannah to Orlando	4–4.5 hrs
Orlando to Miami	3.5–4 hrs

Plotting major train routes across the US, this map is a handy reference for inter-city rail travel. Trip times are given for the fastest available service on each route.

••• Direct train routes

PRACTICAL
INFORMATION

A little local know-how goes a long way in the US. Here you will find all the essential advice and information you will need during your stay.

TIME ZONE

The continental US spans four time zones: PST/MST/CST/EST. Most of Alaska uses AKST; Hawaii uses HST. DST (Daylight Saving Time) is observed everywhere from the second Sunday in March to the first Sunday in November, with the exception of Hawaii and Arizona.

TAP WATER

Unless stated otherwise, tap water in the US should be safe to drink. However, cities such as Flint, Michigan (since 2014), and Newark, New Jersey (2019) have had issues with contaminated water – ask at your hotel if in any doubt.

Personal Security

Crime rates have declined dramatically across the US since the 1990s, and while most places on the tourist trail are reasonably safe to travel, visitors should nonetheless take safety precautions to avoid being a victim of crime. Generally speaking, most crimes occur in neighborhoods or areas not frequented by travelers, and at night. Avoid wearing expensive jewelry, carry only small amounts of cash, wear a money belt under clothing, and always carry cameras, phones, and electronic devices securely.

Natural Hazards

Parts of the US are prone to natural disasters, including earthquakes, forest fires, flooding, tornados/twisters, hurricanes, and, though unlikely, volcanic eruptions (Washington state and Hawaii). With the exception of tornados and earthquakes, which are notoriously hard to predict, local authorities and media outlets should provide plenty of warning for such events (most of which are seasonal at any rate).

With wildlife, your biggest irritations are likely to be with mosquitoes, flies, and blackflies – common in the early summer throughout the US, especially in national parks and wilderness areas. Though attacks are rare, bears are potentially very dangerous – blow a whistle while walking in bear country or invest in a bear spray. If confronted, don't run, make loud noises, or sudden movements, all of which are likely to provoke an attack. Cougar, mountain lion, and puma attacks are very rare. The best strategy with cougars is to try to fight them off with rocks and sticks (they usually avoid groups altogether).

Snake bites are more common in some parts of the US (rattlesnakes are abundant in the West), but only a handful are reported each year and fatalities are rare. Wear proper boots while hiking in the wild and if you do disturb a snake, back away so that it has room to move freely. Even the most venomous bites can be treated successfully with immediate medical attention.

Alligators (seen mostly in Florida) are a lot more docile than they appear, but can still be very dangerous. Attacks on humans are rare, but often fatal, with children especially vulnerable. Most attacks occur in or on the edge of ponds or waterways; the victims are usually alone.

Shark attacks are also very rare in the US (16 per year on average, excluding Hawaii, with 20 fatalities since 2000), though beaches with lifeguards are well patrolled, especially in summer. Due to warming oceans, great white sharks can be seen as far north as New England in summer.

Health

The United States has a private health care system that, though excellent, is extremely expensive. Medical travel insurance is highly recommended in order to cover some of the costs related to an accident or sudden illness. The price of basic care at a hospital emergency room can rise incredibly quickly. Should you be in a serious accident, an ambulance will pick you up and charge later.

Alcohol, Smoking, and Drugs

You must be 21 to drink or purchase alcohol throughout the US; expect to show photo ID. You must be 18 to smoke in the US, but other rules differ from state to state and even city. Some do not regulate smoking at all (such as Oklahoma and Virginia); some ban smoking in certain areas only; and some ban smoking nearly everywhere, even outdoors (California and New York City). As a visitor, assume that most restaurants, bars, and hotels ban smoking.

Unlike Canada, Federal law still prohibits marijuana/cannabis use in the US, but several states have legalized limited amounts for recreational use for anyone over the age of 21, including visitors. Restrictions differ, however, and can be confusing for non-residents (it's usually illegal to smoke cannabis in public places, for example) – check local regulations. Taking any amount of cannabis across state lines or country borders is illegal, and being caught in possession of any other drug will likely result in jail time.

ID

There is no requirement for visitors to carry ID, but due to occasional checks (especially at Federal sites or major office buildings) you may be asked to show a picture ID.

Cell Phones and Wi-Fi

Free Wi-Fi spots are generally available at major airports, libraries, and most hotels. Cafés and restaurants generally permit the use of their Wi-Fi on the condition that you make a purchase.

Local SIM cards ($10 or less) can be used in compatible phones. Some networks also sell basic flip phones (with minutes) for as little as $25 (no paperwork or ID required). Canadian residents can usually upgrade their domestic cell phone plan to extend to the US. Pre-paid phone cards usually offer the best rates for long-distance calls, and are sold in most drugstores.

Post

USPS post offices are generally open 9am–5pm Monday to Friday (though some open earlier), and Saturday from 9am–noon or later.

Taxes and Refunds

Sales taxes vary from state to state, and supplementary local sales taxes may be added. Alaska, Delaware, Oregon, New Hampshire, and Montana have no state sales tax, while California has the highest base rate, at 7.25 percent. Since none of these taxes are levied at a national level, tourists cannot claim sales tax refunds.

Discount Cards

The US National Park Service "America the Beautiful Passes" cover entrance fees for a driver and all passengers in a personal vehicle at all of America's national parks. Over-50s should look into buying an AARP membership (open to non-Americans), which can provide discounts at hotels and on car rentals. Most cities also operate some form of discount card: CityPASS, for example, runs programs for New York, Boston, Chicago, and many others.

WEBSITES AND APPS

InciWeb
This site (www.inciweb.nwcg.gov) offers instant updates on extreme weather.

US National Park Service
Full information on America's national parks can be found at www.nps.gov.

Visit The USA
The USA's official tourist website has useful tips (www.visittheusa.com).

GasBuddy
A must for US road trips, this app locates nearby gas stations and notifies you about deals (www.gasbuddy.com).

INDEX

ACKNOWLEDGMENTS

Dorling Kindersley would like to thank the following people for their contributions to previous editions of the guide: Ruth & Eric Bailey, Bob Barnes, Jyl Benson, Mary Bergin, Eleanor Berman, Jeremy Black, Lester Brooks, Patricia Brooks, Tom Bross, Susan Burke, Rebecca Carman, Richard Cawthorne, Brett Cook, Donna Dailey, Jackie Finch, Bonita Halm, Michelle de Larrabeiti, David Dick, Susan Farewell, Rebecca Poole Forée, Paul Franklin, Donald S. Frazier, Bonnie Friedman, Jennifer Greenhill-Taylor, Rita Goldman, Eric Grossman, Patricia Harris, Ross Hassig, Carolyn Heller, Pierre Home-Douglas, Lorraine Johnson, Penney Kome, Esther Labi, Philip Lee, Helga Loverseed, David Lyon, Clemence McLaren, Guy Mansell, Fred Mawer, Nancy Mikula, Melissa Miller, Kendrick Oliver, Barry Parr, Carolyn Patten, Ellen Payne, J. Kingston Pierce, Don Pitcher, Alice L. Powers, Jennifer Quasha, George Raudzens, Juliette Rogers, John Ryan, Alex Salkever, Litta W. Sanderson, Kem Sawyer, AnneLise Sorensen, Emma Stanford, Brett Steel, Arvin Steinberg, Phyllis Steinberg, Nigel Tisdall, Brian Ward, Greg Ward, John Wilcock, Ian Williams, Marilyn Wood, Paul Wood, Stanley Young.

The publisher would like to thank the following for their kind permission to reproduce their photographs:

Key: a-above; b-below/bottom; c-centre; f-far; l-left; r-right; t-top

123RF.com: bennymarty 35tr; Jon Bilous 216t, 228t; Mariusz Blach 663b; James Byard 377b; coralimages 657br; imagecom 332; jakobradlgruber 8clb, 504b; James Kirkikis 224cra; Nick Kontostavlakis 660–661t; milesbeforeisleep 259cl, 526br; sean pavone 388b; Wasin Pummarin 636b; sorincolac 730–731t; tonobalaguer 462tl.

4Corners: Andrea Armellin 88t; Jordan Banks 50cra, 334t; Massimo Borchi 40tr, 326tr; Kav Dadfar 21bl, 444–5, 448tl; Carlo Irek 35clb; Susanne Kremer 38tr, 316, 495t, 616tl, 717crb, 718; Maurizio Rellini 641bl.

500px: Nina Sauer 102bl.

Alamy Stock Photo: 24BY36 283br; Irene Abdou 331br; Accent Alaska.com 696t; AF archive 301cra; AGE Fotostock / Richard Cummins 683bl, / Steve Dunwell 154bl, / Alvaro Leiva 289br, Dennis Macdonald / *Buffalo Bill—Plainsman* by Bob Scriver 559bc, / George Ostertag 469cl, Alan Majchrowicz Photography 546–7b; AlphaAndOmega 513bl; Tomas Del Amo 715tr; Archive Image 384b; The Artchives 733tc; Barbara Ash 423bc; AugustSnow 501tr; Gonzalo Azumendi 656–7t; © Bill Bachmann 126bl, 531br; Marcus Baker 147clb; D A Barnes 542tl; Carol Barrington 48br; Stephen Bay 432clb; Bruce yuanyue Bi 190t, 364crb; Bildagentur-online / Schickert 655b; Jon Bilous 211t; Pat & Chuck Blackley 41tl, 110tl, 199tr, 229bl, 396–7t, 419tr; blickwinkel / Held 507bl, / McPhoto / SBA 699cla; Bob Colley Photography 261tr; Dimitry Bobroff 245tr, 344tl; Mike Briner 391tr; Bill Brooks 735br; Tim Brown 128clb; Buff Henry Photography 295tl; Ron S Buskirk 337tr; Patrick Byrd 459tr; Susan Candelario 139cla; Cannon Photography LLC /

BrownWCannonIII 606tl, 700–701t, 722–3b; Pat Canova 48–9t; Cavan Images 560cra, / Aurora Photos / Kirk Mastin 49crb, / Josh Campbell 178t, / Andrew Peacock 45clb, / Ethan Welty 697bl; Charles O. Cecil 335cra; Cephas Picture Library / Mick Rock 198tl; Sergey Chernyaev 280cra; Felix Choo 31cla; Chronicle 491tl; Stephen Chung 374bl; Citizen of the Planet / Peter Bennett 632br, / *De L'Esprie and the sculpture was cast into bronze by David L. Spellerberg, National Heritage Collectors Society 1988* 631br; Clarence Holmes Photography 51clb, 230, 352t, 352cl; Classic Image 650clb (1848); Caroline Commins 572–3t; Dennis Cox 463b; Rob Crandall 222–3t, 602tl, / *Cheval Rouge* (1974) by Alexander Calder © 2020 Calder Foundation, New York and DACS, London 2020 196bl; Curved Light USA 8cla; Ian Dagnall 26cr, 42–3t, 66tl, 115tc, 127cra, 234–5b, 260tl, 274bl, 390t, 410cr, 493tl, 554bl, 623cra, 624b, 643tr; Ian G Dagnall 442–3t, 475tl; Danita Delimont / Brent Bergherm 591br, / Jerry And Marcy Monkman 184t, / Walter Bibikow 443cla, / Savanah Stewart 691tr; Danita Delimont Creative / Adam Jones 274–5t, DanitaDelimont.com / Walter Bibikow 461tr; David L. Moore - US SW 529clb; David R. Frazier Photolibrary; Inc. 373tl; dbimages / dbtravel 199tl; / Roy Johnson 356–7b; Phil Degginger 519tl; Clark DeHart 266–7b; Dembinsky Photo Associates / Dominique Braud 419br; Songquan Deng 302bl; Design Pics Inc / Alaska Stock RM / Steven Miley 697crb, / Axiom / Robert L. Potts 23, 574–5, / John R. Delapp 698–9b, / Destinations / Stuart Westmorland 635tl, / Doug Lindstrand 699cra, / Lucas Payne 433tr, / Chip Porter 700br, / Kevin G Smith 39tr; Dinodia Photos RM 82bl; Beth Dixson 725cr; Don Johnston_WU 552cr; Terry Donnelly 250–251b, 593bl; Douglas Peebles Photography / C.Douglas Peebles 727tl; Randy Duchaine 563cla, 66tr, 125tr, 233br; EcoPhotography.com / Jerry and Marcy Monkman 141crb; Education & Exploration 1 124t, 358tc; Chad Ehlers 155tl; Richard Ellis 254tl, 562bl; EmmePi Images 378cla; eye35 482tr, 640–1t; eye35.pix 685br; EyeVisualEyesIt 306tr; David Fleetham 717cla, 737cra; Stephen Flint 46crb; Lee Foster 119crb; Zachary Frank 542cra; Dennis Frates 608–9t; Gabbro 320bl; Gado Images / Smith Collection 200–201b; Gaertner 559tl; Eddy Galeotti 38–9b, 721br; Dylan Garcia 340bl; Larry Geddis 494bl, 606–7b, 610; georgesanker.com 182; Vlad Ghiea 364cr; GL Archive 121bc, 651bc, 653ca, 653br; Glasshouse Images / Circa Images 200br; Goddard on the Go 38br; Bill Gozansky 584br; Granger Historical Picture Archive NYC 200tl, 367tl, / Woolaroc Museum Bartlesville, Oklahoma 53tr; The Granger Collection 55tr; Richard Green 302–3t; Eduard Grjasin 684–5t; guynamedjames 720br; H. Mark Weidman Photography 724bl, 732b; Have Camera Will Travel / David Coleman 218bl, 267tr; Kelly Headrick 737bl; hemis.fr / Walter Bibikow 236t, / Patrick Frilet 37crb, 242–3t, 330tr, 568t, / Marc Dozier 622t, / Stephane Lemaire 483tl, 523bl; Paul Hennessy 301br; Robert Hoetink 298; Bert Hoferichter 112–113t; Keith Homan 675tr; Peter Horree 655cr; George H.H. Huey 451bl; Hum Images 301tr; D. Hurst 198tr; Ian Dagnall Commercial Collection 53br, 428t; Image Professionals GmbH / Hendrik Holler 320–21t; imageBROKER / Norbert Eisele-Hein

480cr, / Horst Mahr 578br, / Michael Szönyi
560–61, / Moritz Wolf 658tl; Images-USA 41crb,
258bl, 268br, 327tr, 547tr, 604cl; incamerastock /
ICP 731br; Interfoto / Personalities 653tr; Rich
Iwasaki 549tl; Eric James 348b, 530t; James Davis
Photography 714tl; Brian Jannsen 180–181b,
301crb, 580bl; Natthaphong Janpum 584crb; Jason
O. Watson (Sports) 111clb; Jeffrey Isaac Greenberg
1 290tc; Jeffrey Isaac Greenberg 3 391bl, 627br;
Andre Jenny 356tl, 596tl; Graham Jepson 29tr; Inge
Johnsson 593crb; Kim Karpeles /Working Model for
Three Piece No.3: Vertebrae by Henry Moore © The
Henry Moore Foundation. All Rights Reserved,
DACS, London / www.henry-moore.org 2020 454bl;
John Kellerman 96–7b, 493br; Don Klumpp 452;
kravka 482tl; Bob Kreisel 659tr; Lake Erie Maps and
Prints 52t; John Lambing 29cla; Lazyllama 46tl;
William Leaman 273clb; Dan Leeth 45cl, 413bl,
571tr; Bruce Leighty 371cra; Martin Leitch 461tl;
Tin Lieu 509t; Chu-Wen Lin 66–7ca; Felix Lipov 85bl;
Littleny 280tl, 284, 566–7b; Look / Hauke Dressler
113br; lucky-photographer 294–5b; Luscious
Frames 142–3t; Dennis MacDonald 111b; Ilene
MacDonald 353bl; MARKA / alberto ramella 57br;
mauritius images GmbH / Walter Bibikow 442bl, /
Christina Czybik 633t; Buddy Mays 191br; Angus
McComiskey 733br; Patti McConville 553br; Brian
McGuire 650br; Jon McLean 672; Troy McMullin
605tl; MediaPunch Inc 215clb; Jordana Meilleur
642cr; Jess Merrill 468bc; Steven Milne 150bl;
Mint Images Limited 651t; Mira 237br; Marc Muench
272tl; National Geographic Image Collection /
Lori Epstein 139tl, / Jonathan Irish 404cr, / Richard
Nowitz 67tl; Native American - Indian culture
485cra; Natural History Library 282tl; Nature and
Science 570–571b; Niebrugge Images 516bl,
693clb, 707br; Ron Niebrugge 641br; NielsVK
44–5t; Nikreates 366tr; North Wind Picture Archives
54br, 253bl; B.O'Kane 440–41b; M. Timothy O'Keefe
280–81t; Oldtime 650clb; OrangeSky 457tr; George
Oze 120b; Efrain Padro 526–7t, 533tr; Panther
Media GmbH / Diana.K 517br; David Parker 651crb;
Sean Pavone 118–19t, 167b, 252t, 262–3t, 313tr,
512–3t, 528–9t; PBpictures 723tl; Philipus 457bl;
Pictorial Press Ltd 271br, 656bc; PixelPod 129tr;
PJF Military Collection 157tr; Chuck Place 573cl;
Susanne Pommer 714–15ca, 716–17b; Chris Poss
31crb; Prisma by Dukas Presseagentur GmbH /
Jose Fuste Raga 487tr; PVstock.com 403t; Raimund
Koch-View 631cla; Ed Rhodes 671tr; Whit
Richardson 450bl; Khristina Ripak 328t;
Robertharding 701br, / Antonio Busiello 544, /
Richard Cummins 594–5b; Stillman Rogers 185crb;
Rolling Stock 497bl; RooM the Agency / tristan
2–3; RosaIreneBetancourt 13 226–7b; Michael
Rosebrock 326tl; Philip Scalia 250tl; James
Schaedig 420b; James Schwabel 706t; Sumiko
Scott 517t; SDM Images 480crb; Florin Seitan
380bl; Galit Seligmann 242tl; Andy Selinger 81t;
sep120 / Stockimo 136crb; Leonid Serebrennikov
666bl; Witold Skrypczak 450–51t, 461cra, 464,
472–3b, 592–3t; Don Smetzer 416bl, 428bl;
Antony Souter 143cl; Spring Images 594tr;
Kumar Sriskandan 140–41t, 185b; Tom Stack
282–3b; Stephen Saks Photography 358–9t;
Charles Stirling 167clb; Stockimo / Birgit Tyrrell
398; Rebecca Stunell 668–9t; Dan Sullivan 676t;
Brigitte Supernova 59clb; Joe Szurszewski 402bl;
TCD / Prod.DB / © Warner Bros 520bl; Stan Tess

138cla, 153tr; 161bc, 166tl; Tetra Images
78–9b, 351br; Andrew Titmus 693br; TMI 586bl;
Rodney Todt 441tr; Tolbert Photo 125bl; Travel
Pictures / Pictures Colour Library 309br; Steve
Tulley 585tr; Tom Uhlman 389tl; Martin Valigursky
663tr; Greg Vaughn 586–7t; Michael Ventura
130bl, 222bl; Elizabeth Wake 71b; Gary Warnimont
386bl; Michael Warwick 674–5b; Mark Waugh
263b; Richard Weber 364bl; WENN Rights Ltd /
Sarah Edwards 375t; Jannis Werner 377crb;
Jim West 41bl, 179br, 235tr, 259t, 394–5b;
Edward Westmacott 151cla; Wild Places
Photography / Chris Howes 534–5t, 555t; Wim
Wiskerke 51tl, 128–9b; World History Archive
429b, 650crb; Jennifer Wright 28cra, 206clb; YAY
Media AS / kamchatka 487clb; Dan Yuen 496–7t;
David Zaitz 33crb, 617tr; Joel Zatz 396br; ZUMA
Press, Inc. / © Sandra Dahdah 449tr, / Mark
Kuhlmann 426cl, / Lexington Herald-Leader /
Mark Cornelison 50cl, / © Marc Nader 13br, /
Southcreek Global / © Steven Branscombe 426–7b.

Audubon Aquarium of the Americas: 2019
Audubon Institute 339tr.

AWL Images: John Coletti 256, 424, 564; Danita
Delimont Stock 410bl, 498; Brent Doscher 678clb;
Michele Falzone 139tr, 416–17t, 736tr; J.Banks 582;
Richard T Nowitz 281cla; Nigel Pavitt 560bl.

Boston Book Festival: Mike Ritter 142bl.

Bua Bar: Rich Wade 87tr.

Courtesy Norman Rockwell Museum: 138tl.

Delta Blues Museum: 351bl.

© Disney: 304t, 304cra, 305tr, 305b.

Dorling Kindersley: Neil Lukas 653crb ; William
Reavell 11br ; Peter Wilson 359br.

Dreamstime.com: Adeliepenguin 86–7b;
Agaliza 100b; Anderm 151t; Mihai Andritoiu
188–9t; Walter Arce 382; Jill Battaglia 563tr; Jay
Beiler 28cla; Bennymarty 491tr, 628tr; Lukas
Bischoff 33cl; Paul Brady 116, 432b; Chrissieracki
418–19b; Sorin Colac 703t, 720–21t;
Coralimages2020 248bl, 630–31t; Davidgn
600–601t; Debsta75 651bl; Deebrowning 10clb;
Donyanedomam 548bl; Anna Dudko 507crb;
Esusek 68cl; F11photo 36tr, 207tr, 244bl, 268–9t,
659b; F8grapher 653bl; Sandra Foyt 43cl; Roberto
Galan 8cl; R. Gino Santa Maria / Shutterfree;
Llc 271tr; Michael Gordon 297tl; Anthony Heflin
381t; Svitlana Imnadze 597b; JaCrispy 26crb;
Jesse Kraft 419tl, 562–3t; Ingus Kruklitis 738–9;
Erik Lattwein 412clb; Lavendertime 84–5t;
Pierre Leclerc 734–5t; Legacy1995 340tl; Chon
Kit Leong 567tr; Littleny 569br; Phillip Lowe
593clb; Lunamarina 300–301t; Maksershov
630br; Marazem 141br; Gerald Marella 430;
Mariakray 281tr; Joshua Mcdonough 168;
Michaelfitzsimmons 79tr; MNStudio 25bl,
710–11; Monkey Business Images 13t; Paula
Montenegro 16c, 62–3; Glenn Nagel 385tl;
Donna Nonemountry 34tl; Yooran Park 601br;
Paulacobleigh 580–81t; Sean Pavone 32bl,

40br, 67tr, 81br, 97crb, 136t, 156cl, 198–9ca, 208t, 232–3t, 248–9t, 254–5b, 264, 270b, 296b, 318–19t, 336b, 344–5b, 372–3b, 386–7t, 401br, 434–5b, 436t, 458–9b, 514–15b, 626–7t; / *Fallingwater in Mill Run; Pennsylvania;* USA by Frank Lloyd Wright / © ARS, NY and DACS, London 2020 26t; Enrico Della Pietra 138cra; Ronniechua 648b; Rudi1976 12clb; 367br; Joe Sohm 12–13b; Spiroview Inc. 106; Andrei Gabriel Stanescu 682t; Sumikophoto 608cla; Tea 367bl; Daniel Thornberg 449cla; Tifonimages 665br; Paul Topp 669br; Tupungato 101tr; Vitalyedush 13cr; Amanda Wanner 261b; Wenling01 448–9ca; Wilsilver77 315clb; Zhukovsky 70tl; Zrfphoto 212bl.

Eastern State Penitentiary: 123tr.

General Porpoise Pioneer Square – Sea Creatures: Aaron Leitz 578cra.

Getty Images: 500px / Dominic Jeanmaire 616–17ca; 500Px Plus / Jeff Clow 520cra; 500px Prime / Diana Robinson 470; AFP / Saul Loeb 215crb, / Mandel Ngan 57tr; Anadolu Agency / Atilgan Ozdil 50crb; Archive Photos 330clb, / Al Greene Archive 660clb, / ClassicStock / H. Abernathy 326–7ca, / Consolidated News Pictures / Ron Sachs 59cl, / Fotosearch 52bl, / GraphicaArtis 53cb, / Hulton Archive 58bl, / David Hume Kennerly 201br, / Lambert 56cla, / MPI 53tl, / PhotoQuest 59cla (Victoria Woodhull), / Stock Montage 54–5t; Aurora / Jeff Diener 543t, / David Hanson 315b, / Daniele Molineris 521; Bettmann 52br, 55clb, 56br, 58clb, 58crb, 543cr; Bloomberg / Scott Eells 68cr, / Mark Kauzlarich 71tl; Menno Boermans 692–3t; Boston Globe / David L. Ryan 158br, / Dina Rudick 186–7b, / John Tlumacki 143br; Boston Red Sox / Billie Weiss 136cr; Andrew Burton 71crb; Rob Carr 30–31b; CBS Photo Archive / Scott Kowalchyk 73br; Stephen J. Cohen 243tr; Corbis Documentary / Atlantide Phototravel 340–41b, / Jon Hicks 243cla; Corbis Historical / Michael Freeman 484bl, / VCG Wilson 59tl; Corbis News / Rick Friedman 10ca; Corbis NX / Andria Patino 99bl; De Agostini Picture Library 55br; Denver Post / MediaNews Group / RJ Sangosti 541tl; DigitalVision / Michael Berman 46–7b; dkfielding 202–203; E+ / DenisTangneyJr 17t, 132–3, 172–3t, / LauriPatterson 47tl, / LPettet 488, / ThePalmer 18cb, 276–7, / wanderluster 11crb; EyeEm / Jared Eygabroad 590–91t, / Benedikt Helmhagen 508bl, / Eric Johnson 438, / Denny Soetiono 616tr; EyeEm Premium / Kevin Chen 6–7; FilmMagic / Roy Rochlin 51cl; First Light / Yves Marcoux 690–91ca; Fototrove / Lambert 201tr; Meera Fox 50cr; Alicia Funderburk 242cra; Noam Galai 72–3t; Gallo Images / Danita Delimont 451crb; Robert Giroux 57clb; Erika Goldring 12t; 339bc; Daniel Grill 140br; Hulton Archive / Culture Club 53cla, / William Philpott 59bl, / Print Collector 54tl, 55cra, / Alex Wong 214bl; Hulton Archive Icon Sportswire / Michael Tureski 30–31t; The Image Bank / Andrew Geiger 550, / Peeter Viisimaa 392; Ingram Publishing 524; jollysiendaphotography 220; The LIFE Picture Collection / Francis Miller 59cb; LightRocket / Pacific Press 51crb; Lonely Planet Images / Eddie Brady 412–13t, / Richard Cummins 342bl, / Mark Daffey 692br, / Jean-Pierre Lescourret 644, / Peter Unger 535cr; MargaretW 540tl; Patrick McMullan / Gonzalo Marroquin 73cla; Michael Ochs Archives 56tl, 491ca;

Moment / Matteo Colombo 480t, / Colors and shapes of underwater world 39cl, / David Epperson 503cl, / Lola L. Falantes 22tl, 476–7; / Larry Gerbrandt 680, / James Atkinson Photography 4, / JeremyMasonMcGraw.com 349tl, / Kathryn Donohew Photography 654tr, / Kelly Cheng Travel Photography 560clb, / L. Toshio Kishiyama 224–5b, / Stewart Leiwakabessy 32–33t, / Luciano Lejtman 24, 612–13, / Eric Lowenbach 520crb, / Mark Brodkin Photography 502–3t, / Naphat Photography 25t, 686–7, / Nick Ocean Photography 679tl, / Photography by Steve Kelley aka mudpig 18tl, 238–9, / Alexander Spatari 10–11b, / Eric Sturdivant 17bl, 192–3,/ Thomas Roche 486tl, / Tony Shi Photography 89bl; Moment Mobile / Jon Lovette 244tr; Moment Open / Carl Larson Photography 20, 360–61, / john finney photography 413cla, / Ratul Maiti 283tr; / Thomas Welborn 28tl, / Tony Shi Photography 108b; Moment Unreleased / Praveen P.N 522t; Bryan Mullennix 556; Scott Olson 331tl; Onfokus 490–91b; Photodisc / Justin Cash 176, / Michele Falzone 534bl; Photographer's Choice / David Madison 702–703b; Photographer's Choice RF / Stephen Frink 44bl; Photolibrary / Maremagnum 95tr, / Marianna Massey 338t, / Sylvain Sonnet 28–9t, 286–7t, / Claire Takacs 68br, / Barry Winiker 215bl; Photonica / Kevin Trageser 638; Pool / Brian Baer 58cra; rappensuncle 50cla; Redferns / Leon Morris 331clb; Sports Illustrated / Erick W. Rasco 51cr; Chad_Talton 542b; Tetra Images 80bl; Toronto Star / Keith Beaty 59br; Universal Images Group 54clb, 59cla, / Education Images 21t, 50clb, 406–7, 421tr, 437bl, / Jeffrey Greenberg 253tr, 300cra, 714tr, / Photo 12 56bl, / Universal History Archive 82ca; Theo Wargo 511tr; The Washington Post 46bl, / Katherine Frey 217br, / Melina Mara 245clb, 245b, / Josh Sisk 196crb; Westend61 716–17t; WireImage / Gary Gershoff 36–7t, / Johnny Nunez 72b.

iStockphoto.com: 400tmax 578t; 4nadia 597cl; 4x6 699tl; Adam-Springer 724–5t; aimintang 121tl; Orbon Alija 97cla; benedek 172bl, 312b, 314tr, 515tl, 617tl; bhojrai 726–7b; BlueBarronPhoto 404–5b; Boogich 68t, 97cra, 290–91b; Lorraine Boogich 410crb; CampPhoto 678b; Chilkoot 690tl; csfotoimages 350–51t, 625tl; CynthiaAnnF 283clb; Dean_Fikar 529bl; DenisTangneyJr 11t, 148bl, 164bl, 164–5t; dhughes9 474bl; diegograndi 86clb; dlewis33 346; dszc 460–61b; E+ / Adventure_Photo 487br, / benedek 482–3, 510, 558b, / DenisTangneyJr 138tr, / ferrantraite 370t, / FilippoBacci 33tr, 486–7b, / franckreporter 581br, / GibsonPictures 540tr, / gladassfanny 45tr, / grandriver 48tc, / IlexImage 34–5b, / JeffGoulden 552–3t, / KenCanning 518br, / LordRunar 506–7t, / mbbirdy 8–9b, / OlegAlbinsky 105t, / S. Greg Panosian 83tr, / Ron and Patty Thomas 22cb, 536–7, 642b, / Shunyu Fan 130–31t, / Spondylolithesis 646t, / stevegeer 422–3t, / ThePalmer 675cb, / twphotos 589cra; edb3_16 310; eternity65 39br; f11photo 174b, 364t, 454–5t; / ferrantraite 456t, / *Cloud Gate* by Anish Kapoor © Anish Kapoor. All Rights Reserved, DACS 2020 26bl; Frankonline 446–7b; GarysFRP 604b; ghornephoto 354; gregobagel 292t; Ivanastar 144–5, 532–3b; janniswerner 160–61t; JMichl 400t; jmoor17 543clb; johnnya123 500b; jonathansloane 181tr; Kirkikis 343tl; kschulze 589tr; Meinzahn 103tr; Melpomenem 620l; milehightraveler 35br, 467t; Joshua Miller 636–7t; miroslav_1 670–71b; mizoula 86tc; OGphoto

503br; OlegAlbinsky 136bl; Eloi_Omella 98tr; S. Greg Panosian 628–9b; Sean Pavone 170t, 212–13t, 273b; Deeterv 74–5, 414, 649tl; Pgiam 19, 322–3; Planet Unicorn 368; Alex Potemkin 109tl; RoschetzkyIstockPhoto 448–9t, 468–9t; sarkophoto 704, 708–9b; Audrey Scripp 114–15b; Seastock 588–9b; stevegeer 366br, 379bl; Ron and Patty Thomas 634–5b; tiny-al 395tr; Torresigner 47cra; urbanglimpses 694, 999t; vernonwiley 581cla; visualspace 56–7t, 97bc; wanderluster 691tl; xavierarnau 90bl; YayaErnst 677b.

The John and Mable Ringling Museum of Art: 319bl.

Le Bernardin: Daniel Krieger Photography 70crb.

LEGOLAND FLORIDA: © 2016 Chip Litherland Photography Inc. 307clb, 307b.

The Maritime Aquarium at Norwalk: Megan Maloy 175tr.

Mary Evans Picture Library: Sueddeutsche Zeitung Photo 660crb.

Mass MoCA: Emma Franco / Zoran Orlić Campus Building 7 / *Wall Drawing 340* by Sol LeWitt © DACS 2020 43crb.

MIM—Musical Instrument Museum: 483tr.

Montparnasse 56 Group: 122–3b.

Mural Arts Philadelphia: *Pedal Thru* by Paul Santoleri. www.paulsantoleri.com. / Steve Weinik 12bl.

Museum of Fine Arts, Boston: 159t.

National Gallery Of Art: 196cr.

National Portrait Gallery, Smithsonian Institution: 210bl.

New Orleans and Company: Paul Broussard 328crb.

New Orleans Historic Voodoo Museum: Charles M. Sandolfo 337br.

New York Botanical Garden: 104br.

Newseum: Sam Kittner 213bl.

The Phillip and Patricia Frost Museum of Science: 188t.

Picfair.com: Andrew Dow 163tr; John Greim 190cr; Ian Martland 92–3t.

Polynesian Cultural Center: 715tl.

Ralph's on the Park: Chris Granger 328cr.

Rex by Shutterstock: Kobal / Black Label Media / Dale Robinette 619t, / Netflix / Alison Cohen Rosa 619crb, / Paramount 618b, UA / Lions Gate 619cl;

imageBROKER / Kohls 652–3t; Moviestore 618cla; Snap Stills 618tr.

Seven Gables: 162clb, 162b.

Shutterstock: JustPix 328bl; Craig Zerbe 480bl.

Smith Tower - Green Rubino: Kip Beelman 578cl.

Smithsonian National Air and Space Museum: 206b; Eric Long 196t.

Superior Bathhouse Brewery: 327tl.

SuperStock: AGE Fotostock / Alan Majchrowicz 598; Biosphoto 419crb; Image Source / Seth K. Hughes 246; Loop Images 690tr.

TopFoto.co.uk: Heritage-Images 651clb; The Image Works / © Underwood Archives 660bc.

Universal Orlando Resort TM: 308–9t, 309clb.

Unsplash: Joshua Earle / @joshuaearle 541tr; Jack Finnigan / @jackofallstreets 60-1; Holly Mandarich / @hollymandarich 540-1ca; Cody McLain / @neocody 728; Ryan Spencer 219br; Todd Trapani / @ttrapani 410t.

The Walrus and the Carpenter – Sea Creatures: Jim Henkens 578clb.

Front flap images
4Corners: Susanne Kremer br; **Alamy Stock Photo:** Michael Warwick cra;
Getty Images: Lonely Planet Images / Jean-Pierre Lescourret cla; Moment / Alexander Spatari c; **iStockphoto.com:** urbanglimpses **t; Unsplash:** Cody McLain / @neocody bl.

Cover images:
Front and Spine: **Getty Images:** EyeEm / Andrei Stoica.
Back: **Alamy Stock Photo:** Littleny cla; **Dreamstime.com:** Monkey Business Images c; **Getty Images:** E+ / DenisTangneyJr tr, EyeEm / Andrei Stoica b.

For further information see: www.dkimages.com

Main Contributors Stephen Keeling,
Donna Dailey, Mike Gerrard,
Taraneh Ghajar Jerven, Patricia Harris,
David Lyon, Paul Oswell, Lisa Voormeij,
Jackie Finch, Andrew Hempstead,
Jamie Jensen, Nancy Mikula, Joanne Miller,
Eric Peterson, Kevin Roe, Kap Stann

Senior Editor Alison McGill

Senior Designer Bess Daly

Project Editor Lucy Richards

Project Art Editor William Robinson

Designers Ben Hinks, Van Le, Sarah Snelling,
Vinita Venugopal, Bharti Karakoti,
Ankita Sharma, Hansa Babra, Chhaya Sajwan,
Simran Lakhiani, Priyanka Thakur

Factcheckers Stephen Keeling, Donna Dailey,
Mike Gerrard, Taraneh Ghajar Jerven,
Patricia Harris, David Lyon, Todd Obolsky,
Paul Oswell, Lisa Voormeij

Editors Matthew Grundy Haigh,
Laure Gysemans, Lucy Sara-Kelly,
Zoë Rutland, Rachel Thompson

Proofreader Kathryn Glendenning

Indexer Hilary Bird

Senior Picture Researcher Ellen Root

Picture Research Harriet Whitaker,
Sumita Khatwani, Rituraj Singh, Vagisha Pushp

Illustrators Arun P, Gautam Trivedi

Cartographic Editor James Macdonald

Cartography Mohammad Hassan,
Rajesh Chhibber and Suresh Kumar

Jacket Designers Maxine Pedliham,
William Robinson

Jacket Picture Research Susie Watters

Senior DTP Designer Jason Little

DTP Designers Tanveer Zaidi, Rohit Rojal

Producer Rebecca Parton

Managing Editor Rachel Fox

Art Director Maxine Pedliham

Publishing Director Georgina Dee

First edition 2004

Published in Great Britain by Dorling Kindersley Limited,
80 Strand, London, WC2R 0RL

Published in the United States by DK Publishing,
1450 Broadway, Suite 801, New York, NY 10018

Copyright © 2004, 2020 Dorling Kindersley Limited
A Penguin Random House Company
20 21 22 23 10 9 8 7 6 5 4 3 2 1

A CIP catalog record for this book
is available from the British Library.

A catalog record for this book is available
from the Library of Congress.

ISSN: 1542 1554
ISBN: 978 0 2414 0863 6

Printed and bound in China.

www.dk.com

**The information in this
DK Eyewitness Travel Guide is checked regularly.**
Every effort has been made to ensure that this book
is as up-to-date as possible at the time of going to
press. Some details, however, such as telephone
numbers, opening hours, prices, gallery hanging
arrangements and travel information, are liable to
change. The publishers cannot accept responsibility
for any consequences arising from the use of this
book, nor for any material on third party websites,
and cannot guarantee that any website address
in this book will be a suitable source of travel
information. We value the views and suggestions
of our readers very highly. Please write to: Publisher,
DK Eyewitness Travel Guides, Dorling Kindersley,
80 Strand, London, WC2R 0RL, UK, or email:
travelguides@dk.com